THE ARCHAEOLOGY OF MOBILITY

Cotsen Advanced Seminar Series

The published results of the Cotsen Advanced Seminars, where scholars explore cross-disciplinary themes in conferences periodically sponsored by the Cotsen Institute.

THE ARCHAEOLOGY OF MOBILITY

OLD WORLD AND NEW WORLD NOMADISM

EDITED BY

HANS BARNARD AND WILLEKE WENDRICH

COTSEN INSTITUTE OF ARCHAEOLOGY
UNIVERSITY OF CALIFORNIA, LOS ANGELES

This book is set in 10-point Janson Text, with titles in 29-point OPTI Forquet Oldstyle.
Edited by Joe Abbott
Designed by William Morosi
Index by Robert and Cynthia Swanson

The picture on the cover was taken in 1998 by pastoral nomad Mohamed Eid, with one of the cameras provided to the Ababda tribe by the Eastern Desert Antiquities Protection Project. It shows his family living in the Eastern Desert, between the Nile and the Red Sea in the border area between Egypt and Sudan.

Library of Congress Cataloging-in-Publication Data
The archaeology of mobility : old world and new world nomadism / edited by Hans Barnard and Willeke Wendrich.
    p. cm. -- (Cotsen advanced seminars ; v. 4)
 Includes bibliographical references and index.
 ISBN 978-1-931745-49-9 (pbk. : alk. paper) -- ISBN 978-1-931745-50-5 (cloth : alk. paper)
 1. Nomads. 2. Human beings--Migrations. 3. Land settlement patterns, Prehistoric. I. Barnard, H. II. Wendrich, Willemina. III. Cotsen Institute of Archaeology at UCLA. IV. Series.

 GN387.A73 2008
 305.9'0691--dc22

2008015350

CONTENTS

CHAPTER 1

THE ARCHAEOLOGY OF MOBILITY:

DEFINITIONS AND RESEARCH APPROACHES

WILLEKE WENDRICH AND HANS BARNARD[1]

THROUGHOUT HISTORY, GROUPS and individuals have traveled the face of the earth for manifold reasons and along a multitude of paths, both in space and in time. Such mobile people, be they hunter-gatherers, pastoral nomads or otherwise, left archaeological traces distinctly different from settled populations. These traces are usually simply characterized as 'ephemeral campsites.' It is frequently stated that mobile people obtain their material culture from neighboring settled populations rather than producing their own and that they do not leave recognizable archaeological traces (Finkelstein and Perevolotsky 1990). From the 24 chapters in this volume, however, and from many more studies that have appeared elsewhere in the recent past (for instance Irons and Dyson-Hudson 1972; Bar-Yosef and Khazanov 1991; Cribb 1991; Chang and Koster 1994; Bar-Yosef and Rocek 1998; Khazanov and Wink 2001; Veth et al. 2005), it must be concluded that there is indeed an 'archaeology of mobility.' By using specific and well-defined methods, which take into account the low density of artifacts and concentrate on regional studies, it is eminently possible to come to a better understanding of mobile people in archaeological contexts.

The archaeology of mobility encompasses more than tracing ephemeral campsites. Much like any other group, mobile people produce, use and discard a distinct material culture that includes functional objects, art and architecture. The latter can be found at the campsites, or at locations in the landscape, where graves or ritual structures have been erected (Betts, Chapter 2; Rosen, Chapter 5; Browman, Chapter 7; Shishlina et al. Chapter 10; Frachetti, Chapter 17; Saidel, Chapter 21). In an archaeological context the traces we encounter are occupation debris but also objects or assemblages that have been left behind,

---

[1] We would like to thank Jelmer Eerkens and Steven Rosen for their comments on earlier versions of this chapter; and William Lovis for the final paragraphs, dedicating this volume to the memory of Margaret Holman.

stored or cached on purpose (Alizadeh, Chapter 4; Milne, Chapter 8; Eerkens, Chapter 14; Barnard, Chapter 19; Wendrich, Chapter 23). Art or written records occur in the form of petroglyphs, rock drawings, landscape signs, group symbols and written texts (Jacobson-Tepfer, Chapter 9). However, most of the written accounts on mobile people have reached us through the eyes and pens of outsiders (Burstein, Chapter 11).

Similar to its predecessors,[2] the Fourth Cotsen Advanced Seminar aimed to stimulate and facilitate the discussion and interaction between scholars of Old World and New World archaeology. As archaeology in the Old World is usually associated with history, languages and the sciences, while archaeologists in the New World have more affinity with social sciences, especially anthropology, this often requires the building of bridges between relatively insular disciplines and, occasionally, the breaching of historical barriers between different archaeological fields of research. Lifting specific subjects out of their customary regional or temporal context, as well as discussing individual studies in a multidisciplinary setting, enable us to approach our research with fresh considerations and to discuss methodologies and results in a wider interpretative framework. That such a multiregional and multidisciplinary approach can be extremely stimulating and lead to surprising new insights is clear from similar initiatives (such as Bailey and Parkinson 1984; Veth et al. 2005), as well as from the chapters presented here.

This volume combines the proceedings of two meetings. The first was a symposium (number 82) during the 69th Annual Meeting of the Society for American Archaeology (Montreal, 2 April 2004); the second was a workshop that took place in the Cotsen Institute of Archaeology at UCLA (Los Angeles, 22–24 June 2004). Presenters were asked to consider three themes: the definition of mobility, the material culture of mobile peoples, and, when applicable, the relations between mobile and settled groups sharing the same geographical area. The discussion centered on the best field methods to record the material traces of mobile groups and the interpretative framework to understand the ancient remains in their cultural context. In addition, contributions are included from scholars who were involved in the discussions, partly through a video conference that took place in June 2004, but could not attend either of the meetings. The chapters in this volume consequently cover a large range of subjects and periods (Figure 1.1; Table 1.1).

---

[2] These seminars are *Theory and Practice in Mediterranean Archaeology: Old World and New World Perspectives* (Papadopoulos and Leventhal 2003); *The Archaeology of Ritual* (8-9 January 2004, convened by Evangelos Kyriakidis); and *Ritual Economy: Untethered by Space, Time, or Economic Form* (2-3 March 2006, co-organized by E. C. Wells and P. A. McAnany).

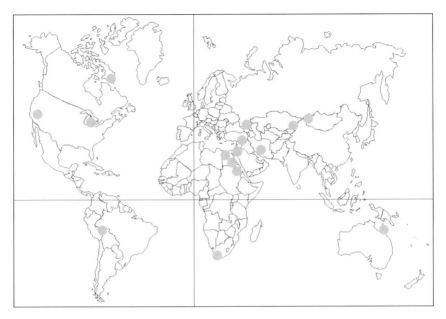

Figure 1.1. World map showing the location of regions discussed in this volume.

This volume is divided into two parts: Part I, 'The Past at Present' provides an overview of the state of the research on a certain area, people or period; Part II, 'The Present and the Future' emphasizes ethnoarchaeology or experimental archaeology and provides outlines or suggestions for further research. Considering the objective of both the meetings and this volume, to stimulate discussions between archaeologists working on different research topics in different areas of the world, the explicit choice has been made to not present the material by region. Instead the focus is on multiregional common themes, as well as obvious differences; thus, the placement of the chapters in the book may invite users to read accounts dealing with different regions and periods. Within each part the chapters are presented in chronological order of the subject matter. A comprehensive table of contents and an extensive index will allow readers to find sections of special interest quickly; an overview of the subject matter of each chapter is presented in Table 1.1; their geographical distribution is illustrated in Figure 1.1.

DEFINITIONS: MOMENT, MOVEMENT AND MOTIVATION

The etymology of the word 'nomad' goes back to the ancient Greek *nomades*, pastoral tribes, related to the verb *nemo*, which means to distribute, to pasture or to graze flocks (Liddell et al. 1958). The term is, therefore, originally linked to pastoralism but has achieved a much broader meaning in which the most

Table 1.1. Overview of the Subject Matter of the Chapters in this Volume:

Chapter/Author(s)	Geographical focus	Subject matter	Time period
Part I: The Past at Present			
2 Betts	Jordan	Overview of several sites and archaeozoological data	7th millennium BCE
3 Bernbeck	Turkey	Theoretical considerations based on the case of Fıstıklı Höyük	6th millennium BCE
4 Alizadeh	Iran	Combining ethnographical and archaeological data for Southwest Iran	5th millennium BCE
5 Rosen	Israel	Theoretical considerations based on the case of the Negev	6th millennium BCE to 1500 CE
6 Buccellati	Syria	State of the research on the Amorites	3rd–2nd millennium BCE
7 Browman	Peru, Bolivia	State of the research on camelid pastoral nomadism in the Andes	2nd millennium BCE to 500 CE
8 Milne	Canada	Models based on lithic finds from several sites on Baffin Island	2nd–1st millennium BCE
9 Jacobson-Tepfer	Mongolia	Survey and interpretation of petroglyphs	1st millennium BCE
10 Shishlina, Gak and Borisov	Southern Russia	Report on several sites and archaeobotanical data	1st millennium BCE
11 Burstein	Egypt, Sudan	Analysis of historical sources	500 BCE to 500 CE
12 A. B. Smith	South Africa	Combining historical and archaeological evidence for the Khoekhoen	0–1500 CE
13 Holman and Lovis	United States	Theoretical considerations based on the case of the Great Lakes Region	500–1500 CE
14 Eerkens	United States	Models based on ceramic and lithic finds in the Great Basin	800–1800 CE
Part II: The Present and the Future			
15 Chang	Kazakhstan	Models based on ethnographical and archaeological data	8th century BCE to 1st century CE
16 S. T. Smith	Sudan, Egypt	Theoretical considerations based on Askut, Tombos and Berenike	1800 BCE to 600 CE
17 Frachetti	Kazakhstan	Models based on several sites in the Koksu River Valley	2nd–1st millennium BCE
18 Szuchman	Syria	State of the research on the Aramaeans	2nd–1st millennium BCE
19 Barnard	Egypt, Sudan	Ceramic analysis and experimental archaeology	4th–6th century CE
20 Magid	Sudan	Ethnohistorical and ethnographical description of the Hadendowa	3rd century BCE to present
21 Saidel	Southern Levant, northern Arabia and the Sinai	Ethnohistorical and ethnographical description of the Bedouin black tent	17th–19th century CE
22 Roe	Northwest Egypt	Resource use by pastoral nomads	20th century CE
23 Wendrich	Southeast Egypt	Ethnohistorical and ethnographical description of the Ababda	20th century CE
24 Cribb	Australia	Conflict management among the Aboriginals	20th century CE
25 Kuznar and Sedlmeyer	World	Computer models for nomadism	21st century CE

important aspect is that of a (residentially) mobile existence. This meaning urges us to further delineate what variations of mobility occur. Here we define 'mobility' as the capacity and need for movement from place to place. This definition takes into account that even though a person's or group's activities may concentrate or depend on movement, there will always be stationary periods, if only to sleep. This is an intentionally broad definition, much more so than, for instance, the one proposed by Holman and Lovis (Chapter 13). It focuses on the movement of humans in the landscape but leaves their organization and motivations to be determined. A further specification of the type of movement is based on the mobile versus settled segment of the group and on the motivation, in the most abstract sense.

Figure 1.2 illustrates four basic types of mobility: the entire group travels from resource to resource (Figure 1.2a); segments of different groups travel to and from specific resource areas (Figure 1.2b); segments of the group gather resources for a base camp (Figure 1.2c); the entire group travels, following a distinct and fixed pattern (Figure 1.2d). These schematic representations focus on the movement of groups in the landscape but leave their motivations, the composition of the population segment, the distance and the time frame to be specified. The length of stationary periods compared to the time of travel is

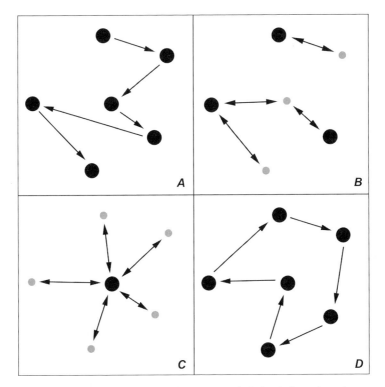

Figure 1.2. Schematic representation of mobility patterns. Black dots indicate the main group; gray dots indicate segments of the group.

equally undefined. Many activities, varying from the slaughtering of animals to the production of textiles or pottery, require such stationary periods. Other activities, such as procuring chert, finding water or collecting mushrooms, are linked to specific locations and seasons. The length of these stationary periods may vary from one night (rest, finding water) or a number of hours (slaughtering, flint knapping) to several years, when the lakes are full of fish or the pastures are lush and green enough to sustain a population for a long period. We can summarize the definition of mobility as a combination of the moment in time, the type of movement and the motivation for mobility.

In his groundbreaking work *Nomads in Archaeology*, Roger Cribb (1991) outlined the differences between hunter-gatherer and pastoral societies (Table 1.2).[3] Cribb's comparison focused on the motivation for mobility, which is either centered on the humans in the group or on the flocks or herds. He also outlined differences in the movement pattern and the resulting archaeological scatter of artifacts. While this comparison, with its clear juxtaposition of features, is probably true for some hunter-gatherer and pastoral-nomadic groups, both archaeological and ethnographic studies have shown many variations that clearly deviate from this pattern (Bernbeck, Chapter 3; Rosen, Chapter 5). By insisting on the forced separation of hunter-gatherers and pastoral nomads, we risk overlooking similarities and overlap. Even the terminology of the two fields of research deviate to the extent that communication about mobility patterns is rendered almost impossible.

Table 1.2. Differences Between Hunter-Gatherers and Pastoral Nomads (after Cribb 1991):

Hunter-gatherers	Pastoral nomads
Procurement and consumption	Production (determined by consumption pattern of livestock)
Moves toward resources or gathers resources for humans	Moves toward resources for flocks (independent of human resources)
Mobility to bring variation in resources	Mobility to maintain access to one resource (grazing)
Consumption immediately after procurement	Human consumption independent of herd
Migration follows complex pattern	Migration track follows simple pattern
Risk minimization for humans	Optimization of pastoral production, minimize risk for herds
Archaeological remains scattered widely	Constrained scatter, less functional variability
Stable and localized migratory patterns	Instability and dramatic shifts in migration tracks

[3] In August 2007, when this volume was in its final stages of production, Dr. Roger Cribb passed away after a protracted battle with cancer. He was only 59 years old and holding an honorary position as Research Fellow at James Cook University (Cairns, Australia) at the time. Roger not only participated in our workshop in Los Angeles (June 2004) and contributed a chapter to this volume, but his seminal work on the archaeology of nomads is quoted in most chapters. He will be sorely missed by his family, friends and colleagues.

TERMINOLOGY RELATED TO HUNTER-GATHERERS

Binford (1980) introduced the term *logistical mobility* to express the movement of part of a hunter-gatherer group to secure provisions (Figure 1.2c). Logistical mobility can consist of a one-day trek or require multiple nights away from the base camp or settlement, which in itself is not necessarily permanent. Usually only part of the group, defined by gender, age, social status or health, embarks on such an expedition (Milne, Chapter 8). In contrast to logistical mobility, the term *residential mobility* has been introduced to indicate a pattern where the entire group leaves and moves the base camp (Figure 1.2a; Kelly 1992). *Tethered mobility* expresses specific limitations to the range or time of movement (Figure 1.2d; Ingold 1980), by dependence on particular resources or by social circumscription. Examples of tethered mobility are found in very different social and environmental circumstances. Caching of pottery by hunter-gatherers can be taken as an indication of tethered mobility (Eerkens, Chapter 14; Kelly 1995).

TERMINOLOGY RELATED TO PASTORAL NOMADS

Pastoral nomadism is the general term for mobility centered on the maintenance and welfare of flocks or herds (Figure 1.2a), while *semi-nomadic pastoralism* denotes a situation where part of the group is settled (Figure 1.2c), or the entire group is settled for part of the year (Figure 1.2b). *Agropastoralism* specifies a combination of agricultural and pastoral activities (Figure 1.2c or 1.2b), and the term focuses on the motivation, not on the mobility pattern (Buccelati, Chapter 6). *Tethered nomadism* indicates a dependence on particular resources, other social groups, or features in the landscape (Figure 1.2d). *Enclosed nomadism* describes the close relation between a nomadic group and the surrounding settled population (Rowton 1974), while *peripheral nomadism* is used for groups that live at the fringes of a settled society. These two latter terms tacitly refer to the relation between the settled and nomadic population rather than to a mobility pattern. They also imply that the studies of mobility are written from the viewpoint of the settled population.

Several terms are used for seasonal migration with flocks or herds, which is determined primarily by weather conditions or scarcity of resources in certain periods of the year (Figure 1.2b). The most general term for this is *transhumance*, but specifications occur, such as *vertical transhumance* (or *vertical mobility*) for seasonal movements in mountainous areas. In this volume authors describe such a process in several different regions: Iran (Alizadeh, Chapter 4), Kazakhstan (Chang, Chapter 15; Frachetti, Chapter 17) and the Andes (Browman, Chapter 7). High-altitude pastures are used in summer, whereas the snow forces the herds to low-lying meadows in winter. *Horizontal transhumance* (or *horizontal mobility*) describes movement at approximately the same elevation over a large area, mostly to find resources in spite of heavy snow cover (Milne, Chapter 8) or drought (Johnson 1969). In the same country, herds are known to follow the winter rainfall (Wendrich, Chapter 23) or relocate in summer to a region where water can be found in wells (Roe, Chapter 22).

The purpose of developing a set of definitions, and a related terminology, is to describe our subject matter in a concise way and to enable communication among scholars. Such definitions and terminology are, in a way, abbreviations and, at the same time, generalizations of detailed descriptions of particular societies at a specific moment in time. There is, however, always the danger that our definitions become blueprints for explaining the variation in human movement through time and space. The same definitions that enable us to speak about the many forms of human mobility ironically also restrict us and render mobility into a set of timeless, static human interactions with the natural surroundings. Ironically, the pinnacle of long-term settled existence, the Near Eastern *tell*, forces us to describe human-settled habitation as a development: the meters of stratigraphical information demonstrate inescapably that human existence is in constant flux. In contrast, the archaeology of mobility has too often focused on static categorizations of human reactions to changing circumstances, a behavioristic approach interpreting the data by resource- or climate-driven human adaptations.

Most authors in this volume argue against such a static concept of pastoral nomadism or hunting and gathering. Since the 1970s focus has shifted from narrowly described modes of resource procurement to the opportunistic use of several supply strategies, sometimes called *multi-resource nomadism* (Salzman 1972). The term *herder-gatherers*, introduced by Rosen (1998, 2002), finds increasingly widespread use and highlights the frequent occurrence of pastoralists who also embark on hunting and gathering (Betts, Chapter 2). Instead of becoming fixated on definitions the authors are concerned with the methodology of studying archaeological remains in a regional setting (Rosen 1992).

By defining *mobility* in terms of 'moment' (length of time, season), 'motion' (mobility pattern charted over time), 'motivation' (resources, but also cultural identity, social or economic circumscription), and 'segment' (the parts of the population defined by gender, age, health or social position), we liberate ourselves from fixed preconceptions. Rather than considering populations as either settled or mobile, recent interpretations, of which several can be found in this volume, emphasize the fluidity of mobility and the role of social organization and agency in the process of mobilization or settlement. The scope ranges from an entire population that is highly mobile to a mostly settled population in which only small groups move around. Mobility should, therefore, be defined

Table 1.3. Factors and Range of Mobility:

	Factor	Range
Moment	Period of movement	Specific day, week, month, season, year
	Length of period of movement	Total no. of nights
	Length of stay in each location	Total no. of nights
	Repetition of mobility pattern	Daily, weekly, monthly, seasonally, yearly, etc.
	Stability of mobility	Repetition over multiple years, decades or centuries
	Variation of mobility over time	Inventory of multiple years, decades, centuries
Movement	Range of movement	Number of km per period of movement
	Pattern of movement	Fixed, flexible, random (specified with map)
Motivation	Purpose of movement	Hunting, gathering, herding (specified with activities)
	External factors	Climate, war, social pressure, illness, etc.
	Decision base for movement	Who decides (group or high-status individual), basis on which decision is made
	Assessment of mobility within the group	Identity, cause for pride, neutral, necessity, compassion, scorn
	Assessment of mobility by outsiders	Identity, cause for pride, neutral, necessity, compassion, scorn
	Mobility integral part of identity	No / Yes (specify how)
Segment	Distribution of mobile population	One group, multiple camps
	Percentage of population in motion	0–100%
	Part of population in motion	Gender, age, social position, profession, cultural identity
	Variation of mobility within the group	Gender, age, social position, profession, cultural identity
	Location of burials / cemetery	Central location (monumental or not), buried 'en route,' cremation, other means

for each population separately according to very specific questions (Khazanov 1984) and over a long period of time. Table 1.3 gives an outline of research questions related to a study of mobility and summarizes the factors involved. It illustrates the complexity of any definition, research program and analysis of human mobility. Several of these factors have been taken into account in the important work of Kuznar and Sedlmeyer (Chapter 25).

From Table 1.3 it is apparent that the segments of a society, the mobility pattern in time and space and, most important, the motivations show an enormous variability in human mobility. Economic or subsistence incentives are by no means the only factors to be taken into account when seeking to explain mobility patterns. Most often the motivations that determine the pattern are a combination of factors, partly dependent on the context and audience, and in constant development and flux. These motivations are manifold, ranging from climatic and subsistence to sociocultural, from economic to religious; and from ideological to a search for personal safety (Cribb, Chapter 24).

RELATIONS BETWEEN MOBILE AND SETTLED GROUPS

There has been much debate on the place of sedentism in the evolution of *Homo sapiens* (Moore 1983; Bender 1985; Marquardt 1985; Cohen 1985; Keeley 1988; Henry 1991; Liebermann 1993; Rosenberg 1998). The vast majority of laymen, politicians and scholars, however, consciously or subconsciously understand settled living as the highest rung on the evolutionary ladder where permanent housing goes hand in hand with agriculture, landownership, social stratification and industrialization. The word *pharaoh*, ruler of one of the earlier complex societies, literally means 'great house,' while in Levantine societies the concept of 'the house' was an all-encompassing social phenomenon (Schloen 2001), so much so that the term is also used for the genealogy by pastoral nomads in the area (Wendrich, Chapter 23). Similar terminology is used by government institutions (the House of Representatives) and rich or noble families (as in Edgar Allan Poe's 'The Fall of the House of Usher'). Without doubt this deterministic point of view is among the reasons that mobile people are under constant pressure to settle down or leave; in our modern and increasingly complex society even more so than in the past.

The relations between mobile and settled groups are relatively well studied (Nelson 1973; Aurenche 1984; Khazanov 1984; Khazanov and Wink 2001). Often this relation is problematic and we should take into account that most of our historical (written) sources on mobile peoples have been recorded by a settled population and usually show misconceptions, either vilifying or romanticizing a mobile lifestyle. In the 1st century CE, Strabo already felt the need to correct this image: "These are nomads and neither many nor warlike, although they were believed to be so by the ancients because of their frequent raids on defenceless people" (Strabo, Geography 17.1.53; Eide et al. 1998).

Nomads are often depicted as raiders or freedom loving adventurers, while the intricacies of social organization, ethnic identity, loyalties and policies are rarely understood (Burstein, Chapter 11; S. T. Smith, Chapter 16). Part of our tendency to oppose sedentary and mobile ways of life stems from the representation of nomadic groups as 'the other' or 'the outsider' by the settled powers. Unsettling accounts of people surviving and even thriving in peripheral areas are, for instance, one way in which the dichotomy between 'the desert and the sown' is maintained (Chang, Chapter 15; Szuchman, Chapter 18; Nelson 1973; Chang and Koster 1994).

As several of the contributions to this volume point out, there is the danger of creating a dichotomy between settled and nomadic life. Humans will adapt their lifestyles to changing circumstances, or proactively decide on changing their way of life, either as a group, as a specific part of the group, or as individuals. No firm delineation can be made between settled and mobile existence. At the same time, we should not imagine the relation between settled and mobile life as a point or range on a scale between 'completely settled' and 'completely mobile.' The decision to move location occasionally, regularly or frequently is in most cases opportunistic. The idea that mobility is an adaptation or a response to (often adverse) changing circumstances is an equally limited view of the different forms of movement and diverse motivations for mobility.

Considering human society through its movements, rather than through its settlements, brings to the fore that even in firmly settled societies there is always a part of the population that is mobile. To mention just a few examples: in many societies trade is in the hands of either separate mobile groups or mobile members of the settled group. Trade inherently requires mobility, varying from farmers traveling to the market town, peddlers and hawkers moving from village to village, to long-distance traders. Religiously motivated traffic is another strong reason for mobility of settled populations but is also a factor in permanently mobile groups. Pilgrimages are known among many of the world's populations and are just a step away from religious orders of mendicants. A third example is the custom of the upper class to move residence to either cooler or warmer regions during part of the year. In 19th century India the British higher ranks moved residence to summer homes in the cooler mountains. Mobility in our modern Western society includes commuters, vacationers, homeless people and refugees (Bernbeck, Chapter 3). And yet, these types of mobility are considered part of the settled mode of living.

MATERIAL CULTURE, LANDSCAPE AND FIELDWORK

Considering the range of potential forms, reasons and objectives for mobility, we should ask how much of these we can actually retrieve from the archaeological record. A number of publications have highlighted the potential of archaeological research of mobility (Monks 1981; Bar-Yosef and Khazanov 1991; Saidel 1998; Rosen 1998, 2002). As Frachetti (Chapter 17) describes vividly, landscape archaeology is essential for understanding mobility (Chang and Koster 1986). Within the landscape the features that are of potential significance for subsistence, resources, ritual and routing are taken into account. The traditional focus on archaeological 'sites' does not answer the questions involved in the study of mobility. Nevertheless, it is inherent to human behavior that most material remains will be left, and can be retrieved, at places where humans stay for at least a short while. In addition, there are traces along the routes, such as specific signs, that denote ownership of resources or other messages to those who pass by. Important sources for studying the material culture of mobile peoples are cached materials: objects that were left behind on purpose to be used during a future stay in a particular location (Figure 1.2d; Eerkens, Chapter 14).

The study of pastoral nomads benefits greatly from the methods developed by prehistorians. Beyond the questions clarifying the nature, scope and scale of mobility, the research focus diverges when concentrating on the specific motivations for mobility. The natural circumstances, subsistence, cultural development as well as the economic and social context of the groups under study differ, as do our sources of information. Archaeologists working on understanding mobility patterns put their efforts into establishing not only the chronology and cultural markers of a region but also the period of stay, the number of recurrent stays, the seasonality of human presence and the activities at each location that has a higher density of material remains than the surrounding landscape. To determine whether a low-density location represents a one-time period of stay, a short-period production site, or a yearly visited campsite is extremely difficult and often impossible. The data have to be placed within the broader context of multisite occupation and landscape analysis (Bernbeck, Chapter 3; Kuznar and Sedlmeyer, Chapter 25). Conclusions on the site use and motivation, literally that which causes these specific people to move or to pause at a particular place for a particular period in a particular time of year, requires a reconstruction of the entire activity pattern. The study of mobility is learning about human interaction with the landscape, its limiting factors, its resources and its meaning.

Different information is gathered from site and regional levels. The most important techniques when studying low-density assemblages are micro-analysis of the taphonomy, the faunal and the botanical remains. Archaeozoological studies potentially provide information on age and size of slaughtered or hunted animals, level of domestication and seasonality (Monks 1981; Brewer 1989; Van Neer 1993; Bar-Yosef and Rocek 1998; Van Neer et al. 2004). Subsistence and climatic information, including seasonal use of sites, can be gained from archaeobotanical research (Shishlina et al., Chapter 10; Holman and Lovis, Chapter 13), while material culture (pottery, metal, textiles, leather, basketry) provides information on activity, date, cultural affiliation, gender, age and organization. Burial sites provide important information on the self-definition and identity of some mobile groups, while for others the inhumation seems to be as fleeting and uprooted as their general existence. The study of sites concentrates on the stationary activities and on the shelters with which mobile groups equip themselves (Magid, Chapter 20). Storage facilities may be indications of recurring visits to the same area (Eerkens, Chapter 14; Akkermans and Duistermaat 1997; Wendrich and Cappers 2005).

On a regional level an inventory of available resources, indications of routing and other remains of the same chronological period enables the reconstruction of a mobility pattern. The study of petroglyphs, geoglyphs (such as cleared areas, stacked stones, border or route indicators) and other visible signifiers is of great importance (Jacobson-Tepfer, Chapter 9). A caveat should be that a mobile group can 'occupy' an area of hundreds of square km, while a yearly track can involve a roundtrip in the 1000 km range (Alizadeh, Chapter 4). Landscape reconstruction, identification of resources and a reconstruction of the climate, weather and ecology are multidisciplinary tasks (Shishlina et al., Chapter 10). Modern archaeological research necessarily involves a team of specialists from different disciplines and in a way mirrors the explorations of the mobile groups in the past. A group's knowledge of resources, such as wells or raw materials, is passed on to the next generation, but when a group has to explore virgin territory, its members embark on a process of 'landscape learning' (Milne, Chapter 8; Rockman 2003). What archaeologists are doing is learning the landscape, with the added difficulty that some facets of the landscape have changed over time. Moreover, particular aspects, such as cultic or symbolic meaning of landscape features, are difficult to deduce or corroborate.

The lack of stratigraphy in low-density assemblages does not represent a lack in development of the mobile society and should not cloud our attempts to understand the complexity of the structure of a society that is highly mobile or spread out over a large area. Communication or planned (and perhaps ritualized) interaction is very important for societies in which meetings cannot take place haphazardly, because the space in which the interaction takes place is not circumscribed or limited (Milne, Chapter 8).

ETHNO-ARCHAEOLOGY

Many contributors to this volume compare data from archaeological, ethnographic and ethno-archaeological studies. Bernbeck's statement that the present state of affairs "cries out for the abandonment of analogical reasoning when dealing with past mobile groups" (Chapter 3) reflects the ongoing discussion of the pitfalls, values, uses and abuses of ethno-archaeology and analogy (Wylie 1985; David and Kramer 2001). The direct historical approach, where present-day populations are considered a continuation or 'survival' of ancient inhabitants of the same area or region, is indeed a dangerous bedfellow for archaeology because it limits the explanatory power of research and denies ancient populations the ability to change. Instead, it should be noted that change is unavoidable and perhaps the only firm given in any archaeological study. Burstein's (Chapter 11) and Saidel's (Chapter 21) contributions to this volume illustrate this clearly from very different perspectives. Often the direct historical approach is connected with an evolutionary slant: a linear development is implicated from hunter-gatherer (a completed stage) to herding (an equally completed stage) to sedentism (a stage still in development). The evolutionary approach is often considered one of gradual improvement with modern (European) humans as the crown of the evolution (Trigger 2006:166–220). The Great Kalahari Debate (Smith, Chapter 12), for instance, is partly based on presuppositions about whether the present inhabitants of the Kalahari are proud hunter-gatherers or pathetic remnants of what once was a number of well-developed cultures. Equally misleading are ethno-archaeological studies that concentrate on very limited, mostly ecological, aspects and use these as a substrate to draw conclusions on a much wider scale. Such a deterministic approach may provide some valuable insights, but it denies agency to individuals and groups and rejects the historical development of group agency, which is often summarized as 'culture.'

The simplified and limiting uses of analogical reasoning are rightly criticized. But analogical reasoning, when done correctly, is not only extremely useful but a method we simply cannot do without (Wylie 1985). Most of us do not have the imagination to formulate the large number of interpretations that could be given to specific archaeological assemblages. Ethnographies and ethno-archaeological studies provide an inventory of known occurrences: a palette of different types of organization, forms of habitation and human reactions to and interactions with a wide range of physical, social and spiritual circumstances. A case in point is the examples of groups with a surprisingly long-distance range of mobility, a yearly round trip that covers more than 1000 km (Alizadeh, Chapter 4). Such an inventory is a source not only of ideas but also of caveats, such as Alan Roe's (Chapter 22) example of two groups that stay in the same area during the same chronological period (late 20th, early 21st century CE) but in different parts of the year. Roe describes the smaller oases around Siwa, where pastoral nomads dwell in summer, while settled agriculturalists go there for the date harvest in fall. Ethno-archaeological research is also used to test specific hypotheses, for instance in relation to depositional and postdepositional processes. Here again the danger looms that we end up with too limited and too deterministic an approach of ancient society. Barnard's (Chapter 19) trials to produce pottery without an existing infrastructure (such as kilns) and with limited availability of water or fuel exemplify the use of experimental archaeology to demonstrate that it is feasible to produce high-quality ceramics in a transient situation. Such experiments do not corroborate a specific production method or locality but refute unwarranted claims that mobile people are incapable of producing ceramics because of a lack of infra-structure (see also Eerkens, Chapter 14).

Related to landscape learning, referred to above, is the notion of the space that one inhabits. This brings us to the cognitive aspects of the archaeology of mobility: there is a large difference between inhabiting a range of campsites, irrespective of the length of stay, and inhabiting the landscape as a whole. Were groups moving from place to place, or did they consider themselves inhabitants of one large space, the landscape through which they moved? Ultimately the question is whether the people we study through the archaeological remains were looking inward, concentrating on their community, or outward, toward the world.

DISCUSSION

The reality of a mobile existence is far more complex than the ordering prin-ciples used to describe them (Figure 1.2). An outline of 'types of mobility' is necessarily a simplification that highlights a number of important aspects but leaves out others. As will be clear from most of the contributions to this volume, such generalizing categories are helpful to the novice, but they should probably be abandoned when interpreting the full range of archaeological or ethnographic data (Table 1.3). This volume gives pointers on how research can do justice to the complexity and developments of past mobile and partly mobile societies. Archaeologists studying the remains of mobile groups require specific methods, which combine a meticulous analysis of 'ephemeral campsites' with a close consideration of the landscape, the availability of resources, as well as the scale, the layout and, often, the borders of the world through which the groups moved. Hunter-gatherers may move more than 500 km to follow the seasonal trek of elk, while settled farmers may temporarily move to a small reed hut on their fields at a distance of 30 km for the summer nights during sowing or harvest time. The traces that they leave reflect the fact that they did not stay in one place permanently but visited the location either one time or repeatedly for shorter periods. On one level there is remarkably little differ-ence in the methods employed in the study of the remains of hunter-gatherers, herder-gatherers, pastoral nomads, or even a settled population that ventured temporarily outside its usual territory. All of these studies can benefit greatly from the methods developed by prehistorians to deal with low-density artifact scatters and landscape archaeology.

Cultures in which mobility plays an integral role are in constant devel-opment. This is not only a result of changing circumstances but also a context-dependent effort to improve the status quo. At the same time, humans are firmly embedded in social relations, as well as ecological, economic and political circumstances. Central to understanding the archaeology of mobility is to refrain from defining mobility in too fixed a set of categories, thereby denying the dynamic and opportunistic development of mobile peoples.

ACKNOWLEDGEMENTS AND DEDICATION

Thanks are due to many people, among whom are two anonymous reviewers, Amber Myers and Kandace Pansire (conference assistants), Sam Aroni (Director of the Special Academic Cooperative Projects, UCLA), William Schniedewind (Chair of the Department of Near Eastern Languages and Cultures, UCLA), Jimmy Suo and Dean Abernathy (Visualization Portal, UCLA), Stein Hitland (University of Bergen, Norway), Sue Rogers (University of Cambridge, UK), Gary Mattison (The Getty Institute, Los Angeles), Magda Yamamoto, Sheryol Threewit, Helle Girey, Ernestine Elster and Charles Stanish (Cotsen Institute of Archaeology, UCLA). Special thanks go to Evangelos Kyriakidis, for sharing his experience; to Louis van Dompselaar, for making the right software available; to Krzysztof Pluskota, for his photographs (Chapter 20); to all participants in Montreal and in Los Angeles, for making the Fourth Cotsen Advanced Seminar a success; and to Lloyd Cotsen, for making it all possible.

The picture on the cover was taken in 1998 by pastoral nomad Mohamed Eid, with one of the cameras provided to the Ababda tribe by the Eastern Desert Antiquities Protection Project (Wendrich, Chapter 23). It shows his family living in the Eastern Desert, between the Nile and the Red Sea in the border area between Egypt and Sudan (Burstein, Chapter 11; S. T. Smith, Chapter 16; Barnard, Chapter 19; Magid, Chapter 20).

This volume is dedicated to the memory of Dr. Margaret B. 'Peggy' Holman, Research Associate at the Michigan State University Museum and Adjunct Faculty in the Department of Anthropology at Michigan State University (Figure 1.3). Throughout her career and despite her research focus on North America, Peggy Holman was a dedicated student of mobile people worldwide, coupling closely their ethnography, ethnohistory and archaeology. Her work fostered cross-cultural approaches rooted in clear use of ethnographic analogues to understand the archaeological record. Peggy contributed substantially to our knowledge of such diverse subject matter as the origin and role of maple sugaring in the upper Great Lakes area, the seasonal and technological implications of caching and storage by mobile hunter-gatherer horticulturalists in the region as well as the seasonal scheduling of mutually desirable resource areas by adjacent mixed economic groups. Moreover, she was always available to provide interested students with her insights and helped to train multiple generations of 'Great Lakes archaeologists.'

Figure 1.3. Margaret B. Holman (center) in the field at the Zemaitis site (Michigan) in 1993, surrounded by her colleagues (from left to right) Janet Brashler, Elizabeth Garland, William Lovis and Terrance Martin.

In April 2006, Peggy succumbed to pancreatic cancer, before she could see the fruit of her work in this volume, a compendium that she greatly anticipated. Peggy's many contributions to the literature of mobile people, including her lead authorship of Chapter 13, testify to her abiding interests in science and people and will certainly endure. We can only regret that the future literature, and our small community, will be the poorer for her absence.

REFERENCES

Akkermans, P. M. and K. Duistermaat
1997   Of Storage and Nomads: The Sealings of the Late Neolithic Sabi Abyad. *Paléorient 22*: pp. 17–32.
Aurenche, O.
1984   *Nomades et sédentaires: Perspectives anthropologiques*. Paris, Éditions Recherche sur les Civilisations.
Bailey, G. and J. Parkinson (eds.)
1984   *The Archaeology of Prehistoric Coastlines*. Cambridge, Cambridge University Press.

Bar-Yosef, O. and A. Khazanov (eds.)

1991   *Pastoralism in the Levant: Archaeological Materials in Anthropological Perspectives.* Madison, Prehistory Press.

Bar-Yosef, O. and T. Rocek (eds.)

1998   *Seasonality and Sedentism: Archaeological Perspectives from Old and New World Sites.* Cambridge, Harvard University Press.

Bender, B.

1985   Prehistoric Developments in the American Mid-continent and in Britanny, Northwest France. In T. D. Price and J. A. Brown (eds.), *Prehistoric Hunter-Gatherers: The Emergence of Cultural Complexity.* Orlando, Academic Press: pp. 21–57.

Binford, L. R.

1980   Willow Smoke and Dog's Tales: Hunter-Gatherer Settlement Systems and Archaeological Site Formation. *American Antiquity 45*: pp. 4–20.

Brewer, D. J.

1989   *Fishermen, Hunters and Herders: Zooarchaeology in the Fayum, Egypt (ca. 8200–5000 BP). British Archaeological Reports, International Series 478.* Oxford, Archaeopress.

Chang, C. and H. A. Koster

1986   Beyond Bones: Toward an Archaeology of Pastoralism. In M. B. Schiffer (ed.), *Advances in Archaeological Method and Theory, Volume 9.* New York, Academic Press: pp. 97–148.

Chang, C. and H. A. Koster (eds.)

1994   *Pastoralists at the Periphery: Herders in a Capitalist World.* Tucson, University of Arizona Press.

Cohen, M. N.

1985   Prehistoric Hunter-Gatherers: The Meaning of Social Complexity. In T. D. Price and J. A. Brown (eds.), *Prehistoric Hunter-Gatherers: The Emergence of Cultural Complexity.* Orlando, Academic Press: pp. 99–119.

Cribb, R.

1991   *Nomads in Archaeology.* Cambridge, Cambridge University Press.

David, N. and C. Kramer

2001   *Ethnoarchaeology in Action.* Cambridge, Cambridge University Press.

Eide, T., T. Hägg, R.H. Pierce and László Török

1998   *Fontes Historiae Nubiorum. Volume III: From the First to the Sixth Century AD.* Bergen, University of Bergen, Department of Greek, Latin and Egyptology: 828-835.

Finkelstein, I. and A. Perevolotsky

1990   Processes of Sedentarization and Nomadization in the History of Sinai and the Negev. *Bulletin of the American Schools of Oriental Research 279*: 67–88.

1991   Foraging, Sedentism, and the Adaptive Vigor in the Natufian: Rethinking the Linkages. In G. A. Clark (ed.), *Perspectives on the Past: Theoretical Biases in Mediterranean Hunter-Gatherer Research*. Philadelphia, University of Pennsylvania Press: pp. 353–370.

Ingold, T.
1980   *Hunters, Pastoralists, and Ranchers*. Cambridge, Cambridge University Press.

Irons, W. and N. Dyson-Hudson (eds.)
1972   *Perspectives on Nomadism*. Leiden, E. J. Brill.

Johnson, D. L.
1969   *The Nature of Nomadism: A* Comparative *Study of Pastoral Migrations in Southwest Asia and Northern Africa. Department of Geography Research Paper 118.* Chicago, University of Chicago.

Keeley, L. H.
1988   Hunter-Gatherer Economic Complexity and "Population Pressure": A Cross-Cultural Analysis. *Journal of Anthropological Archaeology* 7: pp. 373–411.

Kelly, R. L.
1992   Mobility/Sedentism: Concepts, Archaeological Measures, and Effects. *Annual Review of Anthropology 21*: pp. 43–66.
1995   *The Foraging Spectrum: Diversity in Hunter-Gatherer Lifeways*. Washington, Smithsonian Institution Press.

Khazanov, A. M.
1984   *Nomads and the Outside World*. Cambridge, Cambridge University Press.

Khazanov, A. M. and A. Wink (eds.)
2001   *Nomads in the Sedentary World*. Richmond, Curzon.

Liddell, H. G., R. Scott, H. S. Jones and R. McKenzie
1958   *A Greek-English Lexicon*. Oxford, Clarendon.

Liebermann, D. E.
1993   The Rise and Fall of Seasonal Mobility Among Hunter-Gatherers: The Case of the Southern Levant. *Current Anthropology 34*: pp. 599–631.

Marquardt, W. H.
1985   Complexity and Scale in the Study of Fisher-Hunter-Gatherers: An Example from the Eastern United States. In T. D. Price and J. A. Brown (eds.), *Prehistoric Hunter-Gatherers: The Emergence of Cultural Complexity*. Orlando, Academic Press: pp. 59–98.

Monks, G.
1981   Seasonality Studies. In M. B. Schiffer (ed.), *Advances in Archaeological Method and Theory, Volume 4*. New York, Academic Press: pp. 177–240.

Moore, A. M. T.
1983   The First Farmers in the Levant. In T. C. Young, P. E. L. Smith and P. Mortensen (eds.), *Studies in Ancient Oriental Civilization, Volume 36*. Chicago, University of Chicago Press: pp. 91–111.

Nelson, C. (ed.)

1973   *The Desert and the Sown: Nomads in the Wider Society*. Berkeley, University of
        California Press.

Papadopoulos, J. K. and R. M. Leventhal (eds.)

2003   *Theory and Practice in Mediterranean Archaeology: Old World and New World
        Perspectives*. Los Angeles: Cotsen Institute of Archaeology at UCLA.

Rockman, M. A.

2003   Knowledge and Learning in the Archaeology of Colonization. In M. A.
        Rockman and J. Steele (eds.), *Colonization of Unfamiliar Landscapes: The
        Archaeology of Adaptation*. New York, Routledge: pp. 3–24.

Rosen, S. A.

1992   Nomads in Archaeology: A Response to Finkelstein and Perevolotsky. *Bulletin
        of the American Schools of Oriental Research 287*: pp.75–85.

1998   The Development of Pastoral Nomadic Systems in the Southern Levantine
        Periphery: An Economic Model Based on Archaeological Evidence. In M.
        Pearce and M. Tosi (eds.), *Papers from the EAA Third Annual Meeting: Pre-
        and Protohistory. British Archaeological Reports International Series 717*. Oxford,
        Archaeopress: pp. 92–97.

2002   The Evolution of Pastoral Nomadic Systems in the Southern Levantine
        Periphery. In E. van den Brink and E. Yannai (eds.), *In Quest of Ancient
        Settlements and Landscapes: Archaeological Studies in Honour of Ram Gophna*. Tel
        Aviv, Ramot Publishing: pp. 23–44.

Rosenberg, M.

1998   Cheating at Musical Chairs: Territoriality and Sedentism in an Evolutionary
        Context. *Current Anthropology 39*: 5, pp. 653–681.

Rowton, M. B.

1974   Enclosed Nomadism. *Journal of the Economic and Social History of the Orient
        17*: pp. 1–30.

Saidel, B.

1998   Arid Zone Pastoralists in the Early Bronze Age in the Southern Levant.
        Harvard University (PhD dissertation).

Salzman, P. C.

1972   Multi-resource Nomadism in Iranian Baluchistan. In W. Irons and N. Dyson-
        Hudson (eds.), *Perspectives on Nomadism*. Leiden, E. J. Brill: pp. 60–68.

Schloen, J. D.

2001   *The House of the Father as Fact and Symbol: Patrimonialism in Ugarit and the
        Ancient Near East*. Winona Lake, Eisenbrauns.

Trigger, B. G.

2006   *A History of Archaeological Thought*. Cambrigde, Cambridge University Press
        (second edition).

Van Neer, W.

1993   Limits of Incremental Growth in Seasonality Studies: The Example of
        the Clariid Pectoral Spines from the Byzantino-Islamic Site of Apamea
        (Syria, 6th–7th Century A.D.). *International Journal of Osteoarchaeology 3*: pp.
        119–127.

Van Neer, W., A. Ervynck, L. J. Bolle and R. S. Millner

2004   Seasonality Only Works in Certain Parts of the Year: The Reconstruction
        of Fishing Seasons Through Otolith Analysis. *International Journal of
        Osteoarchaeology 14*: pp. 457–474.

Veth, P., M. Smith, P. Hiscock (eds.)

2005   *Desert Peoples, Archaeological Perspectives.* Oxford, Blackwell.

Wendrich, W. Z. and R. T. Cappers

2005   Egypt's Earliest Granaries: Evidence from the Fayum. *Egyptian Archaeology
        27*: pp. 12–15.

Wylie, A.

1985   The Reaction Against Analogy. In M. B. Schiffer (ed.), *Advances in Archaeological
        Method and Theory, Volume 8*. New York, Academic Press: pp. 63–111.

PART I

THE PAST AT PRESENT

CHAPTER 2

THINGS TO DO WITH SHEEP AND GOATS

NEOLITHIC HUNTER-FORAGER-HERDERS IN NORTH ARABIA

ALISON BETTS

For several decades during the mid 20th century CE, after the spectacular discovery of the Pre-Pottery Neolithic A (PPNA) tower at Jericho (by Kenyon) had placed the prehistory of the southern Levant firmly in undergraduate textbooks, the Late or Pottery Neolithic was an orphan period, lost between the cultural riches of the Pre-Pottery Neolithic B (PPNB) and the equally colorful evidence for the Chalcolithic period. For some time it was even suggested that the southern Levant was largely abandoned during the early part of this period (Kenyon 1957; Perrot 1968; Mellaart 1975:67–68; Moore 1985). Only after the 1980s did this picture begin to change (Table 2.1). While increasingly intensive study of the Mediterranean climatic zone has produced evidence for a number of Late Neolithic settlements (Garfinkel 1993; Gopher 1993; Gopher and Gophna 1993; Kafafi 1993; Banning et al. 1994), what has been much more surprising is that extensive surveys in the steppe and desert regions have shown that this period is widely represented from the west Jordan highlands to the Euphrates Valley in Iraq and from the hills around Palmyra to the fringes of the Nafudh desert (Garrod 1960; Akazawa 1979; Betts 1987; Betts and Helms 1987, 1993; Garrard et al. 1994a, 1994b, 1996; Stordeur 2000).

The floruit of the PPNB saw the growth of large villages with elaborate architecture, a rich symbolic corpus, long-range exchange networks and indications of fairly complex social organization (Kuijt and Goring-Morris 2002). The transition from the Middle PPNB to the Late PPNB entailed dramatic shifts in economy and settlement. The occupational focus moved from the core areas of the Mediterranean climatic zone to the steppic interface zone in the east. Concurrently, there is increasing evidence for seasonal or intermittent use of the steppe and desert regions beyond the effective limits of dry farming. By the final PPNB/PPNC a number of the larger settlements declined or were abandoned. Some, such as 'Ain Ghazal in central Jordan, continued, although the period is poorly represented archaeologically. There are also new sites established along

Table 2.1. Chronology of the Neolithic of the Near East (after Horwitz et al. 1999:64–65):

Period	Age BP (uncalibrated)	Age BCE (calibrated)	Millennium BCE
Pre-Pottery Neolithic A (PPNA)	10,200–9400	9800–8400	10th–9th
Early Pre-Pottery Neolithic B (EPPNB)	9400–9200	8400–8100	Late 9th
Mid Pre-Pottery Neolithic B (MPPNB)	9200–8500	8100–7500	Early 8th
Late Pre-Pottery Neolithic B (LPPNB)	8500–8100	7500–7000	Late 8th
Pre-Pottery Neolithic C (PPNC)/Terminal PPNB	8100–7600	7000–6500	Early 7th
Pottery Neolithic/Late Neolithic	After 7600 BP	After 6500 BCE	Late 7th onward

the Mediterranean coast (Gopher 1993; Kuijt and Goring-Morris 2002:414). By the PPNC significant changes in the entire complex of animal resource procurement had occurred in the southern Levant with the introduction of sheep, cattle and, probably, pig to the domestic economy (Horwitz et al. 1999:70; Kuijt and Goring-Morris 2002:417). With the Late Neolithic a very new pattern of settlement emerges. What had been a culturally rich and innovative period devolved into scatters of smaller sites and hamlets in the Mediterranean climatic zone and along the coast, with an unprecedented spread of short-term campsites in previously largely unexploited steppe lands.

Within the steppe, too, the changes were dramatic. During the Mid to Late PPNB the steppe was exploited by hunter-gatherer groups living in seasonal encampments (Betts et al. 1998; Byrd 1992; Garrard et al. 1994a, 1994b, 1996). The large herds of gazelle that roamed the steppe were a favored prey (Betts et al. 1998). Exploitation of the steppe, however, appears to have been restricted to certain ecologically favored locations. In Jordan this included the oasis of al-Azraq and the gorge at Wadi Jilat where deep pools offered out-of-season water supplies (Garrard et al. 1994a, 1994b, 1996), as well as the eastern basalt *harra* where deeply incised valleys (*wadis*) provided seasonal rain pools and the landscape was suited to the mass exploitation of gazelle (Betts et al. 1998). In Syria, PPNB sites have been found in the Palmyrene oasis (Akazawa 1979) and in the region of natural springs at al-Kowm (Stordeur 2000). With the PPNC, and certainly by the beginning of the Late Neolithic, the steppe sites saw the introduction of sheep and goats, a development that heralds the start of the spread of short-term campsites along almost all the wadi systems across the Badiyat ash-Sham. Sites of this period are still also found clustered around the better water sources so that they continue at al-Azraq and Wadi Jilat (Garrard et al. 1994a, 1994b, 1996), while much further east around the seasonal rain pool at Burqu' there is very little evidence for the PPNB, but the Late Neolithic is strongly represented. In Syria and Iraq similar sites can be found along most of the deeper wadis.

The weight of evidence suggests that sheep were first domesticated in southeast Turkey (Peters et al. 1999), spreading out from here and southward (Horwitz et al. 1999:76). In the southern Levant they occur in significant numbers at 'Ain Ghazal by the Late PPNB (Horwitz et al. 1999:71; Martin 1999:88). While goats occur in significant numbers earlier than sheep on southern Levantine sites, there is less consensus on whether they were domesticated there or introduced as a domesticate, although several scholars have at least postulated some form of 'proto-herding' (Horwitz et al. 1999:77; Martin 1999:88; Ducos 1993). In the eastern Jordanian steppe, sheep and goats form a significant part of faunal assemblages by the PPNC (around 6900 BCE calibrated) and are assumed to appear as introduced domesticates from the west (Horwitz et al. 1999:75). This constitutes a fairly dramatic change. Epipaleolithic faunal assemblages are dominated by gazelle with some equid, whereas PPNB sites have mostly gazelle, hare and fox. The introduction of sheep and goats signals a marked change in the nature of steppic economies.

THE END OF THE PPNB

The reasons for the decline of the later Pre-Pottery Neolithic have been debated at some length. Environmental degradation caused by extensive deforestation and overgrazing has been suggested as a strong contributing factor (Rollefson and Köhler-Rollefson 1989; Rollefson et al. 1992). The Pre-Pottery Neolithic saw the rise of the first large population aggregations in the Near East. They required wood for fuel, construction and manufacture of the plaster that was a major feature of their house interiors. As the first mixed farmers in the region, they cleared the woodland for fields and grazed goats on the open pastures surrounding the settlements. It has been suggested that the inhabitants gradually began to find that their immediate environment offered insufficient support to sustain them, slowly bringing about a breakdown of the larger settlements into smaller and more scattered units. This interpretation is disputed by some scholars, however, and in any case should not be considered a monocausal solution to changes that took place over a wide range of environmentally diverse regions (Bar-Yosef 2002:53–54).

Social pressure may also have played a role. The PPNB villages represented the largest sedentary communities ever at that time. Interpersonal stress might have forced apart communities whose social structures, still rooted in a hunter-gatherer tradition, may not have been able to cope adequately with conflict management and large-scale cooperative organization. The complex question of PPNB social structure has been addressed from a number of differing perspectives (Kuijt and Goring-Morris 2002), but the nature of the issue makes it difficult to test against the material evidence. An alternative, or possibly an additional causal factor, may be climate change. Here too the evidence is problematic, with considerable regional disparity in terms of the data. As more information is gathered, there is some consensus in the broader picture but less in the detail. One interpretation is that the Terminal PPNB/PPNC coincided with a cooler and more humid climate (8000–7500 BP uncalibrated; Issar 1998:115), which was followed in turn in the Late Neolithic by increased warming (7500–7000 BP uncalibrated; Issar 1998:115) and reduced rainfall (6400–6200 BCE calibrated; Bar-Yosef 2002; Rosen 1998:229). A variant using much of the same evidence sees a rise in warmer and moister conditions through the early to mid Holocene interrupted briefly by a colder and dryer period between 8000 to 7600 BP (uncalibrated) coinciding with the Terminal PPNB/PPNC (Sanlaville 1997; Wasse 2000). There is also the possibility of a northerly move of the monsoonal belt during the early Holocene, producing summer rainfall that would have a marked impact on land-use potential of marginal steppic regions (al-Moslimany 1994). In general, it is likely that climate change was a factor in the breakdown of the PPNB agglomerating settlements and the subsequent developments in the Late Neolithic, but it is difficult at this stage to define its influence more precisely.

MODELS OF STEPPIC ECONOMIC STRATEGIES

Martin (1999) has presented detailed evidence for the introduction of sheep and goats to the east Jordan steppe by the PPNC/Late Neolithic period. She has also discussed the two main models offered to explain these developments and presented her own alternative model. Köhler-Rollefson (1988, 1989a, 1989b, 1992), arguing principally in relation to evidence from 'Ain Ghazal, suggests that nomadic pastoralism developed in eastern Jordan at some time from the PPNC onward. She proposes that, as a result of environmental pressures on the potential grazing lands in the immediate vicinity of 'Ain Ghazal, groups of herders moved out into the steppe in spring and early summer, eventually becoming specialized pastoralists. She linked this to a shift from meat to milk production to ensure a food supply without diminishing herd size. The model is based both on archaeological evidence and analogy with patterns of seasonal herding practices among modern Bedouin agropastoralists. Byrd (1992) has presented a very different model involving the integration of domestic resources into the economy of indigenous hunter-gatherers. He suggests that expansion and colonization by settled village populations within the fertile Mediterranean climatic zone in the PPNB pushed indigenous hunter-gatherer groups out into the steppe where, in order to survive on reduced resources, they responded by diversifying and exploiting available food sources more intensively. An example of this might be the development of game traps (the so-called desert kites) in this period. They then also selectively integrated domesticated crops and animals into their economic structure to supplement uncertain supplies of seasonal wild produce with a more predictable yearly return.

Martin (1999), countering the model put forward by Köhler-Rollefson, argues that the proportions of 20–50% animal bones in the faunal record on steppe sites does not equate with either the fattening of flocks for slaughter at village sites or total reliance on ovicaprine pastoralism by steppe populations. She suggests rather that the proportion of ovicaprine bones is similar to that of wild animals such as gazelle or hare, which appears to indicate that the steppe peoples did not specialize in any particular form of resource procurement but rather were generalist herders, hunters, foragers, trappers and, possibly occasionally, cultivators as well (Martin 1999:97). Cereal remains have been found at Jilat 13 (Garrard et al. 1996) and chance agriculture is a common practice in modern times in the North Arabian steppe. Martin also discusses the ways in which the flocks may have been managed, specifically whether they were used for milk or solely for meat. Although the evidence is not strong, she believes that a conservative interpretation suggests culling for meat only (Martin 1999:100). She goes further to address the question of whether the Late Neolithic steppe population comprised herders who moved out from the PPNB villages and adopted additional food procurement strategies to survive effectively or PPNB hunter-gatherers who adopted herding. Based on continuity in kill patterns of gazelle and hare across the PPNB/PPNC-LN boundary, she concludes that the latter is more likely and thus broadly supports Byrd's model.

EVIDENCE FROM THE *HARRA* AND THE *HAMAD*

Extensive surveys and a number of excavations by Garrard at Wadi Jilat and al-Azraq and by Betts in the basalt covered steppe (*al-harra*) east of al-Azraq and in the open gravel plains beyond (Figure 2.1; Table 2.2), leading down to the Euphrates in Iraq (*al-hammad*), suggest that Martin's conclusions offer the most reasonable interpretation of the development of herding in the east Jordanian steppe. In the conclusion to her article she reminds us that, as Ingold (1980) has pointed out, the keeping of domestic animals involves different social relationships from hunting, and it also involves different ecological needs. The changes in behavior necessitated by adoption of a major new economic strategy are reflected in markedly different patterns of site type and distribution in the PPNC-LN. Rosen (2002), in a recent overview of the first herders in the Sinai and Negev regions of the southern Levant, also postulates

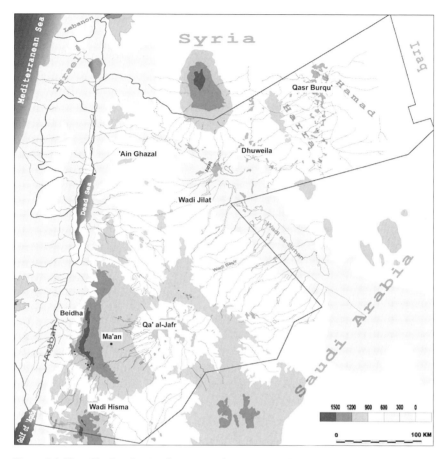

Figure 2.1. Map of Jordan, showing the position of sites mentioned in the text.

a similar interpretation, with a hunter-gatherer phase in the PPNB, followed by a 'herder-gatherer' phase where domesticates are adopted into peripheral systems in the Late Neolithic period.

Although there is wide variety in steppic sites of this period, there is also a broad bipartite division that can be made between sites with a small range of material traces widely dispersed across the steppe and sites with more complex remains that tend to cluster in the vicinity of permanent or semipermanent water sources. Those in the first group are characterized by great frequency, shallow but sometime extensive spreads of artifacts, few or no associated structures and, frustratingly, a tool kit constituting an extraordinarily high proportion of a distinctive chipped-stone artifact, the function of which is unknown. The only use so far clearly identified for this, the concave truncation burin, is as a core for the production of spalls that were then used as drill bits. Bead manufacture

Table 2.2. Radiocarbon Determinations for Sites Excavated by Betts in the East of the Jordanian Steppe:

Site (lab. code)	Age BP	Age BCE (1)[a]	Age BCE (B)[a]	Millennium BCE
Dhuweila 1 (OxA-1637)	8350±100	7500–7270	7540–7140 (0.93)	Mid–late 8th
			7120–7060 (0.07)	
Dhuweila 1 (BM-2349)	8190±60	7260–7170 (0.45)	7420–7350 (0.07)	Mid–late 8th
		7160–7050 (0.55)	7320–7030 (0.93)	
Burqu' 35 (OxA-2770)	8270±80	7470–7250 (0.75)	7480–7460 (0.02)	Mid–late 8th
		7220–7200 (0.06)	7440–7050 (0.98)	
		7180–7140 (0.12)		
		7120–7100 (0.07)		
Burqu' 35 (OxA-2769)	8180±80	7270–7040 (1.00)	7270–7040 (1.00)	Late 8th
			6840–6810 (0.01)	Early 7th
Burqu' 35 (OxA-2768)	8140±90	7280–7010 (1.00)	7420–6990 (0.85)	Late 8th
			6970–6770 (0.15)	Early 7th
Burqu' 27 (OxA-2766)	7930±80	7030–6965 (0.24)	7060–6640 (0.99)	Late 8th
		6950–6930 (0.07)	6620–6610 (0.01)	Early 7th
		6920–6880 (0.14)		
		6860–6850 (0.01)		
		6830–6690 (0.54)		
Burqu' 27 (OxA-2765)	7350±80	6230–6050 (1.00)	6360–6270 (0.14)	Late 7th
			6260–6000 (0.86)	
Burqu' 27 (OxA-2764)	7270±80	6170–6010 (1.00)	6230–5950 (1.00)	Late 7th
Jebel Naja (OxA-375)	7430±100	6380–6170 (1.00)	6430–6040 (1.00)	Mid–late 7th
Dhuweila 2 (OxA-1729)	7450±90	6370–6190 (1.00)	6430–6110 (0.95)	Mid–late 7th
			6090–6050 (0.05)	
Dhuweila 2 (OxA-1728)	7140±90	6050–5930 (0.07)	6160–6140 (0.03)	Late 7th
		5920–5860 (0.30)	6130–5770 (0.97)	Early 6th
Dhuweila 2 (OxA-1636)	7030±90	5950–5780 (1.00)	6010–5690 (1.00)	Late 7th
				Early 6th
Burqu' 03 (OxA-2808)	6900±100	5830–5640 (1.00)	5950–5900 (0.07)	Early 6th
			5890–5590 (0.93)	

[a]Dates are calibrated using CALIB3.0.3.c Data set 1 (bidecadal tree ring data set to 9440 BCE calibrated) and calibration method B (probability method).

was a significant part of the cultural package. The chipped-stone repertoire is normally very restricted, but the tools tend to be fairly large with generous use of raw material. These 'burin Neolithic' sites have been found distributed very widely across the steppe. They are typically located in sheltered positions on terraces overlooking the larger wadi systems, which supply year-round grazing and seasonal water. Depending on rainfall, wadi systems right across the steppe hold water in pools well into the summer months. These act as conduits through the steppe, providing corridors linking the Levant with the Tigris-Euphrates valleys. Sites of this type have been found near el-Kowm (Stordeur 1993) and the Palmyra basin (Akazawa 1979) in Syria, in the wadis of western Iraq (Garrod 1960), and in northern Saudi Arabia (Garrod 1960; Parr et al. 1978) and are widely distributed across eastern Jordan from the Iraq border (Betts et al. 1991) to the edge of the Jordan Valley (Rollefson et al. 1982).

Sites in the second broad category are much more varied. They have stone structures with hearths and pits, a wide range of chipped-stone and other artifacts, imported items and concentrations of faunal and botanical remains. They are relatively rare and cluster around significant sources of water. The main examples are the sites adjacent to the gorge in Wadi Jilat, at the oasis of al-Azraq (Garrard et al. 1994a; b), and Burqu' in eastern Jordan, where an unusually large rain pool may have provided year-round water supplies in prehistoric times (Betts et al. 1990, 1991). Another set of sites has been found in the center of the basalt *harra* at the south end of Dhuweila (Betts and Helms 1987), where large seasonal lakes and deep-cut pools may also have provided long-term water supplies. One more site, which does not fit into any of these categories and can be placed in a group of its own, is the Late Neolithic occupation at Dhuweila that appears to be a seasonal hunting camp (Betts et al. 1998). The sites detailed below are only selected examples of a wider spectrum presented to give a general picture of the range and diversity of Late Neolithic sites in the North Arabian steppe.

JEBEL NAJA

An excavated site of the 'burin Neolithic' type, Jebel Naja had shallow occupation levels with ephemeral hearths, minimal traces of faunal and botanical remains, and an area where bead making was carried out. The chipped-stone tool kit was highly restricted and there were very few other artifacts. The site was located on the edge of the basalt *harra* in a sheltered position on the lower slopes of the massif, overlooking open country with extensive grazing. Water may have been available in pools in the surrounding wadis but no pools were immediately adjacent to the site. Based on the minimum number of individuals, out of a total of eight animals identified from the faunal remains, four were sheep-goat, two were gazelle, and two were hare.

WADI JILAT

A number of Neolithic sites are clustered along the rim of the Wadi Jilat gorge and large open-air Epipaleolithic sites have also been found nearby. The bed of the gorge contains large, deep pools that retain water for long periods after flooding, providing a potential year-round water source. The location is in the limestone steppe on the western edge of the steppe, not far from the modern limits of the Mediterranean climatic zone. The earliest Neolithic sites date to the PPNB; they continue on into the Late Neolithic and possibly later. The sites vary but are generally characterized by subcircular structures made with one or more rows of upright slabs supported by rubble packing. These may well have been covered with an organic superstructure. Each site constitutes a cluster of structures. The chipped-stone tool kits contain a varied array of artifacts, beads were produced at some sites, ground stone artifacts were found in moderate amounts, and there were a small number of imported items. The faunal remains included sheep-goat bones as a significant but not dominant proportion of the total number of animals and the botanical remains included cereals, as well as locally available wild plants.

QASR BURQU'

Qasr Burqu' lies beside a large rain pool that has been augmented in recent times by a dam to create a lake. The number of prehistoric sites clustering around the lake shore indicate that it was always an important water source. The pool is on the eastern edge of the basalt *harra* at the margins of the limestone *hammad*. Apart from a small scatter of Epipaleolithic artifacts, the sites date mostly from the Late/Terminal PPNB to the Late Neolithic. The sites consist of small clusters of stone-built subcircular cells constructed using a combination of dry stone walling and upright slabs supported by rubble packing. They have some depth of stratigraphy (indicating repeated re-occupation), internal hearths and pits and a wide range of chipped-stone artifacts. The chipped-stone tools are moderate in size and there is evidence for increasingly economic use of raw material in the later periods, with greater emphasis on use of poor-quality local sources. The sites also have considerable numbers of ground stone tools and some imported decorative items. The faunal remains from the sites include significant numbers of sheep-goat remains. At Burqu' 27 (McCartney 1992), for example, sheep-goat bones counted for over 50% of the total recovered from the site.

QA' AL-GHIRQA

Qa' al-Ghirqa is a mudflat within the basalt *harra*. Near its southern end, where a fairly deeply incised wadi has carved a long pool, is a string of sites of a particularly distinctive type. None have been excavated, but a number have been extensively surveyed. The sites comprise clusters of circular structures, in some cases linked by enclosing walls. Some structures have corbelled roofs and narrow corridor entrances. There are also some examples of upright slab construction. There are very few ground stone artifacts, but there is evidence of bead making. The chipped stone tool assemblages are moderately varied with a significant proportion of concave truncation burins. The chipped stone assemblages are particularly characterized by the small size of all the artifacts, yet the sites are only 20 to 30 km from plentiful sources of raw material. No faunal or botanical remains have been recovered.

DHUWEILA

Dhuweila was first occupied in the PPNB by hunter-gathers specializing in mass killing of gazelle using large stone-built animal traps called 'desert kites.' The site is located in the basalt *harra* on a low promontory overlooking a large mudflat. There is one main stone shelter built solidly of basalt using a combination of rough dry stone walling and upright slabs with rubble footings. The interior was paved with large flat stones, some of which were used as grinding slabs. The extensive faunal remains consisted of 93% gazelle, with only 5 identifiable specimens (0.2%) of sheep-goat, and the rest of the remains comprising birds, fox, equid and hare. After a period of abandonment the site was re-occupied, but the economy appears to have been similar. Despite the absence of the large PPNB processing areas with hearths, ash and fire-cracked stones, the faunal remains consisted of 94% gazelle, with 39 identifiable specimens (0.5%) of sheep-goat and the rest of the faunal remains as in the earlier period. There is no positive evidence for domesticated animals. The botanical remains were all from wild plants that occurred locally and included edible roots. Evidence suggests that the site was probably occupied seasonally in winter and early spring. There are limited water sources from rain pools in the vicinity, but none are large enough to offer supplies into summer. The large mudflat floods extensively in heavy rain and attracts seasonally migrating birds. Bones from a Little Bittern were found. This bird requires standing water for its natural habitat. Finds included a wide range of chipped-stone tools, numerous ground stone artifacts and some imported decorative items.

DISCUSSION

The North Arabian steppe was used in the later part of the PPNB period by hunter-gatherer groups whose relationship to the peoples in the settled villages is unclear. There is extensive evidence for the Epipaleolithic in the steppe, which is followed by an apparent hiatus in the PPNA. The early to mid PPNB is only found on the margins of the steppe, such as at Wadi Jilat, while the deep steppe was only fully re-used in the Late PPNB. This suggests that PPNB groups had a shared origin with the peoples of the verdant lands to the north and west. Although they shared a common tradition of chipped stone manufacture, there is evidence for culturally distinct practices that suggest that they established independent populations fully adapted to steppic living. Those in the basalt *harra* developed complex hunting techniques using large-scale systems of traps, while the PPNB hunters at Dhuweila produced a distinctive style of rock engraving unique to the steppe. The PPNB groups appear to have been largely confined to the western and northern sectors of the steppe, particularly in areas of more broken terrain. PPNB sites have been found in Wadi Jilat and extensively within the basalt *harra* and in the Palmyrene, but very little evidence for PPNB occupation is known from the open *hammad* to the east. By contrast, most Late Neolithic sites occur around the edges of the *harra* and extensively across the eastern *hammad*. Clearly, there is a complete shift in land-use patterns that must be associated with corresponding changes in economic strategies. Equally clearly, these must bear some relation to the introduction of domestic herds to the traditional hunter-gatherer pattern of subsistence (Table 2.3).

The changes in site location fit closely to the new requirements of herding, specifically a greater need for water and grazing. The locations selected for 'burin Neolithic' sites have been almost invariably re-used by more

Table 2.3. Relative Numbers of Sheep-Goat Remains on Jordanian Steppe Sites, Expressed as 'Minimal Number of Elements' Counts (after Martin 1999:Table 3):

Site	Sheep/goat	Total
Late Neolithic		
Burqu' 27	67	177
Jebel Naja	4	8
Dhuweila 2	38	6355
Wadi Jilat 13-3	143	775
Wadi Jilat 13-2	164	625
Wadi Jilat 13-1	387	1782
Wadi Jilat 25	57	106
Azraq 31	281	1217
Late PPNB		
Azraq 31	2	56
Dhuweila 1	5	2198
Mid/Late PPNB		
Wadi Jilat 7-5	0	79
Wadi Jilat 32	0	155
Mid PPNB		
Wadi Jilat 7-2	0	440
Wadi Jilat 7-3	0	172
Wadi Jilat 7-4	0	233
Wadi Jilat 26	0	12
Early PPNB		
Wadi Jilat 7-1	0	245

recent sheep-goat pastoralists, indicating that herding needs strongly governed the choice of site location. As Martin (1999) points out, however, these people were not exclusively herders. At most, sheep and goats supplied about half of their meat needs while they continued to hunt and collect wild plants, as well as practicing occasional agriculture in wetter areas. Imported items on the sites indicate contact with lands beyond the steppe and imply some form of exchange system, something that was already in place in the PPNB. What is also significant is the marked variety in site types, artifact assemblages and cultural practices. Given the need for wide-ranging movement associated with a hunter-herder-forager lifestyle, this variety cannot be explained in terms of local regional adaptations. What it suggests, rather, is a variety of differing responses on the part of the former hunter-gatherers to the adoption of a new resource. With the increased need for water, it may also mean more marked 'ownership' of dry-season water sources by particular groups who then each begin to develop slightly different cultural signatures. Martin (1999:97–98) is cautious about the faunal evidence for seasonality. The weight of archaeological evidence, however, leans quite strongly toward the likelihood that the steppe did support a population of hunter-gatherer-herders year-round. The burin sites are indicative of wet season use when grazing was plentiful and water pools were widespread across the steppe. The high frequency of sites and low levels of artifacts found there suggest short-term occupation and regular movement. The sites clustered around the more permanent water sources, with more robust structures, greater depth of stratigraphy and a wider range of artifacts, suggest that the steppe was certainly used for a substantial portion of the year when water supplies were limited.

Rightly, much has been made of the problems associated with use of ethnographic analogies to attempt to understand nomadic groups in the archaeological record. However, some of these issues relate to the way in which such evidence is applied. Some authors place stress on the symbiotic relationship between pastoralist and farmer, with the implication that this is a fundamental requirement of successful pastoral practice. Often, too, there is an assumption that the pastoralist is almost fully dependent on the herds, to the exclusion of other economic opportunities. While this may be true for some recent herding groups, it does not necessarily apply in the North Arabian steppe, as has been shown in a perceptive study of the Rwalla Bedouin by Lancaster (1981). Although they appear to have been predominantly pastoralists in the recent past, a closer look at the details of their activities shows a more complex picture. Lancaster stresses the notion of the 'multi-resource nomad,' analyzing all aspects of social and economic life in terms of 'assets and options.' Access to anything from social contacts, to good grazing, to a job opportunity in the trucking business is a potential asset. Balancing these options to maximize economic success in a world of scattered and varied resources is a key skill in Bedouin life and one that makes the Bedouins remarkably adaptable to change while the constant, the glue that holds the system in place, is a particular social system stressing the importance of familial and 'tribal' relationships. This is not to say that the modern Bedouin system is in any way directly comparable to the situation in the Late Neolithic. For a start it is heavily reliant on a complex social structure that has developed over hundreds, if not thousands, of years. The model of a multiresource system, however, where adaptability, choice and variety permit survival in a fairly marginal environment, is a useful one to consider in examining the nature of the Late Neolithic of North Arabia and the introduction of herding as one component among a number of different subsistence strategies.

If Byrd's (1992) model is correct, then the steppe populations were faced with constant adaptation and change from the mid-PPNB onward and apparently managed this condition with a considerable degree of success. In particular, there is no need to assume economic dependence on settled peoples but rather possibly only pragmatic contact for exchange purposes. There is no evidence that the Late Neolithic steppe hunter-herders needed goods that could only be obtained from agriculturalists. Formerly, hunter-gatherers had survived in the region and this form of subsistence strategy continued in parallel with herding. It must also be remembered that even if the climate was as hostile as it is today, conditions would still have been markedly better. The region today is wholly overgrazed and almost completely depleted of the rich array of wildlife it once fostered. In Neolithic times the wadis would have been lined with scatters of pistachio trees and dense shrub vegetation as tall as a person's head, while the open steppe would have teemed with vast herds of gazelle, onager, oryx and flocks of ostrich. Set against this would be the presence of predators: large cats, hyenas and jackals. This abundance would certainly allow the successful survival of small hunter-herder-forager groups in the deep steppe, relying wholly on the wild resources of the land.

This thesis runs counter to the perceived notion of inevitable interdependency between pastoralist and villager that may have developed later as pastoralism became an increasingly important component of the economic system of the steppe. It is helpful to contrast developments in North Arabia with those in the Sinai and Negev region where a similar initial pattern of hunter-herders has been identified (Rosen 2002). However, while the first adoption of domestic animals by steppic groups is similar in both areas, subsequent developments followed different patterns. The Sinai and Negev regions are rich in mineral resources. Transport, trade and possibly primary exploitation are all roles in which the desert/steppe population would be likely to engage and there is evidence to support this. The Sinai Peninsula is also the gateway to Egypt, offering further trade and transport opportunities, while the distances to be covered are not great compared with the land mass of North Arabia. North Arabia is devoid of significant mineral resources, with the exception of chert and basalt, which were in demand in the later prehistoric periods, but these did not offer the same high-market opportunities as the semiprecious stones and metals to be found in Sinai and the Negev. The key advantage of the inhabitants of the North Arabian steppe was command of the shortcut from the Levant to Mesopotamia and to the Middle Euphrates. In the Late Neolithic, although there is evidence for cultural continuity from the Jordan Rift to the Tigris-Euphrates basin, this was of limited significance, but in later times as cultural development in Mesopotamia began to outstrip that of the Levant, this must have had increasing influence on the economy of the steppe. Another point of significance is the size of the steppic periphery. There is evidence for a decline in population in the Negev and Sinai following the demise of the gateway city of Arad (Rosen 2002) in the Early Bronze Age, which Rosen suggests is linked to nomadic dependence. According to Lancaster the options of the North Arabian steppe dwellers were much wider, encompassing an extensive range of peripheral links with great variations in economy, social organization and environment. Failure of one key economic partnership still left many other possibilities to explore.

REFERENCES

Akazawa, T.

1979   Flint Factory Sites in Palmyra Basin. In K. Hanihara and T. Akazawa (eds.), *Paleolithic Site of Douara Cave and Paleo-geography of Palmyra Basin in Syria II*. Tokyo, University Museum: pp. 177–200.

al-Moslimany, A.

1994   Evidence of Early Holocene Summer Precipitation in the Continental Middle East. In O. Bar-Yosef and R. Kra (eds.), *Late Quaternary Chronology and Paleoclimates of the Eastern Mediterranean*. Tucson, Radiocarbon: pp. 121–145.

Banning, E. B., D. Rahimi and J. Siggers

1994   The Late Neolithic of the Southern Levant: Hiatus, Settlement Shift, or Observer Bias? The Perspective from Wadi Ziqlab. *Paléorient 20*: 2, pp. 151–164.

Bar-Yosef, O.

2002   Early Egypt and the Agricultural Dispersals. In H.-G. Gebel, B. D. Hermansen and C. H. Jensen (eds.), *Magic Practices and Ritual in the Near Eastern Neolithic*. Berlin, Ex Oriente: pp. 49–66.

Betts, A. V. G.

1987   Recent Discoveries Relating to the Neolithic Periods in Eastern Jordan. In A. Hadidi (ed.), *Studies in the History and Archaeology of Jordan, Volume 3*. London, Routledge and Kegan Paul: pp. 225–230.

Betts, A. V. G. and S. W. Helms

1987   A Preliminary Survey of Late Neolithic Settlements at el-Ghirqa, Eastern Jordan. *Proceedings of the Prehistoric Society 53*: pp. 327–336.

1993   The Neolithic Sequence in the East Jordan Badia: A Preliminary Overview. *Paléorient 19*: 1, pp. 43–54.

Betts, A. V. G., S. Colledge, L. Martin, C. McCartney, K. Wright and V. Yagodin

1998   *The Harra and the Hamad: Excavations and Explorations in Eastern Jordan, Volume 1*. Sheffield, Sheffield Academic Press.

Betts A., S. Helms, W. Lancaster, E. Jones, A. Lupton, L. Martin, and F. Matsaert

1990   The Burqu'/Ruweishid Project: Preliminary Report on the 1988 Field Season. *Levant 22*: pp. 1–20.

1991   The Burqu'/Ruweishid Project: Preliminary Report on the 1989 Field Season. *Levant 23*: pp. 7–28.

Byrd, B.

1992   The Dispersal of Food Production Across the Levant. In A. Gebauer and T. Price (eds.), *Transitions to Agriculture in Prehistory*. Madison, Prehistory Press: pp. 49–61.

Ducos, P.

1993   Proto-élevage et élevage au Levant sud au VIIe millénaire B.C.: Les données de la Damascène. *Paléorient 19*: 1, pp. 153–173.

Garfinkel, Y.

1993   The Yarmukian Culture in Israel. *Paléorient 19*: 1, pp. 115–134.

Garrard, A. N., D. Baird and B. Byrd

1994a   The Chronological Basis and Significance of the Late Paleolithic and Neolithic Sequence in the Azraq Basin, Jordan. In O. Bar-Yosef and R. S. Kra (eds.), *Late Quaternary Chronology and Paleoclimates of the Eastern Mediterranean*. Tucson, American School of Prehistoric Research: pp. 177–199.

Garrard, A. N., D. Baird, S. Colledge, L. Martin and K. Wright

1994b   Prehistoric Environment and Settlement in the Azraq Basin: An Interim Report on the 1987 and 1988 Excavation Seasons. *Levant 26*: pp. 73–109.

Garrard, A. N., S. Colledge and L. Martin

1996   The Emergence of Crop Cultivation and Caprine Herding in the 'Marginal Zone' of the Southern Levant. In D. Harris (ed.), *The Origins and Spread of Agriculture and Pastoralism in Eurasia*. London, University College London: pp. 204–226.

Garrod, D.

1960   The Flint Implements. In H. Field, *North Arabian Desert Archaeological Survey, 1925–50*. Cambridge, Peabody Museum: pp. 111–124.

Gopher, A.

1993   Sixth–Fifth Millennia B.C. Settlements in the Coastal Plain, Israel. *Paléorient 19*: 1, pp. 55–63.

Gopher, A. and R. Gophna

1993   Cultures of the Eighth and Seventh Millennia B.P. in the Southern Levant. A Review for the 1990's. *Journal of World Prehistory* 7: 3, pp. 297–363.

Horwitz, L., E. Tchernov, P. Ducos, C. Becker, A. Von den Driesch, L. Martin and A. Garrard

1999   Animal Domestication in the Southern Levant. *Paléorient 25*: 2, pp. 63–80.

Ingold, T.

1980   *Hunters, Pastoralists, and Ranchers*. Cambridge, Cambridge University Press.

Issar, A.

1998   Climate Change and History During the Holocene in the Eastern Mediterranean Region. In A. Issar and N. Brown (eds.), *Water, Environment, and Society in Times of Climatic Change*. Dordrecht, Kluwer: pp. 113–128.

Kafafi, Z.

1993   The Yarmoukians in Jordan. *Paléorient* 19: 1, pp. 101–114.

Kenyon, K.

1957   *Digging up Jericho*. London, Benn.

Köhler-Rollefson, I.

1988   The Aftermath of the Levantine Neolithic Revolution in the Light of Ecological and Ethnographic Evidence. *Paléorient 14*: 1, pp. 87–93.

1989a   Changes in Goat Exploitation at 'Ain Ghazal Between the Early and Late Neolithic: A Metrical Analysis. *Paléorient 15*: 1, pp. 141–146.

1989b   Resolving the Revolution: Late Neolithic Refinements of Economic Strategies in the Eastern Levant. *Archaeozoologia 1*: pp. 201–208.

1992   A Model for the Development of Nomadic Pastoralism on the Transjordanian Plateau. In O. Bar-Yosef and A. Khazanov (eds.), *Pastoralism in the Levant: Archaeological Materials in Anthropological Perspectives*. Madison, Prehistory Press: pp. 11–18.

Kuijt, I. and N. Goring-Morris

2002   Foraging, Farming, and Social Complexity in the Pre-Pottery Neolithic of the Southern Levant: A Review and Synthesis. *Journal of World Prehistory 16*: 4, pp. 361–440.

Lancaster, W.

1981   *The Rwala Bedouin Today*. Cambridge, Cambridge University Press.

Martin, L.
1999   Mammal Remains from the Eastern Jordanian Neolithic and the Nature of Caprine Herding in the Steppe. *Paléorient* 25: 2, 87–104.

McCartney, C. J.
1992   Preliminary Report of the 1989 Excavations at Site 27 of the Burqu'/Ruweishid Project. *Levant 24*: pp. 33–54.

Mellaart, J.
1975   *The Neolithic of the Near East*. London, Thames and Hudson.

Moore, A. M. T.
1985   The Development of Neolithic Societies in the Near East. In A. Close and F. Wendorf (eds.), *Advances in World Archaeology, Volume 4*. New York, Academic Press: pp. 1–70.

Parr, P., J. Zarins, M. Ibrahim, J. Waechter, A. Garrard, C. Clarke, M. Bidmead and al-Badr, H.
1978   Preliminary Report on the Second Phase of the Northern Province Survey 1397/1977. *Atlal 2*: pp. 29–50.

Perrot, J.
1968   *La Préhistoire palestinienne*. Paris, Supplément au Dictionnaire de la Bible.

Peters, J., D. Helmer, A. von den Driesch and M. Saña Segumi
1999   Early Family Husbandry in the Northern Levant. *Paléorient 25*: 2, pp. 27–48.

Rollefson, G. O., Z. Kaechele and J. Kaechele
1982   A Burin Site in the Umm Utheina District, Jabal Amman. *Annual of the Department of Antiquities of Jordan 26*: pp. 243–248.

Rollefson, G. O. and I. Köhler-Rollefson
1989   The Collapse of Early Neolithic Settlements in the Southern Levant. In I. Hershkovitz (ed.), *People and Culture in Change: Proceedings of the Second Symposium on Upper Paleolithic, Mesolithic, and Neolithic Populations of Europe and the Mediterranean Basin*. Oxford, Archaeopress: pp. 73–89.

Rollefson, G. O., A. H. Simmons and Z. Kafafi
1992   Neolithic Cultures at 'Ain Ghazal. *Journal of Field Archaeology 19*: pp. 443–470.

Rosen, A. M.
1998   Early to Mid-Holocene Environmental Changes and Their Impact on Human Communities in Southeastern Anatolia. In A. Issar and N. Brown (eds.), *Water, Environment, and Society in Times of Climatic Change*. Dordrecht, Kluwer: pp. 215–240.

Rosen, S.
2002   The Evolution of Pastoral Nomadic Systems in the Southern Levantine Periphery. In E. van den Brink and E. Yannai (eds.), *In Quest of Ancient*

Settlements and Landscapes: Archaeological Studies in Honour of Ram Gophna. Tel Aviv, Ramot Publishing: pp. 23–44.

Sanlaville, P.

1997   Les changements dans l'environment au Moyen-Orient de 20,000 B.P. à 6,000 B.P. *Paléorient 23*: 2, pp. 249–262.

Stordeur, D.

1993   Sédentaires et nomads du PPNB final dans le desert du Palmyre (Syrie). *Paléorient 19*: 11, pp. 187–204.

2000   *El Kowm 2: Une île dans le desert.* Paris, CNRS.

Wasse, A.

2000   *The Development of Goat and Sheep Herding During the Levantine Neolithic.* University College London (PhD dissertation).

CHAPTER 3

AN ARCHAEOLOGY OF
MULTISITED COMMUNITIES

REINHARD BERNBECK[1]

I N THE BIBLICAL story describing Jacob's fate under his father-in-law, Laban, we read: "And Laban set three days journey betwixt himself and Jacob; and Jacob fed the rest of Laban's flocks" (Genesis 30:38). This suggests that Jacob and Laban lived in a spatially dispersed, partly mobile community. Nowhere, however, in the archaeological record of the ancient Near East are such conditions recognized. In this chapter I argue that our sense of communities as social units with strong spatial limits is inadequate. Instead of considering all suprahousehold communities as imagined (Anderson 1991:6), I argue that dispersed, multisited communities are founded on a specific practice, namely mobility. Such an idea could be of importance for 'community' studies in general and for Near Eastern archaeology and history in particular (Canuto and Yaeger 2000). It provides a caveat against reconstructions of social, political or economic processes that are based on a sharp divide between sedentary and mobile populations.

The idea of dispersed communities is not new. Barth (1973), in a treatise on mobile lifestyles, maintained that the multifarious lifeways between full mobility and complete sedentariness can be subdivided into three major categories, based on subsistence activities: 'mixed economies' of herding and agriculture in which all households perform all subsistence tasks in a nonspecialized manner, with relatively low mobility; 'integrated communities' with two segments, one focusing on herding, the other on agriculture; and 'fully separate' herding and agricultural communities, whereby the sedentary and the mobile communities have formal exchange relations. Barth's 'integrated communities' are spatially dispersed groups that are, by necessity, mobile to a certain extent. Anthropology has since shifted its focus, and we find a starkly different view of mobility exemplified in writings about transnational migration, diaspora and refugees (Clifford 1994;

[1.] Thanks are due to Steve A. Rosen and Henry T. Wright for discussions of an early version of this chapter. Geoff Emberling, Gabriela Castro-Gessner, Susan Pollock and Marc Verhoeven gave extensive and essential critiques that improved this chapter throughout.

Table 3.1. Traditional and Current Views of Mobile Groups:

	Traditional view of mobility	Current view of mobility
Moves	Regular, frequent	Infrequent, mostly singular
Reason for moving	Environment	Political enforcement
Goal	Adaptation	Refuge, survival
Expectations	Continuity of moves	Return to origin
Long-term status of migrants	Mobile	Sedentary
Social structure of migrants	Long-term fixed relations	Expediently constituted
Typical groups	Nomads, hunter-gatherers	Diasporic groups, refugees

Lavie and Swedenburg 1996; Daniel 2002). In current anthropology, migrations are described as movements through space, with a result of community dispersal. Displaced people are assumed to live in a continued state of tension. Past experience of a specific origin, or imagined origin, results in the expectation of a return. Cultural anthropology's shift in mobility studies has gone from a 'habitual' to an 'enforced' idea of mobility (Table 3.1). Events of the recent past, and the concomitant creation of *homines sacri* (those who are outside of any social order), fully warrant such a change (Agamben 1998).

Recently, Goldstein (2000) and Preucel and Meskell (2004:221–222) have suggested that ideas such as diaspora are apposite for an understanding of mobility in many past societies. This notion may be adequate to some extent, especially in historical archaeology, but it seems that mobility is too often treated from a 'sedentarocentrist' perspective, which assumes that movement through space is an undesirable state for any community. I will show that mobility and the dispersed, multisited constitution of communities can be a long-term way of life, without any inherent undesirability. I approach the issue of multisited communities and mobility in four steps. First, since I deal with a case from the ancient Near East, I will present a number of reasons for the focus among students of the Near East on either completely mobile or completely sedentary ways of life, and I will examine the restrictive ideas that underlie terms such as *mobility* in this field of research. Next, I discuss methods for empirical analyses of semisedentary and semimobile lifestyles, as well as their temporal scales. Third, I will show, by way of an example from the 6th millennium BCE site of Fıstıklı Höyük in southeast Turkey, how long-term routines or a 'sequential organization' (Walker 2002:164) can be identified archaeologically. Finally, a few indications from Fıstıklı Höyük and surroundings make it possible to reconstruct the dynamics of the multisited community of which Fıstıklı Höyük was one component. My interpretation of the evidence from Fıstıklı Höyük raises a number of questions on theoretical, methodological and practical levels that warrant further investigations. I conclude that multisited communities may have been more widespread than we imagine.

THE MOBILE-SEDENTARY DICHOTOMY

Near Eastern archaeologists and historians, and to a lesser extent also cultural anthropologists, have produced an image of past lifestyles as a stark, unrealistic dichotomy of almost unconnected mobile and sedentary groups. Reasons for this perception include the practices of fieldwork, analogical reasoning and ethnoarchaeology in the Near East, ancient historical sources, Orientalist literature and a simplifying historiography. The following discussion will briefly address these problems.

The structures that govern archaeological fieldwork have an unacknowledged impact on constructions of communities and the complex interplay between sedentary and mobile groups. This is especially the case for scholars based in Western countries. Excavations led by Western archaeologists are almost invariably restricted to a specific time of the year, mainly early summer to early fall. Thus, mobility in winter, when villagers move to towns and cities in search of menial labor, are not experienced. In addition, the physical aspects of fieldwork play into an overly stable perception of village populations, as fieldwork depends on support by relatively sedentary workers. Typically, an employer-laborer relation between researchers and local people develops that shows signs of hire-and-fire politics, including particularly the selection of laborers who show up consistently for work. The idea of the stable, steadily working villager is the result of Western archaeologists' powerful position, which enables them largely to determine relations of production in fieldwork. This working situation is geared toward optimizing the relation between financial resources and scientific results and inhibits close communication with people who pick up work one day and drop it when they see no need for further wages (Bernbeck and Pollock 2004:371–372; Steele 2005:50–52; Pollock, forth.). This dichotomized perspective is reinforced by chance encounters of archaeologists with nonsedentary people. Such encounters occur often on a purely visual basis. On travels, 'nomads' may be identified as those who live in black tents and raise livestock. The construction of a fundamental divide between sedentary people, who depend on agriculture, and pastoral nomads is at least in part due to practical matters of fieldwork combined with ad hoc 'evidential experience' of nomadism. While such impressions may not be explicitly inserted in archaeological interpretations, they have a deep influence on dispositions toward certain kinds of archaeological narratives and against others.

A second factor that influences our mangled perception of the lifeways of 'integrated,' often semisedentary communities in the ancient Near East is analogical reasoning. In its presentist logic this kind of argument produces results similar to those of archaeological praxis, again conflating mobility and pastoral nomadism. There are, however, many ways to construct analogies. In the case of ancient Near Eastern mobility, archaeologists have employed them in an unsystematic fashion. Even a brief overview shows that a mixture of 'historical' and 'formal' analogies prevails (for terminology see Wylie 1985; Bernbeck 1997:85–108). Methodologically, a well-developed historical analogy would constitute a connection between an 'ethnographic present' and a past. Such historical continuity needs to be firmly established in an 'upstreaming' method before resorting to analogical reasoning (Stahl 2001:27–31). When present-day Near Eastern nomadic groups are used as a foil for the past (Hole 1980; Zagarell 1982; Alizadeh 2003), however, the historical continuity is almost invariably assumed rather than researched, and some features typical of modern times are omitted (Gilbert 1975). Geographers such as de Planhol (1968) and Ehlers (1980:154–161) have shown that present Iranian nomadic structures are the result of the Turko-Tartar invasions of the medieval ages (around 1000–1500 CE), while earlier nonpermanent ways of life were characterized by short-range semimobility. There is no direct continuity between Near Eastern prehistoric populations and present-day nomads. A basic condition for historical analogies is missing. Another kind of analogy, dubbed 'formal' by Wylie (1985), is based on an assumption of similarities in environment and technology between present and past. Where identified, the goal of the analogy is to search systematically for recurring characteristics among present and past groups. In such cases one often comes across simplifying assumptions of an 'insignificant' change in natural conditions between past and present (as in Bernbeck 1993). Again, the precondition of some initial similarities between source and subject sides of an analogy are more assumed than researched. For present mobile groups the source side, systematic research using the Human Relations Area Files or the Standard Cross-Cultural Sample (Murdock and White 1969), is rare.[2] One more often encounters anecdotal citations from one or the other present tribe that lives in the same subregion of the Near East as the archaeological mobile group. The closer these subregional connections, the greater the danger is for ecodeterministic arguments, equating similar environments with similar lifeways (Hole 1980).

Analogies have become what Wobst (1978) termed the "tyranny of the ethnographic record," especially in research on past mobility, and this is despite their unsystematic and highly inconsistent use. The reason for such a state of affairs is an unwarranted assumption according to which groups that were not fully sedentary have left only skimpy, unintelligible archaeological remains. In contrast to sedentary village or city life, mobile groups are thought to have

[2] Both standardized data sets of ethnographic sources have been rightly criticized for inherent biases (Conkey and Gero 1991:13–14).

always and everywhere possessed minimal material culture. The underlying idea, again equating mobile life with pastoral nomads as we know them today, leads to further assumptions, for instance that mobile people lived in tents and did not stay for long at any single place (but see Hole 1978:149). While ethno-archaeological research has revealed that even tent dwellers produce significant material remains (Aurenche 1984; Banning and Köhler-Rollefson 1986; Simms 1988; Cribb 1991), ethno-archaeology has focused too much on the analysis of taphonomic detail, site-formation processes and postoccupational documentation of present nomad camps and not enough on the primary task of this field: the investigation of connections between material culture and social practices (David and Kramer 2001:6–14).[3]

Such a state of affairs cries out for the abandonment of analogical reasoning when dealing with past mobile groups (Khazanov 1994:xli). Outside the Near East, geographers and anthropologists have documented a continuum between fully sedentary and fully mobile lifeways. Furthermore, mobility cannot be isolated from a host of other factors such as subsistence strategies, social relations, traditional practices, economic structures, the natural environment and rhythms of life. Mobility and sedentariness need to be inserted into a complex past reality. Linear correlations with one specific factor, especially the adaptationist idea of an increasing length of stay in one place associated with a growing reliance on plant resources rather than animals, do not suffice (Cribb 1991:16). The combining of these two factors, permanence and degree of reliance on plant resources, with linear sociopolitical evolutionism has further reified these anthropological constructs (Sadr 1991:9–11). Such schemes are insufficient because of their restriction of past reality to a few aspects of lifeways and an assumption of simple correlations. There is no place for groups that move their settlements every three to four years (Trigger 1968:56), or for groups in which a few people stay all year-round in a settlement while a substantial part of the population moves out to pursue some kind of subsistence or other activities in a distant location, or for combinations of these. I argue that such elements as partial mobility and spatiotemporal scales of mobility render any categorization based on a linear relationship between poles of mobile to sedentary, agricultural to nomadic, egalitarian to hierarchical unrealistically reductive (Hütteroth 1959; Khazanov 1994:17–25). It follows that a more historical approach to past people's

---

[3.] Despite this criticism of Near Eastern research on mobility, a lot of highly commendable work has been done. This is especially true of recent methods for the identification of seasonality, such as bone isotope analysis (Mashkour 2003) and dental cementum increment analysis (Lieberman 1998). Much of the sophisticated research on the mobility issue is, however, restricted to the Paleolithic and the transition to the Neolithic and focuses almost entirely on aspects of seasonality.

community life is needed and that we have to develop methods that enable us to investigate mobility patterns empirically in the archaeological record.

For an empirical approach to ancient Near Eastern nomadism we are not restricted to archaeological sources. There are ample written documents that mention populations that were not completely sedentary, but written sources cannot be taken at face value (Burstein, this volume). Painstaking investigations into political and ideological circumstances of writing, the scribes, vocabulary meanings and undertones as well as the intent of the documents, need to be taken into account before they can be integrated into a narrative of ancient Near Eastern history. One fundamental bias can never be treated adequately: written sources are the product of sedentary, almost invariably urban, people who not only take an external standpoint when describing mobile populations but also tend to be socially and geographically distant from them (Scholz 1995:50). Overall, written sources from Classical antiquity only contribute to the above-mentioned dichotomy between the 'Desert and the Sown.' Ancient Greek sources depict nonsedentary people in Western Asia as 'barbarian' and 'aggressive' (Briant 1982:19–25). This perspective was anything but new. Older Sumerian and Akkadian texts, although devoid of words for sedentary people and nomads alike, use descriptions such as "those in the steppe" or "the inhabitants of tents" to describe nonsedentary lifestyles (Klengel 1972:17; Szuchman, this volume). Literary texts, for instance the hymn 'Dumuzi and Enkidu,' juxtapose shepherd and farmer in a normative way.[4] The epic of Gilgamesh opposes a civilized urban hero to his wild, bad-mannered counterpart, Enkidu, who lives among animals (Kovacs 1989). Historical inscriptions refer to nonurban groups by using ethnonyms such as Guti, Yaminites and Hanaeans. The problem is that they are known to us from an urban, upper-class scribal perspective and are depicted as wild and basically anarchic. For instance, urban sources on early second millennium BCE Amorite tribes of the Mesopotamian desert depict them as "enemies of the gods," who do not know "ritual or law" and "eat raw meat" (Buccellati 1966:230–232, this volume; Kirsch and Larsen 1996:151). These texts have left their marks on numerous Assyriological interpretations that speak about "waves of invasion" (Winckler 1905), or 'infiltration' of the settled lands by *'reservoirs inépuisables'* of nomads (Kupper 1957), or of *"peuplades . . . turbulentes et pillardes en quête de butin"* (Dossin 1939:995). The derogatory tone of the ancient scribal products has been given an additional Orientalist twist by highly inappropriate translations that use terms such as *sheikh* for the Akkadian word *abu*, suggesting an ahistorical social structure from the second millennium BCE to the ethnographic present (Klengel 1958–59:217; Edzard 1959).

---

[4] *Dumuzid and Enkimdu.* ETCSL translation: t.4.08.33 at http://etcsl.orinst.ox.ac.uk/cgi-bin/etcslmac.ccgi?text=t.4.08.33# (accessed 10 Dec. 2004).

Orientalist literature by travelers, theologians, diplomats and military personnel from the last few centuries adds another problematic dimension to the reconstruction of mobile lifestyles in the archaeological record, reinforcing the impression of a gulf between sedentary and mobile populations. Such travelogs are readily referenced by European archaeologists and function as evidence for a 'timeless' past. The stock of writers cited covers the 18th-20th centuries CE (Niebuhr 1776–80; Musil 1908; Morier 1837; Oppenheim 1939). The implicit logic in citing such works is that before a firm grip of European colonial empires on the Middle East, local people, and especially nonurban people, had no history.

While the polemics of ancient Mesopotamian scribes are nowadays treated in a more sophisticated fashion (Nissen 1980; Buccellati 1990), the general imparted knowledge of the existence of nonsedentary populations in ancient Western Asia has led to problems in historical narratives that work on grand scales, especially those that put a heavy emphasis on long-term demographic trends. The best known works of this kind are survey interpretations of the Mesopotamian lowlands and southwest Iran (Adams and Nissen 1972; Gibson 1972; Johnson 1973; Adams 1981; Wright 1981). Interpretations of aggregate settlement data often resort to nomadism and mobility, as well as the opposite effect of sedentarization as a convenient *deus ex machina* whenever a sudden decrease or increase in sedentary populations cannot be easily explained otherwise (Luke 1965:22). As need be, it is assumed that either nomads settled down or that villagers "voted with their feet" (Johnson 1987:126–127; Grewe 2002:183).

The combination of analogical reasoning, highly biased texts, their uncritical use, and negative demographic evidence as a way of smoothing over discerned abrupt transitions produces a highly biased past of nonsedentary groups. I advocate a more cautious use and interpretation of the mentioned past sources and present evidence, concomitant with a much greater emphasis than hitherto presented on historically specific, archaeological evidence of nonsedentary people. In this way we may obtain a broader view of past ways of living, and dissolve the unfortunate dichotomy of the 'Desert and the Sown'. Past life-ways may have been much more diverse than the limited range documented in historical and ethnographic sources reveals.

ARCHAEOLOGICAL INDICATORS OF MOBILITY

The archaeology of Neolithic and other food-producing societies is, inde-pendently of theoretical orientation, focused on sedentariness. Processual archaeology has always assumed a drive toward sedentariness, based on adaptationist arguments and their underlying instrumentalist reasoning. Such writings speak less about sedentariness, or degrees of sedentariness, than of 'sedentarization,' assuming that the process is inevitable and almost irreversible (Rafferty 1985:113–127; Garel 2004:75–76). Postprocessual archaeologists have their own sedentarocentrist blinkers. A focus on the house as a 'home,' full of connotations of personal protection and (assumed) biographic detail (Hodder 1991; Watkins 1990); on landscape, 'placemaking' and anchoring identities (Preucel and Meskell 2004); and on memory as embedded in constructed landscapes (Pauketat and Alt 2003) is formulated from an implicitly sedentarocentrist perspective. Cultural anthropologists go even as far as suggesting that a lack of movement may amount to resistance (Clifford 1997). Mobility is thus treated for what it is, an ephemeral, passing way of life, while quotidian sedentary life, just as ephemeral, is functionalized and monumentalized.

To investigate mobility, a review of the restricted use of the term in research on the ancient Near East is in order. Most treatises contain three assumptions. First, patterns of movement involve all members of a social group, frequently conceived of as a small community. Second, mobility is seasonal and occurs two or more times per year, while especially longer-term mobility is neglected (Bar-Yosef and Rocek 1998:2–3). Third, and connected to the two other points, evidence for year-round use of a site, derived from faunal and archaeobotanical data, is equated with sedentariness, although this is only a necessary but not a sufficient condition. Unless an intricate spatial analysis is performed, such evidence means no more than that parts of a community were present year-round (Zeder 1994:110–112; Grigson 2003:229).

The idea of a group's dependency on annual or more frequent moves alone does not capture all forms of mobility since it can also work on larger time scales, as is evident from ethnographies (James 1979; Rivière 1995:197–199) and research on the central European Neolithic, for example at Bylany or the Aldenhovener Platte (Soudsky 1969; Lüning 1988). In the latter cases, subsistence-based archaeological indicators of mobility fail because they are geared solely toward seasonality, not toward a system closer to 'swidden' agriculture. Other archaeological indicators are available, however, and have sometimes been used. Large-scale excavations of entire settlement systems are at the basis of the European Neolithic studies mentioned above. In southwestern American archaeology, site size, artifact density, the ratio of internal to external space or the placement of midden areas are taken as correlates for relative mobility (Powell 1983; Rocek 1998:210). The problem with such general measurements is that they allow an assessment of degrees of mobility only by comparison, on a very general level that does not lead to the identification of historically specific practices of mobility.

I propose here that the interpretation of stratigraphies holds much potential to contribute to investigations of long-term mobility if interpreted in the spirit of Walker's (2002) "sequential organization."[5] Archaeological dogma considers that stratigraphies are particular to sites or even single excavation units and that stratigraphic events are random (Ford, cited in Walker 2002). The underlying assumption is that stratigraphies are the result of an entangled mixture of large-scale to small-scale accidental events, ranging from volcanic eruptions and wars to more continuous processes, such as decay and the detritus of quotidian practices of inhabiting a place. The interpretation of stratigraphy, therefore, serves almost always a purely archaeological, comparative purpose, namely the establishment of a sitewide or regional chronology. The sole focus on chronology as well as 'stratigraphic particularism' denies the possibility that stratigraphic sequences could follow a culturally specific diachronic chain of practices that is based on habitual 'life cycles' of inhabiting houses, compounds or whole sites (but see Pauketat 2000; Tringham 2000; Joyce 2004). In a burgeoning 'site abandonment literature' (Cameron 1991; Cameron and Tomka 1993; LaMotta and Schiffer 1999:22–25), however, it is becoming clear that the sudden end of a site or a stratum is not always and necessarily due to site-external forces, whether natural or human. Apart from well-documented ethnographic and archaeological instances of ritual house abandonment from the New World (Walker and Lucero 2000:131–133), similar processes of deliberate abandonment and house burning are read into the evidence from Neolithic sites from southeastern Europe and western Asia (Stevanovi 1997; Campbell 2000; Verhoeven 2000). Most of these events are explained as stages in the life cycle of houses, where the 'death' of a house is intentionally marked, most often by a violent fire.

This is just a beginning in a necessary change in our understanding of stratigraphy as actively produced by site inhabitants. I would extend such interpretations in three directions. First, the focus on house abandonment as a crucial point in the 'life' of a structure overemphasizes one kind of a *rite de passage* of houses. Indeed, the whole 'life history' of buildings should rather be conceptualized according to Kopytoff's (1986) notion of "cultural biography" (Tringham 2000). House trajectories of founding, first use, remaking and finally abandonment are in many societies conceptualized as a mirror of personal biographies or kin-group cycles, and that may well be valid for the past, too (Carsten and Hugh-Jones 1995:39–42). Second, the notion of a biography may apply not only to houses but also to whole sites (Bernbeck

<hr>

[5.] Walker's article on stratigraphy has a terminological flaw: his notion of 'practical reason' is in no way compatible with the general one developed since Kant and applied by social scientists such as Bourdieu. What Walker means by the term is what Horkheimer and Adorno (1989), following in part Max Weber, called 'instrumental reason.'

et al. 2003). In distinction to Kopytoff's 'biographies,' which are based on a one-dimensional, temporal sequencing of contexts of objects, biographies of sites or houses cannot and should not be disentangled from human practices (Joyce and Hendon 2000:155–157). It is rather the dialectical relation between spatial structures and practices that is at the core of such 'biographies.' With regard to entire sites, both foundation and abandonment are still almost invariably envisioned in terms of instrumental reasoning. Sites are founded by groups splitting off from others because of 'scalar stress' (Johnson 1982), resource depletion or other external factors (Bandy 2004) but not because of an unquestioned and unquestionable past and its associated practices. Third, the leap from an analysis of specific processes, such as household cycles (Pfälzner 2001:384–393), to the search for 'typical' biographies, from stratigraphies as a series of singular practices to the inference of practices that constitute recursive sequences, should be part and parcel of any interpretation of the archaeological record. I maintain that, if identifiable, Weberian 'ideal types,' whether of actions or of whole stratigraphies, serve an important heuristic function. As Walker (2002:166) suggests, carefully recorded and evaluated stratigraphies may be representative (socially, temporally and spatially) of a wider realm. In those cases where sequential events transcend discrete deposits, they are part of a past habitus.

Barrett (2000:62–65) has opposed such 'representational' arguments, suggesting an archaeology that is in all aspects particularistic and concerned with concrete situations. Such a reduction of human anticipatory faculties to an immediate future, however, a future that is almost present, reduces past human beings to animals with a practical consciousness. Such beings are caricatures, able to act on their immediate spatial and temporal context without reflexive foresight and oversight (Bernbeck 2003:46). I will try to show by way of a concrete case how a single-site stratigraphy allows the establishment of a site 'biography,' and that an extension beyond it to a whole region allows us to conceptualize the dialectics of mobility and multisited communities.

THE CASE STUDY OF FISTIKLI HÖYÜK

The stratigraphy of Fıstıklı Höyük, a small hamlet from the Halaf period in southeast Turkey, serves as an example for how the biography of a site allows the construction of mobility practices. The Halaf tradition (commonly called a 'culture') dates to the sixth millennium BCE and has sometimes been interpreted as the first hierarchical society in the ancient Near East. Recent work at several Halaf sites indicates a considerable degree of mobility. From the burned remains of a very early Halaf site, Sabi Abyad, archaeologists have concluded that storage buildings were the repositories for the goods of a nonsedentary component of the population (Akkermans and Duistermaat 1997; Verhoeven 1999:203–232). At later Kazane Höyük and sites in the Balikh Valley in Syria, there is evidence for shifting, consecutive settlements that result in a large palimpsest composed of numerous small archaeological sites (Akkermans 1993:163-165; Bernbeck et al. 1999; Akkermans et al. 2006). Investigators have remarked on the generally short occupation span of many Halaf settlements, and the lack of architecture has often been interpreted as evidence for a temporary camp (Hole and Johnson 1986-87:184; Akkermans and Schwartz 2003:119-120, 127; Marfoe et al 2003; Cruells 2004:29). These recent findings cast doubt on earlier assumptions of a hierarchical, sedentary society with a high degree of craft specialization (LeBlanc and Watson 1973; Watson 1983; Campbell et al. 1999).

Fıstıklı Höyük is located at the eastern edge of the wide Euphrates river valley in southeast Turkey, on a small natural elevation (Figure 3.1). It has a shallow stratigraphy no more than 1.5 m deep. Fieldwork at this half-hectare site was undertaken in 1999 and 2000 (Pollock et al. 2001; Bernbeck et al. 2002; Bernbeck et al. 2003). Our initial plans were to investigate seasonal mobility through a detailed spatial analysis of faunal and archaeobotanical remains.

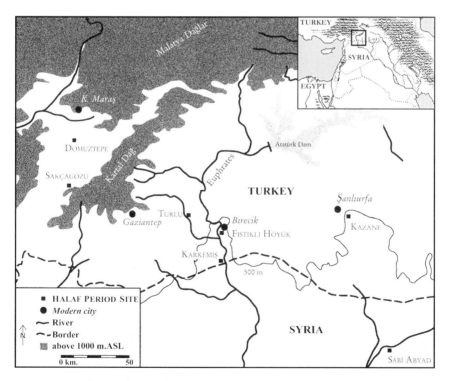

Figure 3.1. Map showing the sites of the Halaf tradition mentioned in the text.

This part of our project is still underway, but longer-term site development provides highly relevant insights into mobility beyond such seasonal patterns. Since Fıstıklı Höyük is both shallow and small, we were able to excavate an estimated 14% of the whole settlement, with 33% of the central area and 8% of its periphery (Figure 3.2). Because of this unusually large percentage of excavated surface, we are confident that the sequence of structures discovered reflects the general 'biography' of the site.

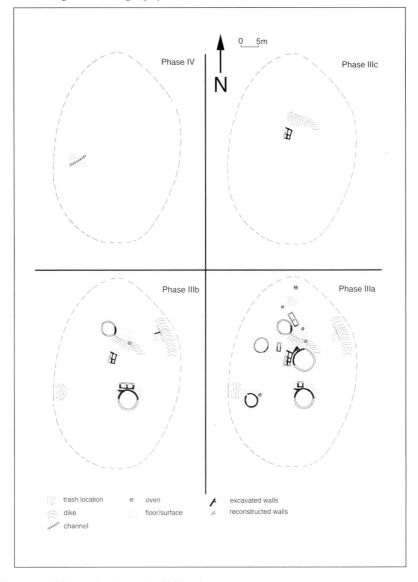

Figure 3.2. Habitation by phase at Fıstıklı Höyük.

Table 3.2. Phases and Their Absolute Dates at Fıstıklı Höyük:

Phase	Date (1σ)[a]	Date (2σ)[a]	Maximum range	Number of samples
IIIx	—	—	5520–5320	2
IIIa	5788–5738	5840–5730	5880–5560	9
IIIb	5780–5733	5800–5725	5800–5660	2
IIIc	5980–5840	5990–5800	5990–5800	2
IV	—	—	—	0

[a] Combined dates per phase.

Despite the shortness of its occupation, Fıstıklı Höyük has a complex stratigraphy. As the site was covered with trees, stratigraphic sequences of separate excavation units could not be linked unequivocally by means of profiles. We therefore used pottery seriation (based on the Robinson coefficient of similarity; Shennan 1988:191–193) to integrate all well-stratified contexts from different units into a single developmental scheme. We used some 13,000 sherds for this purpose. Phase definitions are based on diachronic similarity coefficients, where low coefficients serve as phase dividers. Based on the seriation results, we defined four major phases for the Halaf period at Fıstıklı Höyük, with IV as the oldest, followed by IIIc, IIIb and IIIa (Table 3.2). These phases correlate well with available radiocarbon dates, which were combined by phase for the purpose of comparison with the relative stratigraphy (Bernbeck et al. 2003:17–23).

There are two additional samples that are approximately 400 years later (Bernbeck et al. 2003). At present we have no secure archaeological remains for a Late Halaf phase IIIx of the site and need to investigate in more detail the contexts from which these samples come. There are parallels to later revisiting of other Halaf and Halaf-related sites such as Arjoune (Gowlett 2003), Damishliyya and Umm Qseir (Akkermans and Schwartz 2003:120). The evidence of stratigraphy and of relative and absolute dating provides the framework for a reconstruction of a 'sequential organization.' Initially, in phase IV, Fıstıklı Höyük was used as a tent camp.[6] In this phase the only alteration of the natural rise on which the site was founded consisted of pits and a small ditch, which likely served to divert runoff water from the site. In the subsequent phase IIIc, a small cell-plan building was constructed on the summit of the small hill, prior to any major habitation structure. Such cellular buildings have a long tradition as storage buildings in earlier periods (Kirkbride 1982; Bernbeck

---

[6] Positive evidence for tents consists solely in a few charred wooden sticks driven into a surface and the spatial arrangement of the pits. These remains are typical for the earliest levels of many prehistoric Near Eastern sites, such as Matarrah or Tepe Sarab, and indicate a temporary use of a site that later turned more permanent.

1994:242–243). Associated with this structure was a construction similar to a dike, which we interpret as protecting the storage building from runoff.

In a next step, in phase IIIb, a second dike was built on the eastern limits of the site. Prevention of water damage seems to have been a major concern of the inhabitants of Fıstıklı Höyük, and there was enough foresight to build such structures before any single house. These large structures were likely erected by a group of people larger than a single household, and we may therefore assume that the slow settling in of a community was a 'project' in a Husserlian sense, a practical activity with foresight and planning. Then, two large round 'tholoi,' as the habitation structures of the Halaf tradition are called, were erected. They were located far from each other and, judging by the proximity of storage buildings, each tholos had its own storage unit. We may therefore assume that the social groups that were living in each house stored their products separately.[7]

At the end of this phase a garbage dump was created at the western edge of the site.[8] Since this is the one major space for disposal of garbage that we found, we can again assume a certain amount of intracommunity agreement on its location. An oven, which may have been used communally, was set up on one of the dikes. At Fıstıklı Höyük such ovens likely served to parch grain and turn it into storable material (Clayton 2004). In this early phase of settling in at a site, the detailed reconstruction hints at practical activities that were likely discursively agreed on, such as communal structures, as well as other aspects that served to reproduce an unquestioned and unquestionable lifeworld, such as the specific and standardized forms of cellular storage buildings and round habitation structures.

The next phase, IIIa, is when Fıstıklı Höyük reached is apogee, becoming what we call a 'focal site.' With minimally five tholoi or living structures (Table 3.3), the population was much larger than in the previous phase. The richness of cultural debris was much greater as well, although this might be due in part to sampling bias.[9] This phase, although short in absolute years, consists of an intricate sequence of establishments and abandonment of structures and installations. From the substantial structures that were both newly constructed and repaired, it is clear that some people at least lived for a multiyear duration

---

[7] This does not mean that productive or consumption practices were as segregated. To the contrary, there are good indications that such activities were largely carried out outside of houses in communally accessible areas.

[8] The development of spatially segregated garbage dumps is sometimes claimed as an indicator of semi- or full sedentariness (Panja 2003:115–116).

[9] The excavated volume of phase IIIa deposits is many times larger than that of any other phase.

Table 3.3. Structures and Installations in Use During Each Phase of Occupation at Fıstıklı Höyük:

Phase	Number of tholoi	Number of ovens	Number of storage structures	Ratio of ovens to storage structures
IIIa	5	5	6	1.14
IIIb	2	1	2	0.50
IIIc	0	0	1	0.00
IV	0	0	0	—

at Fıstıklı Höyük. Early in phase IIIa, a small, nonresidential round building was added in the western part of the site, as well as two large tholoi: one in the center, another near the garbage dump. The storage unit of one tholos decreased in size, likely because of less need for such a space because of decreasing numbers of people in that household. Soon after, two more storage buildings were added to the northernmost tholoi at the site, and the old storage building in the center was substantially repaired and extended by at least two rooms. Another tholos was built near the garbage dump. North of the tholoi, a large outside working space with an oven was used intensely. Two other ovens were constructed nearer to the tholoi and the settlement center.

Finally, the site was slowly abandoned, apparently beginning with the entire southern half. In this abandonment process three tholoi disappeared. Between the central one and its large storage structure, a painted vessel was smashed on the final surface. After these events two tholoi were still in use, with only one storage building and three ovens. If the ovens served to process grain into a storable material, this might indicate that fields around the site were still harvested but that the processed food was at least partly stored elsewhere, likely at another site established by people who had moved away from Fıstıklı Höyük. During a final phase IIIx that dates several hundred years later and for which we have so far only radiocarbon dates from problematic contexts, the site, after having been abandoned, was visited again seasonally by a group that did not leave any permanent structures.

To summarize this architectural sequence (Bernbeck et al. 2003), the evidence points toward an early ephemeral use of Fıstıklı Höyük as a location for a camp, then a more substantial, but still temporary, use during which goods were stored at the site, likely leading to sojourns that were longer than before. A relatively permanent establishment of people at the site happened in phase IIIb, which quickly evolved into a full-blown, densely inhabited settlement in the following phase, IIIa. At the end of this phase slow abandonment set in, during which some households stayed while others came back from an unknown new location to process agricultural products that were no longer stored at the site.

PHYTOLITHS AND STONE TOOLS

The sequence outlined above can be supported by other evidence. I restrict myself here to the results of phytolith analyses and some tools that were used in the processing of animals and plants. Among the 40 soil samples from Fıstıklı Höyük that have been analyzed for phytoliths, 26 are from well-stratified contexts (Hassan 2002). Admittedly, interpretive conclusions drawn from such a small sample must remain tentative and acquire their value only in connection with other results that point in a similar direction. Phytoliths from wheat and barley husks occur in variable amounts in these samples. A rough classification into low (including zero), medium and high densities of such phytoliths produces a clear result. Only the latest phase, IIIa, contains any samples with a high density of wheat and barley husks, pointing toward an extensive processing of these plants. All earlier phases, however, also have some evidence of these plant remains (Table 3.4). This should not necessarily be taken as an indication that grain was cultivated in the vicinity of Fıstıklı Höyük from the earliest phase on. Judging by the site's abandonment process, when people apparently continued to practice agriculture and process materials after having moved their houses elsewhere, it is also likely that semiprocessed products were transported to the site in its early use phases. At least from phase IIIc on, storing of such material would have been possible. While sample sizes of different phases may have skewed the outcome in favor of phase IIIa, future analysis of charred plant remains will be used to assess the extent to which plants were processed in the early phases, especially during phase IIIb, when substantial settling-in occurred at Fıstıklı Höyük.

Small finds provide another avenue for investigating the 'sequential organization' indicated by the architectural sequence. Here three items are considered. These are, according to our present knowledge, related to subsistence activities. The most frequently occurring of these are 'jetons,' an enigmatic find typical for the Halaf tradition. Jetons are sherds that have been chipped into a

Table 3.4. Phytolith Samples with Wheat/Barley Husks per Phase:

Phase	Densities of phytoliths of wheat/barley husks			
	High	Medium	Low	Total
IIIa	6	1	13	20
IIIb	—	1	1	2
IIIc	—	—	2	2
IV	—	1	1	2
Total	6	3	17	26

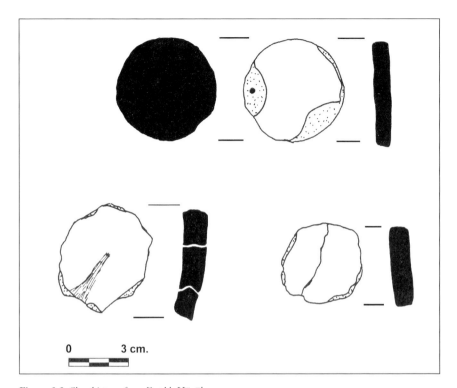

0   3 cm.

Figure 3.3. Sherd jetons from Fıstıklı Höyük.

round shape, sometimes with smoothed edges (Figure 3.3). At Fıstıklı Höyük these items, as well as naturally round, flat river pebbles, have been systematically analyzed for the first time. Costello (2002) has shown that they can be categorized into distinct size and material categories. Of importance in this context is that they are spatially most closely linked to animal bones and are likely mnemonic devices associated with practices of animal keeping (Costello 2002:212–222).

Sickle blades were used for harvesting plants. The Fıstıklı Höyük specimens are irregular, and some of them had double uses as notched tools. In the absence of use-wear analyses of the material, it remains unclear whether the few sickles found were employed to cut cereal plants or reed. We also found a number of round 'calcareous plates' (Figure 3.4). These were coarsely chipped from large pieces of locally available limestone. They were shaped into flat, round disks, some of which have one slightly discolored side, as if they had been exposed to heat. Cracks in the stone, as well as the location of some of the stones near hearths, support this idea (Bernbeck et al. 2003:62–63). These plates may have been used as lids in the preparation of starchy or leafy foods, keeping them at specific low temperatures or controlling the slow cooling of food.

Figure 3.4. Calcareous plates from Fıstıklı Höyük.

Table 3.5. Occurrences of Jetons, Sickle Blades and Calcareous Plates at Fıstıklı Höyük:

Phase	Jetons	Sickle blades	Calcareous plates
	Number		
IIIa	116	12	31
IIIb	13	1	4
IIIc	5	—	—
IV	2	—	—
	Percentage[a]		
IIIa	73	7	20
IIIb	72	5	23
IIIc	100	0	0
IV	100	0	0

[a]Given the small number of finds, especially in the three early phases, the percentage calculations across artifact categories are far from ideal and should be seen as rough quantitative indicators only.

Table 3.5 reveals a clear break in the occurrence of these items between phases IIIc and IIIb. Artifacts that point toward the processing of plant material appear from phase IIIb onward. Not only were plants harvested near the site, but the first parching oven is also documented in this phase. With this inclusion of plant processing and settling in of more permanently resident groups, it became possible to prepare special kinds of food for which heavy cooking utensils, such as the calcareous plates, were needed. This more settled way of life was associated with either a different or a more variable cuisine. Finally, in at least two buildings of phase IIIa, items for processing grain were included in the foundations. I interpret this as an intentional, symbolic re-use of objects that had come to the site initially in phase IIIb. A grinding stone was re-used as a doorsill, and a calcareous plate was turned into a door stone. Both these items marked a liminal space that is neither completely internal nor external. All of the above evidence conforms well with the interpretation of the 'sequential organization' that was derived from the architectural sequence. It is important to note that the results of the phytolith analysis (Table 3.4) seem to contradict the notion of a transformation between phases IIIc and IIIb. I contend that this is due to the fact that plant material was consumed in small amounts at the site from its earliest occupation onward. The tools, and not the plant remains alone, enable us to unravel past practices of production and processing of animals and plants, whereas the biological remains (here only the phytoliths) reveal what was consumed, by animals or by humans.[10]

How do we make the transition from the stratigraphic occurrence of such items to an informed guess about past life in and around Fıstıklı Höyük? This question is essential if narratives about the past aspire to be more than abstract, bloodless models, and to address it requires a theoretical consideration of notions of practice. I will show which kinds of practices we can reasonably infer from the archaeological evidence and what kinds of archaeological fieldwork are needed to further examine the validity of my interpretation.

ANCHORING AND DISPOSITIONAL PRACTICES

Ever since Bourdieu's practice theory was integrated into anthropological discourse, the emergence and continuity of quotidian activities have become a mainstay of theoretical debate. In an important paper, Swidler (2001:81) criticized the prevailing undifferentiated view of practices and asked "whether we are simply awash in practices, each patterned and habitual, each subject to revision as it is transposed or replicated, and none more influential than any other." In her discussion she argues that some practices are "anchoring whole larger domains of practice and discourse" (Swidler 2001:87). I follow this fundamental insight and suggest that at Fıstıklı Höyük those practices that led to the initial use of the site, as well as its occupation and abandonment, were anchoring many but not all other practices carried out, for example different ways of cooking. Thus, much of what I described above in archaeological terms as 'sequential organization' can be imagined as past practices that triggered

---

[10.] In the final analysis of the botanical remains, an effort will be made to distinguish phase by phase between what Hillman (cited in Moffett 2003:243) has called 'producer' and 'consumer' sites.

changes in others. Anchoring practices are more likely than others to have been discursively negotiated. Only the spatiotemporal specificities were negotiable, however, not the anchoring practice itself. For example, the moment and direction of a household move may have been open to dispute but not the necessity of the move itself. Thus, I claim that the 'lifeworld' (in Habermas's sense of *Lebenswelt*) of the inhabitants of Fıstıklı Höyük did not enable them to question whether long-term, spatially small-scale mobility should be continued or abandoned.

It is important to disentangle anchoring, sporadically occurring practices from other habitual activities. Here it is useful to follow Husserl's (1976) distinction between 'protension' and 'project,' where *protension* refers to an immediate future embedded so much in a practice *en cours* that it is asymptotically close to the present, and *project* denotes the future that is physically and temporally distant and more open to reflexivity and discursiveness. Anchoring practices may best be conceived of as projectual, whereas temporally smaller-scale episodes are characterized by protension.[11] Quotidian practices, such as parching grain, cleaning a tholos, leaving the habitation for a nearby field or repairing a wall are, if one wants to adhere to Bourdieu's (1990) terms, 'dispositional,' carried out on an ad hoc, situational basis. Such dispositional practices are not always quotidian. The repair of a damaged house may have happened once a year, or less often, but was carried out in a similarly embodied fashion as that of preparing a meal.

Anchoring and dispositional practices are always dialectically related. Only the expectation of dispositional practices gives the anchoring practices any meaning. Without the anchoring practices' distance from daily routines, however, some aspirations of human life could not be accounted for. Furthermore, anchoring practices are limited to specific fields. In the case mentioned here, the setting up of a tent or the construction of a storage building ground some subsistence and habitation practices but may only marginally influence other activities. I assume that the specific anchoring practices, such as deciding to move to a new site, are recursive, not unique events. They are less particular than many of the daily, improvised activities that were carried out at Fıstıklı Höyük. The reason for this contention is the interlacing of initial settling and abandoning practices. It is clear from the final phase at Fıstıklı Höyük that the majority of the inhabitants had moved on, but some came back to the site for some time, just as the initial settlers of Fıstıklı Höyük still made visits to an older site they had abandoned.

[11.] Swidler (2001) also uses the phrase 'constitutive practices,' which is an unfortunate choice as it implies an undialectical, hierarchic order of practices.

MAKING PRACTICES VISIBLE

These reflections allow an extension of the archaeological organizational sequence at Fıstıklı Höyük to other sites that underwent similar cycles from ephemeral to focal to ephemeral use. Others may have gone through some, but not all, stages identified at Fıstıklı Höyük (Figure 3.5). Thus, when people pitched their first tents at Fıstıklı Höyük, they likely came from another, so far unknown, 'focal site' that was structurally similar to Fıstıklı Höyük in its main phase (IIIa). At the same time, other small groups may have fanned out with herds, carrying agricultural products to other places in the vicinity of a focal site. They also established camps, some on older focal sites, others on potentially viable places for future focal sites. A few simple tools were carried along, including pots and lithics. Camps are likely to have been used only seasonally, and most of the camps never developed into full-blown focal sites.

The whole gamut of practices that were carried out at focal sites is not yet, and never will be, fully reconstructible. Apart from agricultural and herding activities, food processing and crafts are those practices that are most visible in the archaeological record. The drama of daily social relations seems almost impossible to infer from material evidence, but likely generational relationships can be derived from the kind of community that we deal with. It is probable that the population staying year-round at focal sites included children and the elderly, with young adults moving out to more ephemeral sites. Thus, any person would go through an initial stage of life at a focal site, then live a more mobile life, and in old age again stay in such a focal site.

Shifting a focal site to a new place was probably due to events in the social life of the community. The death of an elderly person may have triggered the abandonment of a tholos and the establishment of a new one elsewhere. Slowly, the whole population moved to the new site. The connection between events in the life cycle of families and house establishment or abandonment is well documented (Carsten and Hugh-Jones 1995:39–40; Walker and Lucero 2000:133–134). No close analogy is needed to infer that such times of shift were filled with tensions and potential for dispute and conflict but also anticipation.

FUTURE FIELDWORK AND ITS PROBLEMS

It seems most appropriate to imagine multisited communities as incorporating frequent contacts between people at the focal site and its outliers. The shift to a new focal site therefore did not mean a radical change of the familiar landscape in which people were living. Distances between elements of a community may not have been greater than a few kilometers (Abdi 2003:400–402). This is also

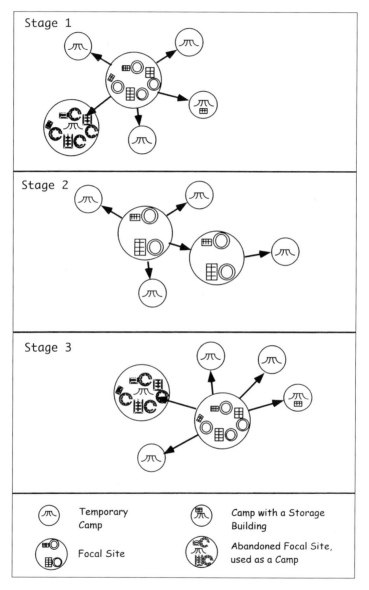

Figure 3.5. Dynamics and structures of a Halafian multisited community on the upper Euphrates.

indicated by two excavations in the vicinity of Fıstıklı Höyük, both with major pre- and post-Halafian components where scatters of Halaf material were found. Zeytinlibahçe is a mere 250 m south of Fıstıklı Höyük (Frangipane and Bucak 2001) and Mezraa is 2 km downstream (Karul et al. 2001:168–169). In neither case do these finds of Halaf artifacts necessarily indicate a campsite established from the focal site Fıstıklı Höyük, since exact dating cannot be established from the little material from those scatters. However, many similar sites can be expected to have been present at the time of Fıstıklı Höyük's phase IIIb and IIIa habitation. In this scenario the site of Fıstıklı Höyük was never a 'community' in and of itself but always a section of a much larger, dynamic one. At the core of a multisited community was a focal site that shifted frequently. From this hub groups left to live temporarily in camps. The archaeological evidence for these communities can only be assembled from a dense web of excavations or a small-scale, high-resolution survey.

At present, such archaeological work has not been carried out around Fıstıklı Höyük. There are several reasons for this. Surveys in the surroundings of Fıstıklı Höyük were geared toward the salvage of major sites threatened by the building of dams (Algaze et al. 1994) and therefore were not designed to identify ephemeral sites. Furthermore, depending on the length of use, such sites would often contain just a few artifacts, with a great likelihood of a complete lack of diagnostic, datable pieces. And even if finds are datable to the Halaf period, it is improbable that they were contemporary with the short occupation span of Fıstıklı Höyük as a focal site. Furthermore, geomorphologic processes have probably destroyed or buried most of these ephemeral sites. For example, the small Halafian site of Tell Amarna, located 25 km downstream from Fıstıklı Höyük on the right bank of the Euphrates, is blanketed by 2 m of erosional material (Cruells 2004:26).

DISCUSSION

If understood as an abstract 'model' of a settlement system, the results of my analysis might not be new. They conform relatively well with Barth's 'integrated communities' mentioned at the beginning of this chapter. Transhumance, however, is in almost all cases interpreted in terms of cultural ecology, as an adaptation to particular natural circumstances rather than as a habitual, socially constructed way of life. My argument here is that mobility is not enforced by external circumstances, such as resource scarceness or patchiness, and that at least in some cases it should be seen as 'community practice.' The stark contrast between real, 'face-to-face' village communities and larger 'imagined' communities (Anderson 1991:6; Isbell 2000) is overly simple. Communities are always both imagined and practiced. 'Practicing community' is the active establishment of what Goffman (1963:17) terms 'co-presence,' the being of several people in one and the same space at the same time (Giddens 1984:64–68). Mobility, as a set of centripetal and centrifugal small-scale moves, is one of the most crucial practices for a community that imagines itself as multisited. Such small-scale mobility is fundamental in both establishing and removing co-presence and, as such, is a deeply dialectical practice. I argue that the establishment of certain structures at a site may be read as an anchoring practice. Mobility is also an anchoring practice, in this case for the field of communicative action,[12] which is constitutive of communities.

Multisited communities may be much more widespread in human history than we think. Recent writings on diaspora, transnational migration and refugees give the overall impression that spatial dispersal of social groups is due to political or religious oppression and dire economic circumstances. This may well be true for the capitalist world system and some older, imperial forms of subjugation. However, neither an ideal of a coherent local (village) community with the closely associated assumption of sedentariness, nor the equally close-knit small group of mobile people is a natural state of being, nor is the stark, constructed contrast between sedentary and nomadic lifeways. Life in dispersed communities is a perfectly 'normal' way of being, not just in hunting-gathering societies but also in communities where agriculture or herding are prevalent. Mobility is an anchor that keeps multisited communities in existence by enabling the face-to-face, spontaneous, frequent and often aimless chat in social encounters; a practice in which means and ends, communication and community, collapse into each other.

REFERENCES

Abdi, K.
2003   The Early Development of Pastoralism in the Central Zagros Mountains. *Journal of World Prehistory* 17: 4, pp. 395–447.
Adams, R. M.
1981   *Heartland of Cities*. Chicago, University of Chicago Press.
Adams, R. M. and H. J. Nissen
1972   *The Uruk Countryside*. Chicago, University of Chicago Press.
Agamben, G. (translated by Daniel Heller-Roazen)
1998   *Homo Sacer: Sovereign Power and Bare Life*. Stanford, Stanford University Press.

[12.] In other contexts practices such as commensality may anchor communicative actions (Appadurai 1981; Pollock 2003).

Akkermans, P. M. M. G.

1993   *Villages in the Steppe*. Ann Arbor, International Monographs in Prehistory. Archaeological Series 5.

Akkermans, P. M. M. G. and K. Duistermaat

1997   Of Storage and Nomads: The Sealings from Late Neolithic Sabi Abyad, Syria. *Paléorient 22*: 2, pp. 17–44.

Akkermans, P. M. M. G. and G. M. Schwartz

2003   *The Archaeology of Syria: From Complex Hunter-Gatherers to Early Urban Societies (ca. 16,000–300 BC)*. Cambridge, Cambridge University Press.

Akkermans, P. M. M. G., R. Cappers, C. Cavallo, O. Neiuwnehuyse, B. Nilhamn and I. N. Otte

2006   Northern Syria: New Evidence from Tell Sabi Abyad. *American Journal of Archaeology 110*: 1, pp. 123–156.

Algaze, G., R. Breuninger and J. Knudstad

1994   The Tigris-Euphrates Archaeological Reconnaissance Project: Final Report of the Birecik and Carchemish Dam Survey Areas. *Anatolia 20*: pp. 1–96.

Alizadeh, A.

2003   Some Observations Based on the Nomadic Character of Fars Prehistoric Cultural Development. In N. Miller and K. Abdi (eds.), *Yeki Bud, Yeki Nabud*. Los Angeles, Cotsen Institute of Archaeology at UCLA: pp. 83–97.

Anderson, B.

1991   *Imagined Communities*. London, Verso (second, revised edition).

Appadurai, A.

1981   Gastro-Politics in Hindu South Asia. *American Ethnologist 8*: pp. 494–511.

Aurenche, O.

1984   *Nomades et sédentaires: Perspectives anthropologiques*. Paris, Éditions Recherche sur les Civilisations.

Bandy, M. S.

2004   Fissioning, Scalar Stress, and Social Evolution in Early Village Societies. *American Anthropologist 106*: 2, pp. 322–333.

Banning, E. B. and I. Köhler-Rollefson

1986   Ethnoarchaeological Survey in the Beda-Area, Southern Jordan. *Zeitschrift des Deutschen Palästina-Vereins 102*: pp. 152–170.

Bar-Yosef, O. and T. Rocek

1998   Introduction. In T. Rocek and O. Bar-Yosef (eds.), *Seasonality and Sedentism: Archaeological Perspectives from Old and New World Sites. Peabody Museum Bulletin 6*. Cambridge, Harvard University Press: pp. 1–8.

Barrett, J.

2000   A Thesis on Agency. In M.-A. Dobres and J. Robb (eds.), *Agency in Archaeology*. London, Routledge: pp. 61–68.

Barth, F.
1973   A General Perspective on Nomad-Sedentary Relations in the Middle East. In
        C. Nelson (ed.), *The Desert and the Sown*. Berkeley, University of California
        Press: pp. 11–21.
Bernbeck, R.
1993   *Steppe als Kulturlandschaft: Das Agig-Gebiet Ostsyriens vom Neolithikum bis zur
        islamischen Zeit*. Berlin, Dietrich Reimer.
1994   *Die Auflösung der häuslichen Produktionsweise: Das Beispiel Mesopotamiens*. Berlin,
        Dietrich Reimer.
1997   *Theorien in der Archäologie*. Tübingen, Francke Verlag.
2003   The Ideologies of Intentionality. *Rundbrief der Arbeitsgemeinschaft Theorie in
        der Archäologie 2*: 2, pp. 44–50.
Bernbeck, R. and S. Pollock
2004   The Political Economy of Archaeological Practice and the Production of
        Heritage in the Middle East. In L. and R. Preucel (eds.), *A Companion to Social
        Archaeology*. Oxford, Blackwell: pp. 335–352.
Bernbeck, R., S. Pollock and C. Coursey
1999   The Halaf Settlement at Kazane Höyük: Preliminary Report on the 1996 and
        1997 Seasons. *Anatolica 25*: pp. 109–147.
Bernbeck, R., S. Pollock, S. Allen, A. G. Castro-Gessner, R. Costello, S. K. Costello,
        M. Foree, M. Gleba, M. Goodwin, P. Horan, S. Lepinski, C. Nakamura, S.
        Niebuhr and R. Shoocongdej
2002   Preliminary Report on the 2000 Season at Fıstıklı Höyük. In N. Tuna and J.
        Velibeyoglu (eds.), *Salvage Project of the Archaeological Heritage of the Ilısu and
        Carchemish Dam Reservoirs: Activities in 2000*. Ankara, Middle East Technical
        University: pp. 1–42.
Bernbeck, R., S. Pollock, S. Allen, A. G. Castro-Gessner, S. K. Costello, R. Costello,
        M. Foree, M.Y. Gleba, M. Goodwin, S. Lepinski, C. Nakamura and S.
        Niebuhr
2003   The Biography of an Early Halaf Village: Fıstıklı Höyük, 1999–2000. *Istanbuler
        Mitteilungen 53*: pp. 9–77.
Bourdieu, P.
1990   *The Logic of Practice*. Stanford, Stanford University Press.
Briant, P.
1982   *État et pasteurs au Moyen-Orient ancien*. Paris, Editions de la Maison des
        sciences de l'homme.
Buccellati, G.
1966   *The Amorites of the Ur III Period*. Naples, Istituto Orientale di Napoli.
1990   "River Bank," "High Country," and "Pasture Land": The Growth of
        Nomadism on the Middle Euphrates and the Khabur. In S. Eichler, M. Wäfler,

and D. Warburton (eds.), *Tall al-Hamidiya. Volume 2*. Göttingen, Vandenhoeck and Ruprecht: pp. 87–117.

Cameron, C. M.

1991   Structure Abandonment in Villages. *Archaeological Method and Theory. Volume 3*: pp. 155–194.

Cameron, C. M. and S. A. Tomka (eds.)

1993   *Abandonment of Settlements and Regions: Ethnoarchaeological and Archaeological Approaches*. Cambridge, Cambridge University Press.

Campbell, S.

2000   The Burnt House at Arpachiyah: A Reexamination. *Bulletin of the American School of Oriental Research 318*: pp. 1–40.

Campbell, S., E. Carter, E. Healey, S. Anderson, A. Kennedy and S. Whitcher

1999   Emerging Complexity on the Kahramanmaras Plain, Turkey: The Domuztepe Project, 1995–1997. *American Journal of Archaeology 103*: pp. 395–418.

Canuto, M. A. and J. Yaeger (eds.)

2000   *The Archaeology of Communities: A New World Perspective*. London, Routledge.

Carsten, J. and S. Hugh-Jones

1995   Introduction. In J. Carsten and S. Hugh-Jones (eds.), *About the House: Lévi-Strauss and Beyond*. Cambridge, Cambridge University Press: pp. 1–46.

Clayton, L.

2004   The Technology of Food Preparation: The Social Dynamics of Changing Food Preparation Styles. Binghamton University, Department of Anthropology (unpublished M.A. thesis).

Clifford, J.

1994   Diasporas. *Cultural Anthropology 9*: 3, pp. 302–338.

1997   *Routes: Travel and Translation in the Late Twentieth Century*. Cambridge, Harvard University Press.

Conkey, M. W. and J. M. Gero

1991   Tensions, Pluralities, and Engendering Archaeology: An Introduction to Women and Prehistory. In M. W. Conkey and J. M. Gero (eds.), *Engendering Archaeology: Women and Prehistory*. Oxford, Blackwell: pp. 3–30.

Costello, S. K.

2002   *Tools of Memory: Investigation of the Context of Information Storage in the Halaf Period*. Binghamton, Binghamton University (PhD dissertation).

Cribb, R.

1991   *Nomads in Archaeology*. Cambridge, Cambridge University Press.

Cruells, W.

2004   Area L: The Soundings. In Ö. Tunca and M. Molist (eds.), *Tell Amarna (Syrie) I: La période de Halaf*. Louvain, Peeters: pp. 15–36.

Daniel, V.

2002   The Refugee: A Discourse on Displacement. In J. McClancy (ed.), *Exotic No More*. Chicago, University of Chicago Press: pp. 270–286.

David, N. and C. Kramer

2001   *Ethnoarchaeology in Action*. Cambridge, Cambridge University Press.

De Planhol, X.

1968   *Les fondements géographiques de l'histoire de l'Islam*. Paris, Flammarion.

Dossin, G.

1939   Benjaminites dans les textes de Mari. In *Mélanges Syriens offerts à M. René Dussaud. Tome II*. Paris, Geuthner: pp. 981–996.

Edzard, D. O.

1959   Altbabylonisch nawum. *Zeitschrift für Assyriologie 53*: pp. 168–173.

Ehlers, E.

1980   *Iran: Grundzüge einer geographischen Landeskunde*. Darmstadt, Wissenschaftliche Buchgesellschaft.

Frangipane, M. and E. Bucak

2001   Excavation and Research at Zeytinlibahçe Höyük, 1999. In N. Tuna and J. Öztürk (eds.), *Ilısu ve Karkamış Baraj Gölleri Altında Kalacak Arkeolojik Kültür Varlıklarını Kurtarma Projesi 1999 Yılı Çalışmaları*, Ankara, ODTÜ Tarihsel Çevre Araştırma Merkezi: pp. 65–132.

Garel, J.-R.

2004   Néolithisation et évolution cognitive au Proche-Orient. *Orient Express 3*: pp. 75–79.

Gibson, M.

1972   *The City and Area of Kish*. Coconut Grove, Field Research Projects.

Giddens, A.

1984   *The Constitution of Society*. Berkeley, University of California Press.

Gilbert, A. S.

1975   Modern Nomads and Prehistoric Pastoralists: The Limits of Analogy. *Journal of the Ancient Near Eastern Society of Columbia University* 7: pp. 53–71.

Goffman, E.

1963   *Behaviour in Public Places*. New York, Free Press.

Goldstein, P. S.

2000   Communities Without Borders: The Vertical Archipelago and Diaspora Communities in the Southern Andes. In M. A. Canuto and J. Yaeger (eds.), *The Archaeology of Communities: A New World Perspective*. London, Routledge: pp. 182–209.

Gowlett, J. A. J.

2003   The AMS Radiocarbon Dates: An Analysis and Interpretation. In P. J. Parr (ed.), *Excavations at Arjoune, Syria. British Archaeological Reports, International Series 1134*. Oxford, Archaeopress: pp. 27–30.

Grewe, C.

2002   *Die Entstehung regionaler staatlicher Siedlungsstrukturen im Bereich des prähistorischen Zagros-Gebirges: Eine Analyse von Siedlungsverteilungen in der Susiana und im Kur-Flußbecken.* Münster, Ugarit Verlag.

Grigson, C.

2003   Animal Husbandry in the Late Neolithic and Chalcolithic at Arjoune: The Secondary Products Revolution Revisited. In P. J. Parr (ed.), *Excavations at Arjoune, Syria. British Archaeological Reports, International Series 1134.* Oxford, Archaeopress: pp. 187–240.

Hassan, A.

2002   Report on Phytolith Samples Taken from the Site of Fıstıklı Höyük, 2000. Unpublished manuscript.

Hodder, I.

1991   *The Domestication of Europe.* Oxford, Blackwell.

Hole, F.

1978   Pastoral Nomadism in Western Iran. In R. A. Gould (ed.), *Explorations in Ethnoarchaeology.* Albuquerque, University of New Mexico Press: pp. 127–167.

1980   The Prehistory of Herding: Some Suggestions from Ethnography. In M.-T. Barrelet (ed.), *L'Archéologie de l'Iraq: Du début de l'époque néolithique à 333 avant notre ère: Perspectives et limites de l'interprétation anthropologique des documents.* Paris, Centre National de la Recherche Scientifique: pp. 119–130.

Hole, F. and G. A. Johnson

1986–1987   Umm Qseir on the Khabur: Preliminary Report on the 1986 Excavation. *Annales Archéologiques Arabes Syriennes 36/37:* pp. 172–220.

Horkheimer, M. and T. Adorno (translated by John Cummings)

1989   *Dialectic of Enlightenment.* New York, Continuum.

Husserl, E.

1976   *Ideen zu einer reinen Phänomenologie und phänomenologischen Philosophie.* Den Haag, Martinus Nijhoff (first published in 1913).

Hütteroth, W. D.

1959   *Bergnomaden und Yaylabauern im mittleren kurdischen Taurus. Marburger Geographische Schriften 11.* Marburg, Selbstverlag des Geographischen Institutes der Universität Marburg.

Isbell, W. H.

2000   What We Should Be Studying: The "Imagined Community" and the "Natural Community." In M. A. Canuto and J. Yaeger (eds.), *The Archaeology of Communities: A New World Perspective.* London, Routledge: pp. 243–266.

James, W.

1979   *Kwanim Pa: The Making of the Uduk People.* Oxford, Clarendon.

Johnson, G. A.

1973   *Local Exchange and Early State Development in Southwestern Iran. Anthropological Papers 51.* Ann Arbor, Michigan Museum of Anthropology.

1982   Organizational Structure and Scalar Stress. In C. Renfrew, M. Rowlands and B. A. Segraves (eds.), *Theory and Explanation in Archaeology.* New York, Academic Press: pp. 389–421.

1987   The Changing Organization of the Uruk Administration on the Susiana Plain. In F. Hole (ed.), *The Archaeology of Western Iran: Settlement and Society from Prehistory to the Islamic Conquest.* Washington, Smithsonian Institution Press: pp. 107–140.

Joyce, R. A.

2004   Unintended Consequences? Monumentality as a Novel Experience in Formative Mesoamerica. *Journal of Archaeological Method and Theory 11*: 1, pp 5–29.

Joyce, R. A. and J. A. Hendon

2000   Heterarchy, History, and Material Reality: "Communities" in Late Classic Honduras. In M. A. Canuto and J. Yaeger (eds.), *The Archaeology of Communities: A New World Perspective.* London, Routledge, pp. 143–160.

Karul, N., A. Ayhan and M. Özdogan

2001   1999 Excavations at Mezraa, Teleilat. In N. Tuna and J. Öztürk (eds.), *Ilısu ve Karkamış Baraj Gölleri Altında Kalacak Arkeolojik Kültür Varlıklarını Kurtarma Projesi 1999 Yılı Çalışmaları.* Ankara, ODTÜ Tarihsel Çevre Arastırma Merkezi: pp. 162–181.

Khazanov, A. M.

1994   *Nomads and the Outside World.* Madison, University of Wisconsin Press (second edition).

Kirkbride, D.

1982   Umm Dabaghiyah. In J. Curtis (ed.), *Fifty Years of Mesopotamian Discovery.* Hertford, Stephen Austin and Sons: pp. 11–21.

Kirsch, E. and P. Larsen

1996   Das Verhältnis zwischen Seßhaften und Nichtseßhaften in Mesopotamien am Ende des 3. und zu Beginn des 2. Jt. v. Chr. In K. Bartl, R. Bernbeck, and M. Heinz (eds.), *Zwischen Euphrat und Indus: Aktuelle Forschungsprobleme in der Vorderasiatischen Archäologie.* Hildesheim, Georg Olms: pp. 148–164.

Klengel, H.

1958–1959 Benjaminiten und Hanäer. *Wissenschaftliche Zeitschrift der Humboldt-Universität zu Berlin: Gesellschafts- und Sprachwissenschaftliche Reihe 8*: 2–3, pp. 211–226.

1972   *Zwischen Zelt und Palast.* Leipzig, Koehler und Amelang.

Kopytoff, I.

1986   The Cultural Biography of Things: Commoditization as Process. In A. Appadurai (ed.), *The Social Life of Things: Commodities in Cultural Perspective*. Cambridge, Cambridge University Press: pp. 64–94.

Kovacs, M.

1989   *The Epic of Gilgamesh*. Stanford, Stanford University Press.

Kupper, J.-R.

1957   *Les nomades en Mésopotamie au temps des rois de Mari*. Paris, Société d'Édition Les Belles Lettres.

LaMotta, V. M. and M. B. Schiffer

1999   Formation Processes of House Floor Assemblages. In P. M. Allison (ed.), *The Archaeology of Household Activities*. London, Routledge: pp. 19–29.

Lavie, S. and T. Swedenburg (eds.)

1996   *Displacement, Diaspora, and Geographies of Identity*. Durham, Duke University Press.

LeBlanc, S. and P. J. Watson

1973   A Comparative Statistical Analysis of Painted Pottery from Seven Halafian Sites. *Paléorient 1*: pp. 117–133.

Lieberman, D. E.

1998   Natufian "Sedentism" and the Importance of Biological Data for Estimating Reduced Mobility. In T. Rocek and O. Bar-Yosef (eds.), *Seasonality and Sedentism: Archaeological Perspectives from Old and New World Sites. Peabody Museum Bulletin 6*. Cambridge, Harvard University Press: pp. 75–92.

Lüning, J.

1988   Frühe Bauern in Mitteleuropa im 6. und 5. Jahrtausend vor Chr. *Jahrbuch des Römisch-Germanischen Zentralmuseums Mainz 34*: pp. 27–93.

Luke, J. T.

1965   *Pastoralism and Politics in the Mari Period*. University of Michigan, Ann Arbor (PhD dissertation).

Marfoe, L., P. J. Parr and C. S. Phillips

2003   The Site and Its Excavation. In P. J. Parr (ed.), *Excavations at Arjoune, Syria. British Archaeological Reports, International Series 1134*. Oxford, Archaeopress: pp. 11–22.

Mashkour, M.

2003   Tracing Ancient "Nomads": Isotopic Research on the Origins of Vertical "Transhumance" in the Zagros Region. *Nomadic Peoples (new series)* 7: 2, pp. 36–47.

Moffett, L.

2003   Wild and Cultivated Plants and the Evidence for Crop Processing Activities. In P. J. Parr (ed.), *Excavations at Arjoune, Syria. British Archaeological Reports, International Series 1134*. Oxford, Archaeopress: pp. 241–250.

Morier, J.

1837   Some Account of the I'lyats, or Wandering Tribes of Persia, Obtained in the Years 1814 and 1815. *Journal of the Royal Geographic Society* 7: pp. 230–242.

Murdock, G. P. and D. R. White

1969   Standard Cross-Cultural Sample. *Ethnology* 8: pp. 329–369.

Musil, A.

1908   *Arabia Petraea. Band III. Ethnologischer Reisebericht.* Wien, A. Hölder.

Niebuhr, C.

1776–1780   *Voyages en Arabie et en D'autres Pays Circonvoisins.* Amsterdam, Chez Baalde.

Nissen, H. J.

1980   The Mobility Between Settled and Non-Settled in Early Babylonia: Theory and Evidence. In M.-T. Barrelet (ed.), *L'Archéologie de l'Iraq: Du début de l'époque néolithique à 333 avant notre ère: Perspectives et limites de l'interprétation anthropologique des documents.* Paris, Centre National de la Recherche Scientifique: pp. 285–290.

Oppenheim, M. Freiherr von

1939   *Die Beduinen, Band I.* Leipzig, Harrassowitz.

Panja, S.

2003   Mobility Strategies and Site Structure: A Case Study of Inamgaon. *Journal of Anthropological Archaeology* 22: pp. 105–125.

Pauketat, T. R.

2000   The Tragedy of the Commoners. In M.-A. Dobres and J. Robb (eds.), *Agency in Archaeology.* London, Routledge: pp. 113–129.

Pauketat, T. R. and S. M. Alt

2003   Monds, Memory, and Contested Mississippian History. In R. M. van Dyke and S. E. Alcock (eds.), *Archaeologies of Memory.* London, Routledge: pp. 151–179.

Pfälzner, P.

2001   *Haus und Haushalt. Damaszener Forschungen 9.* Mainz, Philipp von Zabern.

Pollock, S.

2003   Feasts, Funerals, and Fast Food in Early Mesopotamian States. In T. Bray (ed.), *The Archaeology and Politics of Food and Feasting in Early States.* New York, Kluwer: pp. 17–38.

forthcoming Decolonizing Archaeology: Political Economy and Archaeological Practice in the Middle East. In R. Boytner and L. Swartz-Dodd (eds.), *Filtering the Past, Building the Future: Archaeology, Tradition, and Politics in the Middle East.* Tucson, University of Arizona Press.

Pollock, S., R. Bernbeck, S. Allen, A. G. Castro-Gessner, R. Costello, S. K. Costello, M. Foree, S. Lepinski and S. Niehbuhr

2001 Excavations at Fıstıklı Höyük 1999. In N. Tuna, J. Öztürk and J. Velibeyoglu (eds.), *The Salvage Project of the Archaeological Heritage of the Ilısu and Carchemish Dam Reservoirs: Activities 1999*. Ankara, Middle East Technical University: pp. 1–64.

Pollock, S. and A. G. Castro-Gessner

2004 Engendering Communities: The Contexts of Production and Consumption in Early Mesopotamian Villages. Paper presented in "Que(e)rying Archaeology: The 15th Anniversary Gender Conference" during the 37th Annual Chacmool Conference, University of Calgary, Alberta.

Powell, S.

1983 *Mobility and Adaptation: The Anasazi of Black Mesa, Arizona*. Carbondale, Southern Illinois University Press.

Preucel, R. W. and L. Meskell

2004 Places. In L. Meskell and R. W. Preucel (eds.), *A Companion to Social Archaeology*. Oxford, Blackwell, pp. 215–229.

Rafferty, J. E.

1985 The Archaeological Record on Sedentariness: Recognition, Development, and Implications. *Advances in Archaeological Method and Theory 8*: pp. 113–156.

Rivière, P.

1995 Houses, Places, and People: Community and Continuity in Guiana. In J. Carsten and S. Hugh-Jones (eds.), *About the House: Lévi-Strauss and Beyond*. Cambridge, Cambridge University Press: pp. 189–205.

Rocek, T. R.

1998 Pithouses and Pueblos on Two Continents: Interpretations of Sedentism and Mobility in the Southwestern United States. In T. R. Rocek and O. Bar-Yosef (eds.), *Seasonality and Sedentism: Archaeological Perspectives from Old and New World Sites. Peabody Museum Bulletin 6*. Cambridge, Harvard University Press: pp. 199–216.

Sadr, K.

1991 *The Development of Nomadism in Ancient Northeast Africa*. Philadelphia, University of Philadelphia Press.

Scholz, F.

1995 *Nomadismus: Theorie und Wandel einer sozio-ökologischen Kulturweise*. Stuttgart, Franz Steiner.

Shennan, S.

1988 *Quantifying Archaeology*. Edinburgh, Academic Press.

Simms, S. R.

1988 The Archaeological Structure of a Bedouin Camp. *Journal of Archaeological Science 15*: pp. 197–211.

Soudsky, B.

1969 Étude de la maison Néolithique. *Slovenská Archaeologia 15*: pp. 5–96.

Stahl, A. B.

2001   *Making History in Banda: Anthropological Visions of Africa's Past*. New York, Cambridge University Press.

Steele, C.

2005   Who Has Not Eaten Cherries with the Devil? Archaeology and Politically Problematic Contexts. In S. Pollock and R. Bernbeck (eds.), *Archaeologies of the Middle East: Critical Perspectives*. Oxford, Blackwell: pp. 45–65.

Stevanović, M.

1997   The Age of Clay: The Social Dynamics of House Destruction. *Journal of Anthropological Archaeology 16*: pp. 334–395.

Swidler, A.

2001   What Anchors Cultural Practices. In T. R. Schatzki, K. Knorr Cetina and E. von Savigny (eds.), *The Practice Turn in Contemporary Theory*. London, Routledge: pp. 74–92.

Trigger, B. G.

1968   The Determinants of Settlement Patterns. In K.-C. Chang (ed.), *Settlement Archaeology*. Palo Alto, National Press Books: pp. 53–78.

Tringham, R.

2000   The Continuous House: A View from the Deep Past. In R. A. Joyce and S. Gillespie (eds.), *Beyond Kinship: Social and Material Reproduction in House Societies*. Philadelphia, University of Pennsylvania Press: pp. 115–134.

Verhoeven, M.

1999   *An Archaeological Ethnography of a Neolithic Community*. Leiden, Nederlands Historisch-Archaeologisch Instituut te Istanbul.

2000   Death, Fire, and Abandonment. *Archaeological Dialogues* 7: 1, pp. 46–83.

Walker, W. H.

2002   Stratigraphy and Practical Reason. *American Anthropologist 104*: 1, pp. 159–177.

Walker, W. H. and L. J. Lucero

2000   The Depositional History of Ritual and Power. In M.-A. Dobres and J. Robb (eds.), *Agency in Archaeology*. London, Routledge: pp. 130–147.

Watkins, T.

1990   The Origins of House and Home? *World Archaeology 21*: pp. 336–347.

Watson, P. J.

1983   The Halafian Culture: A Review and Synthesis. In T. C. Young, P. E. L. Smith and P. Mortensen (eds.), *The Hilly Flanks. Studies in Ancient Oriental Civilization 36*. Chicago, University of Chicago Press: pp. 231–250.

Winckler, H.

1905   *Auszug aus der Vorderasiatischen Geschichte*. Leipzig, Hinrichs.

Wobst, M.
1978   The Archaeo-Ethnology of Hunter-Gatherers, or the Tyranny of the
        Ethnographic Record in Archaeology. *American Antiquity 43*: 303–309.
Wright, Henry T.
1981   The Southern Margins of Sumer: Archaeological Survey of the Area of Eridu
        and Ur. In R. M. Adams (ed.), *Heartland of Cities*. Chicago, University of
        Chicago Press: pp. 295–345.
Wylie, A.
1985   The Reaction Against Analogy. *Advances in Archaeological Method and Theory
        8*: pp. 63–111.
Zagarell, A.
1982   *The Prehistory of the Northeast Bahtiyari Mountains, Iran: The Rise of a Highland
        Way of Life*. Wiesbaden, Dr. Ludwig Reichert.
Zeder, M. A.
1994   After the Revolution: Post-Neolithic Subsistence in Northern Mesopotamia.
        American Anthropologist 96: pp. 97–126.

CHAPTER 4

ARCHAEOLOGY AND THE QUESTION OF MOBILE PASTORALISM IN LATE PREHISTORY

ABBAS ALIZADEH[1]

MOBILE PASTORALISM AS a subsistence economy and a way of life is assumed to have developed parallel to the domestication of sheep and goats in southwest Asia (particularly in highland Iran),[2] and possibly elsewhere.[3] But the evidence for interactions between the highlands mobile pastoralist and lowlands settled farming communities in preliterate times in Iran has been elusive. There are now a few lines of evidence available that can shed more light on this problem. The main purpose of this chapter is to present three sets of archaeological data pertaining to the presence of ancient mobile pastoralist societies in southwestern Iran. Since the interpretation of the data is based squarely on inferences from modern-day analogies and social theory, it is necessary to discuss the ethnographic and historical sources of my inferences. The first part of this chapter therefore deals with some introductory

---

[1.] I would like to express my gratitude to Steven Rosen, Reinhard Bernbeck, Barbara Helwing and Nicholas Kouchoukos, who read a preliminary draft of this chapter and made valuable suggestions and criticisms.

[2.] I use the term *mobile pastoralism* instead of *nomadism* to designate the mobile herders of the Zagros Mountains, primarily the Bakhtiyāari and Qashqāaii. Unlike the nomads of the vast steppes or marginal zones (such as the Jazira, Sinai, Negev and Sahara), the Qashqāaii and Bakhtiyāari occupy primary agricultural regions with high population density; they are only highly mobile while migrating; they have high social and economic interactions with the settled farmers; they spend at least a quarter of the year in regions with high population density; they own villages; they routinely practice farming in both winter and summer pastures; and they have developed comparatively complex political organizations and hierarchy.

[3.] See for examples, Adams 1974; Gilbert 1975; Oates and Oates 1976; Thomson Marucheck 1976; Zagarell 1982; Geddes 1983; Levy 1983; Smith 1983; Cribb 1991; Bernbeck 1992; Köhler-Rollefson 1992 and Akkermans and Duistermaat 1996.

remarks on the contemporary mobile pastoralist tribes in southwestern and southern Iran, as well as some theoretical issues pertinent to the present topic. The second part is devoted to the discussion of the archaeological evidence, concluding with remarks derived from the combined ethnographic, historical and archaeological evidence.

Recent studies suggest that ancient mobile pastoralists may have had some measure of influence in the development of complex societies in the ancient Near East, particularly in southwestern Iran (Zagarell 1982; Wright 1987:141-155, 2001). Nevertheless, in the study of the formation of state orga-nizations in the Near East, the role of mobile pastoralist communities is either completely ignored or viewed mostly as a contributing factor. Furthermore, ancient mobile pastoralist communities in southwest Asia are not considered developing societies that could have reached a level of sociopolitical integra-tion, which could then lead to the control of their sedentary farming neighbors. This is understandable, given the difficulties involved in finding pertinent archaeological clues to the presence of ancient mobile pastoralists.

Elsewhere (Alizadeh 1988a, 1988b, 2003b) I have argued that the small settlement at Tall-e Bakun A, in highland Fars, south-central Iran (Figures 4.1–4.3), demonstrates a number of features associated with the level of social complexity attested at some later protohistorical urban centers, but the small size of the site and the regional settlement patterns during the Bakun A phase (4400–4100 BCE) as a whole does not conform to the Central Place theory or tributary economics models, where higher levels of settlements are expected to exhibit more population and more functions. I have suggested that this 'anomaly' may be described, if not explained, if we can demonstrate the under-lying mobile pastoralist structure of the region.

Tall-e Bakun A is not unique. A number of other sites exhibit most of the characteristics of the larger regional centers but are nevertheless too small to have included a large population as a factor. Prominent among these special sites are Tepe Gawra (Tobler 1950),[4] Tell Abada (Jasim 1985), Kheit Qasim (Forest-Foucault 1980; Margueron 1987) and possibly Tell Madhhur (Roaf 1982, 1987). These special sites constitute a category of settlements that does not fit our current models of early urban development in which large, circum-scribed farming populations play a fundamental role in creating socioeconomic and political complexity. In all descriptive and explanatory models the number of sites determines the size of a regional population, and the population of each site is determined by its size. Such estimates obviously account for the settled farming and urban population of a given region. These models, however, do not

---

[4.] Rothman (1988:461, 599–625) considers Gawra an independent specialized site with perhaps a nomadic clientele population.

Figure 4.1. Map of Iran and Mesopotamia.

account for ancient Near Eastern mobile pastoralist communities, though these communities seem to have coexisted for thousands of years with the settled communities as part of the socioeconomic continuum of local polities.

Apart from the problem of archaeologically identifying social groups with residential mobility, it is difficult to attribute to mobile pastoralist communities the degree of social complexity that evolved in farming societies. This is primarily because the scope of internal structural and economic variations is limited in mobile pastoralist societies, where a level of state organization is not expected to develop internally. Nevertheless, in regions with a high degree of interaction between mobile pastoralist and settled farming communities, what Rowton (1981) calls "enclosed nomadism," chiefly aspirations could be realized if that control is extended to include sedentary farming communities. In fact, Rowton (1981:26–27) has shown that in enclosed nomadism it was common

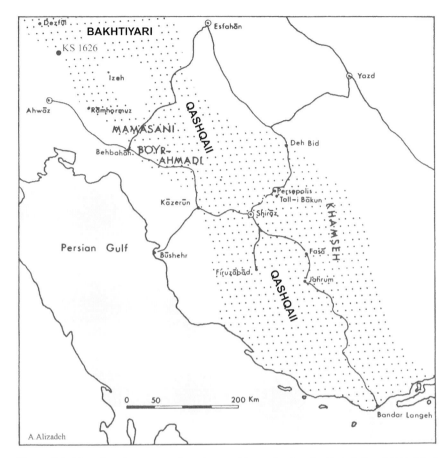

Figure 4.2. Map of southwestern and south-central Iran, showing the Qashqāaii and Bakhtiyāari territories and the distribution of the Bakun A–style ceramics (dotted area).

for the nomadic tribes to include fully sedentary tribes of a regional population. The same is remarkably true of the contemporary mobile pastoralist tribes of the Zagros Mountains.[5] Because of the undiversified pastoral economy and its limitations in accumulating wealth, the desire of mobile pastoralists, particularly the tribal elite, to acquire land-based wealth and power is an important variable in the dynamic relationship between the settled and mobile pastoralist communities in the Middle East. The ethnographic literature abounds with references to acquisition of land by tribal leaders.

To appreciate the comparatively high levels of social and economic interactions between the settled farmers and the mobile pastoralists of southwestern and south-central Iran, it is important to make the fundamental distinction between the latter and the nomads of ecologically marginal zones such as

[5.] See for examples Barth 1961; Garthwaite 1983 and Beck 1986.

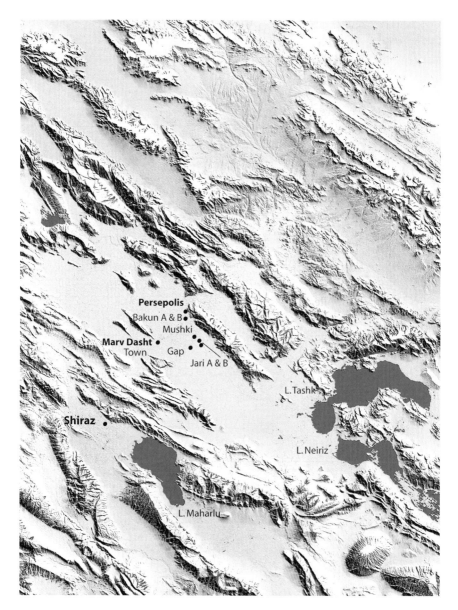

Figure 4.3. Satellite image of northern Fars, showing the intermountain valleys and major sites.

central Asia, the Sahara, the Sinai, the Negev, and the Jazira in northwestern Mesopotamia. Marginal areas unsuitable for grain agriculture but with excellent pasture grounds, and thus with low population density, are rare in southwestern and southern-central Iran. The only winter pastures frequented by the Zagros mobile pastoralist tribes are the fertile intermountain valleys in Fars and the southwestern lowlands of Susiana (modern-day Khuzestan), both with a high density of settled farmers and vast tracks of cultivated lands. This environment must have created a high level of interaction between the Zagros mobile pastoralists and settled farmers not seen in ecologically marginal areas. Thus, regardless of when vertical mobile pastoralism developed in Iran as a specialized way of life, ancient tribesmen must have had comparatively high degrees of interaction with the settled farmers of their winter haunts from the beginning.

An archaeological survey was conducted in northwestern Fars to test the validity of the hypothesis that the spatial distribution of the Fars 5th millennium BCE pottery corresponds to the migration routes of some of the modern-day mobile pastoralist tribes of the Qashqāaii (Figure 4.2). In the 1995 survey in the Qashqāaii territory, many permanent and semipermanent Qashqāaii villages were encountered with strong ties to their pastoralist tribesmen.[6] In such a bipolar socioeconomic and political context the entire settled, semisettled and mobile populations of a tribal territory will have to be taken into consideration.

Moreover, unlike highly mobile nomadic groups of vast steppes (in central Asia) and arid zones (in the Negev and the Sinai), vertical mobile pastoralist tribes of the Zagros Mountains possessed villages with solid architecture in both their summer and winter pastures, in close proximity to the settled farmers and urban centers (Figures 4.4-4.5; Alizadeh 1988a; 2003b; 2004). If this pattern occurred in late prehistory, as argued here, then semipermanent villages cannot be distinguished from permanent farming villages in surface surveys. The assumption that in late prehistoric times such villages existed in the midst of rich agricultural regions is based on ethnographic and historical data, as well as some archaeological clues that are discussed below. This assumption is theoretically significant because it addresses the problem of the economy of scale, which presumably discourages nonpastoral production, especially pottery, among mobile groups.[7]

[6.] These interactions included 'endotribal' marriages between settled and mobile Qashqāaii, settling of noncriminal disputes through the local Qashqāaii chiefs, and economic interaction primarily involving hiring of Qashqāaii shepherds to tend flocks of sheep and goats.

[7.] See Eerkens 2003 for a full treatment of this problem and the question of residential mobility.

Figure 4.4. Semipermanent Qashqāaii village (foreground) and permanent local village (background) near Firuzabad, central Fars (looking west).

Figure 4.5. Woman and children in a mobile pastoralist semipermanent Bakhtiyāari village near Behbahan, showing combined tent and solid architecture common in the region.

Once we assume the existence of semipermanent pastoral villages in antiquity, then the difficult problems of attributing industrial activities to the ancient highland mobile tribes and the spread of certain regional styles of pottery decoration (Figure 4.6) are not as daunting. The spread of the Bakun style of pottery from Fars into the Zagros Mountains, lowland Susiana, and even the Central Plateau may be described as a combined outcome of both segments of the pastoralist society: the client villages where material goods could be manufactured and the mobile population that could carry, use or exchange them. The spread of a specific class of pottery could also have been augmented through marriage alliances, where decorated vessels may have been part of the dowry.[8] Since interregional marriage alliances occur among the ruling elite of societies, then the decorated pottery vessels could serve as symbolically significant.

In ecologically marginal regions the degree of political and economic interaction between mobile and sedentary communities is comparatively low, and raids on farming villages and towns are far more frequent as a way of coping with the highly risky subsistence economy practiced in these regions. Salzman (1994) defines this situation in Iranian Baluchistan as "ecology of raids," where agriculture and animal husbandry are highly risky and demands for grains often outstrip the local supply. Similar ecology and circumstances fostered regular raids on the pueblos of the Tewa by the Comanches in the American Southwest (Ford 1972).

This is in sharp contrast to the territories of the Qashqāaii and Bakhtiyāari, whose winter pastures are in the most fertile and populated intermountain valleys of Fars and in lowland Khuzestan. In these regions both tribal confederations owned not only villages and vast tracks of farmland, but they also provided protection for the populations in their territories against the marauding minor tribes of the Mamasani and Boyr Ahmadi, who occupied the less fertile regions that straddled the Bakhtiyāari and Qashqāaii territories (Figure 4.2). The Qashqāaii and the Bakhtiyāari also had developed complex political organizations that simply did not exist among the nomads of Sistan, Baluchistan, Kerman, and northeastern Iran, even though they all operated within a state society.[9]

The interdependence of settled farming and mobile pastoralist communities created a market from which both societies did benefit. This interaction in turn created a context within which political and economic hegemony was exercised.

[8.] If women were active potters or pot painters in prehistory, and there is no reason not to consider this alternative, interregional marriages in patrilocal societies certainly would lead to the spread of specific pottery styles that in the course of time would become either diluted or would undergo hybridization.

[9.] See for examples Bradburd 1994; Irons 1994 and Salzman 1994

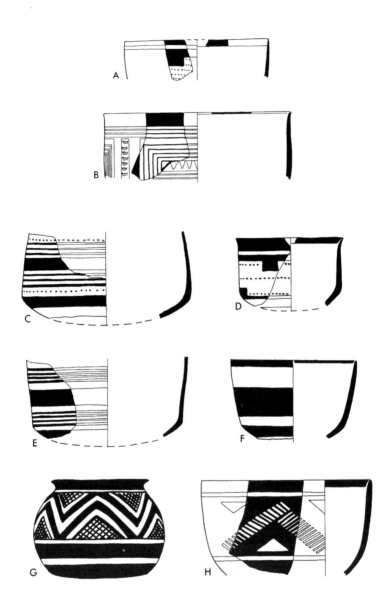

Figure 4.6. Samples of 'dot-motif' pottery vessels of the Late Susiana 1 phase.

It is this interdependence and close proximity of the two societies in highland Iran that underlie much of the sociopolitical and economic development in the Near East in general and in Iran in particular.

Using these insights together with the evidence of surveys and excavations, I propose that a number of mounded sites in late prehistoric Fars and lowland Susiana were established as a result of crystallization of mobile pastoralist socio-economic development (Alizadeh 1988a, 1988b, 2003b, 2004). The Near East has supported rich and complex societies of mobile pastoralists throughout its history.[10] Near Eastern mobile pastoralist communities in general, and those of the Zagros Mountains in particular, have had a high degree of economic and social interaction with the settled farming villages and urban centers. This interaction has been attributed to ecological and geographic factors that force mutually dependent, territorially bound and autonomous entities to share regions that provide the matrix for a web of social, economic and political interactions. Rowton (1973a, 1973b, 1974, 1981) suggests that economic interdependence and territorial coexistence of mobile pastoralists and sedentary agriculturists are major factors in the development of this high degree of integration. Moreover, it is argued that uniting both elements (agriculture and animal husbandry) within the same tribal structure would be advantageous to all concerned (Rowton 1973b:201–215; Adams 1978:329–335). The mobile pastoralist way of life can therefore be seen as an environmental, economic and sometimes political adaptation (Irons 1974).

Until the 1950s the two mobile pastoralist major tribal confederations in southwestern and south-central Iran were the Qashqāaii and the Bakhtiyāari (Beck 1986; Garthwaite 1983). Their socioeconomic and political structures are the best examples of what Salzman (1972) calls "multi-resource nomadism," allowing for a high degree of economic and social complexity and diversity. These characteristics, as noted above, arose from the environmental and geological features of the Zagros Mountains, which impose specific migration routes and a choice of winter and summer pastures.

At this point it is important to outline some aspects of mobile pastoralism in highland Iran, particularly in Fars, that must have contributed to its social and political complexity in highland Iran. The following is a discussion of the four basic features of vertical mobile pastoralism that are particularly important in its socioeconomic development: the complexities of seasonal migration, the agricultural activities, the externalization of tribal pastoral economy, and the political and military potentials.

---

[10] See for examples Mellink 1964; Luke 1965; Roux 1966; Strabo 1969; Herodotus 1972; Bosworth 1973; Lambton 1973; Bottero 1981; Castillo 1981; Digard 1981; Edzard 1981; Malbran-Labat 1981; Postgate 1981; Rowton 1981; Khazanov 1984 and Cribb 1991.

COMPLEXITIES OF SEASONAL MIGRATION

Seasonal migration is of great importance in vertical mobile pastoralism. On average, a tribal family would strike and repitch a tent many times in the course of migration. For example, most of the Qashqāaii tribes travel a round trip of about 1000 km annually. Traveling this long distance requires a great deal of information to conduct the annual migration as efficiently and peacefully as possible (Cooper 1925; Barth 1965; Spooner 1972a; Garthwaite 1983:22). In vertical mobile pastoralism, migration routes are of great importance. Each of the major tribes in Fars follows its own tribal route, the 'Il rāah.' The tribes have a traditional schedule of occupation and departure from a region. A number of factors determine the departure time of the tribes from winter and summer pastures. These factors include the location of the clans in their seasonal pastures; the availability of grass; the possession or lack of farmland; the type and size of the agricultural fields in the tribal region; tribal disputes; the weather and a host of other unpredictable factors such as death and childbirth.[11]

The complexity involved in dealing with these factors requires careful planning, scheduling and cooperation to minimize violent conflicts that might arise if two or more tribes tried simultaneously to follow the same Il rāah (tribal route) or to occupy the same region while migrating.[12] Scheduling and cooperation require large amounts of information processing and decision making by both the tribal elite and camp leaders (Amanollahi-Baharvand 1981:175–81).[13] Barth (1959:9, 1965) argues that the tightly scheduled migration through the bottlenecks required strong and effective coordinating authorities.[14] The allocation of pastures and scheduling of the movement are affairs decided collectively by several tribes or confederacies. A lower level of decision making that involves the location of a camp is equally important in maintaining the

[11] See Varjavand 1967:28 for a detailed discussion of these factors; and Barth 1961:5–7 and Tapper 1979a:95–114, 1979b:84–118 for the relation between grazing rights and social organizations among the Shāahsevan of northwestern Iran.

[12] See Garthwaite 1983:22 for the same situation and arrangements among the tribes of the Bakhtiyāari confederation.

[13] See Cribb 1991:13; Johnson 1978, 1987; Wright 1977a:338, 1977b for a detailed discussion of the processes involved in and the importance of decision making in antiquity.

[14] See Lefébure 1979:115–126 for an examination of the idea that the structure of the authority among the Zagros pastoralists is a direct consequence of environmental constraints. Compare Burnham 1979 and Irons and Dyson-Hudson 1979 for the importance of mobility in the formation of political centralization among mobile pastoralists.

structure of smaller segments of the tribes. For more effective cooperation tribes are divided into smaller segments that usually include wealthy families with large herds and poor families with few or no animals, the poor providing labor for the wealthy (Barth 1959:74 and my own observations). Among the Boyr Ahmadi tribes of southwestern Fars it is the 'rish sefid' (literally, white beard) of the 'māal' (a small segment of a tribe) who coordinates the date of departure with the heads of the families. Thereby the tribesmen reach a consensus that must be consistent with the general guidelines of the confederation that has already been set forth (Husseini-Kazerooni 1973; Garthwaite 1983:44). This lower level of decision making among the mobile pastoralists of the region is deemed an important factor in the social cohesion of these tribes (Barth 1961:25–26, 1965; see also Johnson 1983).

AGRICULTURAL ACTIVITIES

Wide-range anthropological and historical studies have shown that there has never been a totally pastoral society, for grain crops have always been an important part of the mobile pastoralist diet (Spooner 1972b:245–68; Levy 1983:17; Teitelbaum 1984). Though farmers supply the bulk of the grains needed by the mobile pastoralists, the practice of agriculture is also widespread among the latter in highland Iran. Members of many mobile pastoralist tribes invariably rely on dry farming and take advantage of arable lands in both summer and winter pastures.

In the high altitudes of summer pastures, just before leaving the area, some tribesmen sow crops that are covered by winter snow, sprout in the spring, and are ready to be harvested by the time the tribe returns. Similarly, tribal families plant small plots of barley and wheat in December, harvesting them in April just before they depart for their summer pastures in the mountains.[15] At times that the winter crop is not ready, local workers are hired to harvest it for the tribe. In the Bakhtiyāari Mountains, the tribe of Bamadi leaves for the mountains in March or April, a month before the crop is ready. The tribesmen leave some members behind to harvest the crop and to hide it under rocks in makeshift storage, or they hire some sedentary local farmers to harvest it for them while they are gone (Varjavand 1967:19).[16] Stack (1882:68, 100) reports of the same practice among the Qashqāaii: "They leave some men behind to reap their scattered fields which they have ploughed and sown in their Firouzāabāad qeshlāaq or winter haunts. The grain is buried in pits against the return of the

---

[15.] See, for example, Garrod 1946:33 or Amanollahi-Baharvand 1981:47–48, 86–89.

[16.] See Teitelbaum 1984:51–65 for similar practice among the Sudanese mobile pastoralists.

tribe next year." Garthwaite (1983:21, 40) also notes the importance of agriculture among the Bakhtiyāari and that when the tribe moves to its summer and winter pastures some men stay behind to harvest and collect the crop.[17] In addition, some Bakhtiyāari chiefs showed great interest in even large-scale agriculture by investing, building and maintaining irrigation systems in western Iran (Garthwaite 1983:30). This strategically important practice reduces the risk of total dependence on the farming communities and ensures some security if the crop fails in other areas.

EXTERNAL INVESTMENT OF TRIBAL PASTORAL ECONOMY

Among the factors that encourage mobile pastoralists to invest in agricultural land is their awareness of the importance of agriculture as insurance against the danger of losing the entire flock to epidemics and prolonged spells of dry weather (Barth 1961:101–104, 1965; Garthwaite 1983:21, 40). This reinvestment does not mean that mobile pastoralists see any advantage in sedentary life; rather, it is practiced as a measure of security in the event that their livestock breeding should fail (Marx 1980:111). Barth (1961:104–106) notes that sometimes individuals gradually acquire sufficient parcels of land and that once their economy is determined by such possession, sedentarization seems to be the natural result.[18] While the interest of rank and file mobile pastoralists in acquiring farmland may be economic and a response to risk, that of the higher ranking individuals, particularly the chiefs, in acquiring agricultural land can also be seen as politically motivated, for mobile pastoral economy has a limited capacity for furthering political ambitions of tribal chiefs.

The processes of sedentarization do not necessarily lead to sedentism, the outcome of sedentarization. Moreover, sedentism is by no means irreversible and absolute.[19] This is particularly true in times of economic and political uncertainty, when mobile pastoralists keep their options open for shifting from one way of life to another (Adams 1978; Marx 1980:111). In fact, the processes of sedentarization, as argued by Barth, do not constitute a threat to the existence of mobile pastoralism; these processes rather augment pastoralism by maintaining environmental equilibrium through various mechanisms (Barth 1961:124).

[17.] See also the lively description of Freya Stark 1934, who reports the same practice in parts of Lurestan.

[18.] See also Ehmann 1975:113–15, where he reports the same tendency among the Bakhtiyāri tribes.

[19.] For a different view on the processes of sedentarization see Salzman 1980 and Galaty et al. 1981.

Though part-time farming relieves the mobile tribes from total dependence on the agriculturists, it does not satisfy their grain requirement, which is procured either through barter or purchase in market towns. Nevertheless, the mobile pastoralists' practice of agriculture and their knowledge of farming have a strategic significance in that they allow for a greater flexibility in adapting to various environmental and political calamities (Spooner 1972b:245–268). The superior knowledge of mobile pastoralists of environmental resources and geographic features of their vast territories are of strategic importance. Mobile pastoralists are much more familiar with climatic changes, types of soil and the location of water sources and other natural resources, so they can easily shift to a settled way of life. The reverse transition is far more difficult for the sedentary farmers, particularly if they are not related to the mobile tribes of their area. In a favorable environment, with many natural resources and ideal pastures, such as the Zagros Mountains and their piedmonts, the shift from mobile pastoralism to sedentary farming and vice versa seems to have been the major adaptive response to environmental and political pressure.[20] The most recent example is the return of part of the Qashqāaii tribes to mobile life after the Iranian revolution in 1979.

POLITICAL AND MILITARY POTENTIALS

Before they were forced to settle by Reza Shah in the first half of the 20th century CE, the number of mobile pastoralists in Iran fluctuated between one and two million (Barth 1961; Amanollahi-Baharvand 1981; Garthwaite 1983; Beck 1986; Safinezhad 1989). But these numbers, though large, do not indicate the importance of the role of the highland mobile pastoralists in shaping Iranian history. They occupy an important place in the society because they constitute well-organized economic, social, and political units (Sunderland 1968; Ehmann 1975; Briant 1982) that either within a state or in the absence of centralized state organizations could also pose a military threat to farming and urban communities.

As moving targets in rugged terrains, mobile pastoralists are difficult to overwhelm militarily. This mobility, combined with a tribal organization, enabled highland pastoralists to rule supreme over the settled communities in the absence of a strong centralized state (in the history of Iran the rule rather than the exception). In fact, it took the Pahlavi regime several decades of military operations, aided with fighter jets, gunship helicopters and artillery, to politically subdue the Qashqāaii and the Bakhtiyāari. One can envisage that

[20.] See Adams 1974 for the role of mobile pastoralism in environmental and political adaptation; see also Adams 1978.

in prehistoric times bands of mobile pastoralists would have been militarily superior to agriculturists.

It can be argued that the military superiority of mobile pastoralists depended to a large degree on horses and camels and was thus a late development. This is certainly true for the vast steppes of central Asia and regions such as the Sahara. Moreover, in regions with comparatively high population density, such as lowland Susiana and Fars, the sheer superior numbers of settled farmers certainly would be a deterrent to any nomadic intrusion and raids on foot. Nevertheless, in southwestern and south-central Iran, hiding places were readily available to the tribesmen in the nearby Zagros Mountains but were comparatively inaccessible and hazardous to the settled farmers. As the events of the Reza Shah era demonstrate, even a well-organized army with modern technology cannot easily overwhelm the mountain tribes. The military advantage of the vertical mobile pastoralist tribes lies in the geographic and geological features of their surroundings and in the tribes' mobility, fluid subsistence economy and general lack of fixed assets.[21]

It is equally true that without horses and camels, it is not easy to imagine how mobile pastoralist tribes could exert their political hegemony on settled farmers. In the absence of state organizations, or in situations where organized military response cannot be immediate, fleet-footed mobile tribesmen can bring a settled regional population to submission by sheer harassment. It is easy to imagine the vulnerability of farmers during harvest time, when a small band of mobile pastoralists could easily set fire to the harvest and disappear without a trace into the mountains. Similarly, flocks of sheep and goats sent by the farmers to nearby hills could be stolen by the mobile tribesmen, and stories of such events (real or imagined) abound in the major tribal regions in Iran. This inherent military superiority of vertical mobile pastoralists should be considered another factor in their sociopolitical development. As Sáenz (1991) argues in the case of the Tuaregs of northern Africa, the military advantage of vertical mobile pastoralist communities alone can lead to extortion, which in turn may lead to warrior-client interaction and subsequently to stratification and increased social complexity.

Following Earle (1994), one may postulate that because mobile pastoralist groups operate regionally over vast areas on a regular basis, the hierarchy that arises from within can generate overarching levels of social and political organization not present in any one segment of the society. Such levels of organization would then result in the integration of economically and politically segmented groups. The potential military power of the highland mobile pastoralists can, however, be a double-edged sword. As Earle (1994:956) argues, military power can be an equalizing force, which not only coerces submission

---

[21.] See, for examples, Irons 1974; 1994.

but also creates resistance to domination. One may assume that the military aspects of the mobile pastoralist tribes in southwestern Iran in turn became an important variable in the adaptive reorganization of lowland societies of the late 5th and early 4th millennia BCE. In this scenario the military capability of mobile pastoralists could be an important factor in the development of state organization in the region.

THE ZAGROS MOUNTAINS

The above introduction was necessary to provide a context in which mute archaeological evidence can be interpreted. Apart from the archaeological evidence from Fars, three lines of evidence provide additional clues to the presence and activities of ancient mobile pastoralist communities in Iran.

The earliest clues to the presence of socio-economic differentiation among mobile pastoralists in prehistoric Iran is found in the isolated cemeteries of Hakalān and Parchineh in Lurestan, the oldest nomadic cemeteries in Iran and, in fact, in the entire Near East. Louis Vanden Berghe (1973a, 1973b, 1975, 1987) excavated both cemeteries from 1971 to 1973.[22] The cemeteries are located north of Khuzestan, along the Meimeh River in the Pusht-e Kuh region of Lurestan, in the southwestern piedmont of the Zagros Mountains (Figure 4.1). The sites are considered nomadic cemeteries because they are not associated with any known settlements because they are similar in location and tomb construction to the later nomadic Bronze and Iron Age tombs in the same region and also because the region is unsuitable for grain agriculture and almost devoid of permanent ancient, as well as modern-day, villages with agriculture as a subsistence base (Alizadeh 2003a, 2004).

In both cemeteries pottery vessels (about 200) were the most abundant funerary objects. Based on general comparisons to the ceramics of the Early Middle Chalcolithic in central Zagros (Henrickson 1985), Haerinck and Overlaet (1996:27) date the cemeteries in Area A at Parchineh to about 4600–4200 BCE. Pottery vessels from both cemeteries show strong affinities with the pottery of the Ubaid 3 and 4 phases in Mesopotamia and Late Middle and Late Susiana 1 phases (around 5000–4400 BCE) in lowland Susiana. The most interesting characteristic of the cemeteries' artifacts, particularly the pottery vessels, is the specific regional styles that they exhibit, representing Mesopotamia, lowland Susiana and highland Iran.

The obvious continuum of the richness of the funerary gifts deposited in the tombs suggests differential status among those who were buried in the ceme-teries. At this level of social evolution, and with their assumed inherent military

---

[22.] The final report was superbly published posthumously by E. Haerinck and B. Overlaet (1996).

superiority over the settled farming communities, the archaeological evidence suggests that the mobile pastoralist communities of the 5th millennium BCE were in a position to affect the process of social evolution in southwestern Iran.

LOWLAND SUSIANA

Chogha Mish, in lowland Susiana (Figure 4.1), enjoyed a central status in the entire Susiana plain from the Archaic Susiana (about 6900 BCE) through the end of the Middle Susiana period (about 5000 BCE), when its monumental building was destroyed (Alizadeh 1992; Kantor and Delougaz 1996). It is not known whether hostile forces destroyed the monumental building or that the fire was accidental. This event, however, coincided with others that, taken together, suggest a changing organization in the settlement pattern during the first half of the 5th millennium BCE. The destruction of the monumental 'Burnt Building' coincided not only with the abandonment of Chogha Mish but also with the desertion of a number of other sites in the eastern part of the plain, with the appearance of the communal cemeteries of Hakalāan and Parchineh in the highlands and also with the appearance of a specific class of painted pottery with a number of pottery shapes and decorative motifs, including the 'dot motif' (Figure 4.6). These motifs are considered specific to the following Late Susiana 1 phase (the period when Chogha Mish remained unoccupied). The characteristic vessels decorated with the dot motif are found in highland Fars, the Central Plateau and the Zagros Mountains (Vanden Berghe 1975:Figure 5:6, Figure 6:7–8, 17, 20 [Late Ubaid style], Figure 5:13–15, 18, Figure 6:9, 13, 16, 18 [Late Susiana 1 style], Figure 6:11 [Central Plateau style], and Figure 5:2, 12 [Fars style]).

With Chogha Mish lying deserted during the Late Susiana 1 phase, it appears that no single site attained a central status in terms of size and population.[23] The observed westward movement of the Susiana settlements around 4800 BCE and the appearance of the highland communal burials provide a relevant context for the observation made by Hole (1987:42, Table 8) that "...sites were often occupied for only short periods, then abandoned for a time and reoccupied. About half of the sites changed status from occupied to unoccupied or vice versa . . . implying that settlements were unstable and that land was not particularly scarce and therefore not valuable." This westward movement continued until the region east of the Shur River became almost

---

[23.] Site KS-04, about 10 km southwest of Chogha Mish is considered by Kouchoukos (1998) as a large (3–8 ha) population center dating to this phase. Our 2004 excavations indicated that during the Late Susiana 1 phase the site was not fewer than 4 ha with a large mud-brick platform at its summit (Alizadeh et al. 2005).

completely deserted before the Late Uruk phase (about 3400 BCE). Even during the preceding Middle Uruk phase only six sites are reported from this area (Johnson 1973:141–147).

The presumed correlation between the increased activities in eastern Susiana of the highland mobile pastoralists and the westward shift of Susiana settlements at the end of the Middle Susiana period becomes more tenable when we note that the eastern part of the Susiana plain traditionally has been, and still is, the locus of the winter pasture for the mobile pastoralists of the region. If this environmental niche was also used in antiquity, as one might expect, then the westward shift of the settled community may also be taken as an indication of an increase in the activities of the mobile pastoralist groups in the area, and the conflict of interest between the settled and mobile populations of the region, a dichotomy that remains the leitmotif of Iranian history throughout the ages.

Until recently, the above observations had not been contextualized in the field. As part of a joint project by the Iranian Cultural Heritage and Tourism Organization (ICHTO) and the Oriental Institute and Department of Anthropology of the University of Chicago, with a grant from the National Science Foundation (BSC-0120519), geomorphologic surveys in this part of the region were conducted. To gain additional data on the important Late Susiana 1 phase, excavations were conducted at the site of Dar Khazineh (KS-1626) (Alizadeh et al. 2004).

KS-1626 is located some 30 kilometers southeast of the provincial town of Shushtar (Figure 4.2). In this part of the Susiana plain both prehistoric and historical sites are buried under some 2 m of alluvial deposits, a feature that Lees and Falcon (1952) had already noticed. Our excavations in a number of trenches at KS-1626 showed that only certain areas of the site had archaeological remains; the site is mostly formed by the heavy alluvial deposits cut by torrential seasonal floods from the nearby mountains. Tony Wilkinson, Nick Kouchoukos and Andrew Bauer, who conducted the geomorphologic survey, concluded that the construction of a huge irrigation canal (now the Gargar River) during the Parthian/Sasanian period was responsible for this phenomenon. The large-scale Elamite building activities in second millennium BCE Susiana, which required millions of fired bricks, may have greatly contributed to the deforestation of the western foothills of the Masjed Suleiman Mountains; this construction and denuding must have triggered the erosion processes that reached their zenith during the Parthian and Sasanian periods. As a result, the archaeological sites in this region are only visible in the *wadis* (exposed sections of the valleys).

Excavations in the main trench (Figure 4.7, square 379) revealed a peculiar depositional pattern not recorded before in the region. Clayish and sandy sediments 5-10 cm thick superimposed thin lenses of cultural deposits. No solid

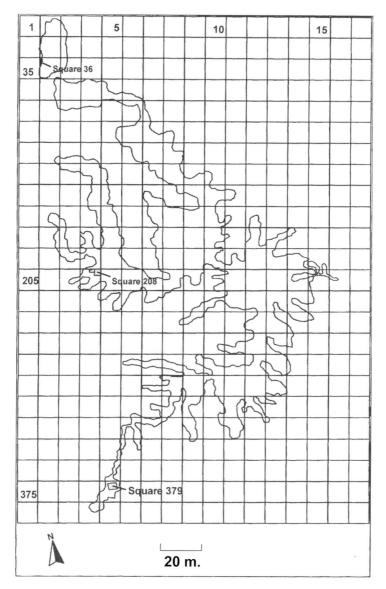

Figure 4.7. Map of KS-1626, showing the location of the excavated areas.

architecture was found except for extremely badly preserved *pisé* partition walls whose faces were usually burnt. Postholes, traces of ash and fireplaces were also encountered. The 'floors' on which these activities took place consisted of alluvial deposits. Thus, in the main area of excavation, when we factored out the alluvial levels from the cultural lenses, we were left with just over 30 cm of deposit for perhaps the entire duration of the 5th millennium BCE. We did not find any extensive organic horizon that would indicate the presence of animal pens. This is hardly surprising as most of the site was destroyed, and our 4x4 m exposure may have been too small to reveal such a feature.

In the other excavation areas (Figures 4.7-4.8) we found three simple grave pits dug into another layer of clayish alluvium. The skeletons were fragmentary and very badly preserved; legs and hipbones were completely absent. Graves 1 and 2 yielded some rubbing stones and pounders. Grave 3, presumably belonging to a female, yielded a saddle-shaped stone mill, stone pounders, and a copper pin that, judging by its position, was used as a hairpin (Figure 4.9). No other archaeological deposit was found below the level of these burial pits. In square 36 (Figure 4.7), again below the top alluvial deposit, we found a fragmentary stone pavement embedded with potsherds of Late Susiana 1 date. Again, we encountered no cultural deposit below this stone pavement.

Dar Khazineh thus seems to be analogous to the modern-day mobile pastoralist campsites (Figures 4.10-4.11). While working at the site, we noticed that the area was used by some mobile pastoralist tribes as a temporary campsite. Specifically, we noticed that the tribes used the western bank of the stream in the *wadi* as an overnight camp. This gave us an excellent opportunity to make some ethno-archaeological observations. After a camp of several families left

Figure 4.8. General view of KS-1626, looking south.

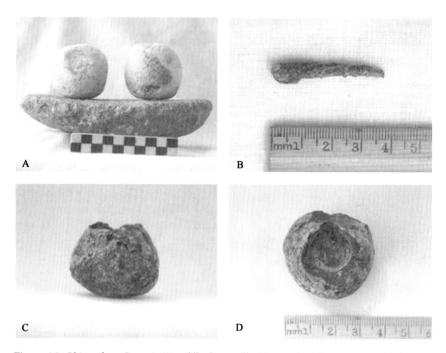

Figure 4.9. Objects from Grave 3: (A) saddle shape mill with pounders; (B) copper pin; (C) bitumen cosmetic vessel? (D) top view of C.

Figure 4.10. Bakhtiyāari spring camp at Chogha Mish (KS-01), looking east.

Figure 4.11. Bakhtiyāari tent in eastern Khuzestan, showing a horseshoe fire pit with low *pisé* surrounding walls and various postholes.

at dawn, we found postholes and three shallow fire pits dug some 10 m apart (Figure 4.12). Twigs and animal droppings were used for fuel. The lumps of clay that had been dug out to make fireplaces were burnt and blackened by the overnight fire, but not much else was left behind. This was very similar to the patterns we excavated in square 379. We also knew that on rainy occasions mobile pastoralists make stone beddings to protect their belongings against moisture and rain, a feature similar to the stone bedding in square 36. In addition, mobile pastoralists use the highest point of natural hills or artificial mounds to bury their dead, a practice analogous to the graves we found in square 208, the highest preserved part of the mound.

SUBSISTENCE ECONOMY

Ms. Marjan Mashkour of the *Centre National de la Recherche Scientifique* in Paris has analyzed the faunal samples. She believes that the faunal assemblage is characteristic of what one expects from a temporary camp of mobile herders. Even though we collected every piece of bone from every layer and feature, only about 400 pieces of bones were found, which is not surprising given the nature of the site. The main domesticated species identified were sheep and

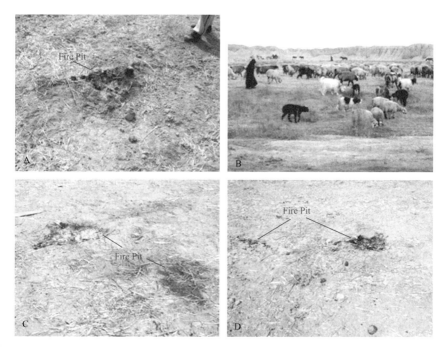

Figure 4.12. Dar Khazineh (KS-1626): (A, C and D) remnants of temporary camp fire pits; (B) Bakhtiyāari encampment.

goats; cattle bones (6–7%) were also present. Wild species included onager (*Equus hemionus* onager), fallow deer (*Dama dama* mesopotamica), medium-size rodents and some mollusk remains.

Ms. Naomi Miller of the Museum Applied Science Center for Archaeology, University of Pennsylvania, analyzed the floral samples. Only a small volume of seeds was recovered, despite the fact that we wet-sieved huge quantities of dirt, especially from the fire pits. Again, the poor recovery of charred botanical remains is consistent with the nature of the site, which was exposed to the elements for much of the year. According to Miller the charred seeds include two plant families, the grasses (*Poaceae*) and the legumes (*Fabaceae*). The only cultivated plant in the grass family was barley (*Hordeum*).[24]

Based on these observations, we concluded that KS-1626 was occupied seasonally by the prehistoric mobile pastoralists of the region, a pattern that is still evident in eastern Khuzestan. The analyses of the flora and fauna samples from the site also corroborate our characterization of the site as a mobile pastoralist camp. It is important to bear in mind that the primary

---

[24.] Mr. Marco Madella of the University of Cambridge is in the process of analyzing the phytolith samples collected from the site.

occupation at Dar Khazineh coincides with the Late Susiana 1 phase, a period we consider to represent the crystallization of a mobile pastoralist mode of production in Iran.

THE CENTRAL PLATEAU

Another line of evidence is now available from the Central Plateau, the primary source of copper in Iran. Remarkable evidence for contact between Fars, lowland Susiana and the highland Central Plateau comes from a series of surveys conducted by Mir Abedin Kaboli (2000) of the Tehran ICHTO. The survey region is located northeast of the city of Qum, some 100 km south of Tehran (Figure 4.1). The unmistakable characteristic ceramics of the Late Susiana 1 phase were found on at least six mounds.[25] Other contemporary prehistoric mounds in the region yielded only the typical late Cheshme Ali pottery.

According to Kaboli (2000:133) mobile pastoralism is still practiced by some families in the region. Sheep and goats are the primary stock, but camels are also raised. In the hot summer months the pastoralists move to the mountains near the provincial town of Saveh, northwest of Qum, or to the nearby Marreh Mountains. While much research is needed to shed light on the dynamics of the appearance in the Central Plateau of the typical 5th millennium BCE ceramics of Fars and Susiana, the available evidence suggests that this development may be related to the demand for copper in south and southwestern Iran. More recent archaeological surveys in the region were conducted by Barbara Helwing, of the German Institute in Tehran, and by Naser Chegini, of the ICHTO, as part of a joint German-Iranian project. In their survey area, between Kashan and Natanz, the region with copper mines, Helwing and Chegini found examples of dot-motif pottery mixed with that of the contemporary late Cheshme Ali phase.[26]

The appearance in the Central Plateau of the typical 5th millennium BCE southwestern and south-central pottery, decorated with the dot motif, is not unilateral. Although no genuine pottery of the Sialk II type (Cheshme Ali phase) has been reported from southwestern Iran, Sialk III type pottery has been reported from surveys and excavations in the heart of the Bakhtiyāari mobile pastoralist tribes of central Zagros regions of Khaneh Mirza (Zagarell 1975:146) and from Godin period VI and the mound of She Gabi in the Kangavar area (Young 1969:Figure 7:1–17; Young and Levine 1974:Figure

---

[25.] See for examples Kaboli 2000:Plates 19:1, 29:1–3, 33:15–16, 36:10, 37:1–5, 39:11.

[26.] I am grateful to Dr. Helwing for generously providing this information.

14:1–20; Levine and Young 1987:Figures 10:50.2–5, 12:10, 17:1–12). This, together with the evidence of the later third millennium BCE gray ware that is found both in the Zagros region and in the central plateau, provides evidence for the continuity of the interactions between southwestern and south-central Iran with areas to the north and the east. These seem to have started in the beginning of the 5th millennium BCE.

DISCUSSION

Admittedly, more specific fieldwork is required to justify the basis of our ethnographic and historical interpretation of the available archaeological records. Nevertheless, we believe that a mobile pastoralist approach is a viable alternative to the existing archaeological interpretations of the events and processes that took place in the 5th and 4th millennia BCE in southwestern and south-central Iran. Specifically, it is within this interpretive framework that the development of small highland sites with the characteristics of large urban centers can be described, if not explained. The unprecedented spread of a specific decorated pottery in the 5th millennium BCE in southwestern and south-central Iran and the Central Plateau, as well as the appearance of copper, lapis lazuli and turquoise in south and southwestern Iran and in northern Mesopotamia, are consistent with our reconstruction of the development and crystallization of mobile pastoralism.

The 5th millennium BCE was a time of rapid population increase and of the development of nascent urban centers in southwest Asia. It is therefore not difficult or unwarranted to assume that mobile pastoralists' mode of subsistence economy and way of life put them in a position to become intermediaries between lowland Susiana, Mesopotamia and highland Iran. Similarly, population increase in the settled farming communities of the lowlands and vast intermountain valleys of Fars would have created a context conducive to the creation of nomadic surplus production, including meat, dairy by-products, leather, wool and possibly *kilims* (carpets). Apart from these tangible products, mobile pastoralist groups could also interact with the settled farmers in providing services such as labor, military protection, scouting and safe-guarding commercial routes (Bates 1973; Black-Michaud 1986; Rosen 2003).

Whether items of exchange included pottery is a question that seems to depend on the degree of residential mobility that imposes restriction on pottery production (Close 1995; Rice 1999; Skibo and Blinman 1999). Arnold (1985), while suggesting that less than a third of mobile societies make and use pottery, argues that a number of practical, logistical and economic (economies of scale) problems are involved in the production of pottery by groups with high residential mobility. In a series of articles, however, Eerkens (2003) and colleagues (Eerkens and Bettinger 2001; Eerkens et al. 2002) discuss a number of strategies through which such obstacles were overcome by the highly mobile tribes of Paiute and Shoshone of the southwestern region of the Great Basin in North America. The pottery manufactured by these Native American tribes is basically simple, crude and limited in shape and accessories (Eerkens et al. 2002:203–205). The same is true of the Negbite pottery of the Negev that has been attributed to the nomadic groups of the region (Haiman and Goren 1992). These observations suggest that even when mobile groups do manufacture pottery, their product is technologically and aesthetically inferior to those produced by sedentary peoples (but see Barnard, this volume).

In the case of the vertical mobile pastoralists of the Zagros Mountains, this distinction need not be made. First, despite their seasonal mobility, the Zagros pastoralists spend only a fraction of the year moving from their summer to winter pastures and vice versa. Whereas in their summer pastures they occupy regions that are not suitable for grain agriculture and are thus sparsely populated, in their winter pastures of Fars and lowland Khuzestan they spend several months in heavily populated and agriculturally rich areas. Some tribes even own villages with solid architecture or a mixture of tents and mud-brick or stone houses. If this situation already existed in the 5th millennium BCE, attributing the manufacture, and thus the spread of the very specific class of the 5th millennium BCE pottery in southwestern Iran to the mobile pastoralist groups is theoretically and practically not far-fetched. Interregional marriages, an important factor in forging interregional alliances through kinship, could also be considered a contributing factor in the spread of some classes of pottery.

In summary, because of their highly specialized and undifferentiated economy, mobile pastoralists would be more interested in trade (either exchanging their own products or serving as intermediaries in long-distance trade) than sedentary people. But self-sufficient farming villages are, by definition, not viable markets for the tribesmen. Mobile herders cannot trade among themselves, however, because of their undiversified economic mode of production. So we know historically, and expect prehistorically, an association between the crystallization of the highland mobile pastoralist communities and the rise of large population centers with diversified economy and a large population not necessarily engaged in subsistence agriculture.

Once the necessary demographic, economic and political conditions were present for a pastoral society to engage in the production and distribution of surplus animal products and material goods, a fixed locus combining production, administration and residential quarters would have to be chosen. Tall-e Bakun A, and similar sites mentioned earlier, may have been the residences of some of the wealthier and higher-ranking individuals whose economic strength and social status allowed them to pursue sedentary trade economy. A common ethnic background, and perhaps kinship ties between the settled and mobile communities in Fars and the Zagros Mountains, may have facilitated processes of economic and sociopolitical development and integration in Fars.

The introduction of the specific Late Susiana 1 pottery in the copper-rich Central Plateau may be linked with exchange activities of southwestern mobile pastoralist tribes in procuring copper, turquoise and lapis lazuli, which began to appear in Fars, lowland Susiana, and Mesopotamia in the 5th millennium BCE.[27] The presence of the typical 5th millennium BCE southwestern pottery in the Central Plateau can also be explained in terms of a reciprocal social system involving pottery vessels and their contents as gifts to gain access in 'foreign' lands (Hodder 1980; Gregory 1982; Earle 1994). Much work in the region, however, is required to shed more light on this inference.

The gradual rise of nascent urban centers with industrial and economic specialization and the rise of a regional elite can be viewed as positive feedback in mobile pastoralist communities. Specifically, the rising demand for wool may be considered a contributing factor (Kouchoukos 1998). In an approach that favors ratios of the number of identified specimens present (NISP) values among taxa, Richard Redding (1981, 1993) has shown that, with the exception of Hassunan and Halafian sites in northern Mesopotamia and Syria, prior to 5500 BCE sheep/goat ratios were more or less uniformly low (< 0.5). By 4500 BCE the ratios changed to 1.5–4.5, indicating a changing trend in herding strategy from a subsistence economy to an economy where animal by-products became important (Kouchoukos 1998:294–301).

By the late Middle Susiana phase (about 5000 BCE) sheep and goats became dominant in Susiana, accounting for approximately 65% at Jafarāabād, with sheep becoming more dominant in the later phase (Kouchoukos 1998:68). Similar developments occurred at the contemporary Chogha Mish. If we consider this development an indication of the increasing importance of wool in Susiana, as well as in southern Mesopotamia,[28] then the concomitant appearance of the large cemeteries of Hakalāan and Parchineh may not be coincidental. We can envisage a situation where the initial development of highland mobile pastoralism in late prehistory was perhaps related to the importance of wool in the economies of both Susiana and southern Mesopotamia.

While small farming villages could provide the necessary grain for these newly developed population centers, items of trade not found in the lowlands were procured through the mobile tribes of southwestern Iran. If, however,

---

[27] The evidence from Mesopotamia is even earlier, except for that found at Gawra: Yarim Tepe I, level 9 (Merpert and Munchaev 1987:15, 17); and Arpachyiah, Half levels (Mallowan and Rose 1935:Plate ivb); and Gawra, level XIII (Tobler 1950:192).

[28] For a detailed study of the importance of wool in the southern Mesopotamian economy during the Uruk period see Kouchoukos 1998.

as a result of population increase and specialization of crafts, more land was brought under cultivation in central eastern Khuzestan, to feed that portion of the population that was not engaged in producing food, one expects to see a reduction in pasturelands in the same area. This situation could have created a context where the mobile tribes may have taken measures to reclaim the lands that they had lost to the farmers. While no direct evidence is available for intensification of agriculture and the subsequent loss of pasture in 5th millennium BCE Khuzestan, the pattern of competition for the available land between the contemporary mobile pastoralist tribes and settled farmers is familiar in Iran.

Growth in both mobile and settled populations can result in an increase in the amount of farming and pasturelands. This in turn would create closer proximity for the two populations and intensification of social interaction. In the context of state organization, or faced with an outside encroaching threat, mobile tribes may forge confederations that, albeit ephemeral, come close to a state-level of political organization. In such a context, social complexity would develop from the constant requirement of the pastoralists for communication and cooperation to maintain economic and social cohesion. This cohesion was usually characterized by a loosely structured centralized system culminating in the single office of chief and welded together by the seemingly dispersed tribes (Barth 1961:71–73).

The available evidence suggests that as craft specialization developed and nascent urban centers became more populated, more organized and differentiated socially and economically in the 5th millennium BCE, the demand for grains, wool, dairy products, animal by-products, timber and exotic goods (copper, turquoise, lapis lazuli, Persian Gulf shells) increased. In this context the mobile pastoralist groups were in a strategic position to become the intermediaries between the lowlands and highlands. I have tentatively attributed this development to the regional conflicts and increasing socio-economic interaction that resulted from the crystallization of mobile pastoralist communities in the highlands.

REFERENCES

Adams, R. M.

1974   Anthropological Perspectives on Ancient Trade. *Current Anthropology 15*: pp. 239–257.

1978   Strategies of Maximization, Stability, and Resilience in Mesopotamian Society, Settlement, and Agriculture. *Proceedings of the American Philosophical Society 122*: 5, pp. 329–335.

Akkermans, P. M. and K. Duistermaat

1997   Of Storage and Nomads: The Sealings from Late Neolithic Sabi Abyad. *Paléorient 22*: pp. 17–32.

Alizadeh, A.

1988a   Socio-economic Complexity in Southwestern Iran During the Fifth and Fourth Millennia BC: The Evidence from Tall-e Bakun A. *Iran 26*: pp. 17–34.

1988b   *Mobile Pastoralism and the Development of Complex Societies in Highland Iran: The Evidence from Tall-e Bakun A.* University of Chicago, Department of Near Eastern Languages and Civilizations (PhD dissertation).

1992   *Prehistoric Settlement Patterns and Cultures in Susiana, Southwestern Iran. University of Michigan Museum of Anthropology Technical Report 24.* Ann Arbor, University of Michigan.

2003a   Report on the Joint Archaeological and Geomorphological Research Expedition in Lowland Susiana, Iran. *Oriental Institute News and Notes 177*: pp. 1–7.

2003b   Some Observations Based on the Nomadic Character of Fars Prehistoric Cultural Development. In N. Miller and K. Abdi (eds.), *Yeki Bud, Yeki Nabud: Essays on the Archaeology of Iran in Honor of William M. Sumner.* Los Angeles, Cotsen Institute of Archaeology: pp. 83–97.

Alizadeh, A., N. Kouchoukos, T. Wilkinson, A. Bauer and M. Mashkour

2004   Preliminary Report on the Joint Iranian-American Landscape and Geoarchaeological Reconnaissance of the Susiana Plain, September–October 2002. *Paléorient 29*: pp. 69–88.

Alizadeh, A., A. Mahfroozi, L. Niakan, A. Ahrar, M. Karami, A. Zalaghi, K. Aqaii, S. Ebrahimi and T. Hartnell

2005   Joint ICHTO-Oriental Institute Excavations at KS-04 and KS-108 in Lowland Susiana, Southwestern Iran. In *Oriental Institute Annual Report 2004/2005.*

Amanollahi-Baharvand, S.

1981   *Pastoral Nomadism in Iran* [in Persian]. Tehran, Bongah Tarjomeh va Nashr Ketab.

Arnold, D. E.

1985   *Ceramic Theory and Cultural Process.* Cambridge, University of Cambridge Press.

Barth, F.

1959   The Land Use Pattern of Migratory Tribes of South Persia. *Norsk Geografisk Tidsskrift 17*: pp. 1–11.

1961   *Nomads of South Persia.* London, Allen and Unwin.

1965   Herdsmen of Southwest Asia. In P. B. Hammond (ed.), *Cultural and Social Anthropology.* New York, MacMillan: pp. 63–83.

Bates, D. G.

1973   *Nomads and Farmers: A Study of the Yörük of Southeastern Turkey. Anthropological Papers of the Museum of Anthropology 52.* Ann Arbor, University of Michigan.

Beck, L.

1986   *The Qashqaii.* New Haven, Yale University Press.

Bernbeck, R.

1992   Migratory Patterns in Early Nomadism. *Paléorient 18*: pp. 77–88.

Black-Michaud, J.

1986   *Sheep and Land.* Cambridge, Cambridge University Press.

Bosworth, C. E.

1973   Barbarian Incursions: The Coming of the Turks into the Islamic World. In D. S. Richards (ed.), *Islamic Civilisation.* Oxford, Cassirer: pp. 1–16.

Bottero, J.

1981   Les Habiru, les nomades, et les sédentaires. In J. S. Castillo (ed.), *Nomads and Sedentary Peoples.* Mexico City, Colegio de Mexico: pp. 89–108.

Bradburd, D.

1994   Historical Bases of the Political Economy of Kermani Pastoralists: Tribe and World Markets in the Nineteenth and Early Twentieth Centuries. In C. Chang and H. A. Koster (eds.), *Pastoralists at the Periphery.* Tucson, University of Arizona Press: pp. 42–61.

Briant, P.

1982   *État et pasteurs au Moyen-Orient ancien.* Paris, Éditions de la maison des sciences de l'homme.

Burnham, P.

1979   Spatial Mobility and Political Centralization in Pastoral Societies. In L'Equipe écologie et anthropologie des sociétés pastorales (ed.), *Pastoral Production and Society/Production pastorale et société, Actes du colloque international sur le pastoralisme nomade, Paris, 1–3 Déc. 1976.* Cambridge, Cambridge University Press: pp. 349–374.

Castillo, J. S.

1981   Tribus pastorales et industrie textile a Mari. In J. S. Castillo (ed.), *Nomads and Sedentary Peoples.* Mexico City, Colegio de Mexico: pp.109–122.

Close, A. E.

1995   Few and Far Between: Early Ceramics in North Africa. In W. K. Barnett and J. W. Hoopes (eds.), *The Emergence of Pottery.* Washington, Smithsonian Institution Press: pp. 23–37.

Cooper, M. C.

1925   *Grass.* New York, G. P. Putnam's Sons.

Cribb, R.

1991   *Nomads in Archaeology.* Cambridge, Cambridge University Press.

Digard, J. P.

1981   A propos des aspects économiques de la symbiose nomades-sédentaires dans
        la Mésopotamie ancienne: Le point de vue d'un anthropologue sur le moyen
        Orient contemporain. In J. S. Castillo (ed.), *Nomads and Sedentary Peoples*.
        Mexico City, Colegio de Mexico: pp. 13–24.

Earle, T. K.

1994   Positioning Exchange in the Evolution of Human Society. In T. Baugh and
        J. Ericson (eds.), *Prehistoric Exchange Systems in North America*. New York,
        Plenum: pp. 419–437.

Edzard, D. O.

1981   Mesopotamian Nomads in the Third Millennium B.C. In J. S. Castillo (ed.),
        Nomads and Sedentary Peoples. Mexico City, Colegio de Mexico: pp. 37–46.

Eerkens, J. W.

2003   Residential Mobility and Pottery Use in the Western Great Basin. *Current
        Anthropology 44*: 5, pp. 728–738.

Eerkens, J. W. and R. L. Bettinger

2001   Techniques for Assessing Standardization in Artifact Assemblages: Can We
        Scale Material Variability? *American Antiquity 66*: 3, pp. 493–504.

Eerkens J. W., H. Neff and M. D. Glascock

2002   Ceramic Production Among Small-Scale and Mobile Hunters and Gatherers:
        A Case Study from the Southwestern Great Basin. *Journal of Anthropological
        Archaeology 21*: pp. 200–229.

Ehmann, D.

1975   *Bahtiyaren-Persische Bergnomaden in Wandel der Zeit. Beihefte zum Tübinger
        Atlas des vorderen Orients, Reihe B, No. 15*. Wiesbaden, Ludwig Reichert.

Ford, I. R.

1972   Barter, Gift, or Violence: An Analysis of Tewa Intertribal Exchange. In E.
        Wilmsen (ed.), *Social Exchange and Interaction. Anthropological Papers 46*. Ann
        Arbor, Museum of Anthropology: pp. 21–45.

Forest-Foucault, C.

1980   Rapport sur les fouilles de Keit Qasim III-Hamrin. *Paléorient 6*: pp.
        221–224.

Galaty, J. G., D. Aronson, P. Salzman and A. Chouinard (eds.)

1981   *The Future of Pastoral Peoples*. Ottawa, International Development Research
        Centre.

Garrod, O.

1946   The Nomadic Tribes of Persia To-day. *Journal of the Royal Central Asian Society
        33*: pp. 32–46.

Garthwaite, G. R.

1983   *Khans and Shahs: A Documentary Analysis of the Bakhtiyari in Iran*. Cambridge,
        Cambridge University Press.

Geddes, D. S.

1983   Neolithic Transhumance in the Mediterranean Pyrenees. *World Archaeology 15*: 1, pp. 51–66

Gilbert, A. S.

1975   Modern Nomads and Prehistoric Pastoralism: The Limits of Analogy. *Journal of Ancient Near Eastern Societies of Columbia University* 7: pp. 53–71.

Gregory, C. A.

1982   *Gifts and Commodities*. New York, Academic Press.

Haerinck, E. and B. Overlaet

1996   *The Chalcolithic Parchineh and Hakalān*. Brussels, Royal Museum of Art and History.

Haiman, M. and Y. Goren

1992   "Negbite" Pottery: New Aspects and Interpretations and the Role of Pastoralism in Designating Ceramic Technology. In O. Bar-Yosef and A. M. Khazanov (eds.), *Pastoralism in the Levant: Archaeological Materials in Anthropological Perspectives*. Madison, Prehistory Press: pp. 143–152.

Henrickson, E.

1985   An Updated Chronology of the Early and Middle Chalcolithic of the Central Zagros Highlands, Western Iran. *Iran 23*: pp. 63–108.

Herodotus

1972   *The Histories*. London, Penguin.

Hodder, I.

1980   Trade and Exchange: Definition, Identification, and Function. In R. E. Fry (ed.), *Models and Methods in Regional Exchange. Society for American Archaeology Papers 1*. Washington, Society for American Archaeology: pp. 151–156.

Hole, F. (ed.)

1987   *The Archaeology of Western Iran: Settlement and Society from Prehistory to the Islamic Conquest*. Washington, Smithsonian Institution Press.

Husseini-Kazerooni, M.

1973   Kuche Mall-e Ka Ebrahim, Il Boyr Ahmadi [in Persian]. In T. Firuzan (ed.), *Ilat va Ashayer*. Tehran, University of Tehran: pp. 63–74.

Irons, W.

1974   Nomadism as a Political Adaptation: The Case of the Yomut Turkmen. *American Ethnologist 1*: pp. 635–658.

1994   Why Are the Yomut Not More Stratified? In C. Chang and H. A. Koster (eds.), *Pastoralists at the Periphery*. Tucson, University of Arizona Press: pp. 175–196.

Irons, W. and N. Dyson-Hudson

1972   *Perspectives on Nomadism*. Leiden, E. J. Brill.

Jasim, S. A.

1985   *The Ubaid Period in Iraq. BAR International Series 267.* Oxford, Archaeo-press.

Johnson, G. A.

1978   Information Sources and the Development of Decision-Making Organizations. In C. Redman (ed.), *Social Archaeology: Beyond Subsistence and Dating.* New York, Academic Press: pp. 87–110.

1983   Decision-Making Organization and Pastoral Nomad Camp Size. *Human Ecology 11*: pp. 175–199.

1987   The Changing Organization of Uruk Administration on the Susiana Plain. In F. Hole (ed.), *The Archaeology of Western Iran: Settlement and Society from Prehistory to the Islamic Conquest.* Washington, Smithsonian Institution Press: pp. 107–140.

Johnson, G. A.

1973   *Local Exchange and Early State Development in Southwestern Iran. Anthropological Papers 51.* Ann Arbor, Museum of Anthropology, University of Michigan.

Kaboli, M. A.

2000   *Archaeological Survey at Qomrud.* Tehran, Iranian Cultural Heritage Organization.

Kantor, H. J. and P. Delougaz (edited by Abbas Alizadeh)

1996   *Chogha Mish. Volume 1: The First Five Seasons of Excavations, 1961–1971. Part 1: Text. Oriental Institute Publications 101.* Chicago, Oriental Institute.

Khazanov, A. M.

1984   *Nomads and the Outside World.* Cambridge, Cambridge University Press.

Köhler-Rollefson, I.

1992   A Model for Development of Nomadic Pastoralism on the Transjordanian Plateau. In O. Bar-Yosef and A. M. Khazanov (eds.), *Pastoralism in the Levant: Archaeological Materials in Anthropological Perspectives.* Madison, Prehistory Press: pp. 11–19.

Kouchoukos, N.

1998   *Landscape and Social Change in Late Prehistoric Mesopotamia.* Yale University (PhD dissertation).

Lambton, A.

1973   Aspects of Saljuq-Ghuzz Settlement in Persia. In D. Richards (ed.), *Islamic Civilisation.* Oxford, Cassirer: pp. 25–26.

Lefébure, C.

1979   Acces aux ressources collectives et structure sociale: L'Estivage chez Ayt Atta (Maroc). In L'Equipe écologie et anthropologie des sociétés pastorales (ed.), *Pastoral Production and Society/Production pastorale et société, Actes du colloque international sur le pastoralisme nomade, Paris, 1–3 Déc. 1976.* Cambridge, Cambridge University Press: pp. 115–26.

Levine, L. D. and C. T. Young Jr.

1987   A Summary of the Ceramic Assemblages of the Central Western Zagros from the Middle Neolithic to the Late 3rd Millennium B.C. In J.-L. Huot (ed.), *Préhistoire de la Mésopotamie: La Mésopotamie préhistorique et l'exploration récente du djebel Hamrin*. Paris, CNRS: pp. 15–53.

Levy, T. E.

1983   The Emergence of Specialized Pastoralism in the Southern Levant. *World Archaeology 15*: pp. 16–36.

Luke, J. T.

1965   *Pastoralism and Politics in the Mari Period*. University of Michigan, Ann Arbor (PhD dissertation).

Malbran-Labat, F.

1981   Le nomadisme a l'époque néoassyriene. In J. S. Castillo (ed.), *Nomads and Sedentary Peoples*. Mexico City, Colegio de Mexico: pp. 57–76.

Mallowan, M. and J. C. Rose

1935   Excavations at Tall Arpachiyah, 1933. *Iraq 2*: pp. 1–178.

Margueron, J.-C.

1987   Quelques remarques concernant l'architecture monumentale à l'époque d'Obeid. In J.-L. Huot (ed.), *Préhistoire de la Mésopotamie: La Mésopotamie préhistorique et l'exploration récente du djebel Hamrin*. Paris, CNRS: pp. 349–378.

Marx, E.

1980   Wage Labor and Tribal Economy of Bedouin in South Sinai. In P. C. Salzman (ed.), *When Nomads Settle: Processes of Sedentarization as Adaptation and Response*. New York, Praeger: pp. 111–123.

Mellink, M. (ed.)

1964   *Dark Ages and Nomads: 1000 BC*. Istanbul, Nederlands Historisch-Archaeologische Institut.

Merpert, N. and R. M. Munchaev

1987   The Earliest Levels at Yarim Tepe I and Yarim Tepe II in Northern Iraq. *Iraq 49*: pp. 1–36.

Oates, D. and J. Oates

1976   *The Rise of Civilization*. Oxford, Elsevier-Phaidon.

Postgate, J. N.

1981   Nomads and Sedentaries in the Middle Assyrian Sources. In J. S. Castillo (ed.), *Nomads and Sedentary Peoples*. Mexico City, Colegio de Mexico: pp. 47–56.

Redding, R.

1981   *Decision Making and Subsistence Herding of Sheep and Goats in the Middle East*. University of Michigan, Ann Arbor (PhD dissertation).

1993   Subsistence Security as a Selective Pressure Favoring Increased Cultural Complexity. *Bulletin of Sumerian Agriculture 7*: pp. 77–98.

Rice, P.
1999   On the Origins of Pottery. *Journal of Archaeological Methods and Theory* 6: pp. 1–54.

Roaf, M.
1982   The Hamrin Sites. In J. Curtis (ed.), *Fifty Years of Mesopotamian Discoveries.* London, British School of Archaeology in Iraq: pp. 40–47.
1987   The 'Ubaid Architecture of Tell Madhur. In J.-L. Huot (ed.), *Préhistoire de la Mésopotamie: La Mésopotamie préhistorique et l'exploration récente du djebel Hamrin.* Paris, CNRS: pp. 425–435.

Rosen, S. A.
2003   Early Multi-resource Nomadism: Excavations at the Camel Site in the Central Negev. *Antiquity* 77: 298, pp. 750–761.

Rothman, M. S.
1988   *Centralization, Administration, and Function at Fourth Millennium B.C. Tepe Gawra, Northern Iraq.* University of Pennsylvania (PhD dissertation).

Roux, G.
1966   *Ancient Iraq.* London, Penguin.

Rowton, M.
1973a   Autonomy and Nomadism in Western Asia. *Orientalia 42*: pp. 247–258.
1973b   Urban Autonomy in a Nomadic Environment. *Journal of Near Eastern Studies 32*: pp. 201–215.
1974   Enclosed Nomadism. *Journal of Economic and Social History of the Orient 17*: pp. 1–30.
1981   Economic and Political Factors in Ancient Nomadism. In J. S. Castillo (ed.), *Nomads and Sedentary Peoples.* Mexico City, Colegio de Mexico: pp. 25–36.

Sáenz, C.
1991   Lords of the Waste: Predation, Pastoral Production, and the Process of Stratification Among the Eastern Twaregs. In T. Earle (ed.), *Chiefdoms: Power, Economy, and Ideology.* Cambridge, Cambridge University Press: pp. 100–118.

Safinezhad, J.
1989   *Nomads of Central Iran.* Tehran, Amir Kabir.

Salzman, P. C.
1972   Multi-resource Nomadism in Iranian Baluchistan. In W. Irons and N. Dyson-Hudson (eds.), *Perspectives on Nomadism.* Leiden, E. J. Brill: pp. 60–68.
1980   *When Nomads Settle: Processes of Sedentarization as Adaptation and Response.* New York, Praeger.
1994   Baluchi Nomads in the Market. In C. Chang and H. A. Koster (eds.), *Pastoralists at the Periphery.* Tucson, University of Arizona Press: pp. 165–174.

Skibo, J. M. and E. Blinman

1999   Exploring the Origins of Pottery on the Colorado Plateau. In J. M. Skibo and
        G. M. Feinman (eds.), *Pottery and People: A Dynamic Interaction*. Salt Lake City,
        University of Utah Press: pp. 171–183.

Smith, A. B.

1983   Prehistoric Pastoralism in the Southwestern Cape, South Africa. *World
        Archaeology 15*: 1, pp. 79–89.

Spooner, B.

1972a   The Status of Nomadism as a Cultural Phenomenon in the Middle East. In
        W. Irons and N. Dyson-Hudson (eds.), *Perspectives on Nomadism*. Leiden, E.
        J. Brill: pp. 122–131.

1972b   Iranian Desert. In B. Spooner (ed.), *Population Growth: Anthropological
        Implications*. Cambridge, MIT Press: pp. 245–268.

Stack, E.

1882   *Six Months in Persia*. New York, G. P. Putnam's Sons.

Stark, F.

1934   *The Valleys of the Assassins and Other Persian Travels*. London, John Murray.

Strabo (translated by H. L. Jones)

1969   *Geography*. Cambridge, Cambridge University Press.

Sunderland, E.

1968   Pastoralism, Nomadism, and Social Anthropology of Iran. In W. B. Fisher
        (ed.), *Cambridge History of Iran, Volume 1*. Cambridge, Cambridge University
        Press: pp. 611–683.

Tapper, R.

1979a   Individuated Grazing Rights and Social Organization Among the Shahsevan
        Nomads of Azerbaijan. In L'Equipe écologie et anthropologie des sociétés
        pastorales (ed.), *Pastoral Production and Society/Production pastorale et société.
        Proceedings of the International Meeting on Nomadic Pastoralism, Paris, December
        1–3, 1976*. Cambridge, Cambridge University Press: pp. 95–114.

1979b   *Pasture and Politics: Economics, Conflict, and Ritual Among Shahsevan Nomads of
        Northwestern Iran*. New York, Academic Press.

Teitelbaum, J. M.

1984   The Transhumant Production System and Change Among Hawayzma
        Nomads of the Kordofan Region, Western Sudan. *Nomadic People 15*: pp.
        51–65.

Tobler, A. J.

1950   *Excavations at Tepe Gawra*. Philadelphia, University of Pennsylvania Press.

Vanden Berghe, L.

1973a   La nécropole de Hakalan. *Archéologia 57*: pp. 49-58.

1973b   Le Lorestan avant l'âge du Bronze: Le nécropole de Hakalan. *Proceedings of the 2nd Annual Symposium on Archaeological Research in Iran*. Tehran, Iranbastan Museum: pp. 66–79.

1975   Luristan: La nécropole de Dum-Gar-Parchinah. *Archéologie 79*: pp. 46–61.

1987   Luristan, Pusht-i-Kuh au chalcolithique moyen (les nécropoles de Parchinah et Hakalāan). In J.-L. Huot (ed.). *Préhistoire de la Mésopotamie*: *La Mésopotamie préhistorique et l'exploration récente du Djebel Hamrin*. Paris, CNRS: pp. 91–106.

Varjavand, P.

1967   *Bamadi, Tayefe-i as Bakhtiari* [in Persian]. Tehran, Tehran University.

Wright, H. T.

1977a   Recent Research on the Origin of the State. *Annual Review of Anthropology 6*: pp. 379–397.

1977b   Toward an Explanation of the Origin of the State. In J. N. Hill (ed.), *Explanation of Prehistoric Change*. Albuquerque, University of New Mexico Press: pp. 215–230.

1987   The Susiana Hinterlands During the Era of Primary State Formation. In F. Hole (ed.), *The Archaeology of Western Iran: Settlement and Society from Prehistory to the Islamic Conquest*. Washington, Smithsonian Institution Press: pp. 141–155.

2001   Cultural Action in the Uruk World. In M. Rothman (ed.), *Uruk Mesopotamia and Its Neighbors*. Santa Fe, School of American Research: pp. 123–148.

Young, C. T., Jr.

1969   *Excavations at Godin Tepe: First Progress Report*. Toronto, Royal Ontario Museum.

Young, C. T., Jr. and L. D. Levine

1974   *Excavations of the Godin Project: Second Progress Report*. Toronto, Royal Ontario Museum.

Zagarell, A.

1975   An Archaeological Survey in the North-East Baxtiari Mountains. *Proceedings of the IIIrd Annual Symposium on Archaeological Research in Iran*. Tehran, Archaeological Research Center: pp. 23–30.

1982   *The Prehistory of the Northeast Bakhtiyari Mountains, Iran: The Rise of a Highland Way of Life. Beihefte zum Tübinger Atlas des Vorderen Orients. Reihe B, No. 42*.Wiesbaden, Ludwig Reichert.

CHAPTER 5

Desert Pastoral Nomadism in the *Longue Durée*

A CASE STUDY FROM THE NEGEV AND THE SOUTHERN LEVANTINE DESERTS

Steven A. Rosen[1]

Archaeological studies of pastoral nomadic systems over the *longue durée*, in this particular case derived from the Negev and surrounding areas, reflect a deeper and more complex dynamic of social and ecological adaptation than is usually acknowledged. Although the inherent adaptive resilience of pastoral nomadic societies has long been recognized as one of its primary attributes, this recognition has been limited virtually exclusively to the short-term ethnographic present. This short-term perspective, on which many historical interpretations have been based, has resulted in a static understanding of the actual history of peripheral nomadic societies. The deep time perspective, the *longue durée*, based on archaeological study as exemplified by work in the Negev and surrounding regions, suggests that some of our basic assumptions concerning these groups are flawed. Re-evaluation of the development of these societies reflects an evolution no less complex than that of their sedentary cousins, places them in a three-dimensional historical context where they are not simply a static given in the landscape, and indeed implies that our very definitions of these societies may be problematic.

With the discovery and excavation of 'kurgans' in the Russian steppe in the early 20th century CE, and the recognition that these monumental burial mounds represented the mortuary activities of ancient nomadic civilizations, archaeologists understood early on that, under certain circumstances, the study of ancient pastoral nomadic societies was an endeavor well worth their while

---

[1.] I am grateful to Emmanuel Marx and Benjamin Saidel who provided important comments on an earlier draft of this chapter. I also thank the organizers and participants of the two meetings from which this volume originated for their input and discussions.

(P'yankova 1994; Koryakova 1998). That these early studies fall unambiguously into the culture-historic paradigm of archaeological research, and that analyses seem to have focused primarily on cultural and ethnic systematics (Belenitsky 1968:45–49; Trigger 1989:148–206; Ochir-Goryaeva 1998; Yablonski 1998), does not lessen the fact that the kurgan builders were understood to be early pastoral nomads. The comparisons with the historic and modern nomad hordes of the Asian steppes were implicit but unambiguous. They were also generally simplistic.

With the adoption of new research paradigms an archaeology of pastoral nomadism, similar in conception to the already extant archaeology of hunter-gatherers, and independent of specific culture-historic frameworks, began to emerge in the 1970s and 1980s (for instance Cohen and Dever 1978; Hole 1978; Watson 1979; Chang and Koster 1986). This archaeology drew especially from cultural-ecological approaches to anthropology and was facilitated by new methods in both fieldwork and laboratory analysis. In the Near East the discovery that herd animal domestication postdated the development of farming societies, contrary to the classic 19th century CE hunter-to-herder-to-farmer evolutionary sequence (Clutton-Brock and Grigson 1984; Davis 1984; Clutton-Brock 1989; Horwitz and Ducos 1998; Horwitz et al. 1999; Zeder and Hesse 2000), sharpened focus on the uniqueness of pastoral nomadic societies and their historical development (Lees and Bates 1974; Khazanov 1984). They were not merely another step on the inevitable progression to complex society but required special explanation since they did not, in fact, fall into the linear evolutionary sequence at all (Gellner 1984). As with hunter-gatherer studies, however, if the crude social evolution, and implied ethnic parallels, of an earlier generation were abandoned, the models, analogues, parallels, and hypotheses generated for understanding pastoral nomadic society and its development were still derived virtually exclusively from comparisons to modern groups. That is, the basic paradigms for explaining the origins of pastoral nomadism and the roles of pastoral nomads in history were still taken exclusively from modern ethnography and ethnohistory.

The insights derived from these comparisons have been tremendous. In most ways they are the engine that has driven archaeological analyses, providing a dynamic set of hypotheses and ideas to be examined against an ever more detailed archaeological record. These ideas have operated at several scales, from the relatively low-level spatial analysis of individual sites and activities (Simms 1988; Cribb 1991), and the understanding of herd management and culling (Payne 1973; Cribb 1987; Redding 1984), to larger scale paradigms, such as sedentary-nomad relations (Lees and Bates 1974; Sumner 1986) and market system mechanics (Wapnish 1981; Wapnish and Hesse 1988; Labianca 1990). Some of these ideas and analyses have proven powerful enough to challenge accepted historical concepts, such as the perpetual struggle between the 'Desert and the Sown' (Banning 1986; Avni 1996), and the use of archaeologically invisible nomads as a deus ex machina for historical explanation (Rosen 1992). These research directions should not be abandoned, but from another perspective it is important to recognize the ultimate limitations of ethnography and history, in the sense of texts (both ancient and modern), for understanding the long-term development of pastoral nomadic societies. In complement, archaeological analysis offers a unique contribution to understanding pastoral nomadic adaptations, most especially over the long term (Hodder 1986; Bintliff 1991).

Three points are to be considered here, none especially new. First, the problems inherent in ethnographic analogy have long been debated in archaeology (Ascher 1961). Hypotheses limited to ideas generated from ethnography may offer little new to be discovered, except by way of re-ordering the components of explanation. In the adoption of some version of archaeo-anthropological uniformitarianism for the explanation of the past, that past social and cultural processes are all recognizable in the present, we ignore the possibility, indeed the probability, of the existence of ancient circumstances for which there is no modern parallel or of modern circumstances with no ancient parallel (Bernbeck, this volume). Given that the scales of archaeological explanation vary, unique historical circumstances abound. Furthermore, the assumption of explanatory uniqueness is rarely warranted. Similar outcomes may have differing and multiple causes. In terms of pastoral nomadism, the herding societies of the 19th century CE, impacted by the armies, technologies, and markets of the developing industrial world system, may not provide ideal models for earlier times and relations. Similar points have been made regarding hunter-gatherers.

A second and related point concerns the actual reliability of our historical and anthropological data. From earliest times, texts dealing with pastoral nomads, deriving almost exclusively from their sedentary neighbors, have almost universally depicted them as 'hostile others' (for instance Burstein, this volume; Kupper 1957; Mayerson 1986, 1989). Yet in the documentation of the complexity of relations between the 'Desert and the Sown' both ethnography and archaeology have demonstrated that such generalized and simplistic characterizations are essentially wrong. The inescapable biases in early textual references to nomads render difficult their incorporation into accounts of pastoral nomadic societies. They reflect the politics and agendas of the state and its citizens rather than objective attempts to describe another society. Even recent historical documents, as for example those of the Ottomans regarding the Bedouin, offer perhaps more in what is not written than in what is actually said (Zeevi 1996). Critical reading is a necessity (Burstein, this volume). The lacunae in early accounts are even more difficult to overcome.

Postmodern critique teaches us that modern anthropology cannot serve as an unbiased observer either.

A third and final point, obviously related to the first two, concerns construction and conception of the actual category 'pastoral nomadism.' In spite of the general recognition of a continuous spectrum of behaviors and adaptations, ranging from fully sedentary full-time agriculturalists (with secondary foddered animal husbandry) to fully mobile nonagricultural pastoralists (Khazanov 1984), and a universal understanding of the geographic variability inherent in the societies falling under this rubric (Bacon 1954), most of us persist in viewing pastoral nomadism as some unique social or economic type whose analytic isolation may have meaning for understanding some larger questions of the human career (Ingold 1980, 1987). By nature of our analytic framework, the conduct of inquiry assumes the existence of threshold values, basic bipolarities in our perception of the structures of human society. Thus, there are groups that are pastoral nomadic and groups that are not; or, alternatively, there is some essential value defining pastoral nomadism, present in varying degrees in different societies, but allowing the measure of the basic 'pastoral nomadicness' of a society. Of course, it is precisely these thresholds and values that allow comparative study, or else we would risk comparing the proverbial apples and oranges. Without addressing, however, the issue of the reality or legitimacy of -*etic* and -*emic* constructions of the units and concepts of anthropological inquiry, their use creates internal analytic dynamics defining research questions and agendas. Having defined pastoral nomadism as distinct from sedentary agricultural systems, and clearly separated from hunting-gathering (itself previously distinguished from farming), further analysis assumes the integrity of the categories. If the hierarchy of categorization is changed, so might the analysis. That is, analysis of pastoral nomadic groups emphasizes comparative study of the groups within the rubric. An alternative approach, à la Leach's (1954) work in Burma, might examine shifting political and ecological patterns incorporating farming, foraging, and herding groups within a region as a single unit rather than as disparate units. Benhke (1980) has noted that tribal configurations in Cyrenaica incorporate a range of adaptations, and numerous scholars have noted the constant shift back and forth between sedentism and mobility, between herding and farming (for instance Barth 1961; Marx 1992).

The ultimate result of this emphasis on ethnography and textual history for our comprehension of pastoral nomadism seems to be its perception as somehow fossilized. Once the basic structure of pastoral nomadism was achieved, at different times in history according to different scholars, there was little or no further fundamental change. Variability is recognized but only within certain limited parameters. In a circular logic, if pastoral nomadic behaviors are basically static, with little postorigins evolution, then the adoption of models from ethnography is all the more justified. A similar tendency has been noted for hunter-gatherers. In somewhat caricatured portrayals, the ethnographies of the mid 20th century CE, looking for models of early hominid behavior, have been viewed as demeaning to modern hunter-gatherer groups in their assumption that somehow these groups represent fossilized Stone Age behavior. Of course, modern hunter-gatherer societies are the result of complex evolution and history no less than the societies of their anthropological analysts, and this is now well recognized by those analysts (Lee and DeVore 1968; Schrire 1980; Headland and Reid 1989; Wilmsen 1989; Solway and Lee 1990). Pastoral nomadism as a phenomenon is no different. It has evolved no less than its village and urban contemporaries. There is a richness of texture to that history that cannot be reproduced through reference to the ethnographic present, in all its variability.

ACHIEVING PASTORAL NOMADISM

There are different ways to define *pastoral nomadism*, and these different definitions define differing perceptions of the evolution of the phenomenon. In particular, four distinct criteria have been cited as defining elements: reliance on herd animals as a primary means of subsistence in contexts of a general scarcity of agriculture (Hole 1978), tribal social organization in association with herding (Tapper 1979), pastoral ideology based on herd ownership (Ingold 1980), and asymmetric economically dependent relations with settled agricultural societies (Khazanov 1984). In modern contexts these four criteria often appear as a package (but see Marx 1992), with major exceptions occurring among some of the African cattle pastoralists whose independence of sedentary agricultural society seems clear. Historically, using the southern Levantine deserts as a case study, this apparently integrated package evolved incrementally over the course of two to three millennia, more or less in the order indicated above. In other regions the definitional trajectory need not be the same.

The earliest evidence for the penetration of domesticated herd animals into the deserts comes from eastern Jordan, where late Pre-Pottery Neolithic B (PPNB) sites show domestic herd animals (sheep and goats) and evidence for opportunistic agriculture in what appear to be seasonal camps (Garrard et al. 1996; Martin 1999). Farther south, in southern Jordan, the Negev, and Sinai, there is no evidence for either herding or agriculture, and the economy was based on hunting-gathering (Tchernov and Bar-Yosef 1982; Bar-Yosef 1984; Dayan et al. 1986). Sometime during the late 7th or early 6th millennium BCE (all dates are calendric absolute dates), the Pottery Neolithic, the first domestic herd animals were introduced into the hunter-gatherer systems of the Negev, Sinai, and southern Jordan. The direct evidence for this penetration (around

6000 BCE) derives from domestic sheep and goat dung layers in Negev rockshelters (Rosen et al. 2005). Indirect evidence, in the form of changes in architecture, reduction in arrowhead percentages, the appearance of Near Eastern sheep and goats in Egypt, and the occurrence of domesticates on the desert periphery, supports this chronology (Goring-Morris 1993; Rosen 2002). Herd animals ultimately replaced hunted animals in the hunter-gatherer subsistence economy, in essence initiating a herder-gatherer economy based on small-band level groups.

By the end of the 6th millennium BCE, formative tribal organization, defined here as a level of demographic organization able to draw on social groups beyond band size for various activities,[2] can be traced in the archaeological record of the desert. It is evident in increasing site sizes at one end of the size spectrum, suggesting seasonal aggregation of multiple bands; in the construction of monumental structures (Avner 1984, 1990; Rosen and Rosen 2003), requiring increased manpower and labor organization; and in cooperative hunting strategies, as in the use of 'desert kites' (Betts, this volume; Meshel 1974, 1980; Helms and Betts 1987). Specifically, settlement patterns seem to have a wider range of size than evident in the preceding periods, suggesting greater social interaction and more complex social patterning (Goring-Morris 1993; Bar-Yosef and Bar-Yosef Mayer 2002; Rosen 2002).[3] The construction of solstice shrines, some of which contain individual blocks of stone weighing up to half a ton, also contrasts with earlier periods and clearly reflects both the ability to create megaliths and the social need to do so. The construction of desert kites, apparently also initiated in this period, reflects a level of planning and cooperative hunting also not evident in earlier periods. The simultaneous occurrence of increased sophistication in hunting and the adoption of domestic herd animals need not be seen as contradictory. Hunting plays a social role among many pastoral groups.

Ingold (1980, 1987) ties the development of pastoral ideologies to fundamental differences between owning a herd and hunting one, between conservation and exploitation. The contrast between these activities translates to basic differences in value systems between hunters and herders. For archaeological purposes it is useful to divide pastoral ideology into two realms: the belief systems and cult;

[2.] The definition of *tribe* is difficult, basically falling between the so-called egalitarian band and chiefdom, with incipient stratification and specialized economies (Buccellati, this volume; Parkinson 2002). My intent is not to plug into a fixed evolutionary framework dictating certain features but to indicate a society beyond the smallest scale, one that has not yet achieved the elaboration of chiefdoms.

[3.] Desert kites are gazelle traps constructed of low walls that funnel the animal into a pit or corral where it can be killed. They were named by British pilots flying over the Near Eastern deserts who saw in them a resemblance to kites.

and the changes in lifestyle reflecting different value systems deriving from the ownership of herds. Although it is difficult to reconstruct the specifics of early pastoral ideologies, it can be no coincidence that a virtual explosion of desert cult arose in the middle to late 6th millennium BCE (Avner 1984, 1990), the late Pottery Neolithic, correlated with what I have referred to as the herder-gatherer phase of pastoral nomadic evolution. This development is reflected most especially in the construction of numerous desert shrines (Avner 1984; 1990; Goring-Morris 1993; Rosen 2002), often with solstice alignments (Rosen and Rosen 2003)[4] and usually in association with mortuary ritual. Many of these seem to have had a megalithic aspect in their size and massiveness. While it is difficult to see the precise symbolic connection between the new ritual behavior, as reflected in these shrines and the 'new' pastoral way of life, this should not really be surprising. First, the -*emic* comprehension of prehistoric symbol systems is one of archaeology's least successful endeavors as a discipline. Second, taking a cue from the preceding agricultural revolution, Cauvin (2000) has emphasized the symbolic aspects, indeed primacy, of symbolic development, yet most of the iconography of the agricultural revolution has little or nothing to do with farming. It is worth noting that attempts to interpret the desert iconography backward in time, from the known symbolism of historical Mesopotamia or the biblical period in the Levant (Avner 1984, 1990), are problematic. The chronological span of thousands of years, and the basic social and cultural contrasts between early desert tribal pastoralism and later sedentary agricultural, urban, and state society, must be accounted for if a set of symbols from one is to be interpretively grafted onto the other. Without detailed consideration of the mechanics of such a transformation, the value of the scholarly wholesale adoption of myth from one society to another must be questioned.

To return to the original point, if we cannot precisely define the belief and symbol systems, it nevertheless seems clear that a transformation occurred and that it can be tied to the rise of herding-gathering. The other half of pastoral ideology, at least from the archaeological perspective, lifestyles reflecting pastoral values, can be seen primarily in the organization of space. On the small scale the architectural changes that accompany the transition to pastoralism in the desert are one of its clearest correlates. The clustered room architecture of the PPNB is replaced, at some point in the Pottery Neolithic or Chalcolithic, by pen-and-attached-room sites (Rosen 2002). This type of structure consists

---

[4.] In the report of the archaeological survey that discovered Ramat Saharonim, this site was dated between the Pottery Neolithic and Early Bronze Age based on cairn construction and design. Radiocarbon and optically stimulated luminescence dates have now established that both the shrine and the cairns are late Pottery Neolithic in date, about 5000 BCE (calibrated; Porat et al. 2006).

of a large central enclosure or enclosures (sometimes inappropriately referred to as courtyards) with the actual habitation structures, or huts, attached to the periphery. The central enclosure has usually been interpreted as an animal pen (Kozloff 1981; Haiman 1992; Rosen 2003), but this functional interpretation is not strictly necessary. The entire organization of the typical occupation has been re-oriented so that the center is now an open space, instead of a densely packed cluster. That this change coincides with the development of pastoralism suggests that the adoption of domestic animals had major effects on the organization of daily life, a trivial conclusion that nevertheless needs to be emphasized. Speculating, and assuming that the enclosures really were animal pens, the centrality of herd animals in these sites dominates their very conception.

On the larger scale, an increase in territoriality is also indicated in the archaeological record, albeit not strongly. The megalithic aspect of the shrines mentioned above, and in particular the development of large tomb fields (*nawamis*, circular vaulted multiple-burial structures, in south and central Sinai; *tumuli* in the Negev), suggests an increased need to demarcate and legitimize claims to territory (Bar-Yosef et al. 1977, 1986). The development of distinct zones of settlement, indicated by the clustering of sites, is matched by the development of two level hierarchies in site size (Haiman 1992), probably both indicating seasonal movement within a territory and tribal organization. This increased territoriality, while tied to tribal organization, can also be attributed to the pressures of herd management (Ingold 1980). Hunter-gatherers are indeed territorial, especially with regard to specific resources such as favored water sources or the famous Kalahari *mgongo* nuts. Although these concerns feature among desert pastoralists as well, their primary source of territoriality is the need for pasture, a far more extensive requirement than control over point source resources (although wells and cisterns may be the focus of dispute). Territoriality may therefore be more marked. On the other hand, extreme variability in climate may render territoriality counterproductive, requiring great flexibility in exploitation of resources. Regardless, evidence for territoriality increases with the adoption of domestic herds.

It is interesting that, to a degree, these archaeological site-distribution patterns parallel those of desert Natufian and Harifian hunter-gatherers, some 5000 years earlier. The terminal Pleistocene culture territories, however, restricted to specific zones within the desert, seem to reflect areas of exploitation rather than areas of ownership or territorial demarcation. That is, there seem to have been neither South Sinai Natufians sharing a border with the Negev Natufians nor any eastern Negev Harifians sharing a border with those of the western Negev and the Negev Highlands. With the rise of herding societies, territoriality also becomes an issue of shared borders. Population increase cannot be ruled out as a factor in the trend toward increasing territoriality, thus explaining the differences between the hunter-gatherer systems mentioned above and the later herder-gatherer and pastoral nomadic systems. It seems reasonable to tie such demographic changes to the transition to food production: herding.

The rise of economic relations between the 'Desert and the Sown' is the final defining characteristic of pastoral nomadism to develop. Unlike the previous criteria, which to a degree can be seen as autochthonous developments, the rise of asymmetric economic relations between tribal groups and sedentary societies is predicated on the evolution of social complexity in the core regions. In the Levant this does not occur until the Early Bronze Age, and the earliest evidence for such relations between core and periphery dates to the end of the 4th and beginning of the third millennium BCE. This period, the Early Bronze Age I–II, saw increased trade between the desert tribes and the urbanizing Mediterranean core region, especially focusing on Arad in the northern Negev, as a gateway town for that trade (Kempinski 1989; Finkelstein 1995:67–86; Amiran et al. 1997; Rosen 2003). Although copper seems to have been the focus of much of that trade, the desert nomads also produced and exported milling stones, beads, seashells, hematite, certain chipped-stone tools, and other trinkets. They seem to have imported grain, based on the common presence of used milling stones with little evidence for agriculture (and, given the environment, little opportunity), some pottery, and other goods. The number of sites that can be attributed to the Early Bronze Age I–II increases tenfold over preceding periods (Rosen 1987), suggesting a major desert population increase.[5] Even with a somewhat ameliorated climate (Rosen 1995), still less optimal than that of the earlier PPNB or the Chalcolithic, it is unlikely that these larger populations could be sustained in the desert based on a herding-gathering subsistence. The Early Bronze Age I–II saw the crossing of the threshold from herding-gathering to pastoral nomadism as reflected in a dependence trade relationship. Without the economic supports of the sedentary zone, especially the import of grain, the Negev pastoral system was not viable. To clinch this case, the abandonment of Arad around 2700 BCE, seems to have entailed the collapse of its pastoral nomadic hinterland, reflected in a virtual absence of sites in the Negev Highlands for several hundred years.

TECHNOLOGICAL DEVELOPMENTS

If the above review somehow defines the genesis of 'pastoral nomadism,' there is nonetheless great developmental variability following the crossing of the threshold. Technological change plays a defining role in some of this

---

[5.] There are not only more sites, but they are also larger, while the period of occupation (Early Bronze Age I–II) is no longer than earlier periods.

development, and indeed some of the postorigins technological changes play as great a role in the common understanding of pastoral nomadism as do the definitions. Sherratt (1981, 1983) has stressed the significance, beginning in the formative period of pastoral nomadism, of secondary product exploitation in the rise of civilization, and this unquestionably play a major role in the evolution of desert tribal societies. Russell (1988) concluded that the energy efficiency of herd exploitation based on dairy products and meat was double that of carnivorous pastoralism. Adding hair and wool to the equation not only increased the efficiency of exploitation but, as a cash crop, must have had significant impact on nomad economics beyond subsistence. Similarly, the domestication of the donkey in the Pottery Neolithic enabled transport of bulk items not previously amenable to long-distance trade. Even given the ability to drag large objects on sledges, as in precontact North America, the exchange system described above for the Early Bronze Age, including large quantities of milling stones, ceramics, metals, and grain, was unquestionably predicated on the earlier domestication of the donkey (Ovadia 1992; Sherratt 1981, 1983). The introduction of domestic horses, especially for riding, into Near Eastern nomadic society, sometime in the late third millennium BCE (Wapnish 1997), must also have had a major impact.

The adoption of the domestic camel as a pack animal, however, was a watershed event in pastoral nomadic history in the Near East. A strong pack camel can carry up to 200 to 325 kg of goods and travel for several days without watering, well beyond the capabilities of any other beast of burden (Gauthier-Pilters and Dagg 1981:110; Bulliet 1990). Although evidence for camel domestication in the Persian Gulf area is as early as the late third millennium BCE, the earliest remains of camels in the Levant date to the Late Bronze Age, the second half of the second millennium BCE, from Tell Jemmeh near Gaza (Wapnish 1981). Found at an *entrepôt* town, these camels probably reflect long-distance, deep-desert trade with Arabia, virtually impossible prior to the camel. Indeed, the ability to traverse the deep desert served both to facilitate previously difficult trade systems and to allow deep retreat into the desert wastes, both characteristics of the classical nomad stereotype. The rise of the Nabateans, the sedentized North Arabian nomads who established a trading kingdom around Petra and the spice route through the desert, was predicated on camel caravans. In addition to its use as a pack animal, the invention and adoption of the North Arabian riding saddle in the latter half of the first millennium BCE provided control of the camel and stability to its rider that allowed fighting from camelback (Bulliet 1990). Thus, desert tribal societies could now constitute a greater military threat, with capabilities well beyond those of earlier nomads (Eph'al 1984). In this context of military technologies the introduction of the composite bow must also have enhanced fighting from camelback, as it did fighting on horseback. Although well documented on the Asian steppe (Shishlina 1997), the subject has been little noted in the Near East.

The invention and adoption of large woven tents should also be considered a technological milestone in the history of pastoral nomadism. Although these tents are usually difficult to trace archaeologically, the total dominance of stone-hut bases as an architectural type throughout the southern Levantine deserts through at least the end of the third millennium BCE suggests a *terminus ante quem* for their introduction. Assyrian sources (Eph'al 1984:10) and biblical references (as in Judges 8:11) to tents as dwelling places suggest presence in the first half of the first millennium BCE. In the Negev the earliest unambiguous evidence for tents can be attributed to the Nabateans, in the first centuries BCE to CE (although it is likely that they were introduced earlier). This evidence consists of stone lines, cleared areas, hearths, and other features in the same general configuration, although not in the specific details, as one can see in more recently abandoned tent camps (Saidel, this volume, 2001; Simms 1988; Avni 1992; Eldar et al. 1992; Rosen 1993). The implications of the adoption of the tent are numerous. On the simplest level, the increased potential for residential mobility enhances the flexibility of the nomadic lifestyle. Besides contributing to the relative ease of striking camps, however, tents allow for great flexibility of spatial arrangements within camps. Indeed, the ability to tent large spaces allows the construction of communal structures far more difficult to build of the brush and stone construction materials usually available in the Levantine deserts. Tents also allow easy internal partition, virtually impossible in the small huts used by nomads in the Negev prior to their introduction (Magid, this volume).

Desert agricultural technologies, both the construction of wells and cisterns and the use of runoff irrigation, have also impacted nomadic societies. Although most of these systems were built during periods of state incursion into the desert, the basic infrastructures remained after the withdrawal of the state. Desert wells and cisterns may serve as major foci for pastoral activities, often structuring movement, serving as borders between tribes or as bones of contention between them, and obviously extending grazing territories, especially for sheep and goats. Even given the disdain often accorded agriculture by nomads, the ability to farm in the desert, as done opportunistically by modern Bedouin, affects both the geographic patterning of tribal territories and the nature of economic relations with sedentary settlements; nomads producing their own grain need not trade for it. Furthermore, nomadic control of farming areas probably increases internal tribal inequalities. As Marx (1967) has noted for the Bedouin tribes of mid 20th century CE Israel, peasant subgroups subservient to the Bedouin often do the actual farming. In the Negev the earliest cisterns, cut into soft loess and lined with stone blocks and mud plaster, are dated to the Iron Age, in the first half of the first millennium BCE. These are accompanied by outposts and small runoff irrigation farms (Bruins 1986). Many of these cisterns still fill with rainwater seasonally. The earliest rock-cut cisterns and wells in the Negev date to the Nabatean period (Glueck 1959:Figure 41) and can be associated with the Nabatean penetration of the Negev. These, too, still fill up regularly. As with the earlier cisterns, these were accompanied by relatively small runoff irrigation systems and associated farmsteads. The major expansion of these systems occurs in the Byzantine and Early Islamic periods, in the middle of the first millennium CE. These terrace field systems are still used by Bedouin today, who farm opportunistically in areas receiving as little rainfall as 100 mm per year, half the usual minimum required for dry farming of barley and one-third for what is needed for wheat.

The introduction of the gun in the late 18th century CE, and its increasing use through the 19th and early 20th centuries CE, also had a tremendous impact on Bedouin society in the Near East (Saidel 2001). It is perhaps difficult to assess the overall effect of this technology on relations between tribal groups and sedentary society since virtually all ethnographic observations postdate the gun. Certainly patterns of warfare must have changed. Saidel (2001) notes that early matchlock muskets could not be used mounted, and Bedouin raiding strategy shifted to the ambush. This, of course, is rather small scale, and whether a real shift in power relations occurred as a result of the introduction of the gun is difficult to ascertain. Even if one did, whether it should be accommodated as part of the ebb and flow of power relations between the 'Desert and the Sown,' or whether it constituted a shift to a new status, is a moot point. The near extinction of such wild herd animals as gazelle, and the local disappearance of other species, like the roe deer and the ostrich, however, can almost undoubtedly be attributed to the increased use of guns. These extinctions and near-extinctions do constitute a major change in ecological balance. In terms of Bedouin adaptations, the social role of hunting, still important in spite of the economic dependence on herds, must have been significantly reduced.

The advent of more recent technologies, such as trucks for transporting animals, wheeled water containers, tractors, and various communication technologies, have had great impacts as well. In fact, whether the most recent pastoral nomads should even be compared with their predecessors as models of nomadic behavior is debatable.

THE IMPACT OF THE OUTSIDE WORLD

Beyond the effects of new technologies, the evolving nature of the adjacent sedentary societies also had profound effects on pastoral nomadic lifestyles, relations, and adaptations. Given the general trajectory of increasing complexity and integration of the external world, with obvious fluctuations, there is also a trajectory to the effects on interactions with and relations to nomadic societies. That is, the impact of sedentary societies, beyond technology, on pastoral nomads evolves over time. These impacts are, on one hand, historically particular but, on another, can be viewed as cumulative and therefore directional, given certain general cumulative trends in historical development. They can be examined from several perspectives, which for our purposes will be classified as territorial, economic, demographic, and ideological.

Although in the myth of the struggle between the 'Desert and the Sown' there is a perception of equality between the forces, in reality, over the long term, sedentary societies have consistently expanded ever deeper into nomad and desert territories, albeit with fluctuations and retreats. Such expansions come at the expense of nomad territories, compressing them and increasing pressure on resources in the even more marginal lands left to the nomads. They are made possible by increasing populations within stable agricultural systems, increasing political integration and military power with the rise of states and empires, and more effective agricultural technologies, allowing better utilization of the desert. Even in the retreat of the state from the desert, the physical infrastructures left behind, as mentioned above in the discussion on technological changes, change the nature of pastoral adaptation. In the Negev, sedentary society has advanced and retreated repeatedly since the origins of pastoral nomadism as a phenomenon. These fluctuations are summarized in Figure 5.1.

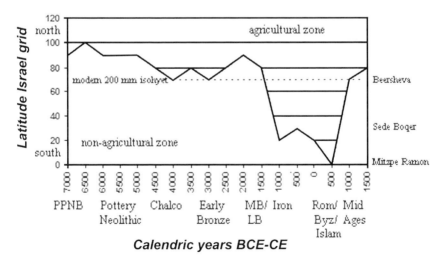

Figure 5.1. Schematic graph of the advance and retreat of the agricultural boundary in the Negev based on data from the Negev Emergency Survey. Vertical scale is in kilometers.

The intent here is not to detail each successive phase of settlement but rather to note that successive incursions by state-level societies from the Early Bronze Age onward extended successively deeper into the Negev,[6] and each such incursion left an ever greater imprint on the landscape and its inhabitants. An additional and crucial point to consider is that although the periods of settlement were punctuated by long periods of retreat from the desert, nomadic presence actually mirrors sedentary presence. During the long periods of reduced state activity in the Negev, the region reverted to peripheral grazing grounds, as opposed to tribal residential territory. Each incursion is accompanied by a resurgence of nomadic activity on its fringes, specifically adapted to the specific circumstances of the incursion.

Obviously partially a function of depth of incursion, the economic impacts of the outside world on nomadic society can be seen to systematically increase through time. It is difficult to measure this increase directly, but to measure trade, for example, petrographic analyses of Early Bronze Age ceramic assemblages from Negev nomad sites show high proportions of local pottery produced by the nomads themselves, in addition to some imports. In contrast, by classical times (Nabatean, Roman, Byzantine, and Early Islamic) 90% or more of the pottery found on the nomad sites was imported, produced by specialists in the towns and sites of the empires of Late Antiquity (but see Barnard, this volume). By recent and subrecent times virtually all pottery used by the Bedouin, the famous black Gaza Ware, is imported, along with a vast array of other manufactured goods. Similarly, one can make a case for the ever-increasing integration of nomad economic activities into the larger economic sphere. On one hand, anthropologists have long been aware that pastoralism is but one in a large set of resources and activities supporting pastoral nomadic societies. Salzman (1972) coined the phrase "multi-resource nomadism" to describe the complex economic base of most of these societies.

The long-term history of Negev pastoral nomadism suggests that with time nomad activities increase in their range, the number of people engaged in them, and their importance to tribal economy. While the earliest developmental phase, that of the herder-gatherers, still exhibits relative economic autonomy, the Early Bronze Age nomads, with a range of cottage industries to supplement their pastoralism (Rosen 2003), seem already to have expanded beyond the threshold of herding-gathering carrying capacity. Certainly by Nabatean times, trade systems played a major role in nomad economies, in some ways providing the raison d'être for their very presence in the Negev. By later classical times,

---

[6.] While Early Bronze Age society in the southern Levant probably did not achieve state level political organization as usually defined, it did achieve a level of secondary urbanism, certainly enough to function as a focus for nomad economies.

in the Byzantine period, local nomads served as guides for the large pilgrimage system to Sinai, raised camels and donkeys for the Byzantine army, received subsidies from Rome for keeping the peace, and may well have been wage laborers in a range of tasks associated with the Byzantine frontier in the Negev. Raiding should perhaps also be seen in this light as an added economic activity (Sweet 1965). The difference between Early Antiquity and Late Antiquity is marked, but difficult to quantify. With modern times the range of nonpastoral activities and their importance seems to increase, with wage labor and warfare playing especially greater roles. The integration of pastoral activities, however, those derived from the animals themselves, also increases with the expansion of access to markets. In the Negev this is difficult to measure archaeologically, but in the 20th century CE, with the direct impact of western markets on local peoples, stock raising emphasized cash returns rather than subsistence.

Although Khazanov (1984) demonstrated some time ago that some form of dependency characterizes most relations between nomads and their sedentary cousins, given the above discussion, economic integration with sedentary societies seems to increase over time. Indeed, in the Near East of recent times, perhaps beginning during the Late Ottoman era, the cash economies tying nomads to sedentary market systems (Black-Michaud 1986) seem qualitatively different from those of earlier eras.

The increasing number of sites in the Negev through time, punctuated by periods of archaeological decline, and their generally increasing size have been well documented in archaeological surveys (Rosen 1987). These trends undoubtedly reflect long-term increases in the population of the Negev, again punctuated by periods of demographic decline, the same fluctuations mentioned above in terms of incursions and pastoral expansions. A large proportion of this long-term increase was in the nomadic populations and can be seen archaeologically in increases in the numbers of base camps, camps, and small campsites, especially in those areas beyond the extent of sedentary and agricultural settlement. An educated guess given the numbers of sites and their sizes suggests a general increase from a few hundred nomads at most, during the herder-gatherer phase of the sequence, to thousands in the Classical era. By way of comparison, the Bedouin population of the Negev in 1947 was approximately 90,000, about double that of 1931 (Abu Rabi'a 2001:80–85). These are changes of orders of magnitude. They must reflect fundamentally different levels of adaptation and integration clearly tied to the evolution of the sedentary societies with which the nomads were associated and to the increasing intensity of the relations between them.

The ideological impact of sedentary societies on their nomadic neighbors can be seen on two levels: in the adoption of new religious beliefs and their effects on aspects of nomadic society and in shifts in nomadic ideologies resulting from sociological changes due to contact and association with external forces. In general it is difficult to assess ideological shifts and impacts confidently because of a paucity of materials (nomads often do not build obvious shrines) and because of the importance of context and meaning for evaluating symbol systems. Furthermore, although 'pastoral ideology' has been cited as a characteristic element in these societies, beyond Ingold's (1980) proposed conceptions of ownership developed primarily to distinguish herding from hunting, there is no consensus on what the defining elements of pastoral nomadic ideology and beliefs might be. In terms of the adoption of religious beliefs, although Avner (1984, 1990) has interpreted the components of many early desert shrines as representing Near Eastern and Mesopotamian pantheons and rites, and hence reflecting the influences of sedentary societies, his claims are unconvincing. Standing stones, in various combinations, are features of societies all over the world; it is not necessary to invoke Mesopotamian imagery to explain them. Furthermore, the chronological (3000 years) and sociological (urban state to desert tribe) distance between the early desert shrines, or even the later ones, and their supposed symbolic cousins is left without any bridging explanation.

The Iron Age cult site at Kuntillet Ajrud (Meshel 1978; Dever 1984) is a better case for external influence, but there is nothing to tie it to pastoral nomadic society. The Nabatean syncretism of the Hellenistic and Roman pantheon with their own is a clear example of external ideological influence, but it is not clear that the Nabateans were indeed pastoral nomads in any standard sense of the word by the time they absorbed Mediterranean religion.

Although there is historical evidence for the adoption of Christianity among some nomadic tribes in the southern Levantine deserts during the Byzantine period (Mayerson 1963), we have little evidence indicating how this adoption affected the tribes socially. The adoption, however, of Islam among desert tribal peoples changed basic social structures throughout the Near East, including those of the Negev, Sinai, and Jordan. While there is some historical question as to the ultimate social and political origins of Islam (Crone and Cook 1977; Donner 1981; Hawting 1982; Crone 1987), the nomads of the Negev adopted Islam early in its history, as evidenced clearly in the large number of open-air mosques found in association with Early Islamic pastoral nomadic camps (Avni 1994; Rosen and Avni 1997) and by hints in some of the texts (Mayerson 1964; Whitcomb 1995). The adoption of Islam provided cohesiveness to nomadic tribes over large expanses never before achieved. Politically the adoption of Islam served as a springboard for major developments in Near Eastern nomadism. The influence of Islam can be seen on a smaller scale as well. Saidel (this volume) has noted how the adoption of Islam affected the organization of space within the tent, deriving especially from the changed roles of women in nomadic Islamic society. The location of mosques in the Islamic sites, always somewhat above and removed from the occupation sites (Rosen and Avni 1997), also differs from that of the preceding pagan shrines, apparently more spatially integrated within the sites.

Ideological shifts occurring as a consequence of contact, without the direct adoption of belief systems, can be seen mostly politically. Although egalitarianism is the nomadic ideal (Sahlins 1968:21; Marx 1967:181), and perhaps observed more in the breach than in practice, contact with the outside world demands leadership, and the greater the demands, and the rewards, from the state or empire, the larger the scale that leadership needs to be. Zimri Lin, king of Mari in the second millennium BCE, created nomadic headmen through his need to govern the tribes under his rule; Rome created the chiefs of large nomadic tribes; and England and France, after the First World War, the kings of nomadic states. There is a trajectory here that belies the stereotypical stasis of pastoral nomadic adaptation.

DISCUSSION

Pastoral nomadism in the southern Levantine deserts is a phenomenon showing intense variation over time. Although we can trace themes and motifs in this variation, and indeed perhaps some cyclicity in their appearance, there is no stability or predictability. Pastoral nomadism seems very much an ad hoc improvisation to meet the special circumstances of each historical context. In this sense the desert tribal societies of the southern Levant, and of course of the Near East in general, should be tied analytically as much to their sedentary complements as they are to some general phenomenon of pastoral nomadism. The basic instability of state adaptations (Marcus 1998) then begins to look structurally similar to that of pastoral nomadic societies. And in this sense we perhaps ought to invoke Leach's (1954) work on the political systems of highland Burma and see the 'Desert and the Sown' as two component parts of an integrated long-term system, fluctuating back and forth between one another. Adams (1978) has suggested a similar perspective in his conceptualization of ancient and modern Near Eastern societies as resilient (meaning adaptable) and shifting between the urban, the rural, and the desert. Rowton's (1977) dimorphic society reflects a similar idea, although it is drawn from 'enclosed nomadism' rather than the geographically peripheral nomadism dealt with here. Of course, in these senses the distinctions drawn above between external and internal impacts and developments are purely relative. If pastoral nomadic societies in the Levant, and in the Near East more generally, should be linked analytically to sedentary societies, then the developmental history of pastoral nomadic societies cannot be static but should exhibit trajectories parallel and linked to the increasing complexities and developments of sedentary societies.

Thus, the developmental changes sketched so briefly in the preceding review should come as no surprise. Furthermore, if pastoral nomadic societies are linked developmentally to their sedentary neighbors, then different pastoral nomadic societies need not show contemporary or parallel developmental characteristics. The idea of set stages of social evolution has been passé for a generation of scholars studying the rise of complex societies. It is reasonable that the concept be abandoned for nomadic societies as well. This is not to say that pastoral nomadic societies cannot be studied as a class. The demands of raising stock and migrating seasonally, without intensively engaging in agriculture, must result in similarities among these societies, if only by definition. But these will constitute only partial explications. In our analytic isolation of pastoral nomadism as a research subject, we risk losing sight of the essential genius of the phenomenon, that ability to achieve ever more impressive adaptations to marginal social and physical environments.

REFERENCES

Abu-Rabi'a, A.
2001   *Bedouin Century*. New York, Berghahn Books.
Adams, R. M.
1978   Strategies of Maximization, Stability, and Resilience in Mesopotamian Society, Settlement, and Agriculture. *Proceedings of the American Philosophical Society 122*: pp. 329–335.
Amiran, R., O. Ilan and M. Sebbane
1997   *Canaanite Arad: Gateway City to the Wilderness* [in Hebrew]. Jerusalem, Israel Antiquities Authority.
Ascher, R.
1961   Analogy in Archaeological Interpretation. *Southwest Journal of Anthropology 17*: pp. 317–325.
Avner, U.
1984   Ancient Cult Sites in the Negev and Sinai Deserts. *Tel Aviv 11*: pp. 115–131.
1990   Ancient Agricultural Settlement and Religion in the Uvda Valley in Southern Israel. *Biblical Archaeologist 53*: pp. 125–141.
Avni, G.
1996   *Nomads, Farmers, and Town-Dwellers*. Jerusalem, Israel Antiquities Authority.
1992   Survey of Deserted Bedouin Campsites in the Negev Highlands and Its Implications for Archaeological Research. In O. Bar-Yosef and A. M. Khazanov (eds.), *Pastoralism in the Levant: Archaeological Materials in Anthropological Perspectives*. Madison, Prehistory Press: pp. 241–254.

1994   Early Mosques in the Negev Highlands: New Archaeological Evidence on
            Islamic Penetration of Southern Palestine. *Bulletin of the American Schools of
            Oriental Research 294*: pp. 83–100.

Bacon, E.

1954   Types of Pastoral Nomadism in Central and Southwest Asia. *Southwestern
            Journal of Anthropology 10*: pp. 44–68.

Banning, E. B.

1986   Peasants, Pastoralists, and *Pax Romana*: Mutualism in the Southern Highlands
            of Jordan. *Bulletin of the American Schools of Oriental Research 261*: pp. 25–50.

Barth, F.

1961   *Nomads of South Persia*. Boston, Little, Brown.

Bar-Yosef, O.

1984   Seasonality Among Neolithic Hunter-Gatherers in Southern Sinai. In J.
            Clutton-Brock and C. Grigson (eds.), *Animals and Archaeology. Volume 3: Early
            Herders and Their Flocks. BAR International Series 202*. Oxford, Archaeopress:
            pp. 145–160.

Bar-Yosef, O. and D. E. Bar-Yosef Mayer

2002   Early Neolithic Tribes in the Levant. In W. A. Parkinson (ed.), *The Archaeology
            of Tribal Societies*. Ann Arbor, International Monographs in Prehistory 15: pp.
            340–371.

Bar-Yosef, O., A. Belfer-Cohen, A. Goren and P. Smith

1977   The Nawamis Near Ein Huderah (Eastern Sinai). *Israel Exploration Journal
            27*: pp. 65–88.

Bar-Yosef, O., A. Belfer-Cohen, A. Goren, I. Hershkovitz, H. Mienis, B. Sass and O.
            Ilan

1986   Nawamis and Habitation Sites Near Gebel Gunna, Southern Sinai. *Israel
            Exploration Journal 36*: pp. 121–167.

Belenitsky, A.

1968   *Archaeologica Mundi: Central Asia*. Geneva, Nagel.

Benhke, R. H.

1980   *The Herders of Cyrenaica: Ecology, Economy, and Kinship Among the Bedouin of
            Eastern Libya*. Bloomington, University of Illinois Press.

Bintliff, J. (ed.)

1991   *The Annales School and Archaeology*. New York, New York University Press.

Black-Michaud, J.

1986   *Sheep and Land*. Cambridge, Cambridge University Press.

Bruins, H. J.

1986   *Desert Environment and Agriculture in the Central Negev and Kadesh Barnea
            During Historical Times*. Nijkerk, Midbar Foundation.

Bulliet, R.

1990   *The Camel and the Wheel*. New York, Columbia University Press.

Cauvin, J.

2000   *The Birth of the Gods and the Origins of Agriculture*. Cambridge, Cambridge University Press.

Chang, C. and H. A. Koster

1986   Beyond Bones: Toward an Archaeology of Pastoralism. *Advances in Archaeological Method and Theory 9*: pp. 97–148.

Clutton-Brock, J. (ed.)

1989   *The Walking Larder: Patterns of Domestication, Pastoralism, and Predation*. London, Unwin Hyman.

Clutton-Brock, J. and C. Grigson (eds.)

1984   *Animals and Archaeology. Volume 3: Early Herders and Their Flocks. BAR International Series 202*. Oxford, Archaeopress.

Cohen, R. and W. G. Dever

1978   Preliminary Report of the Pilot Season of the "Central Negev Highlands Project." *Bulletin of the American Schools of Oriental Research 232*: pp. 29–45.

Cribb, R.

1987   The Logic of the Herd: A Computer Simulation of Herd Structure. *Journal of Anthropological Archaeology 6*: pp. 376–415.

1991   *Nomads in Archaeology*. Cambridge, Cambridge University Press.

Crone, P.

1987   *Meccan Trade and the Rise of Islam*. Princeton, Princeton University Press.

Crone, P. and M. Cook

1977   *Hagarism: The Making of the Islamic World*. Cambridge, Cambridge University Press.

Davis, S.

1984   Climatic Change and the Advent of Domestication: The Succession of Ruminant Artiodactyls in the Late Pleistocene-Holocene in the Israel Region. *Paléorient 8*: pp. 5–15.

Dayan, T., E. Tchernov, O. Bar-Yosef and Y. Yom-Tov

1986   Animal Exploitation in Ujrat el Mehed, a Neolithic Site in Southern Sinai. *Paléorient 12*: pp. 105–116.

Dever, W. G.

1984   Ashera, Consort of Yahweh? New Evidence from Kunitllet Ajrud. *Bulletin of the American Schools of Oriental Research 255*: pp. 21–38.

Donner, F. M.

1981   *Early Islamic Conquests*. Princeton, Princeton University Press.

Eldar, I., Y. Nir and D. Nahlieli

1992   The Bedouin and Their Campsites in the Dimona Region of the Negev: Comparative Models for the Study of Ancient Desert Settlements. In O. Bar-Yosef and A. M. Khazanov (eds.), *Pastoralism in the Levant: Archaeological*

Materials in Anthropological Perspectives. Madison, Prehistory Press: pp. 205–219.

Eph'al, I.

1984   *The Ancient Arabs*. Jerusalem, Magnes Press.

Finkelstein, I.

1995   *Living on the Fringe*. Sheffield, Sheffield Academic Press.

Garrard, A., S. Colledge and L. Martin

1996   The Emergence of Crop Cultivation and Caprine Hunting in the "Marginal Zones" of the Southern Levant. In D. R. Harris (ed.), *The Origins and Spread of Agriculture and Pastoralism in Eurasia*. Washington, Smithsonian Institution Press: pp. 204–226.

Gauthier-Pilters, H. and A. I. Dagg

1981   *The Camel, Its Evolution, Ecology, Behavior, and Relationship to Man*. Chicago, University of Chicago Press.

Gellner, E.

1984   Foreword. In A. M. Khazanov (ed.), *Nomads and the Outside World*. Cambridge, Cambridge University Press: pp. ix–xxvi.

Glueck, N.

1959   *Rivers in the Desert*. Philadelphia, Jewish Publication Society.

Goring-Morris, A. N.

1993   From Foraging to Herding in the Negev and Sinai: The Early to Late Neolithic Transition. *Paléorient 19*: pp. 65–89.

Haiman, M.

1992   Sedentism and Pastoralism in the Negev Highlands in the Early Bronze Age: Results of the Western Negev Highlands Emergency Survey. In O. Bar-Yosef and A. M. Khazanov (eds.), *Pastoralism in the Levant: Archaeological Materials in Anthropological Perspective*. Madison, Prehistory Press: pp. 93–105.

Hawting, G. R.

1982   The Origins of the Muslim Sanctuary at Mecca. In G. H. A. Juynboll (ed.), *Studies in the First Century of Islamic Society*. Carbondale, Southern Illinois University Press: pp. 23–47.

Headland, T. and L. Reid

1989   Hunter-Gatherers and Their Neighbors from Prehistory to the Present. *Current Anthropology 30*: pp. 43–66.

Helms, S. W. and A. V. G. Betts

1987   The Desert "Kites" of the Badiyat esh-Shaur and North Arabia. *Paléorient 13*: pp. 41–67.Hesse, B.

1988   Slaughter Patterns and Domestication: The Beginnings of Pastoralism in Western Iran. *Man 17*: pp. 403–417.

Hodder, I. (ed.)

1986   *Archaeology as Long-Term History*. Cambridge, Cambridge University Press.

Hole, F.

1978   Pastoral Nomadism in Western Iran. In R. A. Gould (ed.), *Explorations in Ethnoarchaeology*. Albuquerque, University of New Mexico Press: pp. 127–168.

Horwitz, L. K. and P. Ducos

1998   An Investigation into the Origins of Domestic Sheep in the Southern Levant. In H. Buitenhuis, L. Bartosiewicz and A. M. Choyke (eds.), *Archaeozoology of the Near East. Volume 3*. Groningen, ARC Publications: pp. 80–94.

Horwitz, L. K., E. Tchernov, P. Ducos, C. Becker, A. von den Dreisch, L. Martin and A. Garrard

1999   Animal Domestication in the Southern Levant. *Paléorient 25*: pp. 63–80.

Ingold, T.

1980   *Hunters, Pastoralists, and Ranchers*. Cambridge, Cambridge University Press.

1987   *The Appropriation of Nature: Essays on Human Ecology and Social Relations*. Iowa City, University of Iowa Press.

Kempinski, A.

1989   Urbanization and Metallurgy in Southern Canaan. In P. de Miroschedji (ed.), *L'urbanisation de la Palestine a L'age du Bronze Ancien. BAR International Series 527*. Oxford, Archaeopress: pp. 163–168.

Khazanov, A. M.

1984   *Nomads and the Outside World*. Cambridge, Cambridge University Press.

Koryakova, L.

1998   Introduction: Some Problems of Nomadic Studies. In M. Pearce and M. Tosi (eds.), *Papers from the EAA Third Annual Meeting: Pre- and Protohistory. BAR International Series 717*. Oxford, Archaeopress: pp. 82–85.

Kozloff, B.

1981   Pastoral Nomadism in Sinai: An Ethnoarchaeological Study. *Production pastorales et société: Bulletin d'ecologie et d'anthropologie des sociétés Pastorales 8*: pp. 19–24.

Kupper, J.-R.

1957   *Les nomades en Mésopotamie au temps des rois de Mari*. Paris, Bibliothèque de la Faculté de Philosophie et Lettres de L'université de Liège.

LaBianca, O.

1990   *Hesban I: Sedentarization and Nomadization: Food System Cycles at Hesban and Vicinity in Transjordan*. Berrien Springs, Andrews University Press.

Leach, E. R.

1954   *Political Systems of Highland Burma*. Boston, Beacon Press.

Lee, R. B. and I. DeVore (eds.)

1968   *Man the Hunter*. Chicago, Aldine.

Lees, S. H. and D. G. Bates

1974   The Origins of Specialized Pastoral Nomadism: A Systemic Model. *American Antiquity 39*: pp. 187–193.

Marcus, J.

1998   The Peaks and Valleys of Ancient States: An Extension of the Dynamic Model. In G. M. Feinman and J. Marcus (eds.), *Archaic States*. Santa Fe, School of American Research: pp. 59–94.

Martin, L.

1999   Mammal Remains from the Eastern Jordanian Neolithic, and the Nature of Caprine Herding in the Steppe. *Paléorient 25*: pp. 87–104.

Marx, E.

1967   *Bedouin of the Negev*. New York, Praeger.

1992   Are There Pastoral Nomads in the Middle East? In O. Bar-Yosef and A. M. Khazanov (eds.), *Pastoralism in the Levant: Archaeological Materials in Anthropological Perspectives*. Madison, Prehistory Press: pp. 255–260.

Mayerson, P.

1963   The Desert of Southern Palestine According to Byzantine Sources. *Proceedings of the American Philosophical Society 107*: pp. 160–172.

1964   The First Muslim Attacks on Southern Palestine (A.D. 633/634). *Transactions and Proceedings of the American Philological Association 95*: pp. 155–199.

1986   The Saracens and the *Limes. Bulletin of the American Schools of Oriental Research 262*: pp. 35–47.

1989   Saracens and Romans: Micro-Macro Relationships. *Bulletin of the American Schools of Oriental Research 274*: pp. 71–79.

Meshel, Z.

1974   New Data About the "Desert Kites." *Tel Aviv 1*: pp. 129–143.

1978   *Kuntillet Ajrud: A Religious Center from the Time of the Judean Monarchy. Museum Catalogue 175*. Jerusalem, Israel Museum.

1980   Desert Kites in Sinai [in Hebrew]. In Z. Meshel and I. Finkelstein (eds.), *Sinai in Antiquity*. Jerusalem, Israel Society for the Protection of Nature and the Israel Exploration Society: pp. 265–288.

Ochir-Goryaeva, M.

1998   Early Iron Age Nomads of Low Volga Region (Model of Cultural Development). In M. Pearce and M. Tosi (eds.), *Papers from the EAA Third Annual Meeting: Pre- and Protohistory. BAR International Series 717*. Oxford, Archaeopress: pp. 129–132.

Ovadia, E.

1992   The Domestication of the Ass and Pack Transport by Animals: A Case of Technological Change. In O. Bar-Yosef and A. M. Khazanov (eds.), *Pastoralism in the Levant: Archaeological Materials in Anthropological Perspectives*. Madison, Prehistory Press: pp. 19–28.

Parkinson, W. A. (ed.)

2002   *The Archaeology of Tribal Societies.* Ann Arbor, International Monographs in Prehistory 15.

Payne, S.

1973   Kill-Off Patterns in Sheep and Goats: The Mandibles from Asvan Kale. *Anatolian Studies 22*: pp. 281–307.

Porat, N., S. A. Rosen, E. Boaretta and Y. Avni

1996   Dating the Ramat Saharonim Late Neolithic Desert Cult Site. *Journal of Archaeological Science 33*: pp. 1342–1355.

P'yankova, L.

1994   Central Asia in the Bronze Age: Sedentary and Nomadic Cultures. *Antiquity 68*: pp. 355–372.

Redding, R. W.

1984   Theoretical Determinants of a Herder's Decisions: Modeling Variation in the Sheep-Goat Ratio. In J. Clutton-Brock and C. Grigson (eds.), *Animals and Archaeology. Volume 3: Early Herders and Their Flocks. BAR International Series 202.* Oxford, Archaeopress: pp. 223–242.

Rosen, A. M.

1995   The Social Response to Environmental Change in Early Bronze Age Canaan. *Journal of Anthropological Archaeology 14*: pp. 26–44.

Rosen, S. A.

1987   Demographic Trends in the Negev Highlands: Preliminary Results from the Emergency Survey. *Bulletin of the American Schools of Oriental Research 266*: pp. 45–58.

1992   Nomads in Archaeology: A Response to Finkelstein and Perevolotsky. *Bulletin of the American Schools of Oriental Research 287*: pp. 75–85.

1993   A Roman Period Pastoral Tent Camp in the Negev, Israel. *Journal of Field Archaeology 20*: pp. 441–451.

2002   The Evolution of Pastoral Nomadic Systems in the Southern Levantine Periphery. In E. van den Brink and E. Yannai (eds.), *Quest of Ancient Settlements and Landscapes.* Tel Aviv, Ramot Publishing: pp. 23–44.

2003   Early Multi-resource Nomadism: Excavations at the Camel Site in the Central Negev. *Antiquity 77*: pp. 749–760.

Rosen, S. A., and G. Avni

1997   *The 'Oded Sites: Investigations of Two Early Islamic Pastoral Camps South of the Ramon Crater. Beersheva XI. Studies by the Department of Bible and Ancient Near East.* Beer-Sheva, Ben-Gurion University Press.

Rosen, S. A. and Y. J. Rosen

2003   The Shrines of the Setting Sun. *Israel Exploration Journal 53*: pp. 1–19.

Rosen, S. A., A. B. Savinetsky, Y. Plakht, N. K. Kisseleva, B. F. Khassanov, A. M. Pereladov and M. Haiman

2005   Dung in the Desert: Preliminary Results of the Negev Holocene Ecology Project. *Current Anthropology 46*: 2, pp. 317–327.

Rowton, M. B.

1977   Dimorphic Structure and the Parasocial Element. *Journal of Near Eastern Studies 36*: pp. 181–198.

Russell, K. W.

1988   *After Eden: The Behavioral Ecology of Early Food Production in the Near East and North Africa. BAR International Series 391*. Oxford, Archaeopress.

Sahlins, M.

1968   *Tribesmen*. New York, Prentice-Hall.

Saidel, B. A.

2001   Ethnoarchaeological Investigations of Abandoned Tent Camps in Southern Jordan. *Near Eastern Archaeology 64*: 3, pp. 150–157.

Salzman, P. C.

1972   Multi-resource Nomadism in Iranian Baluchistan. In W. Irons and N. Dyson-Hudson (eds.), *Perspectives on Nomadism*. Leiden, E. J. Brill: pp. 60–68.

Schrire, C.

1980   An Enquiry into the Evolutionary Status and Apparent Identity of San Hunter-Gatherers. *Human Ecology 8*: pp. 9–32.

Sherratt, A.

1981   Plough and Pastoralism: Aspects of the Secondary Products Revolution. In I. Hodder, G. Isaac and N. Hammond (eds.), *Patterns of the Past: Studies in Honour of David Clarke*. Cambridge, Cambridge University Press: pp. 261–315.

1983   The Secondary Exploitation of Animals in the Old World. *World Archaeology 15*: pp. 90–104.

Shishlina, N. I.

1997   The Bow and Arrow of the Eurasian Steppe Bronze Age Nomads. *Journal of European Archaeology 5*: pp. 53–66.

Simms, S. R.

1988   The Archaeological Structure of a Bedouin Camp. *Journal of Archaeological Science 15*: pp. 197–211.

Solway, J. S. and R. B. Lee

1990   Foragers, Genuine or Spurious: Situating the Kalahari San in History. *Current Anthropology 31*: pp. 109–146.

Sumner, W.

1986   Proto-Elamite Civilization in Fars. In U. Finkbeiner and W. Rollig (eds.), *Gamdat Nasr: Period or Regional Style?* Wiesbaden, Springer Verlag: pp. 199–211.

Sweet, L.
1965   Camel Raiding of the North Arabian Bedouin: A Mechanism of Ecological Adaptation. *American Anthropologist 67*: pp. 1132–1150.

Tapper, R.
1979   The Organization of Nomadic Communities in Pastoral Societies of the Middle East. In L'Equipe écologie et anthropologie des sociétés pastorales (ed.), *Pastoral Production and Society/Production pastorale et société*. Cambridge, Cambridge University Press: pp. 43–66.

Tchernov, E. and O. Bar-Yosef
1982   Animal Exploitation in the Pre-Pottery Neolithic B Period at Wadi Tbeik, Southern Sinai. *Paléorient 8*: pp. 17–38.

Trigger, B.
1989   *A History of Archaeological Thought*. Cambridge, Cambridge University Press.

Wapnish, P.
1981   Camel Caravans and Camel Pastoralists at Tell Jemmeh. *Journal of the Ancient Near Eastern Society of Columbia University 13*: pp. 101–121.

1997   Equids. In E. M. Meyers (ed.), *The Oxford Encyclopedia of Archaeology in the Near East*. New York, Oxford University Press: pp. 255–256.

Wapnish, P. and B. Hesse
1988   Urbanization and the Organization of Animal Production at Tell Jemmeh in the Middle Bronze Age Levant. *Journal of Near Eastern Studies 47*: pp. 81–94.

Watson, P. J.
1979   *Archaeological Ethnography in Western Iran*. Tucson, University of Arizona Press.

Whitcomb, D.
1995   Islam and the Socio-cultural Transition of Palestine: Early Islamic Period. In T. E. Levy (ed.), *The Archaeology of Society in the Holy Land*. London, Leicester Press: pp. 488–501.

Wilmsen, E.
1989   *A Land Filled with Flies*. Chicago, University of Chicago Press.

Yablonski, L. T.
1998   The Nomads of Khwarzem Since the 1st Millennium B.C. to the Middle of the 1st Millennium A.D. In M. Pearce and M. Tosi (eds.), *Papers from the EAA Third Annual Meeting: Pre- and Protohistory. BAR International Series 717*. Oxford, Archaeopress: pp. 133–141.

Zeder, M. A. and B. Hesse
2000   The Initial Domestication of Goats (*Capra Hircus*) in the Zagros Mountains 10,000 Years Ago. *Science 287 (5461)*: p. 2254.

Zeevi, D.
1996   *An Ottoman Century: The District of Jerusalem in the 1600s*. Albany, State University of New York Press.

CHAPTER 6

THE ORIGIN OF THE TRIBE AND OF 'INDUSTRIAL' AGROPASTORALISM IN SYRO-MESOPOTAMIA

GIORGIO BUCCELLATI[1]

B Y THE 19th century BCE, most of Syro-Mesopotamia had come under the political control of dynasties whose rulers, as well as many of their subjects, had common onomastics and presumably a common ethnic origin. The people behind this movement are known to us as 'Amorites,' an English gentilic derived from the Hebrew version of the original name *Amurrum*.[2] The spread of Amorite presence marked a significant break between the third and the second millennium BCE and has been explained in the literature as the result of demographic pressure originating in the Syrian steppe. The Amorites are universally understood as a population in one state or another of nomadism, who came as invaders from the steppe into the fertile valleys of the Euphrates and the Tigris to the north and the east, and of the Orontes to the west. It is part of the generally accepted scenario that the Amorites were a very distinct group, linguistically, ethnically and socially, from the populations of the river valleys. It is further the *communis opinio* that this difference was rooted in their historically having hailed from an equally distinct geographical region, the steppe if not the desert. In other words, they were nomads at the origin, and they went through a progressive series of developmental stages that led eventually to their complete sedentarization. In a series of publications I have

---

[1.] In line with the central topic of this volume, I will present my thesis from the perspective of the origin and development of nomadism in an essay format, without entering into details or providing documentation and without a proper confrontation with the literature. For the evidence that underlies my thesis please see my earlier publications listed in the references (Buccellati 1977b, 1981, 1988, 1990d, 1991, 1992, 1993, 1996a, 1996b, 1997a, 1997b, 1997c, 2004; Buccellati and Kelly-Buccellati 1967, 1986). In this chapter, I will only occasionally refer to these titles.

[2.] The Sumerian equivalent is MAR.TU (Wilcke 1969).

presented an alternative interpretation of the data, from the point of view of history, philology, archaeology and geography. My interpretation revolves around seven major points.

First, the Amorites were originally not nomads but peasants of the long river corridor known today as the *zôr*, the Syrian middle Euphrates from the confluence of the Balikh to a point south of the confluence of the Khabur, where the valley floor becomes extremely narrow and where the current border between Syria and Iraq is situated. This area corresponded to the kingdom of Mari, the only city to control the entire river corridor. Through the early part of the third millennium BCE these peasants had sufficient land for farming and herding within the river valley itself. During that period the steppe remained largely uninhabited.

Second, as the peasant population increased, the limitation of the *zôr* became a major obstacle to any further development. Geography played a significant role: the valley floor is set in a rather deep and narrow canyon that makes it impossible for irrigation to reach the plateau above it, while rainfall is so limited as to render any type of cultivation impossible. As a result of demographic pressure, the peasants took to the steppe, discovering its suitability as a vast rangeland for their donkeys, sheep and goats. Such a 'domestication of the steppe,' as I have called it, began in the first half of the third millennium BCE and reached a level of systemic organization around the middle of the third millennium BCE.[3] In other words, occasional and local exploitation of the steppe would certainly date to earlier periods, while the systematic and macroregional scope that characterizes the agropastoralist system, the domestication of the steppe as a region, would be coterminous with the later expansion of the urban state. This was in turn influenced by the early experience in the steppe of an important segment of the social group.

Third, in the process the peasants developed the potential for an almost total autonomy from the control of the state and its central institutions. At first, this was primarily economic autonomy: the peasants could remain for indefinite periods in the steppe, where the brackish water of the shallow water table, adequate for the animals if not for humans, could easily be tapped through a

---

[3.] The earliest systematic body of evidence pertaining to the Amorites dates to the Ur III period in the last century of the third millennium BCE (according to the middle chronology). Apart from significant, if scattered, attestations in the centuries immediately preceding, several considerations point to an earlier presence of the Amorites. The Ur III evidence comes from southern Mesopotamia, a peripheral area from the point of view of the Amorites, which they must have reached in the later phase of their expansion. Their dialect, in my interpretation, is an archaic form of Akkadian and as such must go back to the period before Akkadian became well established.

network of wells that the peasants learned to dig. A few springs provided enough drinking water for the small human groups of shepherds that accompanied the animals. By remaining with their flocks in the steppe, these groups could easily avoid the taxation that the central urban government was intent on imposing.

Fourth, what followed was a growing military and political independence. Besides taxation, the peasants could avoid conscription as well, all of which is amply attested in the texts of the royal administration of Mari. As they had been trained as soldiers, they would retain these skills and use them for their own needs. This was all the more feasible as the formal urban army of the central government was quite unprepared for the steppe. It is not attested that it ever ventured there, all the military events entailing a confrontation between the regular army and the Amorites taking place in the valley floor.

Fifth, instead of the sedentarization of a nomadic group, we must read these events as a process of nomadization of peasants. Clearly, this nomadization took place under special circumstances: the new nomadic lifestyle developed while its carriers retained strong ties to the 'homeland,' the valley floor, where families and properties were located.[4] Just as important, the raison d'être for the whole process was the expansion of economic opportunities, and these could only be realized if the interaction with the cities remained in force. As a result their nomadization could never be complete.

Sixth, eventually the Amorites swelled back toward the river valleys as invaders from the outside. This is the point where my reconstruction rejoins the traditional view of things: there was indeed an Amorite conquest of the entire arc of urban Syro-Mesopotamia, so that by about 1800 BCE the whole area had come under the control of what are known as 'Amorite dynasties.' The difference is that, in my view, the Amorites are returning to what had always been their original homeland rather than conquering it as total outsiders.

Seventh, linguistically the Amorites remained clearly distinct from the other Semitic populations of Syro-Mesopotamia, and this has universally been considered as reflecting their presumably distinctive geographical origins. In my view the difference can more easily be explained as reflecting a difference in socio-economic background: just as the Amorites are in effect Akkadian peasants, so Amorite is the rural version of the same urban language spoken by the Akkadians. As expected, it retains archaic features that were lost in Akkadian under the influence of Sumerian, a language with which the Amorites had no reason to come in close contact.

[4.] A qualification of nomadism and mobility is the central theme of this volume, and it is not my purpose here to contribute to the pertinent theoretical discussion. See Porter 2000 for a lucid exposition of the basic principles, and the discussions in the literature, as they affect the Amorites.

Against this background I will develop two particular points that I consider of interest for the topic of this volume because they offer a paradigm that is quite at variance with other current models. The first point is the origin of the tribe seen as a political counterpart to the city-state, and the second is the concomitant development of what I would like to call 'industrial nomadism.' First, however, I will briefly review some salient aspects of urban political institutions against the backdrop of which the remainder of this chapter can best be understood.

HISTORICAL BACKGROUND: THE URBAN REVOLUTION

The 'urban revolution' had taken place about a millennium before the events that I propose to consider here. It was the crystallization of a series of phenomena that we like to view today in the light of a process of increased complexity. Long ago I argued that this process is coterminous with the establishment of the state (Buccellati 1977a). In other words, the city is radically different from the noncity (the earlier settlements and their communities) because of its sociopolitical organization. Power was held through vastly different mechanisms and the perception of power so articulated impacted deeply on the worldview of the people who supported it. I will summarize my argument under two headings: functionalization and fragmentation.

First, *functionalization*: the archaeological evidence that signals great changes at the turn of the third millennium BCE consists of three classical phenomena: the vastly expanded size of settlements, the appearance of monumental architecture and the introduction of writing. But how did the transformation that we can so clearly read from what we retrieve in the ground impact the mental template of the people that made it possible? What was the perceptual response of the people affected? Consider the following, for each of the three phenomena just mentioned.

Human groups expanded in size beyond the limits that would make face-to-face association possible, typically placed at 3000 to 5000 individuals. Thus, a new sense of community developed, one based not on personal acquaintance but on territorial solidarity. An individual would identify with another because of assumed shared interests, even if the two individuals had no previous personal knowledge of each other, and this sharing rested on the physical contiguity within the boundaries of the same residential settlement. The tensional factor that made this linkage possible, and desirable, was the awareness that the 'other,' if unknown at the personal level, was known on the level of functionality: if one needed the services of a carpenter, it mattered little whether he was already known as a person or not (Buccellati 2005). Functionality was a new overriding bond, and its efficiency was based on the notion that one would quickly come to expect the availability of, for example, a carpenter, whoever he may be. In this regard the perceptual response to increased community density is the awareness that one can rely on somebody filling any given slot that might be required to achieve a certain end.

The construction of massive new structures entailed a leadership that could identify and, if need be, explain what the intended final result was. It also, of course, entailed the control of financial means that could sustain the operation over protracted periods of time when the end was not in sight. It required, in other words, political will and economic resources. The success of the operation (for instance when a city wall was eventually closed, or a single roof would eventually cover a sprawling building) helped to propel the person who had conceived it onto a pedestal that set him apart from those whose communal effort had in fact made it possible. The single individuals within this anonymous mass would, again, recognize themselves as components of a mechanism that in fact functioned and produced the intended results. Coercion would go hand in hand with a sense of communal, if impersonal, accomplishment.

Writing would codify and project onto an impersonal carrier, a clay tablet, the web of relationships that held this human mass together. The written document is the outward, extrasomatic embodiment of an abstract image that does not as such occur in reality. The subdivision of the human mass into crews, their work assignments for disparate tasks, and the coordination of compensation over long periods of time are nowhere found together in reality. They are found together only as a mental template that acquires a physical embodiment in the written lists. The functionality of the interrelationships is made all the more apparent by their representation as graphic slots in a matrix.

This progressive functionalization of human relationships goes hand in hand with the second major point that I want to make here, which I have called *fragmentation*. There is, in the process of functionalization, an intellectual dimension that comes to the fore, especially in writing, but that is in effect present throughout. Things that in the reality of the physical world are noncontiguous, whether in space or in time, are made contiguous within the framework of a single overarching vision. The seed is seen as the plant, the mud as the brick, the wall as the structure, and so on. Single things that, in their singularity, do not add up to any larger thing are seen instead as potentially constitutive of a meaningful and efficient whole. They are seen as fragments of a larger, as yet unrealized, entity. The emphasis here is on 'seeing': the potential for cohesion among the fragments is not imposed; it is discovered. Hence it is that the fragmentation about which I speak has a twofold dimension. On the one hand, noncontiguous elements are identified as potentially contiguous; and, on the other, mechanisms for bringing about their latent contiguity are set in motion. The perceptual impact of fragmentation is that of widening the hiatus between humans and nature, which had begun the moment the simplest tool was created. When *homo faber* becomes *homo civis*, direct knowledge of nature becomes less important as one learns to rely more and more on an ever greater array of individuals who identify what are, in nature, but fragments and know how to reconstitute their wholeness for the benefit of the community. But the more active the control of fragmentation on the part of some individuals, the tighter their grip on the process that extends their benefit to the other members of he community. The cost of solidarity is the surrender of individual control.

THE GEOGRAPHICAL HORIZON: THE STEPPE AS A PERCEPTUAL MACROREGION

For a proper understanding of the argument that I want to develop with regard to the tribe and the industrial nature of its economy, I must also present some considerations about the landscape and, more specifically, about its perceptual impact as we can presuppose it. My central point is that the geographical horizon of the Amorites, as they were 'conquering' the steppe, came to encompass the landscape not as a marginal area but as an organically perceived macroregion. The landscape is highly differentiated within itself, characterized by prominent mountain ranges, by springs and oases in the piedmont area, by *wadis* punctuated by trees, and, as the single human event that did impact the landscape, by wells. It is, I submit, a major contribution of the Amorites to have introduced this new element of perceptual geography in Syro-Mesopotamia, which impacted not only their own historical development but eventually that of the urban-based states as well.[5] For it is at Mari that the first proper Mesopotamian macroregional urban state came into being. It is characterized by the vast heterogeneous territory that the state controlled only vicariously, as it were, through the Amorites in their dual role as, on the one hand, more or less nominal subjects of the king and, on the other, as those who had discovered the steppe as a region and de facto controlled it. This is reflected in the royal title of 'king of Mari and *Khana*,' where the tribe gives its name to the macroregion. It is the perception of a macroregion that served eventually as the springboard for the dynamics of political development in Mesopotamia from the second millennium BCE onward.

[5.] 'Perceptual geography' is a concept that I have briefly discussed elsewhere (Buccellati 1990b). It refers to the way in which geographical phenomena acquire a physiognomy of their own, which one might call *-emic*, in the mind of the individuals who confront them, potentially different from their objectively measurable, *-etic* dimensions. Thus a given feature in the landscape may be perceived by some as a 'mountain' even if the elevation is objectively minimal.

The notion of a 'macro-region' is important and needs some clarification (Buccellati 1996c). In contrast with it, the landscape of a territorial state established around a city, specifically a city-state, is univocal in the sense that it is homogeneous in terms of geographical features and is dominated by the built environment of a single structural complex: the city with its ziggurat and city walls. It is also perceptually present as a whole to all its inhabitants, since each individual can easily walk across the whole of the urban center and its hinterland while having the ziggurat visible from most points within the territory. Not so with the landscape of the steppe. It is too vast to be viewed as a whole from any given point of view, and it is too differentiated internally to be comprehended univocally. The concept of contiguity is useful in this respect. The spaces within a city-state are all perceived as contiguous because they can be so viewed physically through a minimum of dislocation and because they are uniform. Even a vast space, such as the river valley dominated by Mari, can fit this description because its geographical features remain the same from one end to the other of the long trough. But one cannot perceive of the steppe as contiguous in the same vein, not only on account of its much greater extension but also on account of its greater internal differentiation. That it could nevertheless be so perceived was the accomplishment of the Amorites.[6] They unified in their perception a landscape that the city only sensed as a world beyond. It was through them that the steppe could become an organic whole because of their intimate knowledge of its diverse features. The term *macroregion* refers to just such an organic, unified perception.

It is significant in this respect that there is in Amorite, as there is in today's Syrian Arabic, a proper name for the steppe. In fact, there are two names: *yamina*, for the steppe to the right side of the Euphrates; and *sam'al* for the left side (Buccellati 1990c; the terms are otherwise understood as referring to south and north, respectively). The two areas are known today as *shamia* and *jazira*.[7]

[6.] This bracketing of noncontiguous perceptions I have defined as "meta-perception" (Buccellati 2005). In the case presented here it refers to the vast and internally differentiated expanse of the steppe 'perceived' as a single entity, even though its constituting elements cannot be visually grasped at once as a single unit. The same concept applies to time, as well as space. For instance, the spring season is perceived, or 'meta-perceived,' as a season only because of the juxtaposition that humans can make with the other seasons, which are not at any given time copresent with spring. The concept, if not the term, is a central theme of Porter (2000:32–45, 216), who speaks of the "transcendence of space."

[7.] I have argued that the terms "sons of . . . (*banū* in Amorite, *mārū* in Akkadian) . . . the right (*yamina*)" or ". . . the left (*sham'al*)" steppe are not to be viewed as tribal names but as common nouns equivalent to the English *nomads* or to the Akkadian *mārū ugāarim*, meaning peasants or literally "sons of the irrigation district" (Buccellati 1990c).

This split into two steppes is determined by the Euphrates, perceived not only as a major feature of physical geography, which hinders the movement of the large herds from one side to the other, but also as the locus where the urban world resides, with all of its state controls. In contrast, the proper names for the right and the left steppe are not found in the Sumero-Babylonian south, where even the common noun *ṣērum* has a much more limited use and a more restricted semantic range than in texts relating to Syria.

The territory is seemingly limitless, yet it can be perceived as a whole because of its unhindered openness. Movement along given paths, with stops at fixed and well-known points (especially wells and oases), gives a physiognomy to the landscape that can be grasped as a single entity in spite of its vastness. It can safely be assumed that the peasants in the southern agrarian plains would have hardly any personal knowledge of urban landscapes other than their own. Most of the peasants we are here considering, instead, would travel long distances and subsume the wide expanse of the steppe within a single over-arching perception of its geographical features and resource potential. While no single individual ever had the whole territory immediately within his or her field of vision at any given moment (the way this could happen in a southern city where the ziggurat provided a point of reference visible from most places within the urban territory), people had a relational perception in that they had seen most of it with their own eyes. Such a perception of the steppe was crucial for the impact it had in the political sphere. Control of the steppe's resources rested on the unified perception of its organic quality as a macroregion, and in turn this called for the establishment of new political structures that could match the macroregional challenge. The answer was the tribe.

THE DYNAMICS OF THE SOCIOPOLITICAL PROCESS: THE ORIGIN OF THE TRIBE

It is against the backdrop of the above phenomena that we can appreciate the broader institutional significance of the Amorite movements. Just as the 'urban revolution' coincided with the origin of the state, so the 'steppe revolution' coincided, in my view, with the origin of the tribe. And accordingly, this explains how the tribe emerged as a political institution alternative to the territorial state. The very brief outline above provides the context within which the first proposal, concerning the origin of the tribe, makes sense. The progressive distancing from the urban environment induced an effective state of autonomy from the coercive institutions represented by the central urban government. In the steppe the shepherds could avoid primarily taxation and conscription, yet there were two major ties that remained in effect and kept them bound to their urban origins.

First, they had personal interests they could not possibly jettison, from cultivated land to which they held rights to the family network that retained an essentially agrarian dimension. Second, and more important if less immediately apparent, there was a tensional factor that conditioned their incipient nomadization, namely their factual dependence on the institutional complex found in the city. A significant point to be stressed in this connection is that the villages as they existed in the orbit of the city were by no means 'a-urban.' They were instead fully immersed in urban reality as an institutional complex, however different they may have looked in terms of the built environment in which they lived. Their real estate was secured by deeds sanctioned by the central government; the effective use of resources, from availability of traded goods to control of the river waters by means of canals, was regulated by the state; conflict resolution was ultimately attributed to royal judgment; access to a reality beyond the tangible world, in the form of both communal cultic events and private apotropaic rituals, was in the hands of temple institutions that were essentially urban; and even such a mundane fact as communicating with distant correspondents was in the hands of a few specialized scribes. I have defined this situation as 'para-urban' (Buccellati 1996c). Quite unlike prehistoric settlements, the historical village could not exist apart from its urban context.

As these para-urban peasants began to move away from the villages, the immediacy of the wider urban context was threatened, and the fragility of their situation emerged. How could these para-urban peasants protect property in the steppe? How could they co-ordinate access to resources such as specific pasture grounds or springs and oases? How could they adjudicate conflicts without courts and judges? How could they relate to the divine world without access to either the religious technicians who could perform omens or the organized cultic events unfolding in the temple? How could they send written messages if no scribe was available? These were institutions they had come to depend on but would have had to forgo if wholly isolated in the steppe. As long as their absence from the village was temporary, the problem was all but nonexistent. As nomadization began to develop as a temptingly permanent mode of life, however, its consequences were felt at an ever deeper level. To put it differently, the new situation was undermining the functionalization that the urban revolution had ushered in. In that context it served as the mechanism that made it possible for urban society to retain its cohesiveness and efficiency in spite of its demographic growth. If the pendulum would now swing away from this context, and encourage the development of a properly nonurban, rather than para-urban, society, how could the aggregative power of the new human group be secured? How could group solidarity be maintained beyond the level of face-to-face association, but without the scaffolding of the territorial contiguity that was at the basis of the urban revolution?

The answer, in my view, was the establishment of the tribe. The city had shown that some form of functionalization was necessary if large-scale aggregation was to be achieved and maintained over time. People had come to identify themselves as components of an organism higher than their personal awareness of each other might allow. Each recognized another member of the group not necessarily because of personal acquaintance but because a particular 'other' member would fit a particular functional slot, understood to be of service to the community as a whole. The perceptual link that remained was that of territorial contiguity: all members of the community lived within a single city, whose physical integrity was signaled, among other things, by its city walls or in its immediate hinterland so that each member of the group had a direct perceptual link with the central city. The territory was a perceptual reality that helped the individuals to coalesce into a unified whole.

The tribe emerged as an alternative, in some ways mirroring the city-state, or modeled on it, but in other ways greatly at variance with it.[8] It was modeled on the city-state in that it aimed at serving the same basic needs of political aggregation beyond the level of face-to-face association. But it replaced the perceptual basis of aggregation from territorial contiguity to institutionalized interpersonal relationships. The aspect of mobility, or nomadism, was secondary in this respect on two grounds. First, it was not pervasive, because many members of the groups remained de facto sedentary. Second, it was not permanent, because those who followed the herds in the steppe would retain their roots in the settled areas, to which they would return on a regular basis. Even if partial and occasional, the dislocation of a sizable portion of the group in the steppe did propose an alternative apprehension of what could serve to assure group solidarity. Thus kinship, rather than territorial contiguity, became the bond: a kinship that was not necessarily biological but could be ascribed through social mechanisms.

The sources document an interesting phenomenon that has been much discussed in the literature and that, I believe, can best be interpreted in the light of what I have just said about the origin of the tribe, namely the appearance of people identified as *ha-pí-ru* in the cuneiform sources. The word has been read in a variety of ways and has been related to the Hebrew term ʿibrîm, from which the very English term *Hebrew* derives. I have proposed to read the Akkadian term as ḫābirū, standing for the Amorite ʿābirū, meaning "those who cross over to the clan" (Buccellati 1990b, 1995). I will briefly present both the linguistic and the historical sides of this argument, because it ties in with the larger issue of the origin of the tribe. Linguistically, I view the term as a participle from the same (Amorite) root ʿbr, from which ʿibrum (ḫibrum in

---

[8.] In this sense, viewed as a state, an Amorite tribe is quite different from the prehistoric 'tribal entities' (Bar-Yosef and Bar-Yosef Mayer 2002:360–361).

Akkadian) derives; *'ibrum* is the word for 'clan,' and it can be understood as a noun of action (much like *ilkum*, literally 'the going,' comes to mean 'service'). It can therefore be understood as 'the ingathering,' from which the specialized lexical meaning 'the clan' would have developed. The participle *'ābirum* would then mean 'the one who ingathers.' Given the special lexicalized meaning of *'ibrum* as 'clan,' we can then understand *'ābirum* as 'the one who joins the clan.' The Hebrew correlate *'ibrî* would retain an alternative adjectival formation: instead of a participle, it would be (in its original formation) a gentilic derived from the same word, *'ibrum* and would have the slightly different meaning of 'the one who belongs to the clan,' 'the clansman.'

In my view the term refers, in its Akkadian and Amorite contexts, to those individuals who are outside the original family nexus of the village but who nevertheless aim to join the tribe, which is perceived as a gathering place alternative to the territorial state to which otherwise those individuals would belong. They are, as it were, people in transition between two states, territorial and tribal, taking advantage of the de facto interstices that exist between the two institutions. To this extent they are displaced persons in the process of being assimilated into an alternative, and still rather fluid, sociopolitical institution. This fits quite well with all the references in the texts to the *ha-pí-ru*, in the second millennium BCE, not only in the early part of that period, at the time of the Amorites, but also in the latter part, the so-called Amarna period. The Hebrew usage fits in as well, though semantically the term stresses the result, rather than the starting point, of the process. This is quite consonant with the pertinent historical moment.

In terms of our current interests, the phenomenon of the *'ābirū*, as I understand them, is significant in that it highlights the dynamic pull of the new institution, the tribe. It is quite frankly an escape, an aspect that is presented in particularly vivid terms in the so-called Amarna letters but an escape that has a positive destination. While the motivation would have been in most cases economical, we may also assume a sociopolitical and even a psychological dimension. The tribe embodied a certain nomadic ideal, which is even romanticized in Akkadian literary texts from Gilgamesh to the so-called 'Theodicy.' The escape to the tribe would have appeared to some as a way of eluding not only taxation and conscription but also the deeper and in some ways dehumanizing effects of the urban revolution, the urban functionalization of human beings, and the fragmentation of the relationship with nature. The institutional dimension of this process lies in its serving as a mechanism for the effective ascription of outsiders into the new sociopolitical aggregate. It is interesting that no such mechanism is found for the older state model, that of the city-state, where presumably a simple transference of residence would have been sufficient to qualify a person as a member of the new community. In the tribal state, on the other hand, what was expected was not just immigration but true 'naturalization.'

THE CONCOMITANT ECONOMIC DEVELOPMENT:
THE NATURE OF 'INDUSTRIAL' NOMADISM

The notion of 'industrialization' within such a temporally remote context as that of the third millennium BCE makes sense if we look at it from the point of view of the fragmentation briefly described above (Buccellati 1990b:98). In this light, industrialization is the process whereby the moments of a production sequence are perceived as discrete segments, often at considerable remove one from the other. The urban users of a bronze object are not necessarily aware, much less do they individually control, the long chain of events that has led to the manufacturing of the object. They may know the smith who fashioned it but hardly ever the tradesman who brought the ingots, the craftsman who smelted the component metals, or the miners who extracted the ore. It is only the very few who are aware of the whole sequence who can in fact control it. The impact on perception was enormous. Think of another even more ancient case, the introduction of agriculture. To understand the relationship between the seed and the plant entails precisely such an understanding of, and control over, a fragmented chain of events. It was as if human perception could collapse in one single perceptual moment two very distinct segments that are not in and of themselves perceptually contiguous, temporally (seed and plant) or spatially (ore and object). There is, as it were, an artificial perception (or 'metaperception'), which suspends the rules of natural perception by going beyond them: humans can now bracket in their abstract vision what is not bracketed in their concrete apprehension of things.

The economic impact was equally momentous. It was for the first time that one could give a numeric value to aspects of the human world that previously did not seem to have one. The seed was worth more than what would normally be associated with its immediate use. The seed was now worth the plant that would eventually sprout from it. Thus it was that long-distance trade developed not only for finished products, or for materials in which one could easily see the finished product, such as an obsidian core, but for materials such as raw metals, the potential of which could only be fully realized through a complex series of intermediate steps. And obviously those who could control these intermediate steps would stand to reap benefits incommensurate with the value that one could attribute to each intermediate step by itself.

How does this pertain to our topic? The shepherds who took to the steppe ended up controlling precisely such a chain of discontinuous segments in the utilization of their herds. And they could do so without the interference of third parties, such as merchants, or of the state. The interference of third parties would have come from individuals who, as in the case of the metal trade, would have identified points of origin and organized the transshipment and partial transformation of the desired goods. The Amorites controlled the entire chain, from the breeding and the caring of the animals to the shearing and the supply of dairy products. In fact, they were able to extend, in the process, their mercantile role to the only other critical good found in the steppe, namely salt.[9] The 'Amorite salt,' as it is called in the sources, was the major source of this new commodity so critical for the new urban economy for its use not so much as a dietary supplement but rather as the main preservative of perishable foodstuffs.

The interference of the state had typically taken the form of taxation. This was a way to draw an income from the intermediate steps by assessing a value on the finished product. Hence it is that the pertinent Mesopotamian texts speak at great length of the concern of the state to control the time of shearing, because that was when the finished product, the wool, took concrete shape. But the state had no control over, had in fact no inkling of, the steps that preceded the shearing. This involved a knowledge of the steppe territory, the development of a network of wells, the care for the animals over long periods in these areas of otherwise difficult access. The very remoteness of the territory allowed the shepherds to eschew such interference to the extent that they could avoid returning to the urbanized area of the river valleys.

This vast and autonomous Amorite trading system is what I call 'industrial nomadism.' It was born in the settled areas, and it irresistibly gravitated toward them. It could never have entered in the mind of these shepherds to cut off the ties with their own markets. Quite the contrary, they nurtured the market that they had in fact created and for which they had all interest in maintaining, since they were the only ones who could effectively run it. When these urban markets failed, with the urban demise of the Middle Euphrates (after the collapse of Mari and Terqa), they still did not cut their ties with the cities. Rather, they re-oriented their aims to the west, remaining inescapably linked with the urban dimension. The tribal structure that had developed in the process served as the institutional backbone that kept the system going for centuries, throughout the second millennium BCE. Outsiders, the merchants and the state, were effectively excluded as the tribal organization allowed the Amorites to serve as their own merchants and their own state. The new functionalization provided by the tribe consisted precisely in providing the scaffolding for the ever greater expansion of the economic interests of the group and, in effect, for its ever stronger affirmation of political autonomy as well.

[9.] Truffles are another product indigenous to the steppe, as prized today as in antiquity but obviously not as critical for the urban economy as salt or the produce of the herds.

THE NATURE OF THE EVIDENCE: THE ROLE OF ARCHAEOLOGY

Of central interest to the issue of Syro-Mesopotamian nomadism and mobility is the question of the archaeological evidence, by which one understands in a general sense the material culture emerging from the ground. The evidence on which I have relied so far comes almost entirely from written documents, and although it is true that these themselves have come from the ground, except for the biblical references to the *ibrîm*, they are not typically considered part of the material culture or the archaeological record.[10] We may then ask the question whether, given that we know the actual situation relatively well from the written sources, we can use this as a privileged situation to identify correlative elements in the material culture that can explicitly be linked with the nomadic culture of the Amorites? There are three areas at which to look. The first is the steppe itself, where we might seek evidence of nomadic presence. The second is the reflection of a possible Amorite influence in the material culture of the urban populations. The third is the impact of the geographical environment and the ways in which it conditions today the lifeways of analogous human groups.

The first line of research has proven singularly sterile. We still do not have sites in the steppe that may be called Amorite, not by the numerous wells that dot the steppe, not in the oases where springs provide fresh water, not in the areas of the salt playas of Bouara, Palmyra or the Jabbul. It is interesting that there are no Amorite cities similar to the Aramean cities from the first millennium BCE. One reason behind the research project that centered on my excavations at Terqa was precisely to explore the possibility that this might prove to be some sort of an Amorite border town between Mari and the Amorites. Could there be evidence of a distinctive population that exhibited different traits from those known to us from the excavations at Mari? Nothing in the results could have been farther from this initial hypothesis. In fact, it was especially the evidence from Galvin's (1981) analysis of our archaeozoological remains that started me on a different track, as this suggested that the treatment of the herds was not in keeping with what one would expect if the herders had been large-scale pastoralists originating in the steppe (Zeder 1995). The most probable candidate for the status as an Amorite city is Palmyra, where there may be evidence of an urban settlement as early as the first part of the second millennium BCE (al-Maqdissi 2000) and which would indeed appear to have been structurally quite different from the other urban settlements of Syro-Mesopotamia. An interesting new development is the discovery of a whole new type of evidence, that from petroglyphs in the

---

[10.] Although I disagree with this understanding of the nature of the archaeological record, I retain it here as a premise for my considerations about the relevance of the record for the Amorite question, on account of its being the generally held opinion.

Hemma region (Van Berg et al. 2003). There is no indication that they may be specifically Amorite, and in fact even the date is uncertain, but it is plausible that these may be the work of shepherds who were familiar with the general themes and motifs of the urban world. If so, the petroglyphs would offer a resonance of the iconography that we otherwise know only from the high achievements of the urban workshops. On the other hand, one cannot simply link the Amorites with monuments isolated in the steppe only on account of their location. Thus the stelas of Jebelet el-Beida are more likely to be associated with a political program of the Hurrian dynasties of piedmont cities like Urkesh than with the steppe pastoralists (Dolce 1986).

The second line of research has also limited success, as the interpretations proposed, however plausible, cannot be argued on archaeological evidence alone. Apart from references in the texts to artifacts qualified as 'Amorite,' we have no artifacts in the archaeological record from the pertinent urban settlements that can be interpreted as coming from nomadic populations at home in the steppe, nor is there much in the same record that could be associated with a nomadic origin were it not for what we otherwise know about the broader situation from contemporary textual evidence. Let us consider briefly three specific cases. The diffusion of the iconography of the god Amurru, who became very popular in the early second millennium BCE and who on the face of it would appear to be the eponymous tutelary deity of the Amorites, does not reflect an Amorite religious tradition at all but is rather the projection of the urban perception of their social reality (Kupper 1961). The construction of an 'Amorite wall' (BÀD MAR.TU; Buccellati 1966:327–328) by King Shulgi toward the end of the third millennium BCE attests to an awareness of threat translated into a defensive measure important enough to be the argument of a year name. If there indeed was a wall running along a defensible border, one might expect to find a trace of it in the ground, but none has been found so far. But if it was a string of fortresses, or even a single fortress, strategically placed to confront the incomers, then any archaeological trace of it would be hardly distinguishable from that of other small settlements. The most successful effort at connecting archaeological data from the settled areas to the pastoralists is the one undertaken by Porter (2000, 2002), who attributes to them the building of mortuary monuments serving as markers of tribal territory and social identity. Her insightful interpretation builds on a careful analysis of archaeological data, though it still remains tied to textual information for the finer interpretive points. It is interesting, in this respect, how another segment of the written tradition suggests that the Ur III Sumerian perception of the Amorites was at odds with the self-perception by the Amorites themselves as interpreted by Porter, since a Sumerian cliché about the Amorites is that "on the day of their death they are not buried" (Buccellati 1966:331).

The third line, centering on geography and ethno-archaeology, is productive but limited in its final import. A careful analysis of the landscape shows differences that are not immediately noticeable on maps. This is what I have called "perceptual geography" (Buccellati 1990b), a study of how the perception of the geographical features, assumed to have been the same in ancient times, may legitimately be projected in the past and throw light on the reaction of the ancients to their environment. In our case it is especially the nature of the valley trough, for which the modern perception has a name, *zôr*, that is matched, I have suggested, by the ancient *ah Purattim*. Analogously, a careful consideration of the lifestyles of the shepherds that take to the steppe, in particular the different ways in which they adapt to the winter season, is instructive in showing how the territory can best be exploited by small groups that retain strong ties to a base in the river valleys (Bernbeck, this volume).

DISCUSSION

In point of fact, the archaeology of the material culture in Syro-Mesopotamia, in and of itself, tells us very little about the Amorites. Without the information derived from the cuneiform texts, we would know nothing today of their name as a group and much less of their names as individuals, nothing of their interaction with the urban areas on the valley floors, nothing of their use of the steppe, nothing, in fact, of even their existence. There is, in my understanding of events, a very good reason for this. However 'nomadized' the Amorites may have become in the course of time, they had remained essentially rooted in the rural para-urban areas from which they hailed. The Amorite homeland remained in the alluvial plains, even though they carved out for themselves an ecological niche in the steppe that could be considered as an alternative, or transitional, heartland.[11] Their presence in the steppe was thus not only an extension of village life, but it was also quite ephemeral even by nomadic standards. The herds were tended by minuscule human groups, whose extended family remained in the alluvial areas, where they were eager to return and from whose material culture they amply drew. That they could have given rise to the tribe as an alternative political institution, as I have proposed, is not in contrast with this picture. The tribe echoes the central goal of the city as a territorial state to the extent that it provides effective aggregative means for

---

[11.] As I have argued elsewhere (Buccellati 1990a, in press), it was only in the latter part of the second millennium BCE that the central position of this heartland was established as a whole new type of tribal-territorial state, namely the kingdom of Amurru that I consider to have been centered around Palmyra, resulting in the first proper 'steppe kingdom.'

a population that is larger than the sum of persons known to each other on the basis of face-to-face association. But it does not derive, in our case at least, from a purely endogenous expansion of a family nucleus that is nomadic in origin. Rather, it results from the secondary co-alescing of small human groups that seek effective aggregation outside of the contiguous territorial formula: an aggregation higher than the village but distinct from the state organization that controlled the village from an urban perspective. Hence the very fluid situation that characterizes, in my view, the Amorite movements: they were peasants turned nomads turning urban.

REFERENCES

al-Maqdissi, M.
2000   Note sur les sondages réalisés par Robert du Mesnil du Buisson dans la Cour du Sanctuaire de Bel à Palmyre. *Syria* 77: pp. 137–158.

Bar-Yosef, O. and D. E. Bar-Yosef Mayer
2002   Early Neolithic Tribes in the Levant. In W. A. Parkinson (ed.), *The Archaeology of Tribal Societies Archaeological Series 15*. Ann Arbor, International Monographs in Prehistory: pp. 340–371.

Buccellati, G.
1966   *The Amorites of the Ur III Period.* Naples, Istituto Orientale.
1977a   The "Urban Revolution" in a Socio-political Perspective. *Mesopotamia 12*: pp. 19–39.
1977b   Fugitives and Refugees of the Amarna Age. *Journal of Near Eastern Studies 36*: pp. 145–147.
1981   The Origin of Writing and the Beginning of History. In G. Buccellati and C. Speroni (eds.), *The Shape of the Past: Studies in Honor of Franklin D. Murphy*. Los Angeles, Institute of Archaeology and Office of the Chancellor, University of California: pp. 3–13.
1988   The Kingdom and Period of Khana. *Bulletin of the American Schools of Oriental Research 270*: pp. 43–61.
1990a   From Khana to Laqê: The End of Syro-Mesopotamia. In Ö. Tunca (ed.), *De la Babylonie à la Syrie, en passant par Mari (Mélanges Kupper)*. Liège: pp 229–253.
1990b   "River Bank," "High Country," and "Pasture Land": The Growth of Nomadism on the Middle Euphrates and the Khabur. In S. Eichler, M. Wäfler and D. Warburton (eds.), *Tell al-Hamidiyah 2*. Göttingen, Vandenhoek und Ruprecht: pp. 87–117.
1990c   The Rural Landscape of the Ancient Zôr: The Terqa Evidence. In B. Geyer (ed.), *Techniques et pratiques hydro-agricoles traditionnelles en domaine irrigué. Approche pluridisciplinaire des modes de culture avant la motorisation en Syrie.*

Bibliothèque Archéologique et Historique 86. Tome I. Paris, Geuthner: pp. 155–169.

1990d   Salt at the Dawn of History: The Case of the Bevelled Rim Bowls. In P. Matthiae, M. Van Loon and H. Weiss (eds.), *Resurrecting the Past: A Joint Tribute to Adnan Bounni.* Leiden, l'Institut Historique-Archéologique Néerlandais de Stamboul: pp. 17–40.

1991   A Note on the Muškênum as a Homesteader. In R. J. Ratner, L. M. Barth, M. Luijken Gevirtz and B. Zuckerman (eds.), *Let Your Colleagues Praise You: Studies in Memory of Stanley Gevirtz. Maarav* 7: pp. 91–100.

1992   Ebla and the Amorites. In *Eblaitica. Volume 3.* Winona Lake, Eisenbrauns: pp. 85–106.

1993   Gli Amorrei e l' "Addomesticamento" della Steppa [in Italian]. In O. Rouault and M. G. Masetti-Rouault (eds.), *L'Eufrate e il tempo: Le civiltà del medio Eufrate e della Gezira siriana.* Milan, Electa: pp. 67–69.

1995   Eblaite and Amorite. In E. Eichler, G. Hilty, H. Loeffler, H. Steger and L. Zgusta (eds.), *Namenforschung. Ein internationales Handbuch zur Onomastik / Name Studies. An International Handbook of Onomastics / Les noms propres. Manuel International d'Onomastique.* Berlin-New York, de Gruyter: pp. 856–860.

1996a   Amorite. In J. Turner (ed.), *The Dictionary of Art. Volume I.* London-New York, Macmillan: p. 795.

1996b   Review of M. Anbar *Les tribus amurrites de Mari. Archiv für Orientforschung 42/43*: pp. 233–234.

1996c   The Role of Socio-political Factors in the Emergence of "Public" and "Private" Domains in Early Mesopotamia. In M. Hudson and B. A. Levine (eds.), *Privatization in the Ancient Near East and Classical World. Peabody Museum Bulletin 5.* Cambridge, Peabody Museum of Archaeology and Ethnology: cover page and pp. 129–151.

1997a   Amorites. In *The Oxford Encyclopedia of Archaeology in the Near East. Volume I.* New York, Oxford University Press: pp. 107–111.

1997b   Syria in the Bronze Age. In *The Oxford Encyclopedia of Archaeology in the Near East. Volume 5.* New York, Oxford University Press: pp. 126–131.

1997c   Urkesh and the Question of Early Hurrian Urbanism. In M. Hudson and B. A. Levine (eds.), *Urbanization and Land Ownership in the Ancient Near East, Peabody Museum Bulletin 7.* Cambridge, Peabody Museum of Archaeology and Ethnography: pp. 229–250.

2004   Il secondo millennio a.C. nella memoria epica di Giuda e Israele [in Italian]. *La Rivista Teologica di Lugano 9*: pp. 521–543.

2005   The Perception of Function and the Prehistory of the State in Syro-Mesopotamia. In B. D. Dillon and M. A. Boxt (eds.), *Archaeology Without*

Limits: Papers in Honor of Clement W. Meighan. Lancaster, Labyrinthos: pp. 481–492.

in press Review of Bernard Geyer (ed.), *Conquête de la steppe et appropriation des terres sur les marges arides du Croissant fertile*. *Archiv für Orientforschung*.

Buccellati, G. and M. Kelly-Buccellati

1967   Archaeological Survey of the Palmyrene and the Jebel Bishri. *Archaeology 20*: pp. 305–306.

1986   The Glory of Ancient Syria. *Terra 24*: 4, pp. 6–14; and *Terra 24*: 5, pp. 22–29.

Dolce, R.

1986   Per una Riconsiderazione delle Opere Figurative da Gebelet el-Beyda [in Italian]. *Contributi e materiali di archeologia orientale (Università degli Studi di Roma "La Sapienza")*, *1*: pp. 307–331, Figures 59–60.

Galvin, K. F.

1981   *Early State Economic Organization and the Role of Specialized Pastoralism. Terqa in the Middle Euphrates Region, Syria*. University of California, Los Angeles (PhD dissertation).

Kupper, J.-R.

1961   *L'iconographie du Dieu Amurru dans la glyptique de la Ire dynastie babylonienne: Mémoires de la classe des lettres. 2e Série, Tome 55, Fasc. 1*. Bruxelles, J. Duculot, Imprimeur de l'Academie Royale de Belgique, Gembloux.

Porter, A.

2000   *Mortality, Monuments, and Mobility: Ancestor Traditions and the Transcendence of Space*. University of Chicago (PhD dissertation).

2002   The Dynamics of Death: Ancestors, Pastoralism, and the Origins of a Third-Millennium City in Syria. *Bulletin of the American Schools of Oriental Research 325*: pp. 1–36.

Van Berg P.-L., N. Cauwe, J.-P. Hénin, S. Lemaitre, V. Picalause, K. Ahmo and M. Vander Linden

2003   Fieldwork at the Archaeological and Rock Art Sites of the Hemma Plateau (Hassake, Syria), Season 2002. *Adumatu* 7: pp. 7–20.

Wilcke, C.

1969   Zur Geschichte der Amurriter in der Ur-III-Zeit. *Die Welt des Orients* 5: pp. 1–31.

Zeder, M. A.

1995   The Archaeobiology of the Khabur Basin. *Bulletin of the Canadian Society for Mesopotamian Studies 29*: pp. 21–32.

CHAPTER 7

PASTORAL NOMADISM IN THE CENTRAL ANDES

A HISTORIC RETROSPECTIVE EXAMPLE

DAVID L. BROWMAN

ONE OF THE challenges of this volume is to focus on how pastoral nomadism can be defined, characterized and recognized in the archaeological record. The manner in which researchers began considering livestock management in various regions around the world has influenced the terminology employed and the way the issue has been approached. This chapter looks at one thread of the historical definition and recognition of prehistoric animal management in the Central Andes of western South America. In this region a version of what has been termed 'seminomadic pastoralism' became a principal way of life as early as seven to eight millennia ago (Wheeler 1984; Wheeler et al. 1976) and persists into the 21st century CE with some relict groups from central Peru to northwest Argentina. The essentially treeless grassland expanses of the highland region, along with the sharp vertical ecology of the Andes, significant variations in precipitation and temperature, and the presence of two camelid species with natural seasonal migration behavioral patterns, made the region an ideal locale for development of such seminomadic pastoralism.

Roughly a quarter of the land in the Central Andes is composed of semi-arid and arid grasslands, with the *altiplano* and *puna* constituting the bulk of these areas.[1] Precipitation averages nearly 600 mm per year in the northern part of the Peruvian puna but decreases rapidly as one moves south, to less than 100 mm per year in the southern Bolivian altiplano. This lack of adequate rainfall is one factor that has led to pastoralism. As elsewhere, grazing is a typical means to extract subsistence resources from lands too dry for conventional plant agriculture. But in addition, the Andean altiplano and puna grasslands range in elevation from 3000 to 4800 m. Some of the grasslands that otherwise

---

[1.] The primarily treeless grasslands of the high Andes are known as the *wet puna* in northern Peru, the *dry puna* in southern Peru, the *altiplano* in the wide plateau from Lake Titicaca to central Bolivia and the *salt puna* in southern Bolivia and northwest Argentina.

might potentially receive adequate moisture for plant agriculture are simply too high and too cold to be suitable for plant cultivation. Pastoralism once again becomes the mechanism for extracting resources in these circumstances.

JUNIN SEMINOMADIC AGROPASTORALISM

The original reconstruction of Andean ways of life, by anthropologists half a century ago, described camelid pastoralism developing only as a state industry under the Inca Empire. The great ethnohistorian John Murra and the dean of Andean archaeology, John Rowe, concurred on this interpretation. Although I have written extensively about the nature of prehistoric and ethnohistoric camelid management, the original archaeological field evidence that led to my research in this area has never been appropriately described. So let me present that yet unpublished historic evidence here. It provides the 'hook' for me to describe some of the wider archaeological correlates of Andean pastoralism that are to be observed.

To first follow this example up then, in order to generalize from it later: when I initially located what appeared to be evidence of seminomadic pastoralism in the Andes, a prehistoric pastoralism that existed at least 3000 years before the Inca, my reports were greeted with skepticism by my doctoral dissertation committee. Their view was that the experts had already spoken, and the evidence that I thought I had for pre-Inca pastoralism ran counter to accepted wisdom. I had better go back into the field and re-address my findings. This situation had a career-changing impact because it forced me to learn a good deal about pastoralism in order to convince my committee, as well as other Andeanists, of the considerable prehistoric time-depth of such pastoral lifestyles in the Andean puna and altiplano.

At about this same time Thomas Lynch (1971) was analyzing evidence from his work in northern Peru and shaking up the Peruvianist academy by arguing for Archaic Period seasonal transhumance, in part based on seasonal exploitation of camelid resources. Although the idea of seasonal transhumance and seminomadic pastoralism were outside of the normative paradigm then, within a decade a multitude of Andean scholars had picked up the chase, and today the idea of camelid pastoralism beginning among the Archaic Period populations in the high Andean grasslands is recognized as one of the well-known alternative subsistence exploitation patterns.

One question of semantics that needed to be worked out was what kind of 'pastoralism' the Central Andean peoples displayed. Our early reports spoke of 'nomadic' camelid pastoralism. But Old World pastoralism experts, such as Anatoly Khazanov and others, questioned whether we truly had evidence of *nomadic* pastoralism or whether it was really rather more *seminomadic* pastoralism or even a kind of 'tethered' nomadism. The significant reliance on plant agricultural production, at least in later times, made them question whether this Andean pattern was not better termed 'agropastoralism.'

What was this early evidence? The project research was in the Jauja-Huancayo basin of the Mantaro River drainage in Junin Department in the central highlands of Peru. This basin (about 60 km long and up to 12 km wide) is relatively flat, being an old Pleistocene lake bed, running from 3125–3350 m in elevation. In recent periods it has been utilized extensively for grain and root crop agriculture. Although the majority of the herding activities in prehistoric and ethnohistoric periods took place along the basin slopes and adjacent highland grasslands, at elevations roughly 3500–4000 m, the valley bottom was the locus of some seasonally permanent habitation sites.

The seminomadic pastoralism here is environmentally driven both by temperature and precipitation variation, although because of altitude, temperature is more critical. Rainfall in the basin itself is comparatively abundant, in terms of grassland requirements, ranging from an average of 635 mm a year at the north end to an average of 740 mm at the south end. On the higher slopes the precipitation falls off accordingly with increases in elevation. As is typical for the Andean puna, the rainfall varies considerably between years, with an average variation of ±20%. The area can also experience exceptionally dry years, with precipitation as little as 140 mm, as well as rare abnormally wet years, with precipitation in some restricted locales up to 2000 mm.

Temperature seems to be the more critical environmental variable, with respect to the selection of a pastoral production focus. Diurnal ranges are large, owing to the high elevation, and typically vary more than 20°C in a day. Summer highs may reach 25°C, and winter lows will drop to -10°C, or lower. In the central Peruvian highlands average annual temperature drops off at the standard rate of -0.5°C per every 100 m increase in elevation. For plant agriculture this translates to about two weeks more time required to reach maturity for each 100 m of elevation, as well as increased frost and freeze risk, effectively reducing or eliminating the possibilities of plant agriculture as a subsistence strategy at higher elevations. Thus frosts and freezes drastically reduce the growing season at higher elevations in the Jauja-Huancayo zone, making it difficult to grow crops outside the basin and river valley.

Archaeologically, a radical settlement pattern shift occurred in the Jauja-Huancayo sector of the Mantaro valley with the development of fully agricultural sedentary communities at about 600 CE. But in this basin the development of such fully committed agricultural communities was comparatively late for the Andes. Evidence from the project indicated that for at least the preceding 3000 years (which now of course can be extended much longer), settlements in this area had been seasonally ephemeral. A large number of the earlier localities identified were transitory camps on the hillslopes and flanks and on ridgetops and in the surrounding puna, outside the zone where agriculture was later practiced in the lower valley. In several instances these transitory camps were clearly associated with corral-like constructions. These prehistoric sites looked very comparable to the herding residences recorded for ethnographically documented ovicaprid and camelid herders in this region but, when first found, ran counter to the then-accepted paradigm, as noted above.

Because the original research design had been developed without awareness of this new subsistence pattern variation, the thrust of fieldwork focused on the functioning of the later components of this system rather than on searching for its origins. The basin study region contained most, if not all, of the lower elevation recurrently utilized wet-season pastoral sites but only a small fraction of the more ephemeral higher elevation dry-season herding locales. This initial work did not therefore adequately describe the entire system but rather focused more on the wet-season sites, of which there was a larger sample.

The wet-season sites were small villages, seasonally occupied, situated near a spring, stream or other major water resource. This location supplied sufficient water for the frequent artificially enlarged marshy areas, which provided the softer grasses particularly needed for alpacas, as well as being suitable for wet-season cultivation. Ceramic assemblages indicated continual habitation site utilization for decades or, in the case of the largest settlements, centuries. There were few artifacts related to agriculture at these sites and agricultural tools in general were infrequent. The typical wet-season villages had up to a few score semisubterranean or subterranean pithouses, with mean populations generally estimated in the neighborhood of 100 persons.

There were three to five larger population clusters within the valley basin during this period, spaced from 10 km to 25 km from one another (Browman 1976). In immediately pre-Inca times there were three major ethnohistoric subdivisions of the Wanka peoples living in the area: Hatun-Xauxa, Hanan-Wanka and Lurin-Wanka. But rather than arguing for any direct historical linkages between these larger early prehistoric valley bottom clusters and the later three tribal subdivisions, my interpretation was more general: that population buildup had reached a suitable density that, around 2000–3000 years ago, there were already different political tribal subdivisions among the agropastoralists in the basin, and that these three to five centers most likely correlated to such tribal differentiations.

The wet-season sites were the locus of much of the ritual behavior, as is still the typical pattern among seminomadic camelid herders in the Andes today. Archaeological evidence of ritual behavior (Browman 1970) was seen in the production and utilization of ceramic human and animal figurines, whose examples derived nearly exclusively from the wet-season valley floor sites.

Human figurines were found throughout all phases, from the very earliest identified sites through the Colonial period, but the animal figurines were limited to the pastoral-related sites in early phases.

Animal figurines provided some potential insights into herd management techniques. While among the human figurines male and female variants appeared in about equal numbers, about 80% of the camelid (llama or perhaps llama and alpaca) figurines are female. Typically today, herders prefer only a few males to service a large harem of females; this patterning of figurines suggests a similar prehistoric sex-selection pattern. The archaeozoological techniques available when the research was done did not permit documentation of this pattern in the osteological assemblage, but work in the Central Andes since then by experts such as Jonathan Kent (1982), George Miller (1979), Katherine Moore (1989), and Jane Wheeler (1984) has indicated the importance of sex and age profile ratios in identifying pastoral sites. In addition, all the female camelid figurines depict the udder or teats, but only a few depict any genital features. Hence, although Andean camelids provide too little milk to be utilized as a food supplement by humans, as elsewhere in the world, still the emphasis on desirable female herd animal traits appears to have been on their infant suckling abilities rather than merely the sexual components of fertility and reproduction.[2]

Other livestock management traits similar to modern herding practices were observed in the figurine collection. 'Slashes' comparable to modern ownership marks were observed on some male figurines. These incisions are interpreted as ownership marks not only because they closely resemble the devices employed by modern herders but also because other animal ownership-marking practices are also known in the central highlands at this time. Ear-notching ownership marks, identical in location and type to notching procedures still utilized by today's herders, have been found on prehistoric llama figurines from that period in adjacent areas to the north of the Mantaro, making it abundantly clear that standardized ownership-marking procedures have a history of at least 2500 years in Peru, and probably much longer.

The primitive camelid backpack used for moving goods from field to camp, as well as for transporting goods on the long-distance llama trade caravans, also are depicted on the ceramic figurines. And bone toggles, employed for securing the packing ropes, were recovered during excavation and survey. These artifacts, from wet-season sites, allowed the reconstruction of a robust set of pastoral institutions initially estimated to be three to four millennia duration, now likely much longer.

[2.] One of the distinctive, almost definitive, patterns noted at the onset of domestication of camelids in the Andean region seven millennia ago is the high number of neonate deaths. It is clear that the survival of newborns has long been of considerable concern for herders in this region.

During the dry season the populations dispersed to the surrounding hillslopes, hilltops and puna, where they lived in small hamlets. Dry-season sites were characterized by as few as 3–15 house platforms, rather randomly gathered together. The dwellings built on these short-term, seasonal platforms were constructed of perishable materials. The platforms were most evident on hillslopes where they were utilized to create level living surfaces. The doorways or access for habitations built on the hillslopes faced upslope or uphill, which allowed the resident to enter the structure at ground level rather than having to climb steps or over embankments. The long axis of these oblong to rectangular platforms was often perpendicular to the hillslope. As it would have been considerably easier to construct a platform with the axis parallel to the hillslope, requiring less fill and less revetment, several hypothetical explanations were investigated to explain this orientation. None has so far proved satisfactory.

These temporary habitation sites were characterized by lithic and bone tool assemblages related to hunting and herding activities, and they lacked any agricultural implements. The ceramic assemblages characteristic of this series of sites dated from the earliest ceramics in the area, perhaps as early as 1500 BCE, to the apparent dramatic termination of this settlement pattern variation about 500 CE. Some of the hamlets appeared to lack ceramic assemblages, but it is unknown whether they were preceramic or simply aceramic later sites. The associated occupation debris indicated that the utilization of these house platforms was very short-term, possibly only one season, or more likely a few seasons, and that these grazing-area sites were essentially short-time utilization encampments.

These dry-season herding hamlets were usually situated in locations with good lines of sight. Although the pastoral subsistence pattern was identified in the basin beginning at least by the late preceramic phases, the majority of sites in the survey inventory dated to the Early Intermediate Period of the Peruvian cultural history sequence. The Early Intermediate Period was a time of general political instability in much of Peru, and occupation sites elsewhere in Peru during this period often were relocated to higher, defensible locations. Good sight lines would obviously provide early warning of portending enemy incursions or rustling, so one explanation is that the dry-season site location was selected for defensive purposes.

Considering the rather open and vulnerable locations of the wet-season villages in the valley bottom, as well as the lack of any evidence for substantial outside contact, the idea of defensive location, other than for rustling protection, seems unlikely. A more feasible explanation is that these temporary sites were located at higher elevations to provide the herders with the maximum view for the monitoring of herds from a distance. It also allowed them to make early identification of predators, such as pumas and foxes, and provided them the opportunity to spot, and pursue if they wished, the wild guanaco, deer and smaller mammals with which they supplemented their diets.

This particular pastoral pattern was abruptly terminated at 600 CE, when the Wari imperial conquest resulted in the forcible relocation and resettlement of these valley populations into sedentary communities in maize-growing areas, a pattern reminiscent of situations described for the Middle East in various periods. With the collapse of the Wari Empire about three centuries later, the regional groups then shifted back to a greater pastoral emphasis. The section of the valley under discussion here seems to have controlled a few million head of stock by the Inca period. For example, ongoing ethnohistoric research shows that in the first 15 years of the colonial conquest alone, the Spanish expropriated more than 600,000 llamas and alpacas from two of the three previously mentioned regional Wanka tribal 'kingdoms' that existed here.

ANDEAN PASTORALISM PATTERNS

The evidence supports the proposition that seasonal pastoralism was involved in the prehistoric utilization of the Andes, but to what extent can this pastoralism be subsumed under the category of 'nomadism'? Most current Andean ethnographies and animal management studies have taken to lumping the kind of mixed-plant agriculture and animal herding behavior that is found in the Andean highlands under the general rubric of 'agropastoralism,' which sidesteps the critical issue of the type of movement involved. The fact that in our example the prehistoric pastoralists had regularly utilized permanent wet-season villages, to which they returned on a recurring basis and where they practiced a limited plant agriculture, indicates that these agropastoralist peoples should better be characterized as seminomadic pastoralists or even 'tethered' nomads rather than pure nomadic pastoralists.

Pastoralism frequently involves utilization of land not suitable for plant agriculture, land where moisture often is a critical variable so that herders need to be able to react to local annual precipitation events and vary their exploitation patterns accordingly. This usually requires herders to move their flocks to graze in different areas in different years, depending on which area receives adequate rainfall. To a limited extent this is true of the Andean herders, although, as I have argued above, temperature is a more important environmental factor here.

Under moisture-driven pastoralism, seasonal migrations are sometimes seemingly capricious, driven by reports regarding the locations of rains that season. For the Central Andes, however, the behavioral characteristics of the llamas and alpacas make it easier to adhere to a much more regular and constrained migratory pattern. The wild ancestors of the llama and alpaca migrated seasonally, much like the gazelles formerly did in the Epi-Neolithic

Levant, from winter to summer pastures. Both the wild camelids (guanaco and vicuña) and the domestic camelids (llama and alpaca) mark their grazing territory by voiding their bowels in dung heaps on boundary-marking locales. This activity makes camelid dung collection, for fuel or fertilizer, a relatively easy process in contrast to, for instance, the dispersed ovicaprid pattern.

These behavioral traits can be viewed as making the camelids 'pre-adapted' for pastoral domestication. Early Andean llama and alpaca pastoralism was integrated into, and generally maintained, the ecosystem in which it was introduced. Innovation here was a conservative process, preserving the former way of life by simply making the previously hunted wild guanaco and vicuña more accessible to be sacrificed or harvested when needed, now as herded llama and alpaca, but otherwise maintaining the extant patterns of camelid migration and territorial marking.

The territoriality of these species also leads to the development of what can be viewed as a rather 'tethered' sort of nomadism, as the propensity to return to an established grazing territory has been characterized as tethering the flocks to that pasturage. Thus, because the natural behavior of the camelids resulted in their preferring to return to the same areas, the Andean herders could afford to invest in landscape capital in these pastures, such as enhancing grazing areas through construction of artificial wet meadows, or *bofedales*, and similar improvements. This also made the development of plant agriculture, where possible, a logical component of the pastoral regime. The prehistoric record appears to support the following general evolutionary scenario, evolving from this territoriality: first, hunters following the wild camelids on their annual rounds; second, hunters transitioning into herders of these same animals, managing them on the same rounds; and third, herding groups beginning to supplement their subsistence regime with self-produced domestic plant foodstuffs, thus becoming agropastoralists.

In contrast to Old World pastoral exploitation, Andean camelid herders never employed milk or blood from live animals as food items. The value of the animals was in their wool and hides, their meat, and their transport labor. Over prehistoric time we can observe the principal value of the animals gradually shifting from their utility as meat producers, for the hunters and early herders, to their utility as producers of wool and other animal products for the early agropastoralists, to their more recent prehistoric importance as caravan animals, as well as producers of pastoral goods.

Agropastoralism in the Andes covers a wide range of possible variations.[3] Some of the variants might be subsumed under the "enclosed nomadism" that

---

[3.] I have provided syntheses of the pastoral components in greater detail in other publications (Browman 1984, 1987, 1990, 1998), so I will not repeat all of that information here.

Abbas Alizadeh discusses in this volume for southwest Asia. In some cases of agropastoralism, where the possibility of plant agriculture is severely limited by both temperature and moisture, the groups subsumed under this rubric are mainly pastoral. They maintain a somewhat fictive home community, which they return to on ceremonial occasions, where they store various equipment and goods and where they might practice an extremely limited cultivation, often sowing the seeds and then coming back at harvest time with the hopes of finding something to reap. But for most of the time, the pastoral community is split into smaller herding groups, dispersed across the grazing areas.

At the other extreme are the agropastoral communities that are essentially agricultural but in which the various agricultural families also own livestock, which are permanently kept in the higher grasslands. In some cases these families have only a few animals and combine their holdings with neighbors to make a single viable herd, managed by either hired herding experts or by a relative of one of the families. In other cases the household livestock holdings are larger, with the majority of community households having sizable numbers of animals, herded by relatives on a year-round basis in upper elevation grasslands separated from the village and its fields. In most modern ethnographic examples the location of the flocks is usually within a single day's travel for reprovisioning trips, almost never more than two or three days distant.

In other Andean variations of agropastoral groups the community residents return to the croplands during the wet season, cultivating fields around a permanent settlement while keeping the animals on fallowed lands from previous years. At the end of the growing season the community splits into smaller herding groups, each traveling to their own area of higher elevation grasslands during the dry season. The location of the dry-season camps may vary from year to year, depending on the availability of forage, but are usually situated near some water resource (usually improved as *bofedales*) to which the houschold has traditionally recognized rights. It is this latter pattern, for example, that is evidenced in the archaeological record of the Upper Mantaro basin for the millennia prior to 500 CE.

Because of the apparent extensive utilization of long-distance trade caravan activity, in addition to wet-season fields to secure necessary plant products, the Andean agropastoralists may have been able to live comfortably with fewer 'livestock equivalents' in animals than the theoretical 'pure' nomadic pastoralist. Plant resources seem to have provided a significant part of the annual diet of the recent Andean herding groups, permitting the herders to meet their subsistence needs with fewer animals.

Ethnographic and ethnohistoric estimates of necessary livestock holdings vary considerably, but it appears that the basic 'starter' herd necessary for the newly married couple among heavily pastoral-dependent groups was perhaps no more than roughly 50 camelids. Usually, half of this herd would come from the bride's holdings, accumulated through gifts and natural reproduction growth since her birth, and the other half would come from the groom, accumulated in a similar manner. The 'average' herding family had somewhere between 100 and 200 animals. Only a few 'rich' herders had more than 200 animals, with upper limits on animal holdings usually predicated more on labor access than on pasture access (Browman 1990).

Maximization, and related least-effort analyses, such as optimal foraging and linear program modeling, have presupposed a definition of 'rationality' as applied to 'peasant' agricultural behavior that involves maximizing of production. A logical extension of these analyses is the assumption that 'rational' herders, necessarily involved in maximizing animal holdings, will inevitably overexploit the pasture utilized or held in common. The question of why this 'tragedy of the commons' did not occur with Central Andean agropastoral groups until the late 20th century CE is a puzzling issue under those postulates. As I have argued in detail elsewhere (Browman 1987, 1994, 1998), the indigenous Andean herders dealt with the issues of production uncertainty, both environmental and social, by risk management or risk minimization. Thus the minimization of risk rather than the maximization of production was the operational rationality.

ORIGINS OF CENTRAL ANDEAN PASTORAL LIFESTYLES

There are a number of competing theories regarding the origin of nomadic and seminomadic pastoralism. The most frequently cited origin scenarios for pastoral nomadism include arguments for pastoral nomadism arising from an adaptation to marginal environments (low temperature or low precipitation); pastoral nomadism arising as an economic specialization to exploit interregional markets integrated into more complex states, particularly through control of caravans and transportation; and pastoral nomadism arising as a defensive strategy by less complex societies against expanding encroaching state societies, with the opportunity to 'vote with one's feet' as well as highly mobile resistance allowing one to avoid being unwillingly incorporated into an expanding hegemony. Animals are the vehicles by which all of these nomadic trajectories are seen as being operationalized.

In terms of available evidence, Andean seminomadic pastoralists could fit into the first two of these origin scenarios but not into the third. First, camelids are herded particularly in areas where plant agriculture is not viable, because the lands are too high, too cold, or too dry or because the soils are too poor. This is the pattern observed in Peru since the earliest pastoralists, seven thousand years ago or earlier. Thus the 'marginal environment' origin model is certainly supported. Camelid pastoralism is the principal, and in many cases the only, way that these high-elevation lands can be exploited.

But there may be evidence to support a secondary origin, or at least florescence, of pastoralism in the southern altiplano. In areas such as southern Bolivia and northwest Argentina we have identified archaeological evidence for the growth of polities associated with pastoralism arising simultaneously with the development of large interregional markets in the last millennium and a half. The herding groups owning the transport animals became economic specialists in moving manufactured goods, as well as staples from one exchange network to another. This evidence could be marshaled to support the 'trade and economic specialization' model of pastoral nomadism as a secondary development in response to these conditions.

This secondary florescence in the southern altiplano resulted in a pattern that Núñez Atencio and Dillehay (1978) have called "gyratory mobility" for groups trafficking between Chile and Bolivia (probably a rather misleading appellation). The strategy, however, allowed these pastoralists to thrive during the Inca Empire and to adapt quickly to the needs of the Spaniards, as the European conquerors sought to move silver out and goods into the fabled silver city of Potosi. And even in the late 20th century CE, during periods when truck fuel was in short supply because of embargoes or too costly because of runaway inflation, the remnant herding groups experienced brief periods of resurgence, when their caravan animals once again became a significant means of moving goods.

DISCUSSION

Identification of the complete suite of archaeological pastoral sites in the Andes has proceeded slowly. Archaeologists have been able to identify the main-residence villages, which are the locales of storage and ritual activities, and often the (at least seasonal) residences of groups that produced part of their own tuber and grain foodstuffs. But we have had less success in finding temporarily utilized locales with low archaeological visibility, such as grazing outposts and hunting camps, and in clearly identifying their functions. We know that until very recent times, most of the herding groups continued to kill wild camelids, cervids and rodents on specialized hunting trips, as well as opportunistically taking the same animals when encountered while herding. Because the faunal remains and lithic tools are expected to be similar, if not identical, for these two types of sites, the question arises: how can we distinguish archaeologically between a hunting encampment and a temporary herding outpost? This issue becomes even more complicated as we also have to include the temporary encampments of the trade caravans. Because of the pastoral-derived foodstuffs brought along on caravan trips, we could make a first-order prediction that the archaeological record of an overnight caravan stop might not look much different from that of a hunting camp or a herding station.

Nielsen (2000) has done some pioneering ethno-archaeological work in trying to help sort this problem out. Traveling with contemporary llama caravan groups in the Potosi Department, in southern Bolivia, he investigated the home-based herding locales with main residences, herding posts and grazing area sites. He also collected information along a set of caravan routes, looking at the overnight stops, the rest places and the locations where resources were extracted.[4] In the end Nielsen thought he could identify, at least for this specific contemporary ethnic group, the degree of pastoral specialization, the goods transported, and their caravan stops as contrasted to their seasonal herding stations, as well as the ethnic, sociopolitical and geopolitical context of caravan trade, all based on the specific site context and contents.

More studies of this nature need to be done for other remnant pastoral groups in the Andes before we can hope to define generalized 'rules' for separating these site types in all areas. Lessons from these studies need to be applied to regional surveys. As archaeologists we are currently very good at identifying farmsteads, villages, and so on, but the present archaeological site-surveying projects in the Andes are not yet fine-tuned enough to pick up and differentiate the much more ephemeral herding outpost and caravan stop locations.

The Central Andes is one of the prehistoric locales for independent development of pastoral lifestyle. The Andes may have had 'pure' pastoral nomadism at the onset of domestication of the camelids, but very quickly the pattern evolved into one of seminomadic pastoralism or perhaps tethered nomadism, and in recent historic periods the area is characterized mainly by seminomadic agropastoralism.

A pastoral lifestyle still persists in the Central Andes today in marginal zones, where plant agriculture is severely limited, or impossible, because of climatic constraints. But more recent prehistoric and historic patterns are also based on capitalizing on the need for transport of goods between large state-exchange systems, where the herders control, and have become specialists in, transportation. Thus the Andean example is not 'clean;' it does not fit nicely into an 'either/or' category. The agropastoralism is not a 'pure' pastoral nomadism, and its functioning supports more than one of the popular origin models.[5]

[4.] These *llameros* were involved in a lively trade in rock salt, mined from nearby salt deposits in dried-up Pleistocene lake beds or *salares*.

[5.] Bonavia Berber (1996) has compiled an 850-page volume, in Spanish, on miscellaneous aspects of Andean camelid pastoralism, including an extensive 110-page bibliography of all sources through the early 1990s.

REFERENCES

Bonavia Berber, D.

1996   *Los camélidos sudamericanos: Una introducción a su estudio* [in Spanish]. Lima, Travaux de l'Institut Français d'Etudes Andines.

Browman, D. L.

1970   *Early Peruvian Peasants: The Culture History of a Central Highlands Valley.* Harvard University, Department of Anthropology (PhD dissertation).

1976   Demographic Correlations of the Wari Conquest of Junin. *American Antiquity 41*: 4, pp. 465–477.

1984   Pastoralism and Development in High Andean Arid Lands. *Journal of Arid Environments 7*: 4, pp. 313–328.

1987   Agro-pastoral Risk Management in the Central Andes. *Research in Economic Anthropology 8*: pp. 171–200.

1990   High Altitude Camelid Pastoralism of the Andes. In J. G. Galaty and D. L. Johnson (eds.), *The World of Pastoralism: Herding Systems in Comparative Perspective*. New York, Guilford Publications: pp. 323–352.

1998   Pastoral Risk Perception and Risk Definition for Altiplano Herders. *Nomadic Peoples 38*: 1, pp: 22–36.

Kent, J. D.

1982   *The Domestication and Exploitation of the South American Camelids: Methods of Analysis and Their Application to Circum-lacustrine Archaeological Sites in Bolivia and Peru*. Washington University in St. Louis (PhD dissertation).

Lynch, T. F.

1971   Preceramic Transhumance in the Callejón de Huaylas, Peru. *American Antiquity 36*: 2, pp. 139–148.

Miller, G. R.

1979   *An Introduction to the Ethnoarchaeology of the Andean Camelids*. University of California, Berkeley (PhD dissertation).

Moore, K. M.

1989   *Hunting and the Origins of Herding in Peru*. University of Michigan, Ann Arbor (PhD dissertation).

Nielsen, A. E.

2000   *Andean Caravans. An Ethnoarchaeology (Bolivia)*. University of Arizona, Department of Anthropology (PhD dissertation).

Núñez Atencio, L. and T. D. Dillehay

1978   *Movilidad giratoria, armonía social y desarrollo en los Andes meridionales: Patrones de tráfico e interacción económica* [in Spanish]. Antofagasta, Universidad del Norte.

Wheeler, J. C.
1984   On the Origin and Early Development of Camelid Pastoralism in the Andes.
        In J. Clutton-Brock and C. Grigson (eds.), *Animals and Archaeology. Volume 3:*
        Early Herders and Their Flocks. British Archaeological Reports International Series
        S202. Oxford, Archaeopress: pp. 395–410.
Wheeler, J. C., E. Pires-Ferreira and P. Kaulicke
1976   Preceramic Animal Utilization in the Central Peruvian Andes. *Science 194*:
        pp. 483–490.

CHAPTER 8

COLONIZATION, STRUCTURED LANDSCAPES AND SEASONAL MOBILITY

AN EXAMINATION OF EARLY PALEO-ESKIMO LAND-USE PATTERNS IN THE EASTERN CANADIAN ARCTIC

S. BROOKE MILNE[1]

W HEN DISCUSSING NEW World archaeology, the word *colonization* conjures images of Paleo-Indian sites and Clovis points because these were the first peoples and lithics to enter the North American continent from an Asian/Beringian origin, some 12,000 years ago. Several thousand years later, a second and apparently unrelated pioneering population followed the

[1] Many thanks to Aubrey Cannon and Chris Ellis for reading earlier drafts of this chapter and for offering many helpful comments and suggestions. I am grateful to Chris Ellis for his encouragement over the last few years to undertake such comparative analyses of Paleo-Eskimo and Paleo-Indian material culture. His insights and expertise on Paleo-Indian lithics helped me to formulate several of the ideas presented in this chapter. Thank you also to Lisa Hodgetts for providing another critical northern perspective on Paleo-Eskimo culture and to Robert Park for allowing me to reproduce the map illustrated in Figure 8.1. This chapter was written during my tenure as a postdoctoral Research Fellow in the Department of Anthropology at the University of Western Ontario. Support for this fellowship is generously provided by the Social Sciences and Humanities Research Council of Canada Post-Doctoral Fellowship Program. Funding for my doctoral research, on which part of this chapter is based, was provided by the Social Sciences and Humanities Research Council of Canada Doctoral Fellowship Program, the Association for Universities for Northern Studies Studentship Awards Program, the Northern Scientific Training Program and the McMaster University School of Graduate Studies. It was inspiring to meet, at the Cotsen Institute of Archaeology at UCLA, where this chapter was first presented, with colleagues studying such a unique diversity of cultures, from different periods, centering on issues of human mobility.

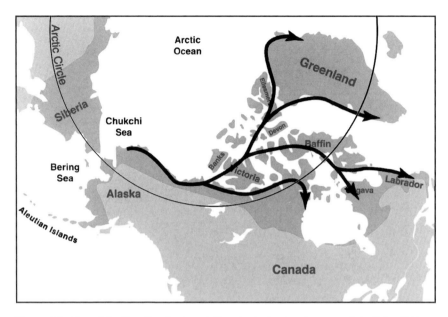

Figure 8.1. Map of the Canadian Arctic and Greenland, showing the route of the Paleo-Eskimos (courtesy of Robert Park).

same entry route into the New World, but instead of moving southward, these peoples came to occupy the previously uninhabited Arctic regions of Canada and Greenland (Figure 8.1). These peoples are known archaeologically as the Paleo-Eskimos.

This movement effectively represents a second discrete colonization of people into a pristine environment in the New World. Despite some obvious similarities between the Paleo-Indians and Paleo-Eskimos in terms of culture origins, small population size, lithic technology and mobility, comparatively little consideration has been given to these early Arctic pioneers when addressing universal archaeological questions of human colonization and adaptation in unfamiliar environments (Ellis 1998). Given the contributions that research on the Paleo-Eskimos can make in addressing questions on these topics, it seems fitting to raise the profile of this culture in the wider field of archaeology. That said, I am in no way implying we presently know all there is to know about these peoples. We can state that the Paleo-Eskimos thrived in the eastern Arctic for roughly 3000 years. We cannot say, though, exactly how they did survive in what initially would have been unfamiliar surroundings. Moreover, how did the Paleo-Eskimos stay in contact with one another given that the average group size is estimated to have been between 10–30 people at any given time of the year (Maxwell 1985:98)? Some archaeologists have argued that to maintain basic biological viability in a population, group size needs to be larger than 25 (for instance Kelly 2003:51). If it is not, frequent and repeated contact with outside groups must be established and maintained, no matter the distance to be traveled (Wilmsen 1973, 1974; Wobst 1974; Mandryk 1993; MacDonald 1998, 1999; MacDonald and Hewitt 1999). With this in mind, social factors take on a more significant role than they have been previously given, especially among small-scale nomadic peoples like the Paleo-Eskimos. In this chapter I consider how colonization, lithic raw material procurement, social contact and landscape learning articulated over time to shape Paleo-Eskimo land-use patterns, particularly those on southern Baffin Island.

To situate this discussion, I begin with an overview of Paleo-Eskimo culture and current interpretations for what sparked their eastward migration from Alaska. To highlight some of the flaws with these cultural characterizations, I draw on Rockman's (2003:4–7) concepts of environmental knowledge and landscape learning. I argue that the establishment of habitual land-use patterns among the Paleo-Eskimos may have been more significantly influenced by demands for lithic procurement and social contact than by subsistence needs. The Paleo-Eskimo migration into the eastern Arctic was fairly rapid, and one of the driving forces structuring this movement may well have been the motivation to secure an adequate and reliable tool-stone supply. As all Paleo-Eskimo groups would have shared similar locational priorities on entering this pristine landscape, a coincidental opportunity for social interaction likely resulted at these tool-stone sources since there would exist a need to acquire locational knowledge regarding their distribution in an unfamiliar landscape. As nomadic peoples, the Paleo-Eskimos did not exist at the mercy of their surroundings, and interpretations of these peoples living a tenuous existence must be reconsidered. As Mandryk (2003:xiii) notes, hunger, cold or adventure can no longer be thought of as the principal driving forces behind human colonization into new lands.

PALEO-ESKIMO CULTURE

Because of poor preservation conditions created by climatic fluctuations, annual freeze-thaw cycles, and moist acidic soils, organic materials generally do not survive in Paleo-Eskimo sites. Consequently, much of what we know about the Paleo-Eskimo culture derives from its lithic remains. The stone tools made and used by these peoples are very distinctive. Typological and morphological similarities, particularly among burins, microblades, microcores and endblades, have led to widespread speculation among Arctic archaeologists that the Paleo-Eskimos originated somewhere in the Old World, most likely Siberia (Giddings 1967). Perhaps the most striking characteristic of Paleo-Eskimo stone tools is their small size (Figure 8.2).

Figure 8.2. Examples of Paleo-Eskimo lithic artifacts illustrating their tiny size. This assemblage is from the Tungatsivvik site (Frobisher Bay, southern Baffin Island) and includes (A) informal tools; (B) burin spalls; (C) microblade fragments; (D) burins; (E) bifaces and biface fragments; (F) scrapers; and (G) core fragments.

Among the Inuit, oral histories claim that the makers of these tools must have been dwarfs precisely because of their small size (Maxwell 1985:40). Several isolated finds, however, indicate that these tiny lithics were mounted into larger hafts, handles and shafts. Given the value of these organic implements in an environment where such materials are often difficult to come by in large pieces, they were rarely discarded with the lithics, thus leaving the impression that only small hands could have used the isolated stone parts. Irving (1957) coined the name Arctic Small Tool tradition (ASTt) and applied it to all Paleo-Eskimo sites from Alaska to Greenland where these tiny stone tools were found. He believed, based on this trait, that they all belonged to a single parent culture.

When exactly the Paleo-Eskimos entered into the New World is a matter of debate largely because of problems with radiocarbon dating Arctic sites.[2] The point of entry, however, is generally accepted as having been on the north shore of Alaska. McGhee (1996:73), Maxwell (1985:37, 39) and Schledermann (1996:39) all speculate that this movement began when several small bands of people crossed the Bering Strait from the nearby Chukchi Peninsula into Alaska via the Seward Peninsula some 5000 years ago. Soon after crossing into Alaska, these people began moving into the eastern regions. Earlier immigrants into the New World, the Paleo-Indians, had not previously colonized the eastern Arctic because the area remained glaciated until roughly 6500 years ago, making it uninhabitable (Maxwell 1985:37; Schledermann 1996:15). Once the ice retreated, human expansion occurred rapidly, with full colonization from Alaska to Greenland being estimated at having been accomplished in 500 years or less (McGhee 1996:73). There remains the question of why the Paleo-Eskimos moved eastward to colonize the last uninhabited region in the New World. As Maxwell (1985:45–47) notes, there is no definitive evidence to explain the impetus for this movement, but there are several theories.

First, it is thought that with the retreat of the glacial ice sheets there occurred a biotic explosion in which plants as well as marine and terrestrial animals thrived in this new environment. Human hunters would have been attracted to these abundant subsistence resources, which would have been easy to hunt, having never seen human beings before. Second, population pressure in Alaska is proposed as a catalyst for colonization. To date, however, there is no direct evidence indicating that population numbers had exceeded the carrying capacity of the local Alaskan environment. Third, it is thought that intergroup tensions or disputes may have resulted in band fissioning, in which those peoples who were shunned or cast out left in search of a new 'homeland' (McGhee 1996:74). Last, the rapid colonization of the eastern Arctic has been closely tied to musk ox hunting. Steensby (1917) proposed that the Paleo-Eskimos followed eastward migrating herds of musk ox from the western subarctic Barrenlands to Greenland. Because of the defensive

---

[2.] The debate in Arctic archaeology surrounding the use of radiocarbon dates deriving from sea mammal fat and bone has spanned several decades (McGhee and Tuck 1976; Arundale 1981; Park 1994). Because of problems with the marine reservoir effect, dates obtained from marine mammal samples are considered less reliable than those obtained from terrestrial sources. Even though efforts have been made to devise correction factors for these marine dates, most researchers still consider them suspect, opting instead for dates obtained from terrestrial species.

tactics of musk oxen, which form a circle or line to protect the herd, all of the animals could be killed at once. Over time this would invariably put pressure on local populations because of their slow reproductive rates (McGhee 1996:55). Therefore, the Paleo-Eskimos would have had to move further and further eastward in search of new herds. Evidence from sites in Greenland, where middens have been found indicating a focused exploitation of musk ox, seems to support this theory. The ethology of musk ox, and their potential for population collapse, suggests that a dependence on this animal as a primary resource would have been extremely risky. Because of this, the musk ox theory remains questionable.

Whatever the catalyst was for the colonization, we know that it was rapid. A plausible explanation for the speed of this process is that the environment, although uninhabited, was not drastically different from the one the Paleo-Eskimos left in Siberia and Alaska. In other words, the Paleo-Eskimos would have been pre-adapted to living in the eastern Arctic environment, having already established sophisticated marine and terrestrial hunting strategies in their place of origin. Despite the probability that the Paleo-Eskimos were pre-adapted to this pristine environment, archaeological interpretations of these peoples' way of life tend to reinforce an idea that Paleo-Eskimo existence was frequently tenuous or 'stressed' (Maxwell 1997:206). They lived year-round in skin tents and snow houses (Ramsden and Murray 1995), enduring winter temperatures of below -40°C. To heat these structures, it is thought that the Paleo-Eskimos burned animal bones and fat in open fires, contained in box hearths, rather than using soapstone lamps (Maxwell 1984:361; Schledermann 1996:8–9). Soapstone lamps are far more efficient as sources of heat and light than open fires are, but few of these items have been found in archaeological sites, leading to speculation that they were not widely used by these earliest Arctic inhabitants (Maxwell 1984:361). Existence in these dwellings would not only be cold but also unpleasantly smoky.

Paleo-Eskimo camps are interpreted as ephemeral given the low density of material remains that characterizes many of them, suggesting that their inhabitants were constantly on the move, most likely in pursuit of animal resources (Andreasen 2000:91; Nagy 2000:144–145). The winter darkness would complicate efforts to hunt, particularly in the highest Arctic regions. Knuth (1967) proposed that to mitigate the long winter months of darkness and isolation, these pioneers may have passed the winter in a kind of semihibernation, during which time little activity of any kind occurred. Presumably, the Paleo-Eskimos cached food outside their skin tents, gathered as much fuel, in the form of musk ox bones, as possible, and crawled underneath heavy skins to sleep the winter darkness away (McGhee 1996:64–65). What reflects the insecurity of this kind of existence are the population estimates for this culture.[3] McGhee (1996:65) states that in the High Arctic, there may have been only 200–300 people scattered over one million km[2]. If these same densities apply to the Low Arctic, then the total Paleo-Eskimo population may have merely comprised 500–1000 people throughout this massive region.[4] When these people were dispersed in winter camps of 10–15 individuals, the loss of any one person, particularly a hunter, could spell disaster for all (Schledermann 1996:101). Moreover, with numbers this small, the loss of a single regional group could seriously hinder the biological viability of the entire population (Park 2000:201).

ENVIRONMENTAL KNOWLEDGE AND LANDSCAPE LEARNING

In the Arctic it is easy to explain away certain patterns of human behavior in the archaeological record, given the sharp seasonal changes experienced in this environment and their effects on the ecosystem. But the Paleo-Eskimos would not have survived long if this was their sole reality. To link these peoples' existence so intrinsically to seasonal shifts in the environment and resource base undermines their ability to think, act and adapt. It denies them agency as human beings and makes them appear as automatons that merely wandered about the landscape, weather permitting, in search of food (Wobst 2000:40). Rockman (2003) recently proposed that to truly understand the process of human colonization in pristine environments, archaeologists must consider how existing knowledge (from a place of origin) and landscape learning (the knowledge that is acquired in a new location) shaped and reinforced the behavior of pioneering populations in unfamiliar surroundings. This kind of analysis facilitates a

---

[3.] Population estimates for the Paleo-Eskimos are highly speculative because large parts of the Arctic landscape remain unexplored. This makes it difficult to devise accurate assessments of Paleo-Eskimo occupation densities. Despite these difficulties, ethnographic accounts by Boas (1964:18, see table for individual settlement numbers) for the southern Baffin Inuit indicate that the overall population numbers for the entire region did not exceed several hundred. Settlement size ranged from 20–82 individuals, and these numbers were wholly dependent on the seasonal availability of subsistence resources. It is acknowledged that the Paleo-Eskimo population was smaller than that of the Inuit (Maxwell 1985). Therefore, it is not unreasonable to speculate that a need for social interaction would have been of critical importance to these earliest peoples both on a cultural level and on a purely biological level (Park 2000:201).

[4.] The Low Arctic is loosely defined as the region south of the Parry Channel. The areas north of the channel are considered High Arctic as this is where the conditions that define the Arctic are at their most extreme (McGhee 1996:44–45).

greater appreciation for how past populations knew and used their environment, and it works to dispel the image of a perilous existence.

Rockman (2003:4–7) acknowledges that "knowing the environment can mean many things," and to simplify discussion, she outlines three basic types of knowledge. *Locational knowledge* includes information relating to the spatial and physical characteristics of particular resources. It also includes the ability to relocate such resources after their discovery. Locational knowledge is considered the easiest form of information to acquire. *Limitational knowledge* refers to familiarity with the usefulness and reliability of various resources, including the combination of multiple resources into a working environment. Development of limitational knowledge depends on the periodicity of the given resource and its intended use. *Social knowledge* is the collection of social experiences that serves as a means of transforming the environment or a collection of natural resources into a human landscape.

Two important factors that must be considered when discussing the process of landscape learning include the means by which knowledge is acquired and the time it takes to acquire that knowledge (Rockman 2003:12). For the Paleo-Eskimos we know that the process of landscape learning occurred rapidly. The way this knowledge was acquired, however, has not been explicitly considered by Arctic archaeologists. Rockman (2003:13–19) proposes four approaches through which knowledge and landscape learning can be incorporated into archaeological investigations. For this chapter I draw on the Resource Modeling Approach, which focuses on the ability of a colonizing population to take information acquired in its original environment and effectively apply it in a new area. The success of transferring this knowledge depends wholly on "the similarity of necessary resources in terms of location and distribution, the limitations in terms of carrying capacity, and the social organization required to access them" (Rockman 2003:18).

In the Arctic the range of subsistence resources is comparatively limited in terms of terrestrial (such as caribou, musk ox, hare, fox, birds) and marine mammals (such as seal, polar bear, walrus, whale). The Paleo-Eskimos would most likely have encountered the same range of species in the eastern Arctic as they would have in Siberia and Alaska. Accordingly, established hunting techniques and knowledge of animal ethology would have been transferable from their old environment to this new one. The social organization required to hunt and process these resources would have been equally applicable. Archaeologists studying Paleo-Indian culture (among which Kelly and Todd 1988; Meltzer 1995; Amick 1996; Kelly 1996) have, over the decades, built on Mason's (1962:243–246) seminal statement that subsistence systems based on the exploitation of large fauna are transferable across long distances and that this transferability would invariably have facilitated the expansion of the

Paleo-Indians throughout the North American continent. This transference of hunting strategies would appear to apply in the Arctic for the Paleo-Eskimos as well. It should be noted that contingent situations, where local faunal resources experienced periodic crashes, would occur. As the same situations would have happened previously, the Paleo-Eskimos likely had existing limitational knowledge on how to deal with them. In effect, the Paleo-Eskimos would have been moving through an environment where the seasonal availability and types of resources would have been similar.

This model posits that information related to nonorganic resources, such as lithic raw materials, may be the least transferable from an old environment to one that is newly colonized (Rockman 2003:19). Lithic raw materials should be considered an exploitable resource in the same sense as plants and animals (Rick 1978:4; Ellis 1984:12; Bamforth 1986:40; Daniel 2001:261; Beck et al. 2002:482). Lithic source areas are not mobile, they are easily manipulated when encountered, and they can be exploited repeatedly once they have been identified on the landscape (Nelson 1991:77). Source areas, however, are directly affected by seasonal conditions where ground cover, such as ice and snow, will reduce their availability (Rolland 1981; Kuhn 1991; Wenzel and Shelley 2001). Lithic raw materials are also not always evenly distributed across the landscape, and their quality can vary greatly among source areas (Andrefsky 1994a, 1994b). With these factors in mind, Paleo-Eskimo toolmakers would have needed to quickly locate tool-stone sources and to assess and access them directly. Consequently, the need to acquire locational and limitational knowledge on lithic source areas in the eastern Arctic would be critical, particularly since the geological distribution of this material resource would be entirely unknown to the Paleo-Eskimos in this pristine environment.

In cases where lithic source areas are highly variable in distribution, quality and seasonal availability, individuals will make every effort to acquire high quality tool stone even if it means having to travel considerable distances to do so (Andrefsky 1994a; MacDonald 1998, 1999). To find lithic sources in a new environment would require exploration, and given the logistical challenges involved in moving a large group of people across the landscape, it would not make sense for the entire group to participate on such journeys. We might expect social organization to change to accommodate long-distance raw material procurement (Binford 2001:465–466). Those individuals most capable of such journeys would include the young and physically fit. These are also the persons who would be looking for prospective mates in other distant groups.

MOBILITY, SOCIAL INTERACTION
AND LITHIC PROCUREMENT

For decades archaeologists studying small-scale nomadic hunter-gatherer cultures have speculated on how these groups survived given their low population densities and the massive territories they came to occupy (Wobst 1974; Kelly and Todd 1988; Mandryk 1993). Wilmsen (1973, 1974) proposed that among such small-scale societies archaeologists should expect to find a reliance on long-distance mating networks to maintain basic biological viability. MacDonald (1998:228–230) recently revisited this issue and, building in part on Wilmsen's (1974:118–119) ideas, he applied this proposition to Folsom Paleo-Indian sites located in the northern and central plains. He found, by tracing the distribution of exotic tool stone throughout these areas, that these Paleo-Indian people not only used mobility as a critical strategy for finding mates but that, in the process of doing so, they were also able to maintain strong social ties with otherwise distant groups, all of whom were living in a recently colonized region. Early land-use patterns among the Folsom Paleo-Indians appear to have been structured in large part by the demands for social contact. And the apparent rendez vous spots were at or near distinct lithic source areas that were, on average, 330 km away (MacDonald 1999:152). In the process of learning the landscape, the Paleo-Indians in this region acquired locational and limitational knowledge relating to tool-stone distribution. Over time this translated into specific social knowledge in which the local environment, or a collection of resources (such as lithics), was transformed into a human landscape where socially determined patterns of activity (such as finding a mate) occurred within and amongst the inhabitants (Rockman 2003:6). Drawing on this example for comparative purposes, I believe that Paleo-Eskimo colonization and the establishment of habitual land-use patterns in the eastern Arctic could have occurred under similar conditions.

In the extreme north, procurement of lithic raw materials is complicated not only by geological patchiness but also by pronounced seasonal restrictions on accessibility. On southeastern Baffin Island, Maxwell (1973:10–11) notes that sources of chert and other stones used in lithic tool production are scarce and that the available sources consist of small, weathered pebbles on the ocean floor. These pebbles can only be obtained during the Arctic warm season, when the shore-fast ice is gone and when the tide recedes to expose the ocean floor. Patchiness and accessibility would have added to the challenges of finding tool stone in this new environment. Stone would have been a highly valued resource, and it is certain that the Paleo-Eskimos were able to find sufficient source locations. Once identified, a source area was likely used repeatedly simply because it was known, not necessarily because it was the best (Kelly 2003:51). With this in mind, all Paleo-Eskimos in the eastern Arctic would have been exploring the landscape in search of tool stone and, in the process of doing so, may have encountered other people exploiting the same source areas. According to MacDonald (1999:152), Folsom Paleo-Indians traveled 160–500 km in search of tool-stone sources. Considering that the population density of Paleo-Eskimos in the eastern Arctic was probably far lower than the estimated figure of 1 person/1000 km^2 for the Folsom Paleo-Indians (MacDonald 1999:154), the former would have had an even greater need for external social contact than the latter.

It is highly unlikely that it would have taken the Paleo-Eskimos a long time to learn the locations of tool-stone source areas. This ties back to Rockman's (2003) concepts of locational and limitational knowledge. As I have mentioned, locational knowledge is considered the easiest form of information to acquire because it can be gathered rapidly in a matter of days, weeks or months (Rockman 2003:4). Limitational knowledge relating to lithic raw materials would not be that different in a new environment because periodicity would be directly linked to the same seasonal restrictions relating to ground cover that would have been previously experienced in Siberia and Alaska. Moreover, the intended use of tool stone, no matter where it was procured, would be the same, since lithics were such an integral component of the Paleo-Eskimo technological inventory. Rockman (2003:4) suggests that it would take roughly a generation to become familiar with such resources in a new environment in terms of "their fluctuations, their potentials, and their carrying capacity." Widely dispersed groups of Paleo-Eskimos would soon locate lithic source areas throughout the eastern Arctic and, in so doing, would invariably encounter other groups or at least see evidence of their existence in the region. This may have provided incentives for these widely dispersed groups to make contact with one another, which in turn may have provided the basis for them to establish long-distance social networks where technological needs would be satisfied, reproductive interests secured, and culture continuity maintained.

Framing the process of Paleo-Eskimo colonization using concepts of knowledge and learning dispels the idea that life for these peoples was perilous. Instead, it acknowledges their unique adaptation to a polar environment and their ability to act on the basis of informed decisions. This approach also looks at how factors other than those tied to subsistence influenced people's behavior and interaction. But how did these patterns change once the Paleo-Eskimos became established throughout the eastern Arctic? Generally speaking, the next phase of colonization involves increasing regionalization, where adaptation takes on a more local or regional focus (Speiss et al. 1998; Mandryk 2003:xiv). Land-use patterns among Paleo-Eskimo sites on southern Baffin Island indicate, however, that these peoples continued to make long-distance journeys to acquire tool stone (Figure 8.3), and it appears that social factors were a major motivation to maintain these long-established patterns.

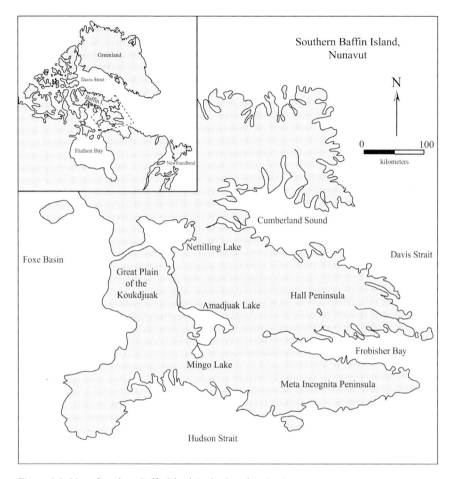

Figure 8.3. Map of southern Baffin Island, in the Canadian Arctic.

THE VIEW FROM SOUTHERN BAFFIN ISLAND

On southern Baffin Island, tool stone is geologically and seasonally restricted (Maxwell 1973, 1985; Odess 1998). In the coastal regions chert occurs in the form of weathered pebbles that can be found only when the shore-fast ice is gone and the tides recede, exposing the ocean floor and coastal headlands. This material is of poor quality and the size of the pebbles restricts the kinds of tools that can be made from them. Fortunately, the interior of the island has a rich and reliable supply of stone fit for tool making in the form of secondary deposits of chert left by retreating glaciers that scoured the inland plains (Stenton 1991; Milne and Donnelly 2004; Milne 2005a). These secondary deposits consist of nodules of varying sizes and are highly variable in quality, color and texture. Amadjuak Lake, one of the large lakes found in the interior, is considered an especially important location for acquiring chert. *Amadjuak* is an English corruption of the Inuktitut word *amaaq* or *angmalik*. *Amaaq* means 'chert,' and 'amaaq lake' means, loosely translated, 'the place chert comes from' (Stenton and Park 1998:25). This attests to the known presence of chert in the interior, and recent archaeological investigations in this area further underscore its abundance and accessibility (Milne 2005a, 2005b).

The most ideal time to acquire stone for tool making is during the warm season when the ground is not covered by ice and snow. Moreover, seasonal food resources like nesting waterfowl and caribou are readily available and can be reliably procured in large quantities with ease (Milne and Donnelly 2004). This would have permitted toolmakers to focus their attention on renewing their tool kits and procuring sufficient raw material supplies to take back to the coast to meet their technological needs for the remainder of the year. Settlement-pattern analyses on southern Baffin Island indicate that the Paleo-Eskimos, like Inuit, spent the winter on the sea ice and outer coastal regions, where they hunted resident populations of ringed seals (Maxwell 1973, 1985; Stenton 1989; Milne 2003a). The distances between the coast and the interior, combined with the challenges of winter travel, would have curtailed frequent trips inland to get tool stone during the winter. Furthermore, procuring terrestrial subsistence resources at this time of year is difficult because migratory species have long since departed for warmer areas. Boas (1964:22) notes that in the past some Inuit have wintered in the interior; however, they only did so for a single season because securing an adequate food supply appeared tenuous. Based on these seasonal factors, procurement of lithic raw material undoubtedly was a planned event during the warm season, and inland travels to get it would have been scheduled accordingly (Milne 2003a, 2005a).

The interior of southern Baffin Island is easily reached from every coastal location via the coastal uplands (Stenton 1989:112). There are major river systems draining from each of the interior lakes out to the coast. As Kelly (2003:48) notes, when foragers are in an unfamiliar area, they rely heavily on prominent landmarks to navigate their way. Following river systems is perhaps the simplest way to explore the unknown "because if one goes upstream on the way out, one simply has to go downstream to return home" (Kelly 2003:48). Parties of explorers sent out to look for lithic source areas could easily find their way to the interior of Baffin Island, and the abundance of local chert there, by following the prominent inland river systems that connect the interior lakes to the outer coastal regions. If distant Paleo-Eskimos in the Cumberland Sound, Hudson Strait and Frobisher Bay regions all ventured inland at the same time, they would most certainly find one another. Ethnographic records document the importance of the interior of southern Baffin Island as a place where the Inuit traveled during the Arctic warm season (Bilby 1923; Soper 1928; Boas 1964).

The southern Baffin Inuit occupy several widely separated coastal districts. During the winter these people experienced a pronounced degree of isolation. Given the centrality of the interior region, it appears to have served as a focal point for seasonal interactions on an interregional level (Stenton 1989:335). Although Inuit populations were larger in the eastern Arctic during the contact period than those estimated for the Paleo-Eskimos, the Inuit were still widely distributed over a large geographic region. Therefore, these warm season interactions were equally critical for maintaining biological viability because during these meetings prospective mates were given opportunities to interact, and group alliances were renewed and strengthened (Stenton 1989:119). It is easy to imagine that the Paleo-Eskimos would have used the interior region for similar social purposes in addition to lithic acquisition, and five inland sites on southern Baffin Island provide archaeological evidence to support this idea. These five sites are variously located along the shores of Nettilling and Mingo Lakes and the Mingo River, which connects Mingo and Amadjuak Lake, and all of them have produced radiocarbon dates associated with the early Paleo-Eskimo period (Milne, in review). These sites are known as Sandy Point, Mosquito Ridge, LdFa-1, LdFa-12, and LeDx-42 (Stenton 1989; Milne 2003a, 2005a, 2005b, in press, in review; Milne et al., in review).

Sandy Point and Mosquito Ridge are located 10 km from one another on the western shore of Burwash Bay, which forms the southern margin of Nettilling Lake (Figure 8.4). Sandy Point is a single-component Paleo-Eskimo site and was excavated by Stenton in 1985. At the time, the site was being negatively impacted by forces of mechanical erosion. Consequently, it is not possible to determine how much of the site was disturbed or how much information may have been lost as a result. Of those artifacts that were recovered, 1176 are lithic debitage and 101 are informal and formal tools. Mosquito Ridge is a large multicomponent site occupied by the Paleo-Eskimos and the later Thule and Inuit cultures. Partial excavation of the Paleo-Eskimo component at Mosquito Ridge yielded a lithic assemblage of more than 20,000 artifacts, of which 97% is lithic debitage (Milne 2003a).

LdFa-1 and LdFa-12 are located 1 km from one another on the northwestern shore of Mingo Lake, which is approximately 250 km south of Nettilling Lake (Figure 8.5). LdFa-1 is a large site containing at least 23 well-defined tent-ring structures, suggesting this location was repeatedly occupied over time. Few Paleo-Eskimo sites on Baffin Island contain this many intact structural features, making this site unusual. Because the topography of southern Baffin Island is characterized by large bedrock outcrops, finding suitable camping spots near favorable hunting locations can be difficult. As a result, more recent populations tend to settle on top of existing site remains, thereby obscuring these earlier occupations. Older tent-ring structures are also occasionally

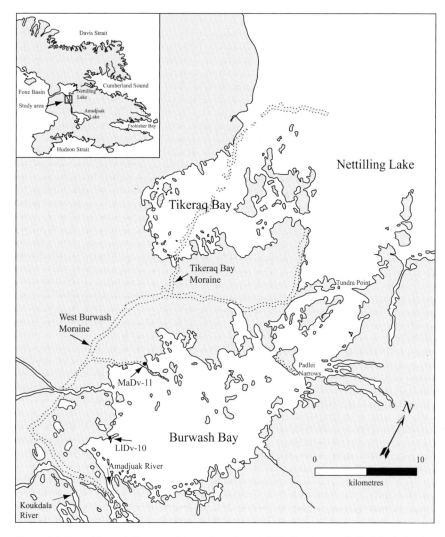

Figure 8.4. Map of Burwash Bay, part of the southern littoral of Nettling Lake on Baffin Island, showing the locations of Sandy Point (LlDv-10) and Mosquito Ridge (MaDV-11) (after Stenton 1989).

dismantled since more recent peoples scavenge perimeter rocks to build new dwellings (Milne 2003b).

Limited testing at LdFa-1 yielded large quantities of lithic and faunal material, which is almost exclusively caribou. Caribou are concentrated in the interior lakes region during the summer and early autumn, and they represent a rich and reliable food source in this area. The incredibly dense concentration of lithic debitage at LdFa-1 made for very slow digging. A total of 13.25 m² were excavated, yielding a lithic assemblage of 18,743 artifacts, 99.7% of which is

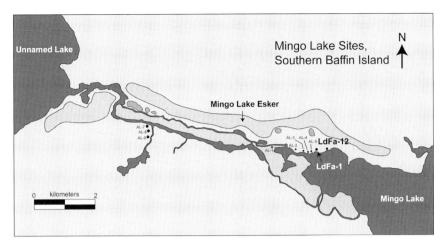

Figure 8.5. Map of the northwest shore of Mingo Lake, showing the locations of LdFa-1 and LdFa-12.

debitage. LdFa-12 is a small single-component Paleo-Eskimo site and it has no visible surface features. The site consists entirely of a 115-meter linear scatter of lithics. LdFa-12 was found serendipitously during a field survey. A well-worn caribou path runs through the center of the site and numerous artifacts and flakes were visible on the surface as a result. While ephemeral sites like LdFa-12 are more difficult to locate given their extremely low archaeological visibility on the Arctic tundra, postdepositional processes, like caribou trampling and frost heave, churn up the surface vegetation to expose underlying deposits. In some instances Paleo-Eskimo deposits are found by accident during the excavation of more recent sites. Despite the ephemeral nature of LdFa-12 and the limited number of units tested (about 5 m^2), it also yielded a comparatively large lithic assemblage of 3743 artifacts, of which 99.5% is debitage. Again, caribou dominate the recovered faunal remains, further indicating the importance of these animals as a subsistence resource in the area.

Last, LeDx-42 is another large Paleo-Eskimo site located on the shores of the Mingo River, approximately 10 km from LdFa-1 and LdFa-12 (Figure 8.6). Like LdFa-12, numerous caribou paths run through the central portion of LeDx-42, and scattered along them were diagnostic lithic artifacts indicating a Paleo-Eskimo cultural affiliation. There is only one possible dwelling structure visible at the site; however, it has yet to be investigated. Extensive testing yielded another large lithic and faunal assemblage, containing caribou remains. The lithics comprise 29,648 flakes, and 87 informal and formal tools.

My analysis of the Sandy Point and Mosquito Ridge lithics was conducted as part of a larger study to assess whether the Paleo-Eskimos followed a seasonal round, similar to that recorded for the southern Baffin Inuit, where winters

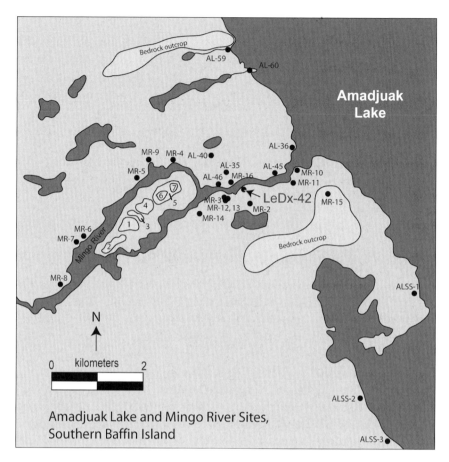

Figure 8.6. Map of the Mingo River, where it drains into the southwest shores of Amadjuak Lake, showing the location of LeDx-42.

were spent in the coastal regions and summers were spent in the interior (Milne 2003a). More than 24,500 lithic debitage and tool artifacts from these two inland sites and four southern Baffin coastal sites were compared. Patterns of tool reduction and use isolated among the inland sites indicate that they were principally used for raw material acquisition. The broad functional interpretation of the Sandy Point site is that it was used for raw material testing, early stage core reduction, and the limited production of tool preforms and blanks (Milne 2005a). These activities would have enabled task groups exploring the area for tool stone to assess its quality and abundance and, in the process, acquire locational and limitational knowledge. By comparison, Mosquito Ridge was used as a lithic acquisition site; however, there is no evidence of raw material testing, just intense early stage reduction (Milne and Donnelly 2004; Milne 2005a).

Stenton (1989) believes that Mosquito Ridge was a focal place in the interior region where later Neo-Eskimo populations would meet and interact for social purposes. I believe that the site had the same significance for the Paleo-Eskimos, in addition to raw material procurement. Mosquito Ridge was occupied very early on in the Paleo-Eskimo occupation of the eastern Arctic given the site's radiocarbon date of 3800 ± 40 BP (Milne and Donnelly 2004:96–97). This date makes Mosquito Ridge one of the oldest Paleo-Eskimo occupations on Baffin Island (Milne and Donnelly 2004:97). While raw-material acquisition may have been the primary incentive leading to the initial occupation of Mosquito Ridge during the colonization of the island, its centrality in the interior and its significance as a meeting place would have further increased its attraction as a place for continuous use. Mosquito Ridge is located beside the Great Plain of the Koukdjuak, one of the largest nesting grounds for snow geese in the world. The faunal assemblage recovered from Mosquito Ridge indicates that the site occupants were intensively hunting snow geese during the Arctic warm season, most likely during the bird's annual molt in early to mid-July. This subsistence resource would have been easy to acquire with little planning or energy investment, and it would have enabled the Paleo-Eskimos to focus more of their time on socializing and tool production rather than hunting (Milne and Donnelly 2004).

Investigations of LdFa-1, LdFa-12, and LeDx-42 were undertaken in 2004. Analysis of the recovered lithic materials is ongoing, but preliminary results do complement those from Sandy Point and Mosquito Ridge, further attesting to the importance of the island's interior as a place for warm season aggregations by the Paleo-Eskimos. Lithic raw-material acquisition was also the principal focus at these three sites. This is most clearly illustrated using flake-to-tool ratios (Milne and Donnelly 2004; Milne 2005a, in press). Flake-to-tool ratios are simple measures used to examine the extent to which lost tool utility at a site was being replaced through tool production activities (Ricklis and Cox 1993:450–451). Ratios are calculated here using all complete and fragmented burins, microblades, cores, bifaces, scrapers, retouched informal tools and burin spall tools. Unretouched flake tools, burin spalls, and bifacial edges were not included since they lack postdetachment modification and, therefore, do not contribute any by-products to the debitage assemblage.

Ratios for LdFa-1, LdFa-12, and LeDx-42 are extremely high (Table 8.1), indicating that tool utility was being replaced by intense tool-stone reduction. Although the ratios for Sandy Point and Mosquito Ridge are low to moderate, the reduction strategies identified through the formal debitage analysis do indicate that acquisition was the focus. In other words, the same reduction and use strategies were employed at all five sites. An obvious reason for these lower figures at Sandy Point and Mosquito Ridge can be attributed to the

Table 8.1. Flake-to-Tool Ratios Identified for Five Inland Paleo-Eskimo Sites on Southern Baffin Island:

Site	Flake/tool ratio	Number of artifacts	Intensity of reduction
MaDv-11	40:1	19,800 flakes | 495 tools	Moderate
LlDv-10	14:1	1176 flakes | 84 tools	Low
LdFa-12	207:1	3725 flakes | 18 tools	High
LdFa-1	406:1	18,691 flakes | 46 tools	High
LeDx-42	593:1	29,648 flakes | 50 tools	High

fact that LdFa-1 and LeDx-42 are extremely large sites that were intermittently occupied for millennia, resulting in larger deposits of reduction debris. Moreover, it is impossible to know how much of the assemblage at Sandy Point was lost as a result of site disturbance. Given the obvious absence of late stage finishing flakes at all five sites, it appears that formal tools were not being made in the interior from start to finish. Rather, reduction strategies isolated in the assemblages indicate that site activities were focused on early and middle-stage reduction, which is more commonly associated with the production of preforms and blanks. Because there are so few finished and intact artifacts in these assemblages, it appears that those implements that were being roughed out were taken away from the site for completion elsewhere. These patterns are entirely consistent with those identified in my earlier study (Milne 2003a), further supporting the inference that the Paleo-Eskimos were traveling inland to procure raw material during the Arctic warm season and then transporting back to the coast sufficient supplies to last them throughout the remainder of the year.

The presence of well-preserved faunal assemblages from LdFa-1, LdFa-12, and LeDx-42 also provides seasonality data in the form of caribou tooth thin sections, indicating these sites were also occupied during the warm season. Last, radiocarbon dates from these three sites further support that seasonal travels to the interior were established early on in the Paleo-Eskimo occupation of southern Baffin Island (Table 8.2). Even more interesting is the fact that additional dates from LdFa-1 and LeDx-42 indicate that these two sites were continuously occupied throughout the entire Paleo-Eskimo period, spanning at least 2400 years (Milne, in review). These dates are important because they coincide with a marked period of climate change experienced in the Arctic beginning around 2600 BP, which impacted the local environment. Winters became longer and harsher, and the extent and duration of the sea ice increased. In response to this the Paleo-Eskimos adopted a more maritime-oriented way of life, focusing on hunting sea mammals, mostly seals. As a result, it can be inferred that the importance of the terrestrial ecosystem decreased in significance to these peoples' way of life and that they spent more of the year in the

Table 8.2. Radiocarbon Dates for Five Inland Paleo-Eskimo Sites on Southern Baffin Island:

Site	Material	Date BP	Designation
MaDv-11	Caribou bone	3800±40	Early Paleo-Eskimo
LlDv-10	Peat	2785±115	Early Paleo-Eskimo
LdFa-12	Caribou bone	3670±40	Early Paleo-Eskimo
LdFa-1	Caribou bone	3530±40	Early Paleo-Eskimo
	Caribou bone	3490±40	Early Paleo-Eskimo
	Caribou bone	3210±40	Early Paleo-Eskimo
	Caribou bone	1230±40	Late Paleo-Eskimo
LeDx-42	Caribou bone	3480±40	Early Paleo-Eskimo
	Caribou bone	2320±40	Middle Paleo-Eskmo
	Caribou bone	2460±40	Middle Paleo-Eskmo
	Caribou bone	2450±40	Middle Paleo-Eskmo
	Caribou bone	1380±40	Late Paleo-Eskimo
	Caribou bone	1330±40	Late Paleo-Eskimo

outer coastal regions. Therefore, finding occupations dating to the middle and late periods in the inland proper of southern Baffin Island is somewhat unexpected. Certainly, the Paleo-Eskimos would continue to need tool stone for their technological needs, but this could be acquired in the coastal regions given the presence of chert pebbles there. The fact that these people continued to travel inland and that they reoccupied the same sites for 2400 years strongly suggests that other factors influenced their seasonal settlement patterns. I believe that social factors and the need for group interaction were among the driving forces that maintained these long-established interior land-use patterns. The Paleo-Eskimos were familiar with this interior landscape and the locations of these specific sites, which were ideal for raw material acquisition and in close proximity to ideal caribou and waterfowl hunting grounds.

The coastal areas of Baffin Island do have accessible sources of chert, although these are in the form of weathered pebbles of inferior quality, and there is also an abundant supply of food resources in these locations throughout the Arctic warm season (Jacobs and Stenton 1985; Stenton 1989). Therefore, the Paleo-Eskimos did not have to keep making these journeys inland purely for subsistence and material needs, particularly during the later periods given the arduousness of adapting to an increasingly colder environment. They would seemingly need to do so for social purposes, however, since the interior remains the most central place to meet. This strongly suggests that a pattern of seasonal mobility and land use, which was established very early on in the Paleo-Eskimo colonization of southern Baffin Island, soon became a habitual part of this culture's seasonal round, in spite of local food and material abundances in the coastal regions. The Paleo-Eskimo cultural landscape on southern

Baffin Island became highly structured by this unique confluence of geese, caribou, stone and social interaction in the interior. This early adaptation to an unfamiliar landscape appears to have helped secure the reproductive success of this population and its cultural continuity over the millennia. Moreover, an abundance of food and people during the warm season would have created a very relaxed atmosphere for social interaction (Milne and Donnelly 2004:108). This stands in sharp contrast to the image of Paleo-Eskimo life being balanced between a constant search for food and a state of semihibernation.

DISCUSSION

The Paleo-Eskimos were the first peoples to occupy one of the most arduous environments in the world. Given their knowledge of the Siberian and Alaskan landscapes, these peoples were essentially pre-adapted for their eastward migration into the pristine eastern Arctic. In this chapter I have argued that the Paleo-Eskimos transferred their existing locational and limitational knowledge from their place of origin to this new environment, which enabled them to successfully colonize it in a short period of time. Moreover, I suggest that the need to find suitable tool-stone sources and to establish social contact were equally if not more important than subsistence in shaping the early exploration of the eastern Arctic and the establishment of subsequent land-use patterns. Tool-stone sources are fixed on the landscape and seasonally restricted in their accessibility. All groups of Paleo-Eskimos would have required this resource to maintain their tool kits. Traveling distances of up to 500 km to access good-quality lithic raw material is not unheard of among Paleo-Indian groups (MacDonald 1999). It is therefore not unreasonable to speculate that Paleo-Eskimos made similar journeys in search of this resource. Once reliable source areas were found, it is highly probable that other distant groups would have been encountered at these locations. This would provide the basis to establish long-distance social and reproductive networks in this massive geographic expanse. Evidence from sites located on southern Baffin Island further indicates that these early land-use patterns were maintained over time, and a significant motivation to do so was a need for social interaction. By shifting my interpretive perspective away from a traditional environmentally deterministic paradigm focused on climate and subsistence, I have presented here a very different interpretation of the Paleo-Eskimo lifestyle from that which pervades the literature. It is not necessary to reduce early hunter-gatherers to the state of automatons to learn about their archaeological past. They knew their environments, and they moved across the landscape making knowledgeable decisions.

REFERENCES

Amick, D.

1996   Regional Patterns of Folsom Mobility and Land Use in the American Southwest. *World Archaeology 27*: 3, pp. 411–426.

Andreasen, C.

2000   Paleo-Eskimos in Northwest and Northeast Greenland. In M. Appelt, J. Berglund and H. C. Gullov (eds.), *Identities and Culture Contacts in the Arctic*. Copenhagen, Danish Polar Centre: pp. 82–96.

Andrefsky, W.

1994a   Raw Material Availability and the Organization of Technology. *American Antiquity 59*: 1, pp. 21–34.

1994b   The Geological Occurrence of Lithic Material and Stone Tool Production Strategies. *Geoarchaeology 9*: 5, pp. 375–391.

Arundale, W. H.

1981   Radiocarbon Dating in Eastern Arctic Archaeology: A Flexible Approach. *American Antiquity 46*: pp. 244–271.

Bamforth, D. B.

1986   Technological Efficiency and Tool Curation. *American Antiquity 51*: 1, pp. 38–50.

Beck, C., A. K. Taylor, G. T. Jones, C. M. Fadem, C. R. Cook and S. A. Millward

2002   Rocks Are Heavy: Transport Costs and Paleoarchaic Quarry Behaviour in the Great Basin. *Journal of Anthropological Archaeology 21*: pp. 481–507.

Bilby, J. W.

1923   *Among Unknown Eskimo*. London, J. B. Lippincott.

Binford, L. R.

2001   *Constructing Frames of Reference: An Analytical Method for Archaeological Theory Building Using Hunter-Gatherer and Environmental Data Sets*. Los Angeles, University of California Press.

Boas, F.

1964   *The Central Eskimo*. Lincoln, University of Nebraska Press (originally published in 1888).

Daniel, I. R., Jr.

2001   Stone Raw Material Availability and Early Archaic Settlement in the Southern United States. *American Antiquity 66*: 2, pp. 237–265.

Ellis, C. J.

1984   *Paleo-Indian Lithic Technological Structure and Organization in the Lower Great Lakes Area: A First Approximation*. Simon Fraser University, Department of Archaeology (PhD dissertation).

1998   The Fluted Point Tradition and the Arctic Small Tool Tradition: What's the Connection? Paper presented at the conference "On Being First: Cultural

Innovations and Environmental Consequences," 31st Annual Chacmool Conference, University of Calgary, November 1998.

Giddings, J. L.

1967   *Ancient Men of the Arctic*. New York, Alfred A. Knopf.

Irving, W. N.

1957   An Archaeological Survey of the Susitna Valley. *Anthropological Papers of the University of Alaska 6*: 1, pp. 37–52.

Jacobs, J. and D. Stenton

1985   Environment, Resource, and Prehistoric Settlement in Upper Frobisher Bay, Baffin Island. *Arctic Anthropology 22*: 2, pp. 59–76.

Kelly, R.

1996   Ethnographic Analogy and Migration to the Western Hemisphere. In T. Akazawa and E. J. Szathmary (eds.), *Prehistoric Dispersals of Mongoloid Peoples*. Tokyo, Oxford University Press: pp. 228–240.

2003   Colonization of New Land by Hunter-Gatherers: Expectations and Implications Based on Ethnographic Data. In M. Rockman and J. Steele (eds.), *Colonization of Unfamiliar Landscapes: The Archaeology of Adaptation*. New York, Routledge: pp. 44–58.

Kelly, R. and L. Todd

1988   Coming into the Country: Early Paleo-Indian Hunting and Mobility. *American Antiquity 3*: 2, pp. 231–244.

Kuhn, S. L.

1991   "Unpacking Reduction": Lithic Raw Material Economy in the Mousterian of West-Central Italy. *Journal of Anthropological Archaeology 10*: pp. 76–106.

Knuth, E.

1967   The Ruins of Musk-Ox Way. *Folk 8–9*: pp. 191–219.

MacDonald, D. H.

1998   Subsistence, Sex, and Cultural Transmission in Folsom Culture. *Journal of Anthropological Archaeology 17*: pp. 217–239.

1999   Modeling Folsom Mobility, Mating Strategies, and Technological Organization in the Northern Plains. *Plains Anthropologist 44*: 168, pp. 141–161.

MacDonald, D. H. and B. S. Hewitt

1999   Reproductive Interests and Forager Mobility. *Current Anthropology 40*: 4, pp. 501–525.

McGhee, R.

1996   *Ancient People of the Arctic*. Vancouver, UBC Press.

McGhee, R. and J. Tuck

1976   Undating the Arctic. In M. Maxwell (ed.), *Eastern Arctic Prehistory: Paleoeskimo Problems. Memoirs of the Society for American Archaeology Number 31*. Salt Lake City, Society for American Archaeology: pp. 6–14.

Mandryk, C. A. S.

1993   Hunter-Gatherer Social Costs and the Nonviability of Submarginal Environ-
        ments. *Journal of Anthropological Research 49*: pp. 39–71.

2003   Foreword. In M. Rockman and J. Steele (eds.), *Colonization of Unfamiliar
        Landscapes: The Archaeology of Adaptation*. New York, Routledge: pp. xiii–xv.

Mason, R. J.

1962   The Paleo-Indian Tradition in Eastern North America. *Current Anthropology
        3*: pp. 227–278.

Maxwell, M.

1973   *Archaeology of the Lake Harbour District, Baffin Island. Archaeological Survey of
        Canada, Paper Number 6*. Ottawa, National Museums of Canada.

1984   Pre-Dorset and Dorset Prehistory of Canada. In D. Damas (ed.), *Handbook of
        North American Indians. Volume 5: Arctic*. Washington, Smithsonian Institution:
        pp. 359–368.

1985   *Prehistory of the Eastern Arctic*. Orlando, Academic Press.

1997   The Canadian Arctic in Transition: Pre-Dorset to Dorset. In G. Gilberg and
        H. C. Gulløv (eds.), *Fifty Years of Arctic Research: Anthropological Studies from
        Greenland to Siberia. Publications of the National Museum Ethnographical Series.
        Volume 18*. Copenhagen, National Museum of Denmark, Department of
        Ethnography: pp. 205–208.

Meltzer, D.

1995   Clocking the First Americans. *Annual Review of Anthropology 24*: pp. 21–45.

Milne, S. B.

2003a   *Peopling the Pre-Dorset Past: A Multi-Scalar Study of Early Arctic Lithic Technology
        and Seasonal Land Use Patterns on Southern Baffin Island*. McMaster University,
        Department of Anthropology (PhD dissertation).

2003b   Identifying Pre-Dorset Structural Features on Southern Baffin Island:
        Challenges and Considerations for Alternative Sampling Methods. *Etudes/
        Inuit/Studies 27*: 1–2, pp. 67–90.

2005a   Palaeo-Eskimo Novice Stone Knapping in the Eastern Canadian Arctic.
        Journal of Field Archaeology 30: 3, pp. 329–345.

2005b   *Archaeological Investigations in the Mingo and Amadjuak Lake Districts of
        Southern Baffin Island. Permit Report covering the Work conducted under Nunavut
        Archaeologist Permit 04-06A*. Manuscript on file with the Department of
        Culture, Language, Elders, and Youth. Government of Nunavut. Igloolik,
        Nunavut.

in press Landscape Learning and Lithic Technology: Seasonal Mobility, Enculturation,
        and Tool Apprenticeship Among the Early Palaeo-Eskimos. In A. Cannon
        (ed.), *Structured Worlds: The Archaeology of Hunter-Gatherer Thought and Action*.
        London, Equinox.

in review Why Go Inland? Palaeo-Eskimo Terrestrial Occupations on Southern Baffin
        Island. *Current Anthropology* (submitted 27 Nov. 2006).

Milne, S. B. and S. M. Donnelly

2004   Going to the Birds: Examining the Importance of Avian Resources to
        Pre-Dorset Subsistence Strategies in the Interior of Southern Baffin Island.
        Arctic Anthropology 41: 1, pp. 90–112.

Milne, S. B., L. Hodgetts and S. Timmermans

in review Pre-Dorset Foragers? New Insights on Pre-Dorset Subsistence Strategies
        from the Interior of Southern Baffin Island. *Arctic* (submitted 3 Nov. 2006).

Nagy, M.

2000   From Pre-Dorset Foragers to Dorset Collectors: Paleo-Eskimo Culture
        Change in Ivujivik, Eastern Canadian Arctic. In M. Appelt, J. Berglund and
        H. C. Gullov (eds.), *Identities and Culture Contacts in the Arctic*. Copenhagen,
        Danish Polar Centre: pp. 143–148.

Nelson, M. C.

1991   The Study of Technological Organization. In M. Schiffer (ed.), *Archaeological
        Method and Theory. Volume 3*. Tucson, University of Arizona Press: pp.
        57–100.

Odess, D.

1998   The Archaeology of Interaction: Views from Artifact Style and Material
        Exchange in Dorset Society. *American Antiquity 63*: 3, pp. 417–435.

Park, R. W.

1994   Approaches to Dating the Thule Culture in the Eastern Arctic. *Canadian
        Journal of Archaeology 18*: pp. 29–48.

2000   The Dorset-Thule Succession Revisited. In M. Appelt, J. Berglund and H.
        Gullov (eds.), *Identities and Cultural Contacts in the Arctic*. Copenhagen, Danish
        Polar Centre: pp. 192–205.

Ramsden, P. and M. Murray

1995   Identifying Seasonality in Pre-Dorset Structures in Back Bay, Prince of Wales
        Island, NWT. *Arctic Anthropology 32*: 2, pp. 106–117.

Rick, J. W.

1978   *Heat Altered Cherts of the Lower Illinois Valley: An Experimental Study in
        Prehistoric Technology. Prehistoric Records Number 2*. Evanston, Northwestern
        University Archaeological Program.

Ricklis, R., and K. Cox

1993   Examining Lithic Technological Organization as a Dynamic Cultural
        Subsystem: The Advantages of an Explicitly Spatial Approach. *American
        Antiquity 58*: 3, pp. 444–461.

Rockman, M.

2003   Knowledge and Learning in the Archaeology of Colonization. In M. Rockman and J. Steele (eds.), *Colonization of Unfamiliar Landscapes: The Archaeology of Adaptation*. New York, Routledge: pp.3–24.

Rolland, N.

1981   The Interpretation of Middle Paleolithic Variability. *Man 16*: pp. 15–42.

Schledermann, P.

1996   *Voices in Stone: A Personal Journey into the Arctic Past. Komatic Series Number 5*. Calgary, Arctic Institute of North America.

Soper, J. D.

1928   *A Faunal Investigation of Southern Baffin Island. Canada Department of Mines Bulletins Number 53*. Ottawa, National Museum of Canada.

Speiss, A., D. Wilson and J. Bradley

1998   Paleo-Indian Occupation in the New England-Maritimes Region: Beyond Cultural Ecology. *Archaeology of Eastern North America 26*: pp. 201–264.

Steensby, H. P.

1917   An Anthropogeographical Study of the Origin of the Eskimo Culture. *Meddelelser om Grönland 53*: pp. 41–228.

Stenton, D. R.

1989   *Terrestrial Adaptations of Neo-Eskimo Coastal-Marine Hunters on Southern Baffin Island, NWT*. University of Alberta, Department of Anthropology (PhD dissertation).

1991   Caribou Population Dynamics and Thule Culture Adaptations on Southern Baffin Island, NWT. *Arctic Anthropology 28*: 2, pp. 15–43.

Stenton, D. R., and R. W. Park

1998   *Ancient Stone Tools of Nunavu: An Illustrated Guide*. Ottawa, Parks Canada.

Wenzel, K. E. and P. H. Shelley

2001   What Put the Small in the Arctic Small Tool Tradition? Raw Material Constraints on Lithic Technology at the Mosquito Lake Site, Alaska. In W. Andrefsky (ed.), *Lithic Debitage: Context, Form, Meaning*. Salt Lake City, University of Utah Press: pp. 106–123.

Wilmsen, E.

1973   Interaction, Spacing Behaviour, and the Organization of Hunting Bands. *Journal of Anthropological Research 29*: 1, pp. 1–31.

1974   *Lindenmeier: A Pleistocene Hunting Society*. New York, Harper and Row.

Wobst, M.

1974   Boundary Conditions for Paleolithic Social Systems: A Simulation Approach. *American Antiquity 39*: pp. 147–178.

2000   Agency in (spite of) Material Culture. In M.-A. Dobres and J. Robb (eds.), *Agency in Archaeology*. New York, Routledge: pp. 40–50.

CHAPTER 9

THE EMERGENCE OF CULTURES OF MOBILITY IN THE ALTAI MOUNTAINS OF MONGOLIA

EVIDENCE FROM THE INTERSECTION OF ROCK ART AND PALEOENVIRONMENT

ESTHER JACOBSON-TEPFER

THE APPEARANCE OF North Asian pastoralism is usually located within the Early to Middle Bronze Age (mid-second millennium BCE), while the emergence of seminomadic pastoralism is associated with the transition from the Bronze to Early Iron Age (early first millennium BCE).[1] This generalized dating is based on evidence from mortuary contexts within the Russian Altai region, the Sayan Mountains of Tuva and the Minusinsk Basin to the north of the Sayan region. That evidence includes the regular appearance of bones of sheep, cattle and horses, apparently part of the funerary feast or intended to be taken to the afterworld, and the regular appearance of ceramic vessels of a shape and substance indicating use for the storing of meat and milk products. What little has remained of worldly goods found in North Asian Bronze Age burials indicates a concern for personal ornament and small items of household utility. Otherwise, there are no clear reflections of mobility:[2] no horse skeletons, no horse trappings associated with riding, and virtually no indication of

---

[1] See Khazanov 1994:19–21 for a provisional understanding of the term *seminomadic pastoralism* within the Eurasian steppe. As he points out repeatedly, the concepts of pastoralism and seminomadism vary from region to region and from period to period. This is certainly the case that will be made here.

[2] Within this chapter the concept of mobility will refer in its most basic form to the regular movement of communities to accompany their flocks. This mobility might have been limited to movement up and down a single mountain or valley, or it might have been truly extensive.

wheeled vehicles as a part of household wealth.[3] Within the same broad region of the Altai-Sayan uplift and the Minusinsk Basin, mortuary evidence from the Late Bronze and Early Iron Ages is abundant. This material indicates an emerging mobility related to a dependency on horse riding. The great burial of Arzhan I, dated to the early first millennium BCE, included the remains of three hundred horses and enough bronze bridle bits to confirm the use of horses for riding (Gryaznov 1980). Later burials at Tuekta in the Russian Altai, dated to the 6th century BCE, had been severely plundered in antiquity, but an abundance of bridle ornaments recovered from the burials attested not only to horse dependency but also to the extent to which exigencies of mobility increasingly influenced cultural aesthetics. This transformation of lifestyle and aesthetic expression is fully demonstrated in the famous burials associated with the Pazyryk Culture, including those excavated by Gryaznov, in 1950, and Rudenko, in 1970, and those frozen burials more recently excavated on the Ukok Plateau (Polos'mak 2001; Molodin et al. 2004). Some of these burials had been partially plundered in antiquity and subsequently frozen. Surviving organic matter indicated the lifestyle of people who were horse-dependent pastoralists and whose way of life involved regular mobility. These burials are all dated between the 5th and third centuries BCE (Alekseev et al. 2001; Slusarenko et al. 2001). In addition to the actual bodies of horses intended to accompany the dead, collapsible stools, small tables and felt horse blankets and carpets were found, all indicating a pastoral and mobile way of life. Rich felted carpets and saddle blankets reflect the central importance of sheep within the economy, while the combination of furs and skins (Polos'mak and Barkova 2005) reveals a continuing dependency on hunting integrated with herding. In the burials of both elite and commoners (Kubarev 1986, 1991) were found wooden and clay vessels of a rough and utilitarian manufacture. Such objects testify to the fundamental need of these Early Iron Age people for portable material possessions and for vessels intended to prepare and transport milk products and meat. Many aspects of clothing and ornament confirm the centrality of horse riding in the life of the Pazyryk Culture (Polos'mak and Barkova 2005).

We do not know the extent to which the pastoralists of the Early Middle Bronze Age actually moved or, if they did, how they moved. Nor is there sufficient evidence to determine the nature and temporality of their habitation sites. We have a much better understanding of the extent to which the Pazyryk

---

[3.] The one exception to this statement is a bronze yoke-shaped object found in a few Karasuk burials and on deer stones (Vadetskaya 1986:Plate V, no. 28; Novgorodova 1989:159–160). Several scholars have suggested that this object was directly related to the driving of chariots (Solov'ev 2001:Figures 50, 51), but others have associated it with bows (Varenov 1984).

Culture engaged mobility. Despite all the signs of mobility embedded in their burial ritual, their log and plank burial chambers took the form of wooden dwellings much like those used by modern Altai dwellers for their winter habitations.[4] This would suggest that Early Iron Age herders had stable wintering sites from where they moved their herds into higher pastures for the summer. Even now in the Mongolian Altai, herders move their dwellings and animals approximately four times a year, cycling from lower to higher pastures and back down again. Similar patterns of movement, perhaps within the same long valleys, most likely characterized the lives of those earlier mobile cultures. Thus it is possible to describe the mobility of Late Bronze and Early Iron Age cultures of the Altai region as horse-dependent and seminomadic or transhumant.

The information so relatively abundant for Bronze and Early Iron Age cultures across a broad swath of South Siberia is virtually absent from the Mongolian Altai. In this vast region jutting westward between Russia and China (Figure 9.1), there have been no excavations until very recently and almost no archaeological surveys relating to settlement sites.[5] Nonetheless, within this archaeological 'silence,' there is abundant evidence of the ancient presence of Bronze and Iron Age cultures. Valleys and ridges are everywhere marked by large and small altars, standing stones, burial mounds and the altars and stone images of ancient Turkic populations (mid-first millennium CE). These surface monuments indicate that the early cultures of mobility attested on the Russian side of the Altai-Sayan uplift were, if anything, even more fully represented on the Mongolian side.[6] A long-range inventory of surface monuments in mountainous Bayan Ölgiy, northwestern Mongolia, however, is revealing the extensiveness of material remains directly relatable to Bronze and Iron Age cultures of mobility.[7] During the summer of 2006, excavations of three burials within the high permafrost zone of Bayan Ölgiy demonstrated conclusively that the seminomadic culture we refer to as Pazyryk was well represented within the Mongolian Altai.[8] These are, however, the only excavations yet undertaken within this critical juncture of North and Central Asia.

[4.] This is vividly indicated in reproductions and drawings by Rudenko (1970), Polos'mak (2001), and Kubarev (1987, 1991).

[5.] But see Derevyanko and Natsagdorj 1990 regarding surveys of Paleolithic sites in northwestern Mongolia.

[6.] The prevailing lack of information regarding that region has much to do with questions of international politics and economy and need not detain us here.

[7.] This is the Mongolian Altai Inventory with E. Jacobson-Tepfer, J. Meacham and G. Tepfer as principal investigators.

[8.] The joint Mongolian/German/Russian project was headed by D. Tseveendorj, H. Parzinger and V. I. Molodin.

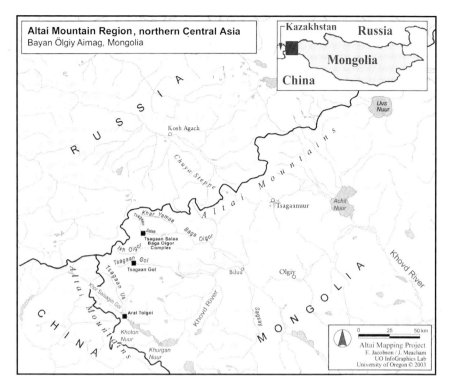

Figure 9.1. Map of the Altai Mountain Region, northern Central Asia (prepared by the Mongolian Altai Inventory and Mapping Project).

Given our present state of knowledge of the relevant archaeology and theoretical constructs for considering the emergence of mobility in North Asia, we are still unable to answer a few simple questions. How did mobility actually happen? Is the model we developed applicable to all regions within the mountain-steppe of North Asia, or were there variations depending on the specific physical setting? Within any inquiry into the emergence of cultures of mobility there is one substantial resource that has hitherto been neglected and that may be useful in responding to these questions. This is rock art or petroglyphs, imagery pecked or engraved into the surfaces of bedrock or boulders. Although the Russian Altai and Tuva have long been known for their rock art sites, that material has rarely been used as documentation for the emergence of pastoralism or horse-dependent seminomadic pastoralism. Within the Mongolian Altai the identification and documentation of rock art sites has occurred much more recently, in a more organized manner, and with a greater concern for the preservation of this cultural resource. As a result, there now exists a vast body of pictorial imagery that could significantly supplement material derived from burials. Moreover, because this material, executed by individual artists perhaps in moments of solitude, disrupts cultural conventions reaffirmed within the mortuary context, it holds the promise of reflecting nuances within cultures of mobility in the ancient Altai (Jacobson 2002). Its use, however, depends on some understanding of its dating; and that dating, in turn, is directly related to the reconstruction of the region's paleoenvironment and its cultural implications.

The larger climatological context of the North Asian steppe and mountain steppe zone is well established. During the late Pleistocene the climate of North Asia was cold and dry and the landscape was characterized by harsh xeric vegetation (Guthrie 1982). Around 10,000 BP (calibrated), increasing humidity and moderately rising temperatures marked the beginning of the early Holocene. Climate amelioration continued into the middle Holocene, a period characterized by the domination of mesic vegetation and the extension of boreal forests. Analyses of radiocarbon-dated pollen and diatom records from Khoton Nuur, the largest lake within the region we are considering, indicate that before 9000 BP (calibrated) this part of Mongolia was characterized by dry steppe vegetation and the absence of boreal conifers. Between 9000 and 4000 BP (calibrated), wetter conditions supported the development of a substantial forest dominated by spruce (*Picea*), pine (*Pinus*), larch (*Larix*) and birch (*Betula*) (Tarasov et al. 2000). Pollen data from Achit Nuur, a large lake on the border between the Bayan Ölgiy and Uvs *aimags*,[9] indicate that the conditions prevailing around Khoton Nuur and one of the sites to be discussed here (Aral Tolgoi) extended across the present-day mountain steppe of northwest Mongolia (Gunin et al. 1999), including two other valleys we will be considering, the Upper Tsagaan Gol and the Oigor drainage.[10] The conditions prevailing through the middle Holocene appear to have dominated until about 4600 BP (calibrated). From then until around 4000 BP, steppe vegetation dominated by mugwort (*Artemisia*), weeds (a variety of *Chenopodiaceae*) and grasses (mostly *Poaceae*) rapidly increased (Tarasov et al. 2000). Forests retreated throughout the region, leading to the present environmental conditions by the late second millennium BCE (Gunin et al. 1999:56). Within our focus region forests were reduced to fragmentary stands on north-facing slopes or somewhat more extensively on slopes north, south and west of Khoton Nuur.

The environmental changes associated with the onset and development of the late Holocene coincided with two profound cultural transformations. Pastoralism dependent on cattle, horses, sheep and goats entered North Asia, probably from western Siberia, at some time beginning in the late third or

[9] Mongolia is divided into 21 *aimag* (provinces), each subdivided into many 'som.'
[10] These analyses are corroborated by paleoenvironmental studies of the Russian Altai in the Ulagan uplands (Blyakharchuk et al. 2004).

early second millennium BCE (Vadetskaya 1986; Anthony 1998; Alekseev et al. 2001). Over the rest of the second millennium, pastoralism based on cattle, as well as on small animals, gradually became established within the Minusinsk Basin and in areas farther south and southwest. Wheeled vehicles were evidently adopted in the same period, but the impact of that innovation on mobility remains unclear.[11] The second major cultural development, the advent of horse riding, seems also to have been brought to North Asia during the Late Bronze Age, although it was known earlier in western Siberia (Anthony 1998:101).[12] One may argue that the apparent coincidence of the advent of horse riding with a greater dependency on large animal husbandry gave rise to several strategic modifications in the lifestyles of steppe and mountain steppe cultures. Horse riding would have permitted the control of considerably larger flocks than would be possible by a herder on foot. By facilitating human movement up to higher pastures, the advent of horse riding would have encouraged the development of more mixed herds, at the same time economizing the energy required of a single herder or small social unit. Sheep and goats grazing their way over slopes could be guarded by a single shepherd on foot. Larger animals, such as cattle, yak, horses and camels, could be driven out to graze on their own. Horse riding allowed the herder to ride out and bring in his larger animals when necessary, even from high pastures, thus extending his animals' access to good pasture. At the same time, the limited carrying capacity of grassland, affected by the drier cooler environmental conditions and impacted by larger herds, must have necessitated an increasingly frequent change of pasture. This, in turn, was also facilitated by the new horse dependency. In other words, climate change, innovative practices and technologies relating to the use of large animals and mobility, and related cultural adaptations to both negative and positive environmental factors functioned together to support the emergence of seminomadic pastoralism at the end of the Bronze Age.[13]

Any discussion of the dating of rock art requires, in advance, a number of qualifications. First, at this time there is no direct way to date petroglyphic rock art at the spatial and numerical scale presented by sites in northwestern

---

[11.] The evidence for the appearance of wheeled vehicles is primarily visual. Images of carts appear on stone slabs associated with the Okunev Culture of the Minusinsk Basin and in association with images of cattle. Novgorodova (1989:173–201) has argued that the spread of wheeled vehicles in North Asia must be associated with the late Bronze Age Karasuk Culture.

[12.] The exact date of the emergence of horse riding remains a subject of debate.

[13.] Such cultural adaptations would have involved the development of the portable dwelling (*gher*), portable furnishings, clothing appropriate for riding, and new forms of food preparation and preservation.

Mongolia.[14] Second, with only a few exceptions, the rock art of the Altai region reflects the real world rather than a world of spirits; or, to be more precise, if the spirit realm was the subject of some of the art we will consider, it was rendered in terms of the real world of knowable animals and activities.[15] Moreover, the pictorial traditions that have been documented in all the major sites of the Mongolian Altai are replicated in sites throughout the Russian Altai and reflected, also, in Bronze Age art of the Altai-Sayan uplift and in Iron Age art of eastern Kazakhstan; it is thus unnecessary to resort to arguments of memory to explain similar subjects and styles across a variety of sites. Shared cultural values and references appear to have supported shared visual and mythic traditions. Finally, given the pictorial basis of Altai rock art in the experience of the real world, any consideration of its dating must acknowledge the constraints imposed by the paleoenvironment.

Dating rock art necessitates a constant tacking back and forth between subject, style, means of execution, environmental constraints, and the information derived from excavation archaeology. Although a thorough discussion of such dating methodology is beyond the scope of this chapter,[16] we can briefly consider how this interreferencing would work. Images of animals that we know disappeared by the end of the Pleistocene establish a period certain for the earliest representations. In the case of the Mongolian Altai, those animals would be megafauna, such as mammoths and rhinoceros, and birds such as ostriches; all clear indicators of a dry, harsh environment and of a Paleolithic pictorial culture. Elk (*Cervus elaphus* sibiricus) depend on the existence of ecotones of open grassland and protective forest. Wild horses and cattle (aurochs, *Bos bos*) presume the existence of integrated extensive steppe, forested steppe and riparian zones. The Altai bear (*Ursus ursus*) requires high mountain meadows, riparian zones and dense forests, while moose (*Alces alces*) require the extensive browse of riparian zones and broken forest. Thus many of the images we have documented can be inserted into a chronology established by

---

[14.] All reliable dating methodologies for the study of rock art refer to pictographs rather than petroglyphs. There have been many attempts to develop reliable dating methods for pecked and engraved art but without results applicable to large-scale studies (Dorn 2001).

[15.] The single exception is offered by a horned, faceless anthropomorphic figure recorded at a number of sites in the Mongolian Altai (Jacobson et al. 2001:II, Plates 77, 106, 207).

[16.] For a more complete discussion of the dating of rock art of the Mongolian Altai see Jacobson 2005 and Jacobson-Tepfer et al. 2007. For a concordance of paleoenvironment, fauna, cultural changes and rock art styles over a period of approximately 12,000 years see Jacobson et al. 2001: I, Chart 1.

environmental factors. Imagery of mammoths, rhinoceros and ostriches reflect a late Paleolithic culture; the style in which these animals were rendered and their outline execution by means of heavy stone implements can be used to propose a date for other, like imagery of individual or overlaid animals. Those early images also offer an understanding of the nature of early visual expression in terms of single, static animals or in terms of overlaid but psychologically unrelated animals. By contrast, the closer that the imagery of animals more dependent on forested zones takes us to and through the Bronze Age, the more significant are indications of psychological interaction. There is a clear correspondence of human representations within apparently narrative settings and a method of execution that reflects finer tools, either stone or metal. Within compositions that by subject, execution and style can be dated to the Bronze Age, we frequently see a considered exploitation of the rock surface in terms of narrative space.

Representations of weaponry offer abundant clues to dating. Excavation archaeology indicates that Bronze Age hunters used a variety of longbows, spears, clubs and bronze daggers and knives (Solov'ev 2001). This weapon set is confirmed by rock art, which also indicates that they carried a kind of tufted stick, probably used for hunting small animals (Jacobson et al. 2001: II, Plates XXVIII, 256).[17] This element disappears entirely with the advent of scenes of riding. The adoption of horse riding carried in its wake a different set of weapons. Bows necessarily became short; to compensate for that change in size, their shape was recurved, thus offering greater thrust to the archer (Solov'ev 2001:Figure 27). This new bow, a particular kind of quiver (*gorytus*) with which it became associated (Jacobson et al. 2001: II, Plates 99, 224, 369), daggers, knives and a particular kind of short sword (*akinakes*) have been amply attested in burials of the Late Bronze and Early Iron Age. Another kind of object looking like a hanging ball appears in rock art imagery together with figures carrying recurved bows and wearing the belted tunic and close-fitting pants of a rider (Jacobson et al. 2001: II, Plate 333). Closely related to the appearance of the recurved bow is a particular kind of stylized deer (Jacobson et al. 2001: II, Plates XI, 141). The combination of these elements (bow, gorytus and deer) is indicated in the great Mongolian tradition of standing stones known as 'deer stones,' dated to the transition period of the Late Bronze–Early Iron (Savinov 1994; Volkov 2002). When this image appears within Altai rock art sites, we can be assured that we are looking at imagery no earlier than the Late Bronze Age and no later than the Early Iron Age (Jacobson-Tepfer 2001).

[17.] This object is replicated today in a small tufted rod worn by Altai hunters of marmots. They claim that by twirling it in front of the animals, they are able to distract and immobilize them.

In the course of a multi-year project in northwestern Mongolia, the Joint Mongolian/American/Russian Project recorded three highly significant rock art complexes.[18] Two of these are among the largest in North Asia, and all three complexes include materials extending over several thousand years. The documentation of North Asian cultures preserved in these materials represents a continuous record from the late Paleolithic, earlier than 9000 BCE, through the Turkic Period (6th–8th centuries CE). Even though all three complexes are in the same general region in northwest Mongolia, it is impossible to ignore significant differences in their topography and in their pictorial records. These differences allow us to consider which visual representations in association with reconstructed paleoenvironments can clarify the conditions for the transition from a hunting to a pastoral dependency and from a pastoral to a mounted seminomadic pastoralism.

LOCATION OF THE COMPLEXES

The three complexes in question are all found within the Altai Mountains of Bayan Ölgiy aimag in northwestern Mongolia (Figure 9.1). The southernmost complex is located at Aral Tolgoi, a small hill at the far western end of Khoton Nuur, near the border of Mongolia and northern China. Aral Tolgoi lies within the floodplain of the rivers Tsagaan Uss and Khar Salaagiin Gol before they empty into Khoton Nuur (Figure 9.2). To the north the narrow valley is bordered by forested slopes leading up to the rocky ridge of a high moraine, to the northwest and west by rocky, inhospitable mountains, and to the southwest by mountains still partially covered by thick forest, the remnant of a far larger forested region in the early and middle Holocene (Gunin et al. 1999). The elevation at the base of Aral Tolgoi is approximately 2000 m. The best grassland in this area, indeed the only extensive grassland at the head of this valley, is that provided by the floodplain itself, from the lake back to the wall of mountains on the west. At present the valley is inhabited permanently only by members of a Mongolian border patrol station, but it is visited during the summer months by vacationing herders. Even now, neither the forested area nor the limited pasture would support the herding of large flocks year-round. Presumably, this constraint would have been considerably greater during the

---

[18.] The Joint Mongolian/American/Russian Project, Altay, functioned between 1994 and 2004. Its purpose was to investigate the ecology of ancient cultures in the Mongolian Altai. Principal investigators in the project included D. Tseveendorj (Institute of Archaeology, Mongolian Academy of Sciences), E. Jacobson (University of Oregon) and V. D. Kubarev (Institute of Archaeology and Ethnography, Siberian Branch, Russian Academy of Sciences).

Figure 9.2. View of Aral Tolgoi from mountains to the south (photograph by Gary Tepfer).

Middle and Late Bronze Age, when the forests around Khoton Nuur were more extensive and the climate somewhat wetter.

The second complex is that of the Upper Tsagaan Gol, located approximately 45 km north of Aral Tolgoi (Figure 9.1). The complex measures approximately 30 km from east to west, including the uppermost end of the river Tsagaan Gol and, to the west, the valleys of its two principal tributaries, the Tsagaan Salaa and the Khar Salaa. Between these rivers rises the sacred mountain, Shiveet Khairkhan, oriented approximately west to east. To the north and south the valley is hemmed in by steep slopes; to the west it is blocked by the glaciated peaks of Tavan Bogd at the intersection of Mongolia, Russia and China. Farther east the Tsagaan Gol descends to its confluence with the largest river in this mountainous region, the Khovd Gol.

Although some ravines within the Upper Tsagaan Gol complex facilitate movement up to the rich pastures on higher elevations, most of the slopes defining the valley are precipitous and characterized by regular rock falls. Indeed, most are passable only by the wild goats that live in this high valley and by their principal predators: wolves and snow leopards. Moreover, the slopes hemming the valley along the whole complex offer little or no real shelter from the cold winds funneled down the Khar Salaa and Tsagaan Salaa. The elevation of the upper Khar Salaa is approximately 2400 m, the summit of Shiveet

Khairkhan is 3320 m, and the highest summit of Tavan Bogd reaches 4374 m. Larch, willow and a few Siberian pine trees can still be found in scattered patches in the upper valley, usually on those slopes so isolated or precipitous that they discourage the wood cutting that has decimated the relic forests in upper valleys throughout the Mongolian Altai. Nonetheless, the rock-pecked imagery in the Upper Tsagaan Gol complex, including representations of elk, bear, wild cattle and even moose, indicates that these forests were more extensive in the past, going back to the Early Middle Bronze Age.

About 30 km north of the Upper Tsagaan Gol is the third complex, Tsagaan Salaa/Baga Oigor (Figure 9.1). This complex extends along the middle flow of the Baga Oigor and its tributary, a small river also named Tsagaan Salaa. The complex stretches approximately 25 km along the valleys, for several hundred meters up south- and east-facing slopes and into deep ravines on the north side of the valley. The valley is broad and open, water is abundant, and grassland is extensive and continuous from the valley floor up over easily negotiated slopes to broad, high pastures (Figure 9.3). Even today the valley includes small ponds with abundant fish and waterfowl. In the not-too-distant past this marshland was much more extensive, spreading in some places to either

Figure 9.3. View looking over the Baga Oigor River up the Tsagaan Salaa River (Ulan Khus *som*, Bayan Ölgiy *aimag*). In the distance are the rocky slopes of Tsagaan Salaa I, II and IV; in the upper center is Tsagaan Salaa III (photograph by Gary Tepfer).

side of the wide Baga Oigor Valley.[19] The valley is now entirely treeless, but a petroglyphic record rich in the imagery of forest-dependent animals indicates that at an earlier period tree cover must have been relatively extensive along the rivers and up the slopes. The elevation of the valley at the confluence of the Tsagaan Salaa and Baga Oigor is approximately 2300 m. Both rivers flow from drainages that begin at the ridge crowned, ultimately, by Tavan Bogd. The most negotiable of the passes over the Tavan Bogd ridge is that of Ulaan Daba at the head of the Oigor river drainage. In contrast to the valleys of Aral Tolgoi and the upper Tsagaan Gol, those of the Tsagaan Salaa and Baga Oigor offer relatively easy routes over the high Altai ridge into the extensive grassland and forests of present-day south Russia, northern China and northeastern Kazakhstan. While the climate is just as harsh as in the valleys of the other two complexes, the physical character of Tsagaan Salaa/Baga Oigor offers much more protection from the weather that comes down from the west and northwest. Deep ravines on both the north and south sides of the large Baga Oigor valley promise shelter from the cold winds, rain and snow in all seasons.

A clear similarity between the subject matter and style of the rock art of the two largest Mongolian Altai complexes, the Upper Tsagaan Gol and Tsagaan Salaa/Baga Oigor, as well as that of recorded sites in the Russian Altai,[20] indicates that Bronze Age and Early Iron Age cultures regularly crossed the mountainous ridge that now forms the international border between Mongolia, China and Russia. In addition, it may be more than accidental that Aral Tolgoi is only about 62 km from the site with the oldest imagery in the Russian Altai, that of Kalgut on the Ukok Plateau (Molodin and Cheremisin 1998). The three Mongolian Altai complexes and their valleys are all in the same mountainous region. Their primary differences lie in a number of specific physical characteristics that would have influenced the way the valleys might have been used by early pastoralists. Ancient migration patterns would have been affected by the proximity of each valley to the high Altai ridge, by the ease of access to and over that ridge, and by passes that could be negotiated by both humans and animals. One must assume that the human- and animal-carrying load of the valleys would have been affected by both the valley width and the existence of natural shelter from wind and weather. The availability of water and the extensiveness of pastureland along the valley floor and on accessible slopes would have qualified the desirability of any valley as a place of temporary or

---

[19.] This is evident in the original air photographs on which the Landscape Model I of Tsagaan Salaa/Baga Oigor was based (Jacobson et al. 2001: II, 17).

[20.] These include, most importantly, Kalbak-Tash, Cheganka, Yelangash and Irbistu, all in the Chuya river drainage (Kubarev and Jacobson 1996; Jacobson and Kubarev 2003).

more permanent residence. Finally, one must assume that access to forested areas, with their promise of ample game and wood, would have rendered some valleys more desirable than others for the purposes of hunting and obtaining timber for dwellings and burial structures. In other words, these three valleys, each with its own pictorial record of early cultures, would have offered different opportunities to peoples of the pre-Bronze, Bronze and Early Iron Ages.

THE ROCK ART AT ARAL TOLGOI

In terms of physical size and number of rock outcrops, Aral Tolgoi is the smallest of our three complexes. It is also the southernmost site and the only one still surrounded by a substantial relic forest, now dominated by pine and larch. The images at Aral Tolgoi are all pecked on the bedrock exposed on the spine of this whale-shaped hill. These surfaces are exceedingly damaged as a result of time, weather and the severity of glacial events in the late Pleistocene. Of the 27 outcroppings on which we have recorded image making (Tseveendorj et al. 2005), approximately seven are so covered with lichen, or are so badly crumbling, that it has been almost impossible to make out the subjects of the imagery. One of the most damaged areas is at the very top of the hill. Interestingly, here are found what appear to be some of the oldest images. These images include large ostrichlike birds (Figure 9.4), massive aurochs (wild cattle), bear, horses and large horned wild sheep. The most significant image is that of a wooly rhinoceros (Figure 9.5) preserved on a fragment of crumbling bedrock. More certainly than any other, this image indicates that the rock art record at Aral Tolgoi began no later than the late Pleistocene and well before forest had become dominant over dry steppe.

Most of the other carved surfaces of Aral Tolgoi are occupied by images of aurochs, horses and elk (Figure 9.6), but there are also a significant number of argali (*Ovis ammon*) and wild goats. Birds other than ostriches are almost entirely absent. Representations of humans are relatively crude, and the contexts in which they occur refer to hunting with heavy clubs, thus indicating a pre–Bronze Age date (Tseveendorj et al. 2005:Figures 41, 60). The animals are almost always treated in a style that might be described as monumental realism. Their representation in terms of static profiles, the frequent appearance of overlay, and the regular indication of the use of heavy stones for pecking reinforce a general date for the Aral Tolgoi imagery in the late Pleistocene and early Holocene. There are only a few images datable to the Bronze Age. One shows archers with longbows (Tseveendorj et al. 2005:Figure 65). There is one image of a rudimentary cart (Tseveendorj et al. 2005:Figure 46) and one pair of stylized deer of the Early Nomadic Period (Tseveendorj et al. 2005: Figure 66). The single horseman dates from the Turkic Period (Tseveendorj et

Figure 9.4. Aral Tolgoi (Tsengel' *som*, Bayan Ölgiy *aimag*): pecked images of large birds (ostriches?) and a horse, late Pleistocene (photograph by Gary Tepfer).

Figure 9.5. Aral Tolgoi (Tsengel' *som*, Bayan Ölgiy *aimag*): pecked image of a wooly rhinoceros, late Pleistocene (photograph by Gary Tepfer).

Figure 9.6. Aral Tolgoi (Tsengel' *som*, Bayan Ölgiy *aimag*): pecked image of an elk (*Cervus elaphus*), late Pleistocene or early Holocene (photograph by Gary Tepfer).

al. 2005:Figure 170). On the terrace immediately south of the hill and to the west, however, are a number of ritual structures and burials indicative of Early Iron Age and Turkic Period dates.[21]

ROCK ART IN THE UPPER TSAGAAN GOL COMPLEX

The rock art in the Upper Tsagaan Gol complex and its state of preservation differ considerably from that at Aral Tolgoi. We have recorded imagery on more than 2400 surfaces, and all of these are sufficiently clear that one may identify either what the imagery represents or what it once represented.[22] Only

---

[21.] A number of artifacts indicative of Paleolithic and Neolithic workmanship have been found in the floodplain around the lower Khar Salaagiin Gol.

[22.] In the Upper Tsagaan Gol complex, as well as at Tsagaan Salaa/Baga Oigor, many images have 'fallen out': the surface, crushed in the process of pecking the contour or silhouette, was weathered and weakened and was subsequently dislodged by freezing and thawing over time. In such cases there remains what might be called a 'ghost image,' clear enough, in most cases, to recognize the subject of the former representation (Jacobson-Tepfer et al. 2007).

Figure 9.7. Upper Tsagaan Gol complex (Tsengel' *som*, Bayan Ölgiy *aimag*): image of an elk, from the pre–Bronze Age, overlaid by a smaller Bronze Age elk (photograph by Gary Tepfer).

a few representations, including aurochs, elk and argali, suggest execution in a period earlier than the Bronze Age. One of these is an image of an elk executed by rough, deeply pecked blows indicative of the use of a heavy stone instrument (Figure 9.7). Its neck is overlaid by an animal pecked with a much finer instrument in the Bronze Age, and its antlers have also been 'finished' (lengthened) at a later date. Images even more archaic in style and execution are located on other outcropping in the Shiveet Khairkhan section of the complex, and a group of clearly archaic animals can be found in the far eastern end of the complex. Although the mode of execution of many of these images (contours pecked with a large, heavy object) and their style (static, in profile and monumental) suggest a date as early as the imagery from Aral Tolgoi, the absence of clearly indicative images (such as mammoths, rhinoceros or ostrich) makes it impossible to be certain when pre–Bronze Age imagery first appeared in the Upper Tsagaan Gol valley.

The vast majority of images in the Upper Tsagaan Gol complex can be dated confidently to the Late Bronze Age, the Early Iron Age and the Turkic Period. These representations include, for the earliest period, extensive scenes of hunts for bear, elk and aurochs (Figure 9.8), compositions showing caravans in which domesticated yak are heavily loaded with children and household goods, and

Figure 9.8. Upper Tsagaan Gol complex (Tsengel' *som*, Bayan Ölgiy *aimag*): pecked scene of hunters attacking an aurochs, Bronze Age (photograph by Gary Tepfer).

some 'household' scenes (scenes with humans and a variety of domesticated animals; Jacobson-Tepfer et al. 2007: II, Plates 505–509, 529).

There are many images of wheeled vehicles with horses and drivers, as well as of vehicles alone (Jacobson-Tepfer et al. 2007: II, Plates 361, 531, 651). Several of these scenes indicate a hunting context (Jacobson-Tepfer et al. 2007: II, Plates 556, 557), but none indicate the use of the vehicle for carrying loads or for combat.[23] Most can confidently be dated to the Bronze Age by style and by the bows and quivers carried by the drivers. The beginning of horse riding in the Bronze Age is well attested in the Upper Tsagaan Gol complex (Figure 9.9). Scenes of herding cattle and horses occur regularly within the complex and on some occasions with considerable artistry (Jacobson-Tepfer et al. 2007: II, Plate 451).

Imagery datable to the transitional Late Bronze–Early Iron Age period includes hunts on foot and on horseback after elk, deer and ibex; some of these scenes appear to reflect mythic traditions (Jacobson-Tepfer et al. 2007: II, Plate 390). The image of a highly stylized elk, datable to the Late Bronze

---

[23.] This is in contrast to the imaginative reconstruction of a war chariot in the North Asian steppe by Solov'ev (2001:Figure 52).

Figure 9.9. Upper Tsagaan Gol complex (Tsengel' *som*, Bayan Ölgiy *aimag*): detail from a larger scene of a deer hunt, showing a pecked image of a rider preparing to shoot his bow, Late Bronze Age (photograph by Gary Tepfer).

Age, appears more frequently here than in Tsagaan Salaa/Baga Oigor; increasingly stylized formulations suggest that it continued until the last centuries of the first millennium BCE (Jacobson 2000a, 2000b, 2001). The number of representations of wheeled vehicles that can be reliably dated to the Early Iron Age is perhaps two (Jacobson-Tepfer et al. 2007: II, Plates 151, 540). There are no scenes of caravans that can be dated to that period with any certainty. The Turkic Period is represented by scenes of riders and hunting, usually for ibex (Jacobson-Tepfer et al. 2007: II, Plates 405–414).

Limited but systematic surveys in the upper Tsagaan Gol valley have allowed us to identify at least two sources of finished Paleolithic tools and related scatter. By contrast, we have not yet identified Neolithic stone artifacts. This, in combination with the recorded rock art, allows us to reach the following tentative conclusions. Artifacts would indicate that the upper valley saw some human habitation, probably seasonal, in the late Pleistocene, but the record for such habitation in the early to middle Holocene is intermittent and uncertain. Beginning in the Middle Bronze Age and extending into the Early Iron Age, habitation, either seasonal or year-round, became more regular. The apparent lacuna in imagery between the late Pazyryk Period (5th to third centuries BCE) and the Turkic Period may be misleading: the people inhabiting this valley at that time may have been uninterested in image making or they may be represented by the many surfaces for which the subject matter and style refer to an indeterminate period in the Iron Age. The Turkic Period is vigorously represented by images on a number of outcroppings as well as by a significant number of ritual sites with carved stone figures, enclosures and other surface structures.

THE ROCK ART AT TSAGAAN SALAA/BAGA OIGOR

Of all three complexes, Tsagaan Salaa/Baga Oigor includes the deepest and most continuous imagistic record, with essentially no cultural interruptions from the late Paleolithic through the Turkic Period.

Four images of mammoths (Figure 9.10) 'pin' the beginning of representational traditions here to a period no later than the late Pleistocene. Representations of wild cattle (Figure 9.11), herds of elk (Figure 9.12), horses, and a few of bear can be dated to the early and middle Holocene. They conjure up an ancient environment in which riparian zones supported thickets of willow

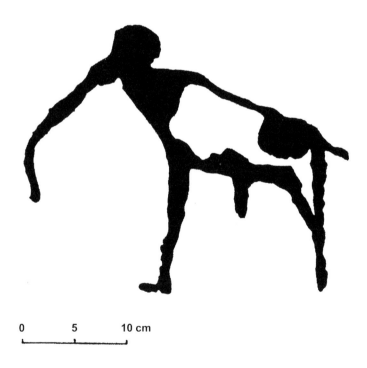

0   5   10 cm

Figure 9.10. Tsagaan Salaa/Baga Oigor complex (Ulan Khus *som*, Bayan Ölgiy *aimag*): drawing of the pecked image of a mammoth, late Pleistocene (BO III; Jacobson et al. 2001: I, Figure 912; drawing by V. D. Kubarev and D. Tseveendorj).

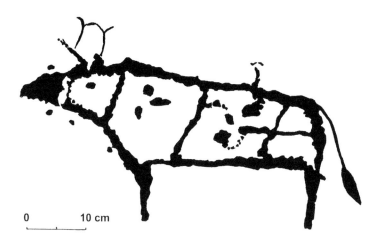

Figure 9.11. Tsagaan Salaa/Baga Oigor complex (Ulan Khus *som*, Bayan Ölgiy *aimag*): drawing of the pecked image of an aurochs, late Pleistocene (BO III; Jacobson et al. 2001: I, Figure 368; drawing by V. D. Kubarev and D. Tseveendorj).

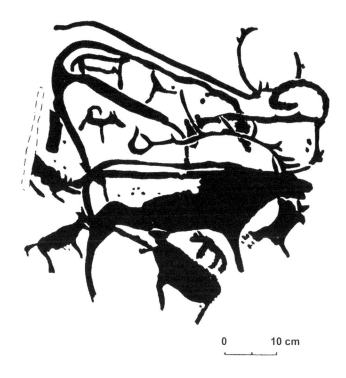

Figure 9.12. Tsagaan Salaa/Baga Oigor complex (Ulan Khus *som*, Bayan Ölgiy *aimag*): drawing of overlaid images of elk and other animals, early Holocene and Bronze Age (TS IV; Jacobson et al. 2001: I, Figure 625; drawing by V. D. Kubarev and D. Tseveendorj).

and other leafy vegetation, while the slopes offered forested shelter. Bronze Age imagery from this complex includes many scenes of hunting wild yak, aurochs, elk, moose, and argali. Representations from the Middle and Late Bronze Age include numerous scenes of family caravans, wheeled vehicles, 'household scenes' and scenes of herding (Jacobson et al. 2001: II, Plates 70, 97, 217, 332). Representations of combat are unusual. Their occasional juxtaposition with scenes of hunting (Jacobson et al. 2001: II, Plate 370) suggests that incursions on clan hunting lands may have been one reason for conflict.

In one superb representation from Baga Oigor IV (Figure 9.13), a large yak bearing a basket, within which can be seen five diminutive figures, is surrounded by a number of figures shooting arrows, while on the sidelines stand two women.[24] There are many Bronze Age representations of wheeled vehicles at Tsagaan Salaa/Baga Oigor. Usually they are shown complete with basket, two wheels, a driver and two horses (Figure 9.14). Sometimes, however, they are represented in a shorthand form: the cart alone, the cart with horses, or the cart and driver but no horses, or even just one or two wheels. In one example a very small cart with driver is shown being pulled by four racing horses (Jacobson et al. 2001:II, Plate 36).

The images of wheeled vehicles here and in the Upper Tsagaan Gol complex raise several perplexing questions. Vehicles could be solid-wheeled (Figures 9.14 and 9.15) or have spoked wheels, with varying numbers of spokes (Jacobson et al. 2001: I, Figures 215a and 680). Given the extremely rocky nature of the terrain in these valleys, it is hard to understand how any kind of wheeled vehicle, solid wheeled or spoked, could have been driven as quickly as the representations suggest. Even more peculiar is the representation of a hunt from a solid-wheeled cart after a fleeing deer (Figure 9.15). This implausibility is all the more striking in that the surface so carved lies on a steep slope strewn with boulders, through which no cart would have been able to negotiate a track, let alone one moving at high speed. Clearly, the scenes with wheeled vehicles so frequently encountered in this complex and in that of the Upper Tsagaan Gol refer to something other than strict reality.[25] Whatever the meaning, it is interesting that none of the images of wheeled vehicles from this complex appear to date to the Early Iron Age.

[24.] Although caravan scenes are relatively more frequently encountered at this large site than in the Upper Tsagaan Gol, scenes of raiding are quite unusual; we have documented no clear representation of the raiding of herds.

[25.] Traditionally, most scholars have tended to see the wheeled vehicle as a sign of Indo-European or Indo-Iranian mythic traditions (Francfort 1998). It is also possible that the wheeled vehicle refers to a sign of status and wellbeing (Jacobson 1993:125–140).

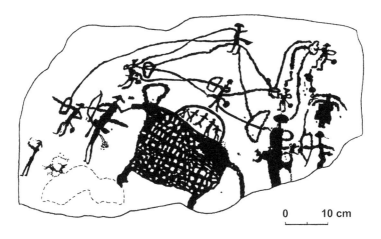

Figure 9.13. Tsagaan Salaa/Baga Oigor complex (Ulan Khus *som*, Bayan Ölgiy *aimag*): drawing of a scene of a raid on a family caravan, Bronze Age (BO IV; Jacobson et al. 2001: I, Figure 1123; drawing by V. D. Kubarev and D. Tseveendorj).

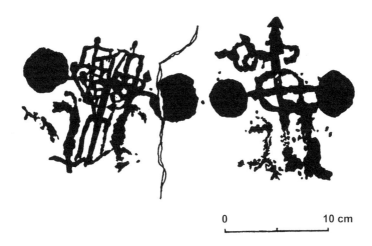

Figure 9.14. Tsagaan Salaa/Baga Oigor complex (Ulan Khus *som*, Bayan Ölgiy *aimag*): drawing of a scene with two wheeled vehicles, Bronze Age (BO IV; Jacobson et al. 2001: I, Figure 1124; drawing by V. D. Kubarev and D. Tseveendorj).

0 cm   40

Figure 9.15. Tsagaan Salaa/Baga Oigor complex (Ulan Khus *som*, Bayan Ölgiy *aimag*): drawing of a hunt scene, Bronze Age (TS IV; Jacobson et al. 2001: I, Figure 590; drawing by V. D. Kubarev and D. Tseveendorj).

Many scenes of hunting, caravanning and herding at Tsagaan Salaa/Baga Oigor refer to the transitional Late Bronze–Early Iron Age. In compositions of this period herding revolves around large cattle and horses (Jacobson et al. 2001: II, Plates 70, 71, 374) rather than the smaller sheep and goats of an earlier stage in the Bronze Age (Jacobson et al. 2001: II, Plates 89, 90). Household scenes datable to this period are of particular interest. These include images of domesticated animals, wild animals, people, dwellings and wheeled vehicles scattered over the surface of a boulder as if offering a slice of contemporary life. Several good examples are found in Tsagaan Salaa IV (Jacobson et al. 2001: II, Plates 187–190), Baga Oigor I (Jacobson et al. 2001: I, Figure 779) and Baga Oigor III (Jacobson et al. 2001: II, Plates 332–334). Like scenes of caravanning, these compositions reflect a world understood as immediately present and vital.

At Tsagaan Salaa/Baga Oigor, as in the Upper Tsagaan Gol, the Late Bronze Age is also represented by the appearance of a highly stylized deer image (Jacobson et al. 2001: II, Plates XI, XII), and this image persists through the early centuries of the Iron Age. The Pazyryk Period is represented primarily by horsemen, hunting scenes and representations of individual animals (Jacobson et al. 2001: I, Figures 939, 1053, 1140; II, Plates 166, 224, 266), but the vigor of Bronze Age art has often been replaced by a studied conventionalization. After the Early Iron Age, imagery of a certain quality and identifiable style falls off. We have documented only a few compositions from the Turkic Period and very few from the Mongol Period, as well as a large number of pecked surfaces of indeterminate date.

DISCUSSION

Rock art of the Bronze and Early Iron Ages in the Mongolian Altai clearly documents the emergence of pastoralism and, later, of seminomadic, mounted pastoralism. These are general patterns that are confirmed by excavation archaeology in a broader region of North Asia. The discussion of three major rock art complexes and the physical character of their valleys suggests how geography and climate qualified those transitions, creating various constraints on the local development of cultures of mobility. Imagery at Aral Tolgoi reflects a region bordering the extensive glaciation of the high Altai valleys and functioning as a transition zone between open woodland and grassland. Such an ecotone supported a hunting economy from the late Pleistocene through the early Holocene. The later, more humid, environment of the middle Holocene supported fauna adapted to a more heavily forested environment. During the early Late Holocene, coinciding with the Early Bronze Age in North Asia, the area around Aral Tolgoi was still sufficiently forested so that emerging pastoralism would have been quite limited. Indeed, imagery reflective of a cultural shift to pastoralism is almost entirely lacking from the Aral Tolgoi repertoire, as is any imagery indicative of the shift to a mounted seminomadic lifestyle at the end of the Bronze Age. Surface structures (burial mounds, ritual altars and stele, Turkic image stones and enclosures) found on the valley floor around Aral Tolgoi and farther west, however, indicate that the valley at the west end of Khoton Nuur offered a zone of transition for small numbers of Iron Age herders moving quite probably toward the passes into present-day China; but the lack of year-round pasture at the west end of Khoton Nuur would have discouraged extended habitation.

The valley of the upper Tsagaan Gol and its proximity to forest and high mountain grasslands offered ideal habitat for aurochs, elk, bear, wild sheep and ibex in the late Pleistocene and early Holocene. The extreme cold of the high valley would not, however, have encouraged regular human habitation. Once a pastoral economy was adopted in the Bronze Age, the precipitous slopes that flank much of the upper valley would have made it difficult to access the rich pastures above, significantly limiting the size of herds that could be maintained year-round in the valley. The lack of sheltered places along the edges of the valley would also have discouraged winter dwelling. Most of the household and caravanning scenes in the Upper Tsagaan Gol complex are east of Shiveet Khairkhan; the relatively small number of such scenes in the upper Khar Salaa and their absence within the Tsagaan Salaa valley suggests that these high subvalleys were neither heavily nor continuously populated through the Bronze and Iron Ages although they were used extensively for hunting and herding.

The depth and extensiveness of the pictorial documentation found at Tsagaan Salaa/Baga Oigor is no accident. Within the Mongolian Altai this valley presented an optimal environment for the emergence of cultures of mobility. The size of the valley and its marshlands would have supported hunting- and fishing-dependent populations in the late Pleistocene and early Holocene. The broad valley floor and forested slopes would have provided ample browsing and grazing for wild animals. By the late-middle Holocene, as forests retreated, grassland became continuous from the valley floor up to the broad ridges of surrounding mountains, and valley wetlands continued to support rich wild bird and fish populations. Folds and draws along the walls of the valley offer shelter from winds from the north and west. In these respects the Tsagaan Salaa and Baga Oigor valleys offered an ideal environment for the cultural transition first to pastoralism and then to a seminomadic and horse-dependent pastoralism.

Scenes representing the herding of cattle, horses and goats vividly reflect the emergence of a pastoral economy in the Bronze Age. Style indicates that many of the finest scenes of caravanning in both the Upper Tsagaan Gol and Tsagaan

Salaa/Baga Oigor were contemporaneous with the herding scenes. They reflect the movement of families up and down the valleys in search of good pasture, at least by the Middle to Late Bronze Age. When we try to understand the appearance of wheeled vehicles, however, many images of which are so clearly contemporaneous with the herding and caravanning scenes, we are faced with a puzzle. The vehicles never occur in conjunction with the caravans, nor are they ever represented as loaded.[26] There are, however, a few instances where they do appear in household scenes. The best example is found on a surface from Baga Oigor III, on which is represented a small family, its domesticated animals and the proximity of abundant wildlife (Jacobson et al. 2001: I, Figures 979, 980; II, Plates XXII, XXIII). Despite such images, however, it remains uncertain how wheeled vehicles participated in an emerging cultural mobility.

The case for the adoption of horse riding is in some respects clearer but not wholly so. Burials from the Pazyryk Period indicate that horses were expected to accompany the dead to the next world and were thus, in a sense, a means of virtual long-range mobility. Reason and experience argue that the development of herds of large animals required horse riding: numbers of horses or yak could hardly be controlled by herders on foot nor, of course, would wheeled vehicles have been any use when the animals were moving up steep slopes. But while the petroglyphic record clearly reflects the use of horses for hunting, it nowhere indicates the use of horses for herding or for carrying burdens.[27]

The final conundrum goes back to the question posed earlier in this chapter: how did mobility actually happen? As far as we can tell from the vast petroglyphic record of the Mongolian Altai, yak were the primary means by which people first engaged in a mobile way of life in the Bronze Age. Yak carried the portable dwellings and all the furnishings, the children and the elderly (Jacobson-Tepfer et al. 2007: II, Plate 530), while adults walked. That, at least, is completely clear through the Late Bronze Age, but the record for the Early Iron Age, or Pazyryk Period, is unclear since there are no caravan scenes that can be certainly so dated. Moreover, although camels are now used extensively in the Mongolian Altai as primary beasts of burden, there is no record whatsoever of their having been so used in the Late Bronze or Early Iron Ages. Again, when they do appear, it is as riding animals, even within a hunt (Jacobson et al. 2001: II, Plate 184). We are left with the conclusion that mobility did occur in

---

[26] The only exception with which I am familiar is from the Russian Altai, from the site of Kalbak-Tash, where a small wheeled vehicle, without horses or driver, is found within a fine scene of caravanning (Kubarev and Jacobson 1996:Figure 449).

[27] See, for example, a fine scene of a family preparing to move camp, from Baga Oigor IV. The animals, including horses, are attached to a lead but only the yak are loaded (Jacobson et al. 2001: II, Plate 332).

the Bronze Age, thanks in large measure to yak as beasts of burden. The role that horses played in the emergence of seminomadic herding can be inferred but not proven; and the actual role of wheeled vehicles within the emergence of mobility is quite unclear, except that they were evidently valued indicators of material well-being. They were signs of mobility but not necessarily the means of large-scale social mobility.

This discussion indicates possible sources for a study of North Asian cultures of mobility and the way in which specific physical contexts may have varied actual experience within any particular region. Even with the materials now available for Bayan Ölgiy, it would be possible to multiply the case studies offered above. Ultimately such a consideration of particular valleys with the Altai Mountains will help to flesh out the theoretical constructs underlying the study of the archaeology of mobility in North Asia.

REFERENCES

Alekseev, A. Y., N. A. Bokovenko, Y. Boltrik, K. A. Chugunov, G. Cook, V. A. Dergachev, N. Kovalyukh, G. Possnert, J. van der Plicht, E. M. Scott, A. Sementsov, V. Skripkin, S. Vasiliev and G. Zaitseva

2001   A Chronology of the Scythian Antiquities of Eurasia Based on New Archaeological and [14]C Data. *Radiocarbon 43*: 2B, pp. 1085–1107.

Anthony, D. W.

1998   The Opening of the Eurasian Steppe at 2000 BCE. In V. H. Mair (ed.), *The Bronze Age and Early Iron Age Peoples of Eastern Central Asia*. Washington, Institute for the Study of Man: pp. 94–113.

Blyakharchuk, T. A., H. E. Wright, P. S. Borodavko, W. O. van der Knaap and V. Ammann

2004   Late Glacial and Holocene Vegetational Changes on the Ulagan High-Mountain Plateau, Altai Mountains, Southern Siberia. *Palaeogeography, Palaeoclimatology, Palaeoecology 209*: pp. 259–279.

Derevyanko, A. P. and S. Natsagdorj (eds.)

1990   *Arkheologicheskie, etnograficheskie i antropologicheskie issledovaniia v Mongolii: Sbornik nauchnykh trudov* (Collection of Research Papers on the Archaeology, Ethnography, and Anthropology of Mongolia) [in Russian]. Novosibirsk, Nauka.

Dorn, R. I.

2001   Chronometric Techniques: Engraving. In D. S. Whitley (ed.), *Handbook of Rock Art Research*. Walnut Creek, Altamira Press: pp. 167–189.

Francfort, H.-P.

1998   Central Asian Petroglyphs: Between Indo-Iranian and Shamanistic Inter-
        pretations. In C. Chippindale and P. S. C. Taçon (eds.), *The Archaeology of
        Rock-Art*. Cambridge, Cambridge University Press: pp. 302–318.

Gryaznov, M. P.

1980   *Arzhan: Tsarskii kurgan ranneskifskogo vremeni* (Arzhan: A Royal Burial of the
        Early Scythian Period) [in Russian]. Leningrad, Nauka.

Gunin, P. D., E. A. Vostokova, N. I. Dorofeyuk, P. E. Tarasov and C. C. Black

1999   *Vegetation Dynamics of Mongolia*. Dordrecht, Kluwer.

Guthrie, R. D.

1982   Mammoths of the Mammoth Steppe as Paleoenvironmental Indicators. In
        D. M. Hopkins (ed.), *Paleoecology of Beringia. 81st Wenner-Gren Foundation
        for Anthropological Research Symposium (Bert Wartenstein, Austria, 1979)*. New
        York, Academic Press: pp. 307–326.

Jacobson, E.

1993   *The Deer Goddess of Ancient Siberia: A Study in the Ecology of Belief*. Leiden, E.
        J. Brill.

2000a   "Emblem" Against "Narrative" in Rock Art of the Mongolian Altay [in Russian
        and English]. *Bulletin of the Siberian Association of Prehistoric Rock Art Researchers
        3*: pp. 6–14 .

2000b   Petroglyphs and Natural History: Sources for the Reconstruction of the
        Ecology of Culture. *Archaeology, Ethnology, and Anthropology of Eurasia 1*: pp.
        57–65.

2001   Cultural Riddles: Stylized Deer and Deer Stones of the Mongolian Altai.
        Bulletin of the Asia Institute. New Series 15: pp. 31–56.

2002   Petroglyphs and the Qualification of Bronze Age Mortuary Archaeology.
        Archaeology, Ethnology, and Anthropology of Eurasia 3: 11, pp. 32–47.

2005   Aral Tolgoi. In D. Tseveendorj, V. D. Kubarev and E. Yakobson (Jacobson)
        (eds.), *Aral Tolgoin Khadny Zurag* (Petroglyphs of Aral Tolgoi) [in English,
        Mongolian, and Russian]. Ulaanbaatar, Institute of Archaeology, Mongolian
        Academy of Sciences: pp. 103–132.

Jacobson, E. and G. Kubarev

2003   Rock Art Complex on the Irbystu River, Altay Republic. *International Newsletter
        on Rock Art 36*: pp. 12–16.

Jacobson, E., V. D. Kubarev and D. Tseevendorj (edited by J. Sher and H.-P.
        Francfort)

2001   *Mongolie du Nord-Ouest: Tsagaan Salaa/Baga Oigor. Répertoire des pétroglyphes
        d'Asie centrale, Fascicule 6* (2 volumes). Paris, De Boccard.

Jacobson-Tepfer, E., V. D. Kubarev and D. Tseveendorj (edited by H.-P. Francfort
        and Y. Sher)

2007 *Mongolie du Nord-Ouest: Haut Tsagaan Gol. Répertoire des pétroglyphes d'Asie Centrale,*
      Fascicule 7 (2 volumes). Paris, De Boccard.

Khazanov, A. M.

1994 *Nomads and the Outside World.* Madison, University of Wisconsin Press.

Kubarev, V. D.

1986 *Kurgany Ulandryka* (Kurgan Burials at Ulandryk) [in Russian]. Novosibirsk,
      Nauka.

1991 *Kurgany Yustyda* (Kurgan Burials at Yustyd) [in Russian]. Novosibirsk,
      Nauka.

Kubarev, V. D. and E. Jacobson

1996 *Répertoire des Pétroglyphes d'Asie Centrale. Sibérie du Sud 3, Kalbak-Tash I*
      (République de l'Altay). Mémoires de la Mission Archéologique Française en Asie
      Centrale. Tome V.3. Paris, De Boccard.

Molodin, V. I. and D. V. Cheremisin

1998 *Drevneishie naskal'nye izobrazheniya ploskogor'ya Ukok* (The Most Ancient Rock
      Art of the Ukok Plateau) [in Russian]. Novosibirsk, Nauka.

Molodin, V. I., N. V. Polos'mak, A. V. Novikov, E. S. Bogdanov, I. Y. Slusarenko and
      D. V. Cheremisin

2004 *Arkheologicheskie pamyatniki ploskgor'ya Ukoka* (Archaeological Monuments
      of the Ukok Plateau) [in Russian]. Novosibirsk, Institute of Archaeology and
      Ethnography, Siberian Section, Russian Academy of Sciences.

Polos'mak, N. V.

2001 *Vsadniki Ukoka* (Horsemen of the Ukok) [in Russian]. Novosibirsk,
      INFOLIO.

Polos'mak, N. V. and L. L. Barkova

2005 *Kostium i tekstil' pazyryktsev Altaia (IV–III vv. do n.e.)* (Costume and Textiles of
      the Altai Pazyryk People of the Fourth–Third Centuries BCE) [in Russian].
      Novosibirsk, INFOLIO.

Savinov, D. G.

1994 *Olennye kamni v kul'ture kochevnikov Evrazii* (Deer Stones in the Culture of the
      Eurasian Nomads) [in Russian]. St. Petersburg, University of St. Petersburg
      Press.

Slusarenko, I. Y., J. A. Christen, L. A. Orlova, Y. V. Kuzmin and G. S. Burr

2001 [14]C Wiggle Matching of the "Floating" Tree-Ring Chronology from the Altai
      Mountains, Southern Siberia: The Ulandryk-4 Case Study. *Radiocarbon 43*:
      2A, pp. 425–431.

Solov'ev, A. I.

2001 *Oruzhie i dospekhi* (Weapons and Armor) [in Russian]. Novosibirsk,
      INFOLIO.

Tarasov, P., N. Dorofeyuk and E. Metel'tseva

2000   Holocene Vegetation and Climate Changes in Hoton-Nur Basin, Northwest Mongolia. *Boreas 29*: pp. 117–126.

Tseveendorj, D., V. D. Kubarev and E. Yakobson (Jacobson)

2005   *Aral Tolgoin Khadny Zurag* (Petroglyphs of Aral Tolgoi) [in Russian]. Ulaanbaatar, Institute of Archaeology, Mongolian Academy of Sciences.

Vadetskaya, E. B.

1986   *Arkheologicheskie pamyatniki v stepyak srednego Yenisey* (Archaeology in the Steppe Region of the Middle Yenisey) [in Russian]. Leningrad, Nauka.

Varenov, A. V.

1984   O funktsional'nom prednaznchenii "modelei yarma" epokhi In' i Chou (Regarding the Function of the "Model Yoke" from the Yin and Zhou Dynasties). In *Novoe v Arkheologii Kitaya* (New Directions in Chinese Archaeology) [in Russian]. Novosibirsk, Nauka: pp. 42–51.

Volkov, V. V.

2002   *Olennye kamni Mongolii* (Deer Stones of Mongolia) [in Russian]. Moscow, Nauchnyi Mir.

CHAPTER 10

Nomadic Sites of the South Yergueni Hills on the Eurasian Steppe

Models of Seasonal Occupation and Production

Natalya I. Shishlina, E. I. Gak and A. V. Borisov[1]

THE ARCHAEOLOGICAL RECORD that was used to reconstruct the economy of the ancient population of the northwestern Caspian Sea steppe consisted of artifacts found in *kurgans* (burial grounds) dating back to the Bronze Age. Although it was argued that seasonal sites were very difficult to identify in the open steppe (Sinitsyn 1931; Shilov 1975; Koltsov 1985), archaeological surveys found sites, as well as different types of artifacts (Minayeva 1955; Koltsov 1985), dating back to the Mesolithic, Neolithic and Eneolithic Periods (Koltsov 1988). The existence of Bronze Age and Early Iron Age sites is still debated. During our archaeological survey in the southern part of the Kalmyk Eurasian steppe (Figure 10.1), we found two sites of the Late Bronze and Early Iron Age: Gashun-Sala and Manych (Figure 10.2).[2] The archaeological excavation of these sites produced new evidence of the seasonal economic cycle of pastoral nomads living in this region during the end of the second into the first millennium BCE.

GEOMORPHOLOGIC AND GEOBOTANIC DESCRIPTIONS

The sites at Gashun-Sala and Manych are located on the southern fringe of a high plateau in the Yergueni Hills. The southern border of the Yergueni Hills is

---

[1] This project was conducted with support of the National Geographic Society, project number 7978-01. We acknowledge the assistance provided by G. Klevezal, I. Kirillova, A. Bobrov, M. Pakhomov, M. Novikova, R. Mimokhod, J. van der Plicht, V. Chichagov and A. Sokolov.

[2] A third site, Chilyuta, was discovered close to Gashun-Sala. Apart from a 1x1 m bore hole, which reached a depth of 3 m, no excavations were performed here.

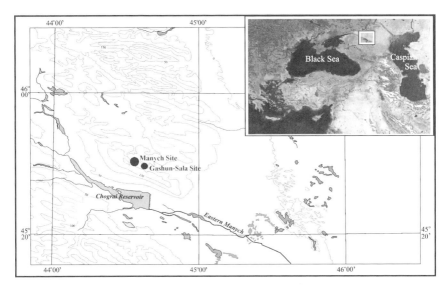

Figure 10.1. Map showing the position of the study area in the north Caspian Steppe.

the local linear uplift of the northwest Choloi-Khamur stretch. An uphill valley of the southern Yergueni Hills stretches to the north of the Shared ravine. Another large ravine, called Ulan-Zukha, is located to the north. At present, all large ravines of the Yergueni Hills are dry and are only sporadically filled with insignificant amounts of water. However, the considerable width of the valleys, the meander belts, and the two terraces above the flood-prone areas indicate that in the past rivers flowed through these valleys.

Throughout the Kalmyk steppe, grazing grounds for sheep and goats are covered with a specific vegetation in which the following plants predominate: cornflower (*Centaurea apiculata* Ledeb.), stickseed (*Lappula heteracantha* Ledeb. *Guerak.*), thistle (*Carduus thoermeri*), yarrow (*Achillea nobilis* L.), *Camphorosma monspeliacum* L., *Xanthium albinum* (*X. Riparium*), different species of *Amaranthus* and other species that grow near sites exploited by humans. The vegetation of the ravines includes belts of mixed grasses in contrast to the more monotonous vegetation that covers the terrace hills. More than a hundred plant species have been identified, with a predominance of annual plants (*Atriplex, Chenopodium, Lactuca, Linum, Polygonum*), mixed perennial plants (*Carduus thoermeri, Galim chumifusum, Phlomis pungens, Potentilla recta, Salvia* sp.), plants growing near water (*Aeluropus littoralis* [Gouan] *Parl., Petrocimonia, Salicornia eurapaea* L.), reeds (*Phragmites communis* Trin.), *Aster tripolium* L. and numerous species of *Artemisia*. There are seasonal variations in the vegetation cover resulting in repeated cycles of vegetation and flowering.

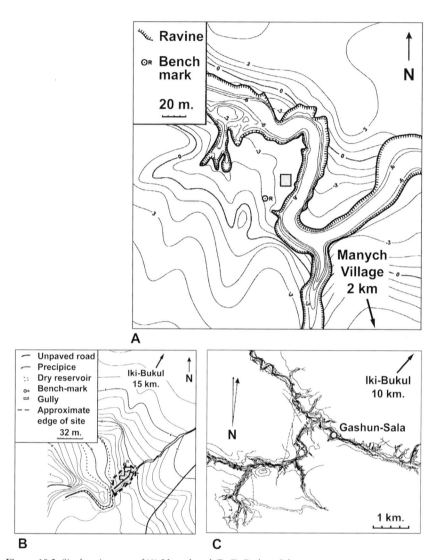

Figure 10.2. Site location map of (A) Manych and (B, C) Gashun-Sala.

Manych, 45°N 40'47.9" / 044°E 33'28.1", is located in the upstream part of a ravine, called Shared, which was a valley of a small plain river (Figure 10.2a). The site is located at the foot of the right bank slope, in the place most suitable for living: an open area, far from the upstream slope and near a river channel of what might have been a full-flow river. These conditions were favorable in several respects. The force of the wind was less than on the steppe. Rain and the runoff from the melting snow were held back by the vegetation and did not flood the settlement. If water reached the flat area of the terrace, it lost its energy, spread out thinly, and receded quickly. No landslides or mudflows were observed near the site, yet traces of many such events were preserved on the opposite slope. A dense network of short tributaries of the Shared River descended from the almost vertical slopes in places where water had taken shortcut routes into the river, subjecting their beds to intensive linear erosion and erosive leakage. All these tributaries appeared to be erosive washouts formed along cattle paths that were exploited for a long time.

Gashun-Sala, 45°N 34'44.6" / 044°E 39'36.3" E, is located near the large Ulan-Zukha ravine (Figure 10.2b, c). The internal part of a large meander, located upstream from the site, is at present a low-lying boggy plain. When the site was occupied, this area may have been an oxbow lake. Judging from the size of the large meanders, and the intensity of the erosion in the valley, the river near Gashun-Sala was a full-flow river with a permanent flow. Both sites, therefore, appear to have been located near valleys of full-flow paleorivers with a permanent inflow and flow rate. The slopes of the Gashun-Sala valley also show many cracks, both ancient and more recent, the result of erosion along ancient and modern cattle paths.

ARCHAEOLOGICAL EXCAVATIONS

At Manych an area of 80 m² was subdivided into 2x2 m squares. Stratigraphy was defined according to natural and anthropogenic layering. Three layers were identified: the turf, the occupation layer, and the rock bed (Figure 10.3). The turf layer was 5–7 cm thick and the anthropogenic layer, between the turf and the rock bed, was as much as 40 cm thick in places. It consisted of dark gray to brown-gray loam. All objects were found in this layer: 58 remains of animal bones; 77 fragments of handmade, thick-walled, sand-tempered pottery; and 29 fragments of wheel-thrown amphorae. Comparison of the potsherds with the Early Iron Age steppe ceramics from adjacent areas (North Caucasus, Don River Valley) showed a similarity with Sarmatian vessels. Five fragments of handmade potsherds of the Late Bronze Age Srubnaya culture were also unearthed (Figure 10.4/2). Another find appeared to be a splash of copper (Figure 10.4/10). No remains of human dwellings were seen. In the rock bed a shallow pit (1.20 x 0.90 m with a depth of 0.38 m) was excavated. This pit was egg-shaped in transect and cup-shaped in cross-section. It contained some animal bone. The recovered Iron Age ceramics (Figure 10.4/1, 4–9) were tempered with coarse sand; had thick, smooth walls; and did not preserve any decorations. The most interesting fragments include four rims, a base, and a massive handle with a worn stamp (Figure 10.4/9). The wheel-thrown amphorae are orange or gray; fragments included two rims and four fluted walls.

Figure 10.3. Manych: (top) the excavation trenches; (bottom left) a shallow pit; (bottom right) a splash of copper.

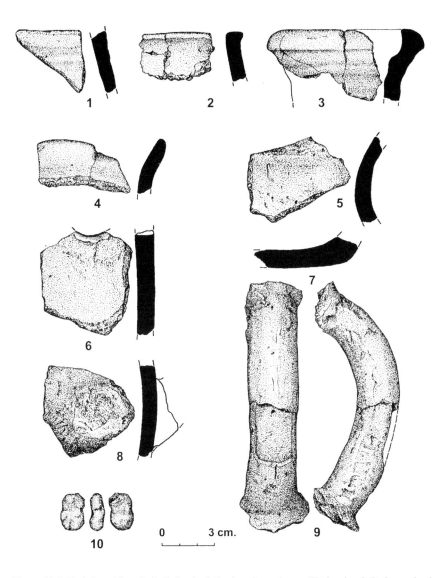

Figure 10.4. Finds from Manych: (1, 3) sherds of wheel-made amphorae; (2) a handmade Srubnaya sherd of the Late Bronze Age; (4–9) Early Iron Age handmade potsherds; (10) a splash of copper.

At Gashun-Sala an excavation area was selected near the bottom of the ravine where a dark gray layer, 0.2–0.3 m thick, with a low content of humus, was visible at a depth of 0.5–0.7 m from the outcrops. During the cleaning of these outcrops, this layer yielded 20 animal bones and teeth, as well as 18 fragments of handmade ceramics, including the rim and base of a large vessel (Figure 10.5/6). Another concentration of animal bones was uncovered near the western cliff, where two fragments of smooth-walled ceramics without decoration were unearthed (Figure 10.6/2–3). Bore holes revealed that this layer, believed to have been anthropogenic in origin, spread along an area of 600 m² adjacent to the western cliff. It has few artifacts and is covered by a thick deluvial sediment.

An area of 128 m² was divided into 2x2 m squares. Four stratigraphic layers were identified according to the natural and anthropogenic layering and the presence of objects. The upper layer (layer 1) was of deluvial origin and consisted of light gray loam 0.20–0.70 m thick without finds. Layer 2 was similar to the layer identified along the cliffs. Its thickness varied from 0.20 to 0.60 m in the southern part of the excavated area. Finds included 271 fragments of animal bones and teeth, 60 fragments of handmade ceramics and large fragments of a wheel-thrown thick-walled red clay vessel. Most handmade ceramics were gray with a smooth wall (Figure 10.6). One of the rims was decorated with slanting notches along the edge (Figure 10.6/12); some walls preserved horizontal line incisions (Figure 10.6/4, 6, 10, 15, 17), large teethlike impressions (Figure 10.6/11), or finger-made pinches (Figure 10.6/9). Other fragments have traces of combing. There were also fragments of a handmade smooth-walled vessel with a flat bottom and a salient body. Its neck, which is not quite obvious, has an ornament in the form of alternating holes and spikes (Figure 10.5/2). Fragments of the upper part of a large handmade pot-shaped vessel were found in the southwestern part of the excavated area (Figure 10.5/1). Similarity of the ceramic assemblage with Srubnaya (Figure 10.5/1, 2, 6; Figure 10.6/8–9, 11–12) and Sarmatian (Figure 6/2–4, 6–7, 10, 12–13, 15–17) vessels suggests these sites were used by representatives of both cultures. Other finds include a fragment of a bone tool (Figure 10.5/4), possibly a skate, typical for the Late Bronze period, a long bone with cut marks (Figure 10.5/3) and a fragment of a clay item with a hole (Figure 10.5/5), possibly a spindle whorl.

Layer 3 consisted of gray to dark brownish loam without anthropogenic insertions; its thickness varied from 0.10 to 0.45 m. Most of the finds were uncovered in its upper part, which yielded 116 remains of animal bones and 62 sherds of handmade undecorated pots with smoothed walls. Their thick walls preserved traces of polishing with grass. The fabric was tempered with small organic inclusions and was poorly fired. A few fragments of decorated ceramics were also present: a rim fragment with a beak (Figure 10.6/1), the wall of a

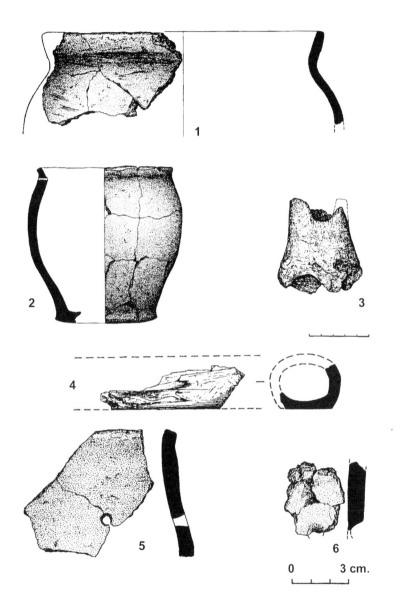

Figure 10.5. Finds from Gashun-Sala: (1, 2, 6) potsherds; (3) a long bone with cut marks; (4) fragment of a bone tool, possibly a skate; (5) a ceramic object, possibly a spindle whorl.

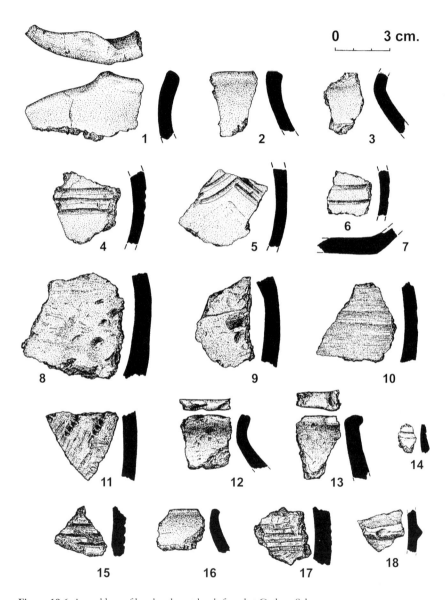

Figure 10.6. Assemblage of handmade potsherds found at Gashun-Sala.

Figure 10.7. Gashun-Sala: (top) the excavation trenches; (bottom left) handmade ceramics in situ; (bottom right) animal bones in situ.

thick-walled vessel decorated with finger impressions (Figure 10.6/18), and several sherds ornamented with incised zigzag lines (Figure 10.6/5, 14). This type of ceramic is very typical for the Late Bronze Age steppe cultures, as well as for the Early Iron Age period. The finds from layer 3 were not distributed evenly across the excavation area: there were concentrations of small fragments of ceramics in the eastern part, where almost no animal bones were present. No remains of human dwellings were found. Layer 3 overlies layer 4, which is a rock bed of yellow to grayish loam (Figure 10.7).

Neither hearths nor the remains of permanent residential buildings or auxiliary houses were found in either of the sites. Most of the finds were animal bones and ceramics dating to the Late Bronze Age, the Srubnaya culture and to the Early Iron Age.

ARCHAEOZOOLOGIC IDENTIFICATIONS

The mammal bones from both Manych and Gashun-Sala were poorly preserved. The taxonomic composition represents a small number of species, but many small or heavily damaged fragments could not be identified. The assemblage contained the remains of domesticated horse, cattle, sheep and goats. Hunted species were also present but in much smaller numbers. The animal bones from Manych included bones of horse, ungulates and domesticated bull. At Gashun-Sala sheep bones predominated, but these were absent among the bones uncovered at Manych. Bones of gazelle, saiga (*Saiga tatarica*) and kulan (*Equus hemionus kulan*) were rarely found at Gashun-Sala.

ARCHAEOBOTANIC DETERMINATIONS

Samples of paleosoil were taken from different occupation layers. Sample 1, from the occupation layer in the southern part of the trench at Manych, contained a lot of poorly preserved pollen. Pollen of goosefoot (*Chenopodiaceae*) predominated, but pollen of gramineous plants (*Poaceae*), asters (*Asteraceae*) and unidentifiable mixed grasses were found in smaller quantities. Remarkable finds included the pollen of lily (*Liliaceae*), pine (*Pinus*) and genuine fern (*Polypodiaceae*). Sample 2, taken just above sample 1, also had an abundance of pollen of goosefoot (*Chenopodiaceae*), asters (*Asteraceae*) and mixed grasses. Wormwood (*Artemisia*) was found in smaller quantities; in rare cases legumes (*Fabaceae*), *Gramineae* plants and *Ephedra* were found. Cattail (*Typha*) was found sporadically; pine (*Pinus*) and alder (*Alnus*) were found rarely. Data of phytolith analysis corroborated the results of the pollen analysis. It should be noted that the soil could have been without vegetation for a long time as a result of overgrazing, pasture digression or wind erosion. Flotation of samples did not yield any results.

A sample from layer 2 at Gashun-Sala had poorly preserved pollen with a low content of pollen of goosefoot (*Chenopodiaceae*), asters (*Asteraceae*), *Brassicaceae*, chicory (*Cichoriaceae*) and mixed grasses. Another sample, from a layer that contained large quantities of bones, contained phytoliths of gramineous plants. Flotation of the subsoil yielded the fruits of chicory (*Cichorium intybus* L.) and amaranth seeds (*Amaranthus* sp.) (Figure 10.8). White amaranth seeds (*Amaranthus albus* L.) were found in a bore pit near the site in another layer with large quantities of animal bones (Novikova et al. 2002). The presence of amaranth, which grows near roads, may indicate that, at the time of the occupation of the site, soils around the site were destroyed. This provides indirect evidence of the possible destruction of the ancient grass and soil cover around the site, which could have been caused by human activity and the overgrazing by domesticated animals. Phytoliths in these samples are predominantly of gramineous plants, characterized by the presence of long cells with wavy edges. The absence of short cells suggests that the vegetation was once mesophyte when the climate was more humid than it is today.

Analysis of the botanical remains indicates that, at the time of the occupation of the site, the area was covered with grasses, amaranth and goosefoot. Plants like ferns and cattail did grow near the water, and it is quite possible that alder grew nearby. The adjacent areas must have been used as permanent grasslands.

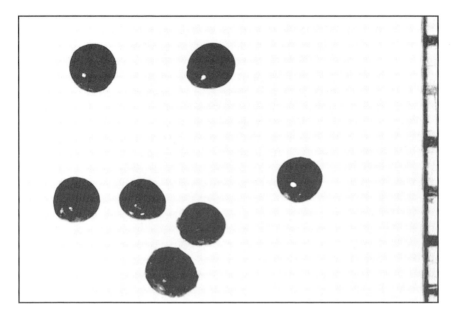

Figure 10.8. Seeds of amaranth found at Gashun-Sala.

ANALYSIS OF THE PALEOSOIL

Morphological properties of the soil profiles were described and soil horizons were identified in the soil profile. Air-dried soil samples were passed through a sieve (2 mm mesh) and chemically analyzed. The soil pH was determined on a saturation paste using a glass electrode pH-meter. The total organic carbon content was determined by oxidizing the humus with 0.4 n $K_2Cr_2O_7$, prepared in a sulphuric acid and water mixture (1/1, v/v). The gypsum content was measured by extracting SO_4^{2-} from the soil with 0.2 n HCl, followed by precipitation of SO_4^{2-} by 10% $BaCl_2$. The content of carbonates (like $CaCO_3$) in the soil was determined by titration. The phosphorus content was measured by determining the concentration of P_2O_5 in carbonate soils with 1% ammonium acetate (the Machigin technique).

In the soil profile at Manych a thin layer (2–3 cm) of yellow-brown loam was discovered at a depth of 12–14 cm. This layer is an outcrop in the domestic pit, indicating the ancient soil surface at the site at the time that this pit was made. The layer above is the gray humus horizon of the modern soil, which has been formed as a result of deluvial processes. This horizon appeared high in organic carbon and phosphorus, with a neutral to slightly alkaline pH. The occupation layer proper is located at a depth of 14 cm and below. The high content

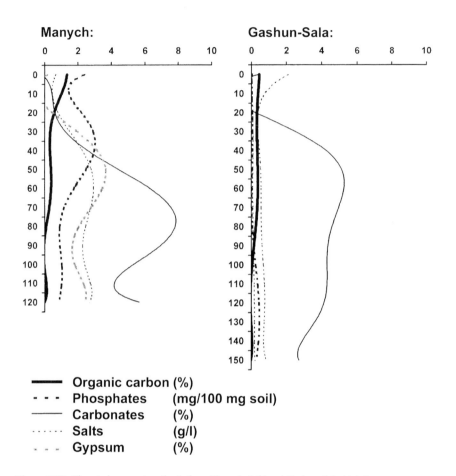

Figure 10.9. Chemical properties of soils from Manych (left) and Gashun-Sala (right).

of mobile phosphorus in the soil should be noted (Figure 10.9). At a depth of 50–60 cm buried soil that formed over alluvial sediments was observed. The site, obviously, has been established in a semihydromorphic landscape on the ancient alluvial calcareous saline soil. A rather thick occupation layer with an insignificant number of artifacts, on the one hand, and the relatively high content of phosphorus and organic carbon, on the other hand, indicates that, most likely, an active accumulation of artifacts occurred in the occupation layer when the site was used during a more humid climate and consequently more intensive water erosion. It can be concluded that the site was used rather intensively during a relative short time.

We also analyzed a soil sample from Gashun-Sala. The upper 30 cm layer was, in fact, the result of sedimentation processes after the site was abandoned. The occupation layer proper was at a depth of 30–80 cm. This horizon had the highest concentration of artifacts. The chemical properties of this layer differ significantly from those of the layers above and below. The organic carbon content of the layer does not vary between 30 and 80 cm, but in the lower horizons it is drastically reduced. At the same time, the phosphorus content is rather low (0.3–0.7 mg/100 g soil). Assuming that phosphorus is an indicator of human occupation, this low phosphorus content can be considered the result of little human activity. In the deeper layers the content of phosphorus is not considerably different (Figure 10.9). The buried soil was deposited below the occupation layer at a depth of 80 cm and below. We suppose that the intense grazing of cattle in the adjacent areas caused the degradation of the vegetation cover and intensified the erosional processes resulting in a rapid growth of the occupation layer. We also think that Gashun-Sala was occupied for a longer, but less intensive, period than Manych.

CHRONOLOGY

The dates of the occupation of the sites were determined by radiocarbon analyses of the animal bones from anthropogenic layers and correlated with the recovered artifacts. The results of the ^{14}C analysis are presented in Table 10.1. Analysis of the data indicates that both sites were actively exploited during the Early Iron Age. As a whole, these dates corroborate the results of the analysis of the ceramic assemblages. Gashun-Sala is likely to have been used more frequently, and for a longer period, from the Late Bronze Age, 1800–1600 BCE calibrated (the Srubnaya culture) until the 1st century CE. The chronology of the Srubnaya culture is based on the ^{14}C analysis of graves in the same area (Mimokhod and Shishlina 2004). The period of the most intensive activity was probably between the 7th-6th centuries BCE and the 1st century BCE. This fits the results of our analysis of the paleosoil, which dated Manych to the 7th-6th centuries BCE. The site could have been visited by local Srubnaya pastoral groups as well.

Table 10.1. ^{14}C Data from Manych and Gashun-Sala:

Sample (lab. no.)	Material	Age BP (uncalibrated)[a]	Calibrated agea
Manych (GrA-19259)	Animal bone from layer 2	2560±40	2746–2559 BP 797–610 BCE
Gashun-Sala (GrA-19226)	Animal bone from layer 3	2495±45	2722–2467 BP 773–518 BCE
Gashun-Sala (GrA-17487)	Animal bone from layer 2	1980±30	37–13 BCE 1–59 CE

[a]Analyses performed by J. van der Plicht at the Groningen ^{14}C Laboratory, the Netherlands.

Table 10.2. Seasonality of the Death of Animals Found at Gashun-Sala and Chilyuta:

Site	Sample[a, b]	Age at death	Season of death	Preservation
Gashun-Sala, layer 2	Ovis aries, left lower jaw with teeth, M_2 and M_3 of the same species (dp_4)	>2 years	Late summer to fall	Satisfactory
Gashun Sala, layer 3	Small ungulate dp4	2 years	Summer	Satisfactory
Gashun-Sala, layer 3	Lower jaw of a small ungulate with dp_4	1–2 years	Summer	Poor
Gashun-Sala, bore hole (1.05 m deep)	A fragment of the left lower jaw of a sheep or goat with premolars, M_1, and M_2	5 years	Spring to late summer	Satisfactory
Gashun-Sala, layer 2	Unknown teeth from the upper jaw of a sheep or goat	3–7 years	Late summer to fall	Satisfactory
Chilyuta, bore hole	M_1 or M_2 from the lower jaw of a sheep or goat with a broken root	2–3 years	Spring to late summer	Satisfactory

[a]Analysis was performed by G. Klevezal and A. Sokolov.
[b]M_1 = first molar; M_2 = second molar; M_3 = third molar; dp_4 = premolar.

Methodological tools to determine seasonality of archaeological sites has been discussed in Kirillova et al. (2000). We selected six animal teeth from the osteological finds from Gashun-Sala and from a bore hole at the adjacent site, Chilyuta. Teeth from the occupation layer at Manych turned out to be unsuitable for dentum and cementum analysis. The results of our analysis are presented in Table 10.2, which demonstrates that Gashun-Sala was used as a seasonal camp from the spring to early fall. Nearby sites that were suitable as seasonal camps, like Chilyuta, could also have been exploited during the warmer periods of the year.

DISCUSSION

The pastoral population of the steppe seemed to have settled in valleys of paleorivers with a continuous flow. They selected flat grounds or the slopes next to low-lying flood-prone terraces. Sites tended to be built in expanded valleys of narrow steppe rivers in areas with large meanders. The sites were conveniently located in shallow open valleys, close to a river and far from the slope above, where winds blew with almost the same force and frequency as on the surrounding plain. The botanical remains indicate that trees such as alders used to grow in the ravines. The vegetation cover was characterized by substantial variations and an abundance of species. This differed significantly from the scarce vegetation of the watershed areas in the open steppe. Many plants identified in the occupation layers were good for fodder; their productivity is at a maximum between May and August. Our determination of the periods of occupation of Gashun-Sala, and nearby Chilyuta, indicates that they were only used during the warmer times of the year. The seasons determined for the occupation during the Srubnaya period, as well as those for the Early Iron Age burials from nearby burial grounds, is consistent with this. Seasonality of the camps fits the results of the analysis of the paleosoil, as well as the climatic characteristics of that time.

The absence of any traces of permanent constructions, dwellings, foundation pits or permanent domestic pits at the sites indicates that they served as temporary campsites. We suppose that both wagons and lightweight constructions of braided mats (such as the 'kibitka' of the historic Kalmyks) were used as dwellings. The study of ancient textiles from the region demonstrates that, from the Bronze Age onward, mats were produced here from whatever materials were available. These mats were used in burial pits but could also have been used as construction material (Shishlina 1999). Soil flotation did not reveal the presence of any domesticated gramineous plants at the sites. The seeds of amaranth and chicory found at Gashun-Sala indicate that its residents were probably gathering plants for their nutritional or medicinal properties. They may also have dried edible plants for the winter. The small number of finds is most likely the result of the temporary use of these sites. The fragment of a spindle whorl and the bone with cut marks found at Gashun-Sala and the splash of copper found at Manych indicate a limited household production (spinning, casting, processing of bones). We can suppose that sheep were sheared, skins and furs were tanned, and carpets were felted in such camps. Indirect proof of this can be inferred from the composition of the animal bone assemblage and the comparison with ethnographic models of pastoral production (Zhitetsky 1893; Tajzscanova 1994).

Bone remains show that the population was engaged in raising domesticated cattle, sheep and horses. Natural water sources appear to have been used as watering places for the animals. Apparently the residents of the sites raised a lot of livestock, and their paths, which must have been used for a long time, eroded into tributaries to the Shared River. The grasslands around the sites must have been used intensively, which led to the depletion of the soils and the appearance of weeds such as chicory and amaranth. The differences in animal species at the investigated sites are also of interest. The absence of sheep and goat bones in the assemblage at Manych points to a certain specialization in raising animals: only cows and horses must have been raised at Manych. Wild animals were absent at Manych, in contrast to Gashun-Sala, where residents hunted wild ungulate in addition to raising cows, sheep and horses. The predominance of sheep and goat bones at Gashun-Sala also indicates that people stayed here for short times only, as sheep overgraze their pastures much faster than other domesticated animals.

The summer campsites of the Gashun-Sala type are without dwellings or domestic constructions. The population was raising domesticated sheep and goats. Nearby pastures, with an abundance of mixed plants, in the rather wide, deep valley, on the slopes, and in the watershed area on the open steppe were used as grazing grounds. Horses and dogs might have been used to facilitate such grazing. The broken soils of the pastures point to overgrazing. In addition to herding, people hunted, gathered wild gramineous and other edible plants, and engaged in simple household productions. Full-flow rivers were used as natural water reservoirs.

Judging by the size of Gashun-Sala (roughly 600 m²) and the nearby wide meanders of the Pra-Gashun River, where ceramics and animal bones were also found, several families could live at this site and the neighboring area at the same time, forming the network of sites observed in the river valley. Another explanation might be that the same group migrated from one pasture to another. Artifacts, ¹⁴C data, and the analysis of the paleosoil indicate that Gashun-Sala was first put to use during the Late Bronze Age, but its more active exploitation occurred during the Early Iron Age. It is quite possible that, as the site was subjected to the impact of floods and wind erosion, some artifacts were displaced. Maybe this is the reason why the dry channel at Gashun-Sala yielded fragments of animal bones and ceramics similar to those found at the site of Gashun-Sala. Pottery, similar to the pottery found in the kurgan burials of the Early Iron Age at the Sharakhalsun burial ground near the Kalaus River in the Stavropol area, indicate that local pastoral groups migrated south. Sheep, which predominated in the herds, are very suitable for long-distance migration. Therefore, such sites as Gashun-Sala and its adjacent area were part of an annual system of seasonal grasslands, with migration from one pasture to the next.

The seasonal campsites of the Manych type are without permanent dwellings and domestic constructions, which indicates that they were used during the warmer periods of the year. Paleoclimatic characteristics suggest that Manych existed in more humid and warm conditions with a higher annual precipitation rate, a likely snow cover, and the impossibility of using this area as pasture in the winter. The population engaged in raising cattle and horses on the terraces, slopes and the nearby watershed areas with grasslands rich in mixed grasses. Excavations in the Shared River valley revealed only small amounts of ceramics and animal bones. The presence of Srubnaya pottery indicates that the campsite was visited as early as the Late Bronze Age. The abundance of artifacts dating to the Early Iron Age in the occupation layer suggests that it was only actively used during that period. Taking all information into account, Manych could only have supported a small group of people, one or two families. Pottery stylistically similar to Manych ceramics, fragments of coarse sand-tempered vessels, were found during surveys along the banks of the Chograi. It is quite possible that pastoral groups migrated there for the winter. Their winter camps could also have been located farther south, in the area of the Stavropolye Hills. Such camps appear to belong to the system of an annual seasonal pastoral cycle economy.

The two types of campsites, Gashun-Sala and Manych, compare fairly well with existing ethnographic models (Zhitetsky 1893; Bulatov 2000). Kalmyk *khotons*, small family groups of pastoralists, consisted of one or two families and several wagons. They were spread out over the entire steppe, spending the winter in permanent sites and the summer in the open steppe. Their number was low, which is why there was no shortage in good winter campsites. The lifestyle of the Kalmyks was predominantly nomadic, using the marginal grasslands of the steppe to raise cattle, horses, sheep and goats. In the morning the women brought the livestock to grasslands near the khoton; right after breakfast the teenagers herded the flocks while the men took the cattle to a watering place. During the day the women were busy with household productions: weaving, spinning, sewing and preparing food. In the evening the men again took the cattle to the watering place. The cattle then spent the night in one place, near a special type of dwelling: the *kibitka*. These consisted of a wooden frame covered by wool bands. When families moved to a different temporary campsite, their kibitkas were dismantled and packed, together with other belongings, on pack animals and the entire khoton moved to a new place. In the spring these moves were short. In the summer, especially in case of droughts, they could last for several days (Zhitetsky 1893:35–37). In a 19th century CE map of the winter and summer migration routes of the Kalmyk, the steppe areas in the south of the Iki-Burul district (north of the area where the campsites that we investigated are located) were used as winter grasslands with migration routes going to the south, across the Kuma and Kalaus rivers (Bulatov 2000:138–139).

Excavations at Gashun-Sala and Manych, located in the South Yergueni Hills, and analysis of the collected data helped us to propose two types of seasonal campsites on the Eurasian steppes in the Late Bronze Age and the Early Iron Age. They correlate with existing historical models of nomadic Kalmyks, who have inhabited this area from the 17th-20th centuries CE. In spite of differences in climatic, social, economic and political conditions, we can definitely note similarities in the seasonal and economic cycles. The ecological niches of the steppe developed from the Eneolithic onward. When a pastoral economy evolved and spread during the Bronze Age, a specific seasonal system of grassland use was developed. This is reflected in the characteristics of the sites. So far we have studied only two camps of the Late Bronze Age and Early Iron Age. We believe that similar studies of other sites in this region will allow us to reconstruct an overall picture of the economy and the household life of the earliest populations of the region.

REFERENCES

Bulatov, V. E.
2000   The System of Seasonal Migrations of the Kalmyks in the Nineteenth Century [in Russian]. In N. Shishlina (ed.), *Seasonality Studies of the Bronze Age Northwest Caspian Steppe. Papers of the State Historical Museum. Volume 120.* Moscow, Poltex: pp. 131–142.

Kirillova, I. V., G. A. Klevezal, K. E. Mikhailov, A. A. Golyeva, Y. E. Trunova and N. I. Shishlina
2000   Complex Methods to Determine the Season of the Bronze Age Graves in Kalmykia [in Russian]. In N. Shishlina (ed.), *Seasonality Studies of the Bronze Age Northwest Caspian Steppe. Papers of the State Historical Museum. Volume 120.* Moscow, Poltex: pp. 30–41.

Koltsov, P. M.
1985   New Neolith and Eneolith Sites of the Black Land [in Russian]. In K. N. Maksimov (ed.), *Ancient Sites of Kalmykia.* Elista, Elistinskoye knizscnoye izdatelstvo: pp. 34–42.
1988   Djangr Site of the Eneolith Epoch [in Russian]. In I. V. Vasilyev (ed.), *Archaeological Cultures of the North Caspian Region.* Kuibyshev, Kuibyshevskoye knizhnoye izdatelstvo: pp. 44–58.

Minayeva, T. M.
1955   Site with Microlith Objects in the Black Lands [in Russian]. *Short Reports of the Institute of the Material Culture 59*: pp. 46–53.

Mimokhod, R. A. and N. I. Shishlina
2004 ^{14}C Data of the Final Catacomb Culture Graves of the Mandjikiny Burial Ground and Problems of the Middle Bronze and Late Bronze Ages Chronology [in Russian]. In L. T. Yablonsky (ed.), *Ancient Caucasus: Retrospection of Culture.* Moscow, Institute of Archaeology RAS: pp. 124–127.

Novikova, M. A., A. G. Devyatov and I. N. Shishlina
2002   Carpological Investigation of the Bronze Age Sites of Kalmykia [in Russian]. In N. Shishlina and E. Tsytskin (eds.), *The Ostrovnoy Burial Mound: Results of the Complex Investigation of the Archaeological Sites of the North-West Caspian Sea Steppe.* Moscow, Elista Tisso Poligraf: pp. 196–203.

Shilov, V. P.
1975   *Essay About the History of the Ancient Tribes of the Low Volga Area* [in Russian]. Leningrad, Nauka.

Shishlina, N. I. (ed.)
1999   *Textile of the Bronze Age Eurasian Steppe. Papers of the State Historical Museum. Volume 109* [in Russian]. Moscow, Poltex.

Sinitsyn, I. V.

1931   Flint Objects from the Dune Sites of the Kalmykia Area [in Russian]. *Bulletin of the Low-Volga Institute of Local Historical Studies Named After M. Gorky*: pp. 83–91.

Tajzscanova, G. E. (ed.)

1994   *The Kazakhs: Historical-Ethnographic Research* [in Russian]. Almaty, Kazakhstan.

Zhitetsky, I. A.

1893   *Essays About the Way of Life of the Astrakhan Kalmyks: Ethnographic Observation, 1884–1886* [in Russian]. Moscow, M. Volchaninov Publishing House: pp. 1–70.

CHAPTER 11

TROGODYTES = BLEMMYES = BEJA?

THE MISUSE OF ANCIENT ETHNOGRAPHY

STANLEY M. BURSTEIN[1]

THE CORRELATION OF textual and archaeological evidence is one of the chronic problems of the historiography of the margins of the ancient world. The eastern deserts of Egypt and Lower Nubia in late antiquity are no exception. Archaeological remains in the Eastern Desert are typically associated with the Blemmyes, who are considered typical desert nomads. This chapter argues that the sources offer little support for this reconstruction; rather, they indicate that in late antiquity the Blemmyes were primarily a sedentary people located in the Nile Valley.

In 1982 Eric Wolf published an influential book entitled *Europe and the Peoples Without History*. Wolf's work was a pioneering effort to re-integrate the experience of peoples on the margins of 'civilizations' into the narrative of modern world history. This volume is part of a similar effort in ancient history. Whether the topic is ancient or modern history, however, the historiography of the margins is beset by similar methodological problems. Two in particular stand out: the correlation of archaeological cultures with specific peoples named in written sources and the validity of the ethnographic present.

The reasons for the persistence of these two problems are clear. The historical record, with all of its problems and deficiencies, seems to provide the basis for a rich and detailed diachronic account of developments within a region, replete with references to individuals and ethnic groups and their conflicts and interactions. By contrast, in the view of historians, the archaeological record cuts a poor figure, with its anonymous architectural, funerary, tool and ceramic assemblages often spread over wide swathes of territory and rarely capable of registering

---

[1] I would like to thank Markus Wiener Publisher, Inc., for permitting me to reprint my translation of Agatharchides' description of the Trogodytes, and Dr. R. H. Pierce, University of Bergen, Department of Greek, Latin and Egyptology, for his comments on earlier versions of this chapter.

change in any mode except the longue durée. The temptation to unite the two kinds of evidence has proved irresistible. One need only think of the endless debate over the archaeological correlates of the Indo-Europeans (Mallory 1989:164–185) or the Celts and Germans (Wells 2001; Burns 2003:18–26); indeed, the latter correlation seems to have ended in the paradoxical conclusion that the distinction between the two peoples is illusory.

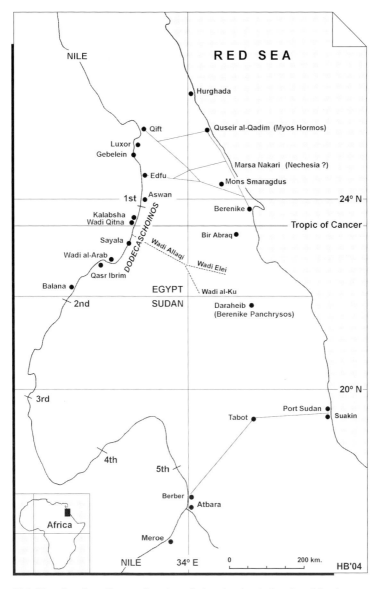

Figure 11.1. Map of southeast Egypt and northeast Sudan, showing the location of the places mentioned in the text (drawn by H. Barnard).

The problem of the ethnographic present is equally vexing. Ideally, historians should have at their disposal multiple and comprehensive ethnographies of the same ethnic group compiled at regular intervals and using the same theoretical frameworks. Comparison would then allow historians to identify and trace over time changes in socio-economic and cultural structures. The reality, of course, is different. For many peoples, and especially those without written native historical traditions, historians are fortunate if they have at their disposal one ethnography and a handful of travelers' accounts, supplemented by accounts in the writings of foreign historians, geographers, and government officials. As a result, the most authoritative ethnography of a people is treated as universally valid for its whole history, creating an impression of changelessness as characterizing the history of peoples living in nonstate societies. The problem was first recognized in North America, where ethnographies of Native Americans, compiled by anthropologists on 19th and 20th century CE reservations, were long erroneously treated as reliable descriptions of the cultures of their precolumbian ancestors (Berkhofer 1978:62–69). Both problems bedevil efforts to reconstruct the history of the peoples of the Eastern Deserts of Egypt and the Sudan.

THE TROGODYTES[2]

The Eastern Desert occupies a vast area bounded by the Nile in the west and the Red Sea in the east and extending from Egypt in the north to Ethiopia and Eritrea in the south. The historical record of this area is long and complex, beginning in the 4th millennium BCE and extending to the present. This record includes texts in numerous languages including Egyptian, Coptic, Greek, Latin, Ge'ez, Arabic and a variety of European languages. The variety of the textual record is as varied as the languages in which it is written, including royal inscriptions, letters, ethnographies, travelers' accounts, histories, geographies, poetry and graffiti in several languages, to mention only the most prominent categories. The one common denominator among these texts is that none of them were written by the people who inhabit the Eastern Desert. All reflect perspectives of the inhabitants of the Nile Valley, to whom the Eastern Desert was a strange and hostile place but whose resources they sought and whose inhabitants they tolerated or feared, depending on whether they needed their services or feared their attacks. Only the meager surviving material record was created by the local populations. Not surprisingly, correlating the material and textual records is a central theme in the historiography of the Eastern Desert. Obvious examples are the identification of the Medjay with the Pan

---

[2.] For the spelling of *Trogodyte* see Burstein (1989:109, note 1).

Grave culture (Lacovara 2001:3, 20); the ascription of virtually all late ancient non-Greco-Roman archaeological material in the Eastern Desert, including Eastern Desert Ware, to the Blemmyes (Pierce 2001:157; Barnard 2002:53–57; Sidebotham et al. 2004:16; but see Barnard 2005); and the closely related controversy over whether the creators of X-Group Culture and the occupants of the elite tombs at Ballana and Qustul, in the Lower Nubian Nile Valley, were Nobatai or Blemmyes (Kirwan 1937:47–62; Adams 1977:419–422; Török 1987:219–221; Welsby 2002:20–23).

The validity and usefulness of such correlations is called into question by the complex ethnography of the Eastern Desert region. Today the Eastern Desert is primarily inhabited by the Beja, a loosely related conglomeration of tribal groups united by geography, a lifestyle based mainly but not exclusively on herding (some Beja are sedentary agriculturalists), and the fact that they speak languages belonging to the Tu-Bedawie language family (Magid, this volume; Paul 1954:12–19). The multiplicity of names for groups supposedly living in the Eastern Desert in antiquity (Medjay, Bega, Bougaeitoi, blhm, Blemmyes, Trogodytes and Megabari, to mention only the most prominent) suggests a similar complexity in antiquity.

Not surprisingly, scholars have long attempted to simplify the ethnography of the region by arguing that, like today, the Beja were also in antiquity the dominant population in the Eastern Desert and that the various ethnic terms mentioned above designated various Beja tribes (Krall 1900:6; Updegraff 1978:156–159). This hypothesis is made more attractive by the fact that the various terms are language specific. Thus, Medjay occurs only in Middle and New Kingdom Egyptian texts; blhm in Demotic texts; Blemmye in Greek, Latin and late Egyptian/Coptic texts; Bega and Bougaeitoi in Aksumite Greek texts; Trogodytes in Greek and Latin texts; Megabari in Greek, Latin and Egyptian texts; and Beja in Arabic texts. The idea that the variety of ethnic terms is the result of individual peoples giving different names to the same ethnic group is an obvious solution to the problem and seemingly supported in the sources. So the linguistic similarities of the terms Beja, Medjay and Bega, the explicit equation of the Bega and Blemmyes by the 6th century CE Christian traveler and geographer Cosmas Indicopleustes (Wolska-Conus 1968, volume 1:63), and the equation of Beja and Blemmye in Arabic and Coptic texts (Plumley and Adams 1974:278) appear to confirm this hypothesis. Finally, since the Bega, Blemmyes and Trogodytes are all attested as possessing livestock (Eide et al. 1998:1094–1100, 1147–1153, 1158–1165), it has seemed safe to assume that, like the modern Beja, the ancient Beja were also pastoral nomads. The principal evidence for this thesis is the description of the Trogodytes preserved among the fragments of *On the Erythraean Sea* of the 2nd century BCE Greek historian Agatharchides of Cnidus (Burstein 1989:62–64, 1998:47–50):

Now the Trogodytes are called 'Nomads' by the Greeks and live a wandering life supported by their herds in groups ruled by tyrants. Together with their children they have their women in common except for the one belonging to the tyrant. Against a person who has sexual relations with her the chief levies as a fine a specified number of sheep.

This is their way of life. When it is winter in their country—this is at the time of the Etesian winds—and the god inundates their land with heavy rains, they draw their sustenance from blood and milk, which they mix together and stir in jars, which have been slightly heated. When summer comes, however, they live in the marshlands, fighting among themselves over the pasture. They eat those of their animals that are old and sick after they have been slaughtered by butchers, whom they call 'unclean.'

They do not assign to any human being the appellation 'parent' but to a bull and a cow, calling the former 'father' and the latter 'mother' and likewise to a ram and a ewe because they do not obtain their daily sustenance from their parents but from these beasts. For drink the mass of the people employs a preparation made from the Christ's thorn plant, but the tyrants drink one that is prepared from a particular flower and is like poor quality sweet wine. They leave the rest of their body naked but cover their loins with a girdle of skins. It is customary for the other Trogodytes to circumcise their genital organs, just as do the Egyptians, but the tribes the Greeks call 'Colobi' have the custom of cutting off with razors during infancy the whole portion that others circumcise. From this practice they gained for themselves the appellation just mentioned.

For armament the tribe of Trogodytes called Megabari have circular shields made of raw oxhide and clubs tipped with iron knobs, but the others have bows and spears.

He says that the Trogodytes deal as follows with the dead. They bind the neck to the legs with withies made from the Christ's thorn plant. Then, after they place the body on a mound, they pelt it with stones large enough to be held in a hand while jeering and laughing until they have hidden the corpse. They then place on top (of the cairn) the horn of a goat and depart free of sadness and completely cheerful. In conducting such a funeral, he says, they act sensibly since to not cause themselves grief on account of those who are free from pain is a sign of intelligence.

They do not fight with each other, as the Greeks do, over land or some other pretext but over the pasturage as it sprouts up at various times. In their feuds, they first pelt each other with stones until some are wounded. Then for the remainder of the battle they resort to a contest of bows and arrows. In short time many die as they shoot accurately because of their practice in this pursuit and their aiming at a target bare of defensive weapons. The older women, however, put an end to the battle by rushing in between them and meeting with respect. For it is their custom not to strike these women on any account so that immediately upon their appearance the men cease shooting.

They do not, he says, sleep as do other men. They possess a large number of animals which accompany them, and they hand cowbells from the horns of all the males in order that their sound might drive off wild beasts. At nightfall, they collect their herds into byres and cover these with hurdles made from palm branches. Their women and children mount up on top of these. The men, however, light fires in a circle and tell traditional tales and thus ward off sleep, since in many situations discipline imposed by necessity is able to conquer nature.

Those individuals who are unable to follow the herds because of age wind the tail of a cow around their necks and willingly free themselves from life. But should one seek to postpone death, anyone has the right to fasten the noose as though from kindness and with a rebuke to deprive him of his life. It is likewise their custom to remove from life those who have been crippled or are suffering from incurable diseases. For they consider the greatest of evils to be for a person to desire to live when unable to do anything that makes life worth living. Wherefore, one can see that all Trogodytes are sound of body and still in the prime of life since none is over sixty years of age.[3]

THE EVIDENCE RECONSIDERED

Despite its brevity, Agatharchides' description of the Trogodytes is unique for its high quality among Greek and Roman accounts of pastoral nomads. It is not, of course, without flaws. It reveals clear evidence of one of the main weaknesses of classical ethnography: the tendency of Greek and Latin writers to moralize about their own societies by holding up supposedly 'simpler' peoples as models of natural behavior (Anderson 1938:ix–xix; Dihle 1962:207–232; Hartog 1988:310–381). It also shows signs of a priori reasoning derived from Agatharchides' use of Peripatetic theories of sociocultural evolution to organize his accounts of Nubian peoples in his work (Burstein 1989:26–28). For example, his insistence on the limited character of Trogodyte marriage, the restriction of property to their livestock, and the fact that warfare among them is directly connected to the protection of their herds' access to pasture are diagnostic features of the pastoral stage that forms the second stage of cultural evolution in the Peripatetic scheme of cultural evolution. The pastoral stage is marked by the breakup of the undifferentiated gatherer society of the 'Golden Age,' which is represented in Agatharchides' work by the Fish-eaters of the Red

---

[3.] Reprinted with permission from the publisher. This translation is a synthesis of the three parallel and overlapping surviving versions of Agatharchides' account of the Trogodytes.

Sea coasts of Egypt and Sudan. More important are two other characteristics of Agatharchides' ethnography of the Trogodytes.

First, Agatharchides' Trogodyte ethnography is almost unique among ancient and medieval accounts of nomads in that it lacks any trace of the two defining characteristics of what the Roman historian Shaw (1982:6) calls "the ideology of the pastoral nomad," namely, "the complete separation of nomads and sedentarists into two polarized and isolated taxonomic compartments" and the characterization of the nomad "as the ultimate barbaric human type who is directly opposed to the 'civilized' sedentary agriculturalist."

Second, and equally important, numerous aspects of his description, such as blood eating, the Trogodyte's quasi-kinship relationship to their animals, the existence of 'pariah' groups such as the butchers mentioned by Agatharchides, and their funerary customs, are all paralleled in later ethnographies of east African pastoralists (Burstein 1989:109–115). Clearly, Agatharchides' claim that his account was based on Ptolemaic explorers' reports is justified, and it is a sound basis for reconstructing the culture of the Trogodytes. But can it also be used to reconstruct the life of the Blemmyes in late antiquity?

The identification of the Blemmyes as a Beja tribe has led scholars to assume it can (Paul 1954:35; Updegraff 1978:192), but there is reason to believe that this is not true. Thus, while it is probable that the Blemmyes were ethnically Beja,[4] not all modern Beja are pastoral nomads, and there is no reason to assume that the situation was different in antiquity.[5] Equally important, no ancient source identifies the Trogodytes with the Blemmyes. Moreover, even if one did, Greek and Roman writers were as susceptible to the pitfalls of the ethnographic present as modern scholars. Once a standard ethnography appeared, it tended to be copied century after century, leaving the described peoples frozen in time and space. For example, India in Greek literature was always north India in the 3rd century BCE (Dihle 1962, 1963), and Gaul was always southern France in the late 2nd and early 1st century BCE (Tierney 1960:189–275; Nash 1976:111–126).

The case is similar for the Trogodytes. Five centuries and hundreds of miles separate the Trogodytes described by Agatharchides from the Blemmyes

---

[4.] For evidence indicating that the Blemmyes spoke a language of the Tu-Bedawi language family see Zhylarz 1940–1941:1–2 and Browne 2004:243–244.

[5.] A good example of the misuse of the ethnographic present with regard to the Blemmyes is Pierce's comment (2001:159) that "the primary reason for believing that the Blemmyes were nomadic in life-style and had a clan-based (segmentary) social structure is the evidence that links them to the Beja, who undoubtedly fit this description," despite the hundreds of years that separate them from the earliest medieval accounts of the Beja.

encountered by the Romans in Lower Nubia and Egypt in late antiquity. The conditions in which the peoples of the Eastern Desert lived changed significantly in those centuries, but Agatharchides' account continued to stand as the standard ethnography of the Trogodytes until the end of antiquity (Burstein 1989:33–36). Agatharchides described the Trogodytes on the basis of the reports of Ptolemaic explorers, who encountered them in the hill country adjacent to the Red Sea coasts of the central Sudan during the early phases of Ptolemaic elephant hunting in the mid-3rd century BCE. Later authors repeated his account for the rest of antiquity. The Ptolemaic footprint in the Eastern Desert at the time that Agatharchides' sources were compiled was light and mostly limited to the road linking Berenike to Koptos, a few forts, the gold mines in Wadi Allaqi and some ports and hunting stations on the Red Sea coast. In contrast, during the Roman period trade caravans and supply convoys regularly crossed the region using one of several roads linking the Nile Valley with the Red Sea coast and with the watering stations, forts, mines, quarries and settlements of various types that were scattered throughout the region. These circumstances make it unlikely that Agatharchides' description of the Trogodytes could also accurately characterize the life of the Blemmyes four or five centuries later.

For almost half a century a number of scholars, including Herzog (1967:57–58), Christides (1980:134–136), and, most recently, the Sudanese scholar Samia Dafa'alla (1987:34–39), have protested against the tendency to reconstruct the culture of the Blemmyes on the basis of their presumed identification with the Trogodytes. The most comprehensive of these critiques is that of Dafa'alla, who argued in an important but little noticed article that there were two groups of Blemmyes, one nomadic and one, more important, sedentary group living near the Nile in Lower Nubia and southern Egypt. Dafa'alla suggested that it was this latter group to which most classical texts referred. Analysis of the evidence for the political organization and location of the Blemmyes in late antiquity confirms the validity of much, but not all, of this reconstruction.

The textual evidence concerning the Blemmyes' political organization in late antiquity is remarkably varied, including texts in Greek, Latin and Coptic, in a wide variety of categories. Included among these texts are tax records, royal decrees, letters, inscriptions, graffiti and allusions in historical and hagiographical works. The picture that emerges from them, however, is clear and consistent.

While it is true that the Greek geographer Strabo (Eide et al. 1996:828–835) included the Blemmyes among the nomadic peoples of Nubia in the late 1st century BCE, it is equally true that the focus of Blemmye life in the 5th century CE had shifted from the desert to a group of towns in lower Nubia. Around

390 CE the theologian Epiphanius (Eide et al. 1998:1115–1121) claimed that the Blemmyes controlled the emerald mines of Mons Smaragdus from their capital at Talmis (Kalabsha), while a quarter of a century later, around 420 CE, the ambassador and historian Olympiodorus (Eide et al. 1998:1126–1128), who visited the Blemmyes, described them as barbarians occupying Talmis and holding also the towns of Primis (Qasr Ibrim), Phoinikon, Khiris and Thapis (Taphis). Later in the century the Nobatian king, Silko (Eide et al. 1998:1147–1153), boasts of seizing Talmis and Taphis from them and conquering their towns from Primis to the first cataract; while the Blemmyan king, Phonen (Eide et al. 1998:1158–1165), demands that Silko's successor, Abourni, return Talmis, and the rest of their territory, to the Blemmyes. There is textual evidence not only for town officials (Eide et al. 1998:1134–1138) but also for various royal officials, who seem to be arranged in a hierarchy including kings (*basiliskoi*), tribal chiefs (*phylarchoi*), subchiefs (*hupotyrannoi*), court officials (*domestici*) and scribes (Updegraff 1978:144, 180–181). The kings had the power to levy taxes and grant exemptions, as well as authority over territory (Eide et al. 1998:1207–1210). As Herzog (1967:58) pointed out almost half a century ago, these features of Blemmye political organization indicate that in late antiquity the Blemmyes were no longer stateless nomads of the type described in Agatharchides' account of the Trogodytes but a people with "a state organization with nobles ruling islands" and "a royal court on the model of a sedentary population with specialized subordinate officials."

The situation is similar with regard to the evidence for the territory of the Blemmyes in the 4th–5th centuries CE. In his important monograph Late Antique Nubia Török (1987:28) claimed that the Blemmyes lived in "the area of the Red Sea hills" and that "late classical sources locate their tribes in the Eastern Desert."[6] The actual situation, however, is exactly the reverse of this statement. With one exception (the 6th century CE historian Procopius) sources consistently place the Blemmyes in the Nile Valley. Five sources are of relevance here: the 4th century CE theologian Epiphanius, the 5th century CE historian Olympiodorus, the late 4th century CE historian Ammianus Marcellinus, the contemporary Latin poet Claudian, and the biography of the Egyptian monk Shenute compiled by Besa. Epiphanius's and Olympiodorus's references to the Blemmyes occupying cities in the Nile Valley have already been discussed. Even more revealing are two passages of Ammianus Marcellinus. In paragraph 14.4.3 Ammianus describes the inhabitants of the Eastern Desert of Egypt, whom he calls Saracens. He treats this term as a synonym for the term Scenitae, 'tent-dwellers' (Ammianus Marcellinus 22.15.2, Rolfe 1935-1939):

[6.] His claim that "some accounts place them falsely 'near the source' of the River Nile" is arbitrary (Török 1987:28).

Among those tribes whose original abode extends from the Assyrians to the cataracts of the Nile and the frontiers of the Blemmyes [ad Nili cataractas porrigitur,
et confinia Blemmyarum] all alike are warriors of equal rank, half-nude, clad in
dyed cloaks as far as the loins, ranging widely with the help of swift horses and
slender camels in times of peace or war. No man ever grasps a plough-handle or
cultivates a tree, none seeks a living by tilling the soil, but they rove continually
over wide and extensive tracts without a home, without fixed abodes or laws.

Two facts emerge from this text. First, Ammianus explicitly excluded the
Blemmyes from the category of tent-dwelling nomads whom he calls Saracens.[7]
Second, his linking of the Blemmyes' territory to the cataracts clearly places it
in the Nile Valley. Confirmation is provided by a passage in paragraph 22.15.24.
Commenting on the disappearance of hippopotami from Egypt as a result of
overhunting, Ammianus observes that "as the inhabitants of these regions
(Egypt) conjecture, they [the hippopotami] were forced from weariness of the
multitude that hunted them to take refuge in the land of the Blemmyes." Given
the hippopotami's need for water, Ammianus clearly implies that the Blemmyes
live near the Nile and not in the desert. The evidence of Claudian and Besa is
similar. The former (Eide et al. 1998:1125–1126), in describing the course of
the Nile, says that the river "winds through Meroe and the fierce Blemmyes and
black Syene," while the latter (Eide et al 1998: 1107–1109) describes a Blemmye
raid on the White Monastery as coming from 'the south,' not the east.

The evidence of the majority of the late ancient sources is clear: the territory of the Blemmyes in the 4th–5th centuries CE lay in the Nile Valley, not in
the Eastern Desert. As mentioned, the only exception is Procopius, but the
exception is only apparent. In describing the distribution of peoples south
of Egypt in his own time Procopius (Eide et al. 1998:1188–1193) says that
"the Blemmyes inhabit the interior of this country (Lower Nubia), while the
Nobatai possess the lands on either side of the River Nile." He points out later
in the same passage, however, that the Nobatai originally lived in the oasis of
Kharga but settled in the Nile Valley at the invitation of Emperor Diocletian,
who wished them "to drive off the Blemmyes." The historicity of Procopius's
account of how the Nobatai gained control of the Lower Nubia is doubtful
(Updegraff 1978:52–54; Eide et al. 1998:1191–1193), but it is clear that he
believed that the Blemmyes originally lived near the Nile and that they took
refuge in the Eastern Desert only after their defeat by the Nobatai, specifically
by Silko and his successors.

[7.] Török's (1987:32) identification of the Saracens with the Nabateans, the inhabitants of northwestern Arabia, ignores Ammianus Marcellinus's explicit statement that
their territory bounded Egypt on the east (Ammianus Marcellinus 22.15.1, Rolfe
1935-1939).

DISCUSSION

The evidence reviewed in this chapter suggests a different course of Blemmye history than that generally found in standard accounts. The emphasis in the sources on Blemmye raids into Egypt has led to the simplistic characterization of them as typical desert nomads, obscuring a more complex historical trajectory. The Blemmyes probably did originate as nomads living east of the Nile in the central Sudan under Kushite suzerainty. That is at least how the geographer Eratosthenes (Eide et al. 1996:557–561) described them in the 3rd century BCE. Aksumite sources indicate that their relatives (the Bega/Bougaeitoi) continued to live that way.

The later history of the Blemmyes, however, differed from that of the Bega. While Strabo (Eide et al. 1996:828–835) in the early 1st century CE and Ptolemy, in Geography 4.7 (Berggren and Jones 2000), in the 2nd century CE still placed the Blemmyes in the central Sudan, by late antiquity they had relocated into the Nile Valley in Lower Nubia, possibly as part of the Kushite colonization of the region. There they underwent a process of sedentarization. As Roman power in the area weakened, the Blemmyes occupied the principal towns of the region, establishing a state based on a mixed agricultural and herding economy that was strong enough by the end of the 4th century CE to seize control of the 'emerald' mines in the Eastern Desert.

This review of the textual evidence concerning the political organization and territory of the Blemmyes supports the identification of a riparian Blemmye population in lower Nubia but not the existence of a separate and distinct population of nomadic Blemmyes in the region as suggested by Dafa'alla. Instead, it suggests that the expansion of Blemmye influence into the Eastern Desert occurred after they had moved into Lower Nubia. This represented their opportunistic adaptation to the opportunities afforded by Roman development in the region, specifically the growth of mining and caravan traffic between the Nile and the Red Sea. It was only after their defeat by the Nobatai in the second half of the 5th century CE that they were forced to abandon the Nile Valley and withdraw into the Eastern Desert. Procopius located them there in the 6th century CE, and other papyri and Arabic sources indicate that they survived as a distinct population until at least the 8th century CE before finally merging with the populations of the region.

If this reconstruction of Blemmye history is correct, it has important implications for the study of archaeological material in the Eastern Desert, including Eastern Desert Ware (Barnard 2002). It is clear that Agatharchides' account of the Trogodytes in east-central Sudan during the 3rd century BCE cannot be used as a basis for reconstructing the life of the Blemmyes living in late antique Lower Nubia. This significantly reduces the ethnographic evidence relevant to Blemmye society. If Eastern Desert Ware, and other Eastern Desert artifacts, was created by the Blemmyes, it was not created by people who were primarily nomads. Alternately, if Eastern Desert Ware was created by nomads, then it cannot be used as diagnostic for the presence of the Blemmyes.

This conclusion should not be surprising. The assumption that the Blemmyes were the sole inhabitants of the Eastern Desert was always a gross oversimplification that obscured more than it explained. As mentioned, Ammianus described the Eastern Desert as occupied by a variety of nomadic tribes that he called 'Saracens.' His account of the Saracens is, unfortunately, marred by 'pastoral ideology,' but the general validity of Ammianus's picture of conditions in the Eastern Desert is not in doubt. Even after they left the Nile Valley, the Blemmyes were only one of the many peoples occupying Lower Nubia and its desert hinterlands. As elsewhere, in the Eastern Desert the correlation of archaeological evidence with peoples mentioned in textual sources is never simple and straightforward but always problematic and uncertain.

REFERENCES

Adams, W. Y.

1977   Nubia: Corridor to Africa. Princeton, Princeton University Press.

Anderson, J. G. C. (ed.)

1938   Cornelii Taciti De origine et situ Germanorum. Oxford, Clarendon.

Barnard, H.

2002   Eastern Desert Ware: A First Introduction. Sudan & Nubia 6: pp. 53–57.

2005   Sire, il n'y a pas de Blemmyes: A Re-evaluation of Historical and Archaeological Data. In J. C. M. Starkey (ed.), People of the Red Sea: Proceedings of the Red Sea Project II, Held in the British Museum, October 2004. Society for Arabian Studies Monographs number 3. BAR International Series 1395. Oxford, Archaeopress: pp. 23–40.

Berkhofer, R. F., Jr.

1978   The White Man's Indian: Images of the American Indian, from Columbus to the Present. New York, Random House.

Berggren, J. L. and A. Jones

2000   Ptolemy's Geography: An Annotated Translation of the Theoretical Chapters. Princeton, Princeton University Press.

Browne, G. M.

2004   Blemmyica. Zeitschrift für Papyrologie und Epigraphik 148: pp. 243–244.

Burns, T. S.

2003   Rome and the Barbarians, 100 B.C.–A.D. 400. Baltimore, Johns Hopkins University Press.

Burstein, S. M. (ed.)

1989   Agatharchides of Cnidus on the Erythraean Sea. London, Hakluyt Society.

1998   Ancient African Civilizations: Kush and Axum. Princeton, Markus Wiener.

Christides, V.

1980   Ethnic Movements in Southern Egypt and Northern Sudan: Blemmyes-Beja in Late Antique and Early Arab Egypt Until 707 A.D. Listy Filologické 103: pp. 120–143.

Dafa'alla, S.

1987   The Historical Role of the Blemmyes in Late Meroitic and Early X-Group Periods. Beiträge zur Sudanforschung 2: pp. 34–40.

Dihle, A.

1962   Zur Hellenistische Ethnographie. In H. Schwabl, H. Diller, O. Reverdin, W. Peremans, H. C. Baldry and A. Dihle (eds.), Grecs et Barbares: Entretiens sur l'antiquité classique. Geneva, Vandoeuvres-Genève: pp. 205–232.

1963   The Conception of India in Hellenistic and Roman Literature. In Proceedings of the Cambridge Philological Society 190: new series 10, pp. 15–23.

Eide T., T. Hägg, R. H. Pierce and L. Török

1996   Fontes Historiae Nubiorum, Volume 2. University of Bergen, John Grieg.

1998   Fontes Historiae Nubiorum, Volume 3. University of Bergen, John Grieg.

Hartog, F.

1988   The Mirror of Herodotus: The Representation of the Other in the Writing of History. Berkeley, University of California Press.

Herzog, R.

1967   Zur Frage der Kulturhohe und der Wirtschaftsform der Frühen Bedja. Paideuma 13: pp. 54–59.

Kirwan, L.

1937   Studies in the Later History of Nubia. Liverpool Annals of Archaeology and Anthropology 24: pp. 69–105.

Krall, J.

1900   Beiträge zur Geschichte der Blemyer und Nubier. In Denkschriften der Kaiserlichen Akademie der Wissenschaften: Philosophisch-Historische Klasse. Volume 47. Vienna, Kaiserlichen Akademie der Wissenschaften: pp. 1–26.

Lacovara, P.

2001   Pan-Grave People. In D. B. Redford (ed.), The Oxford Encyclopedia of Ancient Egypt. Volume 3. Oxford, Oxford University Press, pp. 20–22.

Mallory, J. P.

1989   In Search of the Indo-Europeans: Language, Archaeology, and Myth. London, Thames and Hudson.

Nash, D.

1976   Reconstructing Poseidonios' Celtic Ethnography: Some Considerations. Britannia 7: pp. 111–126.

Paul, A.

1954   A History of the Beja Tribes of the Sudan. Cambridge, Cambridge University Press.

Pierce, R. H.

2001   Past and Present in the Eastern Desert. In K. Krzywinski and R. H. Pierce, Deserting the Desert: A Threatened Cultural Landscape Between the Nile and the Sea. Larvik, Alvheim, and Eide Akademisk Forlag: pp. 143–169.

Plumley, J. M. and W. Y. Adams

1974   Qasr Ibrim, 1972. Journal of Egyptian Archaeology 60: pp. 212–278.

Rolfe, J. C.

1935–1939   Ammianus Marcellinus (3 volumes). Cambridge, Harvard University Press.

Shaw, B.

1982   Eaters of Flesh, Drinkers of Milk: The Ancient Mediterranean Ideology of the Pastoral Nomad. Ancient Society 13: pp. 5–31.

Sidebotham, S. E., H. M. Nouwens, A. M. Hense and J. A. Harrell

2004   Preliminary Report on Archaeological Fieldwork at Sikait (Eastern Desert of Egypt) and Environs: 2002–2003. Sahara 15: pp. 7–30.

Tierney, J.

1960   The Celtic Ethnography of Posidonius. In Proceedings of the Royal Irish Academy (section C) 60: pp. 189–275.

Török, L.

1987   Late Antique Nubia: Antaeus. Communicationes ex Instituto Archaeologico Academiae Scientiarum Hungaricae 16. Budapest, Archaeological Institute of the Hungarian Academy of Sciences.

Updegraff, R. T.

1978   A Study of the Blemmyes. Brandeis University (PhD dissertation).

Wells, P. S.

2001   Beyond Celts, Germans, and Scythians. London, Duckworth.

Welsby, D. A.

2002   The Medieval Kingdoms of Nubia: Pagans, Christians, and Muslims Along the Middle Nile. London, British Museum Press.

Wolf, E.

1982   Europe and the Peoples Without History. Berkeley, University of California Press.

Wolska-Conus, W. (ed.)

1968   Cosmas Indicopleustès: Topographie chrétienne. Tome 1. Paris, Les Éditions du Cerf.

Zhylarz, E.

1940–1941   Die Sprache der Blemmyer. Zeitschrift für Eingeborenen-Sprachen 31: pp. 1–21.

CHAPTER 12

IS ABSENCE OF EVIDENCE, EVIDENCE OF ABSENCE?

PROBLEMS IN THE ARCHAEOLOGY OF EARLY HERDING SOCIETIES OF SOUTHERN AFRICA

ANDREW B. SMITH

THE KHOEKHOEN (KNOWN to the world at large as 'Hottentots') became one of the earliest known 'primitive' people that existed beyond medieval Christendom. While the African "monstrous races" of Pliny (Friedman 1981) seem to have been based on real people, their fanciful descriptions made them more myth than reality. The Khoekhoen, by contrast, although probably within Pliny's category of 'anthropophages'(man-eaters), were people whose 'savage' cultural attributes could be (and were) described and repeated (plagiarized) ad nauseam in the travel literature (Raven-Hart 1967), from the early 15th century CE onward (Smith 1993a). They were initially seen to be closest to what human beings would have been like before the Christian 'original sin' (living in the Garden of Eden), as can be seen in the comparison between Albrecht Dürer's *Adam and Eve* and Hans Burgkmair's people living at the end of Africa (Figures 12.1 and 12.2). Perhaps this is not surprising, since Dürer and Burgkmair were members of the same artist's club in Augsburg, Germany (Smith and Pasche 1997). Later, like Rousseau, Denis Diderot questioned one of the more enlightened travelers among the Khoekhoen, Col. Robert Gordon, in The Hague in 1774 (Cullinan 1989) and used the information to support his ideas on the 'noble savages' in the Pacific. Cullinan (1989:150) shows that there is good evidence that Diderot, contrasting the colonial Dutch lifestyle with that of the Khoekhoen, said the Khoe dwell in "the happiness, innocence, and tranquility of a patriarchal life." The Khoekhoe press, unfortunately, was not able to sustain this mythical aura, and they became archetypical savages up to the 20th century, as the lowest level of humans in the 'Great Chain of Being' (Lovejoy 1942). Even the eminent anthropologist Alfred Kroeber, writing in the 1920s, used them as an example of the argument why no geniuses have shown up in 'primitive' society, whose cultural environment is 'atrophied and sterile,' noting that the extreme southwest of Africa "is in possession of the backward Bushmen and Hottentots" (Kroeber 1923:96).

Figure 12.1. *Adam and Eve* (engraving by Albrecht Dürer, 1504).

The early travel literature is full of descriptions of the large herds of animals owned by the Khoekhoen, and although they were initially eager to trade their stock for pieces of iron, by the beginning of the 17th century the market was so glutted that the Khoe began demanding more valuable metals, such as copper and brass. Sometimes they even refused to trade with the sailors, as seen in the complaint of John Jourdain in 1617:

> In the tyme of our beeinge in this roade wee could not get any refreshinge after the first daie, although the people came downe with great store of cattle and sheepe . . . The next daie after our arrival they brought downe above 5000 head of cattle . . . butt of these cattle they would not sell any unless wee would goe with our people to Cories [a Khoe who could speak English] house . . . when we were come to the toppe of the hill some four miles from the tents, we saw in the valley aboute 10,000 head of cattle (Raven-Hart 1967:87–88).

Even if the numbers were exaggerated, there were no doubt large herds in Khoe hands.

By contrast, the Khoekhoen, so well known in the historic literature, are virtually invisible in the archaeological record. No sites from the period after around 800 BP are recognizable as specifically 'herder' and, with the exception of 17th century CE Dutch colonial structures such as the castle at Cape Town and the redoubt at Oudepost (Schrire 1988), no site has produced large numbers of cattle bones. We can assume that many of the bones found associated with these fortified structures were from animals traded from the Khoe.

Small rockshelters inhabited by aboriginal people on the edge of the coastal plain were occupied during the colonial period. One such site, Voelvlei (Smith et al. 1991), which also yielded colonial artifacts, was probably not occupied by herders, since the cultural material would suggest they were hunters, although

Figure 12.2. Khoekhoe family at Algoa Bay (woodcut by Hans Burgkmair for Balthasar Springer's Journal *Die Merfart und Erfarung nuwer Schjffung und Wege*, published in 1508 in Munich).

one attribute of the herders, large ostrich eggshell beads, was found. This suggests separation, but contact, between hunters and herders even up to the colonial period (Smith 1998).

Extensive surveys for Khoe sites have been carried out, even in areas where they were recorded in the historic literature (Hart 1987), but none have been found. We have to accept that their archaeological 'invisibility' must be due to their mobility and transience across the landscape, as well as the fact that the coastal forelands are also where modern agriculture takes place. Deep plowing of the soil may have obscured signs of transient camps. This appears to have been less so when sheep were the economic base, although the sites are only found on the coast where marine shell makes them more visible (Smith 1987, 1993b; Sealy et al. 2004). A cattle-based economy and the needs of bulk grazers, particularly in a low-nutrient area like the Western Cape, must have meant the herds were probably constantly on the move, and little cultural residue was being left behind.

MATERIAL CULTURE AND ARCHAEOLOGICAL VISIBILITY

Even though the Khoekhoen were massively disrupted by colonial intrusion in the 17th and 18th centuries CE, a picture of their material culture can be gleaned from historic writings. The center of a woman's world was her hut, over which she had absolute control (Smith and Webley 2000). These huts were made from bent saplings, dug into the ground to form a structure across which were placed reed mats to form a dome shape. An encampment in the past would have consisted of a number of these huts laid out to form a ring, leaving an open space in the middle to keep the stock at night (Kolb 1719:Tab XIV, Figure 1, opposite p. 470; Smith 1992:Figure 8.6). Like most modern African pastoralists, the Khoekhoen were very concerned about their personal appearance. As can be seen from the Khoekhoen depicted in Figure 12.3, probably drawn at the end of the 17th century CE, women would have spent a great deal of their time making personal decorative items, which is why copper and brass became so popular as trade items in the 17th century CE.

Robertshaw (1978) was first to recognize that modern Nama (a group of Khoekhoen) camps along the Orange River (the northern border of South Africa with Namibia) were so ephemeral that they quickly leave no trace once they are abandoned. He describes one such encampment at Sendeling's Drift:

> Though the site was occupied within the last twenty years, the position of the dwelling hut or huts could only be estimated from the small amount of wood or matting that remained. As this will undoubtedly perish within a few years no trace

of any huts will survive for future archaeologists to excavate. The hut(s) also leave no post-holes or other features in the ground. A similar situation exists for the kraal in which livestock were kept. Once the perimeter fence has gone and the dung within it decayed nothing will remain (Robertshaw 1978:29).

Figure 12.3. Khoekhoe women interacting with colonists at the Cape. Unknown artist, probably drawn at the end of the 17th century CE (Smith and Pheiffer 1993).

More recent work along the river (Webley 1997; Smith et al. 2001) showed that when stone tools were still being used, herder sites could be identified. In part this was due to massive amounts of silt covering the sites, before flood-control dams were built along the river, and subsequent erosion of the terraces. Once stone cutting tools were replaced by metal ones, the preponderance of wood for making bowls and herding equipment (as well as leather for bags, dress, etc.) all compounded the problem of survival of material culture in the archaeological record. This is exemplified by the Khoekhoe exhibit in the Ethnographic Gallery of the South African Museum, Cape Town, which has only a handful of items surviving from the long history of these people. By the middle of the 18th century CE the Khoekhoen as independent herders were becoming very sparse, and only a few material culture objects of known Khoe manufacture from then have survived in European museums (Rudner and Rudner 1957).

From an archaeological perspective we can assume ceramics would play an important role in identifying Khoe sites. Indeed, when sites of herders can be found during the sheep period, such as at Kasteelberg, there are large numbers of sherds. Away from these coastal areas, however, the distribution of sherds is meager, possibly a result of the more intense use of coastal sites, with the attraction of marine resources (Smith 1993b), but also because of the constant movement across a landscape that today is the main agricultural area of the Cape.

THE EARLIEST HERDERS IN SOUTHERN AFRICA

Having noted the case for the problem of visibility of pastoralists at the Cape, we can turn our attention to a similar problem, that of identifying the earliest food producers in southern Africa. It used to be assumed that the first domestic animals were introduced by incoming Iron Age farmers from the north (Smith 1990a, 1990b). It is now clear, however, that sheep bones found in association with cultural material that indicates aboriginal hunters of the Western Cape predate the arrival of the Iron Age farmers by possibly several centuries. Sites such as Spoegrivier Cave (Webley 2001), Blombos Cave (Henshilwood 1996), Die Kelders Cave (Schweitzer 1979), and Kasteelberg G, an open site (Sadr et al. 2003), all have dates between 2000 and 1900 BP for sheep bones and pottery. The question is: "Were these mostly small cave sites occupied by herders?" Sadr (2003), taking the most parsimonious line with the available archaeological data of sheep bones associated with cultural material that would identify aboriginal hunters (Smith et al. 1991), would say that these were hunters independently becoming shepherds and were thus the earliest food producers at the Cape. But what if the scenario posed above with the later historical Khoekhoen pertained at this early period as well, and there were herders living on open sites who moved across the landscape leaving little archaeological residue, but in turn were the donors of sheep to the hunters? Sadr does not address how the sheep in the caves came to the Cape. He argues that diffusion of stock could have occurred and interprets the advent of small stock in rockshelters in Botswana to support his case (Sadr and Plug 2001). Diffusion among the hunters could have occurred via internal exchange mechanisms, such as *hxaro* (Wiessner 1994) seen among the Ju/'hoansi Bushmen today.

Prior to the advent of food production in southern Africa the entire subcontinent was occupied by hunter-gatherers. These Later Stone Age hunters were part of a hunting lifestyle trajectory that began more than 20,000 years ago. It is into this population that food producers first introduced domestic sheep, and some of these hunter-gatherers at least made the transition to become food producers themselves and became the Khoekhoen. In spite of the fact that all the aboriginal people of southern Africa appear to form a unique biological population, there are three distinct Khoisan languages. All are 'click-based,' but are mutually unintelligible, which suggests a long period of separation. Today these are found among the best known Ju/'hoansi (or !Kung speakers) in the Kalahari and southern Angola, among the few remnants of Cape Bushmen descendants who still remember the language (the !Ui-Taa), and among Khoe speakers in Botswana (where the Khoekhoen existed historically).

Linguistic data suggest that the words for 'ram,' 'milk ewe,' and 'young ram' are loan words only into Khoe languages. According to Ehret (1998) these came via a putative donor East Sahelian language from the north (Ehret 1998), who might be best represented archaeologically by Bambata, a ceramic cultural entity identified in southern Zambia and Zimbabwe. It is unclear exactly what this tradition is, or how it fits with the Early Iron Age, although there appears to be little doubt of its affinity (Huffman 1994). Our 'invisibility' problem may also be at play here. The best evidence for pastoral activity in East Africa comes from Ngamuriak, in Kenya, close to the border with Tanzania (Robertshaw 1978). This site has minimally decorated ceramics with spouts. Pastoral people are often less concerned with decoration on their vessels than agriculturalists, who imbue their pots with symbolic significance (David et al. 1988; Hall 1998). Hodder (1991) has shown how calabash decoration among East African pastoral groups is often more for personal identification than for group symbolism, although certain statements might be made when decoration is used, such as young men and women opposing elder hegemony among the Il Chamus, or possibly resisting male control among the Khoekhoen (Smith and Webley 2000).

The artificial colonial boundary that is the modern state frontier between Kenya and Tanzania would not have inhibited pastoral movement in the past, but we know much less about the archaeology of pastoral societies in Tanzania and Zambia, so any possible southward expansion may have been masked by research into the more dominant, ceramic-rich, Iron Age farming occupations of these countries. One might postulate that small groups of herders colonizing new areas would have been even less likely to leave significant archaeological residues; thus our 'invisibility' scenario may mean this is why we do not see the archaeological contacts between pastoral groups in eastern and southern Africa.

Alternatively, if Bambata is indeed an Iron Age entity, perhaps it is to agrarian societies arriving in southern Zambia and Zimbabwe that we have to look for the donor society. Regardless of the donor, the existence of a tsetse-free corridor from East Africa (Figure 12.4) would have facilitated the southward movement of domestic stock.

Morris (1992) has analyzed skeletal material from both hunting-gathering and farming contexts and has found no Khoisan individuals north of the Zambezi. This may be partially because of the limited number of skeletons available, but it could well mean that the domestic animals had to come to the Khoisan along the Zambezi and into the Caprivi with pastoral groups from the north. Thus, the initial entry would have been from outside groups.

There is no archaeological information to tell us what happened then. The closest we can come is from the distribution of ripple-rim ceramics, which occur across a large area of southern Africa, from northern Namibia to the Limpopo Province of South Africa (Figure 12.4). These are from small,

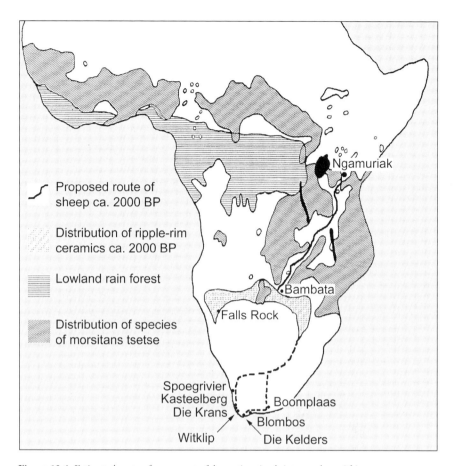

Figure 12.4. Estimated route of movement of domestic animals into southern Africa.

well-made vessels but consist of only a handful of sherds (Smith and Jacobson 1995), and we are unsure how they fit with the Bambata ceramics. We are also not sure if their distribution was the result of spread by Khoe-speakers who took on the package of sheep and pottery and who subsequently spread through the river systems of the Vaal/Orange drainages, ultimately arriving in the Western Cape. Who were these first herders? Is it possible that we have a 'bow-wave' of small numbers of Khoe-speaking herders bringing their stock to the Cape and being the donors of the animals found in the caves?

As an alternative, Sadr (2003) would like to see the local hunters becoming 'Neolithic' food producers independent of Khoe speakers. He uses the open site of Kasteelberg G, which is occupied before and after the appearance of sheep and ceramics around 2000 BP, to support his thesis (Sadr et al. 2003). This pattern is repeated at Witklip Cave, where there is no change in the material culture across the food-production divide (Smith et al. 1991). The beads from the cave sites continue to be small (>5 mm) before and after the appearance of sheep bones (Smith 1998). The small number of sherds (10/ m³), and the fact that none of the rim-sherds can refit, suggests they might be coming in from other groups.

Archaeologically recognizable herding groups with substantial numbers of sheep are visible at Kasteelberg A site by at least 1630 BP (Sealy and Yates 1994) and possibly as early as 1860 BP (Smith 1987). The ostrich eggshell beads from these herder sites are large (<5 mm), and, since they appear abruptly, we might infer that they came via immigrant groups.

THEORIES OF COLONIZATION

The spread of food production and Neolithic farming techniques has been the subject of great debate. Previous assumptions were that farming groups spread out of the Near East and swamped Mesolithic communities in Europe (Piggot 1965). This was seen as an incremental intrusion and colonization by migrants. More recent work has suggested that local Mesolithic hunters adopted farming themselves and transformed the social landscape (Gronenborn 2003). We thus have several models of diffusion or independent adoption of food production. The latter gives credit to indigenes who are capable of adopting new economic ideas and changing their lifestyle. We also have to accept that ideas and commodities do not travel in a vacuum, however, so the people involved may also be spreading and interacting with indigenes. The degree to which incorporation, or not, takes place may depend on competition for resources. Alexander (1984) has suggested that colonization takes place in two steps: *a movable frontier* where small groups of immigrants, initially acceptable to local people, move into new territory (in the case of expansion of early food production this would mean entering areas already occupied by hunter-gatherers); *a static frontier* where the immigrants consolidate their position in the landscape and start to dominate the indigenes (by this time all the best land is being used, and boundaries inhibiting further expansion have been reached; more marginal lands will be progressively occupied, particularly by people being pushed to the periphery of the more dominant society).

This model seemed to conveniently fit the expansion of Europeans into the American West and the subjugation of the Native Americans by a combination of firepower and merchant capital (Turner 1920), although Mikesell (1960) showed how contentious these ideas became and discussed frontiers of assimilation and exclusion. How relevant might the model be for southern Africa? The model of exclusion might fit the expansion of Europeans out of the original settlement at the Cape in the 17th and 18th centuries CE, where, like America, racial attitudes on the part of Europeans kept the cultural groups apart (except for the initial window when there were few European women either on the American or South African frontiers and men would take local or slave wives). In South Africa the power of the church quickly closed ranks against interracial marriages, and a society developed along both class and race lines.

By contrast, polygynous Iron Age farmers have always been quite content to take wives from hunter societies, so there was a far greater potential for integration and assimilation between colonist and indigene, although hypergyny (one-way gene flow) was almost always the result (Morris 1992). Few hunters could have amassed the number of cattle needed for bride-wealth payments to secure farmer wives. There seems to be little doubt that Iron Age farmers had arrived in southern Africa by 1800 years ago, although their initial impact was not very significant along the eastern seaboard of Mozambique and South Africa. Once the central highland was occupied, 1500 years ago, this appears to have been much more intrusive.

Resistance against Bantu-speaking farmers by indigenous hunters certainly took place once the farmers were established (Guenther 1997), but it would seem that most hunters may have been relatively easily subsumed into farming societies elsewhere. This does not explain how domestic sheep and pottery arrived as far as the Cape before Iron Age farmers were in South Africa. There may have been a domino effect, with East Sahelian pastoralists being pushed ahead of expanding farmers out of eastern Africa and local Khoe-speaking hunters being the first Khoisan groups to meet these herders in and around the Caprivi Strip. If they took on sheepherding themselves, this raises the question of how and why this took place. It is in this region that Khoe-speaking groups seem to have established their dominance of the river systems (Cashdan 1986), and such a well-watered, tsetse-free environment would have been conducive to pastoral expansion. The East Sahelian herders could perhaps be seen as a 'bow-wave' of expanding food-producing populations out of East Africa, which was increasingly becoming very diverse in the mixture of different economies. The archaeological problem of identifying the first pastoralists would come from the small size of these initial groups, combined with mobility and the necessary light, portable material culture made from organic materials. Pottery might be the only easily identifiable indicator, and, as suggested above, may not have been particularly heavily decorated and thus easily ignored in archaeological surveys (but see Barnard, this volume). The ceramics that seem to have the strongest association with the earliest pastoralists are usually small, thin-walled vessels (10 cm in height), possibly used for sheep milking, which break up into tiny pieces, making them even more difficult to find on small open sites.

THE TRANSITION TO HERDING

The transition from hunters becoming independent herders, as opposed to hunters becoming encapsulated and subsumed into food producing societies, may depend on a number of factors. Hunters, generally, have a problem competing as equals with food producers (Smith 1998). This does not mean they cannot live separately and maintain their hunting/foraging lifestyle, but this can depend on the hunters having a 'bolt hole': a place they can retreat to out of the way of food producers. The arguments around how and why this might have occurred among Kalahari foragers became very heated in the 1990s and was generally known as 'The Great Kalahari Debate.'

Ranged on one side were researchers who had studied the Kalahari Bushmen (Ju/'hoansi) before massive impact from the outside world (Lee and DeVore 1976; Marshall 1976; Howell 1979; Lee 1979). On the other side were those who, following Wolf (1982), believed that the Ju/'hoansi were a proletariat, whose present condition was part of worldwide colonial expansion and impoverishment of traditional peoples, and that they had been under the hegemony of wider polities since Iron Age times (Wilmsen 1989).

There is no question that many Bushmen were indeed encapsulated by Iron Age people, and once European traders and hunters were involved in the ivory and skin trade, firearms changed the political world forever. The Ju/'hoansi of Nyae Nyae (Marshall 1976) appear only to have been minimally affected by all of these events. The oral traditions suggest black people arrived in Nyae Nyae for the first time as refugees as a result of German genocide against the Herero and as herders in the 1940s (Lee 2002). European traders avoided Nyae Nyae, as it was easier to move around the area (Lee and Guenther 1993). Any contact with the outside by Ju/'hoansi seems to have been on their terms (Lee 2002), and archaeological work in this part of the Kalahari indicates a minimal amount of material culture penetrating from outside (Smith and Lee 1997; Smith 2001).

The archaeological indicators of encapsulation of Bushmen by Iron Age people are clearly stated by Sadr (2002:44), who says that paucity of traditional and prevalence of foreign remains are the clues. These materials include low numbers of stone tools and high numbers of ceramics coming from the more dominant society, as well as shifts in the frequencies of ostrich eggshell and glass beads and metal. Sadr also states that there are clear distinctions between ex-hunters living on the edge of farming communities and those still living in the 'bush.'

Although the Kalahari debate highlighted diverse opinions on the status of modern hunters in southern Africa, it would appear from these studies that it is possible to separate out independent hunters from food producers, the former becoming subsumed into food-producing societies in the archaeological record.

Each of the economic groups had different settlement patterns, which make archaeological visibility variable. Farmers, whose attachment to the land allows accumulation of material goods, particularly ceramics, may be quite dominant in the landscape. Herders, by virtue of their mobility, are really only visible when they repeatedly re-occupy a site, and this is often for reasons other than their pastoral activities, such as fishing or exploitation of marine resources. Hunters are also mobile, but rockshelters are attractive to small groups, and this increases their archaeological visibility.

DISCUSSION

The relations between aboriginal hunters and incoming food producers from the north would appear to have been variable. Some hunters retained their foraging lifestyle, while others took on sheep herding. Still others were subsumed into farming societies.

The archaeological problems of the first herders to southern Africa would appear to stem from a combination of high mobility and small populations, either of people or sheep, entering the region. Since we can make linguistic connections between potential donors of domestic animals outside southern Africa and Khoe speakers, they make the most sense as immigrants to the Cape, as they are ultimately recognizable as the historic Khoekhoen. The questions are: "When did they arrive? Were they the initial donors of stock and ceramics to the cave occupants 2000 years ago, did they arrive when the first herding sites with large numbers of sheep can be seen (around 1800–1600 BP), or did they only appear when large numbers of cattle were introduced to the Cape (sometime after 900 BP)?" To be really contentious, since there is no archaeological evidence for the historic Khoekhoen, Sadr has even suggested that perhaps they only came to the fore once there was a market for the animals when Europeans arrived in increasing numbers after the 16th century CE.

REFERENCES

Alexander, J. A.
1984   The End of the Moving Frontier in the Neolithic of North-Eastern Africa. In
        L. Krzyzaniak and M. Kobusiewicz (eds.), *Origin and Early Development of Food-
        Producing Cultures in North-Eastern Africa*. Poznan, Poznan Archaeological
        Museum: pp. 57–63.
Cashdan, E. A.
1986   Competition Between Foragers and Food-Producers on the Botletli River,
        Botswana. *Africa 56*: 3, pp. 299–318.

Cullinan, P.

1989   Robert Jacob Gordon and Denis Diderot: The Hague, 1774. *Quarterly Bulletin of the South African Library 43*: 4, p. 146.

David, N., J. Sterner and K. Gavua

1988   Why Pots Are Decorated. *Current Anthropology 29*: 3, pp. 365–389.

Ehret, C.

1998   *An African Classical Age: Eastern and Southern Africa in World History, 1000 BC to AD 400*. Oxford, James Currey.

Friedman, J. B.

1981   *The Monstrous Races in Medieval Art and Thought*. Cambridge, Harvard University Press.

Gronenborn, D.

2003   Migration, Acculturation, and Culture Change in Western Temperate Eurasia, 6500–5000 cal BC. In M. Budja (ed.), *10th Neolithic Studies: Documenta Praehistorica 30*. Univerza v Ljubljani, Oddelek za Arheologia: pp. 79–91.

Guenther, M.

1997   Lords of the Desert Land: Politics and Resistance of the Ghanzi Basarwa of the Nineteenth Century. *Botswana Notes and Records 29*: pp. 121–141.

Hall, S. L.

1998   A Consideration of Gender Relations in the Late Iron Age "Sotho" Sequence of the Western Highveld, South Africa. In S. Kent (ed.), *Gender in African Prehistory*. Walnut Creek, AltaMira Press: pp. 235–258.

Hart, T.

1987   Portervill Survey. In J. Parkington and M. Hall (eds.), *Papers in the Prehistory of the Western Cape, South Africa. BAR International Series 332*. Oxford, Archaeopress: pp. 403–423.

Henshilwood, C.

1996   A Revised Chronology for Pastoralism in Southernmost Africa: New Evidence of Sheep at c. 2000 b.p. from Blombos Cave, South Africa. *Antiquity 70*: pp. 945–949.

Hodder, I.

1991   The Decoration of Containers: An Ethnographic and Historical Study. In W. A. Longacre (ed.), *Ceramic Archaeology*. Tucson, University of Arizona Press: pp. 71–94.

Howell, N.

1979   *Demography of the Dobe !Kung*. New York, Academic Press.

Huffman, T. N.

1994   Toteng Pottery and the Origins of Bambata. *Southern African Field Archaeology 3*: pp. 3–9.

Kolb, P.

1719   *Caput bonae spei hodiernum*. Nürnburg, Peter Conrad Monath.

Kroeber, A. L.

1923   *Anthropology*. London, Harrap.

Lee, R. B.

1979   *The !Kung San*. Cambridge, Cambridge University Press.

2002   Solitude or Servitude? Ju/'hoansi Images of the Colonial Encounter. In S. Kent (ed.), *Ethnicity, Hunter-Gatherers, and the "Other."* Washington, Smithsonian Institution Press: pp. 184–205.

Lee, R. B. and I. DeVore

1976   *Kalahari Hunter-Gatherers*. Cambridge, Harvard University Press.

Lee, R. B. and M. Guenther

1993   Problems in Kalahari Historical Ethnography and the Tolerance of Error. *History in Africa 20*: pp. 185–235.

Lovejoy, A.

1942   *The Great Chain of Being*. Cambridge, Harvard University Press.

Marshall, L.

1976   *The !Kung of Nyae Nyae*. Cambridge, Harvard University Press.

Mikesell, M.

1960   Comparative Studies in Frontier History. *Annals of the Association of American Geographers 50*: pp. 62–74.

Morris, A. G.

1992   *The Skeletons of Contact*. Johannesburg, Witwatersrand University Press.

Piggot, S.

1965   *Ancient Europe*. Chicago, Aldine.

Raven-Hart, R.

1967   *Before van Riebeeck*. Cape Town, Struik.

Robertshaw, P. T.

1978   The Archaeology of an Abandoned Pastoralist Camp-Site. *South African Journal of Science 74*: pp. 29–31.

Rudner, I. and J. Rudner

1957   A. Sparrman's Ethnographic Collection from South Africa: Stockholm: Statens Etnografiska Museum.' *Smärre Meddelanden 25*: pp. 5–28.

Sadr, K.

2002   Encapsulated Bushmen in the Archaeology of Thamaga. In S. Kent (ed.), *Ethnicity, Hunter-Gatherers, and the "Other."* Washington, Smithsonian Institution Press: pp. 28–47.

2003   The Neolithic of Southern Africa. *Journal of African History 44*: pp. 195–209.

Sadr, K. and I. Plug

2001   Faunal Remains in the Transition from Hunting to Herding in Southeastern Botswana. *South African Archaeological Bulletin 56*: pp. 76–82.

Sadr, K., A. B. Smith and I. Plug

2003   Herders and Foragers on Kasteelberg. *South African Archaeological Bulletin 58*: pp. 27–32.

Schrire, C.

1988.   The Historical Archaeology of the Impact of Colonialism in 17th-Century South Africa. *Antiquity 62*: pp. 214–225.

Schweitzer, F. R.

1979   Excavations at Die Kelders, Cape Province, South Africa: The Holocene Deposits. *Annals of the South African Museum 78*: pp. 101–233.

Sealy, J., T. Maggs, A. Jerardino and J. Kaplan

2004   Excavations at Melkbosstrand: Variability Among Herder Sites on Table Bay, South Africa. *South African Archaeological Bulletin 59*: pp. 17–28.

Sealy, J. and R. Yates

1994   The Chronology of the Introduction of Pastoralism to the Cape, South Africa. *Antiquity 68*: pp. 58–67.

Smith, A. B.

1987   Seasonal Exploitation of Resources on the Vredenburg Peninsula After 2000 BP. In J. Parkington and M. Hall (eds.), *Papers in the Prehistory of the Western Cape, South Africa. BAR International Series 332*. Oxford, Archaeopress: pp. 393–402.

1990a   On Becoming Herders: Khoikhoi and San Ethnicity in Southern Africa. *African Studies 49*: 2, pp. 51–73.

1990b   *Pastoralism in Africa*. London, Hurst.

1993a   Different Facets of the Crystal: Early European Images of the Khoikhoi at the Cape, South Africa. In M. Hall and A. Markell (eds.), *Historical Archaeology in the Western Cape. Goodwin Series 7*. Cape Town, South African Archaeological Society: pp. 8–20.

1993b   Exploitation of Marine Mammals by Prehistoric Cape Herders. *South African Journal of Science 89*: pp. 162–165.

1998   Keeping People on the Periphery: The Ideology of Social Hierarchies Between Hunters and Herders. *Journal of Anthropological Archaeology 17*: 2, pp. 201–215.

2001   Ethnohistory and Archaeology of the Ju/'hoansi Bushmen. *African Study Monographs*: Supplement 26, pp. 15–25.

Smith, A. B., D. Halkett, T. Hart and B Mütti

2001   Spatial Patterning, Cultural Identity, and Site Integrity on Open Sites: Evidence from Bloeddrift 23, a Pre-Colonial Herder Camp in the Richtersveld, Northern Cape Province, South Africa. *South African Archaeological Bulletin 56*: pp. 23–33.

Smith, A. B. and L. Jacobson

1995   Excavations at Geduld and the Appearance of Early Domestic Stock in Namibia. *South African Archaeological Bulletin 50*: pp. 3–14.

Smith, A. B. and R. B. Lee

1997   Cho/ana: Archaeological and Ethnohistorical Evidence for Recent Hunter-Gatherer/Agro-Pastoral Contact in Northern Bushmanland. *South African Archaeological Bulletin 52*: pp. 52–58.

Smith, A. B. and W. E. Pasche

1997   Balthasar Springer at the Cape (1506). *Quarterly Bulletin of the South African Library 51*: 3, pp. 93–98.

Smith, A. B. and R. H. Pheiffer

1993   *The Khoikhoi at the Cape of Good Hope: Seventeenth-Century Drawings in the South African Library*. Cape Town, South African Library.

Smith, A. B., K. Sadr, J. Gribble and R. Yates

1991   Excavations in the South-Western Cape, South Africa, and the Archaeological Identity of Prehistoric Hunter-Gatherers Within the Last 2000 Years. *South African Archaeological Bulletin 46*: pp. 71–91.

Smith, A. B. and L. Webley

2000   Men and Women of the Khoekhoen of Southern Africa. In D. L. Hodgson (ed.), *Rethinking Pastoralism in Africa*. London, James Currey: pp. 72–96.

Turner, F. J.

1920   *The Frontier in American History*. New York, Henry Holt.

Webley, L.

1997   Jakkalsberg A and B: The Cultural Material from Two Pastoralist Sites in the Richtersveld, Northern Cape. *Southern African Field Archaeology 6*: 1, pp. 3–19.

2001   The Re-excavation of Spoegrivier Cave on the West Coast of Southern Africa. *Annals of Eastern Cape Museums 2*: pp. 19–49.

Wiessner, P.

1994   The Pathways of the Past: !Kung San Hxaro Exchange and History. In M. Bollig and F. Kees (eds.), *Überlebens-strategien in Afrika*. Köln, Heinrich Barth Institut: pp. 101–124.

Wilmsen, E. N.

1989   *Land Filled with Flies*. Chicago, University of Chicago Press.

Wolf, E.

1982   *Europe and the People Without History*. Berkeley, University of California Press.

CHAPTER 13

THE SOCIAL AND ENVIRONMENTAL CONSTRAINTS ON MOBILITY IN THE LATE PREHISTORIC UPPER GREAT LAKES REGION

MARGARET B. HOLMAN AND WILLIAM A. LOVIS[1]

TO BETTER UNDERSTAND the archaeology of late prehistoric mobility in the Great Lakes region of the United States, theoretical concepts of mobility in small-scale societies are used to frame analogies derived from the ethnohistoric record. Despite disruptions associated with European contact, ethnohistoric observations remain relevant for examining late prehistoric mobility. This relevance is a consequence of relative stability in the structure of the environment and the use of seasonal resources across the contact period boundary, which in turn allows the development of analogue models. Local constraints on mobility were highly variable: some territories were essentially filled to capacity with hunter-gatherers, some societies had regular and sustained contact with settled horticulturalists, and all were compelled to respond to the fur trade and consequent interactions with Euro-American settlers. We demonstrate concordance between the late prehistoric archaeological record and ethnohistorically documented flexibility in mobility strategies and integrating social mechanisms that acted to buffer environmental variability.

All of the ethnographically documented native people resident in Michigan during the early years of direct and consistent European contact, around 1650 CE, were mobile to some degree, even after the late adoption of horticulture. Groups regularly moved to obtain seasonally available foods and

---

[1.] Dr. Margaret B. Holman fell victim to pancreatic cancer before the publication of this volume, a synthesis about which she was tremendously excited from its inception as a Cotsen Advanced Seminar. I regret that she is not able to appreciate the publication of our chapter, for which she is largely responsible. I know she would be proud and humbled by the dedication of this volume to her memory, and as her friend, colleague and co-author I am deeply grateful for this kindness.

other resources that were unevenly distributed across the landscape. Some incorporated crops into their subsistence cycle, whereas others grew very little food, if any at all. Mobility patterns depended on the distribution of resources sought and the social constraints on regularly exploited territories. Variations included seasonal aggregation and dispersal of related households, and some degree of sedentation, combined with task-specific logisttic mobility. The Late Woodland peoples (650–1650 CE), immediately preceding European contact, were likewise seasonally mobile and used strategies similar to those seen among historically known groups.

To understand changes in mobility patterns around the Straits of Mackinac and the northern lower peninsula of Michigan (Figure 13.1), we use the established triad of ethnographic analogy, documentary evidence and archaeology. The observed changes that occurred over a millennium range from responses to the use of all available territories by hunter-gatherers, to contact with settled horticulturalists, to disruptions related to the European fur trade, to interactions with American settlers. Thus, we have an opportunity to continually refine our understanding of how mobility in this area was a way of life used to solve problems similar to those faced by nomadic, or mobile, people in other parts of the world.

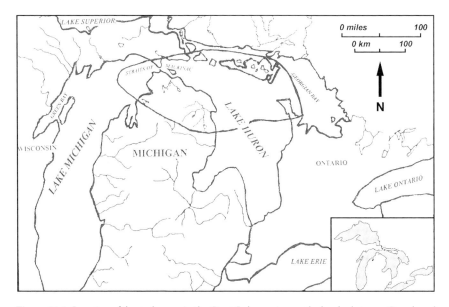

Figure 13.1. Location of the study area, in the Great Lakes region on the border between Canada and the United States.

THEORETICAL FRAMEWORK

We understand mobility as a means by which relatively egalitarian societies secure subsistence when food and other resources are spatially and seasonally separated. Such mobility may be characteristic of people who live entirely on wild foods (hunters, gatherers, fishers) or people who combine hunting, gathering or fishing with horticulture. Movement as part of these kinds of subsistence-settlement systems is through a territory that provides resources throughout an annual cycle. Territories are occupied and 'controlled' by groups whose members usually are extended families related on the basis of primary kinship ties. Territories supplying the subsistence needs of one group may overlap those of other groups (Williams 1968:129; Cleland 1992a:101), suggesting fluid boundary maintenance, and there may be neutral zones available for exploitation by more than one group (Pilling 1968:155).

Mobility may be residential or logistic, or, recognizing that these are extremes of a continuum, a combination of the two (Binford 1980). Residential mobility involves movement of entire households, or groups, to locations where a variety of resources can be obtained nearby and brought back to a base camp for processing. Residential mobility pools the labor of different genders and ages at a single location, where they procure and process food, manufacture tools, construct shelters, make clothing and undertake other tasks. Thus, several needs may be met at the same time and place. Logistic mobility operates in situations where important resources are separated from one another spatially or temporally (Binford 1980:5–10). In such situations one or a few members of a group will move to secure a specific resource to be brought back to the residential base. Task groups, such as hunting parties, may travel considerable distances and be away for extended periods of time before returning with meat and hides that can be processed at the residential location. Binford (1980:14) emphasizes that the structure of the environment—that is, how resources are distributed within it—is critical as to which type of mobility is most likely to characterize the patterning of a group's movements. We take the position that, along with environmental structure, social constraints on the use of territory affect mobility strategies. Emphasis on residential or logistic mobility varied over time within our study area, even though the distribution of wild resources remained constant, as did the potential for growing crops in certain locations. There is evidence for fluctuations in climate, but the structure of these resources within the environment did not change markedly. As the potential for food failure is ever present, mobile people may buffer risk by interacting with their neighbors (Spielmann 1986:280-281; O'Shea and Halstead 1989:124). Co-operative social interactions are important to hunter-gatherers when their normally exploited territory does not supply sufficient food in a given year.

The option of residential movement into adjacent territories, occupied or controlled by other people, is facilitated by good relationships, as is the sharing of overlapping territories. Social constraints and interactions also condition mobility when critical resources are produced or controlled by disparate groups (Spielmann 1986:288–290). Mobility under these circumstances tends to be logistic for purposes of exchange or conflict.

ETHNOGRAPHIC ANALOGY AND LATE PREHISTORIC MOBILITY

The predominant residents of Michigan at the time of contact were three related Algonquian-speaking groups: the Potawatomi in the south, the Chippewa in the north, and the Ottawa, who lived between the other two (Figure 13.2). Each occupied an environment that differed in its configuration from the others, and each employed mobility as part of economic and social strategies that were adaptive to the local environment. Since use of the "direct historical approach" (Strong 1935, 1936; Wedel 1938) is rarely possible, it is these adaptive patterns that form the basis for our inquiries into the mobile lifestyle of prehistoric Late Woodland peoples in the same region (Fitting and Cleland 1969). Our intent here is not to provide a comprehensive overview of the uses of ethnographic analogy in archaeology but rather to historically contextualize its use as a vehicle for explaining late prehistoric mobility within our study region of the upper Great Lakes, particularly Michigan.

As noted, use of a direct historical approach has not been a productive vehicle for such regional explanation, as we cannot normally associate artifacts, or artifact styles, found at a site occupied by a historically documented group with similar artifacts used by their precontact ancestors. We cannot even be confident that these groups, whose initial contact was with the French, were the same Late Woodland peoples who lived in Michigan just prior to contact, early in the 17th century CE (Kinietz 1965:v; Clifton 1984:1). By their own oral traditions the three groups arrived in the region near the end of the Late Woodland period, around 1500 CE. The gap between historically known groups and Late Woodland peoples is attributable to several factors. Continuity and change are apparent in Late Woodland archaeology, but beginning with the arrival of Europeans, the different cultures cease to be archaeologically 'visible' (Cleland 1992b:29). Native Americans adopted European manufactured goods quite quickly. For example, stylistically sensitive pottery was largely discarded in favor of metal kettles (McClurken 1988:8). There was also such widespread disruption and displacement of peoples that pottery known to have been made by a particular group might be found at a site reported to have been occupied by a different group entirely (Fitting 1975).

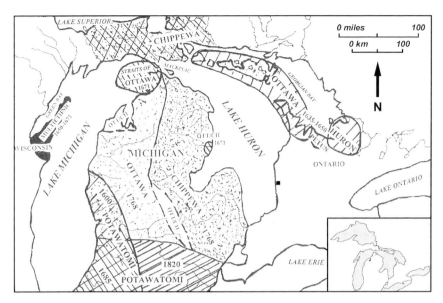

Figure 13.2. Locations of Native American people in the Great Lakes region during the Historic Period (note overlapping and shared territories).

The major disturbances creating such confusion in the Great Lakes archaeological record were one consequence of the warfare between different Native American groups who were competitors in the fur trade (Tanner 1987:1–4). They were variously allied with the French or the British, who themselves were vying with one another for control of the trade. At times, whole areas of the region, including western Ontario and the lower Michigan peninsula, were depopulated, while other areas, such as northeastern Wisconsin, were filled with refugees of differing tribal or ethnic affiliations. The situation is further complicated by the fact that, as a result of this disruption, some groups combined with others in temporary communities, and some formed new multi-ethnic corporate groups. Some populations were so decimated by European diseases, and other consequences of contact, that their sites cannot be identified (Mason 1988:66–67).

The fashion in which Michigan archaeologists have used ethnohistoric accounts to address late prehistoric mobility, particularly on a seasonal basis, owes itself in large part to the now forty-year-old work of G. I. Quimby. In a major chapter of his book *Indian Culture and European Trade Goods*, Quimby (1966) employed the 18th century CE narratives of Alexander Henry, specifically with citations to Henry, to Bain's 1901 editing of Henry (reprinted in 1969), and to Quaife's (1921) annotations of the same narrative. Henry traveled with the Wawatam family of Chippewa for a year, in 1763–1764, and Quimby used the accounts of their travels to both interpret and provide insights into the archaeological signatures that one might expect, including notions of seasonal mobility, technology and resource use. Coupled with other postcontact narratives, such as that of John Tanner (1956) and James Smith (1907), archaeologists refined and developed models that closely reflected their origins in Quimby's original work, situated them in an ecological framework, and applied them to the precontact, late prehistoric past (Fitting and Cleland 1969; Fitting 1975; Holman and Krist 2001, among others).

Deviations from the fundamental model were minor, relatively rare, and incorporated similar elements; there was almost always winter season fission into smaller social units that exploited the interior of Michigan's two peninsulas. In the north, where horticulture was less common and fishing more prominent, seasonal aggregation was primarily during periods of peak fish abundance, spring and late fall; in the south, where horticulture was dominant, general warm season aggregation took primacy. In both cases group territories were viewed as spanning both coastal and interior resource zones, with no independent social or ethnic groups resident in either one or the other and with seasonal movement between zones. In truth, adherence to such derivative models actually explained much, but not all, of what was being observed in late prehistoric context.

Changes in the archaeological view of these more traditional ethnographic analogs have come in the form of altered perspectives on the scale of archaeological inquiry, as well as the role of symbiotic ritual and exchange relationships in fostering more formalized intergroup interactions (Milner and O'Shea 1998; O'Shea and Milner 2002; Howey and O'Shea 2006). While such approaches have not necessarily diminished the ecological perspective that has dominated late-period research, they have nonetheless called into question strict adherence to the primacy of ethnohistoric documents, particularly given the temporal disjunction of more than a century between the arrival of Europeans and the documents on which the models are based (O'Shea 2004). This has given rise in lower Michigan to a competing model of symbiotically interactive coastal horticulturalists and interior foragers, each with relatively separate social territories (O'Shea 2003). These new perspectives, too, have explanatory merit and provide an additional dimension to the approach we take here.

Despite the difficulties caused by confusing archaeological remains and written documents of varying utility, Michigan archaeologists have effectively combined both sources of information to address questions of mobility and changes in mobility strategies over time. These investigations have been productive, in part, because Late Woodland peoples were associated with the same broad environmental zones as the historically documented groups, coped with similar environmental uncertainties, and had similar decentralized social organizations (Quimby 1966:179; Cleland 1992a:97; Holman and Krist

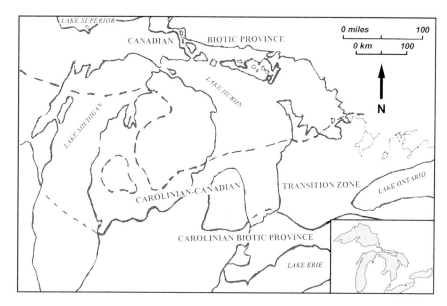

Figure 13.3. Regional environmental zones in the study area.

2001:20). Thus, the patterning of the adaptive strategies employed by the Potawatomi, the Ottawa and the Chippewa in their respective environmental zones have served as a framework guiding archaeological research focused on Late Woodland settlement (Fitting and Cleland 1969:292). But only the patterns of adaptation exhibited by these groups have been traced back into prehistory, not the groups themselves.

THE ENVIRONMENT OF THE STUDY AREA

The Straits of Mackinac and the northern lower peninsula of Michigan are particularly useful for understanding mobility in the Great Lakes region (Figure 13.3). This area occurs at a juncture of environmental zones, where two historically observed adaptive patterns, those of the Chippewa and the Ottawa, were present (Fitting and Cleland 1969). Not only are the subsistence and settlement systems of these groups the best known, but the adaptive use of the broad environmental configuration has also been the focus of surveys and excavations used to test the Late Woodland occurrence of the ethnohistorically derived adaptive patterns (Cleland 1967, 1982; Lovis 1976; Holman 1978; Martin 1989). The environmental zones in the study area are the Canadian Biotic Province and a transition zone between the Canadian Biotic Province and the Carolinian Biotic Province to the south (Albert et al. 1986). Late Woodland and Historic mobility included movement both within and across these environmental zones. Sharing of overlapping territory, as well as movement into environments regularly occupied by other groups, was a significant part of the various adaptations (McClurken 1988). At times, food and other items produced by residents of these zones were exchanged among groups (Kinietz 1965; McClurken 1988; Smith 1996).

People in the Canadian Biotic Province occupy an environment that is highly variable in the distribution of food across the landscape and through the year (Yarnell 1964:5–7; Cleland 1966:9–11). Important differences in food potential can be seen between the Upper Great Lakes and the forests of the interior. There are additional significant differences in habitats between two major forest types. Systematic and scheduled mobility solves the problem of subsistence in the Canadian Biotic Province, where wild resources are unevenly distributed both spatially and seasonally. Great Lakes coastal waters, and the mouths of streams emptying into them, are sources of fish that are particularly abundant and reliable during spawning periods in late spring to early summer and again in the late fall (Cleland 1982, 1989:766–767; Martin 1989:602). For people dependent on wild foods, catching spawning lake sturgeons and suckers can be critical in the spring, when other resources are not yet available. Similarly, fall spawning fish, like lake trout and whitefish, are key to a nutritious supply of food that can be preserved and transported for winter use. Fish found in interior lakes are a source of food throughout the year (Cleland 1966:10; Martin 1999:224). Most soils in the Canadian Biotic Province are too poor, and the growing season too short, to support a reliable horticulture. While some shoreline locations along Lake Michigan and Lake Huron are within the 120 frost-free-day limit for successful aboriginal maize agriculture, they are subject to late frosts in spring and early frost in fall (Yarnell 1964:128–129, 133; Cleland 1966:9–11). When crops are grown in these areas, a successful harvest is so doubtful that crops can only be used as supplements to the wild food supply. Thus, even in favorable locales, lakeshore settings are more significant for catching fish than for planting gardens.

Productivity of the forests in the Canadian Biotic Province varies between the climax vegetation of northern hardwoods, such as beech and maple, and several coniferous subclimax forests, including pines and hemlocks on higher sandier soils and spruce, cedar, fir and birch in swampy soils (Yarnell 1964:5–7). The differences between these various forest compositions are significant because the hardwoods provide foods such as maple sap and beechnuts, as well as forage for a variety of animals. In contrast, vast stands of pine and extensive coniferous bogs and swamps produce little in the way of food for humans or the animals they hunt. Economically important plants do not grow together in the same habitats, nor are they productive at the same times (Yarnell 1964:77). Thus, in order to collect a variety of plants, either concurrently or successively, it is necessary to position oneself in proximity to several habitats. Mobility must also be employed in the Canadian Biotic Province to hunt northern animals such as moose, woodland caribou, bear and beaver (Cleland 1966:10). Most of these animals are essentially solitary, and none are abundant in any one location. Whitetail deer are important game, although they are more numerous in the oak- and hickory-dominated forests and forest edges of the Carolinian Biotic Province (Cleland 1966:65). Unlike southern deer populations, northern deer aggregate, or 'yard' in winter in coniferous forests near cedar swamps, where they are sheltered from the wind and can browse on evergreen vegetation (Doepker and Ozoga 1991). Thus, habitat where deer might be found in the harsh Canadian Biotic Province winter is fairly predictable, and the animals are not necessarily solitary.

The transition zone between the Canadian and the Carolinian biotic provinces is significant for human subsistence because it offers an unusually diverse array of plant and animal foods (Cleland 1966:6–7; Fitting 1966; Hambacher 1992:36). Additionally, the average of between 160 and 140 frost-free days is well above the limit of 120 frost-free days for prehistoric horticulture (Yarnell 1964:127–128). Both biodiversity and the potential for horticulture are most marked along the eastern shores of Lake Michigan and Lake Huron, where climate is ameliorated by westerly winds blowing across the lakes. The westerlies blow lake-warmed air over the land in winter and lake-cooled air in summer. The transition zone is abrupt along the western shore of Lake Huron, where the climate modifying winds have less effect because of the intervening land mass. The transition zone is populated by plants and animals found in the beech, maple and coniferous forests of the Canadian Biotic Province and by plants and animals associated with the oak and hickory forests of the Carolinian Biotic Province (Cleland 1966:224–246; Hambacher 1992:36). Thus, the food supply for mobile hunter-gatherers is characterized by a diversity of species that can be exploited successively through the year. For example, the transition zone yields an abundance of northerly distributed berries along with several species of nuts that are more abundant to the south (Yarnell 1964:78–79). The berries can be obtained as they ripen during the late summer, whereas the nuts can be procured as they become available through the fall. Both foods can be preserved for winter use. Game present in northern portions of the transition zone included more northerly moose and woodland caribou until the 19th century CE (Cleland 1966:10). Whitetail deer and elk were available in lesser numbers than in the Carolinian Biotic Province to the south. Because the various resources of the transition zone occur in patches, movement involves travel to locations where several different micro-environments are in proximity to one another (Yarnell 1964:77–79; Hambacher 1992:36). These micro-environments offer different food plants and, consequently, the animal communities they support. The numerous lakes and streams in the transition zone are sources of multiple fish species, and the rivers in the lower peninsula are transportation routes between the coast and the interior (Hambacher 1992:35). Large portions of the transition zone are south of the spawning grounds of the whitefish, making coastal locations unattractive for fall fishing (Hambacher 1992:35–36).

THE CHIPPEWA AND THE MACKINAC PHASE PEOPLE

The Chippewa were highly mobile people who depended on hunting, gathering and fishing in the Canadian Biotic Province. Chippewa mobility consisted of residential moves by extended family households who moved seasonally to locations where foods were available. The numbers of households residing at a location depended largely on the amount of food available. Always, however, households acted as the basic economic decision-making group that moved together and stayed together throughout the year (Kinietz 1965:321; Cleland 1992b:46–47). Although they planted maize and other crops, the Chippewa could not rely on a harvest sufficient for winter use. Instead, they acquired maize from the sedentary Huron as part of an exchange process mediated by their Ottawa neighbors (McClurken 1988:14). In turn, the Chippewa provided the Huron with meat and hides.

During the warm season the Chippewa hunted, fished, gathered plants, and, in some places, planted gardens (Kinietz 1965:321; Cleland 1992b:46–47). As food was readily available at such times, extended families would come together with related households in settlements often located along the shores of the Great Lakes. Larger aggregations of people occurred at key fall fishing locations along the Great Lakes shorelines and at the rapids of the Saint Mary's River at Sault Ste. Marie. When food was less abundant and more scattered during the winter, households would disperse across the interior landscape. Movement toward winter hunting grounds was often along river systems, where people caught deer and beaver along the way. In spring, households came together again to make maple sugar before returning to their summer settlements. Storage of food procured in each season was an important buffer against times of scarcity (Densmore 1979:40, 119–131). Lined storage or cache pits were dug and filled at settlements, camps and other locations while people were on the move. Scaffolds were used when the ground was frozen in the winter (Smith 1907:35; Tanner 1956:46; Bain 1969:130).

The adaptive strategy proven archaeologically for the earliest phase of the Late Woodland in northern Michigan is comparable to the Chippewa pattern of residential mobility (Holman 1978). During the period between 800 and 1000 CE, known as the Mackinac phase, people were hunter-gatherers who

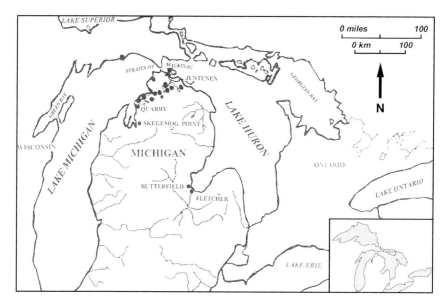

Figure 13.4. Mackinac phase and other early Late Woodland sites mentioned in the text.

systematically moved to obtain the same seasonal resources in the same natural settings as the Chippewa (Figure 13.4). Like communal practices among the Chippewa, social organization in the Mackinac phase was probably characterized by extended family economic units and by seasonal aggregation and dispersal of such families. Unlike the Chippewa, there is no evidence for a formal system of exchange whereby Mackinac phase people provided meat and hides to settled horticulturalists and received maize in return. Although maize was present in the Eastern Woodlands, it was not until about 1000 CE that some Upper Great Lakes peoples became dependent on maize, beans and squash (Murphy and Ferris 1990:261–263, 273; Parker 1996:314; Brashler et al. 2000:570), so there may not have been settled horticulturalists with whom to trade. There were neighbors, however, with whom good relations were maintained in order to buffer risk in an unpredictable environment (Holman and Kingsley 1996). Mackinac phase peoples in the study area were mainly residents of the Canadian Biotic Province, but their sites along the Lake Michigan coast south from the Straits of Mackinac to the north end of Grand Traverse Bay are in the Carolinian-Canadian transition zone. Mobility involved seasonal travel between the coast and interior.

Like the Chippewa, Mackinac phase groups normally spent the warm season at coastal sites, situated near streams populated by spring-spawning fish, where food of all kinds could be found within a relatively short distance (Holman 1978; Martin 1989). In these favorable environmental settings, faunal and floral analyses indicate warm season habitations (Lovis 1973; Holman 1978). As expected from repetitive extended family residential occupations, coastal sites are large, exhibit thick organic midden accumulations, show relatively evenly distributed features (including dwellings), and yield artifacts representing a wide variety of gender- and age-based activities. These activities include hunting, gathering, fishing, cooking, hide scraping, woodworking, manufacturing pottery (including toys) and producing stone tools. This broad range of tasks, and the partitioned spatial structure evident at two sites, indicates that labor was apportioned along age and gender lines similar to that of the Chippewa and other hunter-gatherer groups. At both sites near the source of Norwood chert, stone tools of this material were manufactured in contexts separate from areas where hearths, pottery and other artifacts indicate domestic activities (Lovis 1973; Holman 1978). Mackinac phase domestic areas were arranged along the back edges of lakeshore bluffs in a linear pattern similar to that seen in Chippewa summer camps, where each extended family established its own space (Densmore 1979:122). The absence of more formal partitioning of space suggests that Mackinac phase extended families, like those of the Chippewa, were relatively independent. Flexibility of movement in the season of plentiful food included the option of visiting friends and family at other coastal sites or avoiding social contact altogether by gathering food in the interior (Holman 1978). Mackinac phase coastal sites in the transition zone contain ceramics made by Mackinac phase potters along with pottery made by their neighbors immediately to the south (Lovis 1973). These neighbors shared the use of some transition zone locations with Mackinac phase people, including the Pi-wan-go-ning quarry, where both groups obtained Norwood chert (Lovis 1973; Holman 1978; Hambacher 1992).

The fall component of Mackinac phase settlement centered on the Straits of Mackinac, where whitefish and lake trout came into shallow waters to spawn in late October to early December (Cleland 1966:172). As was the case with the Chippewa, these fish served as a kind of 'survival insurance' for the winter, when food was neither abundant nor reliable. The best known example of a late-fall fishing site is the Juntunen site on Bois Blanc Island, in the Straits of Mackinac (McPherron 1967). Juntunen exhibits intensive occupation along with abundant remains of fish, including sturgeon, whitefish and lake trout (Cleland 1966:157–210). Although plant and animal remains indicate warm-season occupation occurred at Juntunen, this was a particularly desirable site in late fall. Its central location and the abundance of fall-spawning fish created the opportunity for large numbers of people to meet and interact. The intensity of Mackinac phase occupation at Juntunen suggests that it represents an aggregation of local bands comparable to that seen at the Chippewa fall fishery in the rapids at Sault Ste. Marie and fall fishing in the Straits of Mackinac. These gatherings reinforced social ties and were chances to acquire information about winter hunting prospects.

Mackinac phase households occupied winter sites near inland lakes a short distance south of the Straits of Mackinac (Holman 1978:45–48, 149). These sites were situated in sheltered locations where they were surrounded by a wide variety of habitat types and associated game. Such settings increased the probability that winter hunts would be successful. By comparison with coastal sites, excavated Mackinac phase interior sites are characterized by an uneven distribution of materials, fewer features and no developed organic middens. Hearths and postmolds, coupled with abundant pottery and few stone tools, suggest a relatively narrow range of activities focused on domestic concerns.[2] Among the stone tools are projectile points and hide scrapers, both of which are related to capturing and processing game. Plant remains are limited in number and variety, as would be expected from cold-season sites where there was no substantial plant storage as people arrived late in the year with only plant foods they carried with them (Densmore 1979:120). There is no ceramic evidence that interior locations were occupied by anyone other than Mackinac phase people during the early Late Woodland. As expected at winter sites, people lived there in relative isolation.

It is probable that Mackinac phase people, like the Chippewa, made maple sugar at sites temporally and geographically located between winter and summer locales (Holman 1978:154). The sap run provided food in the early spring season of scarcity at a location where related households aggregated after a winter of separation. Evidence for the existence of Mackinac phase sites used for sugaring includes settings with maples distributed so the length of the sugaring season could be prolonged and a site with features such as abundant fire-cracked rock and artifacts probably related to sugaring (Lovis 1978:44; Holman 1984:79).

The early Late Woodland was marked by a pattern of seasonal subsistence that, in most respects, mirrors that of the Historic period Chippewa in the same region. Mackinac phase groups faced the same environmental uncertainties as the Chippewa, but exchange with settled horticulturalists was not a possible solution to potential scarcity of food within their regularly exploited territories. Simply moving into unoccupied land was also impossible because Mackinac phase peoples were surrounded by neighbors who, like them, relied on wild food and faced potential food scarcities. Even though adjacent territories were occupied, people needed to be able to move outside their own primarily exploited territories on an emergency basis. Mackinac phase people and other

---

[2.] Postmolds are organic soil stains remaining after the decomposition of a post, in this case indicative of the remains of temporary dwellings (cf. Chang, this volume).

early Late Woodland peoples of the lower peninsula solved the problem of possible resource shortfalls by engaging in a system of cooperative buffering, whereby they were able to use territories normally within the domain of other groups (Holman and Kingsley 1996:360–361). Cooperative buffering in the lower peninsula is evidenced by joint use of overlapping territory in the transition zone along the northwest coast of Lake Michigan (Holman and Kingsley 1996:361). Some warm-season sites in the transition zone were occupied by Mackinac phase groups and their southern neighbors, while the Norwood chert from the Pi-wan-go-ning quarry in the same area was freely used by both groups (Cleland 1967; Lovis 1973, 1990).

Maintaining good relations through visiting and other interactions is indicated by small amounts of Mackinac phase pottery at the Skegemog Point site near Grand Traverse Bay, which was predominantly occupied during the warm season by a neighboring group (Hambacher 1992). Similarly, the Fletcher site, a warm-season site near Saginaw Bay, belonged to a different set of neighbors and has a few examples of Mackinac phase pottery, suggesting that visiting took place (Brashler 1973; Holman and Kingsley 1996:360–361). The importance of fostering cooperation is seen in a Mackinac phase winter hunting component at the Butterfield site, which is on the northeastern side of the Saginaw Valley, not far from the Fletcher site (Wobst 1968:246). This site is evidence for the option to move into another group's territory in the most problematic season of the year (Holman and Kingsley 1996:363).

THE OTTAWA AND THE JUNTUNEN PHASE PEOPLE

The Ottawa homeland, at the northern end of Ontario's Bruce Peninsula and islands in Georgian Bay (Lake Huron), was at the southern end of the Canadian Biotic Province and, in Michigan and Wisconsin, in the transition zone between the Carolinian and Canadian biotic provinces (Cleland 1966:73; McClurken 1988:12). Mobility related to Ottawa subsistence, including exchange, was both logistic on the part of specific task groups and residential involving entire households. Mobility and social organization among the Ottawa reflected their flexible subsistence strategy centered on the transition zone (McClurken 1988:13–14). The Ottawa raised corn, beans, squash and sunflowers in the fields around their semipermanent villages. In the summer, meat was provided by hunting parties who sought game within 120–160 km from the village (Kinietz 1965:237). When the harvest was good, the Ottawa stored their surplus maize and remained in their villages throughout the winter. Important additional sources of storable foods were the whitefish and lake trout caught in the Straits of Mackinac. Winter stores of maize and fish were augmented by logistic hunting carried out by small parties, usually of men, who would travel long distances in search of game to bring back to the village. Ottawa winter hunts often took place along the river systems in the transition zone of the lower peninsula and in the Saginaw Valley.

Harvests were not always sufficient to provide adequate winter stores as the growing season in the transition zone was subject to late frosts in the spring and early frost at the end of summer (Yarnell 1964:128–129, 133). Additionally, Ottawa crops probably failed during the serious droughts that occurred on average once a decade (McClurken 1988:14). In the winters of years when the harvest was poor, Ottawa subsistence was based on hunting and gathering. At such times, extended family households left their villages and dispersed across the landscape to employ a residential mobility system similar to that of the Chippewa. In addition to seasonal hunting, logistic mobility was employed by the Ottawa in the course of their occupation as middlemen in a system of exchange between neighboring groups (Kinietz 1965:245; McClurken 1988:14). This activity involved the exchange of items that were important for the subsistence of neighbors and for the Ottawa themselves. The Ottawa brokered an exchange of meat and furs, obtained by the northern Chippewa, for maize and other agricultural products grown by the Huron, who cultivated crops in fields around their sizable and relatively permanent villages (Trigger 1969:9–11). Because the territory of the Huron was subject to depletion of game by overhunting, the Huron needed the meat and hides supplied by their trading partners (Smith 1996:285). By virtue of exchange, the Chippewa were able to obtain supplies of maize to augment their food supply, while the Ottawa were able to make their subsistence more secure. Logistic mobility by Ottawa men was a key factor in the exchange network that provided the Chippewa and Huron with food and other items they could not independently produce in sufficient quantities (Kinietz 1965:245; McClurken 1988:23). These men traveled the Great Lakes region in birch-bark canoes along family-controlled routes, where exchange relationships were carefully nurtured by reciprocal gift giving and by the arrangement of marriages with trading partners. Maintaining strong partnerships was important to all parties because the network redistributed key subsistence items throughout the region (Trigger 1969:39).

After the Huron were permanently driven from their homeland by the Iroquois, between 1648 and 1651 CE (Kinietz 1965:2), the old subsistence system depending on trade with the Huron ceased (Smith 1996:105–106). When the threat from the Iroquois had passed, and it was safe to return to the Straits of Mackinac region, many Ottawa established horticultural villages in their old hunting grounds in the transition zone of the northern lower peninsula, where they resumed their pattern of subsistence (McClurken 1988:29–30, 33, 35–36). This included participation in the fur trade, once again as middlemen. The familiar role of broker was employed not between the Huron and the Chippewa but between the French in the east and groups situated to the west of the Ottawa. Once again, logistic mobility was employed to provide furs to the French and European goods to the western bands and tribes. Later, the Ottawa were providers of maize, fish and equipment to French traders passing through the Straits of Mackinac on their way to the interior.

Beginning with the Juntunen phase, about 1200 CE, the region was home to people who practiced a settlement system comparable to the Ottawa pattern (Figure 13.5). Evidence for the Ottawa pattern during the Juntunen phase includes semipermanent horticultural villages, intensive fall fishing locales, long-distance mobility for hunting and exchange and a backup system of residential moves for winter hunting. Whether semipermanent horticultural villages were common during the Juntunen phase and early Historic periods (ca. 1200–1650 CE) is uncertain. There are sites that were intensively occupied during the warm season and through late fall or year-round. The coastal locations of these sites, however, are surrounded by minimal arable land, suggesting that fishing and accessibility, not gardening, were prime considerations in choosing site situations (Cleland 1966:194; Smith 1996:246–252). In all cases maize is found in relatively low densities, whereas the remains of sucker, lake sturgeon, whitefish and lake trout are abundant. Again, the locations of these sites at prime all-season fishing spots, coupled with the faunal evidence, show that the most important foods obtained were fish rather than maize (Cleland 1966; Martin 1989; Smith 1996). The remains of large animals at coastal sites

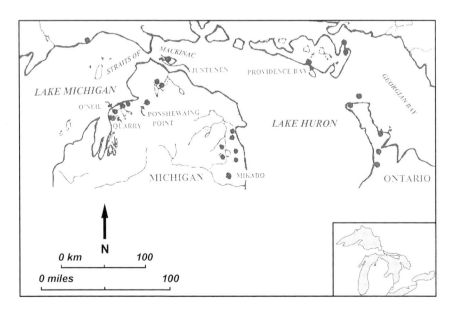

Figure 13.5. Juntunen phase and other later Late Woodland sites mentioned in the text.

reveal that woodland caribou, deer, beaver and bear were desired foods (Cleland 1966:194; Smith 1996:240–241). These animals were not as readily available as fish because they were not present in sufficient numbers to sustain local animal populations in the face of continued hunting pressure (Smith 1996:252). Thus, although some game may have been captured nearby, much must have been obtained by logistic hunting parties or exchange with northern neighbors.

The abundant evidence of fall-season fishing at coastal sites, most likely with the assistance of gill nets, attests to the importance of this activity in the Juntunen phase (Cleland 1966; Smith 1996, 2004). Fall fishing, as part of the Ottawa adaptive pattern, is characterized by the aggregation of smaller, seasonally mobile social units at key fishing locales (Kinietz 1965:239–240; McClurken 1988:13–14). Evidence for aggregation, and consequent displays of more overarching corporate group identity, may be seen in the ossuary burials found at Juntunen (McPherron 1967:229–232; O'Shea 1988). O'Shea (1988:78) notes, "Here the emphasis on territoriality by marking claim to an important seasonal resource location is retained in the mortuary symbolism, although now it is within the context of a large, collective ossuary. Furthermore, within the Juntunen ossuary, the remains of individual family or lineage groups were kept distinct and segregated [...]. This suggests that the deceased from several distinct groups were processed and curated for ultimate interment within the collective ossuary."

While admittedly at a smaller scale, these burials resemble the historically known 'Feast of the Dead' mortuary ritual practiced by Algonquian and western Iroquoian (particularly Huron) groups and documented at the nearby 17th century CE Lasanen site, at the Straits of Mackinac (Cleland 1971). On these occasions all deceased members of a band or tribe were collectively interred in a single pit, at intervals of a few to as many as ten years. Such collective, integrating, rituals re-inforced the social identity of both individuals and smaller social units with the larger regional group by bringing together people whose villages might be located across the broader region. This link to aggregation and associated social ties is underscored by Brown's (2003:219) recent observations that "collective burial is present when communal solidarity is the backdrop for burial rites in communities of a certain size and stability" and "population size has to be of a sufficient size to warrant and to make scheduled or periodic rites possible." In this vein Cleland (1992a:101), consistent with O'Shea (1988), notes that sites like Juntunen, which may be situated at the point where band territories overlap, are natural points of aggregation.

The year-round security of food supplies at semipermanent sites was problematic given the unreliability of harvests and the low density of animal populations nearby. This unreliability implies that subsistence security had to be insured through reciprocal exchange between groups comparable to that seen in the Ottawa adaptive pattern (Milner and O'Shea 1998:199–201; Smith 1996:286). Ceramics and other evidence supports this implication. Later Juntunen phase ceramics have some Huron-like stylistic attributes, as might be expected if the Huron were their trading partners (McPherron 1967:116; Milner and O'Shea 1998:194). Further evidence of reciprocal exchange is presented by Smith (1996:270–273), who suggests that the ritual killing and burial of dogs at upper Great Lakes sites may represent the remains of feasts offered by the hosts of exchange events. Widespread ritual feasting is indicative of the cross-cultural ideology underlying exchange. Dog burials are found at intensively occupied year-round sites such as the Providence Bay site on Manitoulin Island in northern Lake Huron. Providence Bay is a shoreline site easily accessible to traders from the southeast via Lake Huron, from the northwest via the Saint Mary's River, and from the west through the Straits of Mackinac.

Evidence for reciprocal exchange can also be seen at Late Woodland earthwork sites in the northern lower peninsula that date from around 900 to 1500 CE (Milner and O'Shea 1998:181). These sites have earthen berms surmounted by wooden palisades and surrounded by ditches. Many earthworks have gaps in the perimeter facilitating entry for trading parties along with clear areas in the center where exchange could take place (Milner and O'Shea 1998:184, 187). One of the few earthworks to be excavated, Mikado (Carruthers 1969), is characterized by relatively few artifacts, hearths and pit clusters, suggesting short-term usage (Milner and O'Shea 1998:188). The fact that Mikado yielded a large sample of maize, including stems and husk fragments, as well as cobs, points to this short-term use as focused on scheduled exchange. The argument that earthworks such as Mikado functioned as points of exchange is supported by the fact that they lie at ecological and social boundaries (Milner and O'Shea 1998:199). These sites are situated in the headwaters of primary streams near the juncture of interior uplands and coastal lowlands and near the transition between the Carolinian and Canadian biotic provinces. Thus, the products of diverse environments could be brought to these accessible locations for exchange (O'Shea 2003:13).

Ethnographic analogues reveal that exchange between groups often occurred at social boundaries, which constituted safe places that facilitated exchange. A social boundary at Mikado is indicated by the patterning of ceramic attributes on Juntunen ware found there (Milner and O'Shea 1998:199). These attributes indicate distinct stylistic differences with ceramics made by horticultural neighbors to the south (Younge tradition), but there is also a mix of attributes suggesting interaction with these same neighbors. It is noteworthy that Mikado is in a boundary location rather than a central place such as Providence Bay. Milner and O'Shea (1998:200–201) note that such locations provide a place of safety for socially disparate peoples to trade and, like Smith (1996), suggest that feasting and dancing might have taken place in the earthwork 'plazas' to symbolically cement the exchange relationship.

An Ottawa-pattern strategy of residential dispersal into extended family groups to hunt in the winter, as needed, was employed during the Juntunen phase. The same interior sites occupied in winter by Mackinac phase extended family–sized groups were used by Juntunen phase peoples (Holman 1978:45). Again, these sites were situated in relatively isolated and sheltered locations with ecological settings high in potential yield for winter resources. Features and artifacts at interior sites are indicative of domestic activities and hunting, with ceramics limited to Juntunen ware, as would be expected for sites occupied by small groups wintering in isolation. One site, O'Neil, is particularly interesting because it shows that residential mobility on the part of Juntunen phase households was not restricted to winter, nor was it employed only in times of necessity. Thus, households had the ability to make independent decisions with regard to mobility. Lovis (1990:198) has isolated three Juntunen phase occupations at the stratified multicomponent O'Neil site, including an early one, 1200–1300 CE, one about 1440 CE, and a protohistoric occupation about 1700 CE.

O'Neil, located on the Lake Michigan coast south of Lake Charlevoix, was clearly a warm-season habitation (Lovis 1973, 1990). During each Juntunen phase occupation, O'Neil was a spatially partitioned residential site with domestic activities taking place around hearths, separate areas for discarding fish refuse, and still others set aside for the manufacture of stone tools from Norwood chert obtained at the nearby Pi-wan-go-ning quarry (Cleland 1973). Most fish were caught in the spring, and, clearly, the proximity of the quarry was an important factor in deciding to occupy O'Neil during the Juntunen phase. The diverse range of activities represented and the remains of an oval house from the 15th century CE are indicative of residential moves to the O'Neil site during the Juntunen phase. Evidence for logistic occupation at O'Neil by contemporary 'traverse phase' residents of the transition zone shows mutual use of the site, but whether this was scheduled for different times or was concurrent is unknown (Lovis 1990:207). It is noteworthy that O'Neil is the only Late Woodland coastal site south of the Straits of Mackinac that has substantial Juntunen phase residential occupations. In contrast, other sites along the coast were occupied repeatedly in the early Late Woodland Mackinac phase (Holman 1978). Juntunen phase peoples made little use of the Lake Michigan coast south of their fall fishing grounds. Rather, their occupations were concentrated to take advantage of fall fishing and to act as middlemen in the exchange of foodstuffs. Nonetheless, extended families made residential moves in seasons of plenty as well as in times of scarcity and clearly functioned as basic economic units in a decentralized society.

DISCUSSION

Scheduled mobility along the coast and through the interior of the Canadian Biotic Province and the transition zone was consistently used to procure the wild resources of these environmental zones. Historically documented mobility patterns, after about 1650 CE, are also evident in the Late Woodland archaeological record. As predicted from the documents, sites are found in coastal and interior settings where seasonal resources are likely to be found. Furthermore, site structure, features and artifacts reflect site functions and group compositions comparable to those of the historically known patterns, while floral and faunal remains indicate the same seasons of occupation and exploitation of the same resources. Variations in mobility include the Chippewa and early Late Woodland Mackinac phase emphasis on residential mobility in the Canadian Biotic Province and the Ottawa and Juntunen phase use of logistic mobility, coupled with seasonal residential mobility in the transition zone. This variability cannot be explained entirely by environmental differences in the abundance and variety of foods. Like Mackinac phase peoples in the Canadian Biotic Province, early Late Woodland populations in the transition zone probably employed mobility to obtain a range of wild foods (Hambacher 1992). In cooperation with their Mackinac phase neighbors they buffered risk from environmental uncertainties of the transition zone by sharing overlapping territory and by using other groups' territories when necessary (Holman and Kingsley 1996). Thus, the structure of wild resources in the two environmental zones fostered comparable residential mobility strategies in the early Late Woodland, while cooperation between occupants of adjacent territories provided options for movement in times of environmental stress. The differences between the Chippewa and Ottawa patterns are attributable to the fact that coastal areas adjacent to and in the transition zone are more suitable for horticulture than is the Canadian Biotic Province.

The Ottawa pattern appeared in the Juntunen phase, when maize became significant in the Great Lakes region, and is predicated on growing crops and maintaining an active Great Lakes fishery. Both horticulture and fishing were conducted by extended family households at semipermanent coastal sites. These activities acted as tethers for most of the labor force, as did production of trade items such as reed mats (McClurken 1988:24). The Ottawa pattern was a commitment to a semisedentary way of life supported by crops and fish to secure sufficient food in a variable environment. Nonetheless, mobility was critical because harvests were problematic, and fish was not the only source of meat. Subsistence was made more secure by the use of logistic mobility for both exchange and hunting. Such moves, for specific purposes, supplied additional maize and game from more distant sources when neither was plentiful nor available around semipermanent residential sites. Logistic mobility was particularly important after about 1500 CE, when the onset of the 'Little Ice Age' made subsistence even more problematic (Smith 1996; Milner and O'Shea 1998).

Logistic mobility, while critical for subsistence, was also subject to social constraints. These strictures were most apparent in the exchange with settled horticulturalists, like the Huron. The exchange which was a significant benefit to both groups nonetheless required fostering of relationships. This trade was reciprocal, with expectations of an immediate return in foodstuffs and other items of equal value. Actions such as giving of gifts and marrying members of other groups were necessary to ensure the exchange would continue. Without constant effort this trade would fail (McClurken 1988:14–15). Social relations also facilitated logistic mobility for hunting by providing access to territory that was either shared with or controlled by another group. Unlike the case with the Huron, these were relationships with groups such as the Chippewa, who were regarded as close kin and carried the obligations of kinship. Thus, the generosity with which kin treated one another fostered long-term cooperative buffering via the mechanism of mobility. The Ottawa pattern, with its use of residential mobility as a subsistence backup, reflects the continuing importance of maintaining the option to disperse across the landscape. Thus, people were not entirely dependent on reciprocal exchange to make up subsistence shortfalls. The use of residential mobility in turn implies that households had considerable autonomy in economic decision making.

Both the Chippewa and Ottawa patterns of mobility persisted through most of the 19th century CE (McClurken 1988; Cleland 1992b). Until their northern lands were desired for American settlements and industries, such as lumbering and mining, mobility was employed in the same systematic ways to obtain the same seasonal resources in the same natural settings (Quimby 1966:179; Cleland 1983). Additionally, the same social devices were used to buffer risk, especially including kinship ties, that provided access to overlapping territories and reciprocal exchange with Europeans and the first American farmers. Mobility was no longer an adaptive subsistence strategy when both groups ceded most of their land to the United States and, thus, lost ready access to dispersed resources.

Multiple lines of evidence demonstrate concordance between the late prehistoric archaeological record and ethnohistorically documented flexibility in mobility strategies and integrating social mechanisms that acted to buffer environmental variability. This evidence includes site locations, site structures, artifact assemblages and floral and faunal remains. After more than 35 years of archaeological research in northern Michigan and the Straits of Mackinac region, there is no evidence contradicting models based on the historically documented Chippewa and Ottawa patterns. It is critical, however, to carefully, continuously and independently test ethnohistorically derived analogues against regional prehistoric evidence. For example, the prehistoric evidence from southwestern lower Michigan does not support expectations of the 'Potawatomi pattern' in that region. This pattern predicts large and permanent agricultural villages like those inhabited by the Potawatomi, and such large villages have yet to be found (O'Gorman 2003, 2007; O'Gorman and Lovis 2006).

REFERENCES

Albert, D. A., S. R. Denton and B. V. Barnes
1986   *Regional Landscape Ecosystems of Michigan*. Ann Arbor, University of Michigan.

Bain, J. (ed.)
1969   *Travels and Adventures in Canada and the Indian Territories Between the Years 1760 and 1776. By Alexander Henry, Fur Trader*. Rutland, Charles E. Tuttle (originally published in 1809).

Binford, L. R.
1980   Willow Smoke and Dogs' Tails: Hunter-Gatherer Settlement Systems and Archaeological Site Formation. *American Antiquity 45*: 1, pp. 1–17.

Brashler, J. G.
1973   *A Formal Analysis of Prehistoric Ceramics from the Fletcher Site*. Michigan State University, Department of Anthropology (Master's thesis).

Brashler, J. G., E. B. Garland, M. B. Holman, W. A. Lovis and S. R. Martin
2000   Adaptive Strategies and Socioeconomic Systems in Northern Great Lakes Riverine Environments: The Late Woodland of Michigan. In T. E. Emerson, D. L. McElrath and A. C. Fortier (eds.), *Late Woodland Societies: Tradition and Transformation Across the Midcontinent*. Lincoln, University of Nebraska Press: pp. 543–582.

Brown, J. A.
2003   Collective Burial Practices Across the Agricultural Transition in the Eastern Woodlands. In G. Burenhult and S. Westergaard (eds.), *Stones and Bones: Formal Disposal of the Dead in Atlantic Europe During the Mesolithic Neolithic Interface, 6000–3000 BC. BAR international Series 1201*. Oxford, Archaeopress: pp. 207–223.

Carruthers, P. J.
1969   *The Mikado Earthwork: 20Aa5*. University of Calgary, Department of Archaeology (Master's thesis).

Cleland, C. E.

1966   *The Prehistoric Animal Ecology and Ethnozoology of the Upper Great Lakes Region. Anthropological Papers Number 29.* Ann Arbor, Museum of Anthropology, University of Michigan.

1967   *Progress Report on National Science Foundation Grants Nos. GS-1026 and GS-1669: The Environmental Adaptations of the Prehistoric Cultures of the Grand Traverse Bay Area of Michigan.* Report on file at the Consortium for Archaeological Research, Michigan State University, East Lansing.

1971   *The Lasanen Site: An Historical Burial Locality in Mackinac County, Michigan. Publications of the Museum of Michigan State University. Volume 1, Number 1.* East Lansing, Michigan State University.

1973   The Pi-wan-go-ning Prehistoric District at Norwood, Michigan. In H. M. Martin (ed.), *Geology and the Environment: Man, Earth, and Nature in Northwestern Lower Michigan.* Ann Arbor, Michigan Basin Geological Society: pp. 85–87.

1982   The Inland Shore Fishery of the Northern Great Lakes: Its Development and Importance in Prehistory. *American Antiquity 47*: 4, pp. 761–784.

1983   Indians in a Changing Environment. In S. Flader (ed.), *The Great Lakes Forest: An Environmental and Social History.* Minneapolis, University of Minnesota Press: pp. 83–95.

1989   Comments on "A Reconsideration of Aboriginal Fishing Strategies in the Northern Great Lakes Region," by Susan R. Martin. *American Antiquity 54*: 3, pp. 605–609.

1992a   From Ethnohistory to Archaeology: Ottawa and Ojibwa Band Territories of the Northern Great Lakes. In B. J. Little (ed.), *Text-Aided Archaeology.* Boca Raton, CRC Press: pp.97–102.

1992b   *Rites of Conquest: The History and Culture of Michigan's Native Americans.* Ann Arbor, University of Michigan Press.

Clifton, J. A.

1984   *The Pokagons, 1683–1983: Catholic Potawatomi Indians of the St. Joseph River Valley.* Lanham, University Press of America.

Densmore, F.

1979   *Chippewa Customs.* St. Paul, Minnesota Historical Society Press. (originally published in 1929 as Bulletin 86 of the Bureau of American Ethnology, Smithsonian Institution, Washington).

Doepker, R. V. and J. J. Ozoga

1991   Wildlife Values of Northern White Cedar. In *Workshop Proceedings on Northern White Cedar in Michigan: Agricultural Experiment Research Report 512.* East Lansing, Michigan State University: pp. 15–34.

Fitting, J. E.

1966   Archaeological Investigations of the Carolinian-Canadian Edge in Central Michigan. In J. E. Fitting (ed.), *Edge Area Archaeology* (special issue), *Michigan Archaeologist 12*: 4, pp. 143–150.

1975   *The Archaeology of Michigan: A Guide to the Prehistory of the Great Lakes Region. Bulletin Number 56*. Bloomfield Hills, Cranbrook Institute of Science.

Fitting, J. E. and C. E. Cleland

1969   Late Prehistoric Settlement Patterns in the Upper Great Lakes. *Ethnohistory 16*: pp. 289–302.

Hambacher, M. J.

1992   *The Skegemog Point Site: Continuing Studies of Cultural Dynamics in the Carolinian-Canadian Transition Zone*. East Lansing. Michigan State University (PhD dissertation).

Holman, M. B.

1978   *The Settlement System of the Mackinac Phase*. East Lansing. Michigan State University (PhD dissertation).

1984   The Identification of Late Woodland Maple Sugaring Sites in the Upper Great Lakes. *Midcontinental Journal of Archaeology 9*: 1, pp. 63–90.

Holman, M. B. and R. G. Kingsley

1996   Territoriality and Societal Interaction During the Early Late Woodland in Southern Michigan. In M. B. Holman, J. G. Brashler and K. E. Parker (eds.), *Investigating the Archaeological Record of the Great Lakes State: Essays in Honor of Elizabeth Baldwin Garland*. Kalamazoo, New Issues Press: pp. 341–382.

Holman, M. B. and F. Krist Jr.

2001   Late Woodland Storage and Mobility in Western Lower Michigan. In T. C. Pleger, R. A. Birmingham and C. I. Mason (eds.), *Papers in Honor of Carol I. Mason*. (special issue), *Wisconsin Archeologist 82*: 1–2, pp. 7–32.

Howey, M. C. L. and J. M. O'Shea

2006   Bear's Journey and the Study of Ritual in Archaeology. *American Antiquity 71*: pp. 261–282.

Kinietz, W. V.

1965   *The Indians of the Western Great Lakes, 1615–1760*. Ann Arbor, University of Michigan Press.

Lovis, W. A.

1973   *Late Woodland Cultural Dynamics in the Northern Lower Peninsula of Michigan*. East Lansing. Michigan State University (PhD dissertation).

1976   Quarter Sections and Forests: An Example of Probability Sampling in the Northeastern Woodlands. *American Antiquity 41*: pp. 364–372.

1978   A Numerical Taxonomic Analysis of Changing Woodland Site Location Strategies on an Interior Lake Chain. *Michigan Academician 1*: 1, pp 39–48.

1990   Site Formation Processes and the Organization of Space at the Stratified Late Woodland O'Neill Site. In G. E. Gibbon (ed.), *The Woodland Tradition in the Western Great Lakes: Papers Presented to Elden Johnson. Publications in Anthropology Number 4.* Minneapolis, University of Minnesota: pp. 195–211.

Martin, S. R.

1989   A Reconsideration of Aboriginal Fishing Strategies in the Northern Great Lakes Region. *American Antiquity 54*: 3, pp. 594–604.

1999   A Site for all Seasons: Some Aspects of Life in the Upper Peninsula During Late Woodland Times. In J. R. Halsey and M. D. Stafford (eds.), *Retrieving Michigan's Buried Past: The Archaeology of the Great Lakes State Bulletin 64.* Bloomfield Hills, Cranbrook Institute of Science: pp. 221–227.

Mason, C. I.

1988   *Introduction to Wisconsin Indians.* Salem, Sheffield Publishing.

McClurken, J. M.

1988   *We Wish to Be Civilized: Ottawa-American Political Contests on the Michigan Frontier.* East Lansing. Michigan State University (PhD dissertation).

McPherron, A.

1967   *The Juntunen Site and the Late Woodland Prehistory of the Upper Great Lakes Area. Anthropological Papers Number 30.* Ann Arbor, Museum of Anthropology, University of Michigan.

Milner, C. M. and J. M. O'Shea

1998   The Socioeconomic Role of Late Woodland Enclosures in Northern Lower Michigan. In R. C. Mainfort and L. P. Sullivan (eds.), *Ancient Earthen Enclosures of the Eastern Woodlands. The Ripley P. Bullen Series.* Gainesville, University Press of Florida: pp. 181–201.

Murphy, C. and N. Ferris

1990   The Late Woodland Western Basin Tradition of Southwestern Ontario. In C. J. Ellis and N. Ferris (eds.), *The Archaeology of Southern Ontario to A.D. 1650. Occasional Publications of the London Chapter, Publication No 5.* London, Ontario Archaeological Society: pp. 189–278.

O'Gorman, J. A.

2003   The "Agricultural Village" Myth and Recent Research at Moccasin Bluff. *Michigan Archaeologist 49*: 1–2, pp. 91–100.

2007   The Myth of Moccasin Bluff—Rethinking the Potawatomi Pattern. *Ethnohistory 54*: in press.

O'Gorman, J. A. and W. A. Lovis

2006   Before Removal: An Archaeological Perspective on the Southern Lake Michigan Basin. *Midcontinental Journal of Archaeology 31*: pp. 21–56.

O'Shea, J. M.

1988   Social Organization and Mortuary Behavior in the Late Woodland Period in Michigan. In R. Yerkes (ed.), *Interpretations of Culture Change in the Eastern*

Woodlands During the Late Woodland Period. Occasional Papers in Anthropology Number 3. Columbus, Ohio State University: pp. 68–85.

2003   Inland Foragers and the Adoption of Maize Agriculture in the Upper Great Lakes Region of North America. *Before Farming: The Archaeology of Old-World Hunter-Gatherers 2*: pp. 1–21.

O'Shea, J. M. and P. Halstead

1989   Conclusion: Bad Year Economics. In P. Halstead and J. O'Shea (eds.), *Bad Year Economics*. Cambridge, Cambridge University Press: 123–126.

O'Shea, J. M. and C. M. Milner

2002   Material Indicators of Territory, Identity, and Interaction in a Prehistoric Tribal System. In W. Parkinson (ed.), *The Archaeology of Tribal Societies*. Ann Arbor, International Monographs in Prehistory.

Parker, K. E.

1996   Three Corn Kernels and a Hill of Beans: The Evidence for Prehistoric Horticulture in Michigan. In M. B. Holman, J. G. Brashler and K. E. Parker (eds.), *Investigating the Archaeological Record of the Great Lakes State: Essays in Honor of Elizabeth Baldwin Garland*. Kalamazoo, New Issues Press: pp. 307–339.

Pilling, A.

1968   Discussions: Part III. In R. B. Lee and I. DeVore (eds.), *Man the Hunter*. Chicago, Aldine: pp. 155–156.

Quaife, M. M.

1921   *Alexander Henry's Travels and Adventures in the Years 1760–1776*. Chicago, Lakeside Classics.

Quimby, G. I.

1966   *Indian Culture and European Trade Goods: The Archaeology of the Historic Period in the Western Great Lakes Region*. Madison, University of Wisconsin Press.

Smith, B. A.

1996   *Systems of Subsistence and Networks of Exchange in the Terminal Woodland and Early Historic Periods in the Upper Great Lakes*. East Lansing. Michigan State University (PhD dissertation).

2004   The Gill Net's "Native Country": The Inland Shore Fishery in the Northern Lake Michigan Basin. In W. A. Lovis (ed.), *An Upper Great Lakes Archaeological Odyssey: Essays in Honor of Charles E. Cleland*. Bloomfield Hills, Cranbrook Institute of Science: pp. 64–84.

Smith, J.

1907   *An Account of the Remarkable Occurrences in the Life and Travels of Col. James Smith During His Captivity with the Indians in the Years 1755, '56, '57, '58, '59 (with an appendix of illustrative notes by Wm. M. Darlington of Pittsburgh)*. Cincinnati: Robert Clarke (originally published as Ohio Valley Historical Series Number 5).

Spielmann, K. A.

1986   Interdependence Among Egalitarian Societies. *Journal of Anthropological Archaeology 5*: pp. 279–312.

Strong, W. D.

1935   *An Introduction to Nebraska Archeology. Miscellaneous Collections Number 93.* Washington, Smithsonian Institution.

1936   Anthropological Theory and Archaeological Fact. In R. H. Lowie (ed.), *Essays in Anthropology presented to A. L. Kroeber*. Berkeley, University of California Press: pp. 359–370.

Tanner, H. H.

1987   *Atlas of Great Lakes Indian History*. Norman, University of Oklahoma Press.

Tanner, J.

1956   *A Narrative of the Captivity and Adventures of John Tanner During Thirty Years Among the Indians in the Interior of North America*. Minneapolis, Ross and Haines.

Trigger, B. G.

1969   *The Huron Farmers of the North*. New York, Holt, Rinehart and Winston.

Wedel, W. R.

1938   *The Direct-Historical Approach in Pawnee Archeology. Miscellaneous Collections Number 97*. Washington, Smithsonian Institution.

Williams, B. J.

1968   The Birhor of India and Some Comments on Band Organization. In R. B. Lee and I. DeVore (eds.), *Man the Hunter*. Chicago, Aldine: pp. 126–131.

Wobst, H. M.

1968   The Butterfield Site, 20 BY 29, Bay County, Michigan. In J. E. Fitting, J. R. Halsey and H. M. Wobst (eds.), *Contributions to Michigan Archaeology. Anthropological Papers Number 32*. Ann Arbor, Museum of Anthropology, University of Michigan: pp. 173–275.

Yarnell, R. A.

1964   *Aboriginal Relationships Between Culture and Plant Life in the Upper Great Lakes Region. Anthropological Papers Number 23*. Ann Arbor, Museum of Anthropology, University of Michigan.

CHAPTER 14

NOMADIC POTTERS

RELATIONSHIPS BETWEEN CERAMIC TECHNOLOGIES AND MOBILITY STRATEGIES

JELMER W. EERKENS

THERE IS ALWAYS a give-and-take when people, and societies collectively, incorporate the production and use of new material technologies. People usually alter the technology to suit their needs, but they are also often fundamentally changed by the technology as well. Such changes can come quickly and consciously, as deliberate adjustments are made, or they may happen at a slower and imperceptible rate. This chapter examines the interplay between material technology and one aspect of prehistoric lifestyle: settlement strategies, especially residential mobility.[1] Lithic analysis has been heavily engaged in this type of research because stone tools are a common find at archaeological sites spanning the transition between different mobility strategies (Rafferty 1985; Parry and Kelly 1987; Kelly 1988; Basgall 1989; Henry 1989; Lurie 1989; Rosen 1989; Andrefsky 1991; Bamforth 1991; Odell 1996; Thacker 1996). This chapter examines a second, in this context much less studied, technology: pottery. As a case study I draw from the Mojave Desert and the North American Great Basin, or more properly the Basin and Range, where I have been focusing my research for the last decade (Figure 14.1). I will refer to this area simply as the Western Great Basin, although I recognize that it includes parts of the Mojave Desert and the Western Sierra Nevada Mountains, which are technically not part of the Basin and Range geographic province.

The late prehistoric (around 700–100 BP) archaeological record in the Western Great Basin provides an interesting case for examining these relationships for several reasons. First, the aboriginal populations of this area were

---

[1.] In this chapter I focus on residentially mobile hunting-and-gathering populations. However, as discussed during the workshop at the Cotsen Institute of Archaeology at UCLA, June 2004, there ought to be analogous predictions for the material technologies of nomadic pastoralists as well. Some of the discussion in this chapter may apply in such settings, but others, such as the heaviness of technologies, may be less restrictive elements.

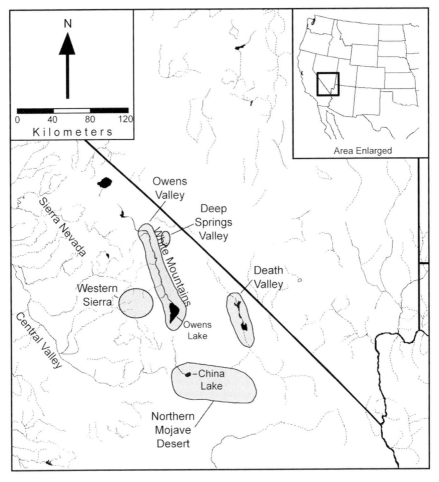

Figure 14.1. Map of the border region between California and Nevada, showing the study areas (in gray).

composed of hunting-and-gathering groups, controlling for a subsistence mode in the study. Second, ethnographic and archaeological data indicate several settlement patterns were found within the region, ranging from nearly sedentary in the Owens Valley to highly mobile in the Mojave Desert. Third, although ethnographic data on pottery making are scarce, pottery is a common component of late prehistoric sites across the entire region and has been the subject of archaeological investigation. Although the coarseness of the archaeological record does not allow us to determine exactly how pottery affected people and vice versa, it does allow us to examine general patterns between pottery making, pottery use, and mobility strategies.

MOBILITY AND POTTERY TECHNOLOGY

There has been a common wisdom or stereotype among many archaeologists that sedentism, agriculture and pottery technologies are necessarily and positively correlated. Indeed, some archaeologists use the presence or absence of pottery in the archaeological record as an independent measure of residential mobility. The presence of potsherds at a site would indicate sedentism, and a lack of pottery would suggest some degree of seasonal transhumance. Although examples of pottery in sites occupied by mobile hunter-gatherers are known (Arnold 1985), as Sassaman (1993:2–3) notes, in such cases the pottery is usually defined as 'crude' and 'technologically unimpressive' thereby relegating it to a status of little or no significance and reinforcing the stereotype (but see Barnard, this volume). There are, of course, good reasons to believe that mobile hunter-gatherers should not make pots. I present five conflicts or problems that hinder the use of pots among mobile societies, both hunter-gatherers and pastoralists. To make pottery a worthwhile technology, mobile societies must resolve these issues.

First, pots are heavy relative to other containers and are taxing to carry around during seasonal movements. This is particularly true for societies that do not have pack animals and societies in which goods must be carried by people on their backs. And even among societies that have pack animals, including dogs, the extra energy required by the animals to move heavy objects requires additional nourishment and grazing time. When lighter alternatives, such as baskets, gourds, animal-skin pouches or other containers are available, such technologies should be more attractive from an energy standpoint than heavy fired clay ones.

Second, because they are relatively fragile, pots are exposed to high rates of breakage when carried around during residential movements. Although they can be insulated from impact shock by being packed in softer materials, each packing up and unpacking of pots increases the chance of breakage. Accidents, such as dropping during transport, increase the risk of breakage. These risks, however small, make ceramic pots inferior relative to other container technologies for mobile groups. Again, baskets and hides are more resistant to impact shock and should be preferable to pots.

Third, mobile peoples may not stay in one place long enough to see the pottery production cycle through. From the collection of clay, to forming a pot, to drying and firing it, the making of a clay pot can take from several days to several weeks (Arnold 1985). In particular, the crucial step of drying an unfired pot may take several days and may require significant oversight to ensure an even and thorough drying. Mobile people, particularly during certain times of the year, may have to move before they can complete the steps necessary to produce pots.

Fourth, and related to the third issue, is that the most opportune time to produce pots, the dry season, is also the time when many seeds, nuts, berries and greens ripen. Time conflicts between gathering food that is only available during narrow temporal windows and the production of ceramic pots may make the latter too expensive. This is particularly true if a significant quantity of plant products must be harvested and stored for later consumption. One way to solve such a time conflict is to divide these tasks by sex or some other societal division. Yet plant gathering and pottery production are both typically performed by women, even among mobile hunter-gatherers.

Fifth, the small population sizes typically encountered among mobile hunter-gatherers tends to limit the demand for pots. As discussed by Brown (1989), one of the significant advantages of pots over other containers is that there is an economy of scale in the production of the former. As multiple pots can be fired at once, this step can be performed almost as easily for one pot as for a dozen. This is not true of other common containers, such as baskets or sewn skins, where each item must be made individually, and making a dozen takes twelve times as long (and twelve times as much raw material) as making one. In arid landscapes, such as the Great Basin, limited fuel resources make this factor of particular importance (Bettinger et al. 1994). Fuel needed for cooking and warmth may be in such high demand that the fuel needed to fire only a small number of ceramic vessels may simply be unavailable.

In sum, ceramic technologies do not lend themselves well to a mobile lifestyle. Yet we know of many archaeological and ethnographic examples of pottery making in mobile societies (Arnold 1985; Barnard, this volume). Indeed, the origins of ceramic technologies often occur within such settings (Ikawa-Smith 1976; Reid 1984; Aikens 1995; Close 1995: Hoopes and Barnett 1995; Rice 1999). So why do these mobile groups engage in pottery production? And when they do, how does their mobility affect the way they organize the production and use of pots? And finally, how do they resolve the conflicts and problems listed above? These issues have not been extensively investigated by archaeologists. Simms et al. (1997; see also Bright and Ugan 1999) have explored some of these questions in the Eastern Great Basin, and Braun (1983) has done so in the eastern United States, but there are few published accounts on this topic. This chapter builds on their work but takes it in a different direction by examining pottery and mobility practices within the Western Great Basin.

Steward (1938) believed residential mobility in the Great Basin to be inversely correlated with population density, which itself was correlated to precipitation and bioproductivity. Residential mobility was necessary to exploit spatially variable and low-density food resources. People followed the distribution and availability of ripening plant foods, especially piñon nuts and

Table 14.1. Population Levels, Average Precipitation and Estimated Degree of Residential Stability for Six Regions of the Western Great Basin:

Region	Population density[a]	Annual rainfall[a]	Mobility rank	Sherds/acre	Sherds/projectile point	Pottery rank
Western Sierra	0.5	57.7	1	N/A	11.9	3
Northern Owens	2.1	16.0	2	0.02	5.2	6
Southern Owens	2.1	14.5	3	0.14	33.9	1
Deep Springs	10.7	15.4	4	0.06	7.9	4
Death Valley	30.0	5.3	5	0.09	17.7	2
Northern Mojave	>30	11.9	6	0.05	7.7	5

[a]The population density is given in persons/square mile (Delacorte 1990; Eerkens 2003a), the annual rainfall in cm/year.

small seeds. Table 14.1 gives the estimated population density (persons/square mile), precipitation (cm/year), and level and density of pottery for six regions, representing a range of different populations within the Western Great Basin, though all are hunter-gatherers practicing some degree of residential mobility. The table ranks residential mobility and the degree of engagement in pottery. It is evident that the degree of residential mobility did not have a predictable or consistent effect on the amount or density of pottery in a region. This suggests that mobility did not affect the degree of reliance on pots in the material culture (Eerkens 2003a).

Although there is variability, vessels from the Western Great Basin are generally medium-sized (18–22 cm high and 18–25 cm wide at the mouth) and undecorated. In most areas, less than 10% of the rim sherds have fingernail-impressed decoration around the rim (Eerkens 2001). Painting, slipping and burnishing are not evident. Straight-sided and direct-rimmed conical boiling pots are the most common vessel type, though spherical bowls with recurved rims are also present, particularly in the eastern part of the Western Great Basin (Bettinger 1986; Pippin 1986; Prince 1986; Lyneis 1988; Touhy 1990). Vessels were constructed mainly by stacking coils of clay onto a circular disk base, welding the coils together by scraping with the fingers, a bundle of sticks or a small object. Sand or crushed rock temper is usually present and was probably part of the local clay matrix. Organic temper is occasionally present in the form of grass blades and other vegetable matter. Vessels were fired at relatively low temperatures (around 600°C) and appear brown-red in color, giving rise to the general category of 'brown wares.' Figure 14.2 shows a nearly complete pot found in Owens Valley, typical for the size and shape of the region. Holes near the rim of the pot were drilled on either side of a crack. Cordage would have been looped through the holes in an attempt to hold the pot together and extend its use life.

Figure 14.2. Whole cooking pot from Owens Valley, California, with repair holes near the rim.

Pottery making is clearly a late technology in the Western Great Basin. Dating of ceramics has not been actively pursued in most regions, but it is clear that they are consistently associated with other artifacts that date to the latest period in prehistory, after 700 BP (Pippin 1986; Rhode 1994; Feathers and Rhode 1998). In Owens Valley, people seem to have been experimenting with ceramic technologies around 1200 years ago (Eerkens et al. 1999), yet the craft does not become commonplace until 500–700 years ago (Delacorte 1999). Pots seem to have been used mainly for boiling seeds and other vegetable products and only rarely were used to process meat (Eerkens 2005). Pots were rarely carried more than 80 km outside their region of manufacture, and production was organized at a small-scale or family level (Eerkens et al. 2002).

RESOLVING CONFLICTS

The presence of pottery among the mobile hunter-gatherers of the Western Great Basin is particularly interesting in light of the problems and conflicts mentioned above. Basketry technologies were highly developed in this region, such that they could perform virtually all the tasks that pots could. Baskets were woven so tightly that they could hold water, were durable and strong enough to boil foods, and were long-lasting enough to store and serve foods. All these activities could be performed at a fraction of the weight of ceramic pots and with much greater resistance to impact stress. Baskets, then, would seem ideally suited to a mobile lifestyle. So why did these people ever get into the business of making pots? Similarly, how did they modify pottery technologies to suit their lifestyle, and how did the use of pottery modify their lifestyle? I address these issues by examining how the Paiute, Shoshone, and the Mojave Desert people of the study area resolved the five problems listed above.

One solution to the heaviness and fragility of pots is simply not to move them at all. Caching pots may have been a way to avoid carrying them during the seasonal round (Eerkens 2003a). In the Western Great Basin two pieces of information suggest that caching was an important strategy used to deal with these problems. First, though uncommon, cached pots from rockshelters and caves have occasionally been recorded and described by archaeologists (Campbell 1931; Wallace 1965; King 1976; Bayman et al. 1996). The discovery,

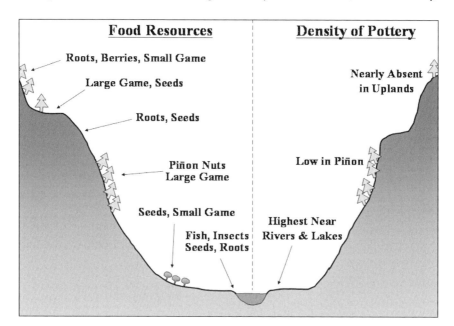

Figure 14.3. Distribution of pottery in Owens Valley (data from Bettinger 1975).

Figure 14.4. The Owens River, near Big Pine.

in March 2002, of a nearly complete pot stowed away in a narrow rock crevice near Little Lake, just south of Owens Valley, is a clear example of a cached pot (Eerkens n.d.). All these caches are in lowland locations. Second, the distribution of potsherds across the landscape is clearly uneven, heavily skewed toward valley-bottom and wetland locations, as shown in Figure 14.3 (Eerkens 2003a). Figures 14.4 through 14.7 depict some of these different environments in and to the east of Owens Valley, California, all within several kilometers of one another. Note the dramatic changes in both the density and makeup of vegetation communities in these different environments.

Alfred Kroeber (1922) recognized this pattern but did not attach any particular meaning to it. Subsequent archaeological investigations have supported his impressions. Surveys in many valleys in the Central and Western Great Basin demonstrate that the frequency of pottery is significantly higher in riverine and lakeside locations on the valley bottom (Hunt 1960; Thomas 1971, 1983; Bettinger 1975; Wallace 1986; Weaver 1986; Delacorte 1990; Plew and Bennick 1990; Gilreath and Hildebrandt 1997; Hildebrandt and Ruby 1999). Table 14.2 shows the results from five regions with comparable survey strategies and coverage. Between 63–100% of the potsherds are located near the valley bottom, even when adjusted for the total number of artifacts found or the area surveyed (Thomas 1971; Bettinger 1975; Delacorte 1990; Gilreath and Hildebrandt 1997; Hildebrandt and Ruby 1999). Despite the fact that archaeological sites from the ceramic period are present in all parts of the landscape,

Figure 14.5. The Owens Valley desert shrub landscape.

Figure 14.6. The Piñon-Juniper landscape of the White Mountains (courtesy of the Far Western Anthropological Research Group).

Figure 14.7. The high altitude alpine desert landscape of the White Mountains.

from valley bottom to alpine zones, pottery is differentially distributed within the former. This suggests that locations across the valley bottom were where people broke, and presumably used, the majority of their pots and that pots were not often carried to other parts of the landscape. Besides the fact that it has all the resources necessary to make pots (clay, sand, water and firewood), a major advantage of the valley bottom is that this is a predictable source of water. As a result, the food resources in these locations are spatially and temporally predictable, particularly when compared with other Great Basin resources such as piñon nuts and dryland seeds (Thomas 1972). Thus, caching only works in areas that have relatively stable and predictable food resources.

Although caching pots would have solved the heaviness and fragility problems, it would have had major repercussions for the lifestyles of people doing so. In particular, since they could not have cached a pot at every spot on the landscape, caching would have tethered people to particular points on the landscape, where they had left their pots. This would result in higher rates of site re-occupation, also referred to as 'occupational redundancy' or 'persistent places' in the literature (Eerkens 2003a). Such tethering may have promoted reliance on foods associated with these locations and may have encouraged the notion of landownership and territoriality. It is also likely that caching behavior would have prompted people to modify pottery technologies to make their products more suitable for storage during the off-season. Thicker and stronger pots may have been the by-product of this behavior.

Table 14.2. Distribution of Pottery by Environmental Zone (adjusted by area surveyed):

	Valley bottom	Piñon/juniper	Above piñon	Reference
Northern Owens	86%	12%	4%	Bettinger 1975
Deep Springs	64%	36%	0%	Delacorte 1990
Northern Mojave	63%	37%	N/A	Gilreath and Hildebrandt 1997; Hildebrandt and Ruby 1999
Reese River	100%	0%	0%	Thomas 1971
Monitor Valley	76%	15%	9%	Thomas 1983

The third conflict, the need to be in one place long enough to see the pro-duction cycle through, may have been solved by remaining in certain spots for longer periods or to occupy them more frequently. Combined with the reasoning above, spending more time at these locations may have led to a positive feedback cycle with the tethering and caching behavior. In particular, spending longer periods of time in places where pots were made and cached may have promoted an increased reliance on the resources available in those areas. If pots had to be constructed for use, and were not already available as cached items, people may have needed to arrive several days or weeks ahead of the availability of such resources to prepare for such activities. Time spent making pots while seed resources were ripe would have subtracted from time that could be devoted to gathering. It is possible that women traveled to valley bottom seed patches several months prior to, or after, the availability of seeds, constructed pots there and cached them for future use. This would have also solved the fourth conflict, namely time conflicts in the dry season between seed gathering and pot production.

All these factors would have forced individuals to alter the way that they made pottery by limiting the amount of time devoted to production. A minimum of time investment is consistent with the ceramic technology seen in the Western Great Basin. The minor amount of decoration, the lack of extensive surface finishing (burnishing, polishing, slipping) and the minimum attention given to symmetry and evenness (rims are often undulating and walls often have a variable thickness) all indicate that pots were hastily made. The use of sand and crushed rock as temper, most likely native to the matrix from which the clay was collected (Schaefer 2003), also indicates little investment in production activities. Moreover, if pots were constructed in the rainy season, there would have been a need for quick-drying pots, to minimize the chances of their getting wet again while drying.

Several methods exist to reduce the time required to dry a pot prior to firing, including addition of fiber temper, roughening the exterior or thinning the pot (Skibo et al. 1989; Schiffer et al. 1994). All of these factors are evident in areas where people were more mobile. Although fiber temper is not dominant in pots from the Western Great Basin, it is present in most sherds in small amounts, again supporting the notion that these pots were constructed to minimize time investment. These findings are consistent with those of Simms et al. (1997), who suggest that mobile foragers invested less in their ceramic pots than sedentary agriculturalists in the Eastern Great Basin. At the same time, there are indications that within the mobile hunter-gatherer groups, greater residential mobility may have fostered greater investment in ceramic technologies, likely because of the greater demands that residential mobility places on the material technology (Eerkens 2003a, 2003b). Pots in regions where people were more mobile are smaller in diameter, thinner, and more often roughened on their exterior surface; they also contain finer temper and are less diverse in size and shape. Although other factors can contribute to these attributes, such as the intended vessel function, the nature and availability of clays, and different learning traditions, there are good reasons to believe that mobility would have an effect on these attributes (Simms et al. 1997). Finally, as Brown (1989) has argued, one of the main advantages of pottery technologies is the economy of scale in production. Pottery is a particularly advantageous technology when large numbers of containers are needed. Unfortunately, mobile societies usually maintain low population densities that do not allow them to take advantage of this attribute of pottery.

All indications from ethnographic and archaeological data confirm that the Western Great Basin was home to low population densities. Although population density certainly varied across the region (Steward 1938), it is clear that areas with higher population did not necessarily produce more pots. Some of the highest densities of pottery in the study area occur in areas where people were quite mobile, and some of the lowest densities occur in areas with semisedentism (Eerkens 2003a). Nor does it appear that pottery production was organized at a higher regionwide level by a few specialists who provided pots to a large area to take advantage of the economy of scale. Pots in the Western Great Basin seem to have been produced on a small scale at a local family or village level (Eerkens et al. 2002).

Low-temperature firing, to conserve fuel, and extensive efforts to increase the use life of pots, for example by repairing cracks (Figure 14.2), may have been responses to the expenses involved in pottery production. These strategies may have been employed to make the costs of production versus artifact use life for pots more equal to that of baskets. Once people were investing in the production of pots, it is likely that pots were put to an increasing range of uses. Analysis of the potsherds from the region suggests an increase in shape and size diversity over time. As people became familiar with the technology, they altered the design to increase heating efficiency and minimize the amount of raw materials needed by making pots thinner (Eerkens 2003b). Once the technology was incorporated into the lives of prehistoric people in the Western Great Basin, it gradually encouraged other changes in day-to-day activities.

DISCUSSION

There are many hurdles for mobile peoples to clear before they can incorporate pottery technologies within their material culture. Overall, these hurdles may account for the general relationship between pottery use and mobility strategies seen worldwide. More specifically, most fully sedentary and semisedentary societies use pots (91% and 75% respectively), but less than a third of mobile nomadic people engage in this activity (Arnold 1985). Yet in some instances mobile groups are able to resolve these issues to make the technology work for them. The Western Great Basin was one of these areas.

Rather than disregard ceramic technologies altogether, late prehistoric societies of the Western Great Basin were extremely inventive and designed ways around the problems that typically beset mobile societies. They actively manipulated aspects of the form, function, use and production of their pots to fit this technology within their mobile lifestyles, that is, to suit their specific needs. It also appears that the use of pots had effects on the lifestyles of these people. It probably tethered people to particular tracts of land, promoted an increased reliance on the resources available in these areas, especially seeds, and may have required much travel and foresight to produce and cache pots ahead of time in patches where high seed yields were anticipated. While tethering may promote decreased mobility or sedentism in the long run (Kelly 1990; 1995), mobile peoples can also be tethered to certain locations by making consistent and repeated use of them (occupational redundancy). Caching and occupational redundancy allowed such groups to take advantage of technologies that are normally reserved for more sedentary groups, including the use of heavy or fragile tools such as ceramic pots. In this respect caching may be an important strategy for mobile pottery-using hunting-and-gathering groups. The success of caching is highly dependent, however, on the spatial predictability of the resources for which the tools are needed.

There is little patterning in the degree of residential mobility versus the amount of pottery (Table 14.1). This suggests that once people resolved the conflicts associated with pottery production, they were free to engage in vessel production to whatever degree was necessary. In other words, once people had figured out how to incorporate pot production and use into their lifestyles (by redesigning shape, temper and texture, as well as by caching), the degree of residential mobility did not have an influence over how many vessels they made. It did, however, affect how they made pots. A design favoring rapid drying, increased postfiring strength, overall lightness and durability was clearly favored.

The above may explain how it was that mobile people were able to make and use pots. A remaining question, of course, is the matter of why they did. Although this question lies beyond the scope of this chapter, I have argued elsewhere that the main reason for this change relates to demands on the time and labor of women (Eerkens 2001; see also Crown and Wills 1995). Prior to the adoption of pottery, stone boiling in baskets was the main method for boiling foods, especially small seeds. Figure 14.8 shows the density of small seeds recovered from flotation studies from house floors in Owens Valley. Clearly, low numbers of seeds were eaten from the 3rd century CE onward (Eerkens 2004). These were probably boiled in baskets; however, around 1350 CE the density of small seeds greatly increased, and seed boiling must have become a major activity. Stone boiling in baskets is an inefficient method because it demands constant attention from women to replace cooled stones with heated ones and to avoid burning holes in the bottom of the basket. Pots may have provided a more efficient boiling container than baskets because they can be set over the fire with little further attention. As a result, greater numbers of seeds could be processed at once.

In conclusion, the restrictions on technology imposed by a residentially mobile lifestyle may force mobile groups to modify technologies in predictable ways. For example, we may expect to see more standardization in certain attributes, especially size, shape and weight. A mobile lifestyle may not allow for a range of shapes to be made and used, and experimentation with new designs

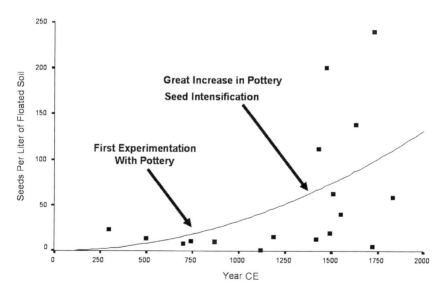

Figure 14.8. Density over time of the concentration of small seeds found on house floors in Owens Valley (after Eerkens 2004).

may not be possible, particularly in more marginal environments where the costs of failure are high. Similarly, we may expect to see a low amount of time invested in these technologies (Simms et al. 1997; Bright and Ugan 1999). Only after people become more sedentary, and the craft becomes established, will we see elaboration in shapes, sizes and styles as the technology is applied to other purposes (Hoopes and Barnett 1995; Simms et al. 1997:783). For items that are cached, we may not see much in the way of decoration or other modifications. While potters may add decoration for their own artistic enjoyment, such effort may not be worth the time if the goal is to transmit social information (such as status or faction membership) when it would be out of view most of the year. It is important to stress that these are expectations only and not blind rules to be applied to the archaeological record. As with all archaeological interpretation, the design, standardization and distribution of material artifacts should help our reconstructions of mobility, but, if at all possible, they should represent just one window on this aspect of prehistoric ways of life.

REFERENCES

Aikens, C. M.

1995   First in the World: The Jomon Pottery of Early Japan. In W. K. Barnett and J. W. Hoopes (eds.), *The Emergence of Pottery*. Washington, Smithsonian Institution Press: pp. 11–21.

Andrefsky, W.

1991   Inferring Trends in Prehistoric Settlement Behavior from Lithic Production Technology in the Southern Plains. *North American Archaeologist 12*: pp. 129–144.

Arnold, D. E.

1985   *Ceramic Theory and Cultural Process*. Cambridge, Cambridge University Press.

Bamforth, D. B.

1991   Technological Organization and Hunter-Gatherer Land Use. *American Antiquity 56*: pp. 216–235.

Basgall, M. E.

1989   Obsidian Acquisition and Use in Prehistoric Central Eastern California: A Preliminary Assessment. In R. E. Hughes (ed.), *Current Directions in California Obsidian Studies. Contributions of the University of California Archaeological Research Facility 48*. Berkeley, University of California Press: pp. 111–126.

Bayman, J. M., R. H. Hevly, B. Johnson, K. J. Reinhard and R. Ryan

1996   Analytical Perspectives on a Protohistoric Cache of Ceramic Jars from the Lower Colorado Desert. *Journal of California and Great Basin Anthropology 18*: pp. 131–154.

Bettinger, R. L.

1975   *The Surface Archaeology of Owens Valley, Eastern California: Prehistoric Man-Land Relationships in the Great Basin.* University of California, Riverside (PhD dissertation).

1986   Intersite Comparison of Great Basin Brown Ware Assemblages. In S. Griset (ed.), *Pottery of the Great Basin and Adjacent Areas. University of Utah Anthropological Papers 111.* Salt Lake City, University of Utah Press: pp. 97–106.

Bettinger, R. L., D. B. Madsen and R. G. Elston

1994   Prehistoric Settlement Categories and Settlement Systems in the Alashan Desert of Inner Mongolia, PRC. *Journal of Anthropological Archaeology 13*: pp. 74–101.

Braun, D.

1983   Pots as Tools. In A. Keene and J. Moore (eds.), *Archaeological Hammers and Theories.* New York, Academic Press: pp. 107–134.

Bright, J. R. and A. Ugan

1999   Ceramics and Mobility: Assessing the Role of Foraging Behavior and Its Implications for Culture-History. *Utah Archaeology 12*: pp. 17–29.

Brown, J. A.

1989   The Beginnings of Pottery as an Economic Process. In S. E. van der Leeuw and R. Torrence (eds.), *What's New? A Closer Look at the Process of Innovation.* London, Unwin Hyman: pp. 203–224.

Campbell, E. W.

1931   *An Archeological Survey of the Twenty Nine Palms Region. Southwest Museum Paper Number 7.* Los Angeles, Southwest Museum.

Close, A. E.

1995   Few and Far Between: Early Ceramics in North Africa. In W. K. Barnett and J. W. Hoopes (eds.), *The Emergence of Pottery.* Washington, Smithsonian Institution Press: pp. 23–37.

Crown, P. L. and W. H. Wills

1995   The Origins of Southwestern Ceramic Containers: Women's Time Allocation and Economic Intensification. *Journal of Anthropological Research 51*: pp. 173–186.

Delacorte, M. G.

1990   *The Prehistory of Deep Springs Valley, Eastern California: Adaptive Variation in the Western Great Basin.* University of California, Davis (PhD dissertation).

1999   *The Changing Role of Riverine Environments in the Prehistory of the Central-Western Great Basin: Data Recovery Excavations at Six Prehistoric Sites in Owens Valley, California.* Report submitted by Far Western Anthropological Research Group to Caltrans District 9, Bishop, California.

Eerkens, J. W.

2001   *The Origins of Pottery Among Late Prehistoric Hunter-Gatherers in California and the Western Great Basin*. University of California, Santa Barbara (PhD dissertation).

2003a   Residential and Pottery Use in the Western Great Basin. *Current Anthropology 44*: pp. 728–738.

2003b   Towards a Chronology of Brownware Pottery in the Western Great Basin: A Case Study from Owens Valley. *North American Archaeologist 24*: pp. 1–27.

2004   Privatization, Small-Seed Intensification, and the Origins of Pottery in the Western Great Basin. *American Antiquity 69*: pp. 653–670.

2005   GC-MS Analysis and Fatty Acid Ratios of Archaeological Potsherds from the Western Great Basin of North America. *Archaeometry 47*: pp. 83–102.

n.d.   Notes on a Cached Brownware Pot near Little Lake, Eastern California. Manuscript in possession of the author.

Eerkens, J. W., H. Neff and M. Glascock

1999   Early Pottery from Sunga'va and Implications for the Development of Ceramic Technology in Owens Valley, California. *Journal of California and Great Basin Anthropology 20*: pp. 275–285.

2002   Ceramic Production Among Small-Scale and Mobile Hunters and Gatherers: A Case Study from the Southwestern Great Basin. *Journal of Anthropological Archaeology 2*: pp. 200–229.

Feathers, J. K. and D. Rhode

1998   Luminescence Dating of Protohistoric Pottery from the Great Basin. *Geoarchaeology 13*: pp 287–308.

Gilreath, A. J. and W. R. Hildebrandt

1997   *Prehistoric Use of the Coso Volcanic Field. Contributions of the University of California Archaeological Research Facility Number 56*. Berkeley, University of California Press.

Henry, D. O.

1989   Correlations Between Reduction Strategies and Settlement Patterns. In D. O. Henry and D. H. Odell (eds.), *Alternative Approaches to Lithic Analysis*. Washington, American Anthropological Association: pp. 139–155.

Hildebrandt, W. R. and A. Ruby

1999   *Archaeological Survey of the Coso Target Range: Evidence for Prehistoric and Early Historic Use of the Pinyon Zone at Naval Air Weapons Station, China Lake*. Report on file with the Naval Air Weapons Station, China Lake, California.

Hoopes, J. W. and W. K. Barnett

1995   The Shape of Early Pottery Studies. In W. K. Barnett and J. W. Hoopes (eds.), *The Emergence of Pottery*. Washington, Smithsonian Institution Press: pp. 1–7.

Hunt, A.

1960   *Archaeology of the Death Valley Salt Pan, California. Anthropological Papers Number 47.* Salt Lake City, University of Utah Press.

Ikawa-Smith, F.

1976   On Ceramic Technology in East Asia. *Current Anthropology 17*: pp. 513–515.

Kelly, R. L.

1988   The Three Sides of a Biface. *American Antiquity 53*: pp. 717–734.

1990   Marshes and Mobility in the Western Great Basin. In J. C. Janetski and D. B. Madsen (eds.), *Wetland Adaptations in the Great Basin. Occasional Papers Number 1.* Provo, Museum of Peoples and Cultures: pp. 233–258.

1995   *The Foraging Spectrum: Diversity in Hunter-Gatherer Lifeways.* Washington, Smithsonian Institution Press.

King, T. J., Jr.

1976   A Cache of Vessels from Cottonwood Spring (Riv-937). *Journal of California Anthropology 3*: pp. 136–142.

Kroeber, A. L.

1922   Elements of Culture in Native California. *University of California Publications in American Archaeology and Ethnology 13*: 8, pp. 257–328.

Lurie, R.

1989   Lithic Technology and Mobility Strategies: The Kosher Site Middle Archaic. In R. Torrence (ed.), *Time, Energy, and Stone Tools.* Cambridge, Cambridge University Press: pp. 46–56.

Lyneis, M. M.

1988   Tizon Brown Ware and the Problems Raised by Paddle-and-Anvil Pottery in the Mojave Desert. *Journal of California and Great Basin Anthropology 10*: pp. 146–155.

Odell, G.

1996   Economizing Behavior and the Concept of "Curation." In G. Odell (ed.), *Theory and Behavior from Stone Tools.* New York, Plenum: pp. 53–81.

Parry, W. and R. L. Kelly

1987   Expedient Core Technology and Sedentism. In J. K Johnson and C. A. Morrow (eds.), *The Organization of Core Technology.* Boulder, Westview Press: pp. 285–304.

Pippin, L. C.

1986   Intermountain Brown Wares: An Assessment. In S. Griset (ed.), *Pottery of the Great Basin and Adjacent Areas. Anthropological Papers Number 111.* Salt Lake City, University of Utah Press: pp. 9–21.

Plew, M. G. and M. Bennick

1990   Prehistoric Pottery of Southwestern Idaho: A Report on the Southwest Idaho Ceramics Project. In J. M. Mack (ed.), *Hunter-Gatherer Pottery from the Far*

West. Nevada State Museum Anthropological Papers 23. Carson City, Nevada State Museum: pp. 107–122.

Prince, E. R.

1986   Shoshonean Pottery of the Western Great Basin. In S. Griset (ed.), *Pottery of the Great Basin and Adjacent Areas*. Salt Lake City, University of Utah Press: pp. 3–8.

Rafferty, J.

1985   The Archaeological Record on Sedentariness: Recognition, Development, and Implications. In M. B. Schiffer (ed.), *Advances in Archaeological Method and Theory*. New York, Academic Press: pp. 113–156.

Reid, K. C.

1984   Fire and Ice: New Evidence for the Production and Preservation of Late Archaic Fiber-Tempered Pottery in the Middle Latitude Lowlands. *American Antiquity 49*: pp. 55–76.

Rhode, D.

1994   Direct Dating of Brown Ware Ceramics Using Thermoluminescence and Its Relation to the Numic Spread. In D. B. Madsen and D. Rhode (eds.), *Across the West: Human Population Movement and the Expansion of the Numa*. Salt Lake City, University of Utah Press: pp. 124–130.

Rice, P. M.

1999   On the Origins of Pottery. *Journal of Archaeological Method and Theory 6*: pp. 1–54.

Rosen, S. A.

1989   The Origins of Craft Specialization: Lithic Perspectives. In I. Hershkovitz (ed.), *People and Culture in Change: Proceedings of the Second Symposium of Upper Palaeolithic, Mesopolithic, and Neolithic Populations of Europe and the Mediterranean Basin*. Oxford, British Archaeological Reports: pp. 107–114.

Sassaman, K. E.

1993   *Early Pottery in the Southeast: Tradition and Innovation in Cooking Technology*. Tuscaloosa, University of Alabama Press.

Schaefer, J.

2003   Petrographic and INAA Analysis of Southern Owens Valley Clays and Brown Ware Ceramics from the Olancha/Cartago Four-Lane Project. In B. F. Byrd and M. Hale (eds.), *Lacustrine Lifestyles Along Owens Lake: NRHP Evaluation of 15 Prehistoric Sites for the Olancha/Cartago Four-Lane Project, U.S. Route 395, Inyo County, California*. Encinitas, ASM Affiliates: pp. 567–605.

Schiffer, M. B., J. M. Skibo, T. C. Boelke, M. A. Neupert and M. Aronson

1994   New Perspectives on Experimental Archaeology: Surface Treatments and Thermal Response of the Clay Cooking Pot. *American Antiquity 59*: pp. 197–217.

Simms, S. R., J. R. Bright and A. Ugan
1997   Plain-Ware Ceramics and Residential Mobility: A Case Study from the Great Basin. *Journal of Archaeological Science 24*: pp. 779–792.

Skibo, J. M., M. B. Schiffer and K. C. Reid
1989   Organic Tempered Pottery: An Experimental Study. *American Antiquity 54*: pp. 122–146.

Steward, J. H.
1938   *Basin-Plateau Aboriginal Sociopolitical Groups*. Washington, Smithsonian Institution Press.

Thacker, P. T.
1996   Hunter-Gatherer Lithic Economy and Settlement Systems: Understanding Regional Assemblage Variability in the Upper Paleolithic of Portuguese Estremadura. In G. Odel (ed.), *Theory and Behavior from Stone Tools*. New York, Plenum: pp. 101–124.

Thomas, D. H.
1971   *Prehistoric Subsistence-Settlement Patterns of the Reese River Valley, Central Nevada*. University of California, Davis (PhD dissertation).
1972   Western Shoshone Ecology: Settlement Patterns and Beyond. In D. Fowler (ed.), *Great Basin Cultural Ecology: A Symposium*. Reno, University of Nevada: pp. 135–153.
1983   The Archaeology of Monitor Valley 2: Gatecliff Shelter. *Anthropological Papers of the American Museum of Natural History 59*: 1, pp. 1–52.

Touhy, D. R.
1990   Second Thoughts on Shoshoni Pots from Nevada and Elsewhere. In J. Mack (ed.), *Hunter-Gatherer Pottery from the Far West*. Carson City, Nevada State Museum: pp. 84–105.

Wallace, W. J.
1965   A Cache of Unfired Clay Objects from Death Valley, California. *American Antiquity 30*: pp. 434–441.
1986   The Pottery of Mesquite Flat, Death Valley, California. In S. Griset (ed.), *Pottery of the Great Basin and Adjacent Areas*. Salt Lake City, University of Utah Press: pp. 71–74.

Weaver, R. A.
1986   Notes on the Production, Use, and Distribution of Pottery in East-Central California. In S. Griset (ed.), *Pottery of the Great Basin and Adjacent Areas*. Salt Lake City, University of Utah Press: pp. 75–81.

PART II

THE PRESENT AND THE FUTURE

CHAPTER 15

MOBILITY AND SEDENTISM OF THE IRON AGE AGROPASTORALISTS OF SOUTHEAST KAZAKHSTAN

CLAUDIA CHANG[1]

EVIDENCE FROM THE Iron Age settlements in the Talgar region of southeast Kazakhstan indicates that the 'fierce horse riding warrior' confederacies such as the Saka (Scythian), Wusun and Yuezhi practiced both farming and herding along the well-watered steppes north of the Tian Shan Mountains (Chang et al. 2003). The splendid kurgan tradition dating from the 8th century BCE through the 5th century CE of the reputed Iron Age nomads also suggests that such pastoral confederacies were hierarchical and stratified (Frachetti, this volume; Shishlina, this volume). To what degree were the members of these confederacies mobile or settled? And how did mobility, or the ability to move with flocks, personnel, military cavalries or caravans, contribute to the social evolution of these chiefdom or incipient state-level steppe societies? I draw on our previously published interpretations of the excavations at three Iron Age settlements in the Talgar region, and the surface surveys conducted in the highland and lowland zones of the mountain-steppe region along the

[1.] The following granting agencies supported the archaeological investigations in the Talgar area: the National Science Foundation, Grant Number BCS-9603661, for fieldwork from 1997 to 2002; the Wenner-Gren Foundation, for fieldwork from 1994 to 1996; and the National Geographic Society, for fieldwork from 1994 to 1996 and in 2003 and 2004. I wish to express my gratitude to the archaeologists of Kazakhstan who contributed to this work: Dr. Karl M. Baipakov, Director of the Institute of Archaeology (Almaty, Republic of Kazakhstan); Fedor P. Grigoriev; Murat M. Nurpeisov; Boris A. Zheleznyakov and Yuri M. Peshkov. Perry A. Tourtellotte helped in all stages of the fieldwork. Over the years I have found Philip Salzman's work an inspiration and his spare prose a model for ethnographic writing and analysis. I share his enthusiasm for Fredrik Barth's (1961) *Nomads of South Persia*, the first and most influential ethnography I know on pastoral nomads.

Tian Shan Mountains in southeast Kazakhstan to put forth a set of questions pertaining to the nature of mobility among these Iron Age agropastoralists (Chang et al. 2002). Did the Iron Age inhabitants of the Talgar region vacillate between 'settled' and 'mobile' lifestyles, and how would mobility or sedentism be apparent in the archaeological record? A set of ethnographic premises, drawn from contemporary pastoral societies in the Middle East, provides a basis for comparison between contemporary and ancient pastoral nomadism. The interface between these two sets of variables is explored: sedentarization versus mobility and hierarchy versus equality.

The Iron Age farmers and herders of the Talgar region appear to have been integrated into a larger ramifying chiefdom or even an incipient state-level society. What role did military mobilization, caravan trade, and predatory raiding play in determining their degree of mobility? Today in southeast Kazakhstan, pastoral nomads practice short-distance pastoral transhumance. Many herders move their flocks of sheep and goats and their herds of cattle and horses between the highland alpine meadows for summer pasture and the lowland steppe areas for fall through spring pasture. Ancient Iron Age pastoralists could have followed similar patterns of transhumance in which at least a portion of the Iron Age population in the Talgar region practiced seasonal mobility. During the Iron Age the Talgar region, just to the north of the foothills of the Tian Shan Mountains, was a node along an east-west corridor used for trade, predatory raiding and military activities. The ancient people occupying this corridor during the first millennium BCE to the first half of the first millennium CE have been labeled the Saka, the Wusun and the Yuezhi nomadic confederacies (Pulleyblank 1970, 1995; Moshkova 1992; Di Cosmo 1994).

In the past the study of nomadic cultures such as the Saka (Scythians) has resulted in the romanticized notions of Iron Age nomads as the perpetrators of social and cultural change across the Eurasian steppe. It has been the assumption that the 'horse riding nomads' governed the steppe regions through their use of mounted archery and their mobility (Pulleyblank 1995). Such romanticized notions of the Eurasian Iron Age nomadic cultures should be evaluated by two empirical lines of investigation: a more informed theoretical view of the variation extant in contemporary pastoral societies, thus the use of better pastoral models, and the application of more rigorous archaeological methods to test such pastoral models. The organization of this chapter follows this programmatic order of investigation. First, the ethnographic models are presented. Second, the current state of archaeological data from Talgar is assessed in light of these models. Finally, future research directions are outlined.

THE STUDY AREA

Since 1994 the Kazakh-American Talgar Archaeological Project has conducted surface surveys and excavations in the Talgar region of southeast Kazakhstan. We have conducted surface surveys in three areas: the Talgar alluvial fan, the highland plateau of Orman, and the valleys of Turgen and Asi (Figure 15.1). The turbulent Talgar River originates in the Tian Shan Mountains and flows northward emptying into the Ili River. This region is called the Semirechy'e or Seven Rivers Area, which extends from the east of the Chinese-Kazakhstan border to the Chu River and is characterized by seven rivers that flow north-ward from the mountains and empty into the Ili River basin (more than 600 km in length). The Talgar alluvial fan is a cone-shaped landform, and its apex is at the base of the foothills where the Talgar River cuts into the valley floor. The fan is situated just north of the highest peak of the Zailiisky Alatau Mountains (in the northern Tian Shan range), Peak Talgar. The steep gradient from the snowcapped Peak Talgar, 5000 m above the semi-arid steppe regions of the Ili River basin, starts at 80–100 km distance. Both the historic and prehistoric herdsmen, who maintained flocks of sheep and goats, as well as herds of cattle, horses and even some camels, probably practiced vertical transhumance moving between highland summer pastures, at 1800–2400 m, and winter pastures at 550–1100 m, just north of the mountain range. Less than one percent of this alluvial fan has been surveyed archaeologically. This relatively small area has yielded a total of more than 500 finds, ranging from settlements and burial mounds to isolated artifacts. Two-thirds of these finds have been dated to the Iron Age. Three Iron Age settlements have been excavated (Chang et al. 2003). Archaeozoological and archaeobotanical analysis (both flotation samples and phytoliths) indicate that the prehistoric inhabitants of these settlements practiced cereal farming (millet, wheat, barley and possibly rice) and animal herding (cattle, sheep, goats, horses and possibly camels).

MODELS OF NOMADIC TRIBES AND CONFEDERACIES

The ethnographic model posited by Salzman (2004) outlines the processes by which contemporary and historic tribes and nomadic confederacies in the Middle East have been encapsulated into regional polities and the nation-state. I have used this model to re-examine the archaeological data on Iron Age settlement and burials from the Talgar region. According to Salzman's (2004) model of encapsulation, any pastoral tribe or confederacy that is incorporated into regional or national markets or has been subjected to the rule of the State will be less capable of maintaining a semblance of egalitarianism and individual autonomy among all the members of the group. The examples used to test these

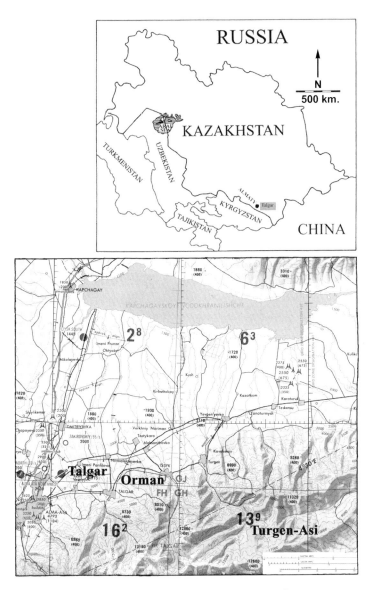

Figure 15.1. Map showing the location of the study area in southeast Kazakhstan.

assumptions include the Yomut Turkmen, the Basseri and the Sarhadi Baluch, as well as other Middle Eastern nomadic tribes that maintain flocks of sheep and goats, and in some cases keep camels as well. The Yomut Turkmen, the Basseri and the Sarhadi Baluch are tribal confederacies that are headed by *khans* (chiefs). Yet these particular groups of nomadic pastoralists also pose a striking contrast to hierarchically ranked tribes or confederacies: each camp group is defined as a group of households that share common pasture resources, govern themselves through consensus rather than coercion, and express egalitarian values, at least in political if not economic arenas. Salzman (2004) then asks why some pastoral tribes remain nomadic while others become settled and why some pastoral societies remain independent and egalitarian while others become hierarchically ordered?

Salzman (2004:34) argues cogently that mobility and sedentism are but opposite ends of a continuum of strategies used by nomadic peoples in response to changing environmental, social or political circumstances. Usually, pastoral mobility is defined as an adaptive strategy allowing herdsmen to maximize the use of dispersed environmental resources such as natural pasture, forage or water. Pastoral peoples traveling with their herds of cattle, sheep and goats, horses or camels across diverse landscapes engage in pastoral productive activities (raising animals for meat, milk, wool or hair), either for subsistence or market consumption. Why do pastoralists 'settle' or restrict their mobility to a fixed location? The usual factors are that they leave herding completely and become farmers; engage in multiresource strategies, including activities that require residence in a fixed location, like agriculture; become wage laborers attached to settled communities; or that they are forced to settle in permanent places as a result of coercive state or government policies. In pre-industrial societies nomadic pastoralism or the periodic movement of humans and their herds, may also have a social and political dimension. Herdsmen may also move frequently in order to escape oppressive regimes, as a military strategy, or to expand social and economic networks.

For Iranian groups, such as the Baluch and the Yomut Turkmen in the 1960s, mobility or sedentism can be seen as adaptive responses to the outside forces of the state (Salzman 2004). The Yomut Turkmen used mobility as a political strategy to avoid Persian control over their wealth and independence (Irons 1974). The Sarhadi Baluch, on the other hand, reduced their mobility in the 1960s and 1970s as they obtained jobs in settlements and began to engage in agriculture (Salzman 2004:35). In both cases the choice to remain mobile or to become settled was an economic and political response to the increasing encapsulation of these nomadic tribes by the larger nation-state.

The image of the fiercely independent and egalitarian nomad is an ethnographically pleasing stereotype. Pastoral nomads, continually confronted with decisions about how to best maintain their individually owned herds on communal pasturelands, are characterized as free agents expressing the ultimate democratic values of self-reliance, independence and autonomy. The opposing ideal, that of the nomadic herdsman or tribal member oppressed by a chief (*khan*) or autocratic leader, suggests that the confederacy or tribal organization is subject to the outside influences of the state or empire (Khazanov 1994).

Yet to what degree does the chief or khan derive his power from the larger sociopolitical hierarchies of the state or centralized bureaucracy? Salzman (2004) challenges Barth's (1961) description of the khan as an autocratic and oppressive ruler who controls the otherwise autonomous and self-sufficient Basseri nomads. He argues that the khan, as the autocratic leader of the Khamseh Confederacy of the Basseri, maintains his coercive and autocratic authority over the Basseri nomads because the herdsmen collude with the leader in order to project the chief's image as an autocratic leader (Salzman 2004:90–91). This act of 'collective impression management' is done to boost the confederacy's position in the multi-ethnic arenas of urban Persian society. Salzman (2004:91) argues that the herdsmen ultimately do maintain their autonomy and self-determination since they exercise 'choice' in selecting their leaders. In fact, the camp group may choose to switch its allegiance to those chiefs who will best 'serve their interests and protect them.' This 'collective' image of the khan as a despot, capable of oppressive and autocratic rule, is a useful fiction promoted by the tribesmen, as a political strategy for maintaining the Khamseh Confederacy's overall clout in the larger multi-ethnic political arena of the Persian state. As Salzman (2004:85) points out, tribesmen could resist coercive and autocratic power but choose not to do so. The khan, with his splendid residency in Shiraz and his extensive networks of political ties to other elites, must serve his subjects by attending to their needs.

MOBILITY AND SEDENTISM IN THE ARCHAEOLOGICAL RECORD

In the Talgar region mixed farming and herding was practiced on the alluvial fan and coupled with short-distance vertical transhumance from the 8th century BCE through the 1st century CE (Chang et al. 2003). Surface surveys of the Talgar alluvial fan demonstrate that the majority of Iron Age places visible on the landscape are burial mounds, 'kurgans' (183 or more), and settlement sites (at least 59). The burial mounds are prominent features of the steppe landscape (Figure 15.2). The high number of kurgans and the low number of settle-ments is due to geomorphologic processes by which the Iron Age settlements are buried under 0.5–1.0 m of deposits. Those settlement sites visible on the surface have been exposed by agricultural plowing or are in erosion cuts or streambed profiles. It is noteworthy that even during ancient times the kurgans must have been dominant features in the landscape while, in comparison, village hamlets were modest in appearance.

Our archaeological excavations at the three Iron Age settlements of Tuzusai, Tseganka 8 and Taldy Bulak 2, from 1994 to 2004, provide another window into the problem of Iron Age social organization (Figure 15.3). At these settlements

Figure 15.2. A Kazakh herdsman and his flock in front of an Iron Age kurgan (burial mound).

the archaeozoological and archaeobotanical remains indicate the presence of agriculture based on millet, wheat and barley and the herding of cattle, sheep and goats, horses and maybe camels. The architecture at Tseganka 8 shows a range of domestic structures, such as at least seven semisubterranean round and rectangular pithouses. At Tuzusai at least 30 circular and rectangular storage pits, a possible pithouse structure and plastered floor fragments associated with stone-lined postholes were identified. At Taldy Bulak 2 several rectangular stone alignments, probably the foundations of houses, postmolds associated with ephemeral dwellings, and overlapping activity areas were found.[2]

Additional features found at all three sites include storage pits, fire pits, hearths, and outdoor activity areas. All three sites have artifact inventories that include grinding stones, small iron or bronze fragments, and red and buff ware utility pottery (bowls, jars, cooking and storage vessels). At Tuzusai there were at least four different occupation periods, including a post–Iron Age occupation, and at Tseganka 8 and Taldy Bulak there were eight to ten occupational levels. These sequences suggest that the village hamlets were semisedentary or year-round sedentary occupations, where a core group of household members stayed to plant, care for, and harvest cereal crops, while others moved with the flocks and herds of cattle, sheep, goats and horses between highland summer pastures and lowland winter grazing. There is insufficient evidence to prove the existence of seasonal occupation, yet the distinct occupation levels at the settlements do seem to indicate intermittent periods of activity at the sites. The

---

[2] Postmolds are soil stains remaining after the decomposition of a post, in this case indicative of the remains of temporary dwellings (cf. Holman and Lovis, this volume).

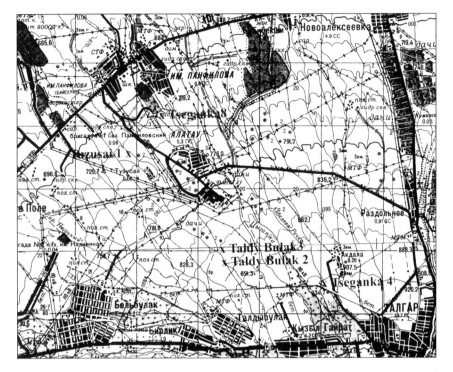

Figure 15.3. Close-up of a topographic map of the Talgar alluvial fan, showing the northern section of the fan where the excavated sites of Tuzusai, Tseganka 8, and Taldy Bulak 2 are located.

artifact inventories, and the relatively unsophisticated nature of the architecture at these settlements, suggest that the inhabitants were common folk, engaged in farming and herding activities. We have not been able to locate the cemeteries or graves of these common folk.

How mobile or sedentary were the Iron Age inhabitants who occupied the small village hamlets of Talgar? An intriguing comparison with the Yomut Turkmen might provide some insight here. The Yomut Turkmen included both nomadic agricultural and nomadic pastoral households that could shift between these occupations (Salzman 2004:33). The ability to shift from a greater emphasis on farming to herding was always a viable strategy for the Iron Age inhabitants of Talgar. At the site of Tuzusai the cultivation of rice increased between 415 BCE and 75 CE, while at Tseganka 8 more emphasis was placed on the cultivation of millet from 775–40 BCE. At Taldy Bulak 2 a paucity of cereal remains in the phytolith samples (Rosen 2003) indicates that animal husbandry might have been favored over cereal cultivation. Households and village communities underwent shifts in their overall subsistence strategies, some favoring cultivation over herding, others herding over farming. This fluctuation between the dependence on crop cultivation or livestock herding at various hamlets in the Talgar region may also signal the shift in and out of nomadic and sedentary lifestyles.

Currently, it is not possible to determine whether these three sites were year-round or seasonal occupations or what kind of mobility strategies were present. Yet some intriguing possibilities exist. The Iron Age village hamlets were used for a wide range of subsistence activities, such as herding, dry farming, irrigation farming and foraging. The local Talgar population may have rotated in and out of these productive strategies based on individual household decisions. Residential mobility, within a single household, might have consisted of several members engaged in vertical transhumant herding while other members engaged in settled subsistence farming. Families or households may have rotated or shifted their places of residence, depending on their reliance on various productive activities at a given point in time. This may have led to preferential migration to Tuzusai, where irrigation agriculture was practiced, or to Tseganka 8, where millet production was favored, or to Taldy Bulak 2, where metal finishing took place.

EQUALITY AND HIERARCHY IN THE ARCHAEOLOGICAL RECORD

The historical data based on texts and inscriptions suggest that the distant Iron Age nomadic confederacies, such as the Saka of the Ili River (Semirechy'e), inhabited territories far from the irrigated desert oases of Chorasmia, Sogdiana, Bactria and Margiana (Central Asian polities) but could have been encapsulated or controlled by such polities throughout the first millennium BCE (Dandamaev 1994). The proposed social structure for the Saka was that of clan and tribal organization. Akishev and Kushaev (1963) divided the 25 burial mounds of Bes Shatyr, a famous megalithic kurgan sanctuary of the Ili River Basin, into three categories: the clan leaders, the aristocratic elite and glorified warriors, and the enlisted warriors. These categories were determined on the basis of burial-mound size and limited information on the burial inventories from each category. Even if we dismiss the criteria on which this three-tiered social stratification was constructed, there still remains sufficient evidence that points to the vast status differentiation between the chiefly leaders and the commoners. For example, the Golden Warrior tomb of Issyk, only 20 kilometers east of the Talgar alluvial fan, was discovered in the side chamber of a tsar kurgan dating to the 3rd or 2nd century BCE. It is the tomb of a youth, robed in a cloth cloak decorated with golden plaques, a magnificent headdress with bird and ram figurines, an inscribed silver bowl, ceramic vessels and other items. At settlement sites in the Talgar fan, with occupation levels from the same time period, there is a lack of any luxury items. When metal objects are found, they usually are utilitarian, such as iron knife fragments, trident arrow points, bronze cauldron fragments, hinges, etc.

Our surveys and excavations on the Talgar alluvial fan have discovered these types of archaeological places: semisedentary village hamlets with simple pottery, metal and farming technology interspersed among the burial kurgans; and a burial cult, as apparent from the large quantity of burial kurgans of different size ranges (heights and diameters) and of different time periods, spanning the first millennium BCE. Is this sufficient evidence to prove the existence of a ramifying clan structure of a chiefdom or incipient state-level society? The artifact inventories at the excavated small hamlets at Tuzusai, Tseganka 8 and Taldy Bulak 2 indicate the vast social differences between the ordinary common folk and the aristocratic elite buried in the burial kurgans. One can infer that, during the Iron Age, there must have been a ranked hierarchy of a chiefly elite group with high-status burial goods buried in the kurgans and the common folk buried in simple graves or cemeteries yet to be located by our surface survey.

In early agricultural states the bureaucracy and elite at the top stratum of society were able to extract valuable economic, political and social resources from the lower classes in the form of tribute or taxation. What kind of resources did the Eurasian nomadic clan chiefs or khans extract from the bottom stratum of society? Furthermore, how did the clan leaders convert simple subsistence resources, animals or grain, into precious luxury items such as gold and silver that in turn became status markers in 'death or burial' cults? Such luxury goods, by their very disposal in burial kurgans, were then effectively removed from everyday circulation. And more important, how did the chiefs or the khans organize the tribesmen, who were the backbone of the internal economic structure of society, into a viable military force? The 'nomadic elite' of the hinterland may have garnered specific localized control through important economic, political and ideological links to the powerful desert-oases kingdoms. Perhaps the kingdoms relied on the far-flung nomadic confederacies as military retainers who controlled distant territories and valuable trade and caravan routes. Therefore, the precious luxury items of gold, silver and bronze found in local burial kurgans were part of a supralocal circulation of elite status items used to bolster the position of the local leaders. Such objects might represent the local leaders' abilities to obtain luxury items through a set of sociopolitical and economic linkages to the more powerful states and kingdoms. This may also explain why the Saka (eastern Scythian) zoomorphic imagery found on precious metals and textiles throughout the first millennium BCE in Eurasia was part of a stylized iconography shared among many disparate local and regional nomadic groups rather than one that represented a single, shared cultural tradition.

The burial mounds, especially those with splendid burial inventories, may have been constructed by the ancient inhabitants as part of a larger 'image-building' strategy to make the leaders of the common herdsmen and farmers appear to be powerful, wealthy and militarily capable, especially in the face of challenges, military and otherwise, from outside nomadic groups. The burial mounds, the largest measure 80–100 m in diameter and are 17 m high, represent the most visible markers of Iron Age occupation of the Talgar alluvial fan. These mounds often form linear patterns along dry streambeds or along the banks of the Talgar River. The human effort invested in building each burial mound, even the smaller ones, is considerable. Many burial mounds have been robbed either in antiquity or in recent history. Certainly these mounds represent a higher investment of labor than the simple domestic architecture of pithouses and simple rectangular room blocks found at the village hamlets.

The archaeological evidence from the three excavated Iron Age settlements in the Talgar region suggests that there was little to no status differentiation among the common folk. The artifact inventories rarely include any luxury or status items, aside from bronze fragments or a jadeite bead or fragments of imported ceramic wares. Within less than a kilometer, however, most of the settlement sites appear to be situated in close proximity to the lines of burial kurgans from contemporaneous chronological periods. Relative egalitarianism existed among the common folk of herders and farmers who inhabited the small village hamlets, while ancestor worship in the form of a mortuary cult emphasized inequality and the presence of hierarchy.

MOBILITY AND HIERARCHY IN THE TALGAR REGION

This following scenario is put forth as a possible interpretation of the Iron Age archaeology of Talgar. How did mobility as a strategy and the nature of hierarchy within the agropastoral population both function on a larger regional level? Did the 'nomadic mobility strategies' and apparent hierarchy within the confederacy contribute directly to processes of state formation? Iron Age social organization might have been egalitarian at the local level and hierarchical at the regional level. The common farmers and herders functioned day to day through a system of equality and relative autonomy. A herdsman might become a farmer, or vice versa, and an entire household or members within the household might engage in seasonal transhumance or practice year-round sedentism. Individuals, households or residential groups operated in a fluid manner alternating between the opposing poles of mobility and sedentism based on rational economic decision making. The elite, emerging out of ranked kin-based units, maintained and cultivated the image of 'nomadism.' Their mobility or nomadism was necessary for the coalescence of larger tribal units, segments or confederacies and for activities such as predatory raiding or military battles that took place on a regional level. Local elites maintained their ability to coerce the common folk into providing labor, tribute or personnel for these activities through 'collective impression management.' An aristocratic leader maintained his charismatic position through the manipulation of obvious status markers, including his ability to participate in an ancestral death cult, which was marked by the linear arrangement of burial mounds along the stream channels of the most productive agricultural and natural pasture areas. The ancestral cult of burying the dead with luxury items way beyond the reach of most commoners reinforced the social and ideological distance between the elite rulers and the rest of society. But was this ideological distance real or fictive? And was some of the rulers' wealth also a display of the leader's allegiance to larger central polities? How were the two worlds, that of the commoner and that of the ranked elite, fused together to form a cohesive whole?

Perhaps the leaders' positions were augmented through another set of mobility strategies unrelated to nomadic pastoralism but instead tied to the group's ability to conduct predatory raiding or to act as a cohesive military force. The hierarchical ranking as apparent from the burial cult preserved the image-building strategy of local elites. They, in turn, relied on the larger nomadic states or empires for their supralocal and regional power. The commoners contributed labor to building this ancestral cult of burial mounds because it served their collective interests to do so. In this way they were guaranteed both access to productive lands and protection from outside marauders. Mighty clan leaders and the aristocratic elite were supported because they could defend and protect the very productive cultivated land and the natural pastures from outside encroachment. Like the Basseri khan, the nomadic elite also best represented the concerns of the tribe or confederacy within larger multi-ethnic, sociopolitical arenas of kingdoms, states and empires. No doubt the herders of Talgar did engage in both long and short distance transhumance, but it was the hierarchical authoritarian organization of the clan or tribe that really defined the nomadic nature of steppe social organization. This hierarchical organization was most necessary at a regional and supraregional level in order to rapidly deploy traders, raiders or warriors. The burial cult was indeed a form of ancestor worship, inscribed on the alluvial fan to commemorate the ancestors of the aristocratic elite and to remind the commoners of their duties and responsibilities toward the larger, regionally organized, tribe or confederacy.

DISCUSSION

This chapter poses far more questions than it answers. Our archaeological research on the Talgar alluvial fan is a first step toward outlining the nature of economic strategies along the northern edge of the Tian Shan Mountains. Archaeological research that links the artifact inventories from the burial mounds to the artifact inventories of the settlement sites needs to be conducted. This will help establish the temporal relationship between the burial cult and the settlements and may also indicate whether or not the burial inventories represent hierarchical ranking and the settlement inventories represent a more egalitarian society. More settlements need to be excavated in the Talgar region to determine the range of variability present in artifact inventories, as well as in faunal and plant remains. As the parameters for the range and variation within settlement sites are more firmly established, such as the occupational histories of such sites and the variation in domestic architecture and artifact inventories, it may be possible to develop a clear method for evaluating whether a given site was used by mobile or settled groups. Surface surveys have been conducted on the Talgar alluvial fan, a nearby highland plateau and a valley at 2400 m above sea level. The survey data from Talgar should be incorporated into large-scale regional studies that will provide a perspective on the Iron Age social organization from several discrete regions of Semirechy'e. Furthermore, the spatial patterning of sites across a large region of diverse environmental zones is necessary for a complete understanding of the range of subsistence strategies practiced during the Iron Age. Finally, we need to redefine Iron Age mobility on the Eurasian steppe, to include strategies for mobility that go beyond subsistence and trading activities such as those tied to militarism and predatory raiding. The interface between the range of mobility strategies and the nature of social hierarchy during this period necessitates an archaeology more closely informed by the fine-grained ethnographic analysis of nomadic pastoral cultures from the contemporary world.

REFERENCES

Akishev, K. A. and G. A. Kushaev
1963   *Ancient Saka and Wusun Culture of the Ili River Valley* [in Russian]. Alma-Ata, Nauka.

Barth, F.
1961   *Nomads of South Persia*. Oslo, Oslo University Press.

Chang, C., N. Benecke, F. P. Grigoriev, A. M. Rosen and P. A. Tourtellotte
2003   Iron Age Society and Chronology in South-East Kazakhstan. *Antiquity 73*: 296, pp. 298–312.

Chang, C., P. A. Tourtellotte, K. M. Baipakov and F. P. Grigoriev
2002   *The Evolution of Steppe Communities from the Bronze Age Through Medieval Periods in Southeastern Kazakhstan (Zhetysu)*. Almaty, Sweet Briar College

and the A. K. Margulan Institute of Archaeology, Ministry of Education and Science of the Republic of Kazakhstan.

Dandamaev, M. A.

1994 Media and Achaemenid Iran. In J. Harmatta, B. N. Puri and G. F. Etemadi (eds.), *History of Civilizations of Central Asia. Volume 2: The Development of Sedentary and Nomadic Civilizations, 700 B.C. to A.D. 250.* Paris, UNESCO Press: pp. 35–65.

Di Cosmo, N.

1994 Ancient Inner Asian Nomads: Their Economic Basis and Its Significance in Chinese History. *Journal of Asian Studies 53*: 4, pp. 1092–1126.

Irons, W.

1974 Nomadism as a Political Adaptation: The Case of the Yomut Turkmen. *American Ethnologist 1*: pp. 635–658.

Khazanov, A. M.

1994 *Nomads and the Outside World*. Madison, University of Wisconsin Press (second edition).

Moshkova, M. G.

1992 *Steppe Region of the Asiatic Part of the USSR in the Scythe-Sarmatski Time* [in Russian]. Moscow, Nauka Izdatel'stvo.

Pulleyblank, E. G.

1970 The Wu-Sun and the Sakas and the Yueh-Chih Migration. *Bulletin of the School of Oriental and African Studies 33 (Special Issue in Honour of Sir Harold Bailey)*: pp. 154–160.

1995 Why Tocharians? *Journal of Indo-European Studies 23*: 3–4, pp. 415–430.

Rosen, A. M.

2003 *Preliminary Report on Phytolith Samples from Taldy Bulak 2*. Unpublished report on file at Sweet Briar College, Department of Anthropology and Sociology (Sweet Briar, Virginia).

Salzman, P. C.

2004 *Pastoralists: Equality, Hierarchy, and the State*. Boulder, Westview Press.

CHAPTER 16

CROSSING BOUNDARIES

NOMADIC GROUPS AND ETHNIC IDENTITIES

STUART T. SMITH

ETHNICITY HAS PROVEN elusive in the archaeological record, causing some archaeologists to despair of ever identifying ethnic groups, especially when dealing with nomads, who often leave only ephemeral traces in the archaeological record. Symbiotic relations with other groups often characterize nomadic peoples, especially pastoralists, producing an assemblage of mixed materials that defies characterization as a distinctive tradition, bounded in space and time. Ethnicity is usually defined this way, with the expectation of a distinct, bounded people with a shared culture and primordial attachments. Ethnic identities are identified through real or perceived commonalities of culture, history and language, but others can also ascribe ethnicity, particularly in contexts like the ones discussed in this chapter. Archaeologists have generally assumed that ethnicity should appear as a distinctive material assemblage, reflecting ethnicity's primordial attachments. This attitude reflects a fundamental misunderstanding of ethnic dynamics. Ethnicity is a powerful phenomenon, affecting us today in fundamental ways that color our perceptions and expectations by creating a focus on ethnic groups. There is, however, an emerging consensus among anthropologists and sociologists that we should not expect to find absolute and bounded ethnic groups either archaeologically or ethnographically. Instead, ethnic identities are situational and overlapping, constructed and negotiated by individuals in specific social contexts. As a result, archaeologists must re-orient their perspective away from the search for neatly bounded groups in favor of an agent-centered approach that focuses instead on ethnic dynamics.

This chapter begins with an exploration of the dynamics of ethnicity, looking at different theoretical models and archaeological examples. The following section examines some different ways in which archaeological evidence can be used to examine ethnic dynamics, using two colonial communities on ancient Egypt's southern frontier, Askut and Tombos, in Nubia, as examples. It will finish with some thoughts on the problems and potentials of studying the ethnicity of nomadic groups with a brief consideration of the potential for documenting ethnicity at Berenike (a Greco-Roman harbor on the Egyptian Red Sea coast).

ETHNICITY, BOUNDARIES AND THE NATION-STATE

Ethnicity is often regarded as a recent phenomenon, linked closely to the dynamics of European colonialism and the nationalist movements of the 19th century CE (Kohn 1944; Handler 1988). Some argue that before this time, an elite made up of a handful of administrators and aristocratic landlords ruled over an agrarian society made up of a larger and more heterogeneous population of peasants. There was no notion that these disparate groups shared a common identity. Elites in many cases shared more in common across state boundaries than with the people they ruled (Banks 1996:123–131). In contrast, Smith (1986) sees evidence for ethnic solidarity, if not nationalism, stretching back into antiquity as *ethnie*, or a combination of a collective name, common myth of descent, shared history, culture, specific territory and sense of solidarity. These ethnie provided the basis and necessary prerequisite for the modern emergence of nationalism. This view reflects the essentialist notion of ethnicity that does not take into consideration the possibility that these features may be constructed post hoc to match the needs of nationalist movements. Nevertheless, Smith's ethnie are a good characterization of the primordial way in which ethnic identities are almost always framed. Smith asserts that ethnie can be traced into the distant past, specifically the ancient Near East, but since the ethnie reside ultimately in people's minds, Banks (1996:129–130) is skeptical that these features can really be identified and traced so far back in time.

The rich historical, artistic and material records of ancient Egypt and the Classical world, however, do provide evidence for the construction of ethnicity. For example, the ancient historian Herodotus defined the Greeks as "the kinship of all Greeks in blood and speech, and the shrines of the gods and the sacrifices that we have in common, and the likeness of our way of life" (Rawlinson 1964: VI, 44). Tonkin et al. (1989) and Hall (1997) note that the ancient Greeks used the term *genos* to refer to themselves, employing *ethnos* primarily for the 'barbaric' other, including animals. Renfrew (1996) points out that Herodotus's focus on genetic, linguistic and cultural foundations for group identity corresponds to modern definitions of ethnicity that emphasize a common territory, descent (or a myth of origins), language, culture and beliefs (especially religion). In this essentialist construction ethnic identity is monolithic and bounded, immutable and self-defined. Tonkin et al. (1989) and Hall (1997) also argue that the 'barbaric' ethnos played a key role in its opposition to the civilized Greek genos. Such 'self/other' oppositions are a fundamental component of ethnic dynamics, so we can see the 'genos-ethnos' terminology as an early expression of ethnicity in spite of some inconsistencies in the etymology of the word *ethnic*.

Ancient Egyptian texts and representations reflect a strong sense of ethnicity (Smith 2003). For example, Pharaoh Akhenaton (1353–1336 BCE) provides a surprisingly modern definition of ethnic groups in the great Hymn to the Aton (Lichtheim 1976:131–132):[1]

> You set every man in his place . . .
> Their tongues differ in speech,
> Their characters likewise;
> Their skins are distinct,
> For you distinguished the peoples.

Such state ideologies demonstrate a strong sense of national identity that is at least theoretically applied to all Egyptians, regardless of social position, and is placed in opposition to ethnic others. The state ideology explicitly linked ethnic groups with territory (Loprieno 1988; Liverani 1990; Smith 2003), creating a sense of Egyptian-ness akin to Anderson's (1983) 'imagined communities' that provide a foundation for the modern nation-state. In spite of extensive conquests and the complete cultural and economic incorporation of Lower Nubia into the Egyptian state during the New Kingdom, the traditional national border of Egypt remained at Aswan in the south and the Mediterranean in the north, coinciding precisely with the Egyptian ethnie, the state ideology's imagined community (Smith 2003).

This evidence contradicts the notion that ethnicity, national borders and national identities are a product of 18th century CE absolutism and the emergence of the modern state (Ratzel 1897; Prescott 1987:1; Wendl and Rösler 1999:7; Parker 2002); in fact, it suggests that all three elements already played a key role in one of the earliest primary states. With this background in mind I will first focus on the identification of ethnicity in the archaeological record, including an examination of ethnic dynamics at two sites (Askut, an ancient Egyptian fortress occupied around 1850–1050 BCE; and Tombos, a cemetery used around 1400–1050 BCE), and wrap up with a consideration of ethnicity among nomadic groups, like the Blemmyes at Berenike.

---

[1] The dates given of the ancient Egyptian dynasties are those suggested by Baines and Malek (2000:36–37).

ETHNICITY AND ARCHAEOLOGY

The ancient view of ethnic groups as distinctive cultures tied to specific territories matches popular perceptions of ethnicity, and indeed ethnic identities are usually constructed in similar terms. Not surprisingly, archaeologists have continued to apply this framework, tending to equate archaeological cultures and ethnic groups in spite of skepticism within both processual and postprocessual approaches (Díaz-Andreau 1996; Hides 1996). This view relies on the essentialist assumption that ethnic groups are bounded and uniform with a set of shared beliefs handed down in a continuous tradition (Jones 1996). Yet, on closer inspection, the seemingly immutable characteristics of ethnicity are surprisingly mutable and socially contingent (Glazer and Moynihan 1963; Royce 1982). The expectation that material culture should fall into consistent, neatly bounded assemblages corresponding to ethnic groups, or indeed international borders, should therefore be abandoned in favor of a more complex model.

Recent studies of ethnicity reject essentialist approaches, instead emphasizing the dynamic nature of ethnic identity. Ethnic groups are subjectively constructed, derived by actors who determine their own ethnicity, regardless of the objective 'reality' of their cultural similarities or differences (Graves-Brown 1996). Barth (1969) observed that the nomadic Pathans founded their ethnic identity on a narrow selection of social elements, not broadly shared cultural features. Instrumentalists argue that actors can shift or create ethnic allegiances for social and economic gain. Royce (1982) documents how the Zapotec of Juchitán manipulated ethnic allegiances to maintain political and economic dominance, shifting between Zapotec and Mexican identities as the situation demanded. In a similar but negative vein the supposedly primordial ethnic polarization that characterized the most recent conflict in the Balkans in reality consisted primarily of post hoc rationalizations (Graves-Brown 1996).

An overly instrumental approach runs the risk of reducing ethnicity to no more than an economic or political strategy, and even instrumentalists point out that ethnic identities are not made up of arbitrary features in order to meet the instrumental needs of a particular situation. Jones (1997) argues that ethnicity is grounded in Bourdieu's (1977) notion of the *habitus*. Jones avoids an extreme instrumental position by arguing that ethnic identity takes on particular forms as a product of the habitus and the instrumental social conditions of a particular context. This approach has the advantage of both allowing for individual agency and acknowledging the important influence of the particular social milieu of those actors.

Most important, ethnic identities are constructed through a consciousness of difference with reference to the specific cultural practices of ethnic 'others.' As a result, competition and conflict sharpen ethnic polarization (Spicer 1962;

Figure 16.1. Ramesses III (1187–1156 BCE) leads ethnic prisoners before the god Amun-Re in this relief at his mortuary temple in Medinet Habu (near modern Luxor, Egypt).

Isajew 1974; Hodder 1979; Royce 1982; Comaroff and Comaroff 1992; Jones 1997). For example, Herodotus reflects a Greek consciousness of both community and superiority (Daugé 1981; Díaz-Andreau 1996). Ancient Egyptian and Near Eastern ideology created and manipulated a positive ethic self juxtaposed with negative ethnic others to legitimize the power and authority of their kings (Loprieno 1988; Liverani 1990; Smith 2003). In each case the king pacified the 'barbaric' foreigners, protecting the inner order and civilization represented by the ethnic self (Figure 16.1). Classical civilization created similar self/other oppositions between the civilized and barbarian.

Kurzban et al. (2001) suggest that this emphasis on difference may have an evolutionary explanation as a by-product of coalition building by our early ancestors. Racial and ethnic stereotypes were easily undermined when the researchers replaced racial categories with an arbitrary yet visible cue correlated with group membership, like shirt color. This is consistent with the notion that racial and ethnic categories are socially constructed rather than having some fundamental biological basis, as some continue to suggest. Constructions of 'us-them' quickly trump physical differences that previously provided the basis for group identity. Kurzban, Tooby and Cosmides later stated on a web-site that "in our experiments, people quickly came to use an arbitrary visual marker to predict coalitional alliances. This happened—with tragic consequences—as soon as it was suspected that Middle Eastern terrorists were responsible for the WTC attacks: hate crimes were perpetrated against individuals (e.g., Sikhs) who had coalitional cues (turbans) reminiscent of headgear worn in the Middle East."[2] On a more positive note, an ethnic group like Latino or Arab can incorporate considerable physical and biological diversity. In a similar way, both the ancient Egyptian and the Classical civilizations avoided the kind of pseudobiological color prejudice characteristic of racism while practicing cultural chauvinism (Smith 2003).

When tied to power relations, the features selected to define the ethnic other are often negative and subordinating, like recent derogatory character-izations about Arab dress and culture in the wake of the World Trade Center attacks or, in the case of ancient Egypt, the assertion that Kush must always be 'wretched' (Smith 2003). In a military context (Figure 16.2) Nubians were cowards, instantly defeated by the king if they even fought at all (Liverani 1990). Not only are foreigners wretched cowards, but they are hardly people at all (Loprieno 1988). At the end of the New Kingdom text *The Instruction of Ani* the student complains that no one could possibly learn everything that Ani presents to him. Ani replies that animals can be trained, and that

> One teaches the Nubian to speak Egyptian,
> The Syrian and other strangers too.
> Say "I shall do like all the beasts,"
> Listen and learn what they do. (Lichtheim 1976:144)

In a similar way Afrikaner settlers called the Tswana of South Africa *skepsels* (creatures), but the Tswana retaliated by calling the Afrikaners *makgoa* (white bush lice) (Comaroff 1978; Crapanzano 1985). The Romans also created negative stereotypes of the groups who resisted them. For example, to Pliny the Blemmyes were headless people with eyes and ears in their chests, and Solinus described them as barbaric savages who simply leaped on their prey like animals when hunting.

ETHNICITY IN THE ARCHAEOLOGICAL RECORD

Given the subjectivity and mutability of ethnicity, how can we get at it archaeo-logically? The first thing to do is to abandon the search for the chimera of neatly bounded ethnic groups corresponding to a particular material culture assemblage. Instead, we need to focus on those parts of the material culture that reflect social contexts where ethnicity is salient. Ethnicity is only one of multiple identities that people assume in different social contexts. At any

[2] http://www.psych.ucsb.edu/research/cep/erasingrace.htm (accessed 6 August 2007)

Figure 16.2. Nubian warriors fall beneath the chariot of Pharaoh Tutankhamun (1332–1322 BCE) in this detail of a painted box found in his tomb (now in the Egyptian Museum, Cairo).

particular time, other forms of identity, like gender or social position, might play a more important role (Meskell 1994). Social arenas where ethnicity might be, but is not inevitably, expressed include foodways, religious practice (especially relating to ancestors) and funerary practice (Santley et al. 1987).

Foodways vary both between and within cultures as a marker of status (Goody 1982). Several archaeologists emphasize the importance of cuisine in the construction of social identities, including ethnicity (Santley et al. 1987; Stanish 1989; Lightfoot and Martinez 1995; Burmeister 2000; Bunimovitz and Faust 2001). Funerals and burial practice demonstrate primordial ties, a key element in the construction of ethnicity (Santley et al. 1987). It is no co-incidence that cemeteries in Bosnia and Kosovo were targeted in campaigns of ethnic cleansing (Chapman 1994). Funerals provide opportunities for the dead to make a final assertion of identity but also, since the dead cannot bury themselves, they allow for an active re-assertion or renegotiation of the social position and identity of their offspring and relatives (Hodder 1982; Morris 1987; Metcalf and Huntington 1991; Meskell 1994). Two case studies reflecting Egyptian-Nubian interactions during the second millennium BCE (Askut for foodways and religion, Tombos for funerary and religious practice) will be used to illustrated how ethnic dynamics can be recognized in specific social contexts (Smith 2003).

ASKUT

At first glance Egyptian colonists in Nubia apparently forged a society identical to the Egyptian core, unlike the northern empire in Syro-Palestine (Trigger 1976; Adams 1977, 1984; Kemp 1978; Higginbotham 2000). The fortress at Askut is no exception. Built around 1850 BCE, this small fortified settlement was occupied continuously through the initial period of Egyptian colonization in the Middle Kingdom, through Nubian control in the Second Intermediate Period (1630–1520 BCE) until the end of the New Kingdom in 1075 BCE (Smith 1995). As is the case elsewhere in Lower Nubia, Askut's whitewashed walls would have symbolized Egyptian dominance and probably Egyptian ethnicity as well. The architecture of the houses and the small chapel also signaled an Egyptian identity (Figure 16.3). Egyptian-style artifacts dominate the material assemblage, as is the case with the contemporary forts in the region. As a result, Egyptologists have emphasized the emulative character of these settlements, either characterizing them as a transplant of Egyptian

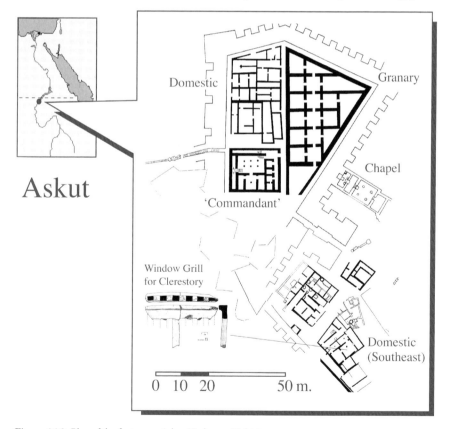

Figure 16.3. Plan of the fortress at Askut (Sudanese Nubia).

culture through colonization or as an indication of the complete assimilative acculturation of native groups.

Archaeological studies of frontier communities caution against equating the overall percentage of native versus colonial artifacts with cultural and ethnic groups, calling instead for a nuanced analysis that focuses on different components of the archaeological assemblage (Stanish 1989; Aldenderfer and Stanish 1993; Lightfoot and Martinez 1995; Stein 1999). Farnsworth (1992) breaks the material culture of California Native Americans incorporated into the Spanish Mission system into a series of subassemblages, examining each for continuity, replacement, and innovation. Similarly, Rogers (1990) breaks down Arikara culture into three contexts: domestic, ritual and funerary. For Askut I will focus on two areas, the domestic ceramic and ritual assemblages.

The ceramics from Askut were divided into three subassemblages: service, storage and cooking pots (Figure 16.4). Nubian and Egyptian pottery differ dramatically in manufacture and decoration, so it is easy to separate even body sherds along cultural lines. As is the case at the other forts, Nubian pottery

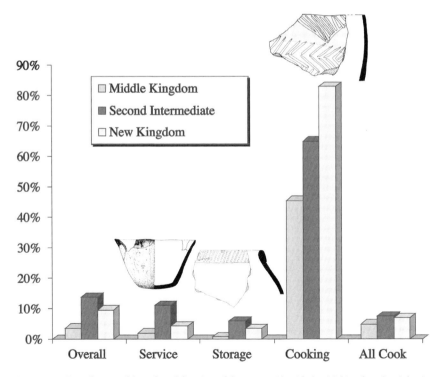

Figure 16.4. Distribution of the inferred function of the pottery identified as Nubian found at Askut in contexts dated to the Middle Kingdom (1975–1640 BCE), the Second Intermediate Period (1630–1520 BCE) and the New Kingdom (1539–1075 BCE).

appears consistently in Askut, in the small numbers that meet the expectations of the Egyptological colonization and acculturation model. When broken down into subassemblages, however, an interesting pattern emerges (Smith 2003). The percentage of Nubian pottery in the service subassemblage fluctuates, starting very low in the Middle Kingdom, increasing substantially in the Second Intermediate Period, when Nubians controlled the area, and declining sharply in the New Kingdom, correlating with the new colonial policy of assimilation. Storage vessels show a similar distribution, but the pattern of cooking pottery is very different. Nubian cooking pots are drastically overrepresented at Askut, starting at nearly half of the cooking subassemblage, growing to two-thirds in the Second Intermediate Period, and dominating during the New Kingdom. Preliminary results of residue analysis using gas chromatography followed by mass spectrometry imply that different Egyptian and Nubian cuisines also existed at Askut. If we suppose, as Egyptian historical sources indicate, that women did most of the cooking, then Askut reflects a kind of counteraccultura-tion, with Nubian women transforming colonial foodways.

The spike in Nubian fine wares during the Second Intermediate Period may reflect an instrumental assertion of ethnic ties demonstrating links between the community and their new Kerma overlords through display during feasting, perhaps driven by the men who helped manage the lucrative trade in luxuries. This might correspond to Goody's (1982:151–152) notion that the elements of foodways that connect to larger political systems tend to change in order to meet political contingencies. Goody also observes that those culinary practices without external entanglements tend to be conservative, and the prominence of Nubian cooking pots and cuisine at Askut may reflect the less overt influence of Nubian women on the community's foodways. The fact that the proportion of Nubian cooking pots, and presumably Nubian cuisine, increases steadily over time, however, implies that this is more than just a passive retention of a Nubian habitus, that it is instead an active assertion of Nubian ethnic identity that eventually came to dominate this particular social context. Although rooted in the habitus, foodways play an important role in engendering and negotiating social identities (Wood 1995). In a similar colonial context native women in Spanish Saint Augustine used local pottery and maintained native foodways (Deagan 1983). Lightfoot and Martinez (1995) argue that native women in California's Russian colony at Fort Ross used cuisine, and the organization of domestic space, to assert their native identity. Foodways and burial practice allowed slaves on southern plantations to maintain a separate ethnic identity, and cuisine continues to play a key role in African American ethnicity (McKee 1999:235). Nubian women within Egyptian colonial communities like Askut may have used foodways to provide an ethnic counterpoint to Egyptian political and cultural hegemony.

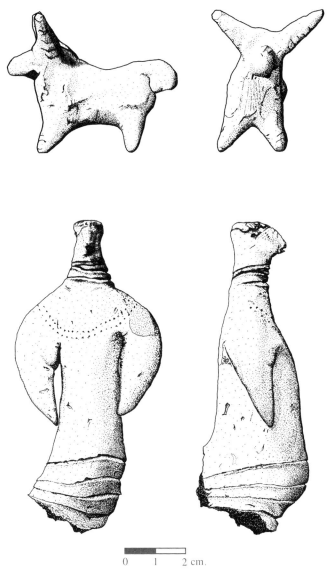

0   1   2 cm.

Figure 16.5. Two figurines from Askut (Sudanese Nubia).

Nubian influence also appears in the presence of Nubian-style fertility and cattle figurines (Figure 16.5). The increasing proportion of the latter may reflect the Nubian religious emphasis on cattle, although the shapes are simple and also appear in Egypt. Less ambiguous is a statuette of a seated pregnant woman in classic Nubian style. It was found adjacent to a typically Egyptian household shrine. Like cooking, fertility magic and household religion were under the purview of women (Pinch 1993, 1994; Robins 1993). This pattern may reflect a transculturation (Ortiz 1940; Deagan 1998) or blending of Nubian elements into an Egyptian ritual setting.

TOMBOS

Located at the headwaters of the third cataract of the Nile, Tombos lay on an important border, marked and explicitly indicated by a number of stelae carved to commemorate the defeat of Kush by Pharaoh Thutmose I in 1502 BCE. It lies only 10 km from Kerma, the former capital of the kingdom of Kush. Preliminary evidence from two seasons of excavation indicates that the cemeteries at Tombos were used from around 1400–600 BCE, and perhaps later, although whether there is continuity between the New Kingdom and the later use of the cemetery is still being investigated (Smith 2003). The location of the Egyptian colonial settlement has also proven elusive. Apart from small amounts of Nubian pottery, funerary architecture and grave goods reflect Egyptian burial practice. An elite area contained perhaps 10 large pyramid tombs of a type popular with high-level bureaucrats during the New Kingdom (Figure 16.6). Like the massive fortresses of Upper Nubia, these impressive structures would provide a symbol of Egyptian control, marking this important internal border within Egypt's southern empire. One of these tombs even had funerary cones dedicated to Siamun and his wife, Weren, a type of decoration rarely found outside Thebes (Ryan 1988). As 'Overseer of Foreign Lands,' Siamun would have played a prominent role in the colonial administration, regulating traffic across the internal border and perhaps assembling the annual tribute in gold, cattle, slaves, ivory and other precious goods from the conquered kingdom of Kush.

In a nearby middle-class cemetery, remains of decorated and inscribed coffins, evidence for mummification, and specialized items (like Ushabti figurines) reflect an Egyptian belief system (Smith 1992). The use of vaulted subterranean chambers as family crypts also reflects Egyptian practices. Objects of daily life, including personal items (like cosmetic equipment), furniture (including the remains of a folding seat), a boomerang for hunting birds, and an almost entirely Egyptian ceramic assemblage demonstrate its overwhelmingly Egyptian cultural orientation. Luxuries like a rare Mycenean juglet attest to the prosperity of the community (Smith 2003).

During the second season of excavation, however, we found burials of four women in Nubian style (Figure 16.7), flexed and oriented with their heads to the east while the bodies above and around them were buried mummified, extended on their back and with their heads to the west in typical Egyptian fashion. Looters had shoved one of these Nubian burials into an unusual position in order to steal valuable jewelry but missed a set of Egyptian style amulets

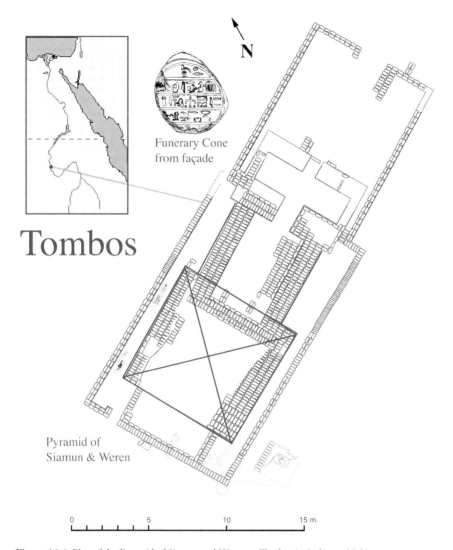

N

Tombos

Funerary Cone
from façade

Pyramid of
Siamun & Weren

0   5   10   15 m.

Figure 16.6. Plan of the Pyramid of Siamun and Weren at Tombos in Sudanese Nubia.

dedicated to the dwarf god Bes, who protects the household from physical and spiritual dangers. A Kerma-style cup was placed at the head of another set of two Nubian burials, but apart from the cup and a couple of shell beads, the grave goods associated with all four burials were Egyptian. Since Egyptian, and presumably also Nubian, funerals were public events, the burial of women in Nubian style at Tombos would make a very overt assertion of ethnic identity against the very Egyptian monumentality of the elite cemetery's pyramids.

Figure 16.7. Nubian-style burial of a woman, found on an Egyptian-style tomb at Tombos in Sudanese Nubia.

Even though, at first glance, both Nubian sites seem to represent the kind of colonial cultural conservatism discussed by Kopytoff (1987), we can see the appearance of both Egyptian and Nubian cultural features as an active social practice, an assertion of ethnic identity by different actors in different social contexts. In settings like Egypt's Nubian frontier, acculturation models oversimplify cultural interactions by emphasizing the transmission of core cultures to peripheral societies with little consideration for individual agency (Lightfoot and Martinez 1995). The evidence of Egyptian and Nubian influence at Askut and Tombos re-inforces the notion that cultural interaction on colonial frontiers is not an either-or proposition of assimilation versus innovation. Individual men and women played a role in cultural and ethnic dynamics that transformed colonial society into a dynamic social field for negotiating cultural differences, not just producing a cultural hybrid. Even in a situation of apparent ethnic polarization, coinciding with political borders and ideological boundaries, we can see the permeability of putative ethnic boundaries and the socially contingent nature of both ethnic identities and cultural interaction.

NOMADS AND ETHNICITY

Pastoral nomads play a special role in their interactions with settled groups, crossing, and in some cases undermining, state and ethnic boundaries. For example, Welsby (1996:204) credits the collapse of the Meroitic state to the infiltration of nomadic Nubians. Ethnic groups like the Nubians often have complex subdivisions that seem to contradict the notion of a consistent, single ethnic group, especially when they include a mobile component that ranges over a wide territory (Barth 1969). Historical sources mention a variety of ethnic groups and subgroups that might be classified as Nubian during the Classical era, including the Nubae, Nobades, Annoubades, Noba, Nuba, Red Noba and the Blemmyes, who may be related to the Pharaonic Medjai. It is not clear to what extent these names refer to the same people or different groups entirely (Burstein, this volume). Even within a single group there are differences. For example, there are indications that factions within the Blemmyes allied with Rome, while others fought against Roman control. Evidence from historical sources and sites like Deir al-Ballas in Egypt point to similar divisions within the Nubian Kerman state.

Given the inconsistencies in terminology and the fact that the terms reflect the construction of 'other' ethnic categories by Greeks, Romans, Byzantines and Arabs, can we even start to investigate the ethnic dynamics of groups like the Blemmyes? Some archaeologists would refute this proposition, but this position represents a fundamental misunderstanding of ethnic dynamics. Perry and Paynter (1999:306–307) note that archaeologists often uncritically adopt an essentialist view of ethnicity, assuming that ethnic groups should be easily visible through bounded sets of material culture. This reflects a highly normative view of culture. Attempts to correlate ethnic groups with archaeological cultures are misguided when they are based on the assumption that material correlates should match a primordial ethnicity. As ethnicity is situational and contingent, we can expect a considerable degree of archaeological variability in the expression of ethnic identity and overlapping rather than mutually exclusive material culture distributions (Hodder 1982; Jones 1996; Hall 1997), especially given the complex interactions that characterize a colonial frontier.

Ethnicity is not constant but dynamic, constructed and negotiated by individual actors in specific social contexts. This requires an agent-centered approach making it necessary to identify individuals in the archaeological record, a difficult task even under ideal conditions, because individuals, and not groups, make decisions about group identities, which can furthermore shift depending on individual interests and desires. This is especially the case for nomadic groups. Barth (1969) describes a considerable degree of heterogeneity among the Pathans, who nevertheless come together as a unified ethnic group, especially in the context of interaction with outsiders. In a similar way we might expect a considerable degree of heterogeneity among groups ranging in the Eastern Desert, between the Nile and the Red Sea, who might nonetheless have exhibited a degree of ethnic solidarity, especially in their interactions with the great powers that controlled Egypt.

BERENIKE

Several lines of evidence point to the presence of nomadic Blemmyes at Berenike (Burstein, this volume; Sidebotham and Wendrich 1996). The following remarks represent some preliminary suggestions for the exploration of ethnic dynamics at this important entrepôt. Pottery now identified as Eastern Desert Ware appears in domestic contexts, increasing in quantity in the last phase of the excavation (Barnard 2002). This change correlates to a shift in the faunal assemblage to large quantities of sheep and goats from the 4th century CE onward. Nubian-style tumulus burials, overlooking the *wadis* (valleys) outside of the city, also appear in this period. But does the presence of distinctive pottery and Nubian burial practice in an Eastern Desert context like Berenike represent an active assertion of ethnicity or just a passive expression of habitus within a cosmopolitan setting?

Pottery, of course, does not necessarily equal the presence of people, but foodways play a central role in enculturation. Meals and dining etiquette are also tied to ethnicity; just think of the importance of 'ethnic' food in the definition of ethnic groups. Ethnic cuisine is often deployed as an active assertion of ethnic identity, rather than reflecting a shared habitus. When displayed during feasts, ceramics can also promote ethnic solidarity both within the group and to outsiders. The correlation of Eastern Desert Ware with changes in the faunal assemblage suggests a shift in cuisine as well as the ceramic assemblage, like that seen at Askut. The possible presence of Nubian religious practices at Berenike may also play a role in the ethnic dynamics of the city. In a lecture, Rob Hughes suggested that a localized version of the Nubian Sol Invectus was worshiped in Berenike's North Shrine. Offering basins from both the North and West Shrines date to the 4th century CE and may also reflect a Nubian influence transmitted by nomads from the Eastern Desert.

Cemeteries like the 4th–6th century CE Nubian tumuli at Berenike provide a clear connection between ethnicity and territory through an emphasis on primordial ties. Against this, Shanna Kennedy argued in a lecture that although Berenike's tumuli superficially resemble tombs at Deraheib and Wadi Qitna attributed to the Blemmyes,[3] the differences in detail, and the widespread use

---

[3] http://www.archbase.com/berenike/UCstudentLA6.html (accessed 6 August 2007).

of similar Nubian practices throughout the Eastern Desert, make it implausible to attribute all of them to a single ethnic group like the Blemmyes. This kind of ethnic diversity, however, is by no means inconsistent with a unified ethnic identity, especially when dealing with a nomadic people that range across a large area and operate within different social and ecological environments (Nile Valley, desert, Red Sea coast). Barth (1969) argued that not every diversification within the group represents a first step in the direction of subdivision. Diversity within an ethnic group, however, can also be approached from a multiscale perspective, with seemingly disparate groups assembling together, especially in the face of a common threat or competitor, only to dissolve into different groups in different social and political settings. Deleuze and Guattari (1987) observe that nomadic clan lineages are essentially segments in action; they meld and divide, and vary according to the ancestor considered, the tasks and the circumstances. So it is in fact quite plausible to associate the tumuli at Berenike with the Blemmyes. Regardless, the tumuli's strategic location along desert ridges outside of Berenike would serve as an active assertion of ethnic territoriality in the context of interaction with Rome.

DISCUSSION

Perry and Paynter (1999:306–307) attribute the tendency for archaeologists and historians to think of ethnic groups as distinctly bounded and exclusive to the very nature of ethnic identities. These are inevitably constructed in essentialist terms that obscure the actual complexity and contextual, gendered nature of ethnicity in frontier communities like St. Augustine, Fort Ross, Askut, Tombos and perhaps Berenike. The key attribute to understand about ethnicity is that although people construct ethnic identities as an essential quality ascribed at birth and immutable, in fact ethnicity is socially contingent and can shift depending on the social and economic interests of individual actors. This has profound implications for the archaeological search for ethnicity, which is often an ultimately futile search for neatly bounded units that can be linked to ethnic groups. We should abandon an overly normative view of ethnicity and look carefully at different social contexts and expect inconsistencies, since ethnic identities can shift in different situations. This means that we need to think as much, if not more, in terms of individual actors than group dynamics in order to get at ethnicity.

Nomads represent a similar dynamic of cultural contact to that between Egypt and Nubia. Nomads generally interact with settled peoples, so we would expect a mixed material assemblage but can still look for key social areas for ethnic expression. For example, Eastern Desert Ware and the persistence of tumulus burials stand out as two areas that might reflect assertions of ethnic identity. The evidence from Berenike suggests a constellation of features, domestic, religious and funerary that points to a possible ethnic influence or perhaps an enclave within a multi-ethnic Berenike toward the end of the settlement. The fact that some features, like the tumuli, are not as distinctive as one might expect, or that Eastern Desert Ware constitutes only one component of the ceramic assemblage, need not bother us. At Askut and Tombos, where one would expect complete assimilation, we see a more complex pattern, with Nubian artifacts as a whole accounting for a small percentage of the overall assemblage but nevertheless with a Nubian ethnic identity emphasized in specific social contexts. The Eastern Desert Ware found at Berenike may operate in a similar way, reflecting the maintenance of ethnic foodways within the settlement at the household level. Other pottery, and even elements of foodways with Egyptian or classical connections, could be more salient to social status. The cemeteries outside of Berenike might represent a primordial claim to territory in line with ethnic dynamics. Like the Pathan, we should expect heterogeneity among the Blemmyes but ethnic expression at boundaries like Berenike, where they came in contact with Romans, Egyptians and others. Regardless, a more detailed examination of the archaeological record at Berenike along these lines will shed light on the ethnic dynamics of this important frontier community and its interactions with desert nomads like the Blemmyes.

REFERENCES

Adams, W. Y.

1977   *Nubia: Corridor to Africa*. London, Penguin.

1984   The First Colonial Empire: Egypt in Nubia, 3200–1200 B.C. *Comparative Studies in Sociology and History 26*: pp. 36–71.

Aldenderfer, M. S. and C. Stanish

1993   Domestic Architecture, Household Archaeology, and the Past in the South-Central Andes. In M. S. Aldenderfer (ed.), *Domestic Architecture, Ethnicity, and Complementarity in the South-Central Andes*. Iowa City, University of Iowa Press: pp. 1–12.

Anderson, B.

1983   *Imagined Communities: Reflections on the Origins and Spread of Nationalism*. London, Verso.

Baines, J. and J. Malek

2000   *Cultural Atlas of Ancient Egypt*. Abingdon, Andromeda.

Banks, M.

1996   *Ethnicity: Anthropological Constructions*. London, Routledge.

Barnard, H.

2002   Eastern Desert Ware: A First Introduction. *Sudan & Nubia 6*: pp. 53–57.

Barth, F. (ed.)

1969   *Ethnic Groups and Boundaries*. Boston, Little, Brown.

Bourdieu, P.

1977   *Outline of a Theory of Practice*. Cambridge, Cambridge University Press.

Bunimovitz, S. and A. Faust

2001   Chronological Separation, Geographical Segregation, or Ethnic Demarcation? Ethnography and the Iron Age Low Chronology. *Bulletin of the American Schools of Oriental Research 322*: pp. 1–10.

Burmeister, S.

2000   Archaeology and Migration. *Current Anthropology 41*: pp. 539–567.

Chapman, J.

1994   Destruction of a Common Heritage: The Archaeology of War in Croatia, Bosnia, and Hercegovina. *Antiquity 68*: pp. 120–126.

Comaroff, J. L.

1978   Rules and Rulers: Political Processes in a Tswana Chiefdom. *Man 13*: pp. 1–20.

Comaroff, J. and J. Comaroff

1992   *Ethnography and the Historical Imagination*. Boulder, Westview Press.

Crapanzano, V.

1985   *Waiting: The Whites of South Africa*. New York, Random House.

Daugé, Y. A.

1981   *Le Barbare: Recherches sur la conception romaine de la barbarie et de la civilisation*. Brussels, Révue d'Études Latines.

Deagan, K.

1983   *Spanish St. Augustine: The Archaeology of a Colonial Creole Community*. New York, Academic Press.

1998   Transculturation and Spanish American Ethnogenesis: The Archaeological Legacy of the Quincentenniary. In J. Cusick (ed.), *Studies in Culture Contact: Interaction, Culture Change, and Archaeology*. Carbondale, Southern Illinois University Press: pp. 23–43.

Deleuze, G. and F. Guattari

1987   *A Thousand Plateaus*. Minneapolis, University of Minnesota Press.

Díaz-Andreu, M.

1996   Constructing Identities Through Culture: The Past in the Forging of Europe. In P. Graves-Brown, S. Jones and C. Gamble (eds.), *Cultural Identity and Archaeology*. London, Routledge: pp. 48–61.

Farnsworth, P.

1992   Missions, Indians, and Cultural Continuity. *Historical Archaeology 26*: pp. 22–36.

Glazer, N. and D. P. Moynihan (eds.)

1963   *Ethnicity: Theory and Experience*. Cambridge, Harvard University Press.

Goody, J.

1982   *Cooking, Cuisine, and Class: A Study in Comparative Sociology*. Cambridge, Cambridge University Press.

Graves-Brown, P.

1996   All Things Bright and Beautiful? Species, Ethnicity, and Cultural Dynamics. In P. Graves-Brown, S. Jones and C. Gamble (eds.), *Cultural Identity and Archaeology*. London, Routledge: pp. 81–95.

Hall, J. M.

1997   *Ethnic Identity in Greek Antiquity*. Cambridge, Cambridge University Press.

Handler, R.

1988   *Nationalism and the Politics of Culture in Quebec*. Madison, University of Wisconsin Press.

Hides, S.

1996   The Genealogy of Material Culture and Cultural Identity. In P. Graves-Brown, S. Jones and C. Gamble (eds.), *Cultural Identity and Archaeology*. London, Routledge: pp. 25–47.

Higginbotham, C. R.

2000   *Egyptianization and Elite Emulation in Ramesside Palestine*. Leiden, E. J. Brill.

Hodder, I.

1979   Economic and Social Stress and Material Culture. *American Antiquity 44*: pp. 446–454.

1982   *The Present Past: An Introduction to Anthropology for Archaeologists*. London, Batsford.

Isajew, W.

1974   Definitions of Ethnicity. *Ethnicity 1*: pp. 111–124.

Jones, S.

1996   Discourses of Identity in the Interpretation of the Past. In P. Graves-Brown, S. Jones and C. Gamble (eds.), *Cultural Identity and Archaeology*. London, Routledge: pp. 62–80.

1997   *The Archaeology of Ethnicity: Constructing Identities in the Past and Present*. London, Routledge.

Kemp, B. J.

1978   Imperialism in New Kingdom Egypt (c. 1575–1087 B.C.). In P. D. A. Garnsey and C. R. Whittaker (eds.), *Imperialism in the Ancient World*. Cambridge, Cambridge University Press: pp. 7–57, 283–297.

Kohn, H.

1944   *The Idea of Nationalism: A Study of Its Origins and Backgrounds*. New York, Macmillan.

Kopytoff, I.

1987   *The African Frontier: The Reproduction of Traditional African Societies.* Bloomington, Indiana University Press.

Kurzban, R., J. Tooby and L. Cosmides

2001   Can Race be Erased? Coalitional Computation and Social Categorization. In *Proceedings of the National Academy of Sciences 98*: 26, pp. 15387–15392.

Lichtheim, M.

1976   *Ancient Egyptian Literature: A Book of Readings. Volume 2: The New Kingdom.* Berkeley, University of California Press.

Lightfoot, K. G. and A. Martinez

1995   Frontiers and Boundaries in Archaeological Perspective. *Annual Review of Anthropology 24*: pp. 471–492.

Liverani, M.

1990   *Prestige and Interest: International Relations in the Near East, ca. 1600–1100 B.C.* Padova, Sargon.

Loprieno, A.

1988   *Topos und Mimesis.* Wiesbaden, Harrassowitz.

McKee, L.

1999   Food Supply and Plantation Social Order: An Archaeological Perspective. In T. A. Singleton (ed.), *"I, Too, Am America": Archaeological Studies of African-American Life.* Charlottesville, University Press of Virginia: pp. 218–239.

Meskell, L. M.

1994   Dying Young: The Experience of Death at Deir el-Medineh. *Archaeological Review from Cambridge 13*: 2, pp. 35–45.

Metcalf, P. and R. Huntington

1991   *Celebrations of Death: The Anthropology of Mortuary Ritual.* Cambridge, Cambridge University Press.

Morris, I.

1987   *Burial and Ancient Society: The Rise of the Greek City-State.* Cambridge, Cambridge University Press.

Ortiz, F.

1940   *Contrapunteo cubano del tabaco y el Azúcar* [in Spanish]. Havana, Montero.

Parker, B. J.

2002   At the Edge of Empire: Conceptualizing Assyria's Anatolian Frontier, ca. 700 BC. *Journal of Anthropological Archaeology 21*: pp. 371–395.

Perry, W. and R. Paynter

1999   Artifacts, Ethnicity, and Archaeology of African Americans. In T. A. Singleton (ed.), *"I, Too, Am America': Archaeological Studies of African-American Life.* Charlottesville, University Press of Virginia: pp. 299–310.

Pinch, G.

1993   *Votive Offerings to Hathor.* Oxford, Griffith Institute.

1994   *Magic in Ancient Egypt*. Austin, University of Texas Press.

Prescott, J. R. V.

1987   *Political Frontiers and Boundaries*. London, Unwin Hyman.

Ratzel, F.

1897   *Politische Geographie*. München-Berlin, Oldenbourg.

Rawlinson, G.

1964   *The Histories of Herodotus*. London, Dent.

Renfrew, C.

1996   Prehistory and the Identity of Europe, or, Don't Let's Be Beastly to the Hungarians. In P. Graves-Brown, S. Jones and C. Gamble (eds.), *Cultural Identity and Archaeology*. London, Routledge: pp. 125–137.

Robins, G.

1993   *Women in Ancient Egypt*. Cambridge, Harvard University Press.

Rogers, J. D.

1990   *Objects of Change: The Archaeology and History of Arikara Contact with Europeans*. Washington, Smithsonian Institution Press.

Royce, A. P.

1982   *Ethnic Identity: Strategies of Diversity*. Bloomington, Indiana University Press.

Ryan, D. P.

1988   The Archaeological Analysis of Inscribed Egyptian Funerary Cones. *Varia Egyptiaca 4*: pp. 165–170.

Santley, R., C. Yarborough and B. Hall

1987   Enclaves, Ethnicity, and the Archaeological Record at Matacapan. In R. Auger, M. F. Glass, S. MacEachern and P. H. MacCartney (eds.), *Ethnicity and Culture*. Calgary, Archaeological Association of the University of Calgary.

Sidebotham, S. E. and W. Z. Wendrich

1996   *Berenike 1995: Preliminary Report of the 1995 Excavations at Berenike (Egyptian Red Sea Coast) and the Survey of the Eastern Desert*. Leiden, Research School CNWS.

Smith, A. D.

1986   *The Ethnic Origins of Nations*. Oxford, Blackwell.

Smith, S. T.

1992   Intact Theban Tombs and the New Kingdom Burial Assemblage. *Mitteilungen des Deutschen Archäologischen Instituts Kairo 48*: pp. 193–231.

1995   *Askut in Nubia: The Economics and Ideology of Egyptian Imperialism in the Second Millennium BC*. London, Kegan Paul.

2003   *Wretched Kush: Ethnic Identities and Boundaries in Egypt's Nubian Empire*. London, Routledge.

Spicer, E.

1962   *Cycles of Conquest*. Tucson, University of Arizona Press.

Stanish, C.
1989   Household Archaeology: Testing Models of Zonal Complementarity in the
        South Central Andes. *American Anthropologist 91*: pp. 7–24.
Stein, G. J.
1999   *Rethinking World Systems: Diasporas, Colonies, and Interaction in Uruk
        Mesopotamia*. Tucson, University of Arizona Press.
Tonkin, E., M. McDonald and M. Chapman
1989   Introduction. In E. Tonkin, M. McDonald and M. Chapman (eds.), *History
        and Ethnicity*. London, Routledge: pp. 1–21.
Trigger, B. G.
1976   *Nubia Under the Pharaohs*. London, Thames and Hudson.
Welsby, D. A.
1996   *The Kingdom of Kush*. London, British Museum Press.
Wendl, T. and M. Rösler
1999   Frontiers and Borderlands: The Rise and Relevance of an Anthropological
        Research Genre. In M. Rösler and T. Wendl (eds.), *Frontiers and Borderlands:
        Anthropological Perspectives*. New York, Peter Lang: pp. 1–27.
Wood, R. C.
1995   *The Sociology of the Meal*. Edinburgh, Edinburgh University Press.

CHAPTER 17

VARIABILITY AND DYNAMIC LANDSCAPES OF MOBILE PASTORALISM IN ETHNOGRAPHY AND PREHISTORY

MICHAEL D. FRACHETTI[1]

PREHISTORIC NOMADIC PASTORALISM presents a unique analytical and theoretical problem for archaeologists, in that often we are trying to explain the prototypical forms of a social and economic way of life that regularly defies a 'typical' classification, even in a given context (Dyson-Hudson and Dyson-Hudson 1980). From the wealth of ethnographic studies concerning contemporary nomadic pastoralists, we may only be able to generalize two rudimentary facts: nomadic pastoralism reflects an intensive engagement in herding of domesticated animals as a primary economic and social way of life; and the strategies and practices (movement, animal management, settlement, trade, warfare, etc.) of nomadic pastoralists are adapted in response to the geographic and temporal dynamics of their environment; their socio-ideological, political and economic relationships; and their individual or group health and well-being. An additional caveat to these observations is that the frequency and amplitude of change across such factors is both irregular and codependent on the nature of the strategies employed.

These conditions can be confounding for the archaeologist, because in the first case the prevalence of domesticated animal remains in archaeological contexts is not sufficient to argue for a nomadic way of life in prehistory. So, although they can be a significant indicator, such data can be easily overvalidated as a requisite aspect of 'nomadic sites.' The second condition presents a frustrating feedback loop, in that the complex layering of environmental, political, and socio-economic considerations that ultimately affects the choices

[1] The research on which this chapter is based was funded by grants from the National Science Foundation and the George F. Dales Foundation. Radiocarbon dates were analyzed by the Arizona AMS laboratory.

and practices of nomadic pastoral societies is impacted and even shaped by the spatial and temporal patterning of those very strategies, thereby indexing a highly dynamic way of life that sometimes appears categorically 'nomadic,' sometimes looks more 'sedentary' and is regularly recast in different places and at different times in different forms. Thus, a paradox lies in the fact that perhaps the only 'regular' aspect of nomadic pastoral lifestyles is the condition of variability. This observation constitutes the first point of this chapter and is illustrated below through some well-developed ethnographic studies of nomadic societies of Western and Central Asia.

Within archaeology the recovery of variation in the layout of domestic contexts, economic strategies, ritual constructions and material culture often leads to typological classifications in the attempt to order distinct social or cultural groupings: A's with A's, B's with B's, and C's with C's. This is especially the case when the relative chronology of sites is in question. Correlating typological distinctions with particular social or economic forms, however, may be the wrong approach in the archaeology of mobile pastoralism, as categorical classifications can mask the potential plurality of strategies employed by a given society. A more useful approach may be to recognize that A's, B's and C's can reflect the variation of strategies, such as different settlement or camp configurations, that enables pastoralists to maintain social cohesiveness and adaptive success within the geographic and temporal fluctuations of their experienced landscape.

The second aim of this chapter is to propose an analytical approach to the archaeology of prehistoric mobile pastoralists that takes the focus away from the identification and categorization of 'nomadic' or 'non-nomadic' data classes and turns it toward the issue of geographic and temporal variability, as reflected archaeologically across pastoral landscapes. The argument here is that prehistoric mobile pastoral societies can be better understood by relating the archaeological variation within various data classes to the optional practices and adaptations relevant to different environmental and social contexts charted across geographic and temporal planes. In other words, this approach advocates modeling how changes in strategy and choice are mapped onto recoverable archaeological landscapes and how the range of options co-varies with other dynamic factors (environment, technology, etc.) over time. Logically, chronological contemporaneity within a range of data is key to the argument, as variation can essentially reflect two scenarios: change over time or variation within a range set. In practice these scenarios combine to produce considerably complex social, economic and political landscapes.

In the final part of this chapter the proposed approach is applied to a case study of Bronze Age societies in eastern Kazakhstan, illustrating that these pastoral groups may have employed a variety of strategies that range across the ideal categories of 'nomadic' or 'sedentary' herders and thereby contributed to the formation of extensive networks of social and economic interaction during the second millennium BCE.

ETHNOGRAPHY OF NOMADISM AS A STUDY OF VARIATION

Nomadic pastoralism is most commonly understood as a way of life based predominantly in the social and economic strategies associated with a routine migratory management of domesticated herd animals (Lattimore 1940:54; Barth 1964:4; Khazanov 1994:17). Etymologically, the words *nomadism* and *pastoralism* both imply pasturing or the raising of herds (Spooner 1973:3; Salzman 2002:245). A number of scholars, such as Barfield (1993:4), however, note that the term *nomadism* is also sometimes used in association with other mobility strategies, such as hunting and gathering. Thus, Barfield distinguishes *nomadic* as a referent to movement, or mobility, and *pastoralism* as a referent to a productive strategy, raising livestock on natural pastures (see also Salzman 2002:245). A number of scholars have long recognized that nomadic-pastoral strategies reflect a considerable degree of variation that makes normative categories, generated on the basis of ideal economic or social types, inadequate as explanatory paradigms. Contemporary ethnographers have noted that a broad definition of *nomadic pastoralism* rather inadequately describes the wide range of socio-economic strategies recorded among societies who rely on herding (Salzman 1972:67; Spooner 1973:4) and does not in itself describe the variability in social and political practices that are documented within these societies (Dyson-Hudson and Dyson-Hudson 1980). Yet they commonly agree that the broad range of pastoral strategies (mobility, multiresource exploitation, etc.) are adaptive in view of specific environmental variations (Bacon 1954:54), human and animal ecology (Barth 1964; Spooner 1973; Koster 1977), and socio-ideological and political contexts (Irons 1974; Tapper 1979). In fact, it is difficult to emphasize one of these contributing factors over the other in forming typological definitions, as ethnographic examples illustrate differing emphasis on each of these factors. In some cases these factors may even fluctuate in their importance to the organization and practices of a particular pastoral group. Dyson-Hudson and Dyson-Hudson (1980:18) summarize this point nicely: "since a unique constellation of ecological, political, economic, and affective factors determines the patterns of movement of each pastoral group, and the specific movements of each independent herd owner within every pastoral society, it is not surprising that there is enormous variation in patterns of mobility."

The ethnographic record exhibits a diversity of adaptations and particular pastoral strategies that confound categorization of ideal types. Migration patterns, for example, are often altered through iterated engagements in productive practices such as agriculture or market trade (Bradburd 1990:34–39), changes in political organization (Shahrani 1979:171–172) or participation in complex and changing routines of social and economic interaction with neighboring populations (Barth 1964:109; Beck 1991). Salzman (2002:256) reiterates this point directly: "shifting between strategies of adaptation [on the part of nomadic societies] in response to changes in conditions has been very common throughout the Middle East and North Africa. We must also keep in mind that 'settled' and 'nomadic,' rather than being two types, are better thought of as opposite ends of a continuum with many gradations of stability and mobility." Ethnographic studies show that nomadic societies often consist of groups who exhibit variously specialized economic practices as part of one sociopolitical structure, thereby defying rigid dichotomies between peasant and nomadic ways of life.

Irons's ethnography (1974:636–637) of the Yomut Turkmen provides a clear example of such a nomadic pastoral system in the Gurgan Plain of Iran. The Yomut Turkmen maintain two occupationally different factions within their tribal organization. These subgroups are called the *chomur* and the *charwa*, the former being primarily agriculturalists, the latter engaged more exclusively in pastoralism. The economic relationship between these groups is supportive, and socially they adhere to a common tribal organization. Both groups employ a degree of mobility in their exploitation of the limited resources of their environment, though the charwa rely more heavily on seasonal migration than do the chomur, even though both groups could feasibly lead far more sedentary lifestyles given their economic demands. Both groups distinguish themselves politically and ideologically from non-Turkmen groups of the same region and use their flexibility in residence as a strategy for resisting political control. Irons (1974:654) contends that the Yomut are strategically able to negotiate multiple political contexts more effectively because their fluctuating patterns of mobility and symbiosis in agricultural and pastoral production enable them to evade taxation and state control, while maintaining viable economic productivity. Irons's example of the Yomut shows that 'nomadic pastoralism' can encompass variations in seasonal migration, settlement, agricultural emphasis and social interaction, making it a highly adaptive strategy.

Salzman (1972:66–67) has proposed that the Yarahmadzai and Gamshadai pastoral tribes of Baluchistan engage in 'multi-resource nomadism,' varying their movement patterns to accommodate the demands of pastoral production and to take advantage of productive date cultivation and the sale of labor in regional markets. Salzman cites these alternative strategies as evidence that pastoralists often maximize their economic and social success in marginal environments by engaging in practices that are not typically associated with societies classified as 'nomads.' Variation in mobile pastoral systems is commonly linked to both the ecology of herding and sociopolitical negotiations (Tapper 1979:111). These factors can contribute to significant changes in the way pastoralists manage territory and lay claim on locations in their landscape (pastures and campgrounds).

Barfield's study (1981:44–46) of the Central Asian Arabs of Afghanistan describes how some nomadic Arabs claim exclusive rights to particular pasture zones, based on rights established through complex political dealings with regional and national political bodies in the early part of the 20th century CE. In light of the environmental variability in pasture quality from year to year, ownership and control of particular locations and resources such as summer and winter pastures (*ailoq* and *qhishloq*) and seasonal cisterns (*yekhdon*) engendered various forms of social interactions, such as trading of resources, political alliances, and land rental, to meet the needs of domesticated herds. Barfield's example describes how the environmental variability of mountainous environments conditioned social practices of greater investment in demarcated locales, contributing to an ecologically ordered but socially negotiable pattern of mobility and pastoral land use.

Pastner (1971:175–180) describes an interesting case where environmental, political and ideological systems of the Makran Baluch of western Pakistan result in various patterns of interactions related to territorial and social affiliations at local and regional scales. Pastner emphasizes how localized patterns of mobility, or the 'micro-pastoral orbit' used by the Makrani nomads to accommodate the demands of herd animals and social groups in a marginal environment, are also extended for purposes of resource exploitation and socioeconomic strategies not specific to herd needs. Alternative aims, such as trade, raiding, itinerant agriculture or the sale of labor, introduce unique mobility patterns and bring nomads into close interactions with sedentary villagers while settling in peripheral residence camps near agricultural villages, often during the time of *haman* (harvest). The nature of camp formation and territorial use in the micropastoral orbit during this time is also affected by ideological concerns that arise from the social pressures associated with the dynamics of interaction around village groups. Islamic concern with 'purdah,' the protection of the honor and purity of women, is a factor that affects economic and practical decisions, as life around imposing sedentary villagers is seen as a risk for the women. Thus, there is an ideological justification for the formation of group camps, where women may be better shielded from sexual predation on the part of outsiders. For the Makrani Baluch, the year-to-year variability of the mobility strategies in their nomadic search for pasture also brings about interaction and overlap between various contiguous micropastoral orbits, forming what Pastner calls a 'macro-pastoral orbit' or territory. This macropastoral orbit generates for the pastoralists a wide range of regional alliances and social affiliations between groups. Such social affiliations become significant in negotiating economic and political relationships when disparate groups come together on the outskirts of sedentary village contexts during *haman*, once again serving the purpose of protecting their ideological concerns. Pastner (1971:182) notes that "it is at this point that social parameters of the macro-pastoral orbit pay off . . . Co-resident encampments of nomads are composed of people united in the web of consanguinity, affinality, and friendship of the macro-orbit . . . These co-resident members of the macro-orbit provide the means of alleviating the apprehensions of men about their women's sexual safety, particularly vulnerable, as it were, during haman." Pastner's example illustrates the overlapping forces of environmental adaptation and political interaction that contribute to the variable scale and pattern of micro- and macropastoral orbits. It also demonstrates how the patterned and variable mobility of the Makrani Baluch results in the formation of social alliances and cohesive social units at camps through the organization of territory along political, economic and ideological lines.

Shahrani's (1979:112–116) study of the Kirghiz of the Wakhan Corridor and Pamir Mountains of Afghanistan describes a case of nomadic pastoralism where pastoral mobility patterns and associated social interactions with neighboring populations were drastically affected by changes in the political geography of northern Afghanistan, China, and the USSR in the early 20th century CE. Shahrani provides a detailed discussion of the ecological impact of the harsh high-altitude environment of the Pamir Mountains on pastoral strategies and illustrates that the ethnic Kirghiz practice an 'intensive' pattern of pastoral mobility, which varies considerably within a confined territory according to the seasonal alpine climate and pasture dynamics. Shahrani (1979:116) notes that "the Kirghiz are intensive pasturage users and the distance covered in their pendular migrations is relatively short but not uniform. The farthest distance between camps occupied by the same herding unit during a year may range from fifteen to thirty-five kilometers. However the distance covered during a change of encampment (e.g. winter to spring) . . . may be less than that suggested above." He further shows that this pattern of mobility was not always typical: prior to 1949 the Kirghiz employed more extensive migrations, moving over 150 km into lowland valleys in present-day China and Tajikistan, interacting with the Wakhi, who are settled agriculturalists of the Wakhan corridor (Shahrani 1979:171). Nevertheless, Shahrani finds historical continuity in the social identity of the Kirghiz in spite of these changes (Shahrani 1979:170). Looking at this case, we observe two scales in which the Kirghiz exhibit variation in their migratory pastoral adaptation. The first is the local and contemporary scale, where their intensive adaptation to the mountain ecology alters their mobility patterns from year to year. The second is the regional and historical scale, whereby their mobility pattern has paralleled considerable change in both environmental exploitation and social interaction over the past 55 years.

The key observation from these ethnographies, among many others, is that mobile pastoral systems often reflect a highly changeable strategy for managing social and ecological demands within a variety of environmentally, politically and ideologically dynamic contexts. Therefore, archaeologists may benefit from the observation that societies engaged in mobile forms of pastoralism commonly construct a social landscape that on the one hand is ordered by their patterns of herd management in response to fluctuating ecological contexts, while at the same time produces variations in social contexts according to the negotiation of social, economic, ritual or political conditions. On this basis typological categorizations of nomadic pastoralism in current ethnography have been superseded by more focused attention on the historical and practical particulars of 'mobile pastoral' ways of life (Humphrey and Sneath 1999), which may lead one to agree with Kavoori's (1999:14) optimistic remark that "we are well past the earlier sterile typological concerns that sought to classify pastoralists as nomads, semi-nomads, transhumants, and so on." Yet oddly, it is still common in archaeological studies to rely on basic categories of economic and social modes of nomadic pastoralism. This is especially the case in studies of the Eurasian steppe (Kosarev 1984; Khazanov 1994), which is the focus of the case study below. Perhaps this is due to the fact that archaeologists often have less refined evidence than ethnographers to describe the complex pressures that contributed to dynamic prehistoric pastoral systems. Yet this complication does not justify a categorically simple description of mobile forms of pastoralism in prehistory. Archaeologists can productively investigate the archaeological signatures of variation in pastoral contexts and benefit from the ethnographic recognition that choice and strategic variability are key aspects to the success and evolution of pastoral societies over time.

THE ARCHAEOLOGY OF MOBILE PASTORALISM

The archaeology of prehistoric mobile pastoralism has suffered from the lack of an approach to target the condition of variability within pastoral systems. Archaeological data such as site layouts, faunal remains and artifact assemblages, which are presented as analogous indicators of socio-economic strategies known from ethnographically recorded 'nomadic' societies, have typically served as the basis for identifying prehistoric nomadic pastoralism in the Near East and Central Asia (Cribb 1991; Bar-Yosef and Khazanov 1992; Kohler-Rollefson 1992). Although these data are compelling evidence for prehistoric pastoral adaptations, they may not present a complete picture if categorically separated from other 'less analogous' archaeological contexts. Even though variations exist in various classes of data across these archaeological landscapes, the approach has more often been to place, for example, tent camps and permanent architecture in categorical distinction, rather than to conceive of these features as part of a range of settlement options reflecting less distinction between pastoralists and others in the fabric of regional prehistoric societies (but see Rosen 2003). Perhaps one rationale for separating nomadic and agricultural populations in Near Eastern archaeological settings lies in the greater formal difference between the archaeological remains of campsites and large urban settlements, and the apparent distinctions in the political economies of protostates and contemporary tribal groups (but see Lamberg-Karlovsky 2003). Even so, archaeologists working in this part of the world are quick to recognize that these groups were likely linked in economic, if not social, symbiosis (Danti 2000), but nomads are still relegated to the periphery in terms of their social and political agency in such contexts.

The relationship between large-scale agricultural settlements and the development of specialized pastoralism is not well documented to date in Central Asia and the Eurasian steppes (Lamberg-Karlovsky 2003). Eneolithic 'culture groups' such as the Atbasar and the Botai of the central steppes reveal little evidence for a developed agricultural economy in the third millennium BCE (Kislenko and Tatarintseva 1999). Like the Atbasar, third millennium BCE societies in Inner Asia, such as the Afanas'ev in the northeastern forest steppes, were primarily hunter-fishers with only limited herding of cattle (Khlobystina 1973; Shilov 1975; Vadetskaya 1986). Faunal evidence in this region indicates that pastoral exploitation of horses, cattle and sheep only became predominant by the end of the third millennium BCE (Tsalkin 1964), such that the model of emerging pastoralism in the Eurasian steppe becomes increasingly dissimilar to that proposed for the Near East. In the western Eurasian steppes, in regions of Southern Russia, North Caucuses, and north of the Caspian Sea, the possibility that specialized pastoralism emerged from mixed agropastoral subsistence strategy is better documented. Settled agricultural practices of societies such as the Srubnaya and Tripolye are well documented for the late third millennium BCE and aggregate sites, such as Sintashta and Arkaim in the southwest Ural region, illustrate that a mixed economy of agriculture and pastoralism was developing by the beginning of the second millennium BCE (Chernykh 1997; Jones-Bley and Zdanovich 2002). Thus, evidence for both agricultural and pastoral economies is known, albeit scantily, in this part of Eurasia.

Archaeobotanical studies in the western steppe region and the Samara Valley, however, have yet to recover any evidence of domesticated plants, even where comprehensive flotation strategies were employed (David Anthony, pers.

comm.). Shishlina (this volume) also notes this trend at Bronze Age sites in the north Caucasus, where her archaeobotanical studies have not revealed domesticated plants. From these results we might propose that 'pastoral' systems in the western steppe reflect a degree of specialization, where some groups were engaged in agricultural production, while other groups, throughout the broader region, were not. Unfortunately, the relationship between these two Bronze Age strategies, either as socially specialized economies or as part of a common adaptive strategy, are still underdocumented. These archaeological debates are hindered by the lack of an approach to situate archaeological data within a framework highlighting the variable social and economic strategies of mobile pastoralists in prehistory. In part, the investigation of variability in prehistoric pastoralism is limited by the desire to match archaeological evidence to the paradigm of set economic modes of production. This approach leaves our understanding of the emergence of prehistoric mobile pastoralism foggy at best. When overly generalized categories are used paradigmatically to explain prehistoric processes, archaeologists are snared somewhat unwittingly within an analytical tautology. Namely, typical categories are used to model prototypical scenarios, which in turn are used to justify the generation of the category itself. To be sprung from this loop, an approach to prehistoric mobile pastoralism is needed that documents the variability of mobile pastoral systems in the past and that accounts for the possibility of unique combinations of ecological, social, political and ideological practices. Landscape archaeology is a useful springboard for developing such an approach.

DYNAMIC PASTORAL LANDSCAPES

Landscape-oriented studies have been part of archaeology long enough that the term alone does not convey a singular approach (Ashmore and Knapp 1999; Stoddart 2000). Anschuetz et al. (2001:158) remark that the imprecise definition of *landscape* is a problem that plagues archaeology, as well as other disciplines such as geography, as all struggle to understand the "fundamental nature of the relationship between people and the spaces they employ." Beyond this observation, most agree that landscape archaeology situates past populations in both an environmental and social milieu, where they create and negotiate the ecological, political, ideological and ritual boundaries of their way of life (McGlade 1995; Knapp and Ashmore 1999; Anschuetz et al. 2001). Ingold (1993:152) constructively points out that 'landscapes' reflect the impact of agents situated in time and space, a vantage point specifically useful for studying mobile pastoralists, whose pattern of life is often synchronous with environmental cycles and whose economic and political activities can be both patterned and flexible (Barth 1969; Beck 1991). From this perspective mobile pastoralism can be studied as the mobile activation of various geographic, economic, ideological, social and political landscapes united into one mode of life.

The landscape approach promoted here assumes that various contexts of pastoral praxis distributed over a given territory contribute to discernible anthropogenic 'footprints' that correspond to specific adaptive practices employed over time, while changing the natural and social environment according to strategic choices (McGlade 1995; Erickson 2000). What is perhaps most appealing about this definition is the allowance for variability in human strategies within periodically different snapshots of the environmental and social context. The creation of landscapes by societies, over lifetimes and longer durations of time, will be reflected by the adaptive stability of certain ways of exploiting the environment and by variations in the social employment of both natural and anthropogenic locales. Ultimately, ecological and archaeological documentation of periods of stability and change in the constructed landscape provides an entrée to discussions of more slippery topics, such as how social, political, economic and ideological frameworks impacted regional populations over time.

As stated by McGlade (1995:114), "we need to understand the conception of nature and the location of humans within its ambit—not simply as a dynamical system, but as part of a social historical process." He proposes that in order to bridge the dialectic between nature and culture, archaeologists should be concerned with 'human eco-dynamics,' which he defines as "the dynamics of human modified landscapes set within a long-term perspective, and viewed as a non-linear dynamical system" (McGlade 1995:126). This use of a nonlinear model of causation loosens the relationship between human strategies and historical outcomes, while taking into account the fact that human actions do result in recoverable and distinctive structures over time. McGlade's paradigm is powerful in that it situates the agent in the foreground of landscape conception yet recognizes that the practice of building social relationships is indeed conditioned by the historically extant structure of the landscape. Thus, the spatial and temporal constraints of the natural environment are conditioned and negotiated through patterns of land use and the variability of human interaction within both the ecological and social affordances of the landscape. Human ecodynamics is a useful concept for tracing mobile pastoralism in that many pastoral activities are economically tied to the potential of the environment, yet strategies are altered to accommodate social, political and ideological pressures applied across those very same territories. Thus, the pastoral 'landscape' represents the amalgamation of these factors into a recoverable, and conceptually real, spatial and temporal entity.

Nevertheless, to deny that the environment has a life of its own is to ignore the visible ecological balance that often defines the natural context of pastoral societies. Many times typical mobility orbits are strategically changed by pastoralists in reaction to short-term fluctuations in the natural environment, such as extremely wet or cold summers in alpine meadows. In such a case upland meadows would not be grazed as usual both because of the inclement conditions at high altitude and the greater abundance of adequate pasture at lower elevations. The effects of this altered plan are then passed back to the environment, as midland pastures become overused and alpine meadows become overgrown. Thus, for each series of reciprocal reactions, there is an anthropogenic ripple effect that lasts longer than the immediate condition. From an archaeological perspective these elemental changes are difficult to document. Thus our 'graphic' for human ecodynamics is necessarily smoothed, and we are constrained by the average case scenario, regardless of our knowledge that human groups are challenged to deal with variability in the actual environment. To better understand the reality of pastoral strategies, and the potential social implications that stem from various modes of interaction, a landscape approach that emphasizes temporal and spatial currents within the human-ecological sphere offers a useful synergy between the fixed archaeological record and the patterns of land use by populations whose resource catchments were variable in terms of distance and accessibility over time.

Human ecodynamics are folded into the pastoral landscape, which encompasses the exploitation and living strategies employed by societies over time and space, within the limits and opportunities of specific environments. Modeling the landscape entails comparing its periodic productivity and identifying potentially successful strategies for its exploitation. This is not to propose a deterministic relationship between environmental productivity and human exploitation. Societies frequently exercise their choice not to utilize certain resources for cultural reasons or to modify their environment to suit their needs given the available technology (Salzman 2002). Pastoral landscapes reflect many practices that are less dependent on the environment, such as the creation of ritual spaces, or patterns of mobility that define routes and boundaries within the landscape not tied to environmental considerations. These spaces may have an equally reflexive impact as the natural setting on the development of patterned occupation of the landscape. We now turn to a concrete archaeological case study, to better understand how variation in economic and social strategies of Bronze Age pastoralists living in the Dzhungar Mountains in Kazakhstan contributed to the formation of a distinct cultural landscape and set into motion wider interregional networks of interaction.

THE PASTORAL ARCHAEOLOGY OF
EASTERN KAZAKHSTAN

The Dzhungar Mountains Archaeology Project (DMAP) was initiated in 1999 to address the nature of Bronze Age pastoralism in one region of the Eurasian steppe, the Semirech'ye and the Dzhungar Mountains (Figure 17.1). The DMAP presents a comprehensive program for scientific archaeological research concerning the economy, social organization, and structure of interregional interaction of Bronze Age societies in the eastern Eurasian steppe zone (Frachetti 2004a). The analytical approach of the DMAP draws from landscape archaeology, which provides a conceptual framework for addressing the distribution of archaeological data from different analytical scales while also considering its spatial variation across a given territory (Frachetti 2006). This approach roots archaeological interpretations in intensive studies of particular locations within the wider distribution of sites across the landscape and justifies them in relation to a number of concomitant factors, such as environmental resources, topography and site-to-site correlations. Spatial analysis of the relative location of settlements, burials and other related locales (such as rock-art sanctuaries), along with detailed scientific analysis of the material culture and archaeobotanical and

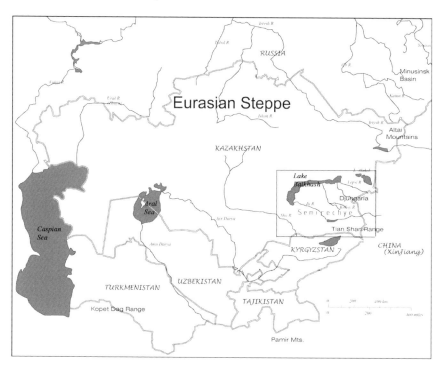

Figure 17.1. Location of the study area in the Eurasian steppe on the border of Kazakhstan and China.

archaeozoological remains, and the chronology of various sites, provides a rich fabric of data at regional, local and site-specific levels. Applying this multiscalar approach, the archaeological methodology included archaeological survey, archaeological excavation, paleo-environmental reconstruction and computer-assisted spatial modeling using a geographic information system. This phase was carried out between 2002 and 2004 and resulted in one of the first contemporary studies of Bronze Age pastoralism in the region (Frachetti 2004b).

Our archaeological survey resulted in the discovery of more than 380 new archaeological sites distributed throughout the study area in the Koksu River Valley in Eastern Kazakhstan (Frachetti 2004b). The Koksu Valley was selected for a number of reasons. First, the environment of southeast Kazakhstan varies drastically from sandy deserts to grassy steppe-lands and alpine meadows within a geographic extent of fewer than 100 km. This geographic variation enabled a concise investigation of different environmental contexts within a logistically reasonable territory and allowed for the correlation between archaeological contexts and their corresponding environmental niches. Second, earlier archaeological research showed that the Koksu Valley had been host to Bronze Age societies engaged in, roughly defined, pastoralism (Mar'yashev and Goryachev 1993; Goryachev and Mar'yashev 1998), while the 'Dzhungarian Gates,' the historical name for the mountain passes through Semirech'ye, are documented trade and travel routes in the region (Bartol'd 1943).

The survey phase of the DMAP documented a variety of site types from different periods within the Koksu Valley, the most common being settlements, burials and rock art, though sporadic finds and unique features were also documented. Within this data set the archaeology of the Koksu Valley dates from the earliest find of a Neolithic flint blade core to the most recent settlements of the past 100 years. Over 80% of the sites can be attributed to the Bronze Age (second and early first millennia BCE). This rough chronology was assigned on the basis of comparable formal characteristics in the construction style of sites, as well as on the basis of datable ceramics and other archaeological materials collected in shovel tests. The chronology was then better justified through archaeological excavations, which produced a more accurate range of absolute dates for these materials on the basis of radiocarbon dating.

Small-scale excavations were carried out at the Bronze Age site of Begash, which contributed material and analytical data concerning the chronology, domestic economy, environment, patterns of land use and burial rituals of Bronze Age pastoral groups (Frachetti 2004b, 2006; Mar'yashev and Frachetti, forthcoming). The excavations included a Bronze Age settlement (Begash), as well as three burials from the nearby cemetery (Begash-2), located 350 m from the settlement (Figure 17.2). Excavations at the settlement provided a sequence of radiocarbon dates that illustrate the site's long-term use throughout the

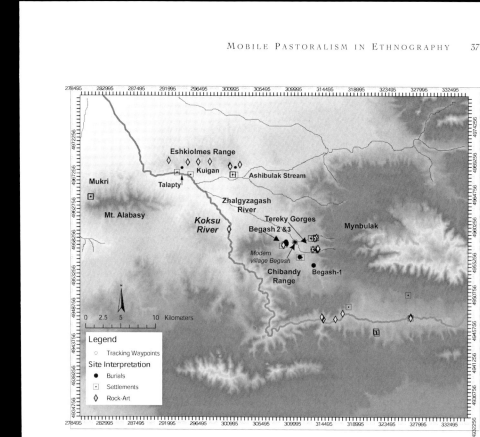

Figure 17.2. Map of the Koksu River Valley, showing the distribution of Bronze Age sites as recorded by the Dzhungar Mountains Archaeology Project.

Bronze Age (2500–1000 BCE calibrated). They also provided archaeobotanical and archaeozoological data, helping to formulate a preliminary picture of the Bronze Age domestic economy in the Koksu Valley. In addition, geological samples were analyzed to establish a local paleoclimatic sequence, which aided in estimating the environmental carrying capacity of pasture resources during the Bronze Age.

The excavations at the associated Bronze Age cemetery provided anthropological data concerning the diet, health, behavior, and rituals of individuals and groups in this region, as well as unique finds of bronze and gold jewelry that, along with ceramics from the settlement excavation, provided a diverse assemblage of artifacts, suggesting an interregional range of interaction for this Bronze Age pastoral population. The most likely economic strategy for societies living in the Koksu Valley during the mid to late second millennium BCE was a vertically transhumant form of mobile pastoralism, predominantly based in herding sheep and cattle between upland pastures in the summer and lowland regions in the winter. This conclusion is based on four lines of evidence (Frachetti 2004b), which will not be discussed in detail here. They include the overwhelming percentage of domestic fauna compared with the limited amount of wild animal remains; the vertical zonality and restrictive nature of the mountain steppe environment in the Koksu Valley, which would promote a strategy of vertical transhumance to support intensive sheep and cattle herding; the provisional 'lack of evidence' from Bronze Age archaeological contexts for alternative subsistence strategies, such as the cultivation of domesticated plants; and ethnohistorical evidence that the traditional economy of the region is characterized by vertically transhumant mobile pastoralism since the 3rd century BCE. Also significant, the archaeological stratigraphy at the settlement of Begash presents evidence for seasonal or stochastic use of winter settlements by mobile pastoralists as opposed to settled herders. At Begash, this interpretation is supported by the iterated infilling shown in the stratigraphy and formation of the site.

Such a general observation about the seasonal pastoral economy is only the starting point for a more detailed understanding of the potential variation in the land-use patterns and social strategies that such a transhumant lifestyle can entail; thus one must examine more closely the variation within archaeological and environmental data to understand the broader impact that such a way of life can have on the cultural geography of the region. In the case of the Dzhungar Mountains, variability in the pastoral strategy of Bronze Age populations was tied to both environmental conditions and sociopolitical choices made on the part of various groups or individuals. These choices and adaptations are reflected in the diversity of archaeological contexts distributed throughout the valley in different environmental contexts.

VARIATION IN THE ENVIRONMENT

It should be noted that the Bronze Age environmental reconstructions are derived from contemporary satellite imagery, adjusted according to data concerning the climatic and environmental changes in the study area. Paleoclimatic studies conducted in the Dzhungar region suggest that the climate and vegetation of the second millennium BCE was broadly comparable with that documented today (Rhodes et al. 1996). This is a topic of debate; paleoclimatologists working in the western steppes and northern Kazakhstan have argued that the climate, not to be confused with the vegetation, of the second millennium BCE was different from today's (Kremenetski 2002). Archaeobotanical research within the scope of the DMAP suggests that the steppe vegetation during the second millennium BCE, at Begash, was comparable to contemporary vegetation (Aubekerov et al. 2003). This conclusion is also supported by archaeobotanical studies in the steppe zone, which argue that in spite of climatic oscillations the general geographic distribution of grassland vegetation in the region has remained unchanged for the past 4000 years (Khotinskiy 1984). Thus, the modern environment may serve as an approximation of the vegetation and environmental geography experienced by pastoralists during the Bronze Age.

Although water sources are abundant throughout the Koksu Valley, soils are poor and generally unproductive for cultivation (Sobolev 1960). More than 80% of the natural vegetation is classified as natural pasture; thus the region has been effectively exploited by mobile pastoralists for millennia. The size and productivity of pastures in the study zone is directly correlated with variations in seasonal climatic conditions and altitude. As a general rule, high-altitude pastures (more than 1400 m above sea level) are three to six times more productive than pastures below 800 m above sea level during the months of June, July and August (Frachetti 2004b). This is because of the aridity in the lowlands during the summer, as well as high summer temperatures in the valley basin. The lowland areas, however, do provide dry fodder in the winter months and are not covered by snow, as are the highland pastures. Therefore, the geography of pasture resources in the study zone can be rectified according to known botanical horizons at different altitudes, and pasture areas can be assigned 'quality' based on their ability to support herd animals during different times of the year. According to range-productivity calculations (Frachetti 2004a), upland pastures are prospective locations for herding during the summer, while lowland areas are more suitable for winter habitation. To summarize the seasonal variations and vertical geography of the valley's resources, as they pertain to the ecodynamics of pastoral populations, we can qualify the environment through a map of seasonal fitness from an economic point of view (Figure 17.3). Naturally, these trends fluctuate both temporally and spatially, meaning that some years are wetter, colder, drier or warmer, and the locations suitable for pasturing or settlement may also change from time to time. Thus, the variation in environmental productivity must be seen as a dynamic factor that contributes to various choices on the part of pastoralists. The impact of periodic environmental variation must also be considered alongside social and ritual concerns; thus, we now turn to some examples of variation in these aspects of the pastoral landscape.

BURIAL AND SETTLEMENT GEOGRAPHY AND FORMS

One of the aims of this chapter is to examine the ways in which societies manipulated and changed the local boundaries of their experienced landscape by recasting economic, ritual, political and social experiences within the temporal and geographic routines of their settlement and migration and through their investments in social contexts such as burials and rock art. As Giddens (1984) argues, structures are never static and, even though the economic, ritual and

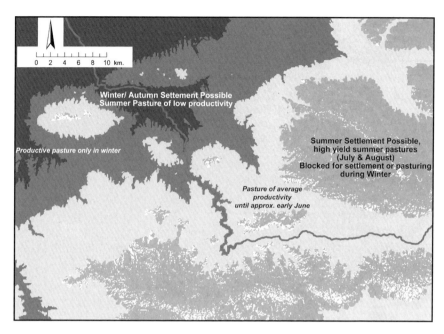

Figure 17.3. Seasonal environmental conditions, related to pastoral activities and settlement, in the Koksu River Valley and surrounding upland meadows.

sociopolitical landscapes of Bronze Age societies do reflect some qualities of regularity, the inherent variation in strategies to negotiate the environmental and social components of the landscape provided scenarios for the boundaries and coherence of that very landscape to constantly be renegotiated. Here I will focus on two archaeological data classes: Bronze Age cemeteries, and settlement typology and geography across the study area.

The burial ground of Begash-2 is located 1.3 km to the northwest of the modern village of Begash on the piedmont terrace of the Chibandy Mountains and roughly 350 m to the northeast of the prehistoric settlement 'Begash.' The cemetery is situated on a flat terrace where a small stream emerges from a steep gorge and consists of 33 stone formations, with multiple burials, and six *kurgan* mounds, likely from later periods (Rosen, this volume; Shishlina, this volume). The Bronze Age burials themselves appear as rectangular, oval or circular stone formations, with 1–5 stone boxlike burial cists with flat capstones inside the stone formation (Figure 17.4). Stone cist burials represent the most common form of burial for the Bronze Age in the region and are common to the other known burial grounds in the Koksu Valley: Talapty, Kuigan and Begash-1 (Goryachev and Mar'yashev 2004). Like Begash-2, Talapty and Kuigan represent a large number of burials constructed at the opening of gorges and are closely associated with substantial settlements and extensive rock art in the

Figure 17.4. Excavated Bronze Age stone cist burial at Begash-2 (Koksu River Valley, eastern Kazakhstan).

nearby cliffs. By contrast, the site of Begash-1 is a cluster of Bronze Age stone cist burials (Karabaspakova 1987). In their construction and material forms the stone arrangements and cist burials at Begash-1 are similar to the other cemeteries in the valley.

Begash-1 significantly reflects a deviation in both its overall scale and geographic context. First, when compared to the other Bronze Age burial groups, Begash-1 is comparatively small. The other burial grounds in the Koksu Valley are large, ranging from 17 burials (more than 35 cists) at Talapty, 35 burials (more than 70 cists) at Begash-2 and at least 40 burials (more than 80 cists) at Kuigan. Begash-1 has roughly 10 stone arrangements, each with two to three cists; thus it is less than half the size of its contemporary cemeteries. A second difference is the geographic context of Begash-1. Unlike the other burials, Begash-1 is located in an open area rather than near a ravine or gorge and, more significant, is not associated with a nearby rock-art site or Bronze Age settlement. From a social perspective it would seem that the group that used Begash-1 as its burial grounds was somehow disarticulated from groups that identified with the larger, more established burials and settlements, such as at Begash-2. One might argue that Begash-1 and Begash-2 are not contemporary and simply represent two distinct periods in the mortuary history of the valley, but from the palimpsest of Iron Age and Bronze Age burials at Begash-2 it is clear that Begash-2 retained its ritual significance for many centuries after the Bronze Age. The burial construction at the two cemeteries is also comparable, which further suggests that they were contemporaneous. Therefore, Begash-1 more likely represents the splintering off, or new arrival, of a social group that decided to establish its own burial ground. The excavations and materials from Begash-1 are not extensively published, so it is difficult to make more detailed statements concerning the root of the variation that may be represented by Begash-1. Regardless of the reasons for the foundation of Begash-1, its disarticulation from other domestic and ritual contexts and its small size represent a geographical and scalar departure from the more common sites of Bronze Age burial grounds in the valley. It may stand as an example of the alternative choices of different groups in the creation of the social and ritual landscape.

In addition to variation in burial contexts there are three different settlement types recovered in the Koksu Valley. Although all seem to have been in use during the Bronze Age, they may reflect various aspects of the economic, social, and political choices of Bronze Age pastoralists. These settlement forms include semi-subterranean houses, small camps and ephemeral settlements. Of the more than 20 Bronze Age settlements recovered in the survey, 50% are classified as semi-subterranean houses, 35% as small camps and 15% as ephemeral settlements. Semisubterranean houses have substantial stone foundations and are multiroom structures. These structures are generally rectangular and the exterior foundation forms a large (as large as 20x20 m) polygon. In addition, individual housing units frequently are arranged in rowlike groups of 5–10 rooms. These house groups are located most often on the flat shoulders and river terraces of small tributary valleys and canyons, such as in the case of the settlement at Begash. The construction of semisubterranean houses includes a stone foundation and wall, typically dug into the earth at a depth ranging from 0.5–1.5 m, with stone coursing mortared with dirt and clay (Figure 17.5). By analogy with similar types of settlements from other steppe contexts, the superstructure was likely made of wood and grass, although there is no evidence for this from excavated settlements in the Koksu Valley. Semisubterranean settlement construction is well known in Semirech'ye from other excavated late Bronze Age settlements such as Talapty (Goryachev and Mar'yashev 1998), as well as from excavated settlements in central Kazakhstan (Margulan et al. 1966). A distinguishing aspect of these substantial settlement contexts is their proximity to large rock-art sites and large Bronze Age cemeteries. Material from excavations at Begash, and shovel tests at a number of these settlements, includes a wide variety of domestic ceramics, burnt and discarded animal bones, grinding stones, stone pestles and metal implements. The detailed excavations at Begash revealed that these structures were likely dug out and re-used on a seasonal basis (Frachetti 2004b).

'Small camps' are similar to semisubterranean houses in some respects, as

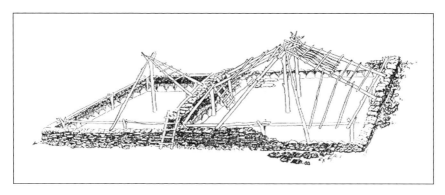

Figure 17.5. Reconstruction of a Bronze Age semisubterranean house in Buguly (central Kazakhstan) comparable to those excavated in Begash (after Margulan et al. 1966).

they often show similar construction techniques, but they are different in terms of size, general shape and geographic location. Small camps are characterized by small stone foundations, most often circular and ranging from 4–5 m in diameter. These smaller structures are found in groups of three to four, often located in small ravines with steep slopes, and are frequently built on small level terrace platforms with little surrounding area. Given their limited spatial extent, these settlements likely serviced smaller groups or were used as short-lived stopping camps for mobile groups. Shallow foundations (often fewer than 0.3 m) and observed thinner cultural strata detected in shovel tests, compared to semisubterranean houses, both support this interpretation. Small camps revealed a mixed assortment of material similar to that of the semisubterranean houses, including handmade ceramics and animal bones. The ceramic material recovered from these settlement types is typical of Bronze Age handmade pottery, which is the primary evidence used to chronologically relate small camps to semisubterranean houses. Although not formally excavated, based on the structural qualities and geography of the small camps, they might be interpreted as satellite habitations or seasonal retreats for smaller groups of the resident populations of the larger settlements. An exemplary group of small camps is located in a steep tributary canyon to the south of the Koksu River. Shovel tests within these structures revealed ceramic fragments clearly associated with known late Bronze Age forms. The settlement area is wedged into a highly inaccessible ravine, although there is a year-round water source. It is likely that this settlement context was not regularly used but rather was either a fail-safe location when more regularly used settlement areas, such as Begash, were undesirable. Alternatively, this instance of small camps might have been occupied by some disarticulated subgroup of the society that was forced, or chose, to make its own settlement outside the more common lowland contexts.

Another example of variation in the settlement geography of the Koksu

Valley is demonstrated by a group of small camps located in the ravines on the western slopes of Mount Alabasy, overlooking the Mukri River. These settlements are located far into the arid lowlands and are nestled into a small ravine that cuts into the terrace plain. The small camp within this settlement group consists of fewer than 10 structures. Unlike the other small camps discussed above, a small group of stone-arrangement burials were constructed near this location, but no rock art was detected. This may suggest that the population that used the area was beginning to invest in it as a more regularly visited location, although a major settlement of the semisubterranean type was not warranted or affordable. Small groups may have used this location in years when settlement zones were inundated by unusually deep snow or when other conditions caused them to extend their domestic and ritual world farther into the lowlands. These small camps are significant in that they reflect the maximum extents to the geographic patterns that characterized the Bronze Age settlement and suggest that either social or environmental factors, or both, could lead groups to introduce variation into the creation of their environment.

Ephemeral settlements are the most difficult to interpret. They do not exhibit any permanent foundations and are known only by the chemical residue they reflect through vegetation. Ephemeral features are typically oval or circular, about 3–5 m in diameter, and are located on the grassy shoulders and open terraces of midland and upland elevations. Often, a nearby rectilinear auxiliary 'footprint,' most likely representing an animal corral, accompanies the oval marking (Figure 17.6). The organization of seasonal summer settlements, in the form of yurt camps, is known from my own ethnographic documentation in the valley (Figure 17.7), as well as from broader ethnographic studies of pastoral settlements (Andrews 1999). At this time, however, we cannot comment scientifically about the chronological antiquity of this settlement type in the Koksu Valley. We can at best suggest that these settlement locations share the consistency over time that is more concretely exhibited in the other types of Bronze Age settlement locales. The distribution of ephemeral settlements illustrates that upland areas have been settled in the past, minimally on a seasonal or transient basis, and that the kinds of structures in this ecological niche likely consisted of nonpermanent foundations.

Different settlement types illustrate a varied pattern of settlement choices in light of practical factors, which suggests that the ecology played a role in the selection and revisitation of particular locales. Groups of semisubterranean houses are located in wide ravines or on nearby wide, flat terraces; small camps are tucked into steep gorges and occupy small tributary terraces; and ephemeral settlements are located in upland zones on flat plains or nearby grassy pastures. In addition, the geographic location and scale of these settlements influenced the way the landscape was experienced in space and time, as larger or smaller

Figure 17.6. Remains of an ephemeral settlement in the Koksu River Valley, evident only by differences in the vegetation.

Figure 17.7. Contemporary Kazakh settlement in the Koksu River Valley, showing the summer yurt and the corral.

groups would come together to various extents at each location.

Semisubterranean houses reflect the largest and most elaborate settlements and are located both in environmentally attractive niches and in socially elaborated spaces, in the proximity of rock art and burials. Small camps, on the other hand, reflect smaller-scale settlements located in areas that cannot support large groups for extended periods of time without frequent relocation. Finally, ephemeral settlements, taken as proxies for the kind of summer highland settlements that may have been constructed by Bronze Age pastoralists, are the most transient or unfixed settlements in the landscape, likely reflecting yearly, or monthly, choices for short-term settlement during summer migrations to higher elevations. Accordingly, the dynamics of social interaction may have been ordered in relation to the social or political identities of Bronze Age groups as derived from the status and scale of domestic spaces. The variation in settlement evidence illustrates that Bronze Age groups employed a number of different habitation types, some of which were geographically permanent, some short-lived, and some of which accommodated frequent movements under changing environmental conditions. These various settlement contexts also suggest dynamic social and political conditions among the valley's populations, though more detailed investigations are necessary to illuminate those factors more clearly. Given the geographic distribution of archaeological sites, however, such as burials and settlements, and the location of pasture resources and ecumenical environmental niches described above, we can now more accurately reconstruct the patterns and extent of mobility of Bronze Age pastoralists. This is a first step toward a better understanding of Bronze Age sociopolitical and economic interactions.

MODELING THE LANDSCAPE DYNAMICS

To model the dynamic engagement of Bronze Age pastoralists, with their constructed and natural landscapes in the Koksu Valley, we must draw from those data sources that we know are relevant to pastoral choices, keeping in mind the likelihood that other, less recoverable, factors also affected the range of archaeological variation presented above. Mobility, for example, is a primary correlate to the archaeological variation of pastoral contexts in the Koksu Valley. The data used to model pastoral mobility patterns include the locales that we can safely assume were visited and exploited by groups and individuals, and where we can link the location and distribution of settlements to other archaeologically recorded social venues (burials, rock-art sanctuaries, etc.) according to the seasonally variable productivity and geographic distribution of natural pastures. On the basis of archaeozoological data, we know that the primary herd animals for Bronze Age groups in the Koksu Valley were sheep and cattle. It is fair to suggest that Bronze Age groups recognized the value in exploiting highland pastures in the summer and the environmental protection of lowland areas in the winter. The archaeology from our survey supports this assumption. Pastoral mobility was at least one practice contributing to the variation in the activation and deactivation of particular loci in the landscape by the Bronze Age population.

Patterns of land use and mobility can be modeled using a geographic information system. This allows for different properties to be emphasized, or diminished, to study their role in mobility patterns while being realistically constrained to the actual data. In this way modeling the dynamics of the Bronze Age pastoral landscape is not left to hypothetical or arbitrary simulation. Patterns of mobility and land use, the examples explored here, can be rooted in the relevant variables that are recovered archaeologically or geographically. The simulated aspect of the model lies in the way 'value' is assigned to various factors, while significant correlation is achieved when independent variables are shown to be mutually significant. In the case of the Koksu Valley, modeling the economic considerations of Bronze Age pastoralists entails understanding the productive capacity of the region's pastures and their geographic proximity to social and domestic contexts. The technical methods used to calculate these figures are discussed elsewhere (Frachetti 2004b; Frachetti 2006).

The capacity of the region's pastures in the height of the growing season is high, such that the pastures located on average 20 km from midland settlements could easily support flocks of more than 20,000 sheep over a given growing season. Thus, the economic pressures on pastoral migration orbits would not demand extensive mobility. In fact, if we return to the site of Begash, there are extremely productive highland pastures within 15 km that could easily provide ample fodder for large herds or flocks (Figure 17.8). Sites located farther into the lowlands may not have been selected for their proximity to summer pasture, however, but for their proximity to ritual sites. The settlement at Talapty is located in an area more than 30 km from rich upland pastures, but the winter settlement area is adjacent to an extensive stone ridgeline in the Eshkiolmes foothills, which contain more than 10,000 rock-art images commonly attributed to the Bronze Age, as well as large cemeteries. It would seem that sometimes the choice to travel farther, and to ignore the economic cost, was justified in terms of the social, ritual or political capital attributed to various territories throughout the broader landscape (Figure 17.9). The construction of a socialized and ritual landscape, demarcated by such features as rock-art sanctuaries, cemeteries, and other socialized spaces, played a role equally significant to that of the environment in affecting the dynamic exploitation of the Koksu River Valley by Bronze Age populations. As noted above, nearly every large settlement in the region of Begash is associated with a group

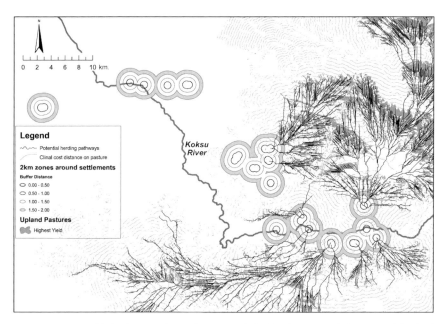

Figure 17.8. Variable land-use pathways between rich highland pasture (dark gray) and lowland settlements, shown as points with 2-km 'activity zones' around them. Routes are calculated based on the quality and productivity of the vegetation. Distance is iterated according to the size and nutritional demand of the herd, ranging between 1000 and 40,0000 animal units to be supported annually. Annual travel, adequate to support even the largest herds, rarely exceeds 35 km.

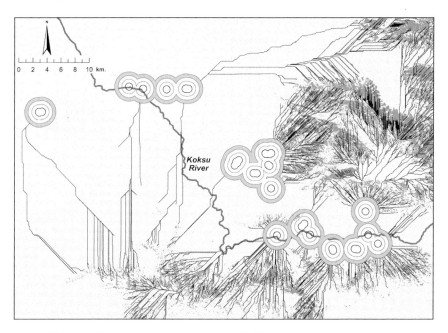

Figure 17.9. Variable land-use pathways between rich highland pasture (dark gray) and lowland settlements, shown as points with 2-km 'activity zones' around them. Routes are calculated to account for pasture quality, terrain (slope) and the location of significant social locales (burials, rock art, etc.). Routes can be more than 50 km to satisfy both herd needs and socioritual practices.

of rock art and a nearby cemetery. The spatial relationship between rock-art, burials, and settlements, coupled with the seasonal economic patterns proposed above, allows for some initial interpretations concerning the land-use schedule and sociopolitical interactions that resulted from group investment in specific locations in the landscape.

The location of settlements provides information concerning the seasonal use of the landscape, which can be tied to social and political strategies. The Bronze Age settlements at Talapty and Kuigan are located in dry lowland areas and likely represent winter or fall settlements, considering the lack of productive pasture in the area during the summer and the favorable winter conditions of the terrace on the south side of the Eshkiolmes range. Begash is located at a slightly higher elevation (around 950 m above sea level) and, given its situation in a protected canyon, probably represents a winter settlement. According to the seasonal economic reconstruction above, these settlements could have been inhabited for 3–7 months, during the late fall, winter and early spring, and would likely have been unoccupied for about 3–6 months during the late spring and summer, while groups migrated to highland pastures. The existence of the complex of burials and rock art near these winter settlements may indicate that investments in the landscape, in part, served to communicate ownership or control over domestic locations while the population was away at highland pastures in the summer. There is little rock art in the upland areas, even though usable rock faces exist there as well. Since the upland pastures are treacherously cold and uninhabited during the winter, it is unlikely that there would be significant human traffic there except during the summer. Logically, there would be no need to protect or mark settlement areas in the highlands. As the nature of the summer pasture resources is much more variable from year to year than winter conditions, marking areas of settlement might actually serve to limit the possibilities of claiming prime locations from year to year. Most likely, the boundaries of summer pastures and settlement zones were negotiated at the time of migration, when pastoralists naturally came together while providing for their herds at the limited territories of highland pastures. Although it may have been unnecessary to mark summer settlement areas, lowland winter settlement areas were accessible to any group passing through the area, so more overt displays of control, power and status, such as symbolic invocations of shamanism, folklore and ancestry (Mar'yashev and Goryachev 2002; Frachetti 2004b), were encoded into the landscape near choice settlements. By socializing these areas with ritual and ideological signs, specific groups could signify their definition of territorial boundaries and could communicate their engagement in specific locations, even though their overall patterns of movement led to periods when these sites were not physically occupied.

DISCUSSION

I have argued that the archaeology of mobile pastoralism is best approached as a patterned yet variable socio-economic strategy. The recovery of this strategy, or strategies, can be facilitated by conceiving of the wider geographic and temporal layouts of pastoral experience and practices within dynamic landscapes, as opposed to categorically rigid paradigms of economic or political systems. The select archaeological examples from the Bronze Age of the Koksu River Valley illustrate that pastoralists of this region were constantly renegotiating the character of their social and economic geography according to the variability of their environmental and social contexts. Ultimately, archaeologists may better understand the wider impact of nomadic pastoral groups in prehistory by documenting the variation within pastoral systems over time rather than by viewing such societies within strict social, economic or political frameworks.

REFERENCES

Andrews, P. A.

1999   *Felt Tents and Pavilions: The Nomadic Tradition and Its Interaction with Princely Tentage*. London, Kölner Ethnologische Mitteilungen Melisende.

Anschuetz, K. F., R. H. Williams and C. L. Scheick

2001   An Archaeology of Landscapes: Perspectives and Directions. *Journal of Archaeological Research 9*: 2, pp. 157–211.

Ashmore, W. and A. B. Knapp

1999   *Archaeologies of Landscape*. Malden, Blackwell.

Aubekerov, B. Z., S. A. Nigmatova and M. D. Frachetti

2003   Geomorphological Particulars in the Region of the Archaeological Monument Begash, Northern Dzhungar Alatau [in Russian]. In *Aktual'nye Problemy Geostistem Aridnikh Territorii*. Almaty, Kazakh National University: pp. 287–289.

Bacon, E.

1954   Types of Pastoral Nomadism in Central and Southwest Asia. *Southwestern Journal of Anthropology 10*: pp. 44–68.

Barfield, T. J.

1981   *The Central Asian Arabs of Afghanistan: Pastoral Nomadism in Transition*. Austin, University of Texas Press.

1993   *The Nomadic Alternative*. Englewood Cliffs, New Jersey, Prentice Hall.

Barth, F.

1964   *Nomads of South Persia*. New York, Humanities Press.

1969   *Ethnic Groups and Boundaries*. Boston, Little, Brown.

Bartol'd, V. V.

1943   *Ocherk Istorii Semirech'ia* [in Russian]. Frunze, Kirgizgosizdat.

Bar-Yosef, O. and A. M. Khazanov

1992   *Pastoralism in the Levant: Archaeological Materials in Anthropological Perspectives.* Madison, Prehistory Press.

Beck, L.

1991   *Nomad: A Year in the Life of a Qashga'i Tribesman in Iran.* Berkeley, University of California Press.

Bradburd, D.

1990   *Ambiguous Relations: Kin, Class, and Conflict Among Komachi Pastoralists.* Washington, Smithsonian Institution Press.

Chernykh, E. N.

1997   *Kargaly: Zabytyi Mir* [in Russian]. Moskva, Institut Arkheologii (Rossiiskaia akademiia nauk).

Cribb, R.

1991   *Nomads in Archaeology.* Cambridge, Cambridge University Press.

Danti, M. D.

2000   *Early Bronze Age Settlement and Land Use in the Tell Es-sweyhat Region, Syria.* University of Pennsylvania (PhD dissertation).

Dyson-Hudson, R. and N. Dyson-Hudson

1980   Nomadic Pastoralism. *Annual Review of Anthropology 9*: pp. 15–61.

Erickson, C.

2000   The Lake Titicaca Basin: A Precolumbian Built Landscape. In D. Lentz (ed.), *Imperfect Balance: Landscape Transformations in the Precolumbian Andes.* New York, Columbia University Press: pp. 311–356.

Frachetti, M. D.

2004a   Archaeological Explorations of Bronze Age Pastoral Societies in the Mountains of Eastern Eurasia. *Silk Road 2*: 1, pp. 3–8.

2004b   *Bronze Age Pastoral Landscapes of Eurasia and the Nature of Social Interaction in the Mountain Steppe Zone of Eastern Kazakhstan.* University of Pennsylvania (PhD dissertation).

2006   Digital Archaeology and the Scalar Structure of Pastoral Landscapes: Modeling Mobile Societies of Prehistoric Central Asia. In T. Evans and P. Daly (eds.), *Digital Archaeology.* London, Routledge: pp. 128–147.

Giddens, A.

1984   *The Constitution of Society: Outline of the Theory of Structuration.* Berkeley, University of California Press.

Goryachev, A. A. and A. N. Mar'yashev

1998   Nouveaux Sites du Bronze Recent au Semirech'e (Kazakhstan). *Paléorient 24*: 1, pp. 71–80.

2004   The Bronze Age Archaeological Memorials in Semirechie. In K. M. Linduff (ed.), *Metallurgy in Ancient Eastern Eurasia from the Urals to the Yellow River*. Lewiston, Edwin Mellen Press: pp. 109–138.

Humphrey, C. and D. Sneath

1999   *The End of Nomadism? Society, State, and the Environment in Inner Asia*. Durham, Duke University Press.

Ingold, T.

1993   The Temporality of the Landscape. *World Archaeology 25*: pp.152–174.

Irons, W.

1974   Nomadism as a Political Adaptation: The Case of the Yomut Turkmen. *American Ethnologist 1*: pp. 635–658.

Jones-Bley, K. and D. G. Zdanovich (eds.)

2002   *Complex Societies of Central Eurasia from the 3rd to the 1st Millennium BC: Regional Specifics in Light of Global Models. Journal of Indo-European Studies. Monograph 46*. Washington, Institute for the Study of Man.

Karabaspakova, K. M.

1987   K Voprosu o Kul'turnoi Prinalezhnosti Pamyanikov Epkhi Pozdnei Bronzy Severo-Vostochnogo Semirech'ya i ikh Svyaz' s Pamyatnikami Tsentral'nogo Kazakhstana [in Russian]. In K. G. Omarova (ed.), *Voprosy Periodizatsii Arkheologicheskikh Pamyatnikov Tsentral'nogog i Severnogog Kazakhstana*. Karaganda, Karaganda University Press: pp. 90–101.

Kavoori, P. S.

1999   *Pastoralism in Expansion: The Transhuming Herders of Western Rajasthan. Studies in Social Ecology and Environmental History*. New Delhi, Oxford University Press.

Khazanov, A. M.

1984   *Nomads and the Outside World*. Cambridge, Cambridge University Press.

Khlobystina, M. D.

1973   Origins et Developpment de la Civilization de Premiere Age du Bronze dans la Siberie de Sud' [in Russian]. *Sovetskaya Arkheologiya 1*: pp. 24–38.

Khotinskiy, N. A.

1984   Holocene Vegetation History. In A. A. Velichko, H. E. Wright and C. W. Barnosky (eds.), *Late Quaternary Environments of the Soviet Union*. Minneapolis, University of Minnesota Press: pp. 179–200.

Kislenko, A. and N. Tatarintseva

1999   The Eastern Ural Steppe at the End of the Stone Age. In M. Levine, Y. Rassamakin, A. Kislenko and T. N. Kislenko (eds.), *Late Prehistoric Exploitation of the Eurasian Steppe*. Cambridge, McDonald Institute for Archaeological Research: pp. 183–216.

Knapp, A. B. and W. Ashmore

1999   Archaeological Landscapes: Constructed, Conceptualized, and Ideational. In W. Ashmore and A. B. Knapp (eds.), *Archaeologies of Landscape: Contemporary Perspectives*. Oxford, Blackwell: pp. 1–30.

Kohler-Rollefson, I.

1992   A Model for the Development of Nomadic Pastoralism on the Transjordanian Plateau. In O. Bar-Yosef and A. Khazanov (eds.), *Pastoralism in the Levant: Archaeological Materials in Anthropological Perspectives*. Madison, Prehistory Press: pp. 11–18.

Kosarev, M. F.

1984   *Zapadnaia Sibir' v Drevnosti* [in Russian]. Moskva, Nauka.

Koster, H. A.

1977   *The Ecology of Pastoralism in Relation to Changing Patterns of Land Use in the Northeast Peloponnese*. University of Pennsylvania (PhD dissertation).

Kremenetski, C. V.

2002   Steppe and Forest-Steppe Belt of Eurasia: Holocene Environmental History. In M. Levine, C. Renfrew and K. Boyle (eds.), *Prehistoric Steppe Adaptation and the Horse*. Cambridge, McDonald Institute for Archaeological Research: pp. 11–28.

Lamberg-Karlovsky, C. C.

2003   Civilization, State, or Tribe? Bactria and Margiana in the Bronze Age. *Review of Archaeology 24*: 1, pp. 11–19.

Lattimore, O.

1940   *Inner Asian Frontiers of China*. Boston, Beacon Press.

Mar'yashev, A. N. and M. Frachetti

forthcoming   The Bronze Age Burials of Begash [in Russian]. *Vestnik, Journal of the Institute of Archaeology, Almaty, Kazakhstan*.

Mar'yashev, A. N. and A. A. Goryachev

1993   Typological and Chronological Questions of Bronze Age Sites of Semirechye. *Rossiyaskaya Arkheologiya 1*: pp. 5–20.

2002   *Rock-Art of Semirech'ya. Volume 2: Updated and Completed* [in Russian]. Almaty, Fond XXI c. Press.

Margulan, A. X., K. A. Akishev, M. K. Kadirbaev and A. M. Orazbaev

1966   *Ancient Cultures of Central Kazakhstan* [in Russian]. Almaty, Nauka Kazakhskoi SSSR.

McGlade, J.

1995   Archaeology and the Ecodynamics of Human Modified Landscapes. *Antiquity 69*: pp. 113–132.

Pastner, S.

1971   Ideological Aspects of Nomad-Sedentary Contact: A Case Study from Southern Baluchistan. *Anthropological Quarterly 44*: 3, pp. 173–184.

Rhodes, T. E., F. Gasse, L. Ruifen, J.-C. Fontes, W. Keqin, P. Bertrand, E. Gilbert, F. Melieres, P. Tucholka, W. Zhixiang and C. Zhi-Yuan

1996   A Late Pleistocene-Holocene Lacustrine Record from Lake Manas, Zunggar (Northern Xinjiang, Western China). *Palaeogeography, Palaeoclimatology, Palaeoecology 120*: pp. 105–121.

Rosen, S. A.

2003   Early Multi-resource Nomadism: Excavations at the Camel Site in the Central Negev. *Antiquity 77*: 298, pp. 749–760.

Salzman, P. C.

1972   Multi-resource Nomadism in Iranian Baluchistan. In W. Irons and N. Dyson-Hudson (eds.), *Perspectives on Nomadism*. Leiden, E. J. Brill: pp. 60–68.

2002   Pastoral Nomads: Some General Observations Based on Research in Iran. *Journal of Anthropological Research 58*: 2, pp. 245–264.

Shahrani, M. N. M.

1979   *The Kirghiz and Wakhi of Afghanistan: Adaptation to Closed Frontiers*. Seattle, University of Washington Press.

Shilov, V. P.

1975   Models of Pastoral Economies in the Steppe Regions of Eurasia in the Eneolithic and Early Bronze Ages [in Russian]. *Sovetskaya Arkeologiya 1*: pp. 5–16.

Sobolev, L. N.

1960   Fodder Resources of Kazakhstan [in Russian]. Moskva, Akademiya Nauk.

Spooner, B.

1973   *The Cultural Ecology of Pastoral Nomads. An Addison-Wesley Module in Anthropology Number 45*. Reading, Addison-Wesley.

Stoddart, S.

2000   *Landscapes from Antiquity*. Cambridge, Antiquity Publications.

Tapper, R.

1979   *Pasture and Politics: Economics, Conflict, and Ritual Among Shahsevan Nomads of Northwest Iran*. New York, Academic Press.

Tsalkin, V. I.

1964   Nekotorye Itogi Izucheniia Kostnykh Ostatkov Zhivotnykh iz Rskopok Arkheologicheskikh Pamiatnikov Pozdnego Bronzovogo Veka [in Russian]. *Kratkie Soobshcheniia Instituta Arkheologii 101*: pp. 24–34.

Vadetskaya, E. B.

1986   *Arkeologicheskie Pamyatniki v Stepyakh Srednevo Yeniseya* [in Russian]. Leningrad, Akademiya Nauk CCCP.

CHAPTER 18

MOBILITY AND SEDENTARIZATION IN LATE BRONZE AGE SYRIA

JEFFREY J. SZUCHMAN

ARCHAEOLOGISTS WHO WORK in Mesopotamia are well aware of the challenges in the archaeology of pastoral nomadism in that region. Wilkinson (2003:50) has pointed to the disappointing record of pastoral nomadic archaeology in the Near East: "Despite the large number of enthusiastic references to the importance of the nomadic element, they continue to be underrecognized in the survey record." One nomadic group that has received special attention despite its absence from the archaeological record is the Aramaean tribes of late second millennium BCE Syro-Anatolia. These tribes were traditionally depicted as the ambassadors of doom for the settled populations of Syro-Anatolia at the end of the second millennium BCE. Roux (1969/1992:275), for example, described the "barbaric Aramaeans" as "originally uncouth bedouins," who "contributed nothing to the civilizations of the Near East." A few years later, Hawkins (1982:375) explained the development of Aramaean kingdoms as the result of "a new and intrusive population group" whose "penetration of Syria . . . must have exerted pressure on the already settled Anatolian peoples." More recently, analyses of textual references to Aramaeans and archaeological surveys in northern Syria have resulted in a reconceptualization of the Aramaean presence in Syro-Anatolia (Schwartz 1989; McClellan 1992; Sader 1992, 2000; Lipinski 2000; Akkermans and Schwartz 2003:367). This new image of the Aramaeans differs from the old view in two important ways.

First, Aramaeans are now understood not as intrusive elements but rather as a local Syrian pastoral people who had been active in the Syrian social and economic sphere for some time before they turned to sedentism. Second, the sedentarization of Aramaeans is no longer assumed to be the result of an organized military campaign against the urban population of Syria and Turkey; rather, Aramaeans became sedentary agriculturists during the Dark Age that followed the demise of the Hittite and Assyrian kingdoms in the final centuries of the second millennium BCE. In doing so, Aramaean tribes filled and exploited a power vacuum that already existed in Syro-Anatolia.

The main evidence for the reconceptualization of Aramaean sedentarization comes from the clear continuity of material culture in areas of Aramaean occupation and the sharp increase in Iron Age settlements in these same areas during the transition from the Late Bronze to Early Iron Age (McClellan 1992; Sader 1992, 2000). The cultural continuity certainly suggests that Aramaeans had been part of the Syrian social landscape for some time before they became sedentary and thus are unlikely to have infiltrated suddenly into northern Syria from the desert (Figure 18.1). However, the notion that Aramaean pastoral tribes sedentarized in Syria during a period of administrative chaos and in the absence of any alternative centralized regime in Syro-Anatolia is less compelling.

Ethnographies of pastoral nomads in the modern period suggest that sedentarization primarily occurs during periods of peace and under relatively stable political conditions rather than in periods of political upheaval (Barth 1961; Cribb 1991:61–64). A famous example of the mechanics of sedentarization shows that an increase in agricultural production will force farmers to expand their cultivated fields into pastoral lands. The pressure now exerted

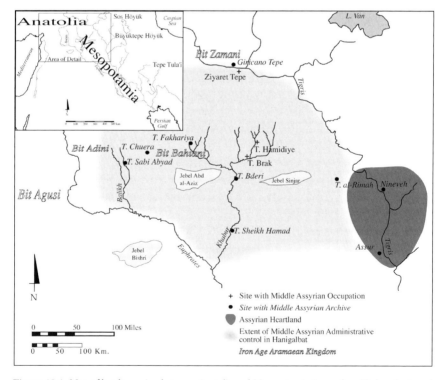

Figure 18.1. Map of border region between Anatolia and Mesopotamia (in modern Turkey, Syria and Iraq), showing the place names mentioned in the text.

on pastoral nomads encourages sedentarization as an alternative to what has become a risky pastoralist venture (Khazanov 1994:212–221). Such a scenario is generally made possible only by a strong central administration that fosters agricultural expansion at the expense of pastoralism. Based on the ethnographic record, Aramaean sedentarization probably began either before or after the upheavals of the late second millennium BCE, when the political conditions of Syro-Anatolia were less volatile. Aramaeans appear to have already established strong sedentary political dynasties in Syria and Anatolia by the time that the Dark Age came to an end at the turn of the first millennium BCE, in the early years of the Neo-Assyrian period (Bunnens 1999). Thus, if Aramaean sedentarization did occur against a backdrop of political stability, it must have begun before the 'Crisis Years' (Ward and Joukowsky 1989) at the close of the Late Bronze Age. It was during this period that the Middle Assyrian kings restored stability to Syro-Anatolia after the fall of the Mitanni kingdom in the 14th century BCE.

WERE ARAMAEANS NOMADIC?

The problem with discussions of Aramaean sedentarization in general lies in the available evidence for Aramaean nomadism. The sources for early Aramaean nomadism are primarily textual and unfortunately scarce. They begin with the description in the annals of King Tiglath-Pileser I of his campaign against the Aramaeans in 1111 BCE:

> With the support of the god Aššur, my lord, I took my chariots and warriors (and) set off for the desert. I marched against the Ahlamu-Aramaeans, enemies of the god Aššur, my lord. I plundered from the edge of the land Suhu to the city Carchemish of the land Hatti in a single day. I massacred them (and) carried back their booty, possessions, and goods without number. The rest of their troops, who had fled from the weapons of the god Aššur, my lord, crossed the Euphrates. I crossed the Euphrates after them on rafts (made of inflated) goat-skin. I conquered six of their cities at the foot of Mount Bišri, burnt, razed, and destroyed [them, and] brought their booty, possessions, and goods to my city Aššur (Grayson 1991:23).

From this and similar statements in the annals of Tiglath-Pileser I, scholars have assumed that, as late as the 11th century BCE, Aramaeans were primarily mobile. Jebel Bišri lies outside the agricultural centers along the Syrian Euphrates, and Tiglath-Pileser I does locate the target of his campaigns in the 'desert.' But the term he uses, *mudbaru* (in line A.0.87.1 45), is also used in Neo-Assyrian texts to refer to the steppe in contrast to the cultivated country. Whether it refers specifically to the desert or to the steppe, the term clearly implies that Aramaeans occupied an environmental zone outside the limits of sedentary irrigation agriculture. The use of the term itself does not, however, rule out the possibility that Aramaeans practiced small-scale cultivation in addition to pastoral activities.

More interesting in regard to the nomadic background of the Aramaeans is their association with the Ahlamu of North Syria. Throughout the inscriptions of Tiglath-Pileser I in the 12th century BCE, the term *Aramaean* is preceded by the term *Ahlamu*. This designation appears sporadically in texts from the second millennium BCE, and it seems to refer to a mobile population in Syria that may have had possession of some lands (Sader 2000; Schachner 2003). As early as the 14th century BCE, King Adad-Nirari I claimed that his father, King Arik-Den-Ili (1319–1308 BCE), had conquered the lands of the Ahlamu (Grayson 1987:132). In the 13th century BCE, during a campaign against a coalition of Mitanni, Hittites and Ahlamu, King Shalmaneser I "became ruler over their lands" and "set fire to the remainder of their cities" (Grayson 1987:184). Ahlamu also appear in second millennium BCE Babylonian sources, which suggests that they had far-reaching contacts with urban kingdoms throughout Mesopotamia (Brinkman 1968:278; Heimpel 2003:28). By the end of the second millennium the term *Ahlamu* probably referred to one or several mobile tribes that may have been attached to a particular territory. Although there is little evidence to suggest that the Ahlamu were the forerunners of the Aramaeans or that a genetic link between the two groups existed (Brinkman 1968:277–278), the association of Aramaeans with Ahlamu by Tiglath-Pileser I may suggest that, if the two groups were not one and the same, the Aramaeans were probably organized either politically, socially or territorially in the same way as the second millennium BCE Ahlamu, so that the two were indistinguishable to the Assyrian rulers.

The association of Aramaeans with Ahlamu and the reference to the *mudbaru* in the Assyrian texts suggests on the one hand that Aramaean tribes were highly mobile. On the other hand, Tiglath-Pileser I boasts of conquering and plundering Aramaean cities and of taking their valuable possessions as booty to his capital Aššur. In these passages he seems to describe a sedentary population, or at least a semisedentary group with assets rich enough to take back to the capital, rather than a primarily mobile people. Furthermore, the language he uses is standard in texts that describe the conquest of cities within an established kingdom. For example, in his account of the conquest of the lands of Katmuhhu and Nairi, to the northwest of Assyria, Tiglath-Pileser I says, "I brought out their booty, property [and possessions]. Their cities, I burnt, razed, [and] destroyed" (Grayson 1991:14). In a later text, Tiglath-Pileser I emphasizes that he crossed the Euphrates 28 times in pursuit of the Aramaeans, which also might suggest a high degree of mobility (Sader 1992,

2000). But it may also reflect the difficulty that Tiglath-Pileser I encountered when he tried to extend his control to such a distance from the Assyrian heartland, where the city of Carchemish constrained Assyrian expansion. That the Aramaeans exhibited such tenacity also indicates their fundamental attachment to their territory, an attachment that may have led to, or been generated by, the establishment of permanent settlements.

The first attestation of Aramaeans in the Assyrian annals, which has traditionally been interpreted as evidence of Aramaean mobility in the 11th century BCE, suggests, in fact, just the opposite: that Aramaean sedentarization had been underway for quite some time before the reign of Tiglath-Pileser I. It may be best, therefore, to think of Late Bronze Age Aramaeans as tribal societies with mobile components rather than as nomads, a term that is too imprecise in this context. This terminology implies that Aramaean tribes also had sedentary components, although the extent and nature of sedentary Aramaean communities in the Late Bronze Age have not yet been addressed. Indeed Middle Assyrian kings had introduced favorable conditions for sedentarization into Syria for over a century before Tiglath-Pileser I ascended the throne.

ARAMAEANS AND ASSYRIANS IN THE LATE BRONZE AGE

Assyria's interest in northern Syria and southeastern Turkey, the land they called Hanigalbat, began when King Ashur-Uballit I (1365–1330 BCE) threw off the yoke of the Mitanni kingdom around 1350 BCE. The newly independent Assyrian king now called himself 'Great King,' although the territory of Assyria remained confined to its traditional heartland and barely extended to the west of the Tigris (Harrak 1987:57). Assyrian occupation of Syria may have begun in the reign of King Adad-Nirari I (1307–1275 BCE). In his first campaigns against Hanigalbat, at the beginning of the 13th century BCE, Adad-Nirari I made the weak Mitanni king an Assyrian vassal. Later, following a failed Mitanni revolt, Adad-Nirari I marched to Waššukanni, the Mitanni capital, and deported the royal family to Ashur. A new Assyrian capital was built at Taidu,[1] securing his control over north Syria and southeastern Turkey from the Tigris to the Euphrates, including the entire Khabur basin.

After the death of Adad-Nirari I, his son Shalmaneser I (1274–1245 BCE) faced another revolt in Hanigalbat that was promptly put down. Following the campaigns of Shalmaneser I, clear evidence of Assyrian settlement in

[1.] Taidu was most likely at, or in the vicinity of, Tell Hamidiye on the Jaghjagh River (Meijer 1986; Harrak 1987), or at Üçtepe, along the Tigris River in Turkey (Kessler 1980).

Hanigalbat appears. At Tell Brak (Oates et al. 1997:13–15), for example, the Mitanni Palace was probably destroyed first by Adad-Nirari and later by Shalmaneser I. Shortly after the second palace destruction, Middle Assyrian occupation began. The earliest texts from Tell Sheikh Hamad date to the time of Shalmaneser I, which suggests that Assyrian occupation of that site also began during his reign (Kühne 2000). In fact, Tell al-Rimah, on the border of the Assyrian heartland, is the only site in Hanigalbat with evidence of Middle Assyrian occupation predating Shalmaneser I (Postgate et al. 1997:56).

Part of what made Assyrian occupation of this territory possible was the administrative structure that Shalmaneser I and his successor, Tukulti-Ninurta I (1244–1208 BCE), instituted. Shalmaneser I removed the king of Hanigalbat to Assyria, along with a large number of other Hanigalbateans. At the same time, people from the north, Assyrians, and others from within Hanigalbat were settled in the now vacant cities of Syro-Anatolia (Machinist 1982:18–19). The entire territory was subdivided into *pahutu* (provinces), each administered by an Assyrian *bel pahete* (official) who reported directly to the Assyrian *sukallu rabu* or *šar Hanigalbat* (king of Hanigalbat), who himself answered to the king of Assyria. Under this system the Assyrian king had direct control over all of the territories west of the Tigris, and Shalmaneser I was able to extend his kingdom as far west as the Balikh River. This system of authority probably remained in place throughout the Middle Assyrian period and probably as late as the 10th century BCE. It is a testament to the success of this system that the Neo-Assyrian kings of the first millennium BCE ruled the entire Near East via an administrative system that was essentially the same as that implemented by Shalmaneser I in the 13th century BCE (Machinist 1982:34).

The administration of the Assyrian provinces and the redistribution of the Syrian population would have had a profound effect on the pastoral nomads of Syro-Anatolia. Since the decline of the Mitanni kingdom in the 14th century BCE, pastoral nomadic groups had not been subject to a strong central administration. The drastic administrative and demographic restructuring of Hanigalbat under the Middle Assyrian kings would have stripped mobile peoples of their relative autonomy and fundamentally impacted their way of life. New urban centers may have altered pastoralist migration routes so that they could benefit from the wealth of the urban elite; a strong military presence would have reduced the ability of nomadic groups to raid villages and towns; conscription may have limited their mobility; taxation and political stability may have expanded agricultural lands into what was previously Aramaean pasture. Irrigation agriculture and a new extensive canal irrigation system (Kühne 1990) would certainly have expanded cultivable areas into lands previously exploited exclusively by pastoral nomads. Any one or combination of these factors might have encouraged the mobile peoples to settle, so that by the time Tiglath-Pileser I encountered them, the sedentarization of the Ahlamu-Aramaeans would have been well under way.

MODELS OF SEDENTARIZATION

That the Ahlamu-Aramaeans became sedentary is not in itself surprising. Since Barth's (1961) groundbreaking work on the Basseri tribe of southwest Iran, ethnographies of Near Eastern pastoral nomads have continued to demonstrate not only the close relationship between nomadic and sedentary society but also the diverse nature of nomadism as a subsistence economy (Salzman 1972; Bates 1973; Marx 1977). In most cases Near Eastern pastoral nomads were neither purely nomadic nor solely reliant on herding sheep and goats as their main economic activity. Salzman (1972) labeled nomads with diverse economic bases 'multi-resource nomads.' Among the Yarahmadzai tribe in Baluchistan, for example, nomads supplement pastoral activities with date palm cultivation, hunting and gathering, and small-scale grain cultivation, as well as raiding (Salzman 1972; 1980a, 1980b). In southwest Iran some Basseri work as hired laborers in village fields (Barth 1961), and a number of Qashqa'i tribe members practice agriculture in addition to pastoralism (Beck 1986, 1991). The diverse nature of their economies enables these multiresource nomads to settle with little effort when pastoralism ceases to be a viable subsistence strategy.

The diversity of nomadic economies and lifestyles corresponds to a similar diversity in the mechanics of sedentarization. Salzman (1980a, 1980b) stresses the voluntary and temporary nature of sedentarization. Nomads move back and forth between degrees of mobility "in response to changing pressures, constraints, and opportunities both internal and external to the society" (Salzman 1980a:14). For archaeologists such flexibility means that historical events alone cannot account for periods of sedentarization or nomadization in antiquity. At best, external factors can only suggest that sedentarization was at least a viable option for those members of a mobile society who saw the shift to agriculture as a necessary alternative to pastoralism.

A number of studies of modern Near Eastern nomads illustrate the variety of sedentarization processes. Despite the diverse impulses toward sedentarization, the ethnographic record makes clear that, in several cases, sedentarization depends on political factors. Barth (1961:118) was explicit about the fact that, although personal wealth is the primary determinant in a Basseri family's decision to settle, sedentarization was more likely to take place in peaceful periods when the central administration was strong. In periods of weak administration a switch to nomadism became much more common. Similarly, the economic effects of land policies instituted by a strong Turkish government led to the sedentarization of Yörük nomads (Bates 1973, 1980). As the government encouraged large-scale cotton, wheat and rice farming, irrigation and cultivation expanded in rural Turkey. This policy reduced the pasturage available to nomads and forced them into a sedentary agricultural lifestyle. Although the presence of a strong central administration does not necessarily lead to sedentarization, the process is certainly more likely to take place against a backdrop of political and economic stability.

A second important archaeological implication of ethnographies of sedentarization is that in most cases, recently settled nomads retain a distinct identity from their sedentary neighbors. This distinction remains, in part, because in order to allow for a return to nomadism if conditions change, the cultural identity of nomads must, to some degree, remain unique. Indeed, for the Basseri, it appeared important to retain some tribal connections as sedentism leads to increased birthrates, and shares of inheritance are not always enough to allow a landowner's children to remain sedentary (Barth 1961). In cases when Basseri settled as a group, tribesmen continued to identify as Basseri and maintained an identity distinct from the villagers (Barth 1961:117). Maintenance of a tribal identity in the case of Yörük sedentarization in Turkey was directly expressed in their material culture (Bates 1973). Permanent dwellings were arranged according to a pattern adapted from the distribution of tents within a campsite and organized according to two branches of one patrilineage. In some cases Yörük families remained mobile but pitched tents as home bases in Yörük village quarters when they grazed their flocks on Yörük fields in the summer. Bates (1973:222) found that, on the whole, although some social changes took place after Yörük settlement, the new adaptations were economic rather than a "massive change in formal institutions or social rules."

Settled Qashqa'i nomads serve as another example of the retention of tribal identity despite a change in residence and subsistence patterns. Sedentary Qashqa'i are as integral a part of the tribe as are nomadic Qashqa'i (Beck 1986, 1991). Sedentarization does not change any of the political affiliations or social relations within the tribe (Beck 1986:185). In some cases tribal cultural affiliation is both tangibly experienced and visually expressed by constructing permanent dwellings over earlier tent sites (Beck 2003:293). Beck (2003:293) describes one striking example of sedentary Qashqa'i tribal identity: a black tent pitched against a permanent dwelling, where a son and his new bride lived and guests were entertained.

The anthropology of sedentarization in the 20th century CE has substantial implications for the archaeology of early Aramaeans. The fact that sedentarization of modern nomads most often occurs when a central administration is politically and economically stable suggests that the same may have been the case for mobile Aramaeans. Mass sedentarization of Aramaean tribes is therefore unlikely to have occurred during the Dark Age that followed the reign of

King Tiglath-Pileser I. Rather, the conditions for successful agriculture and sedentarization had been established much earlier, as Middle Assyrian kings brought political stability and economic control into Hanigalbat. Accordingly, it is in the 14th–13th centuries BCE that mobile pastoralists would have been most inclined to become sedentary. Moreover, because tribal identity is often maintained after sedentarization, and may be expressed in the material culture of sedentarized nomads, Aramaean settlements in Late Bronze Age Syria and Turkey are likely to exhibit a material culture similar to that of their mobile kinsmen but unlike that of their sedentary neighbors.

TOWARD AN ARCHAEOLOGY OF SEDENTARIZATION

Although the literature on nomadism in ancient Mesopotamia recognizes the continuum of mobility and the fluid boundary between nomadic and sedentary lifestyles (Adams 1974; Rowton 1974; Nissen 1980; Zagarell 1989; Finkelstein and Perevolotsky 1990; Cribb 1991; Khazanov 1994), archaeologists have tended to concentrate on one extreme of this continuum and often draw a bold line between sedentism and nomadism in practice (Hole 1980; Cribb 1991; Alizadeh 2003). The result is that, despite a clear awareness of the variations and nuances of pastoral nomadic systems and sedentary-nomadic interaction, the archaeology of nomadism in Mesopotamia is limited to identifying the ancient 'campsite' or 'tentsite.' It is no wonder, then, that the best representative of excavated nomadic sites in Mesopotamia remains Tepe Tula'i (Hole 1974), although its interpretation as a nomadic campsite is disputed (Wheeler Pires-Ferreira 1975). Such controversy over the interpretation of possible nomadic sites is not unique to Tepe Tula'i. The faunal remains of Early Bronze Age Sos Höyük and Büyüktepe Höyük (Howell-Meurs 2001a, 2001b) suggest that the inhabitants of those sites practiced sedentary, rather than nomadic, pastoralism as the excavators originally concluded based on architectural context (Sagona et al. 1996:37).

By searching for only nomadic or sedentary settlements, an opportunity is missed to widen the archaeological perspective to encompass transitional sites or to focus archaeological investigations of ancient nomadism toward the center of the spectrum, to sites of sedentarizing nomads. As they sedentarize, nomads begin to use durable construction materials and to accumulate preservable debris (Cribb 1991; Wendrich, this volume), but they also retain strong cultural connections to their tribes. Thus, the remains of sedentarizing nomads will be more visible than, but not necessarily distinct from, that of their mobile counterparts. Sites of sedentarizing nomads can potentially offer a great deal of information about how their occupants interacted with agricultural village or urban communities. An archaeology of sedentarization can begin to address

Wilkinson's (2003:50) lament over the lack of progress in the archaeology of pastoral nomadism in Mesopotamia. In fact, Wilkinson and Tucker's own survey (1995) of the North Jazira, in Iraq, provides an illustration of how such a methodology might work to determine the extent of Aramaean sedentarization in the Late Bronze Age.

In four seasons, from 1986 to 1990, 497 square km in northwest Iraq were surveyed by Wilkinson and Tucker. The survey region consisted of a shallow basin in the North Jazira, which is drained by small *wadis* (seasonal rivers) in the north and south that empty into the Wadi al-Mur, which itself flows southeast to empty into the Tigris. The basin is flanked by rolling hills to the west, northeast and southeast. In most years dry farming is possible on the North Jazira plain, though the flat wadi basin has a higher agricultural yield than the surrounding hills (Wilkinson and Tucker 1995:7). Wilkinson and Tucker divide the second millennium BCE in the North Jazira into three historical periods: the Khabur period (2000–1500 BCE), identified by a range of Khabur wares; the Mitanni period (1500–1300 BCE), identified by Nuzi ware; and the Middle Assyrian period (1300–1000 BCE), based on characteristic Middle Assyrian pottery (Wilkinson and Tucker 1995:iv, 59). To address the difficulties identifying Nuzi ware and distinguish between Middle and Late Assyrian wares, Wilkinson and Tucker take Khabur wares as generally representative of the first half of the second millennium BCE and Middle Assyrian wares as generally representative of the second half of the second millennium BCE (Wilkinson and Tucker 1995:59). Thus, they effectively collapse the tripartite historical division of the second millennium BCE into two broad archaeological periods based on ceramic indicators: a 'Khabur period' and a 'Middle Assyrian period.' This may well be the best solution, as Khabur ware has since been found in later Mitanni levels at Rimah (Postgate et al. 1997:54). Moreover, Pfälzner (1995), in his analysis of ceramics from Tell Sheikh Hamad, has confirmed that Mitanni wares give way to Middle Assyrian types beginning in the 13th century BCE. One problem with this scheme is that maps of the second half of the Late Bronze Age may conflate the effects on settlement patterns of two significant political developments: the decline of the Mitanni kingdom, beginning in the 14th century BCE, and the subsequent growth of the Middle Assyrian kingdom. Thus, the overall thinning of the number of settlements in this period probably reflects the ruralization, perhaps accompanied by an increase in pastoral nomadism, that followed the collapse of the Mitanni kingdom and not the expansion of Middle Assyrian control.

Further complicating the settlement picture in this period is the fact that any increase in settlement that may have occurred during the Middle Assyrian period is dwarfed in comparison to the dramatic settlement growth that took place in the first millennium BCE (32 new settlements). Wilkinson and Tucker

(1995:62) conclude that at least some of these new Late Assyrian settlements may have been occupied by sedentarized tribesmen, who they suggest turned to agriculture in this period. A close look at the changes in settlement between the Khabur and Middle Assyrian periods, however, shows that sedentarization may have begun as early as the Middle Assyrian period. In the Khabur period in the North Jazira, several new settlements appear along wadis or as satellites of large urban centers. These locations are appropriate for an agricultural economic base, and the small sites that emerge associated with large centers may indicate a general growth in urbanization in the first half of the second millennium BCE. In the Middle Assyrian period, by contrast, fewer new settlements are established, compared with the preceding period. Whereas in the Khabur period 25 new sites appear, in the Middle Assyrian period there are only seven new sites. Like the new sites of the Khabur period, some of these new Middle Assyrian sites occur along wadis, which is consistent with primarily agricultural activities. Some of these new sites, however, are established at some distance from the wadi beds and urban centers of the region, a trend that is new in the Middle Assyrian period. Two Middle Assyrian period sites (numbers 69 and 157) are located on the western and eastern slopes of the large wadi basin, on land that is not as productive as the flat terrain on the floor of the basin. A third site (number 105) is located in an area that was entirely devoid of settlement in the preceding period. Whereas in the Khabur period settlement was concentrated in the northern and southern ends of the survey region, these three new Middle Assyrian settlements fill the space between these two poles. Furthermore, all three of these sites are quite small, site 157 being 1.2 ha and sites 69 and 105 only 0.8 ha. Might these new Middle Assyrian period sites be home to sedentarizing pastoral nomads, transitioning from temporary to permanent settlements?

DISCUSSION

As the Middle Assyrian regime introduced the political stability that made sedentarization feasible, along with the economic stability that intensive irrigation agriculture demanded, the pastoral nomads of the region would have pursued agriculture more intensively. As the pastoral activities that had required seasonal campsites gave way to year-round cultivation, these temporary settlements may have taken on more permanent fixtures and, by the end of the Late Bronze Age, may already have become productive agricultural communities integrated economically and politically into the provincial landscape of the Middle Assyrian kingdom. In the Late Assyrian period, settlement continued in this central area, and the whole region became more densely occupied. Sedentarization of nomads certainly may have played some role in the Iron

Age settlement increase (Wilkinson and Tucker 1995:62), but this should not be understood as a sudden and explosive event. The cursory re-evaluation presented here of the North Jazira Survey shows that Aramaean sedentarization began in the Middle Assyrian period at the end of the Late Bronze Age. A much more detailed study of the abundant surveys of Late Bronze Age Syro-Anatolia will be required to confirm these suggestions, but the aim of this chapter has been to advocate for an archaeology of sedentarization as a way to approach the survey data. The disappointing record of the archaeology of pastoral nomadism in Mesopotamia stems in part from the fact that the implications of the anthropology of sedentarization have largely been ignored by archaeologists in practice, if not in theory. In the case of early Aramaean nomads, Middle Assyrian occupation of Syro-Anatolia created the political and economic conditions that tend to encourage sedentarization. Once we move away from a false nomadic-sedentary dichotomy in terms of settlement types by investigating sites of sedentarizing nomads, the survey record appears to correspond with those anthropological implications. The archaeology of sedentarization may be one way to confront the challenges of pastoral nomadic archaeology in Mesopotamia.

REFERENCES

Adams, R. M.

1974   The Mesopotamian Social Landscape: A View from the Frontier. In C. B. Moore (ed.), *Reconstructing Complex Societies: Supplement to Bulletin of the American Schools of Oriental Research 20*: pp. 1–13.

Akkermans, P. M. M. G. and G. Schwartz

2003   *The Archaeology of Syria*. Cambridge, Cambridge University Press.

Alizadeh, A.

2003   Some Observations Based on the Nomadic Character of Fars Prehistoric Cultural Development. In N. F. Miller and K. Abdi (eds.), *Yeki Bud, Yeki Nabud: Essays on the Archaeology of Iran in Honor of William M. Sumner*. Los Angeles, Cotsen Institute of Archaeology: pp. 83–97.

Barth, F.

1961   *Nomads of South Persia*. Boston, Little, Brown.

Bates, D.

1973   *Nomads and Farmers: A Study of the Yörük of Southeastern Turkey. Anthropological papers of the Museum of Anthropology 52*. Ann Arbor, University of Michigan.

1980   Yoruk Settlement in Southeast Turkey. In P. C. Salzman (ed.), *When Nomads Settle: Processes of Sedentarization as Adaptation and Response*. New York, Praeger: pp. 124–139.

Beck, L.

1986   *The Qashqa'i of Iran*. New Haven, Yale University Press.

1991   *Nomad: A Year in the Life of a Qashqa'i Tribesman in Iran*. Berkeley, University of California Press.

2003   Qashqa'i Nomadic Pastoralists and Their Use of Land. In N. F. Miller and K. Abdi (eds.), *Yeki Bud, Yeki Nabud: Essays on the Archaeology of Iran in Honor of William M. Sumner*. Los Angeles, Cotsen Institute of Archaeology: pp. 289–304.

Brinkman, J. A.

1968   *A Political History of Post-Kassite Babylonia (1158–722 B.C.)*. Rome, Pontificium Institutum Biblicum.

Bunnens, G.

1999   Aramaeans, Hittites, and Assyrians in the Upper Euphrates Valley. In G. del Olmo Lete and J.-L. Montero Fenollós (eds.), *Archaeology of the Upper Syrian Euphrates, the Tishrin Dam Area*. Barcelona, Institut del Pròxim Orient Antic: 605–624.

Cribb, R.

1991   *Nomads in Archaeology*. Cambridge, Cambridge University Press.

Finkelstein, I. and A. Perevolotsky

1990   Processes of Sedentarization and Nomadization in the History of Sinai and the Negev. *Bulletin of the American Schools of Oriental Research 279*: pp. 67–88.

Grayson, A. K.

1987   *Assyrian Rulers of the Third and Second Millennia BC. Volume 1 (to 1115 BC)*. Toronto, University of Toronto Press.

1991   *Assyrian Rulers of the Early First Millennium BC. Volume 2 (1114–859 BC)*. Toronto, University of Toronto Press.

Harrak, A.

1987   *Assyria and Hanigalbat: A Historical Reconstruction of Bilateral Relations from the Middle of the Fourteenth to the End of the Twelfth Centuries B.C.* Hildesheim, Georg Olms.

Hawkins, J. D.

1982   The Neo-Hittite States in Syria and Anatolia. In J. Boardman (ed.), *Cambridge Ancient History. Volume 3, Part 2*. Cambridge, Cambridge University Press: pp. 372–441.

Heimpel, W.

2003   *Letters to the King of Mari: A New Translation with Historical Introduction, Notes, and Commentary*. Winona Lake, Eisenbrauns.

Hole, F.

1974   Tepe Tula'i: An Early Campsite in Khuzistan. *Paléorient 2*: pp. 219–242.

1980   The Prehistory of Herding: Some Suggestions for Ethnography. In M. T. Barrelet. *L'Archéologie de l'Iraq: Du début de l'époque néolithique à 333 avant notre ère: Perspectives et limites de l'interprétation anthropologique des documents.* Paris, Editions du Centre National de la Recherche Scientifique: pp. 119–128.

Howell-Meurs, S.

2001a   Archaeozoological Evidence for Pastoral Systems and Herd Mobility: The Remains from Sos Höyük and Büyüktepe Höyük. *International Journal of Osteoarchaeology 11*: pp. 321–328.

2001b   *Early Bronze and Iron Age Animal Exploitation in Northeastern Anatolia: The Faunal Remains from Sos Höyük and Büyüktepe Höyük. BAR International Series 945.* Oxford, Archaeopress.

Kessler, K.

1980   *Untersuchungen zur historischen Topographie Nordmesopotamiens: Nach keilschriftlichen Quellen des 1. Jahrtausends v. Chr. Beihefte zum Tübinger Atlas des Vorderen Orients B 26.* Weisbaden, Ludwig Reichert.

Khazanov, A. M. (translated by Julia Crookenden)

1994   *Nomads and the Outside World.* University of Wisconsin Press.

Kühne, H.

1990   The Effects of Irrigation Agriculture: Bronze and Iron Age Habitation Along the Khabur, Eastern Syria. In S. Bottema, G. Entjes-Nieborg and W. van Zeist (eds.), *Man's Role in the Shaping of the Eastern Mediterranean Landscape.* Rotterdam, A. A. Balkema: pp. 15–30.

2000   Dur-katlimmu and the Middle Assyrian Empire. In O. Rouault and M. Wäfler (eds.), *La Djéziré et l'Euphrate syriens de la protohistoire à la fin du IIe millénaire av. J.-C. Subartu* 7. Turnhout, Brepols: pp. 271–279.

Lipinski, E.

2000   *The Aramaeans: Their Ancient History, Culture, Religion.* Leuven, Peeters.

Machinist, P.

1982   Provincial Governance in Middle Assyria and Some New Texts from Yale. *Assur 3*: pp. 1–37.

Marx, E.

1977   The Tribe as a Unit of Subsistence: Nomadic Pastoralism in the Middle East. *American Anthropologist 79*: pp. 343–363.

McClellan, T. C.

1992   The 12th Century BC in Syria: Comments on H. Sader's Paper. In W. A. Ward and M. S. Joukowsky (eds.), *The Crisis Years: The 12th Century B.C.: From Beyond the Danube to the Tigris.* Dubuque, Kendall-Hunt: pp. 164–173.

Meijer, D.

1986   *A Survey in Northeastern Syria.* Istanbul, Nederlands Historisch-Archaeologisch Instituut te Istanbul.

Nissen, H.

1980   The Mobility Between Settled and Non-settled in Early Babylonia: Theory and Evidence. In M. T. Barrelet. *L'Archéologie de l'Iraq: Du Début de l'époque*

Néolithique à 333 avant Notre Ère. Paris, Editions du Centre National de la Recherche Scientifique: pp. 286–290.

Oates, D., J. Oates and H. McDonald

1997   *Excavations at Tell Brak. Volume 1: The Mitanni and Old Babylonian Periods.* Cambridge, McDonald Institute for Archaeological Research.

Pfälzner, P.

1995   *Mittanische und mittelassyrische Keramik: Eine chronologische, funktionale, und produktionsökonomische Analyse. Berichte der Ausgrabunki Tall Šeh Hamad / Dur-Katlimmu. Band 3.* Berlin, Dietrich Reimer Verlag.

Postgate, C., D. Oates and J. Oates

1997   *The Excavations at Tell al-Rimah: The Pottery.* Wiltshire, British School of Archaeology in Iraq.

Roux, G.

1969/1992   *Ancient Iraq.* London, Penguin.

Rowton, M. B.

1974   Enclosed Nomadism. *Journal of the Economic and Social History of the Orient 17*: pp. 1–30.

Sader, H.

1992   The 12th Century BC in Syria: The Problem of the Rise of the Aramaeans. In W. A. Ward and M. S. Joukowsky (eds.). *The Crisis Years: The 12th Century B.C.: From Beyond the Danube to the Tigris.* Dubuque, Kendall-Hunt: pp. 157–163.

2000   Aramaean Kingdoms of Syria: Origin and Formation Processes. In G. Bunnens (ed.), *Essays on Syria in the Iron Age. Ancient Near Eastern Studies Supplement 7.* Louvain, Peeters Press: pp. 61–76.

Sagona, A., M. Erkmen, C. Sagona and I. Thomas

1996   Excavations at Sos Höyük, 1995: Second Preliminary Report. *Anatolian Studies 46*: pp. 27–52.

Salzman, P. C.

1972   Multi-resource Nomadism in Iranian Baluchistan. In W. Irons and N. Dyson-Hudson (eds.), *Perspectives on Nomadism.* Leiden, E. J. Brill: pp. 60–68.

1980a   Introduction: Processes of Sedentarization as Adaptation and Response. In P. C. Salzman (ed.), *When Nomads Settle: Processes of Sedentarization as Adaptation and Response.* New York, Praeger: pp. 1–19.

1980b   Processes of Sedentarization Among the Nomads of Baluchistan. In P. C. Salzman (ed.), *When Nomads Settle: Processes of Sedentarization as Adaptation and Response.* New York, Praeger: pp. 95–110.

Schachner, A.

2003   From the Bronze to the Iron Age: Identifying Changes in the Upper Tigris Region. The Case of Giricano. In B. Fischer, H. Genz, É. Jean and K. Köroğlu (eds.), *Identifying Changes: Proceedings of the International Workshop "The*

Transition from Bronze to Iron Age in Anatolia and Its Neighbouring Regions." Istanbul, 8–9 November 2002. Istanbul, Türk Eskiçag Bilimleri Enstitüsü.

Schwartz, G. M.

1989   The Origins of the Aramaeans in Syria and Northern Mesopotamia: Research Problems and Potential Strategies. In O. M. C. Haex, H. H. Curvers and P. M. M. G. Akkermans (eds.), *To the Euphrates and Beyond: Archaeological Studies in Honour of Maurits N. van Loon*. Rotterdam, A. A. Balkema.

Ward, W. and M. S. Joukowsky (eds.)

1989   *The Crisis Years: The 12th Century B.C.: From Beyond the Danube to the Tigris*. Dubuque, Kendall-Hunt.

Wheeler Pires-Ferreira, J.

1975   Tepe Tûlâ'i: Faunal Remains from an Early Campsite in Khuzistan, Iran. *Paléorient 3*: pp. 275–280.

Wilkinson, T. J.

2003   Archaeological Survey and Long-Term Population Trends in Upper Mesopotamia and Iran. In N. F. Miller and K. Abdi (eds.), *Yeki Bud, Yeki Nabud: Essays on the Archaeology of Iran in Honor of William M. Sumner*. Los Angeles, Cotsen Institute of Archaeology: pp. 39–51.

Wilkinson, T. J. and D. J. Tucker

1995   *Settlement Development in the North Jezira, Iraq. Iraq Archaeological Reports 3*. Wiltshire, British School of Archaeology in Iraq.

Zagarell, A.

1989   Pastoralism and the Early State in Greater Mesopotamia. In C. C. Lamberg-Karlovsky (ed.), *Archaeological Thought in America*. Cambridge, Cambridge University Press.

CHAPTER 19

SUGGESTIONS FOR A *CHAÎNE OPÉRATOIRE* OF NOMADIC POTTERY SHERDS

HANS BARNARD[1]

AMONG THE MORE enigmatic, and sometimes controversial, aspects of a nomadic, mobile lifestyle are the desire and the ability of people that have not (yet) settled to manufacture, or even use, ceramic vessels. Current, well-balanced opinions on the subject of pottery production by mobile people are reflected in several other contributions to this volume.

> There has been a common wisdom or stereotype among many archaeologists that sedentism, agriculture and pottery technologies are necessarily positively correlated. Indeed, some archaeologists use the presence or absence of pottery in the archaeological record as an independent measure of residential mobility. The presence of potsherds at a site would indicate sedentism and a lack of pottery some degree of seasonal transhumance. Although examples of pottery in sites occupied by mobile hunter-gatherers are known . . . in such cases the pottery is usually defined as 'crude' and 'technologically unimpressive' thereby relegating it to a lesser or unimportant status and reinforcing the stereotype (Eerkens, this volume).

[1.] I would like to thank David Verity for sharing some of his vast experience with me; Steve Sidebotham, Roberta Tomber, Pamela Rose, Anwar Abdel-Magid, Richard Pierce, Knut Krzywinski, Eugen Strouhal, Jana Součková, Jitka Barochová, Manfred Bietak, Elfriede Reiser-Haslauer and Roswitha Egner for making the necessary material available; John Bintliff and Steve Rosen for their stimulating remarks; Jelmer Eerkers and Paul Nicholson for their comments on earlier versions of this chapter; Anna Barnard-van der Nat for her financial and logistical support; and Willeke Wendrich for her unending encouragement. The license to excavate the site of Tabot was issued by the Department of Antiquities and National Museums, Khartoum, Sudan, to Dr. Anwar Abdel-Magid. Test excavations carried out by the license holder in 1994 and 1995 were sponsored by the Committee for Development Research and Education (NUFU) of the Norwegian Council of Universities within the framework of their Sudan Program (Phase II: Archaeology Project). The license holder authorized Hans Barnard to study and publish the pottery from Tabot.

There seems to be consensus, among the authors contributing to this volume, that a fraction of mobile people will produce their own pottery and that this pottery will usually be of poor quality.

> These observations suggest that even when mobile groups do manufacture pottery, their product is technologically and aesthetically inferior to those produced by sedentary peoples. Arnold (1985), while suggesting that less than a third of mobile societies make and use pottery, argues that a number of practical, logistical and economic (economies of scale) problems are involved in the production of pottery by groups with high residential mobility (Alizadeh, this volume).

The relative low quality and inferior aesthetics of the vessels produced by mobile people usually extends to a lack of decoration of the vessels. This adds to the difficulty of identification, in an archaeological context, if remains of such vessels are found at all.

> Pastoral people are often less concerned with decoration on their vessels than are agriculturalists, who imbue their pots with symbolic significance . . . The ceramics that seem to have the strongest association with the earliest pastoralists are usually small, thin-walled vessels (10 cm in height), possibly used for sheep milking, which break up into tiny pieces, making them even more difficult to find on small open sites (A. B. Smith, this volume).

Over time, the character of residential mobility may have changed, slowly losing some of the properties of hunting-gathering or herding-gathering, including the production of pottery, and growing more dependent on the surrounding settled communities.

> It is difficult to measure this directly, but to measure trade, for example, petrographic analyses of Early Bronze Age ceramic assemblages from Negev nomad sites shows high proportions of local pottery produced by the nomads themselves, in addition to some imports. In contrast, by classical times (Nabatean, Roman, Byzantine and Early Islamic), 90% or more of the pottery found on the nomad sites was imported, produced by specialists in the towns and sites of the empires of Late Antiquity. By recent and subrecent times, virtually all pottery used by the Bedouin, the famous black Gaza Ware, is imported, along with a vast array of other manufactured goods (Rosen, this volume).

Despite these intricacies, the pottery used and left behind by mobile people can, in specific circumstances, be recognized and used to show, and even date, their presence.

> Sherd scatters of coarse gray pottery identified as 'Gaza Ware' have been found at many abandoned Bedouin tent camps in the Negev and Sinai. Such sherd scatters

at archaeological sites in the Negev Highlands constitute the only evidence that these settlements were re-used by Bedouin . . . Dating Gaza Ware is problematic because it has not been the subject of systematic typological and chronological research. Current studies indicate that the production of Gaza Ware may have begun as early as the second half of the 17th century CE, or the beginning of the 18th century CE, and that it continued to be manufactured until the end of the 20th century CE . . . This suggests that the abandoned Bedouin tent camps situated in the Negev Highlands should be dated between the 17th-20th centuries CE (Saidel, this volume).

In this chapter I will deal with the production aspect of a corpus of ceramic vessels, Eastern Desert Ware, that does not fully fit the above characteristics. Although these vessels are believed to have been handmade by pastoral nomads in the arid landscape between the Nile and the Red Sea, during the 4th-6th centuries CE, most vessels are not only rather well finished but also distinctively decorated (Figure 19.1). This makes it possible to identify even small sherds of Eastern Desert Ware among many sherds of 'imported' wheel-thrown

Figure 19.1. Examples of Eastern Desert Ware, believed to have been made by pastoral nomads, during the 4th-6th centuries CE, in southeastern Egypt and northeastern Sudan (Figure 19.2). EDW 17 is from Berenike (on the Red Sea coast); EDW 234 is from Wadi Sikait (in the *Mons Smaragdus* area); KHM 76918 is from Sayala (in the Nile Valley, courtesy of the *Kunsthistorisches Museum* in Vienna); and P 840 is from Wadi Qitna (just west of the Nile Valley, courtesy of the *Náprstek Museum* in Prague).

vessels. This special case may indicate that the production of pottery less recognizable than Eastern Desert Ware may have been more common among mobile groups than is usually suggested.

Given the dearth of additional archaeological finds and the ambiguous historical sources (Burstein, this volume; Barnard 2005) Eastern Desert Ware may remain our only source of information about its producers, the dwellers of the Eastern Desert (Figure 19.2). Next to a careful study of the ancient artifacts, currently undertaken from the macroscopic to the molecular levels (Barnard and Strouhal 2004; Barnard et al. 2006), additional insights may be acquired through experimental and ethno-archaeological studies (Shepard 1976; Rye 1981; P. J. Arnold 1991; Arnold et al. 1991; Stark 1991; Gosselain 1992; Longacre and Stark 1994; Schiffer et al. 1994; Rice 1996; Kramer 1997; Deal 1998; Arthur 2002).[2] At present the inhabitants of the area do not produce any pottery, rendering an ethno-archaeological study pointless. Therefore, this chapter reports on my experimental work trying to reproduce vessels similar to Eastern Desert Ware, in a setting as close as possible to that of the ancient pastoral nomads. Based on these experiments, I put forward a *chaîne opératoire* (operational sequence) with an archaeological rather than an ethnographic perspective (Table 19.1). Archaeologists typically deal with sherds rather than vessels and usually do not attribute separate meanings to sherds or whole vessels. The chaîne opératoire that I suggest, therefore, aims to explore the processes resulting in the sherds of handmade burnished and decorated vessels recently found in the Egyptian and Sudanese Eastern Deserts. In no way is it meant as proof that Eastern Desert Ware vessels were indeed made by pastoral nomads rather than by settled desert dwellers or inhabitants of the Nile Valley; it serves only to show that it would have been feasible for them to do so.

EASTERN DESERT WARE

During the first survey and excavation season at the Greco-Roman harbor Berenike, on the Egyptian Red Sea coast, in 1994, a number of remarkable potsherds were found (Figure 19.1). These were of handmade cups and bowls with burnished surfaces and incised decorations (Rose 1995). The closest parallels for this pottery are described at sites in the Nile Valley, most notably in Kalabsha, Wadi Qitna and Sayala (Kromer 1967; Bedawi 1976; Strouhal 1984:157–177; Barnard and Strouhal 2004; Barnard and Magid 2006; Barnard et al. 2006; Barnard and Rose, in press), a considerable distance across an arid landscape to the west. Since then, similar sherds have been recognized at sites

---

[2] An excellent overview of the recent literature on these related, and sometimes confused, subjects can be found in Stark 2003.

in southeastern Egypt and northeastern Sudan (Luft et al. 2004; Nordström 2004; Sidebotham et al. 2005; Barnard and Magid 2006; Barnard, in press; Barnard and Rose, in press), always in small quantities among many sherds of late-Roman (Byzantine) Egyptian or Meroitic (X-group) vessels (Figure 19.2). These, combined with a few other datable finds (like coins) and radiocarbon

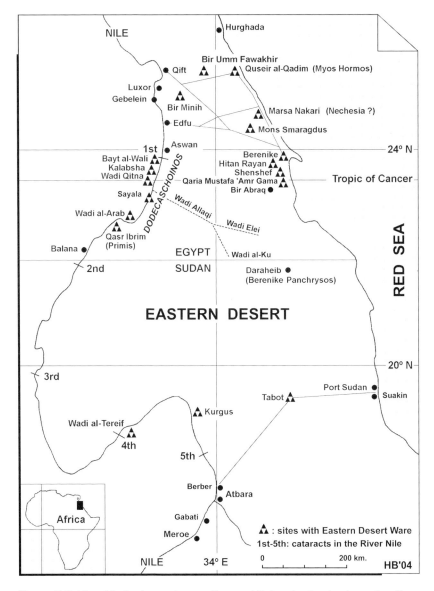

Figure 19.2. Map of the border area between Egypt and Sudan, showing the places where Eastern Desert Ware has been described.

Table 19.1. A Possible *Chaîne Opératoire* for Archaeologically Recovered Sherds of Eastern Desert Ware:

Phase	Tools	Skill[a]	Time[b]
Vessel as concept			
obtaining raw materials (clay, temper, water, fuel)	receptacles (shovel, axe)	+	++
preparation of the paste (sieving, mixing, levigating?, drying)	receptacles, sieve?	++	++
shaping the vessel (coiling, pinching)	none	+	+
surface treatment (wiping) and decoration (impressing)	cloth, pointed tool	+	+
drying until leather hard	none	-	+
Vessel as creation			
surface treatment (smoothing) and decoration (incising)	abrasive, blade	++	+
drying until bone dry	none	-	++
decoration (slipping) and surface treatment (burnishing)	brush, slip, pebble, oil?	++	+
heating, prefiring	none	++	+
firing, refiring	saggar?	++	+
Vessel as object			
first use, seasoning	sealant	+	+
intended use	none	-	+++
re-use (for instance as grave gift)	none	-	+++
Vessel as tool			
breaking of the vessel	none	-	+
repair and re-use or utilization of (some of) the sherds	drill, thread, adhesive?	+/++	+
discarding the remains of the vessel	none	-	+++

[a]Skill levels: - = no skills required; + = limited skills required; ++ = expert skills required.
[b]Time estimates: + = phase may take 0–6 hours; ++ = phase may take 0.5–7 days; +++ = phase may last years.

dates (Strouhal 1984:265; Sadr et al. 1995:227; Magid 2004:157–159), allow the conclusion that these vessels must have been produced between at least the end of the third and the beginning of the 8th century CE. Given its distribution the corpus is now identified as Eastern Desert Ware (Barnard 2002).

The majority of Eastern Desert Ware vessels are made of an orange to rusty-red fabric with few organic but abundant poorly sorted mineral inclusions (identified in petrographic thin sections as angular quartz and feldspars). Macroscopic and microscopic inspection of this fabric places it outside the 'Vienna System' that classifies the common clay sources used for pottery in Ancient Egypt (Arnold and Bourriau 1993). The technology, shape and decoration of the vessels also make it unlikely that they were produced by the permanent inhabitants of the Nile Valley as the pottery is very different from that usually encountered. Preliminary interpretation of the elemental composition of more than 140 Eastern Desert Ware sherds, obtained by laser ablation inductively coupled plasma mass spectrometry (LA-ICP-MS),[3] indicate that these vessels were made in several geologically different areas, all most likely outside the Nile Valley. A comprehensive discussion of the origin of Eastern Desert Ware falls outside the scope of this chapter, but based on the technical research summarized above, the distribution of the finds (Figure 19.2), and the fact that the Eastern Desert at the time was inhabited by pastoral nomads (Burstein, this volume; Magid, this volume; Barnard 2005), as it is today (Magid, this volume; Wendrich, this volume; Murray 1935; Paul 1954), it is now assumed that Eastern Desert Ware was made and used by the pastoral nomads roaming the area in the 4th-6th century CE (Rose 1995; Barnard 2002, 2005). When used, most likely as serving vessels as suggested by their shape and size, the vessels, so different from those used by the settled people in the region, must have also acted as cultural, and possibly even ethnic, markers (S. T. Smith, this volume). The identification of these ancient nomads is elusive because of the lack of material remains other than the pottery and because historical sources on the area are both scarce and ambiguous for this period (Burstein, this volume; Barnard 2005). Several explanations can be proposed for the occurrence of such small numbers of remarkable potsherds, always mixed with large numbers of sherds from imported vessels, in such a large area. These explanations range from a demand-driven production, by settled or traveling professionals, to a household production taking place where and when the need arose or the opportunity presented itself. The validity of the latter explanation depends on whether it is feasible for mobile people to produce pottery as well made and finished as Eastern Desert Ware. The aim of this chapter is to investigate this feasibility for which I tried to reproduce Eastern Desert Ware, giving particular attention to the problems and possibilities likely to be encountered by mobile people.

EXPERIMENTAL POTTERY PRODUCTION

The pastoral nomads in the region today, the Ababda and the Bisharyyin,[4] do not produce any pottery but instead use imported ceramic cups and coffeemakers (*djabana*) alongside metal and plastic containers (Wendrich, this

---

[3.] This research was done on the GBC Optimass Orthogonal Time-of-Flight ICP-MS, with attached New Wave LUV Laser Ablation System, owned by the Institute for Integrated Research in Materials, Environments, and Society (IIRMES) at California State University, Long Beach, and sponsored by Dr. Hector Neff (IIRMES) and the Cotsen Institute of Archaeology at UCLA.

[4.] Both groups claim to be among the many tribes of the Beja (Paul 1954), along with the Hadendowa (Magid, this volume) and the Beni Amer.

volume). Modern pottery most like Eastern Desert Ware, in technology and appearance, is at present regularly manufactured in the southwestern United States and northwest Mexico (LeFree 1975; Bell 1994; Wisner 1999).[5] For a while I therefore joined longtime amateur potter David Verity in his endeavor to master the ceramic techniques that are most famously practiced in Mata Ortiz (Chihuahua, Mexico). Using this experience, and data obtained in some more experimental settings, I suggest the following archaeologically focused chaîne opératoire for the sherds of Eastern Desert Ware (Table 19.1),[6] assuming the presence of the necessary tools, skills, and time (Shepard 1976; Rye 1981; Bourriau et al. 2000). Not all sherds or archaeological vessels, which are the end products of this sequence, necessarily see all phases or go through the phases in the exact order as given, as will be explained below. Both in Arabic, the language currently spoken in the area where Eastern Desert Ware is found, and in English, *clay* means different things to geologists, potters and archaeologists; this is even more so for *temper* (Rice 1987; Hertz and Garrison 1998). A prospective nomadic potter in a familiar landscape, however, will need to see how the raw materials present themselves only once or twice to be able to find and recognize them. In the desert (Figure 18.3), clay and materials that can be utilized as inorganic temper are usually found in the same area, and they are frequently naturally mixed in adequate proportions. As these areas are often devoid of water and fuel, it will be necessary to either bring those or to carry out clay and temper. Settled potters typically do the latter (P. J. Arnold 1991; Gosselain 1992; Deal 1998; Wisner 1999), while mobile people may do the former as they will usually be carrying water and fuel for other purposes.

Although clay and potential temper are relatively easy to recognize, their behavior when shaped and fired is impossible to predict. It is therefore very likely that mobile people, like their settled counterparts, returned to sources that had proven to yield good raw materials, or at least raw materials with known properties (P. J. Arnold 1991; Arnold et al. 1991; Gosselain 1992; Deal 1998; Wisner 1999). They may have included such valued sources in their routes, as they will almost certainly have done with sources of special supplies, such as temper rich in mica or clay suitable for slips. After collecting clay, water and temper, these are combined into a paste that can be shaped and fired. One way of doing this is to break up the raw clay, which will be a mixture of

---

[5.] The closest local, but ancient, parallels are the vessels of the C-Horizon, produced by Nubian groups that inhabited the Nile Valley from the first to the third cataract between 2300–1500 BCE.

[6.] A *chaîne opératoire* is typically used as a way to describe the production process of a class of objects. I use it here as one of many tools to study the sherds or complete vessels of Eastern Desert Ware found in archaeological context.

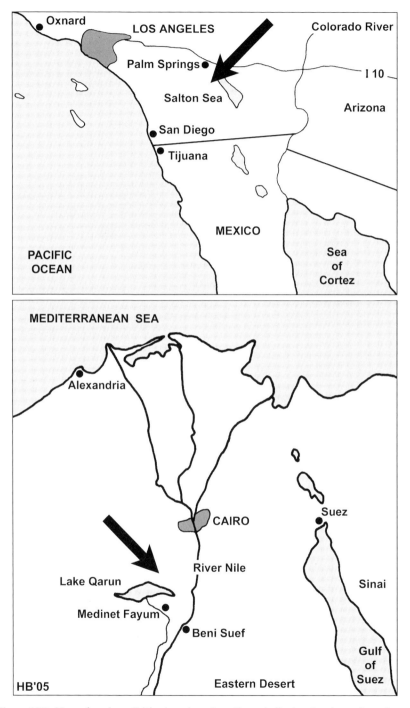

Figure 19.3. Maps of southern California and northern Egypt, indicating the places where clay and (inorganic) temper were collected for the experiments described in this chapter.

clay, silt and other inclusions, and suspend the actual clay particles in water. As these particles are very small, by definition,[7] they will remain suspended for hours while larger particles will quickly sink to the bottom. After a while the suspension is carefully decanted into a second receptacle through a sieve, if available, or cloth and allowed to settle. As this technique requires much time and water, naturally levigated clay sources (at the bottom of dry lakes or ponds) would have been preferred and may have been used exclusively. Pure clay, however, is not suitable for the production of pottery because it will shrink dramatically while drying, causing cracks and breaks. Therefore, not all inclusions should be removed from the raw clay, or some 'filler' should be added to the paste. These nonplastic materials will be cemented by the clay particles, forming a network that will sufficiently reduce, but not completely eliminate, shrinkage. Many materials can be used as filler, including silt,[8] dung, volcanic ash, chopped straw, crushed shells or pottery (grog), each with its own effect on both the technological process and the appearance of the vessel (Shepard 1976; Rye 1981; Arnold et al. 1991; Schiffer et al. 1994; Bourriau et al. 2000). I chose to add about one part of silt (Figure 19.4), by volume, to four parts of clay and allowed them to settle together. It is unclear whether some of the inclusions in Eastern Desert Ware were added in a similar way, as necessary in Santa Clara, New Mexico (LeFree 1975), or if they were naturally present, as in Mata Ortiz, Mexico (Wisner 1999). Experience would have shown which sources naturally produced clay and temper in a favorable ratio. These would have attracted mobile people to return, especially as such raw material required much less preparation.

After clay and silt have settled, which may take several days, the water is removed and the paste dried to a workable plasticity. This is best done on a slab of plaster of paris (Figure 19.4), or by wrapping the paste in cloth, to slow down the drying process, but can also be done in the sand and probably even on the move. Once the paste is fit to be shaped, which can again take several days, it can be modeled into the desired form by connecting two, or more, rings to a base (coiling) or by pinching a ball into the right shape (Figure 19.5). The surfaces can be smoothed with a wet finger, or a damp wad of cloth, and decorations can be impressed into the wet surface. Impression can be made with, among many other things, a fingernail, a blade, a shell, an animal bone or a potter's 'comb' (Shepard 1976; Rye 1981). Experiments have shown that many of the decorations on Eastern Desert Ware were made with thorns of a

---

[7.] Depending on the scientific context, clay is defined as platy particles weathered to smaller than a 2–4 µm (0.002–0.004 mm) diameter.

[8.] Again depending on the context, silt is defined as particles weathered to a diameter between 2–4 µm (0.002–0.004 mm) and 0.05 mm.

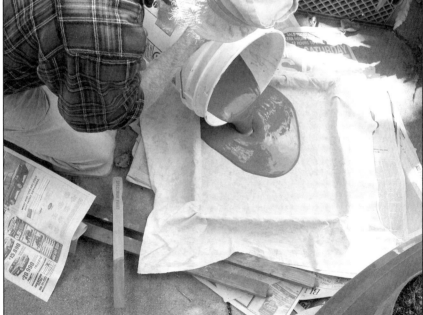

Figure 19.4. Preparation of potter's clay (by David Verity).

date palm (*Phoenix dactilifera*), which are the underdeveloped leaves at the base of a palm frond (Barnard, in press). In the Nile Valley, palm fronds are often used for fuel, and their thorns would have been readily available to potters. In the desert, where there are no palm trees, they may have been imported. The shaping and decorating of a vessel takes 30–60 min, after which the vessel is allowed to dry until it is 'leather hard:' when the paste has lost its plasticity but still holds 20–30% free water (Shepard 1976; Rye 1981; Bourriau et al. 2000).

Once a vessel is leather hard, which may take several hours, its shape can no longer be changed, but small repairs and additional decorations can be made (LeFree 1975; Shepard 1976; Rye 1981). It is also possible to further smooth the surface with a piece of damp cloth or leather (Bell 1994:53). It is likely that the potters who made Eastern Desert Ware did either of these, but I worked on my vessels only in the plastic and in the 'bone dry' stages. This latter stage is reached after all the free water has evaporated from the fabric. This can take several days but may be accelerated by carefully warming the vessel, for instance by placing it in the sun and regularly turning it around (Shepard 1976; Gosselain 1992; Kramer 1997; Deal 1998; Wisner 1999; Bourriau et al. 2000). Between the leather-hard and the bone-dry stages the vessel is susceptible to damage from handling and spontaneous cracking. Until firing, the production process can be completely reversed by adding enough water. Minor repairs can be made, or the paste can be completely recycled. It also means that the drying vessel must be shielded from water and sweat. When bone dry, the vessel can be smoothed, with sandpaper or another abrasive, slipped and burnished (Figure 19.5). If they did not do so when the vessel was still leather hard, the potters working on Eastern Desert Ware may have smoothed their bone-dry vessels with sand or an abrasive stone, like pumice or vesicular basalt, a technique reminiscent of burnishing. Slipping is the application of a thin suspension of clay with a distinctive color (naturally or because of an added pigment) by pouring or brushing this on the desired areas (Shepard 1976:67–69). Clays that make a good slip, bonding securely while delivering a bright color, are rare and would have been collected when encountered, or even warranted a detour, and carried around until needed. Burnishing is the polishing of a vessel by rubbing it with a hard object, like a pebble or the back of a spoon, after wetting the surface with slip, water or oil. The frequent combination of the slipping and burnishing of Eastern Desert Ware makes it likely that these were joined actions. The high luster of many Eastern Desert Ware vessels indicates that these were fired at relatively low temperatures (below 750–800°C or 1400–1500°F) as such luster tends to fade on exposure to higher temperatures.

The next stage of pottery production, the firing of the clay vessel, is the shortest and most dramatic. When the paste reaches sufficiently high

Figure 19.5. The shaping and smoothing of vessels.

temperatures, it will mature: the clay minerals irreversibly lose their ability to turn back into a plastic paste. Another important effect, depending on the conditions during the firing, is the burning off (oxidation) or deposition (reduction) of carbon, which greatly influences the color of the vessel (Rye 1981:114–118). At higher temperatures the iron oxides in the clay can also be reduced or oxidized, changing between black and red, respectively (Bourriau et al. 2000). If Eastern Desert Ware was indeed produced by nomadic potters, it was most likely fired in an open fire, unless space and time were negotiated in kilns belonging to settled potters in the Nile Valley. As is apparent from their results, several undesirable effects of firing vessels in an open fire were evidently circumvented by the nomadic potters. An important difference between a kiln and an open fire is that the temperature in a kiln can be better controlled and reach a higher maximum. As the water bonded to the clay minerals needs to be driven out gently, to prevent blistering, cracking or even exploding of the vessel, an open fire needs to be carefully monitored. The choice of fuel can facilitate this: dry wood will burn swift and hot, while animal dung or charcoal will take longer to heat up. At present, the pastoral nomads in the area use camel dung for cooking when wood is scarce and burn charcoal where wood is plentiful. The former is possible since the spread of the camel in Egypt during the last centuries BCE, and I saw the latter still done in the late 1990s. The dung of donkeys or sheep and goats may also have been used. A method to prevent the vessels from being destroyed by the firing is to force most of the water out first, by heating the vessel to a moderate temperature for a prolonged period. One or two summer days in the desert sun may be hot enough to do so (Shepard 1976; Wisner 1999). Alternatively, the vessels may have been buried in heated sand, as is currently the way that the nomads in the area bake their unleavened bread (Wendrich, this volume).

Another crucial difference between an open fire and a kiln is the contact between the vessel and the fire (flames and ashes). In a kiln the fire is separated from the vessels, which are heated by the hot gasses released by the fire. Allowing more or less air into the kiln generates an oxidizing or a reducing environment, respectively. Placing a clay vessel directly into an open fire allows the flames to create color differences on the fired surfaces, leaving so-called 'fire clouds,' while the collapsing fire will create a reducing environment. This will induce the paste to take up carbon, released by burning organics outside and inside the fabric, turning the vessel black. As most Eastern Desert Ware vessels do not show fire clouds or reduction, the ancient nomadic potters must have found ways to prevent them from appearing. The simplest way to reverse some of the fire clouds and most of the reduction is to take the hot vessel out of the fire, before it collapses, and allow it to cool in the open air (Rye 1981). A better method is to protect the vessel with a 'saggar' or *quemador* (Wisner 1999). A

Figure 19.6. Saggars used in California (above, photograph by W.Z. Wendrich) and in Egypt (below, photograph by the author).

saggar can be interpreted as a very simple kiln. It consists of a metal or ceramic container, holding the clay vessel, which is placed in or on top of the fire. I have successfully used an upturned terracotta flowerpot, an old paint drum (with a few holes to secure an oxidizing environment) and a perforated cookie tin (Figure 19.6). Ancient potters could have separated their vessels from the fire with larger vessels, such as cooking vessels, or may have constructed ad hoc saggars with the sherds of broken vessels or slabs of stone (LeFree 1975). Like the receptacles used for the preparation of the paste, such items would have been relatively easy to clean and to re-employed for their original function.

For this study I made about a dozen vessels and fired them using a variety of techniques. Put directly into an open fire, vessels did not survive, and vessels buried below an open fire did not mature (they failed to lose their ability to suspend in water). Clearly the temperature must be raised slowly, to gently drive out the water and reach a maximum above 360°C or 680°F (Figure 19.7). The vessels fired in a saggar in a slowly started open fire did mature without cracking or reducing but lost some of their luster. The same was true for vessels fired in the controlled environment of an electric kiln set to switch off at 866°C or 1591°F (using pyrometric cone 012). The optimal temperature for Eastern

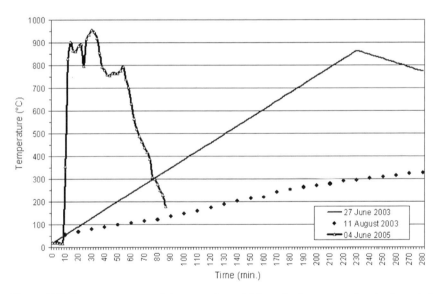

Figure 19.7. Temperature curves of three experimental firings, the first representing the theoretical temperatures inside an electric kiln controlled by a kiln-sitter (with pyrometric cone 012), on 27 June 2003; the second showing the measured temperatures below a slow-started bonfire failing to mature three buried vessels, on 11 August 2003; the third showing the measured temperatures in the center of a fast-started bonfire destroying not previously heated vessels, on 4 June 2005. Measurements were performed with an Omega Type K thermocouple (kindly made available by Dr. Brian Damiata, University of California, Riverside), which has a Chromel (nickel-chromium) positive and an Alumel (nickel-aluminum) negative lead, attached to a RadioShack digital multimeter. A plastic thermos flask with melting ice (0°C = 32°F) was used as external reference.

Desert Ware must therefore have been 410–810°C (770–1490°F) but probably closer to the latter (Shepard 1976; Rye 1981; Gosselain 1992; Schiffer 1994; Bourriau et al. 2000).

A vessel placed on top of a small fire of 2 kg (about 4.5 lb) charcoal, kindled with kerosene (paraffin) after the vessel was in place, also matured without cracking (Figure 19.8). This setup appeared to allow enough oxygen to reach the vessel to prevent absorption of reduced carbon released by the fuel. In places where olive oil was applied to the vessel, the surplus of carbon could not be oxidized, leaving a black surface (Figure 19.9). This carbon was later removed, turning the surface reddish brown, by firing the vessel again in a fully oxidizing environment. Some fire clouds remained, however, especially on the bottom of the vessel where it had been in direct contact with the glowing embers.

The resulting unglazed earthenware, quite similar to Eastern Desert Ware, will be more or less porous, especially when new or if used relatively little. To reduce this property, such vessels are often 'seasoned' by heating, for instance, milk, oil, butter or honey (with beeswax?) in a new vessel. This saturates its walls and diminishes the permeability of the fabric.[9] Resin or bitumen may also have been used to this effect or to repair broken vessels (Eerkens 2002). Little is known about the intended use of the vessels, but given their size and shape, they most likely functioned as serving vessels. At the same time, they probably acted as cultural, or ethnic, markers as they are markedly different, in technology and appearance, from the vessels of the settled population in and around the region (Sidebotham et al. 2002; Luft et al. 2004).

Many Eastern Desert Ware vessels were recovered from graves, where they had been placed as grave goods for the deceased, to whom they probably belonged during life (Habachi 1967; Strouhal 1984). A very similar custom is still practiced by the pastoral nomads now living in the area, despite centuries of Christian and Islamic discouragement (Barnard 1998; Wendrich, this volume). Sherds of many other vessels were found in private and public buildings in settlements in the Nile Valley and in the Eastern Desert. It takes little skill and time to break a vessel, but this should not always be interpreted as an accident. The intentional breaking of vessels can be part of a *rite de passage* or be an expression of joy or mourning, for instance during a Jewish wedding, a Greek dance, or in the context of the ancient Egyptian ritual 'breaking the red pots,' where the breaking was usually followed, and sometimes replaced, by the burial of the vessels (Ritner 1993:144–153). There are no indications that

---

[9] This technique is still widely practiced in modern Egypt and should be taken into account during the analysis and interpretation of ancient organic residues (Bourriau et al. 2000:128; Barnard et al. 2007).

Figure 19.8. Firing vessels in California (above, photograph by W.Z. Wendrich) and in Egypt (below, photograph by the author).

Figure 19.9. Examples of the vessels produced in California (above) and in Egypt (below).

Eastern Desert Ware was ever deliberately broken, but given the importance evidently attached to the vessels, it certainly cannot be ruled out.

There are indications that attempts were made to repair broken Eastern Desert Ware vessels, not by using an adhesive (such as a resin or bitumen) but rather by 'stitching' the sherds by threading holes drilled along the breaks, a technique commonly used (Eerkens, this volume). Eight of the 290 sherds that I studied in detail preserved a small hole, some of which may have been intended to suspend the vessel; others may be repair holes. No traces of adhesives, wire or string were ever seen. As the vessels must have been highly valued, it is hardly surprising that attempts were made to extend their functional life as long as possible, albeit possibly for a different task. After a broken vessel was judged beyond repair, its sherds may have been used as cover, scraper, toy, gaming piece or as a surface to receive writing (*ostrakon*). Finally, the remains of the vessel may have been crushed to serve as temper for a vessel still to be made (grog), or they may simply have been discarded to be studied by archaeologists centuries later.

DISCUSSION

There is sufficient archaeological and experimental evidence to conclude that the production of pottery, including vessels as nice as Eastern Desert Ware, by mobile people, and certainly by pastoral nomads, is eminently possible. Apart from a substantial investment in time and resources, however, ceramic vessels are relatively heavy, fragile and uneconomical to produce in small numbers (Alizadeh, this volume; Eerkens, this volume). The discussion of whether mobile people could produce pottery, therefore, is replaced by the question of what would make them decide to do so. The value of the specific properties of ceramics, for the completion of certain tasks, is clearly appreciated by mobile people worldwide, as is apparent from their propensity to use vessels acquired from settled outsiders. Among the few things that the nomads currently roaming the area where Eastern Desert Ware is found will always carry with them are the essentials for their 'coffee ceremony,' including a terracotta coffeemaker (made by settled potters in Sudan) and several small porcelain cups (industrially made in China). These fragile, but not very heavy, ceramics are stored in custom-made containers of basketry, leather or wood to prevent breakage (Wendrich, this volume).

One reason for mobile groups to produce their own pottery may be a limited availability of imported vessels. Settled potters, or other possible sources of pottery, may be far away or difficult to reach. These will likely be associated with other cultural, religious, or ethnic groups, which may obstruct the necessary contacts, and the available material can be of limited practical use or too expensive, in terms of currency, barter or otherwise. Any of these factors may prompt members of the mobile group to produce some of their own pottery. Modern developments have decreased the need to produce pottery, replacing it with metal or plastic containers and providing access to ceramics produced in places as distant as China. During the 4th-6th centuries CE there was certainly no shortage of imported ceramic vessels in the Eastern Desert. The number of vessels that passed through as containers for trade items can only be guessed, but an abundance of vessels is found at the ancient harbors, road stations, mines and quarries throughout the region (Sidebotham et al. 2001, 2002). Some may have been intended for long-distance trade but remained behind because they were damaged or appropriated; others would have contained supplies for those temporarily working and living in the desert. It seems unlikely that the pastoral nomads could not somehow have obtained a sufficient number of vessels from this copious source, and they must have had other, and obviously important, reasons to produce their own.

Mobile potters can try to emulate vessels produced by settled potters, especially when they are already using their imported products, or develop their own type of vessels. The technology will be similar, but nomadic potters will have to develop their own techniques to adjust to their specific environment and needs. Such adaptations are likely to differ from place to place, according to the local situation and the availability of the necessary materials. Features that are not essential, like micaceous temper or red slip, can be omitted, and decorations preferably made with the thorn of a date palm can be made with the thorn of an acacia instead. Several acacia species, such as *Acacia nilotica* and *A. raddiana*, occur in the region where Eastern Desert Ware is found, and several Eastern Desert Ware vessels appear to have been decorated with a round tool. This has left less distinctive marks than the triangular thorn of the date palm but may well have been another thorn, for instance one of the *Acacia* species mentioned above.

The apparent use of date palm thorns on many Eastern Desert Ware vessels is remarkable. As palm fronds are often used for fuel by potters in the Nile Valley, their triangular thorns are readily available to them.[10] In the desert there are very few palm trees, and the use of palm thorns seems therefore indicative of production in the Nile Valley. However, this is not concurrent with the origin of the

---

[10.] Fronds of the doam palm (*Hyphaene thebaica*), rather than those of the date palm (*Phoenix dactylifera*), can also be used for fuel. Doam palms were more abundant in the Nile Valley in ancient times; they have been slowly replaced by date palms because of climatic changes and human intervention. Doam palm fronds carry real thorns on their stem, reminiscent of a rose or bramble branch, with an oval rather than a triangular cross-section.

clay matrix, outside the Nile Valley, as suggested by petrographic and chemical analysis of the fabric. Furthermore, the use of palm thorns to apply incised or impressed decorations on pottery is rarely attested for vessels originating in the Nile Valley after the C-Horizon (2300–1500 BCE). Like Eastern Desert Ware, vessels of the C-Horizon are handmade, partly burnished and decorated with incised decorations, but there is no evidence to suggest continuous production during the 1800 years that separate them, nor of a revival of the C-Horizon culture after Lower Nubia had been under more or less long-lasting Egyptian, Napatan, Meroitic and Roman influence. We must therefore assume that either the clay for Eastern Desert Ware was brought into the Nile Valley, where the vessels were subsequently made and fired, or that palm thorns were taken from the Nile Valley into the desert, to be used for the decoration of Eastern Desert Ware and probably primarily other chores. Many of the current inhabitants of the Eastern Desert live, at least part of the time, in dwellings made of rugs and mats over a dome-shaped wooden frame (Magid, this volume; Wendrich, this volume). These mats are made of palm leafs (from *Phoenix dactylifera* or *Hyphaene thebaica*), to which inhabitants obviously have access, held together by wooden pegs not unlike date palm thorns. Such dwellings appear to be mentioned in Egyptian Middle Kingdom and Late Kingdom texts, while Strabo reports, in the 1st century CE, that the nomads in the desert live in dwellings made of interwoven split pieces of palm leaves (Magid, this volume).

In the period during which Eastern Desert Ware was produced, the 4th–6th century CE, there was a substantial influx of outsiders into the arid landscape between the Nile and the Red Sea. A network of trade routes connected the Mediterranean Basin and the Nile Valley with the Red Sea coast, Arabia, sub-Saharan Africa and India (Sidebotham and Wendrich 1996; Wendrich et al. 2006). Next to these transient traders, the Eastern Desert was more permanently inhabited by numerous quarrymen, miners and early Christian hermits (Sidebotham et al. 2001, 2002, 2005). The resulting infrastructure of settlements, tracks and supplies, not equaled until the development of the Red Sea coast for tourism in the 1990s, allowed the pastoral nomads to settle temporarily when they accepted employment as laborers, guards, guides or prostitutes. Even more fleeting contacts, including those with a hostile nature, must have introduced the indigenous inhabitants of the Eastern Desert to the pottery of the more recent immigrants. Both groups would have benefited from the large volume (attested by the quantity of recovered sherds) of pottery imported into the region. That the mobile inhabitants of the Eastern Desert apparently chose this period of relative plenty to produce their own pottery may be attributed to the following three points.

Being in the same place for a longer period than they probably would have been previously may have enabled the pastoral nomads to see the pottery production process, as reflected in Table 19.1, through for the first time (Eerkens, this volume). The infrastructure that allowed this would also have provided them with the necessary surplus of water and fuel.

Some of the immigrants (traders, miners and quarrymen) may have given more or less detailed instructions, suggestions or inspiration to the nomadic potters. Despite the possibility that they were educated by outsiders, the nomadic potters decided to create their own corpus rather than imitate imported vessels. This decision seems to have been based on their desire to separate themselves from the more recently arrived inhabitants of the Eastern Desert. The growing number of immigrants and their increasing influence, partly fueled by the changing politics of the Roman Empire toward ethnic and cultural minorities, would have increased this need, which sometimes gave rise to violent confrontations (Eide et al. 1998; Barnard 2005).

Finally, sherds of Eastern Desert Ware will necessarily be concentrated near the settlements of its producers and users. The more significant settlements, like those associated with mines, quarries and harbors, will attract the attention of archaeologists prior to the ephemeral campsites of pastoral nomads. Many isolated sherds of Eastern Desert Ware vessels may lay scattered unobserved over the vast stretches of arid landscape between the places where it has so far been found (Figure 19.2; A. B. Smith, this volume). These could date from periods well before and after the time of contact between the indigenous nomads and the immigrant traders, miners and quarrymen. More research, including a more systematic survey of the area, will be necessary to understand the relation between Eastern Desert Ware and the pastoral nomads of the Eastern Desert between the 4th-6th centuries CE.

REFERENCES

Arnold, D. and J. Bourriau (eds.)
1993   *An Introduction to Ancient Egyptian Pottery. Deutsches Archäologisches Institut Abteilung Kairo Sonderschrift 17.* Mainz am Rhein, Verlag Philip von Zabern.
Arnold, D. E.
1985   *Ceramic Theory and Cultural Process.* Cambridge, Cambridge University Press.
Arnold, D. E., H. A. Neff and R. L. Bishop
1991   Compositional Analysis and "Sources" of Pottery: An Ethnoarchaeological Approach. *Journal of Archaeological Method and Theory* 7: pp. 333–375.
Arnold, P. J.
1991   *Domestic Ceramic Production and Spatial Organization: A Mexican Case Study in Ethnoarchaeology.* Cambridge, Cambridge University Press.

Arthur, J. W.

2002   Pottery Use-Alteration as an Indicator of Socioeconomic Status: An Ethnoarchaeological Study of the Gamo of Ethiopia. *Journal of Archaeological Method and Theory 9*: pp. 331–355.

Barnard, H.

1998   Human Bones and Burials. In S. E. Sidebotham and W. Z. Wendrich (eds.), *Berenike 1996: Report of the 1996 Excavations at Berenike (Egyptian Red Sea Coast) and the Survey of the Eastern Desert*. Leiden, Research School CNWS: pp. 389–401.

2002   Eastern Desert Ware: A First Introduction. *Sudan & Nubia 6*: pp. 53–57.

2005   Sire, il n'y a pas de Blemmyes: A Re-evaluation of Historical and Archaeological Data. In J. C. M. Starkey (ed.), *People of the Red Sea: Proceedings of Red Sea Project II. British Archaeological Reports International Series 1395*. Oxford, Archaeopress: pp.23–40.

in press   Eastern Desert Ware from Marsa Nakari and Wadi Sikait. *Journal of the American Research Center in Egypt*.

Barnard, H., S. H. Ambrose, D. E. Beehr, M. D. Forster, R. E. Lanehart, M. E. Malainey, R. E. Parr, M. Rider, C. Solazzo and R. M. Yohe II

2007   Mixed Results of Seven Methods for Organic Residue Analysis Applied to One Vessel with the Residue of a Known Foodstuff. *Journal of Archaeological Science 34*: pp. 28–37.

Barnard, H., A. N. Dooley and K. F. Faull

2006   New Data on the Eastern Desert Ware from Sayala (Lower Nubia) in the Kunsthistorisches Museum, Vienna. *Ägypten und Levante 15*: pp. 49–64.

Barnard, H. and A. A. Magid

2006   Eastern Desert Ware from Tabot (Sudan): More Links to the North. *Archéologie du Nil Moyen 10.*: pp. 15-34.

Barnard, H. and P. J. Rose

in press   Eastern Desert Ware from Berenike and Kab Marfu'a. In S. E. Sidebotham and W. Z. Wendrich (eds.), *Berenike, 1999–2000: Report of the 1999 and 2000 Excavations in Berenike, Siket, and Wadi Kalalat and the Survey of the Egyptian Eastern Desert, Including the Beryl Mines in Wadi Sikait*. Los Angeles, Cotsen Institute of Archaeology.

Barnard, H. and E. Strouhal

2004   Wadi Qitna Revisited. *Annals of the Náprstek Museum Prague 25*: pp. 29–55.

Bedawi, F.A.

1976   *Die Römische Gräberfelder von Sayala-Nubien. Berichte des Österreichischen Nationalkomitees der UNESCO-Aktion für die Rettung der Nubischen Altertümer VI. Philosophisch-Historische Klasse Denkschriften 126*. Vienna, Verlag der Österreichischen Akademie der Wissenschaften.

Bell, J.
1994   Making Pottery at Mata Ortiz. *Kiva: Journal of Southwestern Anthropology and History 60*: 1, pp. 33–70.

Bourriau, J. D., P. T. Nicholson and P. J. Rose
2000   Pottery. In P. T. Nicholson and I. N. Shaw (eds.), *Ancient Egyptian Materials and Technology*. Cambridge, Cambridge University Press: pp. 121–147.

Deal, M.
1998   *Pottery Ethnoarchaeology in the Central Maya Highlands*. Salt Lake City, University of Utah Press.

Eerkens, J. W.
2002   The Preservation and Identification of Piñon Resins by GC-MS in Pottery from the Eastern Great Basin. *Archaeometry 44*: 1, pp. 95–105.

Eide, T., T. Hägg, R. H. Pierce and L. Török
1998   *Fontes Historiae Nubiorum: Textual Sources for the History of the Middle Nile Region Between the Eighth Century BC and the Sixth Century AD. Volume 3: From the First to the Sixth Century AD*. University of Bergen, Department of Greek, Latin, and Egyptology.

Gosselain, O. P.
1992   Technology and Style: Potters and Pottery Among Bafia of Cameroon. *Man (New Series) 27*: pp. 559–586.

Habachi, L.
1967   Tongefässe. In H. Ricke (ed.), *Ausgrabungen von Khor-Dehmit bis Bet El-Wali. The University of Chicago Oriental Institute Nubian Expedition Volume 2*. Chicago, University of Chicago Press: pp. 46–68.

Hertz, N. and E. G. Garrison
1998   *Geological Methods for Archaeology*. New York, Oxford University Press.

Kramer, C.
1997   *Pottery in Rajasthan: Ethnoarchaeology in Two Indian Cities*. Washington, Smithsonian Institution Press.

Kromer, K.
1967   *Römische Weinstuben in Sayala (Unternubien). Berichte des Österreichischen Nationalkomitees der UNESCO-Aktion für die Rettung der Nubischen Altertümer IV. Philosophisch-Historische Klasse Denkschriften 95*. Vienna, Verlag der Österreichischen Akademie der Wissenschaften.

LeFree, B.
1975   *Santa Clara Pottery Today. School of American Research Monograph Series Number 29*. Albuquerque, University of New Mexico Press.

Longacre, W. A. and M. T. Stark
1994   *Kalinga Ethnoarchaeology: Expanding Archaeological Method and Theory*. Washington, Smithsonian Institution Press.

Luft, U., A. Almásy, M. A. Farkas, I. Furka, Z. Horváth and G. Lassányi

2004   Preliminary Report on the Fieldwork at Bir Minih, Arabian Desert. *Mitteilungen des Deutschen Archäologischen Instituts Abteilung Kairo 58*: pp. 373–390.

Magid, A. A.

2004   The Site of Tabot: An Old Waystation in the Southern Red Sea Hills, Sudan. In S. Wenig (ed.), *Neueste Feldforschungen im Sudan und in Eritrea: Akten des Symposiums vom 13 bis 14 Oktober 1999 in Berlin*. Wiesbaden, Harrassowitz Verlag.

Murray, G. M.

1935   *Sons of Ishmael: A Study of the Egyptian Bedouin*. London, George Routledge.

Nordström, H.-Å.

2004   Pottery Production. In D. A. Welsby and J. R. Anderson (eds.), *Sudan, Ancient Treasures: An Exhibition of Recent Discoveries from the Sudan*. London, National Museum: cat. no. 255 (p. 269).

Paul, A.

1954   *A History of the Beja Tribes of the Sudan*. Cambridge, Cambridge University Press.

Rice, P. M.

1987   *Pottery Analysis: A Sourcebook*. Chicago, University of Chicago Press.

1996   Recent Ceramic Analysis. *Journal of Archaeological Research 4*: pp. 133–202.

Ritner, R. K.

1993   *The Mechanics of Ancient Egyptian Magical Practice. Studies in Ancient Oriental Civilization 54*. Chicago, Oriental Institute of the University of Chicago.

Rose, P. J.

1995   Report on the Handmade Sherds. In S. E. Sidebotham and W. Z. Wendrich (eds.), *Berenike 1994: Preliminary Report of the 1994 Excavations at Berenike (Egyptian Red Sea Coast) and the Survey of the Eastern Desert*. Leiden, Research School CNWS: pp. 41–43.

Rye, O. S.

1981   *Pottery Technology: Principles and Reconstruction. Manuals on Archaeology 4*. Washington, Taraxacum.

Sadr, K., Alf. Castiglioni and Ang. Castiglioni

1995   Nubian Desert Archaeology: A Preliminary View. *Archéologie du Nil Moyen 7*: pp. 203–235 .

Schiffer, M. B., J. M. Skibo, T. C. Boelke, M. A. Neupert and M. Arenson

1994   New Perspectives on Experimental Archaeology: Surface Treatments and Thermal Response of the Clay Cooking Pot. *American Antiquity 59*: pp. 197–217.

Shepard, A. O.

1976   *Ceramics for the Archaeologist*. Washington, Carnegie Institution (fifth printing of the 1954 manuscript).

Sidebotham, S. E., H. Barnard, J. A. Harrell and R. S. Tomber

2001   The Roman Quarry and Installations in Wadi Umm Wikala and Wadi Semna. *Journal of Egyptian Archaeology 87*: pp. 135–170.

Sidebotham, S. E., H. Barnard, L. A. Pintozzi and R. S. Tomber

2005   The Enigma of Kab Marfu'a: Precious Gems in Egypt's Eastern Desert. *Minerva 16*: 1, pp. 24–26.

Sidebotham, S. E., H. Barnard and G. Pyke

2002   Five Enigmatic Late Roman Settlements in the Eastern Desert. *Journal of Egyptian Archaeology 88*: pp.187–225.

Sidebotham, S. E. and W. Z. Wendrich

1996   Interpretative Summary and Conclusion. In S. E. Sidebotham and W. Z. Wendrich (eds.), *Berenike 1995: Preliminary Report of the 1995 Excavations at Berenike (Egyptian Red Sea Coast) and the Survey of the Eastern Desert*. Leiden, Research School CNWS: Figures 1–2, 1–3 (pp. 3–4), pp. 441–452.

Stark, M. T.

1991   Ceramic Production and Community Specialization: A Ceramic Ethno-archaeological Study. *World Archaeology 23*: pp. 64–78.

2003   Current Issues in Ceramic Ethnoarchaeology. *Journal of Archaeological Research 11*: 3, pp. 193–242.

Strouhal, E.

1984   *Wadi Qitna and Kalabsha-South: Late Roman-Early Byzantine Tumuli Cemeteries in Egyptian Nubia. Volume 1: Archaeology*. Prague, Charles University.

Wendrich, W. Z., R. S. Bagnall, R.T. J. Cappers, J. A. Harrell, S. E. Sidebotham and R. S. Tomber

2006   Berenike Crossroads: The Integration of Information. In N. Yoffee and B. L. Crowell (eds.), *Excavating Asian History: Interdisciplinary Studies in Archaeology and History*. Tucson, University of Arizona Press: pp. 15–66 (an earlier version appeared in the *Journal of the Economic and Social History of the Orient 46*, 1; 2003: pp. 46–87).

Wisner, M.

1999   The Ceramic Technology of Mata Ortiz. In S. Lowell (ed.), *The Many Faces of Mata Ortiz*. Tucson, Rio Nuevo Publishers: pp. 187–197.

CHAPTER 20

HISTORY OF THE NOMADIC ARCHITECTURE OF THE HADENDOWA IN NORTHEAST SUDAN

ANWAR ABDEL-MAGID[1]

T HE HADENDOWA IS the largest and politically dominant group among the Beja tribal confederation. The other main groups are the Bisharyyin, the Amarar (Paul 1971:18-19, 21; Vaagenes 1990:35; Egemi 1994:2; Manger 1996:19; Nautrup 2004:11), and the Atman (Vaagenes 1990:35; Hjort af Ornäs and Dahl 1991:1). All of these tribal groups are believed to be indigenous inhabitants of the area between the Nile River and the Red Sea Hills in the Sudan (Figure 20.1). They speak an unwritten Cushitic language called *Tu-Bedawie* (Walker 1987; Vaagenes 1990:35, 1998:1; Hjort af Ornäs and Dahl 1991:2; Egemi 1994:2).

There is a fifth tribal group, called the Beni Amer, that is believed to be among the indigenous inhabitants of the Southern Red Sea Hills in Sudan. As they speak a different language, *Tigre*, their connection to the Beja remains a controversial issue. Some researchers, like Egemi (1994:2), regard them as a separate group, whereas others, like Manger (1996:19), Paul (1971:21) and Vaagenes (1990:35), consider them one of the Beja tribal groups. The Beja, especially the Hadendowa, do not consider the Beni Amer as one of their tribal groups. Nautrup (2004:11) assumes that the Beni Amer are part of the Beja tribal confederation but emphasizes that their language difference creates a 'symbolic difference' between them and other Beja groups.

More Beja tribal and subtribal groups live in the Red Sea Hills area and further south in Kassala State and along the River Atbara. Detailed accounts on these, including their origins and their history, are presented in several

[1.] I am grateful for the help that I received during the process of data collection and the writing of this chapter from Professor Leif Ole Manger and Professor Richard Holton Pierce of the University of Bergen (Norway), from Hans Barnard of the University of California, Los Angeles (USA) and from Krzysztof Pluskota.

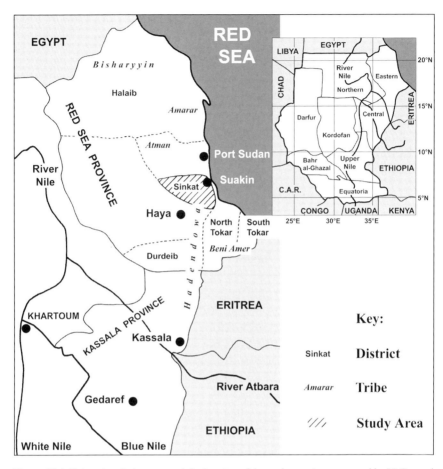

Figure 20.1. Beja main tribal groups and the location of the study area (map prepared by H. Barnard after Manger et al. 1996:204).

publications (Seligmann 1913:593–705; Owen 1937:183; Murdock 1959:315; Arkell 1961:170; Paul 1971:12–37, 137–139; Holt and Daly 1979:1). Nomadic pastoralism based on the rearing of livestock has always been the basic element of the economy of the Beja (Egemi 1994:84). They are probably one of the earliest pastoral groups, not only in Northeast Africa (Grigg 1974:119) but in Africa at large (Murdock 1959:314). Egemi (1994:86) believes them to be "the first pastoralists to inhabit Sudan." Fattovich (1993:445) suggests that in 2000–1500 BCE the pastoral Gash Delta Group people "spread to the east and north, as far as the Red Sea coast, occupying the whole northern Ethiopian-Sudanese borderland." Fattovich did not, however, engage in discussing the relationship between the Gash group and the Beja. In his book *Surat al-ard*, written in 988 CE, the Arab geographer Ibn Haugal described the Beja as pastoral nomads wandering about with their animals in search of good pasture and water in the area extending from the Nile River to the Red Sea and from Egypt to Eritrea (Ibn Haugal 1979). Historically, the emergence of the Hadendowa (as well as the Bisharyyin and Amarar) can be traced to the 15th–16th centuries CE (Paul 1971:25).[2]

The Beja and the Hadendowa can hardly be studied without taking into account the role of the camel and its impact on their lifestyle. There is no doubt that the introduction of the camel and the spread of its use in the Beja territory was a landmark that redefined pastoral economic strategies, demographic mobility, social structure and political power. Most of these issues are beyond the scope of this chapter, which will focus on the effects of the introduction of the camel on the nomadic architecture. The camel has been used as a pack and riding animal in the Eastern Deserts of Egypt and Sudan since the 3rd century BCE (Prussin 1995:14). As the oldest pastoral groups roaming the area, the ancient Beja must have been owners and breeders of camel since the 3rd century BCE, if not earlier. The earliest direct evidence for the camel's being used as a pack animal for the nomadic dwellings of the Beja dates to the 14th century CE (Burckhardt 1822:182; Vantini 1975:621). This, however, cannot be considered the earliest date for the use of the camel in the Beja territory.

The introduction of the camel greatly facilitated the transport of the dwellings and belongings of the Beja across their otherwise impenetrable territory. It enabled them to reach far pastures, to keep larger herds of livestock, and to obtain new building and furnishing materials from the wool and hides of those herds. Ethnographic and anthropological research among the Hadendowa has shown that the camel is indispensable to transport their nomadic dwellings, furnishings and baggage whenever they travel "distances in excess of a dozen kilometres" (Ausenda 1987:192). When traveling shorter distances than that, donkeys are also used, especially in the southern part of the Hadendowa area (in Kassala State). It takes four to six trips with a donkey to move all parts and furnishings of a dwelling. It has been reported that, in emergency situations like floods or fire, a man can move his dwelling over a maximum of one kilometer taking at least fifteen trips to bring all components of the tents to safety (Ausenda 1987:192). This clearly illustrates that it is labor intensive and time consuming to move nomadic dwellings, even over limited distances, without the help of a camel.

Until the late 19th and early 20th centuries CE the Hadendowa had large herds of cattle and smaller herds of camels in their territory, which extends from the Sinkat District in the Southern Red Sea Hills to the Gash Delta in

---

[2.] Egemi (1994:86) implies that the Hadendowa have been known since the 10th century CE.

Kassala State (Seligmann 1913; Sadr 1991). Paul (1971:16) also reports that large herds of cattle were kept in these areas. Repeated droughts and increased aridity, especially in the northern part of their territory, forced the Hadendowa, like many other pastoral groups in the Sahel zone, to abandon cattle herding and to rear camels, sheep and goats instead. They also cultivate *Sorghum vulgare* (*durra* in Arabic) after the infrequent rainfall. The subtribal groups of the Hadendowa who inhabit Kassala State still keep small herds of cattle. As they are more settled, they practice flush-irrigated cultivation of sorghum on a regular basis. Nevertheless, the characteristic feature of Hadendowa life is mobility, in search for water and pasture. The type of dwellings they use reflects their economic and environmental adaptation to the landscape, as well as their customs. It is in the area of the northern Hadendowa (in the Sinkat District) that I carried out archaeological, ethnographic and ethno-archaeological research. This included a study of the Hadendowa past and present nomadic architecture.

NORTH AFRICAN NOMADIC TENT DWELLINGS

Theoretically and academically, *tent* has been defined as "an eminently practical, completely portable house demonstrating all the principal elements of permanent architecture" (Cribb 1991:85). Architecturally, a tent may be defined as "a prefabricated structure consisting of a flexible covering and structural supports temporarily brought together to form an integrated architectural unit" (Cribb 1991:85). Both definitions encompass a variety of architectural units ranging from extremely temporary and disposable to more permanent, and all combine a tent form with a house function. The Hadendowa nomadic dwelling fulfills all the elements and variables of these definitions. The data collected during my fieldwork show that the Hadendowa people know and distinguish between a tent form and a house function, yet they consider and call their nomadic dwelling 'a house' (*beit* in Arabic). One is tempted to suggest that such use and understanding are meant to emphasize a functional rather than an architectural purpose. My Hadendowa informants, however, offered a cultural explanation, asserting the distance and distinction between the Hadendowa and other nomadic groups residing in the area and neighboring territories (like the Rashaida Arabs). We do not know whether similar tendencies existed among past Beja populations. The name of the nomadic dwelling of the contemporary Hadendowa is *Badaigaw*, meaning 'mat-house' (*beit al-birsh* in Arabic). This is self-defining and explicitly proclaims such a dwelling to be a house made from mats. These 'houses' are contrasted to 'mud houses,' 'sun-baked brick houses' and 'burnt-brick houses' emphasizing that houses have a range of which the Hadendowa dwelling is one form. The Hadendowa conception and naming of their dwelling as houses is consistent with the definition of a house as "a building intended for human habitation, especially one used as residence of a family" (*Merriam-Webster's Dictionary*) or "a building which people, usually a family, live in" (*Cambridge Dictionary*). Owen (1937:204–205) seems to have been one of the first authors to describe the Hadendowa dwellings as 'houses' rather than as 'tents' indicating his understanding of their culture. Murray (1978:80) reports that the Bedouin of the Sinai call their tent a 'hair house' (*beit al-sha`ar* in Arabic), while they use 'tent (*kheima* in Arabic) to denote a European-style canvas tent.

In the literature on the nomadic groups and their dwellings in North Africa the reader often encounters confusion in the use and meaning of the terms *house*, *tent*, *hut*, *dwelling*, *shelter*, and so forth. For instance, Nicolaisen (1963:327, 332–349), in his ethnographic study of the Tuareg of the Sahara Desert, uses the term *hut* to denote three types of permanently built dwellings. Lewis (1969:67) uses the same term to describe both the portable skin- and mat-covered dwellings of the Somali nomads in East Africa and the permanent dwellings of farmers in the same region (Lewis 1969:85). In other instances, different terms are used to describe a single type of portable nomadic dwelling. Murray (1978:81) called the portable nomadic dwellings of the Beja 'huts' while Prussin (1995:5) calls the same dwellings 'tents.' Another confusing use of the terms is evident in the work of Oliver (1971:25–35) who used the terms *shelter* and *tent* to describe the dwellings of the nomadic Kababish nomadic group in western Sudan. I propose the term *tent-dwelling* (*maskan* in Arabic) when referring to the ancient and present nomadic architecture of the Beja and the Hadendowa, particularly those dwellings in which mat coverings are used. In this chapter the term *tent-dwelling* denotes 'a temporary and spacious structure meant for human habitation, architecturally designed to meet a particular need to suit a mobile pattern of exploitation of natural resources and, at the same time, to symbolize an expression of cultural personality.'

The oldest and simplest form of human-made dwellings is probably a frame of one, or several, poles, or rods, covered with bark, skin, grass, reeds or mats. Prehistoric hunter-gatherers were perhaps the first to invent this type of dwelling, which continues to exist among contemporary hunter-gatherer groups (Rosen, this volume). Skins are among the rewards of hunting; bark, reeds, grass or leaves were used where available. All these materials are flexible and can be folded or rolled and neatly packed and moved. Similar to early hunter-gatherer practice, early pastoral nomadic groups most likely took the covers and left the frame (the heavy and nonflexible poles or rods) behind when they moved as "it is easier to cut new poles than to carry the old ones along" (Faegre 1979:60–61). Obviously, if people moved in areas where wood is scarce, the frame must have been taken along as well, their poles or rods lightened as much as possible. As the tent-dwelling is set up and dismantled many times, systems making the disassembling, transportation and subsequent assemblage easier undergo continual improvement and modification to adapt to changing environments, building materials and resources, as well as to meet cultural and individual preferences (Faegre 1979:60–61).

Prussin (1995:54) divides the tent-dwellings of the African pastoral groups into two basic types: tensile structures and armatures. A tensile structure consists of a central pole (or system of poles) kept in position by stretching a sheet (or sheets) of membranous covering or coating tightly over the pole. One form of tensile structure, commonly called a tent, is architecturally based on the structural interdependence between the pole(s) and the covering(s). The armature has a system of poles that, unlike those of the tensile, can stand up independently without any tight covering. The type or form of covering, or the tension it puts on the pole(s), has no structural function (Faegre 1979; Prussin 1995).

Some have suggested a simple evolutionary development from an armature to a tensile structure without providing cultural, economic or environmental reasons for such development. Others, like Prussin (1995:55), note that the architecture of the dwellings of African nomadic groups does not always follow this evolutionary sequence. Sometimes the transitions are retrograde, and in other instances both types, tensile and armature, co-exist. There are also forms of African nomadic architectural structures that appear to be composites between armature and tensile structures. The contemporary Hadendowa dwellings, portable structures consisting of a frame of wooden poles covered with mats, can be regarded as such a composite type because they combine the structural interdependence between the wooden frames (of the tensile structure) and the independent coverings that characterize the armature structure.

THE HADENDOWA TENT-DWELLING

The emphasis of this chapter is on the history of the Hadendowa nomadic architecture, its development and its economic, social, symbolic and environmental implications. A few problems were encountered during the process of data collection and analysis. First, previous research on the history of the Hadendowa nomadic dwellings was scarce and fragmentary. Furthermore, the Hadendowa nomadic dwellings were, and still are, made of perishable building materials of organic origin. These materials (wood, leather, wool, etc.) decay and perish over time. It is therefore difficult to find the evidence of ancient dwellings or settlements. The settlements and campsites of the Hadendowa are often occupied for a short time, which does not allow for the accumulation, and recovery, of indicative cultural debris. Because of their continuous movement, pastoral groups tend to have few possessions or tools, most of which are multifunctional and lightweight. When a nomadic dwelling is moved, what is left behind is a hearth, a few shallow postholes, some stones and perhaps fragments of broken pottery or grinding stones. These will get buried, blown or washed away by wind, rain or the water running off the mountains in a gully or stream (*khor* or *wadi* in Arabic). The Hadendowa area is predominantly mountainous, which adds to the other constraints on finding archaeological evidence of nomadic dwellings. The mobile settlement pattern of the Beja, the perishable nature of the building materials of their dwellings, and the rocky nature of the Red Sea Hills are the three main reasons for the lack of archaeological evidence for this people (but see Saidel, this volume).

The research questions of this study of the Hadendowa tent-dwellings include the following:

— Did the Hadendowa once have types of dwellings other than the contemporary mat house (the *Badaigaw*), and, if so, what was the nature and architectural structure of these dwellings?

— How far back can we trace the history of the contemporary *Badaigaw* and the other types of dwellings, if any existed?

— What are the forms and designs of the earlier types of dwellings, and how did they develop over time?

— Were these forms of dwellings subject to change as a result of external influence after contacts with other regions?

— How is the development associated with the changes in environmental conditions and the Hadendowa economy?

In the course of discussing these questions, I will also deal with issues related to the history of the ancient nomadic architecture, such as the building technology, the transportation technology and the symbolism associated with these structures. There is textual and archaeological evidence indicating that the history of the nomadic dwellings in the Beja territory is much older than the emergence of the contemporary Beja tribal groups, including the Hadendowa. It should also be emphasized that the contemporary Beja nomadic dwellings as used by the various tribal groups seem to be closely related, exhibiting similarities in frame structure, form, coverings and building material. Therefore, the present study deals with the ancient history of the nomadic dwellings in the Beja territory as a whole.[3] Mention is made where there is any concrete evidence of specific names or areas.

The study of the ancient nomadic dwellings in the territory of the contemporary Beja would not be complete without considering the history of similar

---

[3] Whether past population(s) that lived in the territory of the contemporary Beja are related to or different from the present Beja population is a question beyond the scope of this chapter (see Burstein, this volume).

and related ancient dwellings within the wider context of North Africa. The first written evidence for tent-dwellings in Egypt is found in royal correspondence from Dynasty VI (2325–2175 BCE), in which no information on the shape of these dwellings is provided (Prussin 1995:7).[4] Textual evidence from around 1500 BCE indicates that the tent became part of Egyptian military equipment because all references are in a military context (Drew 1979:5). Reliefs in Luxor and Abu Simbel clearly show Egyptian royal and military tents, but no information is available on the materials from which these were built, how they were built, or if any tents existed that were used by ordinary people (Prussin 1995:7). Other textual sources indicate that the ancestors of the contemporary Beja tribal groups first came to the attention of the Egyptians around 1900 BCE. The first depiction of a 'Bejawie' (probably related to the modern Beja) appears in a Dynasty XII (1991–1786 BCE) tomb-chapel in Upper Egypt, but there is no reference to any type of Beja dwellings or to the name of the owner of the tomb (Prussin 1995:6). It is possible that the ancient Bejawie resided in tent-dwellings as mentioned in the Egyptian texts and even that the Egyptian tent was adopted from the tent-dwellings used by the Bejawie people.

Later archaeological and textual evidence provides us with more, although still incomplete, information on the history of the Beja tent-dwelling. The available data indicate that the area has had a pastoral nomadic population since times immemorial (Burckhardt 1822; Seligmann 1913; el-Maqrizi 1922; Owen 1937; Paul 1971; Hasan 1975; Vantini 1975; Updegraff 1978; Egemi 1994). Their dwellings were characterized by their simple design, their light weight and the ease with which they could be dismantled, moved and reconstructed. The contemporary Beja mat tent-dwellings illustrate these characteristics. Several sources mention skin, hair and mat tent-dwellings (Burckhardt 1822; el-Maqrizi 1922; Paul 1971; Vantini 1975; Prussin 1995). The mat tent-dwelling is the only type that has survived and has continued to be commonly used by the modern Beja. A detailed documentation on the contemporary Hadendowa mat tent-dwelling will be the subject of an in-progress ethnographic study on the social and spatial symbolism of the contemporary nomadic architecture of the Hadendowa tribal group in northeast Sudan. Therefore, the following focuses on the ancient skin, hair and mat tent-dwellings.

SKIN TENT-DWELLINGS

One of the earliest mentions of leather tent-dwellings in North Africa, used mainly by soldiers, dates to the Egyptian Middle Kingdom (1975–1640 BCE).

[4.] The given dates of the ancient Egyptian dynasties are those suggested by Baines and Malek (2000:36–37).

Of interest here is a remark in the story of Sinuhe, around 1875 BCE, in which it is mentioned that Sinuhe stayed with the Bedouin who live in tents in the desert between Egypt and Palestine (Helck and Otto 1983:1372). It is implied that these tents were made of leather. Other textual evidence indicates that these Bedouin were living in present-day northeast Sudan and southeast Egypt (Sadr 1991). Leather tents may also have been used by the Libyans who came to Egypt around 1194–1188 BCE, but it is not clear whether they brought these tents or used tents that they found in Egypt (Roe, this volume; Helck and Otto 1986:1372). Egyptian accounts on military campaigns against the Syrians also mention tents. In 1274 BCE the Egyptians captured the son of the Syrian king of Qadesh and took the tent in which he was found. Assyrian reliefs on this event include drawings that clearly show what this tent looked like. An intriguing remark by Prussin (1995:7–8) states that the mat tent-dwellings of the contemporary Hadendowa "bear close resemblance to the structure of the ancestral Assyrian tents." In addition, Prussin states that the two Egyptian terms used in Dynasty XIX texts (1292–1190 BCE) imply that the Nubians, against whom the Egyptians were fighting, used mats and leather as coverings for their tents (Prussin 1995:7). On the basis of this evidence Prussin argues that the Egyptian army, finding the southern Nubian tent suitable to their needs, may have adopted and used it.

The earliest archaeological evidence of leather tent-dwellings in North Africa dates to Dynasty XXI (1075–945 BCE) and consists of a large leather tent found among royal mummies in what was originally a Dynasty XI tomb complex (Brugsch 1891). The hieroglyphic texts on the leather indicate that the tent belonged to Isimkheb, a princess and high priestess, and that it was a funerary symbol of a high-ranking office (Prussin 1995:7–8). This tent was made of the skins of hundreds of goats and gazelles (Prussin 1995:7). An intriguing question has been raised regarding the possibility of its being related to the Beja (Prussin 1995:8). As no information is available on its supports and its shape when erected, the nature of its relation to the Beja, as suggested by Prussin, remains unclear.

The first and second centuries CE were the period of contact between the Romans and the indigenous pastoral tribes in North Africa. These contacts involved exchange and adaptation of the type of dwellings these pastoral groups used at the time. It has been reported that during their military campaigns in Africa, the Roman soldiers slept in skin tents. These tents consisted of a velum made of a number of calf or goat skins, stitched together to form rectangular coverings. These were fixed to a pole and held taut with ropes (Prussin 1995:7–8). A 310–330 CE mosaic showing hunting scenes and tents was found at Hippo Reguis on the Mediterranean coast. Tents are also shown on a mosaic from around 300 CE, found at Oudna in Tunisia, depicting a rural scene.

When the Arabs arrived in North Africa, during the 7th century CE, a large network of trade routes was developed linking the West African coast to the Red Sea and further east across the Red Sea into modern Saudi Arabia. These trade routes provided a stimulus for the spread, exchange and adaptation of nomadic architectural knowledge and technology. By the 11th century CE nomadic dwellings were in use all over this vast area (Prussin 1995:7–8). At present, the northern Tuareg of the Sahara are renowned for their skin tent-dwellings (Faegre 1979:29; Prussin 1995:6). Skin tents are also used by other contemporary nomadic groups roaming the western Sahara, for instance the Teda. Skin and mat tent-dwellings are also reported to be in use by pastoral groups living in the deserts of Egypt, Sudan, Ethiopia and Somalia (Faegre 1979:64).

During my archaeological survey and excavations in the southern Red Sea Hills, mainly in the Hadendowa area, I neither saw skin tent-dwellings nor was I told about the presence of this type of dwelling anywhere in the area. The archaeological survey and excavations conducted in the southern Red Sea Hills area did not yield any evidence of exclusively nomadic camp or settlement sites. Thus, our only sources are the fragmentary accounts of historians, early travelers and geographers who traveled in the area. Among these is the medieval Arab historian el-Maqrizi (around 1300 CE) who described the Beja as a nomadic people living in tent-dwellings made of skin. He also stated that they kept large numbers of 'well-bred, long horned' cattle, as well as camels, sheep and goats, and that they roamed the area searching for good pasture for their animals (el-Maqrizi 1922). On the basis of this account one could infer that, contrary to the present time, the climatic conditions were less arid and more favorable for large herds of cattle, camel, sheep and goats. Even though el-Maqrizi tells us that the tent of the Beja magician has a dome shape (Vantini 1975:631), he does not specify what type of hides was used, if the hides used were treated (tanned), or how many hides were needed to build this or other types of tent-dwellings.

The archaeological evidence for the presence of cattle, sheep and goats in the Beja territory predates the account of el-Maqrizi by thousands of years, suggesting a population of cattle pastoralists in what was then a savannah environment (Sadr 1991). A text dating about 2575 BCE states that the Egyptian king Snofru invaded the land of the Beja and Nubia and returned to Egypt with 200,000 head of cattle (Sadr 1991:93). Excavations at the site of Tabot in the southern Red Sea Hills, west of Sinkat, revealed bones of cattle, sheep and goats with a radiocarbon date of 225 CE ±60 (Magid 1998). A large rock drawing found at the site of Samadi, also situated in the southern Red Sea Hills, west of Sinkat, portrays a large number of herds of long-horned cattle. The date of this drawing is unknown, but burial tombs found in its vicinity have been dated to the 3rd century CE (Magid et al. 1995). This is consistent with the fact that the Beja tribes owned large herds of cattle and camels until a hundred years ago (Seligmann 1913; Paul 1971; Sadr 1991). Historical sources (Paul 1971:16), oral history (Dirar 1992:731), and field observations (Nautrup 2004:268) also report that the Hadendowa bred cattle and that it was the women who did the tanning and built the tent-dwellings.

Complementary evidence includes the undated rock paintings in the mountain massif of Tassili and Ajjer in the central Sahara. These show accurate "renditions of the nomadic ethnographic present" (Prussin 1995:4). One of the paintings shows a woman, surrounded by herds of cattle, holding a bent wooden frame used for an armature tent-dwelling in a form similar to that of the contemporary Rendille nomads, in Somalia, and the contemporary Hadendowa. Another painting portrays an accurate elevation of a tent armature (Prussin 1995:4). It has been stated that the dome frame, made of bent poles, is not only the most commonly used frame for the African nomadic tent-dwellings but also that it is "undoubtedly the oldest" (Faegre 1979:62) in both West and East Africa. The women of the contemporary nomadic Tuareg and Teda in the Sahara are known for their outstanding skills as leather workers. They produce both the skin tent-dwellings and the leather farthings of these dwellings (Faegre 1979:65). The most commonly used skin for the cover of the skin tent-dwelling is that of goats, but sheepskin is also used. Cattle skin is used where available (western Sudan). Treatment and preparation of the skin includes the removal of the hair and tanning with fruits and bark of the *Acacia arabica*. It is smeared with butter or tar to make it water resistant, soft and foldable. Ethnographic studies among contemporary pastoral nomads in Africa show that cattle hide is less desirable because it shrinks and hardens when it dries after being exposed to (rain)water (Faegre 1979:70). The coverings of very large Tuareg tent-dwellings are made of as many as 150 goatskins, while an average size tent-dwelling is made of 30–40. The tent-dwelling of a typical contemporary nomadic Danakil in Ethiopia has a diameter of around 3.3 m and is about 1.3 m high at the center (Faegre 1979:75). Such a dwelling can be made with only 10–15 goatskins.

From the archaeological evidence of nomadic dwellings from the central Sahara, and the ethnographic parallels from both the Sahara and East Africa, it can be inferred that the ancient skin tent-dwellings of the Beja were dome shaped with a wooden frame and that women were responsible for both processing the building materials and building the actual dwelling. The tradition of such skin tent-dwelling probably dates back thousands of years. Classic sources and accounts of travelers and geographers on the Beja attest to the presence of skin tent-dwellings in the Beja territory at least six to seven centuries after the arrival of the Arabs. There are strong indications that skin tent-dwellings used by the 'ancient' Beja were similar to those used by the ancestors of the contemporary Tuareg and by other nomadic groups in West and East Africa. Accordingly, there are reasons to assume that the African skin tent-dwelling (including that of the 'ancient' Beja) was one of the products of an indigenous African nomadic architecture.

Neither the written sources, the archaeological evidence, nor the oral tradition indicate when and why the use of the skin tent-dwellings was abandoned. A steady decrease of the rainfall may have been the main factor that led to a marked reduction in both the size and composition of the herds leading to the abandonment of skin tent-dwellings for which substantial numbers of skins are required.

HAIR TENT-DWELLINGS

Information on the ancient hair tent-dwellings of the Beja is mostly obtained from the accounts of early travelers and geographers writing about the region. The earliest of these are by Arab writers like al-Istakhari (932–950 CE), Ibn Haugal (around 977 CE) and al-Hamadhani (Vantini 1975:112, 151, 633; Ibn Haugal 1979). They report that the Beja live in hair tent-dwellings but do not name the animal(s) providing the hair or the shape of the tent, although al-Hamadhani describes the hair of the tent as being 'woven.' Two centuries later, el-Maqrizi wrote about the Beja territory, its environment, wildlife, vegetation, its people and their food, economic strategies, spiritual life and some of their customs and habits (el-Maqrizi 1922:280). Of interest here is their diet, which consisted of only milk and meat. This indicates the importance of the animal herds that they owned. El-Maqrizi also made a general remark on the dwellings of the Beja, describing them as tents made of hair and skin.

Reporting on his visit to a Beja, and most likely Hadendowa, encampment in the early 19th century CE, Burckhardt tells us that he found tents of woven hair supported by bent poles (Ausenda 1987). Although Burckhardt did not provide detailed information on the structural architecture or form of these dwellings, his general description of the frame as having bent poles suggests that the hair tent-dwellings have a dome shape. If this inference is correct, then there is reason to believe that, similar to the skin and the contemporary mat tent-dwellings, the frame structure of the ancient Beja hair tent-dwelling was a product of an indigenous nomadic architecture. During my survey and archaeological excavations in the southern Red Sea Hills, I did not see hair tent-dwellings, nor did I find any archaeological evidence or traces indicating the presence of these in the past. Knowledgeable informants from the Hadendowa area could not recall having ever seen or having ever been told about Beja dwellings made of animal hair.

Unlike the Beja, some of the pastoral nomadic groups in North Africa replaced their traditional dome-shaped skin and mat tent-dwellings with a modified form of the Arabian rectangular 'black tent' (Saidel, this volume; Faegre 1979:62). Examples of these groups in Sudan are the al-Rashaida in East Sudan,[5] the Kababish in West Sudan and other pastoral groups in North Africa, such as the Berber of the Djebel Nefousa in Tunisia. They have introduced some modifications that gave the tent an African "characteristic profile of a high curved ridge line instead of the Arabian flat roof" (Faegre 1979:29). This means that the history of the 'black tent' in North Africa is not older than the arrival of the Arabs in Africa, in the 7th century CE. The black tent is a tensile structure that requires few vertical wooden poles and few tension bands. Goat hair is predominantly used for making the black tent, which explains its name, but sheep wool and camel hair are often added. Women design and make the black tent. It casts adequate shade, while its loose weaves allow good ventilation. The hair provides warmth during cold winter nights (Faegre 1979:7–12).

Accounts on the Beja territory in the 10th-19th centuries CE describe plants and animals similar to those existing today in the savannah zone, at least 700 km further south. This shows that the climatic conditions were once less arid than today. Because a hair tent-dwelling will leak after prolonged rain and become too heavy for its frame structure, it is likely that such dwellings were not desirable in such a wet climate (Faegre 1979:12). The earliest date for the presence of hair tent-dwellings in the Beja area is from the 10th century CE, almost three centuries after the Arabs arrived in North Africa. The dome-shaped type of the hair tent-dwelling continued to be used in the Beja area until, or shortly after, the late 19th century CE.

Available sources do not show who was responsible for building the hair tent-dwelling in the Beja territory. But the building of other ancient and contemporary Beja types of tent-dwellings is assigned to women. Ethnographic studies among North African pastoral groups show that the collection, preparation and processing of the building material, as well as the building and maintenance of the hair tent-dwelling, are performed by the women. It is therefore most likely that building and maintaining the hair tent-dwelling of the Beja was also performed by women. The history of the hair tent-dwelling in the Beja area is short compared to that of the skin and mat dwellings. The construction resembles the older tent-dwellings in form and frame structure (a dome shape on a bent wooden frame). Goat hair was probably the preferred fiber to make the tent covering, but sheep wool and camel hair may also have been used. It is not possible to infer the size of the dwellings or the amount of hair needed to build each type of dwelling.

[5.] The Rashaida are an Arab pastoral group who migrated from Saudi Arabia to the Sudan about 150 years ago (Egemi 1994).

The presence of a dome-shaped hair tent-dwelling in the Beja area can be explained in two ways. The Beja may have borrowed the idea and technology of making a woven-hair covering for their traditional dome-shaped frame structure. Unlike other North African pastoral groups who adopted the Arabian rectangular hair tent, the Beja were apparently reluctant to embrace this dwelling, despite their gradual Islamization and intermarriage with the Arab invaders. This resistance may, on the one hand, have been based on sociocultural or political reasons. On the other hand, the Arabs who settled in the Beja territory and intermarried with the Beja may have adopted the traditional dome-shaped frame structure, while retaining the hair covering of their Arabian black tents. In other words, the Arabs who settled in the Beja area may have adapted the hair covering of their rectangular nomadic dwellings to the dome-shaped frames used by the Beja.

MAT TENT-DWELLINGS

The contemporary mat tent-dwelling is the most common, if not the only, form of housing used by the present nomadic Hadendowa and other Beja nomadic groups (Figure 20.2). The archaeological survey and test excavation carried out in the southern Red Sea Hills yielded no evidence of any form of mat tent-dwellings. Textual sources and ethnographic sources, however, provide some information about the history of the mat tent-dwelling of both the Beja and the Hadendowa.

Figure 20.2. Typical Hadendowa *Badaigaw* (mat tent-dwelling).

The earliest mention of mat tent-dwellings occurs in a text dated to Dynasty XIX (1292–1190 BCE), which suggests that the Nubians used both mat and skin tent-dwellings (Prussin 1995:7). Although there is no reference in the text to dwellings of the population inhabiting the territory of the contemporary Beja, it is likely that they used similar dwellings. This assumption is based on the suggestion that the Egyptian skin tent-dwelling of Dynasty XXI (1075–945 BCE) was a modified version of the Nubian or Beja skin tent-dwelling and that mat tent-dwellings were known in Egypt since the Old Kingdom (Helck and Otto 1986:1372; Prussin 1995:8). In the 1st century CE Strabo reports that the Beja nomadic housing was "built by interweaving split pieces of palm leaves" (Prussin 1995:6). But Strabo stopped short of pointing out who was responsible for building the mat dwellings or of describing their form and frame structure.

Evidence, both archaeological and ethnographic, from elsewhere in North Africa provides pointers that may help fill in these gaps in our knowledge. This evidence includes ethnographic studies that show that the Beja mat tent-dwelling is closely related to that of the contemporary pastoral Tuareg and Teda in the Sahara Desert (Faegre 1979:75). The archaeological evidence from Tassili and Ajjer, in the central Sahara, indicates that the contemporary Tuareg and Teda mat tent-dwelling is a product of a building practice that existed at the time when these rock paintings were made. It has been stated that the form of the present Hadendowa mat tent-dwelling bears close resemblance to that of an Assyrian tent depicted on an Assyrian relief (Prussin 1995:8). Furthermore, the oral tradition among the Hadendowa indicates that the contemporary building practice, as well as the form and frame, of the mat tent-dwellings has been known in the area since time immemorial. Accounts of early Arab travelers and compilers, as for instance el-Maqrizi, include description of different species of trees that may have provided the raw materials for a mat tent-dwelling. These include the doam palm (*Hyphaene thebaica*) and *Ziziphus spina-christi*. The accounts also contain detailed descriptions of species of plants concurrent with conditions similar to a savannah type of environment (el-Maqrizi 1922:270; Vantini 1975:151).

Unlike the skin and hair tent-dwellings, the mat tent-dwellings continued to be widely used in the Beja territory. Among the reasons for its survival are the availability of the necessary building materials in the local environment; the simplicity of its construction, dismantling and transport; and its durability in all types of weather. Mat tent-dwellings were probably used in the region of the contemporary Beja since the first millennium BCE, and a direct association of these dwellings with the Beja was first made in the 1st century CE. The ancient mat tent-dwellings had a dome shape similar to those used at present. They were built of the same materials, mats made from leaves of the doam palm and bent wood.

REED HUTS, CAVES AND ROCK SHELTERS

Historians often refer to the description by the 5th century BCE Greek historian Herodotus of the portable dwellings, made on reeds and rushes, in the region of the ancient city Meroe (Prussin 1995:5). Indirect association of these reed dwellings with the ancient Beja was first indicated in the inscription of the Aksumite king Ezana in recording his military campaign against Meroe, and his destruction of their royal capital, in 350 CE. The inscription mentions the 'Noba' people's dwelling in reed huts and the fact that the army arrived at the frontier of the 'Red Noba.' Trimingham (1949:45) suggested that the 'Red Noba' might be the Blemmyes, who probably owned and used the same type of reed dwellings. The earliest direct evidence of reed dwellings in the Beja territory dates to around 1267 CE, when the Arab traveler el-Maqrizi wrote that the majority of the houses in the Red Sea Aydhab were made of reeds (Vantini 1975:148). No description of similar dwellings is known from anywhere else in the Beja territory. It should be emphasized that el-Maqrizi identified these dwellings as 'houses' and not 'tents' indicating that the Aydhab dwellings were probably permanent rather than pastoral ones. As Aydhab was at the peak of its activities as a sea port for pilgrims and trade caravans crossing the Red Sea during the 12th–13th centuries CE, it seems likely that some, if not all, of these houses were owned by Beja to rent out to outsiders passing through the port (Trimingham 1949:13).

Based on archaeological and ethnographic data from the southern Red Sea Hills, caves and rock shelters were, and still are, used in the Beja area as temporary shelters (Magid et al. 1995:163–190). Two caves and one rock shelter were located during our survey. The size of the rock shelter and the two caves appeared too small to accommodate more than one person comfortably. Rock paintings of circles, some with a cross inside, were found on the walls of the caves. Several fireplaces in and just outside one of these caves were excavated, revealing a few potsherds in three different layers, each 10 cm thick. These cultural layers were thin and badly eroded. The quantity and type of these remains indicate that the cave was occupied for short and discontinuous periods. Radiocarbon analysis of charcoal samples from the oldest, bottom layer of the cave (about 30 cm below the surface) showed them to date to the 13th century CE. The second cave was surveyed, and one recent fireplace, but no other cultural remains, was found. Our informants believe that such types of shelters have been used since time immemorial during cold nights or periods of rain.

The scarcity of archaeological material in the caves and the infrequent mention of reed huts in the accounts of classic writers and early Arab travelers indicate that both types of dwellings seem to have been used for purposes other than those connected with livestock and herding. The reed huts were used for accommodation of outsiders, pilgrims and traders, while the rock shelters were used by Beja travelers and passersby for temporary protection. One may therefore cautiously conclude that reed huts and caves are not common forms of Beja nomadic dwellings, nor were they regularly used by the ancient population of the Beja territory.

EUPHORBIA STEM-DWELLINGS

These dwellings (*bokar* in Hadendowa) were first reported, in the Hadendowa area, at the beginning of the 20th century CE by Seligmann (1913). They are made by driving the dead stems of *Euphorbia abyssinica* into the ground to form circular or oval structures slanted in such a way that they produce walls and domes (Figure 20.3). Mat tent-dwellings usually are dispensed with when a *Euphorbia* stem-dwelling is built. As these dwellings are more permanent, their nomadic owners often use them as base dwellings for most of the year while using mat tent-dwellings during seasonal movements. The *Euphorbia* stem-dwellings are still used by contemporary Hadendowa but only in a limited area where *Euphorbia* is relatively abundant (in the area of Erkweit, east of

Figure 20.3. A *Euphorbia* stem-dwelling in the north of the study area; note the stone supporting wall (photograph by Krzysztof Pluskota).

Sinkat, in the eastern part of the Hadendowa territory). This area receives summer and winter rain and is characterized by its high elevation (about 1000 m above sea level).

Our informants confirmed that they use *Euphorbia* stems because they survive the humid climate better than mats or other types of building material. The ancient dome-shaped design, which is traditionally associated with the ancient skin, hair and mat tent-dwellings, is retained in the *Euphorbia* stem-dwellings. We observed that many Hadendowa living in *Euphorbia* stem-dwellings have settled and have completely abandoned a pastoral nomadic lifestyle. There are dwellings in the area of Erkweit, Sinkat, and farther west that are similar in architectural design but with frames made of curved wooden beams and covered with mats of doam-palm leaves. These are also called *bokar* in the Hadendowa language.

LITTERS AND PALANQUINS

Palanquins and litters (*howdaj* and *shibria* in Arabic) are inseparable parts of the traditional nomadic dwelling (Prussin 1995:17). Both consist of a superstructure fastened on top of a packsaddle and set on a camel's back to transport people, mainly women and children, and baggage (Figure 20.4). They are also used to shelter infants when the nomads take a break during the day or camp overnight during their journey. Thus, litters and palanquins can be considered dwellings in transit (Prussin 1995:46–47, 107). The frame of the superstructure of the litter and palanquin is commonly made of wood, bent in the shape of a bow, which is assembled over a pad so that they form a dome. Mats of doam-palm leaves or of wool and sheets of cloth cover the frame. Slight differences are observed in the details of the frame design or the ornamentation of litters and palanquins among the different North African nomadic groups. With the covers put over the frame, the litter and the palanquin give the impression of an armature (Prussin 1995:52). The materials for the litters and palanquins are collected and processed by women, who are also responsible for the dismantling, re-assembling and mounting of the litter (Prussin 1995:42).

Litters and palanquins are commonly used among many North African nomadic groups like, for instance, the Tuareg and the Teda in the Sahara; the Kababish, the Hassanyia and the Beja nomads in the Sudan; and the Somali in East Africa. Our informants state that the palanquin has been used in the Hadendowa area since time immemorial and that the technological knowledge and experience of its manufacture is passed on from mothers to daughters. The available sources provide no information on the history of litters and palanquins in the Beja territory. The depiction of several camels carrying palanquins on

Figure 20.4. Detail of a 16th century CE bronze map of the world, showing camels carrying palanquins in *Nubia Sarracenorum* (currently kept in the Vatican Museum, Rome; photograph by Krzysztof Pluskota).

a 16th century CE bronze map of the world, currently in the Vatican Museum (Rome), proves that palanquins were used in Nubia, and probably by the Beja as well, by that time and probably earlier.

THE PACKSADDLE

In the history of the camel as a means of transport of the Beja people, their dwellings, furnishings and other possessions, the packsaddle has played an important role. The difference in loading a camel with a person or a dwelling, combined with the anatomy of the camel, dictated the development of two different types of saddles, the riding saddle (*makhlufa* in Arabic) and the packsaddle (*haweya* in Arabic). It is noteworthy that the packsaddle is multi-functional (it can also be used for transporting individuals), while the riding saddle is function-specific (it cannot be used for moving loads). As nomads require a packsaddle more than a riding saddle, it seems safe to assume that the packsaddle was invented first and that the riding saddle was a later develop-ment. The earliest archaeological evidence in Sudan of a camel packsaddle is a figurine that was found in Meroe and has been dated to the 1st century BCE (Epstein 1971:566; Murray 1978:104; Bulliet 1990:117). One of the earliest, and often cited, literary references to the camel in North Africa dates to 46

BCE and tells us that when the Romans defeated King Juba of Numidia, at the battle of Thapsus, they captured twenty camels. These may have been pack animals normally used for agriculture (Gauthier-Pilters and Dagg 1981:117). Evidence from North Africa for the distinction between the packsaddle and the riding saddle is found on a frieze in a Roman house at al-Djem, in Tunisia, dated to 140–160 CE. The frieze shows "a camel being ridden on what appears to be a saddle with two side panels" (Prussin 1995:14). Other evidence consists of Assyrian reliefs in Egypt and terracotta figurines of loaded camels dated to the Greco-Roman period in Egypt (332 BCE–395 CE).

Similar to the structure of several African camel saddles, that of the contemporary Beja and Hadendowa is characterized by a framework put together as a permanently assembled unit. The assembly of the packsaddle, as well as that of the riding saddle, requires adequate knowledge of the camel anatomy and thorough experience with knots and the rawhide used to fasten the wooden components of the saddle (Prussin 1995:51). All literary and archaeological evidence indicates a continuity of the nomadic building practices, as well as the materials and production techniques of packsaddles. It is therefore likely that the procedures of loading and unloading, used by the contemporary Hadendowa, is also a continuation of ancient practices.

DISCUSSION

Limited research has been done on the Beja, and Hadendowa, ancient nomadic architecture, its development and its socio-economic and environmental context. Our archaeological and ethnographic research aimed at studying these largely neglected issues, but the results remain inadequate to draw comprehensive conclusions. Other sources of information are therefore included to construct a historical account on the nomadic architecture of the Beja. These sources consist of textual evidence, accounts of classic writers and early Arab travelers and geographers, historical and ethnographic studies and oral history. Combining the data from these sources suggests that there has been a continuity of forms and building practices of the nomadic dwellings in the Beja territory for at least the last 2000 years. The dome shape and the building materials, mainly plant material and to a lesser degree leather and hair, of the dwellings has continued to be the same. There are reasons to assume that the building practices and the form of the dwellings are products of indigenous knowledge and experience. Skin, mats and hair were used to cover the frame structure. The use of skin and hair coverings, evident in rock drawings and historical accounts, attests to the presence of large herds of livestock in the recent past. Combined with the accounts of the ancient flora and fauna in the Beja territory, these large herds indicate that the climate was once less arid. The disappearance of the skin and hair as coverings for the Beja nomadic dwellings may be attributed, at least partly, to the loss of the herds as a result of decreasing rainfall. The mat tent-dwelling continued to be used by the Beja because of the availability of its building material. Similar to ancient nomadic groups in North Africa, the Beja women were the collectors, processors and producers of building materials, as well as the architects, builders and maintainers of the nomadic dwellings. There are reasons to suggest, therefore, that the dome shape of the dwellings was the reflection of gender skills and a marker of both the production process and the final product.

Although little is known about the origins and history of the palanquin in the Hadendowa and the Beja area, it bears witness to the creative process of nomadic architecture in general. It is built of the same materials, retains the same form, and serves the same functions as the tent-dwelling: protection and privacy. It illustrates the relationship of the nomadic dwellings during movements and reflects the proficiency and practicality of the nomadic technology of transport. The combination of the camel and the packsaddle provided an efficient nomadic vehicle, enabling the Beja and the Hadendowa to break physical and geological barriers and allowing them to reach new and better natural resources. It also enabled them to keep larger herds of cattle, sheep and goats, which in turn supplied them with wool, hair and leather for covering and furnishing their dwellings.

REFERENCES

Arkell, A. J.

1961   *A History of the Sudan from the Earliest Times to 1821*. London, Athlon Press.

Ausenda, G.

1987   *Leisurely Nomads: The Hadendowa (Beja) of the Gash Delta and Their Transition to Sedentary Village Life*. University of Columbia (PhD dissertation).

Baines, J. and J. Malek

2000   *Cultural Atlas of Ancient Egypt*. Abingdon, Andromeda.

Brugsch, H. K.

1891   *A History of Egypt Under the Pharaohs*. London, John Murray.

Bulliet, R. W.

1990   *The Camel and the Wheel*. New York, Columbia University Press.

Burckhardt, L.

1822   *Travels in Nubia*. London, John Murray.

Cribb, R.

1991   *Nomads in Archaeology*. Cambridge, Cambridge University Press.

Dirar, M. S.

1992   *Tareikh Sharaq al-Sudan: Mamalik al-Beja, Qabaelaha wa Tareikhaha: Al-Juzu al-Awal wa al-Tnai* [in Arabic]. Cairo, Maktab Abkass.

Drew, P.

1979   *Tensile Architecture*. London, Granada.

Egemi, O. A. M.

1994   *The Political Ecology of Subsistence Crisis in the Red Sea Hills, Sudan*. University of Bergen, Department of Geography (PhD dissertation).

el-Maqrizi (edited by M. Gaston)

1922   *El-Mawaiz wa`l-I`tibar fi Dhikr El-Khitat wa`l-Athar* [in Arabic]. Cairo, Imprimerie de L'Institut Français.

Epstein, H. (with I. L. Mason)

1971   *The Origin of Domestic Animals of Africa*. New York, Africana Publications.

Faegre, T.

1979   *Tents: Architecture of the Nomads*. London, John Murray.

Fattovich, R.

1993   The Gash Group of the Eastern Sudan. An Outline. In L. Krzyzaniak, M. Kobusiewicz and J. Alexander (eds.), *Environmental Change and Human Culture in the Nile Basin and Northern Africa Until the Second Millennium B.C.* Poznan, Poznan Archaeological Museum: pp. 439–448.

Gauthier-Pilters, H. and A. I. Dagg

1981   *The Camel: Its Evolution, Ecology, Behaviour, and Relationship to Man*. Chicago, University of Chicago Press.

Grigg, D. B.

1974   *The Agricultural Systems of the World: An Evolutionary Approach*. Cambridge, Cambridge University Press.

Hasan, Y. F.

1975   *Dirasat fi taryikh Al-Suodan: Aljuzu Al-Awal* [in Arabic]. Khartoum, Khartoum University Press.

Helck, W. and E. Otto

1986   *Lexikon der Ägyptologie. Volume 6*. Wiesbaden, Otto Harrassowitz.

Hjort af Ornäs, A. and G. Dahl

1991   *Responsible Man: The Atmaan Beja of North-Eastern Sudan*. Stockholm-Uppsala, Stockholm Studies in Social Anthropology in cooperation with Nordiska Afrikainstitutet.

Holt, P. M. and M. Daly

1979   *The History of the Sudan from the Coming of Islam to the Present Day*. London, Weidenfeld and Nicolson.

Ibn Haugal, A. G.

1979   *Surat al-Ard* [in Arabic]. Hairout, Al-Haiat Publishing House.

Lewis, I.

1969   *People of the Horn of Africa, Somali, Afar, and Saho*. London, International African Institute.

Magid, A.

1998   Ancient Waystations in the Southern Red Sea Hills, Sudan: A New Discovery. *Sudan Notes and Records 15*: pp. 5–15.

Magid, A., R. H. Pierce and K. Krzywinski

1995   Test Excavations in the Southern Red Sea Hills (Sudan): Cultural Linkages to the North. *Archéologie du Nil Moyen 7*: pp. 163–190.

Manger, L.

1996   General Introduction. In L. Manger, H. Abd el-Ati, S. Harir, K. Krzywinski, and O. R. Vetaas (eds.), *Survival on Meagre Resources: Hadendowa Pastoralism in the Red Sea Hills*. Stockholm, Gotab: pp. 18–36.

Murdock, G.

1959   *Africa: Its Peoples and Their Culture History*. New York, McGraw-Hill.

Murray, G. W.

1978   *Sons of Ishmael: A Study of the Egyptian Bedouin*. New York, AMS Press (reprint of the 1935 manuscript).

Nautrup, B. L.

2004   *Gender, Society, and Religion: Changing Everyday Life Among the Hadendowa-Beja of the Gash Delta, Eastern Sudan*. University of Copenhagen, Institute of Anthropology (PhD dissertation).

Nicolaisen, J.

1963   *Ecology and Culture of the Pastoral Tuareg: With Special Reference to the Tuareg of Ahaggar and Ayr*. Copenhagen, National Museum.

Oliver, P.

1971   *Shelter in Africa*. London, Barrie and Jenkins.

Owen, T. R.

1937   The Hadendowa. *Sudan Notes and Records 20*: 2, pp. 183–208.

Paul, A.

1971   *A History of the Beja Tribes of the Sudan*. Cambridge, Cambridge University Press.

Prussin, L.

1995   *African Nomadic Architecture: Space, Place, and Gender*. Washington, Smithsonian Institution Press and the National Museum of African Arts.

Sadr, K.

1991   *Development of Nomadism in Ancient Northeast Africa*. Philadelphia, University of Pennsylvania Press.

Seligmann, C. G.

1913   Some Aspects of the Hamitic Problem in the Anglo-Egyptian Sudan. *Journal of the Royal Anthropological Institute of Great Britain and Ireland 63*: pp. 593, 705.

Trimingham, J. S.

1949   *Islam in the Sudan*. London, Oxford University Press.

Updegraff, R. T.

1978   *A Study of the Blemmyes*. Brandeis University (PhD dissertation).

Vaagenes, V.

1990   *Women Going Public: Social Change and Gender Roles in the Red Sea Hills, Sudan*. University of Bergen, Department of Geography (Candidacy thesis).

1998   *Women of the Interior, Men of the Exterior: The Gender Order of Hadendowa Nomads, Red Sea Hills, Sudan*. University of Bergen, Department of Geography (PhD dissertation).

Vantini, G.

1975   *Oriental Sources Concerning Nubia*. Heidelberg-Warsaw, Society for Nubian Studies, the Polish Academy of Science and the Heidelberger Akademie der Wissenschaffen.

Walker, P.

1987   *Food for Recovery: Food Monitoring and Targeting in the Red Sea Province, Sudan, 1985–1987*. Oxford, Oxfam.

CHAPTER 21

THE BEDOUIN TENT

AN ETHNO-ARCHAEOLOGICAL PORTAL TO ANTIQUITY OR A MODERN CONSTRUCT?

BENJAMIN A. SAIDEL[1]

O NE OBJECTIVE OF ethno-archaeological research is to record human behavior in traditional communities in order to shed light on ancient societies. Kramer (1979:1) states that "observations of contemporary behavior can facilitate the development and refinement of insights into past behaviors, particularly when strong similarities can be shown to exist between the environments and technologies of the past and contemporary sociocultural systems being compared."[2] In the Old World, ethno-archaeological investigations of Bedouin campsites have been conducted in the southern Levant, northern Arabia and on the Sinai peninsula (for instance Zarins et al. 1980:23, Plate 11; Bar-Yosef 1984:155; Banning and Köhler-Rollefson 1986, 1992; Simms 1988; Avni 1992; Eldar et al. 1992; Zarins 1992; Goren-Inbar 1993). These projects demonstrated that the campsites of pastoral nomads are archaeologically visible and that the archaeological signature of tent camps is influenced by the nature of the surrounding terrain (such as Rosen 1992:76, 1993:443; Saidel 2001). Ethno-archaeological fieldwork carried out on the tent camps of modern pastoral nomads was performed on the assumption that

[1] An early version of this chapter was presented as part of Symposium 82, *Nomads in Archaeology*, during the 69th Annual Meeting of the Society for American Archaeology (Montreal, 2 April 2004). I thank Anna Belfer-Cohen, Laura Mazow and Steven Rosen for their incisive comments on the earlier drafts of this chapter. I also thank Edna Sachar for her meticulous copy editing. This paper was written during my tenure as the Ernest S. Ferichs fellow at the W. F. Albright Institute of Archaeological Research in Jerusalem in 2004/2005, and I thank the Albright Fellowship Committee for its support.

[2] See David and Kramer (2001:12, Table 1.1) for additional definitions of *ethno-archaeology*.

this research would provide insights into ancient forms of mobile pastoralism (for example Hole 1979:196, 1980:120–121). In particular, it was assumed that these structures are comparable in form and function to similarly shaped tensile structures in antiquity. This perspective is represented, for example, in a preliminary report of a survey carried out in the central and southwestern provinces of Saudi Arabia: "This best modern parallel to the post-Neolithic sites comes from a recently abandoned (last ten years) Bedu tent encampment in Qatar (al-'Uqda) where multiple stone cobbles were used to clearly anchor the entire tent walls . . . leaving a clear rectangular tent outline" (Zarins et al. 1980:23). In this example the basis for drawing the comparison between the Bedouin tent and post-Neolithic tents is that both types of structures are rectangular (Zarins et al. 1980:23, Plates 11, 10A, 31A). The shape of the Bedouin tent, combined with recent ethnographies describing the sedentarization of the Bedouin, has been used to identify the sedentarization of nomads in the archaeological record of the early Iron Age I in the southern Levant (for example Finkelstein 1988:237–258, 1995:46–49). The methodological approaches outlined above are problematic because no one has yet considered the age of the Bedouin tent and the customs carried out inside of this structure. Implicit in much of the research is the premise that the Bedouin tent is a relic from a primordial past.

In this chapter I use various lines of evidence to propose two possible dates for the age of the Bedouin 'black tent.' The first is based on the organization of space within this structure; the second is based on some of the material culture found inside it. The latter is significant as a means to establish the age of some of the customs and material culture found inside the black tent as described by Western and non-Western travelers and ethnographers. By dating the material culture, we can also provide relative dates for some of the social customs carried out inside this tent. This study does not investigate the origins of tensile architecture in the southern Levant or in the Old World. Rather, its purpose is to ascertain the age of a specific type of tent, namely the Bedouin 'black tent' (for example Magid, this volume; Musil 1928:61–76; Dickson 1951:66–80; Simms 1988), and some of the activities carried on inside it. The geographical focus of this study is primarily the southern Levant, northern Arabia and the Sinai, with data also drawn from other parts of the Near East. This research relates to Bedouin black-tent dwellers who are, or have been defined by others as, Bedouin (Burckhardt [1831] 1967:3; Musil 1928:xiii, 44; Kirk 1941:60, zone 2; el-Aref [1944] 1974; Simms 1988).

Table 21.1. Selected Examples of the Size of Bedouin Tents:

Location or tribe	Tent dimensions (m) or size (m²)	Reference
Petra, Jordan	15x4 m	Simms 1988:202
Petra, Jordan	51.5 m² (main tent)	Bienkowski and Chlebik 1991:Table 3
Petra, Jordan	18.4 m² ('second tent')	Bienkowski and Chlebik 1991:Table 3
Wadi Fatima, Saudi Arabia	10x4 m	Katakura 1977:73
Rwala tent without main pole (*harbus*)	4–6x2.5–3 m	Musil 1928:72
Rwala tent with one main pole (*katba*)	12x3.5 m	Musil 1928:72
Rwala tent for children or the 'poorest inhabitants of the camp' (*tuzz*)	4x2 m	Musil 1928:72

THE BEDOUIN BLACK TENT

The Bedouin black tent, the *beit sha`ar* or 'house of hair,' is defined as a rectangular structure that varies in length and width (Table 21.1) (Weir 1976:1).[3] This type of tent was found throughout the Levant, northern Arabia, and the Sinai, as well as in other parts of the Near East and North Africa (Andrews 1990). The Bedouin black tent is primarily used during the winter months because it is water-repellant and, when it rains, the fabric expands, making the tent waterproof (Burckhardt [1831] 1967:37, 67; Musil 1928:61; Dickson 1951:66; Weir 1976:1; Kay 1978:11). During the summer months, those Bedouin who could afford to purchase a second tent, one made of lighter materials such as cotton, did so, but 'poverty' compelled others to continue to live in the black goat-hair tent (Jabbur 1995:249). The Bedouin had various means to acquire the panels of goat hair that were sown together to make a tent. Some Bedouin women wove their own tent panels; however, this was not possible for the mobile pastoralists who lived in deserts because goats could not survive in such arid conditions (Weir 1976:46). Goat-hair panels, or entire tents made of goat hair, were purchased by the Bedouin from towns or itinerant merchants (Musil 1928:61; Dickson 1951:73; Weir 1976:49). Many towns in the Levant manufactured Bedouin tents. According to Weir (1976:49), during the British Mandate in Palestine, tents were manufactured in Safad, Majd al-Kurum, Samakh, Beisan, Anabta, Tulkarm, Nablus and Hebron. Tents were also

[3] It is acknowledged that some Bedouin, such as the Jebaliya, use tents that are not rectilinear and that during the summer they do not use the *beit sha`ar* at all because it is too hot (Bar-Yosef 1984:155; Goren-Inbar 1993:418). Aside from tents, the Bedouin use a variety of other types of spaces for shelter, such as caves and rock shelters (Magid, this volume; Bienkowski 1985; LaBianca 1990:83, 87, 222, 232; Simms and Russell 1997).

made in the village of Shhim, in Lebanon (Weir 1976:49; Jabbur 1995:250). According to Jabbur (1995:250) a major tent-producing center was located in the Syrian town of Yabrūd: "In this small town there were about 2000 people who earned their living making tents. There are about 300 looms there, and these supply the Bedouins of Syria and export to Jordan, Iraq, Najd, Kuwayt, and the oil companies."

Bedouin tents are often physically divided, by using a curtain or rug, into two sections; one for men (*al-shigg*) and one for women (*al-mahram*) (Burckhardt [1831] 1967:40; Musil 1928:64; Dickson 1951:71–73; Cole 1975:64–65; Weir 1976:17). The men's, *al-shigg*, side of the tent is used primarily for entertaining guests and other tribesmen (Musil 1928:64, 97). Items found in this area include a hearth, an assortment of rugs and cushions and camel saddles for sitting and reclining. One of the more important activities carried out on this side of the tent is the preparation of coffee for consumption by guests and friends (Musil 1928:100–102; Dickson 1951:195–201; Weir 1976:7–10). In general, the men's section of the black tent contains fewer material culture items than the women's side. Most household chores like cooking, however, are carried out in the women's, *al-mahram*, side of the structure, where domestic items and baggage are stored (Table 21.2) (Doughty [1888] 1979:267–268; Musil 1928:100; Weir 1976:17). Lancaster (1997:61) observes that the division of the Bedouin tent into two parts is a reflection of the duality of Bedouin society: the men's part of the tent is associated with the public aspects of society, whereas the women's side is restricted to 'private' aspects of Bedouin life. The gendered division of space inside the Bedouin tent is attributed to Islamic beliefs and customs that determine how space is used and where activities are conducted (Insoll 1999:62, 72, 90).

Table 21.2. Objects Found in the Bedouin Tent as Recorded by Burckhardt, Musil and Dickson

Reference	Found in *al-shigg* (men's section)[a]	Found in *al-mahram* (women's section)[a]
Burckhardt (1967)	Camel bags and packsaddles (for comfort), Persian carpet, wheat sacks (cushion)	Butter, cooking utensils, water skins
Musil (1928:64)	Camel saddle, pillows	Barley, butter, carpets, copper utensils, coffee, coverlets, dates, litters, loom, rice, sâğ (iron sheet for baking bread), salt, spindle, sugar, wheat, wooden utensils
Dickson (1951:76–77)	Carpet, case for coffee cups, coffeepots, incense burner, mattresses, men's camel saddle, mortar and pestle for coffee, peg for stirring coffee beans, pillows, rifle	Blankets, camel saddles, cardamom, coffee, cooking utensils, dates, flour, hand loom, litters, rice, rifle ammunition, spare rifle, salt silks, spindles, sugar

[a]Only major material culture items are presented.

Concerning this division of space within, Insoll (1999:62) writes: "The primary and over-riding concern is with privacy and the protection and seclusion of women (in certain cultural contexts referred to as *purdah*) and the sanctity of the family. Both wife and domestic space are to be protected, and domestic life is linked to ideas of purity." In this context there is a well-defined etiquette that describes how a stranger should approach a Bedouin tent, as recognized by Bedouin and Western travelers alike (for example Doughty [1888] 1979:39–40; el-Aref [1944] 1974:108; Diqs 1969:18). El-Aref ([1944] 1974:136–137), for example, describes how a guest should behave on entering a Bedouin tent:

> There are strict rules of social conduct to which the guest must conform if he would not be considered ill mannered and undeserving of kindness. Facing the entrance to a *Bedawi* tent, the *hareem* is always on the right. On the left of the tent is the *Shigg* where the guest is entertained. It is very distasteful and offensive to a *Bedawi* to have another man even pass closely to his harem, therefore it is incumbent on a visitor to approach the tent from the rear and to keep the tent on his left as he comes to the front. That is rule (1).

> Rule (2) is that he shall not take undue notice or peer at a woman moving about in the tent. He should appear to ignore their presence.[4]

Given the gendered division of space within the Bedouin tent, Musil (1928:64) recorded an anecdote that demonstrates how the Rwala manipulated these rules to disarm their guests when they entered the men's section of the tent: "The master of the tent and his guests remove their shoes or boots, which they place behind them against the dividing wall, while they hang their rifles on the main pole in the women's compartment." Although the interpretation is speculative, this behavior appears to be one mechanism for defusing potential tensions between host and guests: while their shoes are kept in the men's section, their firearms are stored in the women's part of the tent, which is off-limits. If a violent disagreement arose between a host and his guests their rifles would, at least theoretically, be inaccessible. I suggest that the Bedouin black tent as we know it today emerged some time after the mid 7th century CE, that is to say, following the Islamic conquest of Palestine. This *terminus post quem* is based on the division of space and gender roles assigned to men and women in Islamic societies.

[4.] Aref el-Aref was born in Jerusalem and educated in Istanbul. During the period of the British Mandate in Palestine he held various administrative posts, including governor of Beersheba (Abu-Rabiʿa 2001:86–87). As a result, he became well acquainted with the Bedouin who lived in the Negev and wrote a number of books on this population (such as el-Aref 1938, [1944] 1974; see also Abu-Rabiʿa 2001:87).

COFFEE, TOBACCO AND POTTERY

Another means to determine the age of the Bedouin tent is to establish relative dates for some of the objects found inside these structures. In the following section I propose relative dates for the accoutrements associated with coffee consumption and tobacco smoking among the Bedouin. Both activities are well attested in Western travelogues and in the ethnographic literature (such as Conder 1879:282). The presence of pottery known as Gaza Ware is another line of evidence that can be used to date Bedouin tents.[5] According to historic and ethnographic accounts, coffee is an important part of Bedouin society. Coffee is the only foodstuff prepared in the men's part of the Bedouin tent, and the equipment used to prepare it is usually stored there. The preparation of fresh coffee is a hallmark of hospitality among the Bedouin (Doughty [1888] 1979:289, 290; Musil 1928:469; Dickson 1951:195; Weir 1976:10). Both sexes in Bedouin society consume coffee (Musil 1928:100; el-Aref [1944] 1974:36; Dickson 1951:76–77, 84, 198–199). The social value of coffee is illustrated by the accoutrements used for coffee preparation and consumption (Musil 1928:100), as well as by the many poems extolling the virtues of this beverage (Musil 1928:102–114). The grinding of coffee beans is also considered an art and a means of personal expression: "The noise made by the mortar and pestle, *hess al-mihbas*, is heard everywhere in the vicinity, and the people give their opinion as to whether these sounds are regular and artistic or not. The pounding of coffee is an art, and musical ability is judged according to the way in which it is done" (Musil 1928:101).

Information contained in travelogues and ethnographies indicates that both Bedouin of humble means and tribal leaders spent considerable portions of their income on coffee consumption. One travel account from the early 19th century CE indicates that one Bedouin spent as much as 29% of his yearly income on luxury goods that included coffee (Burckhardt [1831] 1967:70).[6] The Rwala leader, An-Nûri eben Šaʿlân, spent an appreciable portion of his income on the purchase of coffee and sugar (Table 21.3). Dickson (1951:78) notes that the Bedouin in Kuwait hide their coffee with other valuables: "Treasures such as money, coffee beans, cardamom, sugar, salt, silks and special holiday attire are kept by the housewife locked up in a small tin or wooden box. The key of this she always keeps on her person, and tied to a portion of her head veil or *milfa*."

[5.] Firearms are problematic chronological indicators because some Bedouin continued to use obsolete weapons for economic or social reasons, while others had the means to procure modern rifles (Saidel 2000:197–213). They are therefore excluded from this discussion.

[6.] Other luxuries purchased included a "dried apricot jelly" and "a sweet jelly made of grapes" (Burckhardt [1831] 1967:70).

Table 21.3. Prices of Foodstuffs by 'Load.'

Foodstuff[a]	Cost per 'load' (in $)	Amount spent (in $)
Butter (no number of loads given)	247.50	247.00
Burrul (husked wheat)	1.60	11.25
Camel (for consumption)	45.00	225.00
Coffee	60.00	90.00
Flour	36.00	1440.00
Rice	6.00	18.00
Sugar	12.50	25.00
Sheep (for consumption)	2.70	270.00
Wheat	0.68	13.50

[a]Livestock purchased for human consumption is included for comparison; foodstuffs for animals are excluded (data drawn from Musil 1928:59).

The introduction of coffee to the Middle East provides a relative date for the introduction of this beverage to Bedouin society. The use of coffee as a beverage did not become widespread in the Ottoman Empire until the 17th century CE (Arendonk 1978:450–451; Baram 1996:120, 1999:140). According to Baram (1999:142), by 1610 CE, coffee and coffeehouses were present throughout the Ottoman Empire. Because coffee is a stimulant, there were times during the 17th century CE when consumption was banned on religious grounds (Arendonk 1978:451; Baram 1999:141; Insoll 1999:106). Archaeologists have interpreted the finds of small porcelain coffee cups at archaeological sites in the southern Levant as evidence of the import and consumption of coffee in this region (for example Edelstein and Avissar 1997:133; Baram 2000:147, 154; Boas 2000:553–554; Ward 2000:189–190; Kletter 2004:198–200). Therefore, the dating of the objects necessary to prepare coffee, and its social role within Bedouin society, cannot be earlier than the 17th century CE. This only applies to the use of coffee, however, and does not mean that other (hot) beverages were not offered as expressions of hospitality

Tobacco, another stimulant used by both men and women in Bedouin society, was exported from the New World, also during the 17th century CE (Von Gernet 1995:79; Baram 2000:149). The adoption and use of tobacco among the Bedouin is well documented for the 19th and early 20th centuries CE (Doughty [1888] 1979:355–356; Musil 1928:127; el-Aref [1944] 1974:36). They acquired tobacco from various sources, by means of purchasing it in markets in towns or from itinerant tobacconists, casual exchange and personal cultivation (Doughty [1888] 1979:355, 487, 525; el-Aref [1944] 1974:36). Like coffee, tobacco was often a subject for Rwalan poetry (Musil 1928:128–131).

In the Ottoman period the Bedouin acquired tobacco pipes both through purchase and by making their own from local stone. According to information contained in travel accounts and provided by pipe collectors, the Bedouin in northern Arabia and Sinai crafted their own pipes (Doughty [1888] 1979:288; Baram 1996:192, 193, figure 9). Citing Musil, Baram (1996:192–194) points out that male and female smokers among the Rwala Bedouin use different types of tobacco pipes. Tobacco pipes, dating from the 17th–20th centuries CE, have been found, in archaeological surveys, along the coast of northern Sinai (Cytryn-Silverman 1996:147–149) and in the Negev Highlands. Examples of the latter, however, are either poorly illustrated or not illustrated at all, making it impossible to date them at this time. Given the origin of tobacco, and the archaeological evidence of tobacco smoking, the Bedouin could not have adopted it prior to the 17th century CE.

Sherd scatters of coarse gray pottery identified as 'Gaza Ware' have been found at many abandoned Bedouin tent camps in the Negev and Sinai. Such sherd scatters at archaeological sites in the Negev Highlands constitute the only evidence that these settlements were re-used by Bedouin (Rosen 1981, 1994:21–22). Dating Gaza Ware is problematic because it has not been the subject of systematic typological and chronological research. Current studies indicate that the production of Gaza Ware may have begun as early as the second half of the 17th century CE or the beginning of the 18th century CE and that it continued to be manufactured until the end of the 20th century CE (Rosen and Goodfriend 1993; Ziadeh 1995:211, 220; Bulle and Marmiroli 2000:93). This suggests that the abandoned Bedouin tent camps situated in the Negev Highlands should be dated to the 17th–20th centuries CE.[7]

[7.] Legal definitions of what constitutes an archaeological site vary, and the implications are significant for the preservation of abandoned tent campsites. In Israel, remains of human activities that date to before 1700 CE are considered archaeological sites and are accordingly given legal protection (Rosen and Goodfriend 1993:147). Publication of archaeological materials dating after 1700 CE is dependent on each excavator. For example, the excavation of archaeological deposits in Jaffa from the "late nineteenth to early twentieth centuries" was not published because the sediments and artifacts are not "considered as antiquities by Israeli law" (Kletter 2004:205–206). In contrast, Ustinova and Nahshoni (1994:176) published the results of their excavations of farmsteads located in Beersheva, which they dated from the 1930s to the late 1940s CE. In contrast to the antiquities laws in Israel, the Archaeological Resources Protection Act of 1979 in the United States of America defines an archaeological site as any traces of human activities that are at least 100 years old.

THE BEDOUIN TENT IN ARCHAEOLOGICAL CONTEXT

Ethno-archaeological investigations in the southern Levant have identified the archaeological remains of recently abandoned tent camps (for example Simms 1988; Avni 1992:242–247; Saidel 2001). At present there are no published examples of excavated Bedouin tent camps in the southern Levant that predate the 20th century CE. The best published example of a Bedouin tent and tent camp in an archaeological context is Ras Abaruk Site 5 in Qatar (Garlake 1978). This site contains the outlines of at least six tents. The pottery from surface collection and test excavation indicates that occupation at this settlement spanned the 17th–19th centuries CE (Garlake 1978:166). Although surveys in the Negev have documented the presence of Bedouin tents in this region, no Bedouin tents dated to the 6th–18th centuries CE have as yet been excavated. However, Gaza Ware pottery at these tent sites, as well as in locations where there are no architectural remains of tents, is visible evidence of Bedouin occupation from the 17th–20th centuries CE (Rosen 1981, 1994:21–22). Archaeological and historical data have been used to posit a Bedouin presence in the northwestern Negev during the Mamluk period (Schaefer 1989:54–56). Sherd scatters of Mamluk pottery, hearths and a lack of architectural remains are interpreted as evidence that these 'camps' were occupied by Bedouin (Gazit 1996:18). The data are problematic, however, as many of the Mamluk campsites have evidence of multiple-period occupations (Gazit 1996:40–41, 50). Caution needs to be exercised in the identification of these sites as 'Bedouin camps,' because the site formation processes may be misleading. Citing this problem in relation to Chalcolithic sites in the northwestern Negev, Gilead (1992:31) writes, "The dried mudbricks were made of local silt, identical to the natural soil. When they decay, it is sometimes impossible to separate them from the natural soil. This may give the wrong impression that such sites featured no architecture, and were, therefore, nomadic camps."

Therefore, the 'Bedouin campsites' identified by Schaefer (1989) need to be investigated further to determine whether they are indeed the remains of tent camps or rather deflated farmsteads. Stone outlines of ancient and modern rectilinear tents were documented at the sites of Har 'Oded and Nahal 'Oded, located to the south of the Ramon Crater (Rosen and Avni 1997:22–23, Figure 4.2, 44, 54, 55, Figure 5.12, Figure 5.13, 59, 70). At both of these sites pottery attributed to the 6th–8th centuries CE was found adjacent to the stone outlines of rectilinear tents. This is tantalizing evidence for the emergence of the Bedouin black tent.

The best example of rectilinear tents in an archaeological context in the southern Levant is represented at the site of Giv`ot Reved in the Ramon Crater. Rosen's (1993:448) research at this site identified a series of rectangular tents, arranged in a row, dated to the second and third centuries CE. While the stone foundations of these structures do provide evidence of the existence of rectilinear

tents in pre-Islamic periods, their presence in these archaeological contexts does
not constitute evidence for the Bedouin tent per se as it remains to be determined
if the use of space inside both types of structures is similar or dissimilar to one
another (Doughty [1888] 1979:267–268; Musil 1928:64–68, 97, 100; Insoll
1999:62, 72, 90).[8] The results of such research, however, indicate a relatively
shallow time-depth for the Bedouin tent and its related material culture and has
immediate methodological implications for archaeological and ethno-archaeological research in the southern Levant, as well as in the wider Middle East.

From an archaeological perspective our knowledge of the antiquity of the
Bedouin tent is hindered by several issues. Scholars working in the southern
Levant have traditionally not been interested in conducting archaeological
investigations at sites from the Ottoman period (1515–1917 CE), although this
no longer is the case (for instance Ziadeh 1995; Schick 1997–1998; Baram and
Carroll 2000). The paucity of archaeological research on historic and ancient
forms of pastoralism can also be attributed to the commoditization of archaeological sites and data as sources of prestige for scholars and their institutions.
In practical terms this is illustrated in at least four forms that are neither mutually exclusive nor the sole purview of any subdiscipline of archaeology. First,
the excavation of large urban sites, by virtue of their size, is more prestigious
than fieldwork carried out at smaller settlements, be they farmsteads, forts or
pastoral encampments. Second, importance is often attached to sites, regardless
of their size, that are mentioned or described in documents and literature from
antiquity. Third, prestige is bestowed on some archaeological sites because they
were excavated in the early 20th century CE by a prominent archaeologist and
therefore merit further investigation. Fourth, inherent importance is attached
to research that makes a contribution, or is perceived to make a contribution, to
subjects that are deemed 'sexy' in Western civilization, such as the biblical flood
story (for example Wilford 1999, 2001; Leary 2000).[9] These forms of prestige
are projected in scholarly and popular media for academic and lay audiences.
As Homan (2002:4) notes, the habitations of pastoral nomads, be they from
prehistoric or historic periods, are generally not of interest to archaeologists:
"even when practicable, excavating tent fragments and elliptical settlement
patterns is less romantic and fruitful in both publications and fundraising than

---

[8.] Archaeological research conducted in the Negev Highlands demonstrated that
most tents from the Chalcolithic through the Early Arab periods were circular (Rosen
1984:119, 1994:18-20; Haiman 1989; see also Magid, this volume).

[9.] This phenomenon is not unique to Old World archaeology or sub-branches of
Near Eastern archaeology like biblical archaeology. For an example of the commodifi-
cation of archaeological research in the New World, consider the title of Adovasio and
Page's (2003) book: *The First Americans: In Pursuit of Archaeology's Greatest Mystery.*

digging a massive urban center."[10] In other words, it appears that archaeological research on mobile pastoralists is perceived to generate less academic currency than fieldwork carried out at ancient urban centers.

THE ETHNO-ARCHAEOLOGICAL VALUE OF THE BEDOUIN TENT

In archaeological studies of the southern Levant some scholars have argued that the pillared houses of the Iron Age I, also known as the 'Israelite four-room house' (Figure 21.1), are copies in stone of the Bedouin tent (Figure 21.2), with the pillars mirroring the position of the wooden tent poles (Herzog 1984:76–77; Finkelstein 1988:257). This analogy is based on three factors. First, the inhabitants of these sites were Israelite pastoral nomads in the process of sedentarization (Herzog 1984:76–77, 82–83; Finkelstein 1988:74–80, 238). Second, ethnographic information is cited indicating that when the Bedouin construct houses made of stone or cement, the layout of these homes mirrors the design of their tents: "It is widely accepted that nomads in the process of sedentarization retained traditions from their pastoral existence, at least initially. An obvious example is the transference of their tradition of dwelling in portable tents made of perishable materials to their permanent architecture" (Finkelstein 1988:245). Third, it is proposed by Finkelstein (1988:248) that the rectilinear shape of the four-room house and its division of space are based on the Bedouin tent: "From our hypothesis that the elliptical site originated in the nomadic encampment, it follows that the individual unit of construction—a broadroom or 'casemate'—reflected the individual desert tent. In this connection, it should be stressed that the tradition of the tent shape was apparently even stronger than stone construction, for it was deeply rooted in centuries of an unchanging lifestyle and consistent geographical setting . . . It is therefore unlikely that the shape of the desert tent in our region was altered over the course of time."

The parallel drawn between the four-room house and the Bedouin tent is methodologically flawed. There are no similarities between the layout and use of space inside the Bedouin tent and in the pillared houses of the Iron Age I period in the southern Levant other than that both structures are rectangular. Furthermore, the division of space inside Bedouin tents, and in their

---

[10.] It should also be mentioned, however, that the publication of fieldwork carried out at pastoral encampments is relatively easy, given the limited amount of material culture and small size of these settlements. Moreover, in the arid zones of the southern Levant it is also relatively easy to draw the architectural plan of an entire mobile-pastoralist site, which cannot be said of tells and other sites containing complex stratigraphy.

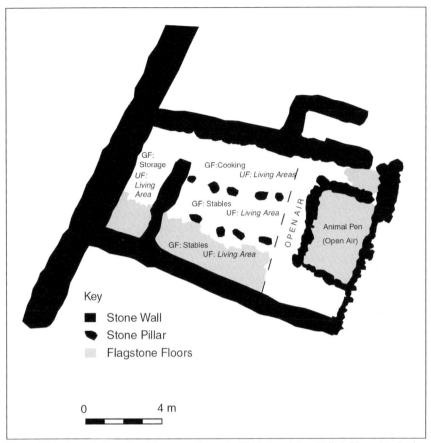

Figure 21.1. An early Iron Age I four-room house in Fields A and B at Tall al-'Umayri in Jordan (redrawn and modified after Clark 2003:36). The function of the interior spaces follows Clark's (2003:37) reconstruction of this building as a two-story structure. The activities conducted on the ground floor (GF) are indicated in regular font; those carried out on the upper floor (*UF*) are in italics.

homes made of durable materials, such as mud brick (Figure 21.3), are totally different from the layout of the four-room house. The analogy proposed by scholars such as Finkelstein also does not take into consideration that the division of space within the Bedouin tent and the manner in which it is used are directly impacted by gender relations and social distances predicated on Islamic sensitivities.

The implications of this for the ethno-archaeological research on Bedouin tents are profound. Based on information contained in historic and ethnohistoric sources, it is apparent that tent camps recorded by ethno-archaeologists over the past 20 years have few similarities in size and layout to Bedouin encampments from the 19th–20th centuries CE. At the beginning of the 19th

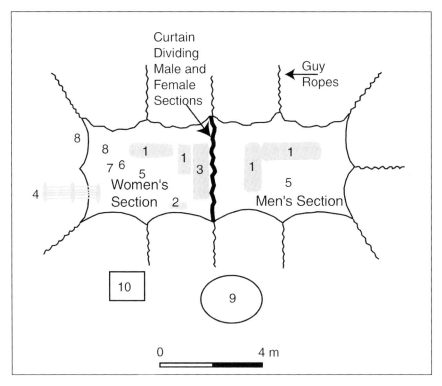

Figure 21.2. Plan of a Bedouin tent in Wadi Fatima, Saudi Arabia (redrawn and modified after Katakura 1977:75). The interior contents include (1) mats; (2) a manual sewing machine; (3) a closet box; (4) a loom; (5) lamps; (6) an incense burner; (7) a coffeepot; (8) kitchen utensils; (9) a pen made of thorny branches for sheep and goats; (10) a twig shelter to cover leather water bags.

century CE the campsites of the Aeneze, of which the Rwala were a subtribe, varied in size from 10–800 tents (Burckhardt [1831] 1967:32). By the turn of the 20th century CE, the Rwala distinguished three sizes of tent camps: those comprising fewer than ten structures (*ferîz*), those containing 10–29 tents (*neǧe*), and those exceeding thirty tents (*nezel*) (Musil 1928:77). Ethno-archaeological research conducted in Israel, Jordan and Egypt has seldom documented tent camps comprising more than two contemporaneous tents (Banning and Köhler-Rollefson 1992; Eldar et al. 1992).[11]

Travel accounts and ethnographies from the Ottoman period demonstrate that Bedouin tent camps also changed in layout. By the beginning of the 19th century CE, Aeneze tent camps were arranged in both circular and linear

[11.] Studies of larger tent camps have been conducted by Cribb (1991) in Turkey and by Evans (1983) in Iran.

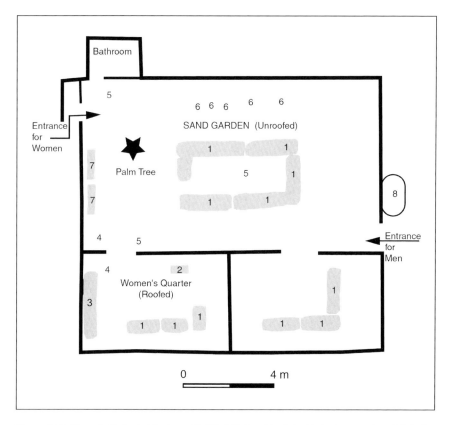

Figure 21.3. Plan of a Bedouin 'clay house' in Wadi Fatima, Saudi Arabia (redrawn and modified after Katakura 1977:75). The following domestic items are located in the open courtyard and in the rooms: (1) mats; (2) a manual sewing machine; (3) a closet box; (4) kitchen utensils; (5) lamps; (6) water vessels; (7) a chicken coop; (8) a pen made of thorny branches for sheep and goats.

alignments. In some instances tents were arranged in multiple rows, as many as three or four tents deep. Historic and ethnographic sources indicate that the layout of the tents in Bedouin encampments was influenced by two factors: animal husbandry and security. Bedouin who raised sheep and goats tended to arrange their tents in the shape of an ellipse, whereas those who herded camels pitched their tents in parallel lines (Musil 1928:180). Musil (1928) observed, at the turn of the 20th century CE, that the layout of Rwala tent camps was influenced by security conditions. In areas with no threat of physical attack tents were scattered or arranged in parallel rows. When the Rwala were expecting an attack, tents were grouped together to form larger concentrations, although Musil does not specify shape.

None of this information is hinted at in the current ethno-archaeological literature as this describes a relict population of pastoralists whose spatial organization of tent camps has changed significantly over the past 110 years and bears little resemblance in plan to the tent camps from the Ottoman and Mandate periods. A major problem with ethno-archaeological research on the Bedouin is the presumption that the Bedouin black tent and tent camps are unchanging relics from a chronologically undefined past. What is often overlooked, however, is that the lifestyle, economy and settlement patterns of the Bedouin have been impacted by political events and governmental programs aimed at controlling and settling them since the end of the 19th century CE and continuing to the present day (for example Marx 1967:6, Map 1, 36–58; Lewis 1987:124–147; Perevolotsky et al. 1989; Bienkowski and Chlebik 1991:162–177; Kressel and Ben-David 1995:119, 138; Rogan 1999:180–182, 249–250).

DISCUSSION

The information presented above indicates a relatively shallow time-depth for the Bedouin tent. At this stage of research it appears that the division of space within this structure should be attributed to gender relations in Islam, suggesting that the use of space inside the Bedouin black tent most likely developed sometime after the 7th century CE. Based on the fact that the adoption of coffee, tobacco and pottery by the Bedouin in the southern Levant, and the activities and social customs associated with them, cannot be older than the 17th–18th centuries CE, the parallels drawn by Finkelstein, and others, between the four-room house of Iron Age I Palestine and Transjordan and the Bedouin tent are baseless because the main evidence for this analogy is that both structures are rectilinear. The Bedouin of the past 200 years are a powerful icon for ethno-archaeologists working in the southern Levant and wider Near East, regardless of their academic training and discipline (Bernbeck, this volume). In a number of publications on the Bedouin, the first chapter is devoted to a description of the Bedouin tent (for instance Weir 1976:1–6; Kay 1978:11–32). A common observation on the Bedouin made by 19th–20th century CE travelers and archaeologists was that, except for their use of coffee, tobacco and firearms, the Bedouin were essentially living fossils (for example Conder 1879:282; Glueck 1970:11). Ironically, ethno-archaeological research on these populations has fallen into the same seductive trap. In reality, disparities in the size and shape of contemporary Bedouin tent camps, as recorded by ethno-archaeologists, with those from the19[th]–20th centuries CE demonstrate that Bedouin encampments in the southern Levant and northern Arabia have changed significantly over the past 100 years.

REFERENCES

Abu-Rabiʿa, A.
2001   *A Bedouin Century: Education and Development Among the Negev Tribes in the Twentieth Century.* New York, Berghahn Books.

Adovasio, J. M. and J. Page
2003   *The First Americans: In Pursuit of Archaeology's Greatest Mystery.* New York, Modern Library.

Andrews, P. A.
1990   *Vorderer Orient Nomadenzeltformen.* Wiesbaden, Dr. Ludwig Reichert Verlag.

Arendonk, C. van
1978   Kahwa. In E. Donzel, B. Lewis and C. Pellat. *The Encyclopedia of Islam (New Edition. Volume 4: IRAN-KHA.* Leiden, E. J. Brill: pp. 449–453.

Avni, G.
1992   Survey of Deserted Bedouin Campsites in the Negev Highlands and Its Implications for Archaeological Research. In O. Bar-Yosef and A. M. Khazanov (eds.), *Pastoralism in the Levant: Archaeological Materials in Anthropological Perspectives.* Madison, Prehistory Press: pp. 241–254.

Banning, E. B. and I. Köhler-Rollefson
1986   Ethno-archaeological Survey in the Beda Area, Southern Jordan. *Zeitschrift des Deutschen Paläestina-Vereins 102*: pp. 152–170.
1992   Ethnographic Lessons for the Pastoral Past: Camp Locations and Material Remains Near Beidha, Southern Jordan. In O. Bar-Yosef and A. M. Khazanov (eds.), *Pastoralism in the Levant: Archaeological Materials in Anthropological Perspectives.* Madison, Prehistory Press: pp. 181–204.

Baram, U.
1996   *Material Culture, Commodities, and Consumption in Palestine, 1500–1900.* University of Massachusetts, Amherst (PhD dissertation).
1999   Clay Tobacco Pipes and Coffee Cup Sherds in the Archaeology of the Middle East: Artifacts of Social Tension from the Ottoman Past. *International Journal of Historical Archaeology 3*: pp. 137–151.
2000   Entangled Objects from the Palestinian Past: Archaeological Perspectives for the Ottoman Period, 1500–1900. In U. Baram and L. A. Carroll (eds.), *A Historical Archaeology of the Ottoman Empire: Breaking New Ground.* New York, Kluwer: pp. 137–159.

Baram, U. and L. Carroll (eds.)
2000   *A Historical Archaeology of the Ottoman Empire: Breaking New Ground.* New York, Kluwer.

Bar-Yosef, O.

1984   Seasonality Among Neolithic Hunter-Gatherers in Southern Sinai. In J. Clutton-Brock and C. Grigson (eds.), *Animals and Archaeology. Volume 3:, Early Herders and Their Flocks. BAR International Series 202*. Oxford, Archaeopress: pp 145–160.

Bienkowski, P.

1985   New Caves for Old: Beduin Architecture in Petra. *World Archaeology 17*: pp. 149–160.

Bienkowski, P. and B. Chlebik

1991   Changing Places: Architecture and Spatial Organization of the Bedul in Petra. *Levant 23*: pp. 147–180.

Boas, A. J.

2000   Pottery and Small Finds from the Late Ottoman Village and the Early Zionist Settlement. In Y. Hirschfeld (ed.), *Ramat Hanadiv Excavations: Final Report of the 1984–1998 Seasons*. Jerusalem, Israel Exploration Society: pp. 547–580.

Bulle, S. and B. Marmiroli

2000   Gaza, une ville en Devenir. In J.-B. Humbert (ed.), *Gaza Méditerranéenne: Histoire et Archéologie en Palestine*. Paris, Ministère des Affaires Étrangères: pp. 87–100.

Burckhardt, J. L.

1967   *Notes on the Bedouins and Wahabys: Collected During His Travels in the East (Reprinted Edition)*. New York, Johnson Reprint (originally published in 1831).

Clark, D. R

2003   Bricks, Sweat, and Tears: The Human Investment in Constructing a "Four Room" House. *Near Eastern Archaeology 66*: pp. 34–43.

Cole, D. P.

1975   *Nomads of the Nomads: The Al Murrah Bedouin of the Empty Quarter*. Chicago, Aldine.

Conder, C. R.

1879   *Tent Work in Palestine: A Record of Discovery and Adventure*. London, Palestine Exploration Fund.

Cribb, R.

1991   *Nomads in Archaeology*. Cambridge, Cambridge University Press.

Cytryn-Silverman, K.

1996   The Islamic Period in North Sinai: The Pottery Evidence. Hebrew University of Jerusalem (Master's thesis).

David, N. and C. Kramer

2001   *Ethnoarchaeology in Action*. Cambridge, Cambridge University Press.

Dickson, H.

1951   *Arab of the Desert: A Glimpse into Bedouin Life in Kuwait*. London, George Allen and Unwin.

Diqs, I.

1969   *A Bedouin Boyhood*. New York, Praeger.

Doughty, C. M.

1979   *Travels in Arabia Deserta (Reprinted Edition)*. New York, Dover. (originally published in 1888).

Edelstein, G. and M. Avissar

1997   A Sounding in Old Acre. *'Atiqot 31*: pp. 129–136.

el-Aref, A.

1938   *Die Beduinen von Beerseba: Ihre Rechtsverhältnisse, Sitten, und Gebräuche*. Luzern, Verlag Räber und CIE.

1974   *Bedouin Love, Law, and Legend: Dealing Exclusively with the Badu of Beersheva (Reprinted Edition)*. Jerusalem, Cosmos Publishing Company (originally published in 1944).

Eldar, I., Y. Nir and D. Nahlieli

1992   The Bedouin and Their Campsites in the Dimona Region of the Negev: Comparative Model for the Study of Ancient Desert Settlements. In O. Bar-Yosef and A. M. Khazanov (eds.), *Pastoralism in the Levant: Archaeological Materials in Anthropological Perspectives*. Madison, Prehistory Press: pp. 205–217.

Evans, C.

1983   On the Jube Line: Campsite Studies in Kurdistan. *Archaeological Review from Cambridge 2*: pp. 67–77.

Finkelstein, I.

1988   *The Archaeology of the Israelite Settlement*. Jerusalem, Israel Exploration Society.

1995   *Living on the Fringe: The Archaeology and History of the Negev, Sinai, and Neighbouring Regions in the Bronze and Iron Ages*. Sheffield, Sheffield Academic Press.

Garlake, P.

1978   An Encampment of the Seventeenth to the Nineteenth Centuries on Ras Abaruk, Site 5. In B. de Cardi (ed.), *Qatar Archaeological Report: Excavations 1973*. Oxford, Qatar National Museum: pp. 164–171.

Gazit, D.

1996   *Map of Urim. Archaeological Survey of Israel 125*. Jerusalem, Israel Antiquities Authority.

Gilead, I.

1992   Farmers and Herders in Southern Israel During the Chalcolithic Period. In O. Bar-Yosef and A. M. Khazanov (eds.), *Pastoralism in the Levant: Archaeological*

Materials in Anthropological Perspectives. Madison, Prehistory Press: pp. 29–41.

Glueck, N.

1970   *The Other Side of the Jordan*. Cambridge, American Schools of Oriental Research.

Goren-Inbar, N.

1993   Ethno-archaeology: The Southern Sinai Bedouin as a Case Study. In A. Biran and J. Aviram (eds.), *Biblical Archaeology Today: Proceedings of the Second International Congress on Biblical Archaeology, Jerusalem, June–July 1990*. Jerusalem, Israel Exploration Society, Israel Academy of Sciences and Humanities: pp. 417–419.

Haiman, M.

1989   Preliminary Report of the Western Negev Highlands Emergency Survey. *Israel Exploration Journal 39*: pp. 173–191.

Herzog, Z.

1984   *Beer-Sheba II: The Early Iron Age Settlement*. Tel Aviv, Tel Aviv University, Institute of Archaeology.

Hole, F.

1979   Rediscovering the Past in the Present: Ethnoarchaeology in Luristan, Iran. In C. Kramer (ed.), *Ethnoarchaeology: Implications of Ethnography for Archaeology*. New York, Columbia University Press: pp. 192–218.

1980   The Prehistory of Herding: Some Suggestions from Ethnography. In M.-T. Barrelet (ed.), *L'Archéologie de l'Iraq: Du début de l'époque néolithique à 333 avant notre ère: Perspectives et limites de l'interprétation anthropologique des documents*. Paris, Centre National de la Recherche Scientifique: pp. 119–127.

Homan, M. M.

2002   *To Your Tents, O Israel!* Leiden, E. J. Brill.

Insoll, T.

1999   *The Archaeology of Islam*. Malden, Blackwell.

Jabbur, J. S.

1995   *The Bedouins and the Desert: Aspects of Nomadic Life in the Arab East*. Albany, State University of New York Press.

Katakura, M.

1977   *Bedouin Village: A Study of a Saudi Arabian People in Transition*. Tokyo, University of Tokyo Press.

Kay, S.

1978   *The Bedouin*. New York, Crane, Russak.

Kirk, G. E.

1941   The Negev, or Southern Desert of Palestine. *Palestine Exploration Quarterly 73*. pp. 57–71.

Kletter, R.

2004   Jaffa, Roslan Street. *'Atiqot 47*: pp. 193–207.

Kramer, C.

1979   Introduction. In C. Kramer (ed.), *Ethnoarchaeology: Implications of Ethnography for Archaeology*. New York, Columbia University Press: pp. 1–20.

Kressel, G. M. and J. Ben-David

1995   The Bedouin Market-Corner Stone for the Founding of Be'er-Sheva: Bedouin Traditions About the Development of the Negev Capital in the Ottoman Period. *Nomadic Peoples 36/37*: pp. 119–144.

LaBianca, Ø. S.

1990   *Sedentarization and Nomadization: Food System Cycles at Hesban and Vicinity in Transjordan*. Berrien Springs, Institute of Archaeology and Andrews University Press.

Lancaster, W.

1997   *The Rwala Bedouin Today*. Prospect Heights, Waveland Press (second edition).

Leary, W. E.

2000   Found: Possible Pre-Flood Artifacts. *New York Times*, 13 September: p. A4.

Lewis, N. N.

1987   *Nomads and Settlers in Syria and Jordan, 1800–1980*. Cambridge, Cambridge University Press.

Marx, E.

1967   *Bedouin of the Negev*. ManchesterUniversity of Manchester.

Musil, A.

1928   *The Manners and Customs of the Rwala Bedouins*. New York, American Geographical Society.

Perevolotsky, A., A. Perevolotsky and I. Noy-Meir

1989   Environmental Adaptation and Economic Change in a Pastoral Mountain Society: The Case of the Jabaliyah Bedouin of the Mt. Sinai Region. *Mountain Research and Development 9*: pp. 153–164.

Rogan, E. L.

1999   *Frontiers of the State in the Late Ottoman Empire: Transjordan, 1850–1921*. Cambridge, Cambridge University Press.

Rosen, S. A.

1981   Observations on Bedouin Archaeological Sites near Ma`aleh Ramon, Israel. *Forum for Middle East Research in Anthropology 5*: pp. 11–14.

1984   Kvish Harif: Preliminary Investigation at a Late Neolithic Site in the Central Negev. *Paléorient 10*: 2, pp. 111–121.

1992   Nomads in Archaeology: A Response to Finkelstein and Perevolotsky. *Bulletin of the American Schools of Oriental Research 287*: pp. 75–85.

1993   A Roman-Period Pastoral Tent Camp in the Negev, Israel. *Journal of Field Archaeology 20*: pp. 441–451.

1994   *Map of Makhtesh Ramon. Archaeological Survey of Israel 204.* Jerusalem, Israel Antiquities Authority.

Rosen, S. A. and G. Avni

1997   *The 'Oded Sites: Investigations of Two Early Islamic Pastoral Camps South of the Ramon Crater.* Beersheva, Ben-Gurion University of the Negev Press.

Rosen, S. A. and G. A. Goodfriend

1993   An Early Date for Gaza Ware from the Northern Negev. *Palestine Exploration Quarterly 125*: pp. 143–148.

Saidel, B. A.

2000   Matchlocks, Flintlocks, and Saltpetre: The Chronological Implications for the Types of Firearms Used by the Bedouin During the Ottoman Period. *International Journal for Historical Archaeology 4*: pp. 191–216.

2001   Ethnoarchaeological Investigations of Abandoned Tent Camps in Southern Jordan. *Near Eastern Archaeology 64*: pp. 150–157.

Schaefer, J.

1989   Archaeological Remains from the Medieval Islamic Occupation of the Northwest Negev Desert. *Bulletin of the American Schools of Oriental Research 274*: pp. 33–60.

Schick, R.

1997–1998   The Archaeology of Palestine/Jordan in the Early Ottoman Period. *ARAM Periodical 9/10*: pp. 563–575.

Simms, S. R.

1988   The Archaeological Structure of a Bedouin Camp. *Journal of Archaeological Science 15*: pp. 197–211.

Simms, S. R. and K. W. Russell

1997   Tur Imdai Rockshelter: Archaeology of Recent Pastoralists in Jordan. *Journal of Field Archaeology 24*: pp. 459–472.

Ustinova, Y. and P. Nahshoni

1994   Salvage Excavations in Ramot Nof, Be`er Sheva. *'Atiqot 25*: pp. 157–177.

Von Gernet, A.

1995   Nicotian Dreams: The Prehistory and Early History of Tobacco in Eastern North America. In J. Goodman, P. E. Lovejoy and A. Sherratt (eds.), *Consuming Habits: Drugs in History and Anthropology*. London, Routledge: pp. 67–87.

Ward, C.

2000   The Sadana Island Shipwreck: A Mid-Eighteenth-Century Treasure Trove. In U. Baram and L. Carroll (eds.), *A Historical Archaeology of the Ottoman Empire*. New York, Kluwer: pp. 185–202.

Weir, S.

1976   *The Bedouin: Aspects of the Material Culture of the Bedouin of Jordan*. London, World of Islam Festival Publishing.

Wilford, J. N.

1999   Plumbing Black Sea for Proof of the Deluge. *New York Times*, 5 January: p. F3.

2001   Scholars Find Further Signs of Big Flood Evoking Noah. *New York Times*, 1 October: p. A14.

Zarins, J.

1992   Pastoral Nomadism in Arabia: Ethnoarchaeology and the Archaeological Record, a Case Study. In O. Bar-Yosef and A. M. Khazanov (eds.), *Pastoralism in the Levant: Archaeological Materials in Anthropological Perspectives*. Madison, Prehistory Press: pp. 219–240.

Zarins, J., N. Whalen, M. Ibrahim, A. J. Mursi, and M. Khan

1980   Comprehensive Archaeological Survey Program: Preliminary Report on the Central and Southwestern Provinces Survey 1979. *Atlal 4*: pp. 9–36.

Ziadeh, G.

1995   Ottoman Ceramics from Ti'innik, Palestine. *Levant 27*: pp. 209–245.

CHAPTER 22

Naming the Waters

NEW INSIGHTS INTO THE NOMADIC USE OF OASES IN THE LIBYAN DESERT OF EGYPT

Alan Roe[1]

IN RECENT DECADES substantive progress has been made toward interpreting the unique archaeological footprints of nomadic societies. Ethno-archaeological methods have been valuable tools where the archaeological record of such societies has proven more fragmentary or dispersed than that of sedentary societies. While strides have been made in understanding the material culture of nomads and, to a lesser extent, their social and economic organization, however, we know much less about the ways in which this organization may find political and territorial expression. This chapter constitutes an ethnographic study of pastoral nomadic resource use in the northern part of the Libyan Desert of Egypt, with a specific focus on a group of small, currently uninhabited, oases of the interior. The fieldwork for this study was undertaken as part of an investigation of traditional natural resource use in the area, to better inform the participatory protection and conservation of these oases. Accordingly, it had a strong historical orientation, drawing heavily on oral histories and corporate memories that extended back more than a century, well before the introduction of modern technologies or the administrative impact of the modern Egyptian State. The study describes a stable system of nomadic resource use and political interaction that has spanned at least a century (some secondary sources indicate even longer).

The objectives of this chapter are twofold. First, the case study of nomadic ecology provides an insight into how this part of the Sahara has been historically used by pastoral nomads and considers the distinct archaeological signatures of this use. Second, the chapter describes an unusual nonconsensual relationship of resource-sharing that historically existed between nomads and the population of the oasis of Siwa. This historical relationship is utilized to demonstrate the potential difficulties of drawing conclusions from the archaeological record alone.

[1.] The research on which this chapter is based was undertaken under the auspices of the Egyptian-Italian Environmental Program.

APPROACHES TO OLD WORLD NOMADIC PASTORALISM

With the realization that most pastoral nomads do indeed leave identifiable archaeological residues (Hole 1978), there has followed considerable research utilizing ethno-archaeological methods to examine the material cultures of contemporary nomads to assist in the identification and interpretation of ancient occupation sites (Simms 1988; Cribb 1991; Avni 1992; Banning 1993). While the Near East and the Levant have been a major geographical focus for these studies, ethno-archaeological investigations of nomadic campsites have also been undertaken in a wide range of locations, including Iran (Evans 1983), southern Arabia (Zarins 1992), Sudan (Bradley 1992) and Africa (Robertshaw and Collett 1983).

Although nomadic life is not normally consistent with a rich material culture (Finkelstein 1995), ethno-archaeological investigations have identified a range of architectural features and structures associated with pastoral camps and may even allow researchers to distinguish between mobile and sedentary pastoral populations (Cribb 1991). Researchers have further found that nomads exhibit distinct preferences in the selection of occupation sites with respect to features of landscape (Banning and Kohler-Rollefson 1992). Despite methodological advances in recognizing and interpreting the archaeological signatures of nomadic occupation, there are recognized limitations on the extent to which archaeological materials alone allow for reconstructing nomadic societies (Bar-Yosef and Khazanov 1992). In contrast to urban settlements, the archaeological record for nomads rarely allows investigation through a cross section of society, to establish a wide socio-economic representation, or of longitudinal development sequence at a single site. For this reason archaeologists have looked increasingly to available ethnographic studies of nomadic societies to provide possible analogies for societal organization and function (Hole 1979; Smith 1985; Cribb 1991; Levy 1992).

Many researchers define pastoral nomadism as a distinct form of food-producing economy. In its purest form pastoralism can be characterized as subsistence-level livestock production in the absence of any form of supplementary activity (Khazanov 1984). Economic specialization to this degree has been associated with social and economic risks and instability (Cribb 1991), however, and it is correspondingly scarce. More commonly, mobile pastoralism has been practiced as the dominant activity within a wider portfolio of economic activities, combining elements of agriculture, trade, waged labor and raiding (Barfield 1993).

Early modern ethnographic studies of pastoral societies (Evans Pritchard 1940; Baxter 1954; Gulliver 1955) focused primarily on endogenous human and social adaptation to remote marginal environments. Consequently, their accounts tended to enforce precolonial and colonial perspectives of pastoral

nomads as isolates sustained by their herds and socially structured by ecological and environmental determinants. Such models tended to limit nomadic
articulation with wider society and structures such as markets. If anything,
this interaction was characterized by an unrelenting animosity between the
'Desert and the Sown' (Reifenberg 1950). Contemporary models of Old
World pastoral nomadism have been revised on the basis of later ethnographic
studies. Researchers now increasingly recognize relations of exchange between
nomads and sedentary populations (Khazanov 1984). Both groups have been
portrayed as mutually interdependent, where animals, animal products and
services are exchanged for nonpastoral products, such as grain and manufactured commodities (Barth 1973). This new understanding of complexity in
nomadic-sedentary interactions, exchange and the possibility of transition
between productive modes comes as some assistance to archaeologists and
anthropologists working with archaeological materials. Some, however, have
questioned the extent to which modern ethnographies (often 'development'
focused and thus highlighting socio-economic and sociopolitical change) may
be utilized as the basis for assumptions about the more distant past.

A great deal of ethno-archaeological research has been undertaken in the
Near East and Levant. In contrast, comparatively little is known about the
ecology and organization of pastoral nomadism among the Egyptian oases.
Although these 'Islands of the Blessed' have constituted an important pastoral
resource for millennia and have sustained diverse nomadic cultures, the scarcity
of contemporary analogues for ancient nomads and rapid rate of development
in the oases has severely restricted the potential for this kind of research.
Likewise, there has been only very limited investigation of the archaeology
of pastoral nomads in the Libyan Desert. In the absence of archaeological
evidence from the area of study, assumptions about nomadic societies are
currently based on incomplete and possibly ethnocentric Egyptian primary
sources and on ethnographic analogies drawn from other parts of North Africa.
The evidence offered in this chapter provides an ethnographic and ecological
baseline against which these assumptions may be reassessed.

THE PHYSICAL ENVIRONMENT

The Libyan (or Western) Desert of Egypt (Figure 22.1), apart from the north
coastal fringe, is largely hyperarid.[2] In this respect the ecology of the area

---

[2] The terms *Libyan* or *Western Desert* may be used interchangeably to describe the
hyperarid desert west of the River Nile. The term *Libyan Desert* is adopted here to
emphasize the biophysical integrity of the desert, crossing modern state borders in the
eastern part of the Sahara.

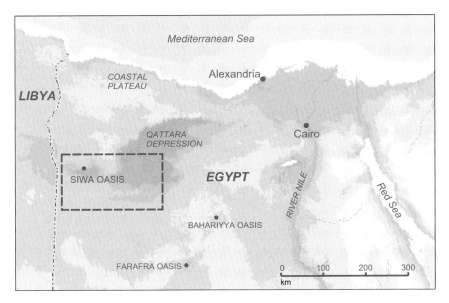

Figure 22.1. General location of the study area in Egypt.

differs significantly from the regions of the Near East and Levant, where much of the archaeological study of nomadism has been centered. Negligible rainfall over much of the desert interior means that life is largely concentrated in and around the various oasis depressions, where the water table is proximate to ground level. The ecology of the region is thus dominated by groundwater.

The principal geomorphic features of the north Libyan Desert are the coastal plateau, the Qattara Depression, the oasis depressions and the Great Sand Sea (Figure 22.2). The Qattara Depression encompasses an area of 19,500 km² of playas, saltpans and sand plains at a mean elevation of about 60 m below sea level (Masini 2001). Two small oases exist within the depression, fed by brackish springwater: Al Qara in the west and Moghra in the east. Outside the Qattara Depression to the south and east are other oasis depressions: (from east to west) Shayata, Jirba, Siwa, Tabaghbagh, Al Araq, Bahrein, Nuweimisa and Sitra. These are bounded to the south by the high dunes of the Great Sand Sea. Only Siwa and Al Qara are currently populated, and all lie 300–350 km south of the Mediterranean coast. The closest of these oases to the Nile Valley lies about 400 km west of the Nile and the farthest about 600 km.

Although the Mediterranean coast receives up to 200 mm annual rainfall, precipitation diminishes rapidly moving south across the coastal plateau. Rainfall over the desert interior is negligible, amounting to no more than 9 mm annually at Siwa. Mean maximal monthly temperatures range from 20°C in January to 38°C in July (Kassas 1955). The oasis depressions support a diversity of vegetation,

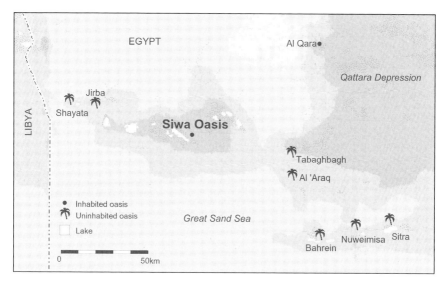

Figure 22.2. The oases of the northern Libyan Desert.

and some 37 species (typical of the species found elsewhere in the Libyan Desert oases) have been identified (Sinibaldi 2002). Around the brackish lakes grow dense reed thickets, typically *Phragmites australis*. Low-lying moist areas affected by saline soils are dominated by *Arthrocnemum macrostachyum*, *Juncus rigidus* and *Alhagi graecorum*. Elsewhere, *Nitraria retusa* and *Cressa cretica* dominate. The sandy margins of the oases support xerophytes such as *Zygophyllum coccineum* and *Cornulaca monocantha*. Most oases also host communities of the date palm *Phoenix dactylifera*. Evidence suggests that the northern Libyan Desert reached its present condition of hyperaridity during the later Holocene (from about 5000 BP). A series of moist intervals has since occurred during the Quaternary, however, the most recent corresponding to the Greco-Roman period (332 BCE–395 CE) of occupation in Egypt (Hassan and Gross 1987).

THE HUMAN ENVIRONMENT

There is evidence for a long period of resource use at the oases of the north Libyan Desert.[3] Lithic assemblages from the area indicate occupation by hunter-gatherer cultures between 10,000–7000 BP (Hassan and Gross 1987). The distribution of sites throughout the area suggests dry season occupation in the

---

[3] Research in the area has hitherto been confined to Siwa, Al Qara and Al Araq oases (Hassan and Gross 1987). The full extent of prehistoric occupation will be determined only through more extensive studies.

vicinity of oasis springs and marshes and the establishment of dispersed hunting camps beyond the rim of the oasis depressions during the season of higher rainfall. Egyptian primary sources refer to the peoples of the Libyan Desert from the middle of the third millennium BCE onward. Ancient Egyptians described the peoples of areas west of the Nile as 'Tjehenu' and later also as 'Tjemehu.'[4] The former group perhaps occupied areas adjacent to the Nile Delta, whereas the latter may have been distributed farther south (Osing 1980). Later, during the second millennium BCE, the names of 'new' populations enter into the Egyptian record, principally in declarations of military victories (Kitchen 1990).[5] There is some evidence that the Tjemehu peoples of the second millennium BCE were pastoral nomads or possibly seminomads. Records attest to their cattle breeds being known and husbanded in Egypt during the 14th century BCE (Kitchen 1990:16), while later Egyptian accounts, possibly exaggerated, describe the capture of many thousands of livestock during New Kingdom wars and skirmishes. In common with many nomadic cultures, the Tjemehu society left little archaeological evidence (Knapp 1981), and most knowledge of its material culture comes from Egyptian pictorial and textual sources.

Comparatively little is known about the geographic range or extent of these Libyan tribes. Current assumptions, based on the archaeological evidence of minor coastal trading sites (White 1990) and modern ethnographic studies from neighboring Cyrenaica, have led to the belief that the ancient nomads would have summered in better watered coastal areas and moved inland into the desert during the cooler winter season. Ancient Egyptian inscriptions describe the roaming bands moving into the western delta, Nile Valley, and to the oasis of Bahariya, and possibly Farafra (Kitchen 1990:20). Fakhry (1974:61), accepting this Egyptian evidence, viewed the occupation of the Egyptian oases in terms of aggressive military incursions, although more recent interpretations suggest that more gradual, socio-economic processes may have been the mechanism behind these population movements (O'Connor 1990). The settlement of Libyan nomads along the western borders of Egypt was significant in that, by the early first millennium BCE, Libyan chieftains not only controlled the inner oases but, with the foundation of Dynasty XXII (945–715 BCE), had assumed the government of the whole country. These developments, however, lie outside the scope of the current discussion.

[4.] The earliest reference to the Tjemehu comes from Dynasty VI (2325–2175 BCE), the reign of Pharao Pepi I (Kitchen 1990).

[5.] The 'Meshwesh' tribe is first mentioned during the reign of Amenhotep III (1390–1353 BCE), while the 'Libu' are only mentioned by name on inscriptions dedicated to Ramses II (1279–1213 BCE). Numerous other small bands or tribes are listed by Bates (1914) and Rowe (1948).

Pastoral tribes are known to have utilized the interior of the Libyan Desert throughout classical antiquity and are described in sources such as Herodotus and Pliny. These Libyan or Berber groups remained in the desert interior long after the Arab expedition of Amr ibn el Asi invaded Cyrenaica in 643 CE and may not have been displaced until the 'Beni Suleim' Bedouin tribes moved west from Arabia in the 11th century CE. At the end of the 18th century CE, 'Awlad Ali' tribes from Cyrenaica migrated east across the coastal plateau to displace the 'Hanadi Arabs.' Both of these groups were descendants of the original 'Beni Suleim' (Murray 1935). Today, the Awlad Ali Bedouin remain the predominant Arab tribe of the northern Libyan Desert and coastal plateau. Many are now settled at coastal locations and in the western delta (a small community has also settled on the outskirts of Siwa Oasis), where they are largely integrated into Egyptian political and economic life (Cole and Altorki 1998). The traditional exploitation of desert resources through nomadic pastoralism was continued, however, into the latter part of the 20th century CE, and a few households still practice a modified form of this. As in other segmentary tribal systems, the Awlad Ali are segmented into a number of clans and descent groups by gene-alogy. The 'beit' is the minimal lineage group and is the basic camping and economic unit, encompassing 20–50 people. The maximal lineage (or tribal section) is known as the *ashira* and is headed by a senior *sheikh*.

The traditional nomadic economy of the Awlad Ali draws together a number of elements. These include camel and ovicaprid (sheep and goats) herding, some barley cultivation on the coastal plain, the provision of commercial and transport services, and other forms of waged labor (Bujra 1973). Bedouin livelihoods in the northern part of the Libyan Desert have historically been constructed around these combined activities and were thus shaped not only by ecological but also socio-economic determinants. The following information describing nomadic ecology has been elicited on the basis of direct observation of current pastoralism, discussion with individuals currently engaged in pastoral production, and discussions with elders possessing personal recollections or historical knowledge of production conditions spanning the 20th century CE.

PASTORAL MIGRATION

Traditionally, the Awlad Ali have herded both camels and ovicaprids, species subject to very different management systems. While ovicaprid production has been orientated to supply external markets, camels tend to be raised for more subsistence functions (milk, transport and meat). Over recent decades, with the growth of markets, there has been an increase in economic specialization in production and overall growth in the size of the herds. Informants recall that, at traditional subsistence levels of production, households would usually manage stock at a ratio of about ten ovicaprids per camel. This chapter focuses exclusively on ovicaprid management, since these have a much longer history of domestication and management in the study area.[6]

The ovicaprid production ecology of the northern Libyan Desert is closely linked to seasonality. The annual cycle begins on the coastal plateau, where there is generally some rainfall during the winter months. In a good year this may occur from October or November through March and stimulate the growth of grasses and succulent annuals. These pastures provide a rich source of nutrition for ovicaprids during the important lambing, kidding and milking seasons. Synchronous with these first rains, households traditionally sow well-watered areas (runoff channels and depressions) with barley. Except in years of exceptionally high rainfall, these pastures are exhausted with the onset of the summer heat, after which the barley is grazed in situ.[7] In years when northern pastures are poor (cited as two or three years out of five), all forage and fodder resources are exhausted by early June. Under these conditions some sections of the Awlad Ali tribe send their livestock deep into the Libyan Desert to the oases of the interior, ranging from Moghra in the east to Jaghabub in the west. This grazing migration has a long historical precedent, extending back many generations to the arrival of the tribe in the area.

Being groundwater rather than rainwater dependent, the desert oases host a largely perennial flora. Indeed, some of the key forage species in the oases, such as *Alhagi*, appear to blossom during the summer months. The summer availability of water and proximity of forage make the Libyan Desert oases indispensable resources for pastoralists. Today herds are (and were historically) kept in the vicinity of the desert oases for three to five months, until the return of the rains on the northern fringes of the desert.

Ovicaprids require constant shepherding, both to direct the herd's movement and to protect them from predators like foxes, jackals and hyenas. According to modern shepherds, the optimal management ratio is about one shepherd to 200 animals. More animals, and the herd would become unmanageable, while a smaller herd results in an inefficient use of labor. Given that even today, with generally larger herd sizes than in the past, many livestock owners own considerably fewer than 200 animals, it is common practice for the livestock of kinsmen to be combined to create larger management units for

[6] There is evidence that camels were not widely managed in Egypt until the end of the first millennium BCE (Wilson 1984). A good overview of the available data for the prehistoric spread of animal domestication across Saharan North Africa is presented by Gautier (1987).

[7] When seasonal conditions were conducive to barley maturing full term, some was generally held back from livestock for household supply of grain.

migration. Many households hire professional shepherds for herd management as livestock owners may have other social and economic commitments over the period of the migration. Until the recent past, migration herding was always done by male kinsmen or family members, if not by the owner himself.

Throughout living memory, migration to the inner desert oases has been the sole preserve of men with expert knowledge because of the scarcity of water fit for human consumption, extreme summer temperatures and other dangers of the long journey across the northern part of the desert.[8] Individuals or small groups of men carrying supplies by donkey or camel would escort the herds, while the remainder of their household and kin groups remained at coastal encampments. Tribal elders indicate that the migration of complete household units would have been more common prior to the 20th century CE, especially at times of drought on the north coast. Owing to the scarcity of forage and water resources in the desert beyond the Qattara Depression, herds move directly from oasis to oasis, stopping to drink and graze for a couple of days at each water source before moving on. The final destination of the herds and the duration of their visit to each oasis is partly determined by the tribal affiliation of the owners and their grazing rights as recognized under traditional tribal law, the *'urf*. According to senior Awlad Ali informants, traditional grazing entitlements to the oases of the northern Libyan Desert are divided among four tribal sections: the 'Asheibat,' the 'Arawa,' the 'Qatifa,' and the 'Samalus.'[9]

The Asheibat are recognized among Bedouin as holding primary grazing rights to the oases of Shayata and Jirba, west of Siwa. The Arawa hold *'urfi* rights (by tribal law) to the spring of Tabaghbagh and oasis of Al Araq; the Samalus have these entitlements to Bahrein oasis; and the Qatifa lay claim to distant Nuweimisa and Sitra oases (Figure 22.3). According to tribesmen encountered among these oases in summer 2002, these lineage groups would traditionally restrict their herds to the areas over which they held *'urfi* rights, although there was open, short-term, access to water and grazing for moving herds between oases. Under certain conditions tribal sections may also trade longer-term grazing rights if mutually advantageous.

[8.] The journey droving sheep and goats from the coast to the inner oases reportedly took about 20 days (today the trip to Siwa is often made by truck) and was only possible in stages utilizing water sources and sparse perennial forage en route. These locations and routes were known to experienced drovers, but still animals were regularly lost in transit.

[9.] While the Asheibat, Arawa and Qatifa are each sections of the Awlad Ali, the Samalus were originally a separate tribe (Murray 1935). Today the distinction is largely overlooked and the Samalus act as a section of the Awlad Ali.

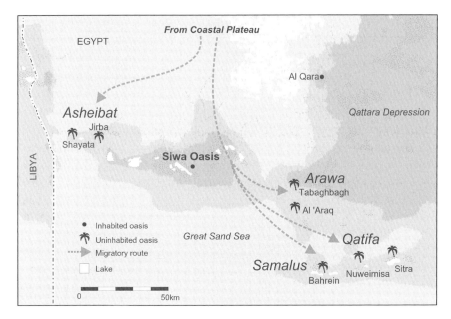

Figure 22.3. Traditional migratory destinations in the northern Libyan Desert.

PASTORAL ECOLOGY

The feeding behavior of sheep shows a clear preference for grazing on succulent material, principally annual grasses and herbs, while goats combine grazing with browsing on bushes and woody shrubs. In practice, however, the Awlad Ali nearly always manage both species in combined groups (other than small numbers of goats maintained permanently at the home encampment to supply milk). The oasis depressions of the Libyan Desert offer a range of forage opportunities for nomadic herds. On the basis of observations made at the oases of Al Araq, Bahrein and Sitra, and the reports of Asheibat shepherds, important forage species were identified and ranked in order of importance (Table 22.1). These observations demonstrated that the reeds and rushes (*Phragmites* and *Juncus* sp.) of the oasis wetlands constituted the most important grazing resource. Not only do the thick stands provide the greatest density of edible material, but it was reported that early in the life cycle of the plants they are highly palatable and thirst quenching for ovicaprids.[10] As mature stands, however, the oasis reeds and rushes are unpalatable. The normal practice adopted by desert herders is therefore to burn off mature stands to stimulate

---

[10.] This claim of the Asheibat has not been scientifically verified. Shepherds insist, however, that sheep and goats thrive on the young shoots of *Juncus acutis*, even where standing water is too brackish for them to drink.

Table 22.1. Ovicaprid Oasis Forage Species Ranked by Importance:

Rank	Species	Location
1	*Phragmites australis*	Oasis wetlands
2	*Juncus acutis*	Oasis wetlands
3	*Alhagi graecorum*	Oasis fringe
4	*Nitraria retusa*	Oasis fringe
5	*Cornulaca monocantha*	Sand
6	*Zygophyllum coccineum*	Sand

regrowth. Young shoots rapidly emerge from burnt ashes and are ready for grazing within three or four weeks.

Burning was observed at the oasis of Bahrein, and it was noted that this was carefully managed and was, in this event, restricted to relatively small areas of *Juncus acutis*. Herders must judge from experience how large an area to burn to sustain their herds for a given duration. They must also time each successive burning so that new shoots reach the required level of maturity just as the previous area of grazing is exhausted. Ideally, each successive burning should occur at different parts of the oasis, or at different oases, so that animals cannot stray between grazing areas. According to Bedouin elders, the burning of reeds and rushes has been practiced annually for generations and is a basic management tool for the pastoral utilization of the desert oases. Asheibat herdsmen reported that under this system of management, ovicaprids would maintain condition without additional feeds. On the basis of observations, and the reports of herders, it is estimated that the western oases of Jirba and Shayata could support a population of 1500 ovicaprids. The larger eastern oases (Al Araq, Bahrein, Nuweimisa, Sitra) were reported capable of supporting about three times this number through the summer season. Migrant herds are normally kept at the oases of the desert interior for about five months during a migration year. They return to the north coast when the first winter rains there stimulate pasture growth. Pastures of annual grasses are known to be of superior nutritional value, highly desirable for lambing and milking, and (after winter fattening) stock becomes available for sale to coastal markets.

During the period of annual sojourn at the desert oases, the living conditions of herders are arduous. They endure extreme summer temperatures, often without direct access to fresh water, forcing them to regularly fetch water from neighboring springs or oases on pack animals. Furthermore, the Libyan Desert oases are infested with flies and fever-bearing mosquitoes. The only protection against these insects is to remain enshrouded in fire smoke. Food is largely restricted to durable supplies of grain, brought from the coast, and immature dates picked locally. This food is often mixed with the milk of lactating goats or camels and supplemented by occasional hunting of gazelle (*Gazella dorcas*) and hares (*Lepus capensis*). The activities of preparatory burning, regularly accessing water potable to stock, and exploiting local food and fuel sources results in a pattern of frequent localized movements within individual (and between neighboring) oases as *'urfi* rights allow. Under these difficult conditions of occupation, herders have few of the regular chattels of the permanent Bedouin camps of the coastal plateau. Commonly, they find shelter in caves or build simple shelters from the most widely available material: bundled reeds and rushes. Even today herders have very few material possessions, just water-skins and maybe a jar, knives, old weapons and some basic utensils.

RELATIONS WITH THE OASEANS

At present only the oases of Siwa and Al Qara support permanent populations. Historically and culturally these populations have been isolated from broader Egyptian society and are believed to be the settled descendants of the original Libyan peoples of the desert. Even today, they maintain their distinct Berber language and cultural practices (Fakhry 1973). Since antiquity, these oaseans have built their livelihoods around the cultivation of dates, olives and lesser crops in their irrigated gardens (Kuhlman 1998). Consequently, the Siwans have developed a sophisticated understanding of soil and water management. At both Siwa and Al Qara, oasis populations have historically constructed fortified mud-brick settlements, elevated high above the oasis depression floor with high exterior walls and narrow entrances to facilitate their defense. This defensive architecture was adopted partly owing to the feuds and battles that characterized the fractious medieval society of Siwa but also because the oases have been historically subject to regular raids by desert nomads (Fakhry 1973).

The historical relationship between the Awlad Ali tribes and the sedentary oaseans of the north Libyan Desert has been complex. On the one hand, the oases towns have presented possibilities for plunder.[11] On the other hand, with their camels the desert tribes have largely controlled the transport of oasis products to the markets of the Mediterranean coast and Nile Valley. The ambiguity of this relationship is nowhere more apparent than in the respective claims of both groups to the uninhabited oases of the study area. Senior sheikhs of the Siwan and Al Qara tribes relate how, in the past, parties of oaseans would travel with donkey caravans to collect the fruit of wild date palms (*Azowi*) from the isolated desert oases during the annual winter harvest season.[12] This practice ended in the early part of the 20th century CE, after which the extension

[11] According to Fakhry (1973:19), Bedouin predations on Siwa ended with the conquest of that oasis by the troops of Muhammed Ali in the 19th century CE.

[12] The dates of the *Azowi* palm are deemed to be of the lowest quality of several varieties harvested at Siwa. Only about a third is considered fit for human consumption.

of irrigation and intensification of date cultivation at Siwa itself made these hazardous desert journeys redundant. This long tradition of resource management is enshrined, however, in traditional Siwan lore and in the old historical manuscripts of Siwa, which claim the uninhabited oases as the property of the Siwan tribes. Specifically, the Al Qara people historically owned and harvested the oases of Tabaghbagh and Al Araq, while the Siwa tribes harvested their *Azowi* palms at the oases of Shayata, Jirba, Bahrein, Nuweimisa and Sitra.

While some Siwan elders maintain that Bedouin tribes have no rights to oases resources, and therefore are prohibited from visiting them, other opinion posits that Siwan ownership of the oases means exclusive control of their products (dates and potable water) but that little could be done to actually prevent seasonal Bedouin grazing. Consequently, visiting Bedouin herds should be tolerated. This concession comes with a remarkable caveat: while nomads may drink from oasis waters and (if necessary) clear and scrape out shallow water holes, they are not permitted to assign names to water sources they dig. According to old Siwan law manuscripts, 'naming the waters' would signify creation of a permanent well and thus infringe on ownership rights. Through much of the 20th century CE discrepancies existed between the respective resource claims to the uninhabited oases (Figure 22.4). At the time of this study the Siwan claims expressed perceived

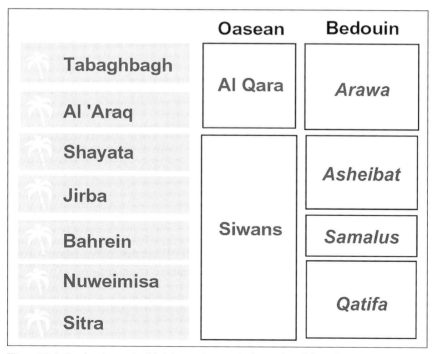

Figure 22.4. Overlapping territorial claims to the oases in the northern Libyan Desert.

historical and symbolic rights of ownership, which they no longer actually used, while the Awlad Ali claims were related to actual management and use.

In practice, Bedouin and oasean groups have tended to overlook their respective claims as there is little incongruency between these claims. As long as the former do not challenge Siwan symbolic rights of ownership and the latter are not in a position to prevent Bedouin herds from grazing, mutual toleration of the status quo exists. In effect, ambiguity over resource ownership serves the purposes of both groups; their sheikhs have never formally met and refuse to do so.[13] Apparent inconsistencies in the political relationship between desert nomads and oaseans were explained thus: where co-operation has occurred between groups (as historically in the transport of harvested oasis products to the coast), these transactions had been arranged on personal bases between individuals. It was reported that no wider structural or cooperative agreements had ever existed between Bedouin and Siwans, which seems consistent with historical evidence for almost simultaneous conflict and commerce between the groups.

ARCHAEOLOGICAL SIGNATURES

What does the information gathered during this study indicate about the archaeological signatures of nomadic use and occupation of the Egyptian oases? One of the most significant findings of the study, previously unrecorded in the Libyan Desert, relates to the evidence for the long-standing practice of managing key oasis forage species with fire. Evidence for past fire management of this type should be observable in the strata of oasis sediments, notably in wetland (or former wetland) areas of oasis depressions. At this juncture it is worth referencing some findings of the Combined Prehistoric Expedition in the southern Libyan Desert. Geo-archaeological investigations conducted at remote oasis depressions have revealed layers of burnt reed charcoal deposits resting on Aeolian sand at the base of ancient lake beds. The accumulated evidence seems to suggest the periodic burning of *Phragmites* and *Typha* (a species akin to *Juncus*) along the margins of the ancient lakes (Haynes 1987).[14] In the absence of other evidence it was speculated that this

---

[13.] This has changed since a group of Asheibat Bedouin settled at Siwa about a century ago. Siwan sheikhs still refuse to meet Awlad Ali sheikhs from outside the oasis but now include the local Bedouin sheikhs within their own council. The Siwan Asheibat sheikhs have links to both the Siwans and their kinsmen on the north coast.

[14.] Burnt-reed charcoal deposits have been identified at the uninhabited oases depressions of Oyo, Merga and Selima (Haynes 1987). In terms of geomorphology and ecology these oases are similar to their counterparts in the northern Libyan Desert.

burning was undertaken "by Neolithic pastoralists to provide better access to lake water" (Haynes 2001:129). Whether the modern practices recorded at Al Araq, Bahrein, Sitra and Nuweimisa may have relevance to this conclusion is not yet clear.

The material residues of modern herding camps are sparse, related to the fact that at present only specialist male shepherds undertake migrations through the desert. Shelters are usually temporary, owing to the necessity of regularly relocating the herd between prepared grazing areas, and constructed from local perishable materials such as reed stems and palm leaves. Exploration of caves in the escarpment overlooking the oasis of Bahrein revealed evidence of use including stores of old water jars, packsaddles and other equipment. Heavy smoke-soot residues on the walls and roof of the cave suggested occupation, as well as storage functions, smoke providing some necessary relief from swarming insects. Whether these caves were used by shepherds or represent periods of occupation when entire household units migrated was not possible to establish through superficial observation.

A further activity associated with oasis occupation is hunting, which brings some variety to the diet of herders. Compared with coastal areas, the wildlife of the oases is relatively abundant. Contemporary hunters utilize vintage firearms together with a variety of more traditional techniques for trapping birds and small mammals. Metal blades are useful for butchering, as well as for cutting cords and ropes associated with packsaddles. Although sparse, all the manufactured artifacts associated with migratory Bedouin seem to have been acquired via the broader market economy, from population centers on the north coast.

As reported by Siwan informants, the desert oases have also historically been the destination of donkey caravans from the populated oases with the purpose of collecting *Azowi* dates. The eldest living Siwans had participated in the last of these expeditions in the early part of the 20th century CE. There are some important differences between these visits and those of Bedouin to the oases. Siwan caravans would stop only briefly at each oasis, requiring just a few days to harvest dates from the palm groves at each site. Although it is possible that past Bedouin migrations to the oases involved full household groups, it is known with certainty that Siwan date-collecting camps were exclusively male. Finally, the material culture of the Siwa oasis is highly distinct from that available through regional markets and a majority of items were manufactured within the oases.

Collectively, the above observations lead to a further point with respect to interpretation of the archaeological record at the desert oases. While a future investigator might identify the residues of regular occupation and resource use by two contemporary (yet distinct) cultural groups over a long period of time, it may be more difficult to accurately discern the duality in this use or the complex social and political relationship between users. Although this hypothetical investigator would find evidence for successive visits and occupations through long historic periods, it may be less obvious that nomadic pastoralists were usually in occupation during summer months, while Siwan campsites were established only at the time of the date harvest during the winter months. Despite the apparent archaeological proximity of residues, the two groups were rarely, if ever, present simultaneously, and it may be misleading to assume any kind of formalized relationship between them. As ethnographic research has indicated, the historic relationship between oasis-using groups has effectively been one of nonconsensual resource sharing manifest in a reluctant toleration of respective activities. This reflects the current ambiguity, and the historic volatility, of the relations between Bedouin and Oasis dwellers.

NOMADIC USE OF THE EGYPTIAN OASES

The system of traditional Awlad Ali migration described in this chapter constitutes a journey that could exceed 400 km (each way) across arid desert terrain. That such a pattern of regular pastoral migration with sheep and goats existed historically is of itself noteworthy. It has long been known that camel herding tribes made regular migratory journeys to and between the Egyptian oases (Murray 1935), but hitherto there has been little evidence for similar migratory use by herders of small stock. This study demonstrates that the interior oases of the Egyptian desert have been and continue to be utilized as an important reservoir of forage against conditions of drought or summer scarcity elsewhere. That groundwater-dependent forage resources are available year-round indicates that they could potentially complement pasture and migration regimes at both northern (winter rainfall) and southern (summer rainfall) fringes of the Libyan Desert. This study further suggests that the prospect of several months of supply of forage is considered sufficient incentive to attract pastoralists over long distances, enduring considerable hardship and risks.

The evidence of this study thus contributes additional data to help us understand the behavior of past nomadic societies under comparable resource conditions. It is worth noting that contemporary speculations about how ancient Libyan pastoralists may have utilized natural resources through migration describe nomads moving inland during the winter from summer coastal camps. This model draws heavily on ethnographic observations made in neighboring Cyrenaica and does not take into account the possibility of summer migrations to inland oases or the forage resources available there. While oasis resources, under the management system described, hold the potential to support ovicaprid herds at maintenance for several months, it is a normal practice for herds to return to rain-stimulated annual pastures for the vital lambing, kidding and milking season, thus putting an upper limit on the duration of pastoral occupation of oases over any given year; unless, of course, coastal pastures fail completely. In this latter eventuality it is possible that herding groups could occupy oasis sites as long as necessary until pasture conditions improved elsewhere. It is probable that more-sustained periods of occupation would be visible in the archaeological record. If sustained drought in coastal areas drove large numbers of pastoral groups to seek permanent forage resources in the desert interior, this would possibly exceed the capacity of resources in the study area and require herders to spread further into the Libyan Desert. This type of strategy seems consistent with primary Egyptian sources (dated to around 1213–1204 BCE) that document the arrival of starving Libyan bands at the Bahariya Oasis, apparently searching for productive land (Magid, this volume; Kitchen 1990:20).

It is also noteworthy that, in the case of both Bedouin and (historically) Siwan resource use, resources are divided into subunits under the management of individual descent groups. General recognition of territorial rights is of particular importance for Awlad Ali fire management: it enables herders to plan and implement burning regimes within their own territorial unit, first preparing and then setting aside areas for future use, without risk of other resource users depleting these first. With respect to access rights, fire management practices at the oases are closer to agricultural practice than the 'open access' grazing of seasonal pastures. Most ethnographic studies note that where Bedouin invest labor and other management inputs into the preparation of land for cultivation, such as plowing and sowing, this investment confers exclusive access to the product of these labors. Long-term sustained inputs can result in recognition of territorial rights under traditional law.[15] Similarly, the recognized management inputs at the uninhabited oases seem to have conferred exclusive access rights to resource-using Awlad Ali descent groups.

DISCUSSION

The ethnographic work undertaken in the northern Libyan Desert may contribute to our understanding of nomadic societies and pastoral resource use in two distinct ways. The first relates to the production of ethnographic analogy for historic and prehistoric pastoral resource use in the specific region of study. The second relates to the practical constraints of interpreting the archaeological record of nomadic occupations.

---

[15] See Lancaster and Lancaster 1999 for a wider discussion of traditional Bedouin systems of access to resources and territoriality.

This study has described how the Arab Bedouin groups of the northern Libyan Desert traditionally exploit and manage resources in the isolated and currently uninhabited oases of the interior. It has provided the first description of this form of migratory resource use and demonstrated both the significance of groundwater-sustained oasis resources to pastoralists and their capacity to access and utilize them. It has been postulated that these observations have relevance not only to understanding the ecology of pastoral groups in the northern part of the desert but also to those groups utilizing the southern margins bordering the Sahel. Developmental change has now made it difficult to observe traditional systems of resource management by pastoralists at other Egyptian oases.

The case study further highlights the complexity of relationships that may exist between nomads and other groups. At present, while the Awlad Ali articulate effectively with the broader regional political economy, there is considerable local variation in how specific relationships are managed. Similarly, archaeological evidence may allude to temporary occupations by small groups of Bedouin and Siwan resource users at the uninhabited oases, but this does not necessarily represent co-residence, nor should it be interpreted as the basis for any kind of broader structural relationship. The mobility fundamental to the nomadic lifestyle will always present challenges for the investigator (archaeological, ethnographic or other) in drawing general conclusions from the data and will always require exhaustive explorations of all potential interpretations.

REFERENCES

Avni, G.
1992   Survey of Deserted Bedouin Campsites in the Negev Highlands and Its Implications for Archaeological Research. In O. Bar-Yosef and A. Khazanov (eds.), *Pastoralism in the Levant: Archaeological Materials in Anthropological Perspective*. Madison, Prehistory Press: pp. 241–254.

Banning, E.
1993   Where the Wild Stones Have Gathered Aside: Pastoralist Campsites in Wadi Ziqlab, Jordan. *Biblical Archaeologist 56*: pp. 212–221.

Banning, E. and I. Kohler-Rollefson
1992   Ethnographic Lessons for the Pastoral Past: Camp Locations and Material Remains Near Beidha, Southern Jordan. In O. Bar-Yosef and A. Khazanov (eds.), *Pastoralism in the Levant: Archaeological Materials in Anthropological Perspective*. Madison, Prehistory Press: pp. 181–204.

Barfield, T.
1993   *The Nomadic Alternative*. Englewood Cliffs, Prentice Hall.

Barth, F.

1973   A General Perspective on Nomad-Sedentary Relations in the Middle East. In C. Nelson (ed.), *The Desert and the Sown: Nomads in Wider Society*. Berkeley, University of California Press: pp. 11–22.

Bar-Yosef, O. and A. Khazanov

1992   Introduction. In O. Bar-Yosef and A. Khazanov (eds.), *Pastoralism in the Levant: Archaeological Materials in Anthropological Perspective*. Madison, Prehistory Press: pp. 1–9.

Bates, O.

1914   *The Eastern Libyans: An Essay*. London, Macmillan.

Baxter, P.

1954   *The Social Organization of the Boran*. University of Oxford (PhD dissertation).

Bradley, R.

1992   *Nomads in the Archaeological Record: Case Studies in the Northern Provinces of the Sudan. Meroitica 13*. Berlin, Akademie-Verlag.

Bujra, A.

1973   The Social Implications of Development Policies: A Case Study from Egypt. In C. Nelson (ed.), *The Desert and the Sown: Nomads in Wider Society*. Berkeley, University of California Press: pp. 143–157.

Cribb, R.

1991   *Nomads in Archaeology*. Cambridge, Cambridge University Press.

Cole, D. P. and S. Altorki

1998   *Bedouin, Settlers, and Holiday-Makers: Egypt's Changing Northwest Coast*. Cairo, American University in Cairo Press.

Evans, C.

1983   On the Jube Line: Campsite Studies from Kurdistan. *Archaeological Review from Cambridge 2*: 2, pp. 67–77.

Evans-Pritchard, E.

1940   *The Nuer: A Description of the Mode of Livelihood and Political Institutions of a Nilotic Tribe*. Oxford, Clarendon Press.

Fakhry, A.

1973   *The Oasis of Egypt. Volume 1: Siwa Oasis*. Cairo, American University in Cairo Press.

1974   *The Oasis of Egypt: Volume 2: Bahariyah and Farafra Oases*. Cairo, American University in Cairo Press.

Finkelstein, I.

1995   *Living on the Fringe: The Archaeology and History of the Negev, Sinai, and Neighbouring Regions in the Bronze and Iron Ages*. Sheffield, Sheffield Academic Press.

Gautier, A.

1987   Prehistoric Men and Cattle in North Africa: A Dearth of Data and a Surfeit of Models. In A. Close (ed.), *Prehistory of Arid North Africa*. Dallas, Southern Methodist University Press: pp. 163–187.

Gulliver, P.

1955   *The Family Herds*. London, Routledge and Kegan Paul.

Hassan, F. and T. Gross

1987   Resources and Subsistence During the Early Holocene at Siwa Oasis, Northern Egypt. In A. Close (ed.), *Prehistory of Arid North Africa*. Dallas, Southern Methodist University Press: pp. 85–103.

Haynes, V.

1987   Holocene Migration Rates of the Sudano-Sahelian Wetting Front, Arba'in Desert Eastern Sahara. In A. Close (ed.), *Prehistory of Arid North Africa*. Dallas, Southern Methodist University Press: pp. 69–84.

2001   Geochronology and Climate Change of the Pleistocene–Holocene Transition in the Darb al Arba'in Desert, Eastern Sahara. *Geoarchaeology: An International Journal 16*: 1, pp. 119–141.

Hole, F.

1978   Pastoral Nomadism in Western Iran. In R. Gould (ed.), *Explorations in Ethnoarchaeology*. Albuquerque, University of New Mexico Press: pp. 127–167.

1979   Rediscovering the Past in the Present: Ethnoarchaeology in Luristan, Iran. In C. Kramer (ed.), *Ethnoarchaeology: Implications of Ethnography for Archaeology*. New York, Columbia University Press: pp. 192–218.

Kassas, M.

1955   Rainfall and Vegetation Belts in Arid North-East Africa. In *Plant Ecology: Proceedings of the Montpellier Symposium*. Strasbourg, UNESCO: pp. 49–59.

Khazanov, A.

1984   *Nomads and the Outside World*. Cambridge, Cambridge University Press.

Kitchen, K.

1990   The Arrival of Libyans in New Late Kingdom Egypt. In A. Leahy (ed.), *Libya and Egypt, c. 1300–750 BC*. London, Centre for Near and Middle Eastern Studies: pp. 15–27.

Knapp, A.

1981   The Theran Frescoes and the Question of Aegean Contact with Libya During the Late Bronze Age. *Journal of Mediterranean Anthropology and Archaeology 1*: pp. 249–279.

Kuhlman K.

1998   Roman and Byzantine Siwa: Developing a Latent Picture. In O. Kaper (ed.), *Life on the Fringe: Living in the Southern Egyptian Deserts During the Roman and Early Byzantine Periods*. Leiden, Research School CNWS: pp. 159–180.

Lancaster, W. and F. Lancaster

1999   *People, Land, and Water in the Arab Middle East: Environments and Landscapes in the Bilad ash-Sham*. New York, Harwood.

Levy, T.

1992   Transhumance, Subsistence, and Social Evolution in the Northern Negev Desert. In O. Bar-Yosef and A. Khazanov (eds.), *Pastoralism in the Levant: Archaeological Materials in Anthropological Perspective*. Madison, Prehistory Press: pp. 65–82.

Masini, A.

2001   *Environmental Amelioration in Siwa: Technical Report*. Gland, International Union for the Conservation of Nature.

Murray, G. M.

1935   *Sons of Ishmael: A Study of the Egyptian Bedouin*. London, George Routledge.

Osing, J.

1980   Libyen, Libyer. In W. Helck and E. Otto (eds.), *Lexikon der Ägyptologie, Volume 3*. Wiesbaden, Otto Harrassowitz: pp. 1015–1033.

Reifenberg, A.

1950   *The Struggle Between the Desert and the Sown* [in Hebrew]. Jerusalem, Mosad Byalik.

Robertshaw, P. and D. Collett

1983   The Identification of Pastoral Peoples in the Archaeological Record: An Example from East Africa. *World Archaeology 15*: pp. 67–78.

Rowe, A.

1948   A History of Ancient Cyrenaica. In *Cahiers des annales du service des antiquités de l'Égypte 12*. Cairo, Department of Antiquities.

Simms, S.

1988   The Archaeological Structure of a Bedouin Camp. *Journal of Archaeological Science 15*: pp. 197–211.

Sinibaldi, I.

2002   *Proposal for the Establishment of the Siwa Protected Area*. Siwa, Egyptian-Italian Environmental Programme.

Smith, A.

1985   The Ethnoarchaeology of Pastoralism in Saharan and Sahel Zones of West Africa. In M. Liverani, A. Palmieri and R. Peroni (eds.), *Studi di paletnologia in onore di Salvatore M. Puglisi*. Università degli Studi di Roma "La Sapienza": pp. 57–70.

White, D.

1990   Provisional Evidence for the Seasonal Occupations of the Marsa Matruh Area by Late Bronze Age Libyans. In A. Leahy (ed.), *Libya and Egypt, c. 1300–750 BC*. London, Centre for Near and Middle Eastern Studies: pp. 1–14.

Wilson, R.

1984   *The Camel.* Essex, Longman.

Zarins, J.

1992   Pastoral Nomadism in Arabia: Ethnoarchaeology and the Archaeological
        Record: a Case Study. In O. Bar-Yosef and A. Khazanov (eds.), *Pastoralism
        in the Levant: Archaeological Materials in Anthropological Perspective*. Madison,
        Prehistory Press: pp. 219–240.

CHAPTER 23

FROM OBJECTS TO AGENTS

THE ABABDA NOMADS AND THE
INTERPRETATION OF THE PAST

WILLEKE WENDRICH

T HIS CHAPTER REFLECTS nine years of interaction with the *Ababda* nomads
(singular: *Abadi*; feminine: *Abadiyya*), living in the southern part of the
Eastern Desert, between the Nile Valley and the Red Sea in Egypt (Figure
23.1). From 1994 to 2002 a group of up to 80 Ababda excavated the ancient
harbor town of Berenike, supervised by an international crew of approximately
40 archaeologists (Sidebotham and Wendrich 1995, 1996, 1998, 1999, 2000,
2007). The Ababda way of life is currently under pressure. Discussions during
and after the work often centered on the rapid change of Ababda culture in
recent times. These changes are the result of an increase of tourism along the
Red Sea coast and the fact that the Egyptian government would like to see
the Ababda settle. For this purpose several villages were built along the main
road along the Red Sea coast. The village layouts are spacious: the houses were
built in flat desert areas with much space between the buildings. Each house
contained two units, each with two rooms. Each Ababda nuclear family was
given a two-room unit, which one entered from a gated courtyard. Water tanks
were placed near areas where traditional Ababda dwellings were concentrated,
and the government provided drinking water for these communities. Apart
from these housing projects on the Red Sea coast, Ababda have settled in the
Nile Valley, mostly in the region around Kom Ombo, which was developed
to house the Nubians displaced by Lake Nasser in the 1960s. The younger
generation of Ababda whose parents had settled in Wadi Khareet expressed
a keen interest in saving a record of their culture. They asked if I could not
write a book about them, much like the books about the ancient inhabitants
of the region. I suggested that they should write such a book themselves, with
my assistance, a project that is still ongoing.

In relation to this writing project a group of Ababda and several members of
the excavation team started to record the Ababda culture and created a collection of Ababda material culture. As part of the process of awakening interest in
the cultural heritage of the Ababda, the Eastern Desert Antiquities Protection
Project (EDAPP) was granted a substantial contribution by the Cultural Fund

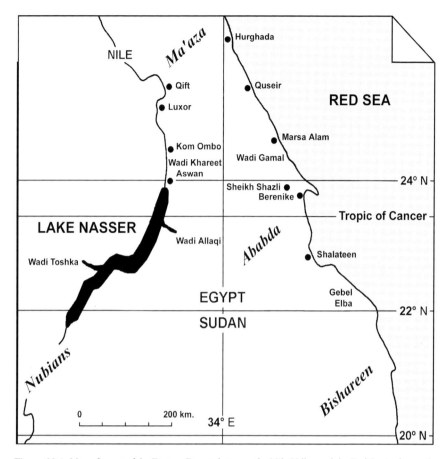

Figure 23.1. Map of a part of the Eastern Desert, between the Nile Valley and the Red Sea in the south of Egypt and the north of Sudan, with the location of different groups of nomads indicated, as well as the place names mentioned in the text (map prepared by H. Barnard).

of the Royal Netherlands Embassy in Cairo. This grant was used for training in archaeological techniques and to build a site museum where the collection could be housed. Part of the collection was displayed in this site museum; another part was arranged into a small exhibit in one of the towers of the restored Ottoman fort in Quseir. A third collection traveled to the Netherlands and formed the core of an exhibition in the Wereldmuseum Rotterdam.[1]

The exhibit in the Netherlands contrasted two collections: one composed by the Ababda, and one collected by the Egyptologist L. Keimer, purchased by the Wereldmuseum in the 1950s. The 'collection philosophies' behind these

---

[1.] This exhibit was entitled *Nomaden tussen Nijl en Rode Zee* (Nomads Between the Nile and the Red Sea) and ran from April 2002 through March 2003.

two, and therefore also the objects, are very different. Keimer was interested in making a 'museum quality' collection of the finest Ababda arts and crafts representing the life of 'the other.' The EDAPP collection is made by the Ababda to represent their own cultural identity and to give a representative image of what Ababda life is like to future Ababda, who will live in a changed world, and to inform outsiders (Egyptians, foreign tourists) about Ababda culture and heritage. In 2006 the Royal Netherlands Embassy in Cairo donated funds to build an exhibition center that will form the core of the *Beit al-Ababda* (Ababda House) in the Wadi al-Gemal National Park.

Keimer published extensive descriptions of the Eastern Desert cultures (1951, 1952a, 1952b, 1953a, 1953b, 1954a, 1954b). His specific interest was to outline 'survival' of the material culture of the Beja from the Pharaonic period to the present. In a series of articles he highlighted a wide range of aspects such as the use of headrests, amulets, kohl eye protection, makeup, hairstyles and gazelle traps. During the work in 1998 it was clear that my interest in Ababda culture was different from that of Keimer. As an archaeologist I was fascinated by the recent history, the material culture and present way of life, of the Ababda from an ethno-archaeological perspective. The strategies of the Ababda to cope with periods of drought and to survive successfully in an arid region provided important information on potential use of tactics to cope with similar circumstances by the ancient inhabitants of Berenike and by the nomadic Eastern Desert Dwellers, for which we found evidence in the excavation. Both Keimer's and my interest in Ababda culture and history differ, therefore, from that of the group of Ababda, working on the EDAPP collection.

What follows is a brief introduction into the Ababda way of life, highlighting those aspects that are of interest to me as an archaeologist: their complex social structure, their notion of personal ownership, and their impact on the landscape. The physical traces that the Ababda way of life may leave for future archaeologists may serve as a reminder that the sparse material traces of mobile people can represent complex social systems and ideas of identity, belonging and ownership. This chapter is partly descriptive because little information has been published on the present-day Ababda. The discussion focuses on multiple interpretations of the past, which can be identified in the various attempts that have been made to describe and interpret Ababda history and culture.

THE ABABDA

The Ababda are perhaps best characterized as multiresource pastoral nomads roaming the valleys (*wadis*) of the Eastern Desert and the Red Sea coast, although a substantial number of them have permanently settled in the Nile Valley. Their identity is strongly connected to the landscape they inhabit; the camels, sheep, and goats they own; their material culture; and their social ceremonies. The Ababda are generally classified as a subgroup of the Beja nomads, which occupy an area stretching from Quseir, in Egypt, to Eritrea. The Beja include the Bishareen, the Hadendowa, the Amarar, the Atman and the Beni Amr (Magid, this volume; Murray 1923; Paul 1954; Salih 1980; Morton 1988; Hobbs 1990). The Rashaida, who live around Shelateen and can be recognized by their purple outfits, have migrated from Saudi Arabia relatively recently. The same is true for the Ma'aza, who live north of Quseir (Hobbs 1990). In contrast to most of the Beja, the Ababda speak a dialect of Arabic (De Jong 2002).

Several authors have claimed that the Beja have lived in the region of the Eastern Desert of Egypt and the Red Sea Hills of Sudan since time immemorial and that they are to be considered identical with the ancient Bulahau, Blemmyes, Bega and Bougaites (Eide et al. 1998; Pierce 2001).[2] These names are known from Roman texts from the 4th to 6th centuries CE in which these groups are invariably presented as untrustworthy, unruly and uncontrollable (Updegraff 1988; Eide et al. 1998). This identification, however, is based on the uncritical use of the ancient sources and a disregard of two millennia of development (Burstein, this volume; Barnard 2005). The Greco-Roman sources are internally incoherent, and it is obvious that for most ancient authors the Blemmyes and other peoples were diffuse groups, perceived as 'the other,' and representative of the diversity of inhabitants of the areas south of the Roman border. Archaeological evidence for nomadic activities in the region seems to indicate, in the late Roman period, a population well rooted in both the desert and settled society. A distinctive type of pottery, which may have served as a cultural or ethnic marker, was possibly produced in the desert (Barnard, this volume; Barnard and Strouhal 2004; Barnard et al. 2005). There is no extensive literature on the Ababda. The most comprehensive are the publications of Louis Keimer (see above).

SOCIAL ORGANIZATION

The Ababda are organized patrilineally and claim to descend from Abad, who came to Egypt from Saudi Arabia and was the son of Zubeyr (ibn al-Awwam), 'a friend' of the Prophet Mohamed (Murray 1923). At the same time, they consider themselves to belong to the Beja. In contrast to their closest southern neighbors, the Bishareen, the Ababda call themselves 'Arabs.' This, however, does not in the first place refer to Saudi Arabia as place of origin, and is not an

---

[2] Bigeh, an ancient name for the harbor of Berenike appearing on several medieval maps, is thought to refer to the Bega who took control of the region in the 6th century CE (Murray 1967; Eide et al. 1998).

ethnic designation, but instead refers to a lifestyle in contrast with the settled inhabitants of the Nile Valley (Morton 1988). The Ababda lineage is subject to mystification by the Ababda themselves. Identity is specified at different levels, depending on the context, and a person can be Beja, Ababda, 'Ogada (one of the Ababda 'clans'), and his father's and grandfather's son. A young Ababda participant in the project, who made an inventory of what several older persons had to say on the subject, provided a chart in which the Ababda are divided into 16 *qabila* (tribes), each belonging to one of three family or clan groups that all use a distinctive *wasm*, or clan sign (Table 23.1).

The family and tribal relations of the Ababda as recorded by Murray in the early 20th century are very different (Murray 1923). The 'Ogada, who are the most prominent Ababda group at present, do not feature in his overview (Table 23.2). The Arabic terms *'aila* (family, plural *'ayaal*), *qabila* (tribe, plural *qabayil*) and *beit* (house, plural *buyut*) can be utilized at different levels, to indicate various group compositions. These words are used where English would employ terms such as *lineage, tribe, clan, family, house, extended family* or *nuclear family*. The terms as used by the Ababda differ from the way they are employed by the *Ma'aza*, in the northern part of the Eastern Desert and the *Awlad Ali*, a Bedouin group that moved from Saudi Arabia into the Sinai, the Mediterranean coastal area and the Western Desert, probably around the 11th century CE. The Ma'aza are divided into approximately 20 clans (*aila*, most

Table 23.1. Overview of Ababda Families and Tribes:

Family or clan (*wasm* = brand and sign of clan ownership)	Main center of 'residence'	Qabila ('tribe')[a]
al-Habshee	Arab Saleh	Haranaab
		Kerdjaab
		'Ogada
		Nuffa'
		Saadalaab
		'Amaraab
ar-Rasaan	Manazig, Khuda', Hemeira	Billalaab
		Batranaab
		Zeydaab
		Timeen
		Farhanaab
		Kimilaab
		Djahalaab
al-Khortaam	Hamata, Abu Greya, Abu Khusun	Greidjaab
		Hamidaab
		Farradjaab

[a]Data recorded by Gamaa Hussein.

often translated as 'family'), stemming from the same lineage (an often mythical forebear), and divided into households (Hobbs 1990). The Awlad Ali have a subdivision in *qabila* (tribe), which in turn is divided into other *qabila* (clan), subdivided into *aila* (family, the maximal lineage), subdivided into *beit* (house, minimal lineage), which in turn is subdivided into *aila* (extended family) and *beit* (household) (Cole and Altorki 1998). These translations may perhaps lose the most important organizational aspect of the nomadic interrelationships, which are determined by real, mythical or invented lineage. In theory, mobility does not affect these relationships, because the group identity is not linked to a geographical region, nor is it defined by land ownership. In practice, the Ababda tend to cluster in groups of the same families, clans or tribes, and multiple groups are found to share the same region.

LAND AND RESOURCE OWNERSHIP

The Eastern Desert is an arid region, with an annual rainfall between 20 and 200 mm occurring mostly in the winter and often causing flashfloods (*seyl*, plural *seyul*). These floods create temporary lakes near the shoreline and fill up the water holes, while a subterranean water flow fills the aquifers, providing the region with enough water to last for at least two or three years without additional rainfall. Aridity is determined by the lack of precipitation, by the rate of evaporation and, most important, by the irregularity of the annual rain (Krzywinski 2001; Cappers 2006). This means that in some years the Ababda can embark on opportunistic agriculture, but regular agricultural pursuits are impossible. In the past the Ababda cultivated only *durra* (*Sorghum* sp.). Today corn (*Zea mays*, also called *durra* in Arabic) or barley (*Hordeum vulgare*) is sometimes also sown. Growing wheat, the staple of the Ababda diet, is not feasible. Dry farming of barley requires about 200 mm of annual rainfall, just on the border of moist years, and wheat needs approximately 300 mm rain per year (Cappers 2006). Stable agricultural fields are therefore not a feature of the landscape. The notion of ownership and claims on land are often considered to depend on a settled lifestyle and the need to protect crops. Although this may sound like a plausible supposition, it is clear that mobile populations also have territorial claims and rights of ownership. These claims are not focusing as much on a specific plot of land as on resources. They are obtained and maintained by a complex social system of reciprocal observation of rights, which enables mobile peoples (hunter-gatherers, pastoral nomads or mobile agriculturalists) to leave property behind without the risk of losing it to other groups or individuals.

Although landownership has not become an issue until recent infringements of the Egyptian government into Ababda territory (Cole and Altorki 1998), ownership of resources has always been recognized. A *wasm* is a symbol used

Table 23.2. Overview of the Ababda Tribe and Its Subdivisions (after Murray 1923:423):

Forebear	Group	*Qabila* ('tribe')
Muhammad, son of Ashab, son of Abad	Muammad-ab (northern section)	'Abdein-ab
		'Amran-ab
		'Atiya-b
		'Adwalla-b
		Edidan-ab
		Faraj-ab = Farradjaab
		Fisheij-ab
		Hameid-ab = Hamidaab
		Jâral-ab
		Jubran-ab
		Malak-ab
		Rahal-ab
		Seidan-ab
		Shaf-ab
		Shein-ab
		Shuweim-ab
Bilal, Son of Jama, son of Ashab, son of Abad	Bilal-ab = Billalaab (southern section)	'Amîr-ab = Billalaab
		Batran-ab = Batranaab
		Firhan-ab = Farhanaab
		Hamud-ab
		Jahad-ab
		Jidal-ab
		Kirj-ab
		Rajab-ab
		Saadalla-b = Saadalaab
		Selîm-ab
		Taman-ab = Timeen?
		Zeid-ab = Zeydaab
Haran, son of Jama, son of Ashab, son of Abad	Haranaab	Haranaab
Harein, son of Jama, son of Ashab, son of Abad	Harein-ab	Harein-ab
		Nafa-b = Nuffa'
Meleik, son of Abdalla, son of Abad	Meleik-ab	Meleik-ab
		Fuqara
Jimeil, son of Abad?	Jimeiliyîn	
'Ibud, son of Abad		'Ibudiyîn
		Shanatir
'Broken tribes'		Anqar-ab
		Hamej
		Heteimiya
		Hukm
		Kimeil-ab
		Qireij-ab = Kerdjaab

as a burn mark for camels, but it can also be scratched in stone or laid out with sticks and rocks as an explicit sign of land and resource ownership. It is a 'signature' recognized by all Ababda to secure an *aila*'s claim on the resources of a particular area and form a material trace of social organization. Members of the family are allowed to use the scarce water resources, hunt and gather plants or wood. Outsiders have to ask permission and can be denied access in times of resource stress. The *wasm* is also known from other nomadic groups, such as the Ma'aza, who arrived in the Egyptian Red Sea Mountains around 1700 CE, and the Rashaida, who arrived in the border area between Egypt and Sudan in the early 20th century CE (Hobbs 1990; Roe, in press).

Although the Ababda are usually described as pastoral nomads, whose existence was based on the possession of camels, sheep and goats (Paul 1954; Morton 1988), much of their activities, as known from descriptions dated to the 19th–20th centuries CE, could perhaps better be described as hunting and gathering. The women were responsible for the herds, while the men went out into the desert to hunt gazelle or ibex and collect wood (for charcoal production) or medicinal plants. The latter activity is still important, and the economic importance of herbs sold in the Nile Valley is undiminished. For their own use the Ababda collect the pods of the *Acacia nilotica* (used for tanning), the wood of the *Acacia tortilis* (to make coffee mortars) and *Lagenaria siceria*, a gourd used as a container (*loza*) for cosmetic hair grease (Christensen 2001; Cappers 2006).

Men traveled to the Nile Valley to sell their products and to assist with the harvest, especially in Lower Nubia, where many men had left to work in Cairo as cooks, guards and servants. The Ababda received sorghum or wheat in exchange for their help and after the harvest the flocks were allowed to graze on the abandoned fields. This activity came to an abrupt end with the closing of the Aswan High Dam, and the subsequent filling of Lake Nasser, in the 1960s. The Ababda along the Red Sea shore also procured fish and mollusks. Central to the survival strategy of the Ababda is their superior knowledge of resources that are not easily accessible.

At present, the Ababda women still mostly lead a traditional life. They set up temporary residences in the wadis of the Eastern Desert with their children and flocks. Women are not allowed to milk the sheep, goats or camels, nor are they permitted to slaughter animals. If no male relatives are present, the animals are not milked and the lambs, kids and young camels drink their full share. When a man grows rich, meaning that his flock is getting too large to be tended by his wife, he can marry a second, third or fourth wife, who then takes part of the flock to a different area. There is a direct relationship between the size of the flock and the carrying capacity of the land (Roe, in press). If the amount of grazing needed cannot be found within a day's walk, then part or all of the flock is moved to a different area.

THE OVERNIGHT BAG AND THE PORTABLE RESIDENCE

An 'overnight bag' of an Abadi, the minimal resources that a man will take on a short trip, of two or three days' walking, consists of two sheep's skins, open at the neck, the legs connected with a leather strap to form a carrying sling. The smaller bag (*girbi*) contains water, while the other (*giraab*) holds a knife, approximately a kilogram of flour, some salt, a plastic mixing bowl, matches, a globular coffeepot (*djabana*) in a protective basket (*kabuta*), a metal coffee roaster, a pestle and mortar, a cylindrical basket containing three or four tiny Chinese cups, a wooden stand with hollows to hold the cups, raw coffee beans, sugar, ginger root and a stick of *meshwak* (*Salvadore persica*: 'toothbrush bush'). An archaeologist, finding such a collection of coffee-production equipment may conclude that we must be dealing with a permanent campsite because no person in his right mind would bring all this stuff on a walking trip. An inventory of what an American, making a similar trip, would bring shows that 'traveling light' is a relative notion. He or she might carry two gallons of water, in a plastic container, and a backpack with a Leatherman all-purpose tool, a torch, spare batteries, clean underwear, clean socks, sleeping bag, disinfecting nonwater soap gel, toothbrush and toothpaste, deodorant, snakebite kit, camera, notebook, pain killers, bandages, trail mix bars, Nescafe, a can of tuna, a can of tomato paste, macaroni, processed cheese triangles and an aluminum pot. Both travelers bring their essential equipment and supplies, but the understanding of what is essential differs substantially.

For the Ababda, drinking coffee is an important, almost ceremonial, activity any time of day. It is closely connected with basic hospitality. When meeting, or taking a break, the Abadi will build a small fire and boil water. In the meantime the coffee beans are roasted over the fire and crushed in the mortar with some ginger root. The crushed coffee is carefully guided into the narrow opening of the *djabana*, which is filled with hot water, and put back in the ashes to brew. A small bung of date-palm fiber is stuffed in the opening as a strainer. A guest is offered three, seven or nine cups of this strong, spicy coffee, which is served in tiny cups, half filled with sugar. Part of the sugar is dissolved by stirring the coffee with the end of a match. The second and third cups are poured onto the remaining sugar. Figures 23.2–23.6 present an overview of the chaîne opératoire of making *djabana*.

The *djabana*, and the importance of serving coffee as part of a hospitality ritual, is not restricted to the Ababda. Similar use is known in a large region encompassing the east of Sudan, Ethiopia and Eritrea. The Ababda form the northernmost group that uses the globular coffeepots. Emphasis on the importance of serving coffee to guests is also found at the other side of the Red Sea, in Yemen, but there the coffee is prepared in preferably heavy, silver coffeepots.

Figure 23.2. Preparation of *djabana*: pouring water into a tin can.

Figure 23.3. Preparation of *djabana*: roasting coffee beans in a tin can with a handle.

Figure 23.4. Preparation of *djabana*: pounding the roasted coffee beans in a wooden mortar with a length of reinforcement steel.

Figure 23.5. Preparation of *djabana*: pouring the ground coffee into the narrow opening of the coffeepot (also called *djabana*).

Figure 23.6. Preparation of *djabana*: the coffee with ginger is ready and the coffeepot (*djabana*) rests on a ring stand. Small Chinese cups are half filled with sugar, which will last for at least three servings. The strong, ginger-flavored coffee is poured and a new batch is started immediately. The guests drink either three, seven or nine cups, depending on the length of the meeting.

Figure 23.7. Headrest (*mutir'is*), acacia wood with aluminum repair; the saddle is approximately 20 cm wide.

Figure 23.8. Headrest (*mutir'is*), leather over wooden frame; the height is 35 cm.

Figure 23.9. A milking basket (*kahel*) made of finely coiled doam palm leaf.

There are more striking correlations with Ethiopian and Eritrean material culture, for instance the use of headrests (*mutir'is*; Figures 23.7–23.8), rather than pillows, and the extensive use of finely coiled basketry, often decorated with overlays of leather strips (*kahel*; Figure 23.9).

In contrast to the extensive inventory brought on short trips, the entire family's residence fits on two camels. Extended families live in small groups of mat houses (*beit al-burush*) built by the women. The only contribution to the house by the men is during the wedding, when the husband brings all the materials needed to build the first mat house. The Ababda could be characterized as 'matrilocal,' at least for the first year of the marriage. In the early evening of the first day (*al-farta*) of the wedding ceremony, which usually takes five days, the husband visits the family of his wife. With a stick (*assaia*) he draws the outline of the place where the house should be built. The actual building of the house is done by the older women of the wife's family. First they sprinkle sugar over the area where the house is to be built, to invoke a life of sweetness and happiness. Then, using digging sticks, they excavate nine postholes forming a roughly rectangular ground plan, oriented east-west, with an extra post for the entrance at the long side of the house facing south, away from the mostly northerly winds. Forked acacia branches are placed in these postholes, and three or four curved roots of the acacia are tied to the forked ends to form the skeleton of the roof (Figure 23.10). All branches are tied together with a special plaited rope, made with eight white and eight black bundles of wool (Figure 23.11). The effect is a decorative plait of white and black V-shapes. The house skeleton is clothed with woven woolen carpets, called *shamla* (Figure 23.12), on the inside, and with mats, sewn from plaited doam palm leaf (*Hyphaene thebaica*), on the outside (Figure 23.13). Each mat of the house is approximately 3x1.5 m and consists of 11 strips sewn together, each strip plaited of 13 strands of doam palm leaf, approximately 20 mm wide. These mats are molded over the frame and kept in place by wooden pegs used much in the way that pins keep together fabric (Figure 23.14). These pegs are approximately 300 mm long and pierce through the edges of two mats and sometimes also the underlying carpet.

The entrance of the house is formed by the nicest looking carpet. The mats forming the roof of the house form a slight overhang at the south, which gives the entrance some protection from the sun. The entrance carpet, effectively the south wall of the house, can be taken up, to open up the entire house (Figure 23.15). The house has no visible internal division, but the area to the east, away from the entrance, is considered the women's side, while the western side is regarded as the male side (Saidel, this volume). The house is used mostly by the women who cook, make coffee or bake bread in front of the entrance. Women's tasks include spinning wool and weaving carpets, both the heavy but mostly undecorated *shamla* and more supple blanket-like carpets that are used to sleep on (*farsha*) or under (*hemel*). Carpets are woven on simple horizontal looms, consisting of four pegs in the ground to which two cross bars have been tied to hold the warp under tension. The warp is of coarse wool twine; the weft traditionally consists of natural colored wool. At present, a *shamla* is mostly undecorated, whereas a *farsha* sometimes has a simple striped decoration. The *hemel* (blanket) has patterns varying from simple stripes in natural colors (white and shades of brown to almost black) to elaborate patterns of triangles. These are now often made with very brightly colored wool, or synthetic fibers, bought at the market.

Tanning leather, with acacia pods, is also a woman's task, as well as manufacturing leather products, such as water-carrying bags (*gurbah*), leather buckets to haul water from a well (*dalwa*), leather tanning vessels (*garrad*), decorative bags in which to keep the household's belongings (*dabiya*) and a large variety of decorative camel gear. It is the children's task to fetch water from wells (*bir*), or natural rain collection basin (*galt*), and to take the animals out to browse.

Figure 23.10. Building a *beit al-burush*: forked acacia branches and roots are secured into the ground and tied into a frame.

Figure 23.11. Building a *beit al-burush*: a special rope plaited of black and white string is employed for the bindings.

Figure 23.12. Building a *beit al-burush*: the inner walls of the house consist of tightly woven goat-hair carpets.

Figure 23.13. Building a *beit al-burush*: the outer walls of the house are made of large doam palm leaf mats.

Figure 23.14. Building a *beit al-burush*: the mats are stitched together with sharp pegs of acacia wood.

Figure 23.15. Building a *beit al-burush*: the box-shaped mat house is oriented with its back to the north to protect the entrance from the prevailing wind.

FOODWAYS AND COOKING UTENSILS

The traditional Ababda diet was mostly dependent on milk of the flocks and cereals exchanged or bought in the Nile Valley. The staple food was *aseeda*, a porridge made from water and flour (originally ground sorghum, more recently wheat). If available, salt, butter or milk were added to the mixture that was cooked for an hour in a *burma* (a vessel cut from *hamr*, steatite quarried at Abu Gurdi, Rod al-Gamr and other places in the Eastern Desert). The porridge was eaten with the right hand from a communal wooden bowl. These large wooden bowls (*gaddah*) were a precious possession and hard to come by; therefore, almost all *gaddah* show extensive repairs.

A fast way to prepare food was to make dough of water and ground sorghum (*durra*) and bake bread (*rudaaf*) on top of heated stones in a shallow depression, approximately 20 cm in diameter, lined with flat stones. A fire was built in this and then removed to reveal the hot stones onto which the dough was poured, which was then covered with the hot charcoal. When sorghum was replaced by wheat, around 1950, the dough was smoother and could be baked directly in the sand. This bread, known as *kaburri* or *gurs* (disk), is baked for 15 min, after which the charcoal is removed, the bread turned and baked for another 15 min. After having the sand and ashes wiped off, the bread is ready to eat. Apparently an adoption from a Nile Valley tradition is the production of *ruqaaq*, thin bread, rolled out on a table and baked on the metal lid of an oil barrel, balanced on three stones over a fire.

Meat and vegetables were not regularly added to the meal. Occasionally gazelle or ibex were hunted and consumed. At present, hunting is illegal, although it still occurs, not only by the Ababda but also by mostly Arab tourists (Cole and Altorki 1998). The flocks of female sheep and goats were kept intact, and the male animals were sold off immediately after the rainy season. Sheep, goats and camels are rarely slaughtered for consumption. Occasions when this takes place are weddings and the *karama*, a festive gathering of the *aila* at which each *qabila* slaughters one or more animals. The meat is prepared much like the bread: large stones are heated, and the meat is spread out on top and covered by charcoal. This procedure is called *salaat* and is considered a highlight of celebrating the community. Outsiders are invited (*karama* is from the root *krm*, 'being generous'), but they are not allowed to slaughter animals. They can contribute by giving money. Generosity is not just a positive characteristic but a serious religious obligation.

PERSONAL CARE, CLOTHING AND ADORNMENT

Ababda men wear wide cotton breaches with a very low crotch, over which they have a simple shirt to their knees, also of white cotton, and a dark colored waist-coat. The women wear very colorful flowery dresses, covered with equally colorful but monochrome wraps. This is the modern equivalent of traditional Ababda-style clothing, which existed of large sheets of cotton wrapped around the body for both men and women (Keimer 1953b). Leather sandals are nowadays mostly replaced by plastic flip-flops, although sturdy leather sandals with soles made of old car tires are worn as well. When, however, the going gets tough, especially on mountain paths with treacherous sharp rocks, shoes and sandals are usually taken off.

The Ababda and Bishari men were most famous for their hairstyles, which consisted of long curly hair on top of the head and curled tresses or plaits hanging down framing the face and neck, and for the wooden combs they wore as adornment (Keimer 1954b). This gained them the derogatory nickname 'fuzzy-wuzzies' by the British in the 18th–19th centuries CE. The hair is rubbed with fragrant sheep's fat, which helps to prevent it from drying out in the wind and sun. The combs, the main function of which is to decorate the hair, are still made of acacia wood, but Afro-style plastic combs are bought at the market as well. The use of headrests (Figures 23.7–23.8), rather than pillows, is possibly intended to preserve the elaborate hairstyle.

Like that of the men, the hair of the women is carefully greased and plaited. Gold-foil 'coins' are worked into the hairdo, lining the forehead. Colorful beads, red berries and shells decorate the plaits. They make the hair heavy and enhance dancing movements. Jewelry is considered very important by the women. Heavy silver anklets (khul-khal) are a woman's savings. Gold is used for earrings and nose ornaments, the most traditional ones drilled through the top of the nose and covering its largest part with a lozenge-shaped decorated plate of gold. Necklaces and bracelets are usually made of cheaper materials such as shells or glass, clay or plastic beads. A woman's adornment concentrates on the head. The men do not wear jewelry but may be seen wearing leather necklaces or upper armbands containing an apotropaic amulet.

GENDER PRIORITIES

While creating the EDAPP collection, to be housed in the *Beit al-Ababda* in the Wadi al-Gemal Nature Park, a group of men and women were asked to list the objects that were essential to represent their culture. The priorities were, perhaps not surprisingly, quite different, with one exception: everything related to the *djabana* was considered the most important by both men and women (Table 23.3).

Table 23.3. Priority List for the Collection of Ababda Objects:

Men[a]		**Women**[a]	
djabana	globular coffeepot	*djabana*	globular coffeepot
muhmas	coffee roaster	*muhmas*	coffee roaster
hohn	mortar and pestle	*hohn*	mortar and pestle
kabuta l'il djabana	basket for coffeepot	*kabuta l'il djabana*	basket for coffeepot
kabuta l'il findjaan	basket with cups	*kabuta l'il findjaan*	basket with cups
masaanab	coffee cup stand	*masaanab*	coffee cup stand
lauwaya	ring stand for coffeepot	*lauwaya*	ring stand for coffeepot
hababa	fire fan	*hababa*	fire fan
sarg	camel saddle	*hegel*	ankle band
sarg sennaar	back-bladed riding saddle	*zumam*	nose decoration
howiyya	packsaddle	*loza*	hair fat container
feraya	leather leg protector	*mukhala*	kohl (eye paint) holder
mukhlaya	decorative saddlebag	*mutir'is*	headrest
hemel	camel blanket	*amud*	forked wood for house
zumam	nose ring for camel	*amud*	roof spans
rasaan. .	head gear	*mereiya*	rope for house
mahakaba / m. fardateen	front decoration with 1 or 2 tassels	*shamla*	carpet: inner house walls
lebab	back decoration	*birsh, burush*	mats: outer house walls
assaia	stick (camel driving)	*farsh*	floor mat
gurda	goat-hair saddle band	*hemel*	decorated floor carpet
auwkaal	camel hobble	*rihaya*	mill
gurbadj	whip	*gaddah*	wooden serving bowl
kahel	basket for milking	*mufrak*	stirring utensil
daraga	shield	*burma*	cooking pot, ceramic
seyf	sword	*giddur*	cooking pot, stone or copper
khandjar, shutaal	dagger	*dabya*	decorated leather bag
shutaal	curved dagger	*gurbah*	undecorated leather bag
ganad	fire maker	*gurbet el-moya*	leather water bag
		dalwa	leather bucket
hulaal	hair comb	*gur*	leather tanning bag
loza	hair fat container	*abreek*	metal or ceramic water jug
hegaab	leather bound amulet	*mukhlaya*	decorative saddlebag
gurbah	undecorated leather bag	*muhakkaba*	tasseled decoration
tambura	musical instrument, lute	*hemel*	saddle blanket
tabla	drum	*do'a*	wedding saddle
taar	large drum		
		fustan, khalaga, toob	dress, wrap
sirwal, budja	long, baggy underpants	*shibshib*	sandals
aragi	long overshirt		
sawakni	vest		
shash	white cotton turban		
shibshib	sandals		

[a]Data were collected in 1999 in Berenike, Arab Saleh and Manazig (Figure 23.1).

The men listed all different parts of camel gear as the second-most important group of objects. Every tassel, belt and bag is identified by an individual name. It is the mother of an adolescent boy who produces these items, to deck out the camel of the proud youth. Most of the camel gear is purely decorative: the saddlebag can hardly contain goods, but its long colored tassels enhance and exaggerate the swinging motion of a running camel and make for a handsome sight. The women's equivalent, the wedding saddle, was not mentioned with the same sense of urgency as the men's camel decorations. Wedding saddles are a spectacular sight, built up of a palm leaf basketry core, covered with red velvet, and decorated with a carpet of kauri shells, waving ostrich feathers and beads of glass and silver. The women did mention camel gear, the production of which is their responsibility, but only after the household utensils. The women concentrated on items for adornment, which were mentioned immediately after the *djabana* gear. Jewelry is embellishment and at the same time a woman's capital.

For the men, shield, sword and dagger came immediately after the camel adornments and saddles. Symbols of hunting, warfare and feasting, these items are considered an integral part of Ababda male identity. Clothing was initially not mentioned by men or women, even though the Ababda attire is very different from what is worn in the Nile Valley. Hair combs, however, were considered an important part of Ababda identity. The wooden, and at present also plastic, combs are often hardly visible in the large shocks of hair; nevertheless, they are an integral part of the outfit. A drawing made by Saad Mansur in 1998 summarizes the quintessential young Ababda male: on camelback traveling through the wide desert landscape with mountains and acacia trees, bearing shield and sword, comb in hair, riding a well-decked-out camel (Figure 23.16). The women, instead, mentioned all parts needed to build a house.

IMMATERIALITY OF ABABDA CULTURE

The strong social organization of the Ababda is not expressed by impressive monumental architecture, representing social stratification in palaces for the living or in mausoleums for the dead, but rather by feasting. The social integrity is safeguarded by *karama*, irregular meetings at which several sheep or even camels are slaughtered and consumed. At such a feast everybody shares in the wealth; even those who could not afford to slaughter take part in the sumptuous meal, consisting of sand-baked meat and bread. The location of these feasts is not fixed, but some areas are considered more suitable than others. *Karamas* are mostly celebrated on the wadi floor, where there is sand suitable for baking bread and stones for roasting the meat. The remains of the feast, stacks of bones (the skins are taken) and concentrations of charcoal, will leave a material trace.

Figure 23.16. Drawing by Saad Mansur of Ababda men and their camels in an Eastern Desert landscape. Note the whips, shields, swords, *feraya* (leg protection covering the camel's shoulders), tassels and decorative hair combs.

One episode of rainfall and the subsequent flash flood, however, will probably be sufficient to wash away most of the evidence of a feast.

The *karama* is not a religious phenomenon, although religious festivals are sometimes combined with a *karama*. A good example is the *maulid* (birth festival) of Sheikh Shazli, who reportedly discovered coffee. His tomb is hidden deep in the Eastern Desert in a wadi surrounded by steep mountains. The simple tomb has recently been adorned with a mosque and amenities for the thousands of visitors that come and stay here every year during a pilgrimage of several days. The architecture of the tomb of Sheikh Shazli is unlike the Ababda tombs in the area. These are isolated rings of stone, often with an installation indicating the direction of Mecca (*qibla*).

The Ababda are Muslims and trace their ancestry back to Saudi Arabia, but they have their own take on Islam. Religion, magic and medicine are one continuum. The great esteem in which deceased holy men are held, such as Sheikh Shazli who died on his return trip from the *hadj* (pilgrimage to Mecca), reflects their potential as mediators between humanity and God. In addition, it is the local sheikh who is not only judge and adviser but also provider of amulets against snakes, scorpions and other dangers. These amulets (*higab*) are personal and nontransferable. Herbs play some role in medicinal treatment of illness, but more important is the intervention of the sheikh, who can place *kyet bi-an-nahr* (fire-signs), burn marks on the skin made with red-hot nail heads (Barnard 2000). Protection against infant mortality is provided by putting a miniature sword, in a miniature scabbard, in the crib. This allows the baby to fight off the large mythical bird that preys on infants.

Swords used to be important in daily life and are still worn regularly by almost every man who owns one. Sword and shield stand for masculinity and protection. They are also used in dancing and form an important part of every festivity, be it a birth, a wedding or a *karama*. The sword dance is performed by two men, each holding a shield, made of elephant hide, in his left hand and raising a sword in the air with his right hand. While stamping and jumping to the rhythm of the accompanying instruments and songs, each man shakes the flexible steel sword with short jerky movements so that it is kept in constant vibration (Figure 23.17). The swords are never used for mock attacks. The dance lasts for one to two minutes, after which the two dancers quickly put down their accoutrements and return to the ring of onlookers. Two others speedily take their place. When asked why the dancers were only allowed such a short period, the answer was that everybody in the company wanted to have his turn.

Figure 23.17. The Ababda sword dance is performed by two men making their swords vibrate in the air while accompanied by the clapping and singing of other men. They quickly give up their place to a new pair of dancers.

The instruments used to accompany the singers are a small or a large drum (*tabla* and *taar* respectively) and a kind of lute with four strings (*tambura*), the resonance box of which is traditionally made of the shell of a turtle. Alternatively, a plastic bucket or a broken jerry can functions as drum, and a *tambura* can be made out of scraps of wood. Songs sung with the sword dance are called *hoseeb* or simply *seyf* (sword). These are heroic songs in which the sword is said never to rest in the scabbard. The *bir* (well) songs tell about clean water in abundance. Adolescent boys have a different set of songs, such as the *bagraab*, which accompany a different type of dance in which the dancers jump straight into the air with both feet held together.

All dances are strictly segregated by gender and age. The girls sing *harkaak* songs, which are mostly about the beauty of the camel. The women's dance is only performed in isolation, with no men present. One woman will move to the center of the circle, while the others sing and clap the rhythm. She pulls back the *toob* from her head and reveals her magnificent hairdo, decorated with coins, shells and beads. Then she flicks her head and arms backward and curves back slowly to her starting position. The accent of the music corresponds with the repetitive backward jolt (Figure 23.18). Women also sing songs called *donub*, which express the wish that there will be rain, or celebrate the prospect

Figure 23.18. The dance of Ababda women is performed by one woman rhythmically throwing back her head and arms while accompanied by the clapping and singing of other women.

of getting together with others. These two subjects are closely related. The women are often living an isolated life in separate wadis until the rain enables or forces them to come together in one area. This has the added benefit of enabling social interaction.

MOBILITY, DISTANCE AND SOCIAL LIFE

The rain in the Eastern Desert is usually concentrated in the winter and in the south, in the Gebel Elba region near the Egyptian-Sudanese border. Although the Ababda groups claim ownership of resources, there are no rules on the grazing in a period in which rainfall is limited. If grazing is insufficient to maintain the herds, when the rains have failed for a number of years, the herds move to the south (Roe, in press). Mobility is triggered by natural circumstances and does not follow a pre-established pattern, nor is it limited to certain periods of the year (Morton 1988). Physical proximity of individuals and groups is, therefore, mostly an effect of the carrying capacity of the land. Families come together in the rainy season, in those regions that receive the rain. This mobility prevents the dry regions from being overgrazed and provides a period of recuperation of the local flora and fauna.

Because the rainfall is often very localized, knowledge of the situation in the entire Ababda region is of the utmost importance. As recorded for the Bishareen (Morton 1988), the Ababda exchange information from person to person. Travelers are expected to take the time to provide news on rainfall, feed growth and movements of people. The communication system, in a region that until today is devoid of (cellular) telephones, functions with surprising accuracy and speed. Morton (1988) recorded from oral history that in 1914 "a party of Ababda had walked 500 km through mountain and desert on the accurate information that work was available." Our archaeological project, in the 1990s, relied on this network to attract a group of up to 80 Ababda workmen. After our unannounced arrival it would take no more than three days for groups of Ababda to arrive at our campsite. At least 30 came from Wadi Khareet in the Nile Valley. In contrast to 1914 they arrived by bus and pickup truck, but they had received the 'accurate information' about the availability of work in the same way.

The other opportunities that Ababda, especially the women, have to interact are during special occasions, such as weddings and *karamas*. One woman, living 60 km from the nearest asphalt road, and about the same distance from any other Ababda camp, informed me that she would travel "from the end of the world" to participate in these occasions, especially if they involved a member of her family.

IMPACT ON THE LANDSCAPE

The impact of the Ababda on the landscape is limited. Although all their economic activities employ natural resources (grazing, charcoal burning, collecting medicinal plants), the Ababda are selective in where and when they collect these resources. During a collection trip to gather wood for a *beit al-burush*, two Ababda first went to speak to the head of the family who owned the resources. He gave his consent and joined the two others to help with (and control?) the wood collecting. Nine forked branches of acacia were needed, to function as the 'pillars' of a house. This involved visiting four different clusters of trees, spread out over a distance of approximately 7 km in the same wadi. Only one branch was taken from each tree and not more than two from the same cluster. This method of sustainable tree use, which concentrates on browsing, is called *ewak* (Krzywinski 2001). The curved pieces of wood for the roof of the house, actually tree roots, are only collected opportunistically after being laid bare by a flash flood. They are kept and moved from campsite to campsite until needed.

The Ababda will once in a while embark on hunting trips or will try to trap animals, although bird hunting is increasingly rare. Part of the Ababda territory has recently been made a national park, and some of the Ababda have been trained as rangers. The hunting of protected species, such as ibex and gazelle, is now officially illegal in the entire region of the Eastern Desert, but such activities, especially when instigated and financed by tourists from Saudi Arabia (Cole and Altorki 1998), are very difficult to monitor.

Since the 1960s the Ababda have increasingly been able to purchase light pickup trucks. With the exception of transport to some hard-to-reach areas, the Toyota Hilux has mostly replaced the camel as beast of burden. Ababda drivers are masters in negotiating the sandy wadis, knowing the types of sand that require slow driving and the kinds that call for fast driving. There is a distinct impact of these pickups on the wadi floor and flora, especially because no tracks can be established: driving in the same path is a certain recipe to get stuck. Increasingly, however, the Ababda are faced with churned-up wadi floors, which challenge even the best of drivers, where tourist companies and individuals have ventured out to enjoy a desert safari. The much heavier terrain vehicles are far more destructive, not only because of the churning wheels but also because they enable larger groups of people to reach more remote areas. Ignorant of the cultural and natural rules and requirements of the region, these visitors often behave like trespassers, cutting wood that 'belongs to nobody' in an 'empty land' for a fuel-devouring fire that gives the city dweller a safe and romantic 'into the wild' experience. Impact on the cultural and natural landscape of the Eastern Desert is, therefore, mostly the result of recent changing modes of transportation and land use.

ABABDA MATERIAL TRACES

Our work with the Ababda has provided insights into the traces that are left behind and how these can be used to understand ancient mobile populations. The Ababda do not leave extensive garbage deposits, however, and much of the refuse is eaten by sheep and goats. When a mat house is taken up and moved to another location, a rectangular clearance, where stones and pebbles were removed from the inside of the house, is clearly visible. Traces of the shallow postholes can sometimes be discerned, but the precious wood is taken along or, if no longer in usable condition, burnt as fuel. Concentrations of animal dung are rare, as this too is used as fuel.

The most recognizable signs of Ababda presence are the things that have been left behind on purpose. At wells and water holes leather buckets are left, to enable other women and children tending the sheep, or thirsty travelers, to haul up the water. In addition to communal property there are also personal belongings. Such possessions are the things that can be carried, on foot or camelback, or were left behind in a conspicuous place, often in trees. Similar behavior has been attested elsewhere (Eerkens, this volume), but the personal belongings of the Ababda are usually not hidden. Sometimes wooden platforms are built on which individuals or families leave their possessions until they return to the same area. These platforms are 1–2 m above the ground to keep the items safe from sheep, goats and flash floods. The Ababda social code prevents anybody from touching these unguarded 'deposits,' even if the person has died and will not return to claim his or her belongings (Figure 23.19).

Tombs are another material sign of Ababda presence, but they are difficult to interpret because they are widely dispersed and often consist of only a ring of stones or a headstone. The tombs of important men are decorated with a low stone enclosure and colorful flags. Green, the color of Islam, is dominant, bleaching to a tattered white over time. Inside the enclosure a deposit of personal belongings and provisions are placed: cigarettes, sandals and one or two cooking vessels (Figure 23.20).

Even the immaterial aspects of Ababda life, such as celebrations, feasting and religious beliefs, leave material traces in the form of bone scatters, amulets and other apotropaic items, such as the miniature swords and scabbards. The impact of the nomadic groups on the landscape in earlier periods was probably equally limited and can be difficult to trace archaeologically. It is interesting to note that at present the traces that are most obvious are those left on purpose, such as the ones outlined here and the *wasm* resource ownership signs introduced above.

Figure 23.19. An acacia tree with an Abadi's belongings: a platform of sticks tied together holds a plastic jerry can and several items wrapped in a checkered blanket. At the foot of the tree sits a metal can with water; to the right lies a crate of the type in which fruits from the Nile Valley are transported.

Figure 23.20. An Ababda tomb, decorated with flags and a few grave goods. This tomb had two soapstone vessels and a pair of sandals.

DISCUSSION

This description of the Ababda culture was made with the help of our Ababda team members. Although they participated in the process, the chapter at hand is based on the features that I consider of importance to include and undoubtedly differs from what the Ababda writers' team would have selected. The purpose of their original request to me, to write a book about them, stemmed from a notion that their way of life was under pressure and on the verge of changing forever. The collection of Ababda artifacts was the starting point for discussions on the less tangible aspects of Ababda way of life, including social values and history. I will try to outline here at which points the various Ababda histories diverge.

The Ababda refer to two types of history: the history of the Ababda origin and the cultural memory of the Ababda way of life. The first is reflected in a great interest in genealogical trees (Tables 23.1–23.2). The main purpose of the genealogy is to trace the Ababda to Saudi Arabia and establish a firm link with the birthplace of Islam and, preferably, a direct relation to the prophet Mohamed. A secondary purpose of the virtual map of tribal relations is to establish communality. Through common forebears, along patrilineal connections, every individual can define his or her relation to the larger group. The Ababda consider themselves part of the Beja and related to the Bishareen, but at the same time they clearly distinguish themselves. They also see themselves as being fundamentally different from the Nubians and the Egyptians. The latter term is not only used to indicate the settled population in the Nile Valley, and now also along the Red Sea, but also to indicate power relations. The 'Egyptians' with whom the Ababda have direct dealings are mostly representatives of the army or the civil administration. The cultural memory of the Ababda is related to landscape, location of resources, economic strategies and cultural contacts. More recent oral history, of encounters with German and British military during World War II or British and Italian representatives of mining companies, are mingled with stories about fathers and grandfathers who booked successes in the hunt. The recent history of the Ababda does not consist of golden memories, remembering a blissful period. The drawbacks of their poor existence without many resources are all too clear.

The historical interest of the Ababda differs greatly from that of Keimer, the Egyptologist who visited the region in the late 1940s. His main interest in the history of the Ababda was to emphasize a cultural continuity with ancient Egypt. Keimer was certainly a keen observer, but the object of his studies was the material culture of the Ababda rather than the Ababda culture as an entity within its own specific context. His rather simplistic use of analogy between ancient and modern cultures, based on random ethnographic parallels, failed to take into account the cultural development and historical context of both Pharaonic and Ababda culture and preserved a biased, static view of each civilization. Keimer's approach objectified and had no interest in giving a voice to the Ababda and Bishareen.

My own approach of Ababda history originated in a working relationship and discussions during our work. It was fueled by questions about the activities of the ancient inhabitants of the region, the Ptolemaic and Roman settlers who came from the Nile Valley, and the nomadic population of which we found evidence in our excavations. Trying to gain an understanding of the factors that determine Ababda mobility, while observing the ingenuity and improvisation with which the Ababda make things work with a minimum of possessions, was very helpful in thinking through our own interpretations of the past. At the same time, observations of residual material traces, the expression of social networks, and the material overrepresentation of certain aspects of the culture (in the case of the Ababda all the equipment needed for the 'coffee ceremony') gave important caveats to prevent too simple an explanation of archaeological data. For instance, Eastern Desert Ware, a specific type of ceramics found in the harbor town of Berenike in Late Roman deposits, was interpreted as a cultural or ethnic marker, based on the shape, decoration, fabric, context and distribution of the vessels. The importance of the *djabana* in Ababda culture does not by any means constitute 'proof' for such an interpretation. It does, however, provide an example of a mobile culture in which specific objects, which may seem like 'ballast' to an outsider, constitute an essential part of the material culture and are carried around at all times.

Thus we have at least four distinct interpretations of an Ababda past: its Pharaonic roots, its Islamic base, its recent daily life history, and its ethno-archaeological or ethnohistorical value. These interpretations are not necessarily in conflict with each other, but it would be unsophisticated to propose that they consist of four sets of 'objective' observations, coated with different interpretations, which can be combined or harmonized to flesh out the complete picture. At the outset each of these histories started with particular explicit or implicit concerns and, more important, with different definitions of what constitutes a valid method to reach conclusions. Multiple interpretations of the past are an inherent effect of the scholarly discourse but also of the recognition that scholars and scientists present a very specific set of approaches. Even though the debate on its significance and consequences has scarcely started, multivocality allows nonacademic voices to be heard. That is why it is important that the Ababda write their own books.

REFERENCES

Barnard, H.

2000   Geneeskunst geïnspireerd door armoede [Medicine Inspired by Poverty, in Dutch]. *Nederlands Tijdschrift voor Geneeskunde 144*: pp. 949–951.

2005   Sire, il n'y a pas de Blemmyes: A Re-evaluation of Historical and Archaeological Data. In J. C. M. Starkey (ed.), *People of the Red Sea: Proceedings of the Red Sea Project II, Held in the British Museum, October 2004. Society for Arabian Studies Monographs number 3. BAR International Series 1395*. Oxford, Archaeopress: pp. 23–40.

Barnard, H., A. N. Dooley and K. F. Faull

2005   New Data on the Eastern Desert Ware from Sayala (Lower Nubia) in the Kunsthistorisches Museum, Vienna. *Ägypten und Levante 15*: pp. 49–64.

Barnard, H. and E. Strouhal

2004   Wadi Qitna Revisited. *Annals of the Náprstek Museum Prague 25*: pp. 29–55.

Cappers, R. T. J.

2006   *Roman Foodprints at Berenike: Archaeobotanical Evidence of Subsistence and Trade in the Eastern Desert of Egypt*. Los Angeles, Cotsen Institute of Archaeology.

Christensen, A.

2001   Charcoal and Coffee. In K. Krzywinski and R. H. Pierce (eds.), *Deserting the Desert: A Threatened Cultural Landscape Between the Nile and the Sea*. Bergen, Alvheim & Eide Akademisk Forlag: pp. 109–132.

Cole, D. P. and S. Altorki

1998   *Bedouin, Settlers, and Holiday-Makers: Egypt's Changing Northwest Coast*. Cairo, American University in Cairo Press.

De Jong, R.

2002   Notes on the Dialect of the 'Ababda. In W. Arnold and H. Bobzin (eds.), *Sprich doch mit deinem Knechten aramäisch, wir verstehen es. 60 Beiträge zur Semitistik: Festschrift für Otto Jastrow zum 60*. Wiesbaden, Harrassowitz: pp. 337–359.

Eide, T., T. Hägg, R. H. Pierce and L. Török

1998   *Fontes Historiae Nubiorum: Textual Sources for the History of the Middle Nile Region Between the Eighth Century BC and the Sixth Century AD. Volume 3: From the First to the Sixth Century AD*. Bergen, University of Bergen, Department of Greek, Latin, and Egyptology.

Hobbs, J. J.

1990   *Bedouin Life in the Egyptian Wilderness*. Cairo, American University in Cairo Press.

Keimer, L.

1951   Notes prises chez les Bišarîn et les Nubiens d'Assouan: Première partie. *Bulletin de l'Institut d'Égypte 32, Session 1949–1950*: pp. 49–101.

1952a   Notes prises chez les Bišarîn et les Nubiens d'Assouan: Deuxième partie. *Bulletin de l'Institut d'Égypte 33, Session 1950–1951*: pp. 42–84.

1952b   Notes prises chez les Bišarîn et les Nubiens d'Assouan: Troisième partie. *Bulletin de l'Institut d'Égypte 33, Session 1950–1951*: pp. 85–136.

1953a   Notes prises chez les Bišarîn et les Nubiens d'Assouan: Quatrième partie. *Bulletin de l'Institut d'Égypte 34, Session 1951-1952*: pp. 329–400.

1953b   Notes prises chez les Bišarîn et les Nubiens d'Assouan: Cinquième partie (1). *Bulletin de l'Institut d'Égypte 34, Session 1951-1952*: pp. 401–449.

1954a   Notes prises chez les Bišarîn et les Nubiens d'Assouan: Cinquième partie (2). *Bulletin de l'Institut d'Égypte 35, Session 1953-1954*: pp. 447–470.

1954b   Notes prises chez les Bišarîn et les Nubiens d'Assouan: Sixième partie. *Bulletin de l'Institut d'Égypte 35, Session 1953-1954*: pp. 471–533.

Krzywinski, K.

2001   Cultural Landscapes: An Introduction. In K. Krzywinski and R. H. Pierce (eds.), *Deserting the Desert: A Threatened Cultural Landscape Between the Nile and the Sea*. Bergen, Alvheim & Eide Akademisk Forlag: pp. 9–60.

Morton, J.

1988   Sakanab: Greeting and Information Among the Northern Beja. *Africa: Journal of the International African Institute 58*: pp. 423–436.

Murray, G. W.

1923   The Ababda. *Journal of the Royal Anthropological Institute of Great Britain and Ireland 53*: pp. 417–423.

1967   Troglodytica: The Red Sea Littoral in Ptolemaic Times. *Geographical Journal 133*: 1, pp. 24–33.

Paul, A. M.

1954   *A History of the Beja Tribes of the Sudan*. London, Cass.

Pierce, R. H.

2001   Past and Present in the Eastern Desert. In K. Krzywinski and R. H. Pierce (eds.), *Deserting the Desert: A Threatened Cultural Landscape Between the Nile and the Sea*. Bergen, Alvheim & Eide Akademisk Forlag: pp. 143–166.

Roe, A.

in press   A Preliminary Investigation of the Parameters of Premodern Economic Production and Exchange in the Desert Hinterlands of the Berenike Archaeological Project Area. In S. E. Sidebotham and W. Z. Wendrich (eds.), *Report on the 2001 Excavation Season at the Greco-Roman Harbor of Berenike (Egyptian Red Sea Coast) and Excavations at Abu Greiya*. Los Angeles, Cotsen Institute of Archaeology.

Salih, H. M.

1980   Hadanduwa Traditional Territorial Rights and Inter-population Relations Within the Context of the Nature Administration System (1927–1970). *Sudan Notes and Records 61*: pp. 118–133.

Sidebotham, S. E. and W. Z. Wendrich

1995   *Berenike 1994: Preliminary Report of the 1994 Excavations at Berenike (Egyptian Red Sea Coast) and the Survey of the Eastern Desert.* Leiden, Research School CNWS.

1996   *Berenike 1995: Preliminary Report of the 1995 Excavations at Berenike (Egyptian Red Sea Coast) and the Survey of the Eastern Desert.* Leiden, Research School CNWS.

1998   *Berenike 1996: Report of the 1996 Excavations at Berenike (Egyptian Red Sea Coast) and the Survey of the Eastern Desert.* Leiden, Research School CNWS.

1999   *Berenike 1997: Report of the 1997 Excavations at Berenike and the Survey of the Egyptian Eastern Desert, Including Excavations at Shenshef.* Leiden, Research School CNWS.

2000   *Berenike 1998: Report of the 1998 Excavations at Berenike and the Survey of the Egyptian Eastern Desert, Including Excavations at Wadi Kalalat.* Leiden, Research School CNWS.

2007   *Berenike 1999–2000: Report of the 1999 and 2000 Excavations at Berenike and the Survey of the Egyptian Eastern Desert, Including the Survey of Sikait.* Los Angeles, Cotsen Institute of Archaeology.

Updegraff, R. T.

1988   The Blemmyes I: The Rise of the Blemmyes and the Roman Withdrawal from Nubia Under Diocletian. In W. Haase and H. Temporini (eds.), *Augstieg und Niedergang der römische Welt, Volume 2 (10.1).* Berlin, Walter de Gruyter: pp. 44–97.

CHAPTER 24

NO ROOM TO MOVE

MOBILITY, SETTLEMENT AND CONFLICT AMONG MOBILE PEOPLES

ROGER L. CRIBB

WHEREAS MOBILE PEOPLE have usually been studied in terms of their ecology and patterns of migration, I will focus on the implications of mobility for the formation of temporary settlements. It is suggested that mobile people are typically able to form communities of optimal size and composition, thereby minimizing the level of interpersonal conflict: "So there was not enough pasture land for the two of them to stay together, because they had too many animals. So quarrels broke out between the men who took care of Abram's animals and those who took care of Lot's animals. . . . Then Abram said to Lot, 'We are relatives and your men and my men shouldn't be quarreling. So let's separate. . . . You go one way and I'll go the other way'" (Genesis 13:5–9). The consequences of permanent, fixed settlement for people with a tradition of mobile lifestyles are considered here in relation to the stress caused by unfamiliar housing and higher density living and the problems of regulating conflict. Australian Aboriginals and Near Eastern pastoral nomads are considered as examples.

Ethnographers and archaeologists dealing with mobile peoples have tended to focus on those aspects of mobility connected with subsistence and to neglect its sociopolitical dimensions (but see Tapper 1979 and Bates 1973). In this chapter I explore the implications of a mobile lifestyle for social organization and particularly for the management of conflict. Nomadic pastoralists and those with a nomadic tradition, as well as mobile hunter-gatherers and those with a hunter-gatherer tradition, are considered. While the economies and logistics of mobility in nomadic-pastoralist and hunter-gatherer cases are very different, there appear to be certain properties inherent in the practice of a mobile lifestyle that cut across differences in subsistence, economy, ecology and social organization.

CONFLICT AMONG CONTEMPORARY
ABORIGINAL POPULATIONS

In the 1970s James O'Connell wrote a paper called *Room to Move* (O'Connell 1979). It described an Aboriginal desert camp in Central Australia that had been set up adjacent to a pastoral property, where some of the people worked. These people, the Alyawara, had not been long in contact with white settlers; two generations at most. The camp, consisting of various 'humpies' constructed of tarpaulins and corrugated iron, was an informal affair, laid out according to Alyawara custom in clusters of households arranged loosely according to kinship distance. The camp was characterized by an open layout and low density. O'Connell reported that the level of interpersonal conflict was low. Disputes, mainly of a domestic nature, were usually solved by one of the antagonists moving to a different household—often the woman moving into an all-female household, for some time at least. The level of alcohol consumption was low. Though partly integrated into the mainstream economy, these people were living in a 'tribal' society. By virtue of voluntary associations and appropriately spaced dwellings, however flimsy and dilapidated, they were able to maintain a reasonably well integrated and peaceful community. They had room to move.

In the city of Cairns, in north Queensland, Aboriginal people originally from the communities in Cape York Peninsula are currently living an equally 'tribal' lifestyle. Kinship reckoning is paramount for them as well, but the outcomes are quite different. They wander the streets in search of hidden nooks and crannies where they can drink or sleep. Some find accommodation at a designated night shelter or in one of the diversionary centers for those too intoxicated to help themselves. Relatives with access to flats or houses in the city are overwhelmed. There are large areas of the city center where they dare not go. Ragged camps spring up on small lots of vacant land on the city's outskirts (Cribb 2003). People are hemmed in and crowded together. Disputes escalate and frequently become violent. They have no room to move.

HORIZONTALLY AND VERTICALLY
INTEGRATED SOCIETIES

By 'tribal society' I mean one in which overlapping kinship ties determine the allocation of resources, as opposed to one based on allocation through some kind of division of labor. Tribal societies are a good example of what I will call 'horizontal integration,' where all people live much the same lifestyle and there is little specialization in economic pursuits. In contrast, a vertically integrated society is one in which there is a great range of lifestyles, and economic activity is organized around a wide range of economic specializations. For the most part the allocation of resources does not occur along kinship lines but through specialized institutions and markets. This is not to say that tribal people do not interact with or participate in much wider economic and social systems. They frequently do. Degrees of mobility and population density affect horizontally organized societies far more than those that are vertically organized. Whereas in the former case solutions are found in two dimensions, the latter allows multidimensional solutions.

Mobile people are to a very large extent organized horizontally and live in tribal societies; however, not all tribal people are mobile. There is a wide range of tribally organized people who are settled horticulturalists, are agriculturalists, or practice some form of limited transhumance. Many tribes in the Middle East are divided into mobile pastoral and settled sections with some interchange of personnel between the two (Cribb 1991). The Yanomamö horticulturalists in the Amazon basin are village dwellers who move their entire communities in response to ecological factors and intervillage conflicts (the two are often related), as do many other 'slash-and-burn' horticulturalists for similar reasons (Chagnon 1976). The last two cases may be 'mobile,' but they are not strictly speaking 'nomadic' because they do not move their productive capital with them (Cribb 1991).

Whereas vertically organized societies offer many contexts for interpersonal interaction (household, workplace, clubs and other voluntary associations) with different sets of people, those organized horizontally allow far fewer such contexts. Everyone is playing much the same game, doing much the same thing within much the same context and within the same kin-related sets. This is illustrated in Figure 24.1, which models a network of intersecting kin groupings. This horizontal organization has important implications in relation to conflict avoidance and resolution. Whereas the urban dweller can escape family stress at work and work stress at home, those who are tribally organized generally have access to far less variety in their choice of associations, the primary ones being kin-based. Vertically organized societies, in short, offer not only manifold domains of interaction but also more nooks and crannies in which to hide from conflicts and potential conflicts.

TOLERANCE THRESHOLDS RELATING TO CONFLICT

Although kinship networks can be a vital source of support, they can also generate stress and conflict. Tribal societies handle this in various ways, for example by means of tribal councils, groups of elders or elected headmen presiding over spatially discrete groups or different levels of organization. It has been suggested that optimal group sizes for different purposes may be somehow wired into human interaction. After many years of research in the

Figure 24.1. Aboriginal painting by Timmy Japangardi (Papunya, central Australia), showing the relations between individuals in a group, mapped onto the paths between water holes in the landscape.

New Guinea highlands, Anthony Forge concluded that "*Homo sapiens* can only handle a certain maximum number of intense social relationships, successfully distinguishing between each. When the number of relationships he is involved in rises above this figure he can only continue by classification of relationships to cut down the total number of different relationships he has to act in and carry information about around in his head" (Forge 1972:375).

There are optimal sizes for boards of directors, classrooms, councils and military organizations (section, platoon, company, battalion), each of which has its own tolerance threshold. It is precisely at these tolerance thresholds that communication tends to break down and conflicts develop that will frequently result in subgroups forming and going their separate ways. Where such groups are engaged in the exploitation of resources and involve potential population growth, other factors come into play. Those fracture points where organizational breakdown occurs are often associated with breakdowns in the management of resources. Tensions generated at these organizational thresholds often coincide with ecological crises, as with the budding off of Yanomamö villages as neighboring resources become exhausted, giving rise to intracommunal strife or the splitting of herding camps among nomadic pastoralists as conflicts come to a head over pasture or migration tracks. Those tribal groups who lead mobile lifestyles have the inherent capacity to manage such tensions and information overload and to avoid or defuse any resultant conflicts by simply translating social distance into physical distance.

Tapper (1979) has followed up the biogenic argument and considered the implications of this important property of mobile territorial systems. He has drawn attention to the way in which mobile people are able to map out their social organization on the ground, by way of fluidity in their settlement systems, in a way that settled people cannot, even if the latter are tribally organized: "It will be among nomads rather than among settled peoples that we can expect the emergence and evidence of any inherent social dynamic processes generating interactional communities of a certain size and character . . . The same factors may operate in settled societies . . . but it is sooner in mobile and flexible than in stationary and fixed societies that we can expect them [biogenic factors] to express themselves in social groupings" (Tapper 1979:61).

As I suggested earlier, mobility, whether among pastoral nomads or hunter-gatherers, is usually treated by ethnographers in terms of economic objectives and access to resources, but mobility has other vital implications. While attention is commonly paid to sociopolitical factors, researchers rarely explain how these affect or are affected by mobility. Whereas those occupying permanent settlements are frozen into a fixed pattern, be it kinship based or not, mobile people may exercise the option of not only choosing the location of their settlements but also of adjusting the density of these settlements so that households and wider kin-based groups do not impinge unduly on each others' activities or privacy. They also have the option of choosing their immediate neighbors. Whereas vertically organized societies achieve privacy through enclosure, horizontally organized ones achieve it by spreading out.

Mobility between settlements therefore contains the possibility of mobility within settlements in terms of the location of households over time. Mobile people are able to choose their immediate neighbors on a seasonal basis so

that temporary settlements closely reflect the existing pattern of social relations (Bates 1973). An excellent illustration of this, though on a small scale,
is an incident reported by Frederick Barth among the Basseri nomadic pastoralists in southwest Iran. During an overnight stop on the migration trail,
two families were involved in a dispute over a choice tent site. The dispute
culminated in each family's dragging its tents and belongings to opposite
ends of the camp, thereby literally defusing a conflict by means of physical
distance (Barth 1961).

Different cultures display different tolerance levels for crowding. Vertically
organized urban societies are able to withstand extremely high population
densities in contrast to those societies that are horizontally or tribally organized. In the latter, tolerance levels may be much lower for crowding by
strangers than by those who are bound by close ties of kinship. For tribally
organized or 'segmentary' societies even kin groups, or groups based on
kinship, may exhibit different degrees of density tolerance for different levels
of tribal organization.

RESPONSES TO SETTLEMENT DENSITY

The obverse of the proposition that mobility acts to defuse conflict is what
happens when people are forced together in fixed settlements. Increases in
tension and potential conflict are accommodated by putting up walls, in both a
literal and figurative sense. This process is taken to its extreme in the case of the
modern city, where the privacy so obtained is reinforced through anonymity.
The beginnings of this process can be seen in the sedentarization of nomadic
pastoralists. First the settlement pattern becomes fixed. Next, storage structures
spring up, and eventually a permanent dwelling may be constructed, although
the family may continue to spend most of its time in the tent (Watson 1966),
what I have called elsewhere a 'composite settlement' (Cribb 1991:154–157). In
many cases courtyards with walls are constructed or houses begin to abut each
other as the settlement grows (Nissen 1968; Sweet 1974). In this way kinship
structures may still be preserved, though in a fixed spatial form unresponsive
to generational changes in household composition.

In *Nomads in Archaeology* I developed a model called the 'domestic complex'
for examining intrasite spatial organization (Cribb 1991). This model examines
the internal organization of household units in which the pattern of structures
and activities tends to be remarkably consistent across households. For nomadic
Yörük, in southern Turkey, the complex occupies a rectangular area of about 10
by 20 m, aligned according to slope, terrain, aspect, prevailing wind direction
and location of water bodies. Crucially, no two domestic complexes overlap,
and they are usually separated by a distance over which a conversation can be

held. Tent sites and other features, such as external hearths and storage facilities (fixtures), remain until re-occupation the following year and may be occupied and used by different households. Such settlements are highly resistant to crowding, which may partly account for the generally low levels of interpersonal conflict observed within nomadic communities (Swidler 1972; Watson 1979). It is of great interest that, while an increase in interpersonal conflict has been observed among sedentarizing pastoral nomads (Swidler 1972), the process occurs within the framework of a single culture.

In the Near East the internal structure of a tent site has much in common with the living room of a village house occupied by members of the same ethnic group, as has the etiquette of household life. As sedentarization proceeds, the former is converted with relative ease into the latter. Indeed, settlement most commonly occurs within the framework of a wider tribal entity in which the majority of households are settled. It is true that some forcibly settled nomads are known to abandon the houses that have been built for them because they do not conform to cultural norms. This, however, presupposes the existence of a blueprint for household organization. Pastoral nomads are part of a wider tradition of which housing is a vital part. This is where the sedentarization of nomadic pastoralists differs fundamentally from that of mobile hunter-gatherers.

Mobile people from a hunter-gatherer tradition undergoing sedentarization possess no such architectural blueprints. They are part of a tradition in which fixed and permanently occupied housing with a standardized floor plan has no place. Although temporary shelters of various kinds were employed, the organization of activities and space depended very much on the immediate environment, including wind direction, shade patterns and ground surface. We lack significant data on the settlement patterns of precontact or contact Aboriginal societies. Excavations in Australia have been of insufficient extent to throw much light on this question. The accounts of early historical ethnographers or observers tend to focus on aspects such as material culture, food procurement, spirituality or the formal properties of kinship systems. Modern regional archaeological studies have thrown some light on broad patterns of seasonal movement, as have modern ethnographic and ethno-archaeological studies. But neither gives very much attention to intrasettlement organization. There are, however, a few clues from casual observations by settlers. A plantation owner who settled on the west coast of Cape York Peninsula established a working relationship with the local Aborigines, who formed a number of camps along the adjacent beach (McLaren 1926). Over time the camps began to merge into a single large camp, and this process was accompanied by a marked increase in interpersonal tension, arguments and violence.

THE IMPACT OF FIXED HOUSING

Social psychological studies of postcontact Aboriginal settlements have drawn attention to the highly stressful nature of social interactions in which the fixed nature of the European housing provided, together with its inadequacy, inhibit the spatial expression of the realities of social relations, including constant violation of explicit kin avoidance rules (Reser 1979). Household space, designed along functional lines, breaks down as all rooms are used in much the same fashion. In many cases the family and its visitors camp outside, using the house itself for storage. After at least four generations of settlement many houses in Aboriginal contemporary communities are abandoned because they are incompatible with the social life of the inhabitants. Attempts to conform to aspects of traditional culture frequently result in neglect and damage such as chopping up furniture to be used as firewood. A good deal of research has been done on the provision of housing in Aboriginal communities (Reser 1979). Some radical designs have been put forward, with or without consultation with Aboriginal people, and some have actually been implemented, with varying degrees of success.

In a community in central Australia I came across a group of fiberglass hexagonal huts, each with three alcoves for nuclear families, a door and storage space. The central portion of the roof was open to the sky, enabling smoke to escape from a central fireplace. The design had a certain logic. The singular fact, however, was that all the complexes were empty and had been abandoned some time ago. Presumably the former occupants were now part of a large camp of people located in the dry streambed adjacent to the official settlement. While I could not identify these people to ask why they had left the complexes, their reasons were clear enough. Three nuclear families could not comfortably occupy such a space. Dogs would be a nuisance, snakes could not move through without being trapped and becoming dangerous, the enveloping walls would prevent the wind from blowing through and, most important, the occupants could not see what was happening in neighboring dwellings or notice the approach of visitors until the latter were on top of them.

CONTEMPORARY COMMUNITIES
ON CAPE YORK PENINSULA

Cape York Peninsula, lying in the extreme northeast of Australia, contains about a dozen settlements of Aboriginal people who have been in contact with European culture for approximately a century. In the early 20th century CE the people were either encouraged or forced to live in settlements (missions) and to reside in permanent dwellings laid out in lines or squares in European fashion, with little or no attempt to accommodate kinship considerations. Since the 1970s the missions have been transformed into local authorities run by community councils, and one of the key functions of the community council is to provide housing that varies little from the standard European plan of lounge room, kitchen, bathroom and three bedrooms.

During the mission days households (read nuclear families) were generally accommodated in small huts assigned by missionaries to families in an arbitrary manner. An exception was the old settlement at Lockhart River, where housing was organized in hamlets occupied by members of each separate clan group, located at a distance from each other. This made for a reasonably harmonious community. When the community was relocated after the Second World War, however, housing was arranged in a radial pattern centered on the European compound (council office, store, post office, European households) and assigned on an arbitrary basis rather than in accordance with kinship distance (Chase 1980; Figure 24.2). Tensions within the community increased dramatically until in recent times Lockhart has come to be regarded as one of the most dysfunctional communities on Cape York Peninsula.

It is remarkable that many of the inhabitants of Lockhart preferred, and continue to prefer, camping on the nearby beach during the dry season. Temporary makeshift dwellings of corrugated iron and canvas were arranged in clusters in a line at regular intervals along the beach, each cluster occupied

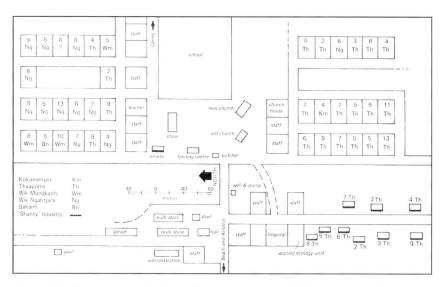

Figure 24.2. Plan of the new Lockhart River settlement around 1973. Note the radial plan and schematized arrangement of dwellings (after Chase 1980:Map 3).

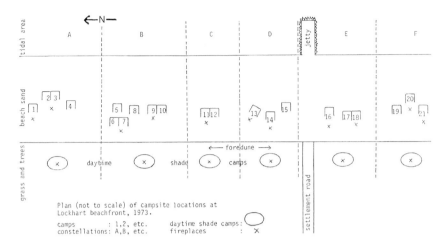

Figure 24.3. Dry season beach camp at Lockhart River (after Chase 1980:Figure 21).

by closely related people (Figure 24.3). Senior persons in adjacent clusters also tended to be close relatives. Each cluster had a day camp or day shade on the dunes above the beachfront. It is immediately obvious that such a community conforms much more closely to the realities of kinship organization than did the nearby permanent settlement and, while the overall population density of the beach camps may be greater than that of the settlement, the mapping out of kinship relationships made for a more harmonious settlement.

During fieldwork near Aurukun in 1985 our research party consisted of myself, two anthropologists, a local couple, two middle-aged male traditional owners and one elderly woman (Cribb 1986). Every evening we made camp in much the same manner: a flat area on a salt pan, dune or sandy riverbank was selected, and swags and blankets were laid out in a consistent linear pattern. The couple camped together near the center with the elderly woman at one end and the single males at the other end. Individuals were separated by a distance of at least 2 m, and sometimes fires were maintained between adjacent individuals. This pattern, even though not organized along kinship lines, was indicative of the kinds of protocols that are of great significance in Aboriginal culture. Larger numbers of people spending longer periods of time together would tend to spread out in a low density settlement pattern composed of such modules.

THE CAMP AT CHINAMAN CREEK

Between 2001 and 2003, members of the Lockhart community and others from adjacent areas staying in the regional city of Cairns, together with other kin, constructed a similar kind of camp on the bank of Chinaman Creek, a mangrove creek on the outskirts of Cairns. The area had been used as a dumping ground and was littered with garbage and rusted car wrecks. Such a location would not have been chosen by Aboriginal people given any choice in the matter. There was no sanitation and the nearest water supply was approximately 100 m distant. The camp was located parallel to the mangrove fringe and consisted of four clusters of makeshift dwellings constructed of timber, canvas and plastic tarpaulins. It was bounded on the other side by stands of long grass. One couple occupied an abandoned van. The area, approximately 10x40 m, was occupied by up to 20 people at any one time. People would come and go, though there was a core of around 10 people. Related groups would visit and congregate in large groups in which a good deal of heavy drinking would occur. Such camps are known as 'drinking camps' and the people as 'long grass people.' These are common on the outskirts of northern Australian cities (Day 1999; Sansom 1980).

The singular feature of the camp at Chinaman Creek was the high level of interpersonal conflict and frequent violence, certainly fueled by alcohol but deriving partly from the fact that people were living virtually on top of one another. As many as 20 adults were sharing the space that would normally be occupied by a single family. Unlike the beach camps at Lockhart River, where clusters were separated by a reasonable distance, the Chinaman Creek clusters were closely juxtaposed with no room for activity areas or day shades. Frequent arguments erupted through individuals invading another's personal space or sleeping area. Domestic disputes were frequent and often violent, leaving the woman with nowhere to take refuge. Other arguments centered on kinship issues with one person disputing the ancestry or relationships of another.

PUBLIC SPACE AND CONFLICT

Whereas some anthropologists maintain that 'traditional' Aboriginal culture is dying, I would counter that no culture is 'traditional' and that no culture 'dies.' What we are seeing is change, or metamorphosis, together with continuity (Chase 1980). Technologies are replaced and songs, stories, preferential marriage systems and even whole languages may be lost; but the core of the culture, the kinship system, remains strong and other aspects of life are arranged around it. Touch this web at any point and one is quickly entangled. Establish even a putative relationship with one person (as a 'brother') and one suddenly has a house full of sisters, nephews and aunts.

One very important feature of Aboriginal culture is the tendency for all disputes to become public, exposed to the full range of people who may have an interest in them and tending to involve more and more people arraigned along kinship lines. A certain amount of space is required for this. In contemporary communities such disputes can surge up and down a street and spill over into other public areas, causing a great deal of noise but usually resulting in few injuries. The Royal Commission of Inquiry into Aboriginal Deaths in Custody (RCIADC) acknowledged the great difference between the ways in which Aboriginal and Western societies cope with the issue of conflict and unacceptable conduct, particularly the intervention of certain kin in disputes, the public nature of most disputes, and the general acceptance of fighting and swearing as an integral part of disputes. Above all, 'avoidance and mobility' are solutions that are far less available now than they were in earlier times, something also acknowledged by the RCIADC. Under modern conditions, even within Aboriginal communities, nearly all forms of overt conflict are likely to develop into public-order issues.

Particularly for tribal people living in towns and cities, problems arise through the expression of conflict in an urban setting. Disputes often take the form of very loud shouting and swearing across a city street as if there were no mainstream city life going on around them, reflecting the conduct of disputes in tribal Aboriginal communities. Such disputes are typically aired in public, where others may be aware of the nature of the dispute and the grievances involved, so that potential allies can be mobilized or mediators brought in. The disputes, which may appear chaotic, have an underlying structure and require a great deal of space for their resolution.

DISCUSSION

While there is no way that the degree of conflict can be measured through archaeological evidence, there are ways in which archaeological data can have a bearing on settlement density, which in turn relates to cultural factors such as tolerance thresholds for crowding. On the basis of the above arguments we would expect that tentlike house plans, arranged in a low density pattern, could indicate the sedentarization of nomadic pastoralists accompanied by certain changes in the degree and kind of social integration. Or it could reflect marginalization and stress among nomadic people forced into diminishing life space, similar to the present-day marginalization of nomad settlements on the outskirts of a village or town. Or the clustering together of floor plans may indicate a transition to a more permanent settlement.

Wherever the tolerance thresholds in Aboriginal social organization may occur, they are not permitted full expression in the kinds of community or urban situations dealt with above. While much of the technology and ideology of past Aboriginal society has been irrevocably lost, this is still a horizontally and tribally organized culture. The tendency in such a culture to give expression to the state of play of social relations has been severely constrained by fixed settlements and loss of control over living space. In the past one may imagine populations in a more or less continual state of flux, scheduling their movements around broad changes in the availability of resources but also responding to the vicissitudes of social life. The need for sociability was constantly balanced by avoidance of those situations and those people likely to give rise to interpersonal conflict. Settled life in fixed communities has severely strained the tolerance thresholds of a traditionally mobile and flexible society, and many of the dysfunctional features of contemporary Aboriginal society (violent crime, domestic violence, communal strife) may derive in no small measure from this source.

Perhaps clues may be found along the coast of Cape York Peninsula in the linear distributions of occupation sites in the form of clearings on the coastal dune systems and large, mounded shell heaps strung out along the salt pans and silt plains (Cribb 1986). Such sites would have accommodated kinship groups of various sizes moving from place to place in response to resource depletion and the state of play of interpersonal relations with alternative settlement sites being available close by.

REFERENCES

Bates, D. G.

1973   *Nomads and Farmers: A Study of the Yörük of Southeastern Turkey. Museum of Anthropology Publications 52*. Ann Arbor, University of Michigan.

Barth, F.

1961   *Nomads of South Persia: The Basseri Tribe of the Khamseh Confederacy*. Boston, Little, Brown.

Chagnon, N.

1976   *Yanomamö: The Fierce People*. New York, Holt, Rinehart and Winston.

Chase, A. K.

1980   *Which Way Now? Tradition, Continuity, and Change in a North Queensland Aboriginal Community*. University of Queensland, Department of Anthropology and Sociology (PhD disseration).

Cribb, R.

1986   Archaeology in the Aurukun Region: A Report on Work Carried Out in 1985. *Queensland Archaeological Research 3*: pp. 133–158.

1991   *Nomads in Archaeology*. Cambridge, Cambridge University Press.

2003   *Getting to Know the Mob*. (unpublished manuscript)

Day, B.

1999   Forgive Us Our Trespasses: Finding Space for Aboriginal Fringe Dwellers in Darwin. *Canberra Anthropology 22*: 2, pp. 62–69.

Forge, A.

1972   Normative Factors in the Settlement Size of Neolithic Cultivators. In P. J. Ucko, R. Tringham and G. Dimbleby (eds.), *Man, Settlement, and Urbanism.* London, Duckworth: pp. 363–376.

McLaren, J.

1926   *My Crowded Solitude.* New York, McBride.

Nissen, H. J.

1968   Survey of an Abandoned Modern Village in Southern Iraq. *Sumer 24*: pp. 107–114.

O'Connell, J. F.

1979   Room to Move: Contemporary Alyawara Settlement Patterns and Their Implications for Aboriginal Housing Policy. In M. Heppell (ed.), *A Black Reality: Aboriginal Camps and Housing in Remote Australia.* Canberra, Australian Institute of Aboriginal Studies: pp. 97–120.

Reser, J. P.

1979   A Matter of Control: Aboriginal Housing Circumstances in Remote Communities and Settlements. In M. Heppell (ed.), *A Black Reality: Aboriginal Camps and Housing in Remote Australia.* Canberra, Australian Institute of Aboriginal Studies: pp. 65–96.

Sansom, B.

1980   *The Camp at Wallaby Cross: Aboriginal Fringe Dwellers in Darwin.* Canberra, Australian Institute of Aboriginal Studies.

Sweet, L.

1974   *Tell Toqaan: A Syrian Village. Museum of Anthropology Publications 54.* Ann Arbor, University of Michigan.

Swidler. W. W.

1972   Some Demographic Factors Regulating the Formation of Flocks and Camps Among the Brahui of Baluchistan. In W. Irons and N. Dyson-Hudson (eds.), *Perspectives on Nomadism.* Leiden, E. J. Brill: pp. 69–75.

Tapper, R. L.

1979   The Organization of Nomadic Communities in Pastoral Societies of the Middle East. In L'Equipe écologie et anthropologie des sociétés pastorales (ed.), *Pastoral Production and Society/Production pastorale et société. Proceedings of the International Meeting on Pastoralism. Paris, December 1976.* Cambridge, Cambridge University Press: pp. 43–65.

Watson, P. J.

1966   Clues to Iranian Prehistory in Modern Village Life. *Expedition 8*: pp. 13–23.

1979   *Archaeological Ethnography in Western Iran. Viking Fund Publications in Anthropology number 57.* Tuscon, University of Arizona Press.

CHAPTER 25

NOMAD

AN AGENT-BASED MODEL (ABM) OF PASTORALIST-AGRICULTURALIST INTERACTION

LAWRENCE A. KUZNAR AND ROBERT SEDLMEYER[1]

And Hamor and Shechem his son came unto the gate of their city, and communed with the men of their city, saying, these men [the sons of Jacob] are peaceable with us; therefore let them dwell in the land, and trade therein . . . And it came to pass that on the third day . . . two of the sons of Jacob, Simeon and Levi . . . took each man his sword, and came upon the city boldly, and slew all the males. They took their sheep, and their oxen, and their asses, and that which was in the city, and that which was in the field, and all their wealth, and all their little ones, and their wives took they captive, and spoiled even all that was in the house (Genesis 34:21–29).

Cathay's great general, Prince Fu-hsing, advised his king . . . And if these cities are forced to fight the Mongol army they'll most likely surrender to them. I say we should offer tribute to the Khan of the Mongol for now . . . Let's give one of your daughters to their Khan. Let's give the men of their army heavy burdens of gold, silver, satins, and other goods . . . And our soldiers carried off as much satins and goods as their beasts could hold and went on their way, securing their bundles with ropes of silk (Kahn 1998:147–148).

WHETHER THE DRAMATIC annihilation of the Shechemites by Jacob's nomadic sons or the smug satisfaction expressed by Mongol chroniclers; propagandists, historians and anthropologists alike often portray contentious pastoral-to-agricultural interactions (Goldschmidt 1979). The scenario reads as follows: Pastoral nomads are free, violent and rapacious; agriculturalists are wealthy and vulnerable, and inevitably, the martial nomads conquer the hapless, effete city folk. The earliest written records concerning pastoralists,

---

[1.] The authors gratefully acknowledge the indispensable computer programming efforts of Allyson Kreft (who, at the time of this study, was Research Assistant at the Department of Computer Sciences, Indiana University–Purdue University at Fort Wayne).

dating from 18th century BCE Mesopotamia, indicate that relations between pastoralists and sedentary folk have been contentious since the birth of the state (Simon 1981). But ancient writers also note that pastoral nomads and urbanized agriculturalists are symbiotically linked through trade, each providing what the other needs or desires. Anthropologists reinforce this linkage by documenting mutualism, pastoral domination or domination of pastoralists by agricultural states (Asad 1973; Barth 1973; Gellner 1973; Dyson-Hudson and Dyson-Hudson 1980; Simon 1981; Barfield 1989; McCorriston 1997). Sources ancient and modern suggest counteracting forces between the need to trade and the constant threat of domination by one's trading partner in these societies. The central problem for understanding cultural processes like these is that anthropologists usually only observe the results of process, not the processes themselves. Since many culturally interesting phenomena, such as cycles of conquest, growth of family wealth and settling into village life (sedentarization), take place over decades or longer, it is not possible for anthropologists to witness firsthand the processes that generate these phenomena. Researchers must infer the mechanism that caused an observed set of affairs, much like an archaeologist must infer the prehistoric processes that generate archaeological remains (Cronk 1998). Relatively recent advances in computer science provide anthropologists with a means of addressing this methodological difficulty.

Agent-based models (ABMs) use advances in object-oriented programming and increased computing power to model the independent actions of numerous individuals, allowing emergent phenomena to occur. ABM simulations permit researchers to program theoretical processes and to test whether or not these processes lead to observed phenomena in the context of simulated social systems (Epstein and Axtell 1996). Anthropologists use ABM simulations to explain the rise and fall of civilizations (Dean et al. 1999; Axtell et al. 2002; Lazar and Reynolds 2002), to model the emergence of ethnic groups (McElreath et al. 2003), and to simulate complex ecological systems (Kuznar 2006). ABM simulations have the added benefit of forcing researchers to specify all variables necessary for the functioning of a theory, enabling them to appreciate where their empirical understandings of the world are inadequate and suggesting future field research. In this chapter we demonstrate how ABM simulations can be used to test theories of interest to anthropologists studying pastoral nomads and their agricultural neighbors.

PASTORAL NOMAD–SEDENTARY AGRICULTURALIST DICHOTOMY

Many researchers have challenged the pastoral nomad–sedentary agriculturalist dichotomy, noting that there are many exceptions (Bates 1971; Salzman

1972; Spooner 1972). Even so, logistical incompatibilities exist often enough between pastoral and agricultural production, the former leading to a focus on mobile animal herding and the latter to sedentary agriculture, to allow the distinctions to persist (Bernbeck, this volume; Barth 1973; Gellner 1973; Goldschmidt 1979). Nomadic pastoralists specialize in animal husbandry that requires mobility (Dyson-Hudson and Dyson-Hudson 1980:17). Furthermore, pastoral production is particularly distinguished by its volatility (Barfield 1993:13). Even though pure pastoralists independent of agricultural society do not exist, Barfield (1993:4) recognizes that enough people in many societies do fit the description of nomadic pastoralists to be singled out for categorical study. Historians have detailed clear and profound interactions between sedentary agricultural states and pastoral nomads, shaping the history of East Africa, the Middle East and China (Lattimore 1951; Ibn Khaldun 1967; Simon 1981; Barfield 1993). The persistence of the pastoral nomad–sedentary agriculturalist distinction warrants current investigation of its use. Instantiating these two general modes of production in computer models allows both the testing of the validity of the concepts (do they work, or do these distinctions fall apart?) and of theories based on these distinctions (do pastoralists and agriculturalists interact in the ways and for the reasons hypothesized?).

Our aim in this chapter is to demonstrate how computer modeling can aid in establishing the usefulness of these concepts and their associated theories. We begin this discussion by reviewing theories of the cyclic history of pastoralist-agriculturalist interaction. Then we turn to anthropological theories that specify the mechanisms that may produce these historical cycles. We outline a computer model designed to capture these mechanisms. The model is then used to see whether the theorized mechanisms produce the historical cycles and ethnographic patterns researchers propose. The chapter concludes with a discussion of results and future directions for research.

CYCLES OF CONQUEST AND PASTORAL NOMADS

The first theorist to examine the interaction of pastoral nomads and agriculturalists closely was the medieval scholar Ibn Khaldun. In the Muqaddimah, published around 1381 CE, he proposed a systematic cycle of pastoral conquest, sedentarization, social decay and subsequent conquest that largely held until the modern era (Barfield 1989). He argued that because of the differences in the material conditions faced by desert nomads and urbanites, they develop different subsistence systems, psychologies and ideologies. Ibn Khaldun notes a fundamental interdependence between nomads and city dwellers; "while [the Bedouins] need the cities for their necessities of life, the urban population needs [the Bedouins] for conveniences and luxuries" (Ibn Khaldun 1967:122).

He also argues that urban concerns, such as keeping up with inflationary prices and engagement in commerce, distract agriculturalists from maintenance of the martial skills necessary to defend their lifestyles (Ibn Khaldun 1967:276, 278, 285–286). The ultimate result is conquest by nomadic pastoralists who, attracted to the ease of urban life, sedentarize. These recently sedentarized folk are eventually conquered by another group of pastoral nomads, culminating in historical cycles of conquest and settlement by pastoral dynasties.

> Sedentary culture was always transferred from the preceding dynasty to the later one. The sedentary culture of the Persians was transferred to the Arab Umayyads and 'Abbâsids. The sedentary culture of the Umayyads in Spain was transferred to the Almohad and Zanâtah kings of the contemporary Maghrib. That of the 'Abbâsids was transferred, successively, to the Daylam, to the Saljuq Turks, to the Turks in Egypt, and to the Tartars in the two 'Iraqs' (Ibn Khaldun 1967:140).

Ibn Khaldun (1967:107) concludes with the same stereotypes echoed in antiquity: "'[D]esert life no doubt is the source of bravery, [and] savage groups are braver than others. They are, therefore, better able to achieve superiority and to take away the things that are in the hands of other nations . . . Whenever people settle in fertile plains and amass luxuries and become accustomed to a life of abundance and refinement, their bravery decreases to the degree that their wildness and desert habits decrease . . . This is exemplified by dumb animals, such as gazelles, wild buffaloes, and donkeys, that are domesticated."

Lattimore (1951) described the rise of pastoral nomadism as an economic specialty on the central Asian steppes, its characteristics and the cyclical rise and fall of Chinese agrarian kingdoms in terms reminiscent of Ibn Khaldun. He recognized that a continuum exists between pure pastoral and pure agrarian societies but that, because of environmental differences in agrarian potential, one or the other subsistence system would dominate a region, setting up a dynamic interaction between nomadic pastoral societies of the steppe and Chinese civilizations of the irrigated valleys that would permeate East Asian history (Lattimore 1951; see also Barfield 1989; Khazanov 1994:60). This interaction alternated among trade, extortion, raiding, conquest and vassalage (Lattimore 1951:332, xlvii, 333, 77 and 547 respectively). Lattimore notes that pastoral and agrarian societies are linked through interdependent trade relations, although he argues, contra Ibn Khaldun, that nomads needed Chinese luxury goods more than Chinese needed pastoral products (Lattimore 1951:69). Pastoral nomads enjoyed a military advantage by virtue of their mastery of the horse and their constant practice of martial skills while protecting their flocks (Lattimore 1951:63–66, 333). The successful domination of Chinese society by nomads, however, undermined the very abilities that enabled the nomads' success: "the protected oasis immobilized its protectors and, if it became too wealthy and its protectors insufficiently mobile in the warfare of the steppe, it was always overwhelmed by raiders" (Lattimore 1951:77, 333). And so, echoing Ibn Khaldun, Lattimore demonstrates that a similar cycle of nomadic conquest, transformation into agrarian society, and subsequent conquest characterized Chinese history.

More recent scholarship largely reinforces these historic trends in pastoral-agrarian interaction. Khazanov (1994) provides an encyclopedic comparison of pastoral nomad histories from the Middle East, North Africa, East Africa and the Asian steppe. He describes the modes of nomadic adaptation to agrarian societies as sedentarization, trade, submission to states, and the subjugation of agrarian states. His thorough review of many historical examples from throughout the Old World does justice to the diversity of pastoral lifestyles, although certain basic patterns clearly emerge. Until the modern era, pastoral nomads generally enjoyed a military advantage over sedentary societies: "nomadic raids have been recorded in all regions where nomadism is widespread" (Khazanov 1994:222, 263). The pattern persists even when pastoralists have historically been encapsulated and forced to submit to states (Burnham 1979; Irons 1979; Krader 1979; Lattimore 1979). One of the more forceful denials of this pattern is Asad's (1973) analysis of Bedouin history in the Middle East, although in each of his examples state domination of nomads is either incomplete or the result of modern military technology. While these historians describe general patterns, and even provide some mechanisms, they cannot provide detailed studies of the actual mechanisms by which individual nomadic pastoralists would decide to settle. Ethnographic studies of contemporary pastoral societies are necessary to identify the actual mechanisms of sedentarization and its effects.

ETHNOGRAPHY AND SEDENTARIZATION

Ethnographies in the 20th century CE have both reinforced the basic trends noticed by Ibn Khaldun and Owen Lattimore and exposed the diversity of the ways that pastoral-agricultural interaction takes place and the local factors that influence these contingent variations (Goldschmidt 1979; Dyson-Hudson and Dyson-Hudson 1980; Barfield 1993). Despite this variation, a number of basic generalizations appear to hold concerning pastoralists who rely on large animals in arid lands. Herds are a volatile source of wealth, fluctuating wildly from wealthy to poor levels based on environmental (weather, pasture) and social (raiding, demography) factors (Goldschmidt 1979:20; Barfield 1993). The key to long-term success is the building of large herds, fostering entrepreneurial behaviors and attitudes among pastoralists (Goldschmidt 1979:23). Citing Edgerton's research on culture and personality, Goldschmidt argues that these situational factors reinforce a set of personality traits, including aggression, use of violence and capacity to suffer physical hardship (Goldschmidt 1979:24). These generalities lead to the following tendencies that have influenced the interactions of pastoral nomads and agriculturalists for millennia.

First, the pastoral combination of mobility and familiarity with weapons has preserved pastoral nomads' military pre-adaptation (Irons 1965, 1972; Salzman 1979). Second, pastoral nomadism as an economic specialization exists only in conjunction with sedentary agricultural societies, so nomads must acquire the primarily grain crops they need for food as well as other goods necessary for their existence (Dyson-Hudson and Dyson-Hudson 1980). Third, this interaction varies from raiding to extortion to trading, based on the relative military and political strengths of nomads and villagers (Irons 1972; Asad 1973; Berntsen 1976; Swift 1979). Pastoral nomads and sedentary agricultural villagers, however, are not forever locked in either their ways of life or battles. Instead, there has always been a continuum between pure nomadic pastoralism (which has always been a rare occurrence) and fully agricultural life, and there have always been avenues for social mobility and trade between the two extremes.

Barth (1961) proposed two pathways that pastoralists might take in transforming into sedentary villagers either through economic success or failure: "radical departure from the middle range of wealth . . . cannot be accommodated within the [pastoral] organization" (Barth 1961:110). In the case of economically successful herders, once their herd becomes too large for them to manage, they must hire poor shepherds to watch them (Roe, this volume). Despite contractual agreements, however, the productivity of these herds is decreased because of a hired hand's inattentiveness toward a flock that is not his own (Barth 1961:13, 111). Ethnographers have noted similar problems in pastoral societies in both the Middle East and East Africa (Barth 1961; Dahl 1979; Hannoyer and Thieck 1982). Consequently, wealthy herders realize that investing their surplus in land and settling is the more profitable strategy, and they become agrarian villagers, analogous to the transformation nomadic elites often made after conquering agrarian states. The other pathway to sedentism is poverty. Once a herder is so impoverished that his herd can no longer sustain himself and his family, he has no choice but to drop out of the pastoral game and attach himself to an agrarian village, finding work as a tenant farmer or some other form of laborer (Barth 1961). Barth (1961) notes that statistically, this is the more usual route to sedentism. Glatzer (1982), working in Afghanistan, notes that sedentarization can also be a two-way street, with particularly successful agriculturalists investing surplus wealth in livestock to the point where they spin off pastoral families.

Barth's general scheme, although subject to contingencies such as land availability and the influence of state-level governments (Bates 1971; Irons

1972), has nonetheless been largely corroborated in the past 40 years. Beck (1991, 1998) has recorded the sedentarization of most Qashqa'i pastoralists in Iran, which has occurred as the result of a combination of legal changes in land tenure that made nomadism difficult and the introduction of vehicular transport that made moving with animals obsolete. In Afghanistan most sedentarization has occurred among pastoralists impoverished through poor herd management, drought and warfare (Glatzer 1982; Barfield 2004). War, drought and colonial domination have led to mass sedentarization of many pastoralists worldwide (Asad 1973; Ben-David 1990; Fratkin and McCabe 1999; Kuznar 1999; Adano and Witsenburg 2003). While economic success is less often the route pastoralists take to sedentism, Irons (1972) noted that this occurred in the early 20th century CE among Yomut Turkmen in Iran, and Swift (1979) documents such a shift in Somalia in the late 20th century CE.

This dual route to sedentarization is driven by the characteristic volatility of pastoral production. Pastoralism is notably risky, leading to extremes of failure and success in pastoral societies through the world (Barth 1961; Irons 1972; Schneider 1979; Browman 1987; Cribb 1991; Kuznar 2001). Very successful herders will be faced with unmanageable herds, and these herders are likely to reinvest surplus stock in sedentary agrarian and urban enterprises. For the destitute, pastoralism is no longer viable, and they must seek employment and support from the larger settled agrarian and urban sectors. Because of pastoral volatility, the interaction between agricultural and pastoral sectors is likewise uncertain and dynamic. In summary, researchers have identified several relatively simple principles that influence pastoral-agriculturalist interactions. Members of both parties must acquire goods that the other has. Pastoralists have historically been militarily superior to sedentary villagers. Pastoralism is riskier than agriculture and the very wealthy and poor tend to sedentarize, becoming villagers. Variations on these themes exist, owing to the contingencies of ecological particularities and the presence or absence of a strong state. These few simple rules have the potential to interact in very complex ways. Our aim is to instantiate these few rules in a general but relatively realistic agricultural-pastoral scenario in order to see if their interaction will produce the rich and varied historical trends researchers have noticed. Given the historical dimension of these processes, computer simulations are necessary to model how the behavior of individual pastoralists and agriculturalists may lead to historical patterns.

SIMULATING PASTORALIST-AGRICULTURALIST INTERACTIONS

ABM simulations are computer programs that allow individual agents to interact, in a virtual setting, with other agents and their environment according to programmed rules (Epstein and Axtell 1996). Researchers can test theories of environmental influence or social interaction by programming these conditions and rules into the model, and they can then verify if the model produces lifelike results (Kuznar 2006). Compared with most mathematical or statistical analyses, often based on aggregated or averaged data, these models provide for more realistic results because the agents and their actions remain discrete. Therefore, the possibility for nonlinear interactions exists, shifting the model into varied and unexpected states and mirroring the complexity of real-life systems (Axelrod 1997; Terna 1998). In our case we will employ ABMs to capture the dynamics of pastoral nomad–sedentary agriculturalist trade and conflict. Our ABM uses the Java-based ABM programming framework called 'Swarm' (Terna 1998), which facilitates the programming of independent agents, the assignment of behavioral rules, and the graphical display of agent behavior.

Our primary aim is to demonstrate the potential usefulness of ABMs for theory testing and the direction of field research. Therefore we have created a simple scenario of pastoral-agriculturalist interaction that mimics the sorts of environments and behaviors anthropologists have recorded in the arid environments of the Middle East and East Africa. To instantiate a reasonable simulation of pastoral-agricultural interactions, we need to create an environment, place resources in that environment, place pastoral and agricultural agents in that environment, and provide the agents with decision-making and behavior rules. For the sake of simplicity we have left out important factors, such as the effect of a strong state government with the ability to garrison troops or the ability of agriculturalists to invest in pastoral enterprises. We also had to simplify some social interactions (such as inheritance rules and trade scenarios) in order to focus on some essential aspects of pastoralist-agriculturalist interaction. In the future, simplified aspects of the simulation can be sophisticated to more accurately reflect social realities. Also, more contingent factors can be programmed into the simulation, testing the strength of their effects in generating the diversity of pastoral lifestyles. Despite these simplifications, our simulation still provides realistic interactions between relatively militarized pastoral nomads and relatively vulnerable sedentary agriculturalists, such as has recently been starkly demonstrated in the Darfur region of Sudan (Kuznar and Sedlmeyer 2005). The various components of the model that must be specified include time, environment, productive resources, the human element and behavioral rules.

Since agrarian and pastoral rhythms occur ubiquitously on a seasonal basis, each iteration of the simulation will represent one season: spring, summer, fall or winter. The environmental setting is reminiscent of the typical arid environment of the Middle East or East Africa in which agriculturalists inhabit a watered valley while pastoralists migrate among highland and lowland pastures scattered throughout the rest of the landscape. Some pastoralists migrate over distances of 10–20 km (Shepardson and Hammond 1970; Kuznar 1995; Sidky 1995), others over hundreds of kilometers (Barth 1961; Cribb 1991). Because migrations are usually between these extremes, as among Yomut Turkmen of Iran (Irons 1972), we model an environment that is 50x50 km. A river cuts across this environment, with agricultural land occurring along its course. Pastures are scattered about the landscape, with summer pastures occurring in the eastern portion of the environment (mountain pastures) and winter pastures scattered nearer the river course (lowland pastures). Glatzer's work (Glatzer and Casimir 1983) in western Afghanistan provides a fairly representative distribution of agriculture and summer and winter pastures and is the basis for the geography of our model. Each land type needs a level of productivity, a hazard rate and a hazard effect in order to model environmental fluctuations that impact both agriculturalists and pastoralists.

Following experimental work, agricultural productivity for traditional Middle Eastern fields growing emmer wheat would be 500 kg/ha primitive wheat, providing 3300 Kcal/kg (Casimir 1988; Hillman 1990:169). We use a drought hazard rate of 50%, given 40–60% recorded for Luristan, Iran (Hole 1978:141). The effect of a hazard would be a 50% loss felt during autumn, reflecting the decreased yield experienced during harvest time after a drought, consistent with figures provided by Dean et al. (1999:187) for decreased yields in arid lands. Pasture productivity varies considerably from extremely low, in Afghani and Iranian deserts, to relatively high in the lush alpine pastures of South America (Kuznar 1991a, 1995). A reasonable median would be 500 kg dry matter/ha/yr as recorded for desert scrub in the American Southwest (Cook and Sims 1975). Pastures beginning to grow in the spring typically do not achieve full productivity at this time, so spring productivity will be reduced by 20%. Summer productivity will be 100%, while fall and winter productivity will amount to the vegetation left over after grazing, following data from the Sahel in Mali (Diarra and Breman 1975). The annual hazard rate (percent drought years) for pastures in arid environments typically varies from lows around 10% (Dahl and Hjort 1976:116) to highs of 40% (Cook and Sims 1975) and ranges between 15–30% in the Sahel in Mali (Diarra and Breman 1975). We use a median figure of 25%. Since the key periods of stress are spring and summer, we divide this hazard evenly between these two seasons. Hazard effects are often high, ranging from 50% animal loss in Iran (Barth 1961:7), to 80% dry matter loss for the U.S. Western Range prairie (Cook and Sims 1975), and a moderate 51–57% dry matter loss (severe drought compared to moderate drought) in Mali (Diarra and Breman 1975). Given the more severe effect of drought on pasture, we use 65% dry matter loss for the pasture hazard effect.

We have already specified the agricultural resource levels in terms of traditional wheat production in the Middle East. Herd animals present more complex demographics, including dry matter assimilation rates, disease and mortality rates, body mass, butchering percentage, meat and milk production, and herd reproductive rate. We elaborate on each in turn. As a simplification, we ignore fiber production because of the varied return rates for fiber throughout the world and the volatility of the fiber market. It would be more reasonable to include fiber production for a specific application. The amount of food necessary to produce cattle, sheep and goats is about 3.5% of their weight in dry matter/day (Devendra 1978; Iannelli 1984; Gatenby 1986). Herd mortality rates (mostly from disease and predation) amount to 8% in North Africa (Dahl and Hjort 1976:265) and the Peruvian highlands (Kuznar 1995). For herds in the Middle East, Hole (1978:144) reports rates of disease of 30–50% of a herd every three to seven years. As we are modeling a herd based on small stock, the standard live bodyweight per animal is roughly 40 kg, and the standard meat takeoff is 20 kg/animal (Devendra 1978). Dahl and Hjort (1976:209) estimate that the takeoff rate for a flock is 8% per year, providing 60,525 Kcal and 1500 g protein/head. Sheep, goats and other livestock also produce milk, however, and Dahl and Hjort (1976:212) estimate an expected milk production of 45 kg per ewe/year for human consumption. In a herd of 40% ewes this would produce 1100 Kcal/kg ewe and 65 g protein/kg ewe (Dahl and Hjort 1976:212, 216). This equals, per head of herd, 19,800 Kcal/yr and 1690 g protein/yr. The herd reproductive rate, only assessed during the spring, should average 18% (Dahl and Hjort 1976:231). Cribb (1991:28) notes that this results in a comparable 0.7 to 0.9 births per ewe/yr in the Middle East.

THE HUMAN DIMENSION

We have instantiated an environment with resources and have characterized the seasonal and random variations in those resources. Now we must create human agents who will populate and interact in this environment. Some agent attributes will be common to all agents, such as basic nutritional demands. Others will be specific to pastoral or agricultural ways of life, such as fertility rates, mortality rates and life spans. Also, economic factors will be specific to ways of life, including labor demands, access to resources and raiding mortality rates. We adopt the basic nutritional demand figures used by Kohler et al. (1999:160) in their ABM of the rise and fall of Anasazi civilization. Nutritional demands are broken down to two basic requirements: Kcal and protein. Nutritional protein demands are 63 g/day for males and 50 g/day for females and children. Nutritional Kcal demands are 1872 Kcal/day for males, 1560 Kcal/day for females and 1000 Kcal/day for children. Other biological and economic attributes are different for agricultural and pastoral populations.

Sedentary agriculturalists tend to have higher fertility than mobile pastoralists (Roth 1986). We use a total completed fertility rate of 6 children/female, as commonly observed for sedentary agriculturalists (Thomas 1973:147). Comparison of morbidity and mortality between agriculturalist and pastoral populations in Mali indicates that the agriculturalist disease rate should be about 3% while the childhood (age 1–5) mortality rate should be around 25% (Fratkin et al. 1999:157). Recorded total completed fertility rates in pastoral societies in Africa range from 3.2 among the Himba to 4.7 for the Pokot (Fratkin and McCabe 1999:8). The fertility rate of the Basseri, in the Middle East, was probably around 4 (Barth 1961:12). We use a fertility rate of 4 for pastoral groups. Pastoral disease rates are probably closer to 2% (estimated from the figure in Fratkin et al. 1999:157). A recurrent pastoral childhood mortality rate would be around 40%, as recorded in surveys of pastoral groups in the Sahel (Fratkin et al. 1999:154; Gray et al. 2003:S8; Roth 1986:71).

Each agriculturalist household operates as a corporate entity that farms land to produce grain for consumption, tax payments and trade. A reasonable labor rate for arid land farming would be 1 ha per adult and half that per child, as suggested by figures presented by Hillman (1990:169) and consistent with the amount of agricultural land typically cultivated in south central Asian agriculturalist communities (Lewis 1965:100; Sidky 1995: 23). Labor is a constant constraint on pastoral production (Swidler 1972; Dyson-Hudson and Dyson-Hudson 1980; Kuznar 1991b). Basseri herding labor rates were about 300 animals/adult and 150 animals/child (Barth 1961:6), and this figure is reinforced cross-culturally (Cribb 1991:28).

Raiding mortality has been directly observed among East African pastoral communities. Gray et al. (2003) provide detailed demographic data on raiding mortality among the Karimojong during different periods of raiding intensity and weapon use. In the 1950s an escalation of cattle raiding among Karimojong led to violence, accounting for 22% of all male deaths (Gray et al. 2003:S15). It was 12% in the two previous decades. Since the 1970s, and the introduction of firearms, it has gone up to 33%. Unfortunately, they provide no data on the number of raids a man does during his life. However, a man's raiding life span is probably not more than 20 years and is probably intense while trying to acquire bride wealth (Gray et al. 2003:S18). Assuming one raid per year (probably more before and less after marriage), we divide the mortality rates by 20 to get the probability of death on a raid. The annual probability of dying on a raid was therefore 0.0060 during the peaceful period while still using spears. This would increase to 0.0110 during periods of intense raiding with spears. The introduction of automatic rifles increases the mortality rate to 0.0165. A reasonable, prefirearm long-term raiding death rate would be somewhere in between intense and peaceful periods of raiding with spears: 0.0085. These raiding data were derived from armed herders attacking other armed herders; the rate for a herder raiding an unarmed agriculturalist would obviously be lower. We will assume that the mortality rate for pastoralists would be twice as low when attacking an agriculturalist, and the agriculturalist's mortality rate from being attacked would be twice as high. Therefore, the per capita death rates per raid are adjusted to 0.00425 for pastoral nomads and 0.01700 for agriculturalists.

THE RULES OF THE GAME

After instantiating an environment, resources and agents with essential attributes, these various entities must interact and we must provide them with rules that will govern their interactions. The rules can be divided into demographic rules, movement rules and social rules (inheritance, trade and raiding). For simplicity's sake we use straightforward demographic rules. We already noted the childhood mortality rates. Adulthood for agents begins at age 20. All agents die at age 65, unless already dead. If an adult agent dies, his or her household disappears as it is no longer viable. Women have a 20-year reproductive life span, between age 20 and 40, and their probability of conceiving in any year is their fertility rate divided by 20. When an agent reaches the age of 20, that agent marries the next nearest agent who is of marriageable age. They then form a new pastoral family herding unit.

Since pastoralists are the only agents who are mobile, the movement rules will concern only them. Each pastoral agent has an adjustable vision of 10 grid squares (roughly 5 km), allowing the agent to know what is near his or her location. Once 80% of the pasture production is consumed, the agent moves in the direction (determined by vision) of increased yield. If no direction is obvious then the agent moves randomly. If an agent has a metabolic need (Kcal store is at two seasons minimum yearly resource level for the family), the agent moves toward an agriculturalist for trade. Agriculturalists don't move, but they need to acquire sufficient fields for their sustenance. When an agricultural family's needs exceed its field production, the family acquires new fields. It begins by adding field plots contiguous to current fields. If that is not possible, it acquires the nearest new fields. A new family acquires the nearest open agricultural land to the adult male head of household. If all land is exhausted, then these new families exit the program: we assume they migrate away.

Herds are collectively owned and pastured by families. Mirroring the widespread tendency of pastoralists to practice patrilineal descent, we will assume patrilineal inheritance (Barfield 1993). When a child matures, at age

20, inheritance occurs. The simulation calculates the parents' family's herd size needs, plus adult child's herd size needs. If the parent has a herd adequate for the family needs plus that child's, then the program calculates and awards the basal herd needs for all and bequeaths the remaining portion to the child proportionately (so if there are four children, each will receive 25% of the excess herd). If the parent's herd is not large enough to bequeath, then the child remains stuck at home. It is customary for women in the Middle East and Central Asia to receive a dowry, which is essentially her inheritance, given to her, or her husband, at marriage, and is a form of portable wealth (Martin and Voorhies 1975; Dyson-Hudson and Dyson-Hudson 1980; Barfield 1993). While a woman may not typically receive animals, her dowry is nonetheless wealth, and her parents need to be wealthy enough in animals to afford it. Our model simply gives a woman her portion of the herd at marriage, which she then combines with her husband's herd as though they combined their wealth assets. Children tend to stay at home in agricultural societies and often care for their elderly parents (Handwerker 1983). When a parent dies, wealth and field possessions are divided equally among children.

In order to determine whether two agents would trade, and at what rates of exchange, we use the trade rule developed for the Sugarscape ABM (Epstein and Axtell 1996). Trade occurs when mutually beneficial to both parties. If not, either the pastoralist attempts a raid or, if unsuccessful in the attempt or execution, goes without. This models the risks that agents incur in holding out for a better price, with the possibility of retribution. Agents will choose the nearest neighboring potential partner, and each will estimate his own marginal rate of substitution for the goods potentially traded. In our model the two goods at issue are Kcal and protein. An agent's marginal rate of substitution (MRS) of Kcal for protein is simply calculated as Kcal stored/Kcal needed for a family per year divided by protein stored/protein needed for the year (Epstein and Axtell 1996). In our case, if a pastoralist's marginal rate of substitution for Kcal is greater than an agriculturalist's marginal rate of substitution for Kcal, then trade can occur. MRSs establish a range of feasible prices (quantities that can be exchanged). If we have two agents, P (pastoral nomad) and A (agriculturalist), the range of prices at which they will trade is [MRSp, MRSa]. While these may be theoretically agreeable prices, they will not normally be considered 'fair' because an agent wealthy in one good may 'gouge' another who is needy for that good. To limit the effect of such price gouging, we follow Epstein and Axtell (1996) and use the geometric mean of the endpoints of the feasible price range:

$$p(MRS_p, MRS_a) = \sqrt{MRS_p MRS_a}$$

in which MRSp is the pastoralist's marginal rate of substitution and MRSa is the agriculturalist's marginal rate of substitution. The amount exchanged is equal to p units of Kcal if $p>1$, and $1/p$ units of Kcal if $p<1$. Altering MRSs by taking this geometric mean was important in the model because during preliminary model verification, price gouging emerged that would probably not be tolerated in any culture, thus reinforcing Epstein and Axtell's general intuition.

In Epstein and Axtell's simulation, if mutually beneficial terms of trade are not possible, agents seek other trading partners. In our simulation we more realistically model the harsh constraints of satisfying need in the short-term: sometimes trading partners cannot be found. Consequently, people either suffer resource depletion and starve, or they use violence to obtain what they need. Berntsen (1976) provides a description of just such raiding where Maasai choose to raid agriculturalists too poor to trade. If a nomad has a nutritional need yet cannot trade, then the nomad may raid an agricultural household. In most tribal societies raids are considered unsuccessful if a member of the party is killed (Chagnon 1992). If any raiders die, then the raid is unsuccessful and nothing is gained. If the raid is successful, then the raiders divide the spoils equally.

Following Barth's (1973) hypothesis, there are two routes to sedentarization for herders: success and failure. In the case of success a herder's flock becomes so large that he can no longer manage it profitably, even with hired help. In that case the herder invests surplus wealth in fields and becomes an agriculturalist. In a related way pastoral raiders gain so much sedentary wealth, such as fields, that they likewise must settle down to enjoy the fruits of their success. To model this route to sedentarization, we define a maximum herd size that a family can manage. If herd size becomes twice this maximum herd size, pastoralists often have mitigating strategies for very large herds; then the pastoral family becomes agricultural and settles on unused agricultural land, purchased with their animals. We estimate the purchase price of land by taking the average price of protein in the previous iteration and multiplying this by the bodyweight of the herder's livestock. This wealth is used to buy the amount of land required to grow the amount of grain that could be purchased with that herder's liquid capital. Failure also results in sedentarization. In this case pastoralists whose wealth falls below the family's minimum needs can become agriculturalists, if they manage to migrate to unused land before their resources fail. These pastoralists will also liquidate their livestock and buy land, as described above. In this manner we expect to more realistically model the impoverished nature of failed pastoral turned agriculturalist life.

EXPECTATIONS

We have produced a model based on available empirical data on arid land ecology as well as pastoral and agriculturalist demography, economics and lifestyles. We have provided a set of rules that mirror historically important theories of pastoral decision making and pastoralist-agriculturalist interactions. If these theories can actually explain the phenomena they purport to explain, then our simulation should produce those patterns. If they do not, then either the theories are incorrect or important variables in the model are wrongly specified, indicating future research directions to correct these deficiencies. The primary research question we explore in this chapter is: "Do the interactions among pastoral nomads and sedentary agriculturalists result in cycles of raiding, pastoral aggrandizement, pastoral settlement and subsequent pastoral conquest as suggested by Ibn Khaldun, Owen Lattimore, and Thomas Barfield?"

To test these propositions, incidents of raiding and sedentarization are recorded per iteration, as well as the population numbers of pastoral nomads and sedentary agriculturalists. If historical theories of cycles are correct, then periods of intense raiding should be followed by periods of relative peace, until pastoral numbers grow to a size where they again pose a more constant threat to the agricultural population. If theories of sedentarization are correct, pastoralists should run into problems with excess wealth and excessive poverty, and poverty should be more common than enrichment. If these patterns emerge from model runs, then not only will this confirm the validity of these theories, but also, we can examine the model variables to gain a clearer understanding of which were important in bringing about the results.

MODEL RUNS AND RESULTS

Twenty model runs were performed to explore the range of resulting histories and to test the sensitivity of the model's parameters. An advantage of ABM simulation is that every event is recorded so that when a particular outcome emerges, such as the death of an agriculturalist family, the data log of the ABM can be queried for the precise cause of the event. This capability allowed us to derive the relationships among system variables we describe below. Overall, the resulting pastoral-agricultural societies that we generated appeared similar to ethnographically known societies, although the broad historical trends researchers have recorded failed to emerge. We examine the possible reasons for the model's successes and failures. The following data illustrate a typical run. Over a 200-season (50-year) period, the average nomad population was 43 (composed of families including a husband, wife and two immature children at any time), and the agriculturalist population was 115 (with a family size of about 10). These figures capture the relative family size differences between nomads and agriculturalists cited above, although the agriculturalists are perhaps slightly more fertile than ethnographically observed. The average family herd size was 113 sheep and goats. The average herd figures match the ethnographic observations very well (Cribb 1991:35, Table 3.1a). Mobility patterns exhibited a seasonal transhumance between summer pastures in highlands away from sedentary villages and fall-winter settlement near agriculturalist trading partners (Figure 25.1).

In a typical run, trading precedes raiding, but raiding begins to take precedence over trading, being inversely related until both activities stabilize (Figure 25.2). In the run we are analyzing, the average trade/season/family was 0.09,

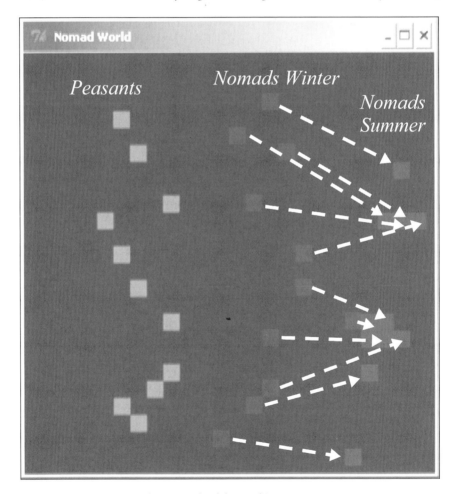

Figure 25.1. NOMAD screenshot: seasonal mobility graphics.

and the average raid/season/family was 0.15, or 0.36 trades and 0.6 raids/
year/family. Both activities typically took place during the harvest in the fall
(Figure 25.3). This was due to the availability of goods during the harvest
time of the year. It is important to note that nomads could trade or raid whenever a need arose, and indeed occasional off-season interactions took place.
However, an initial fall trade set a precedent for yearly seasonal trade and raid

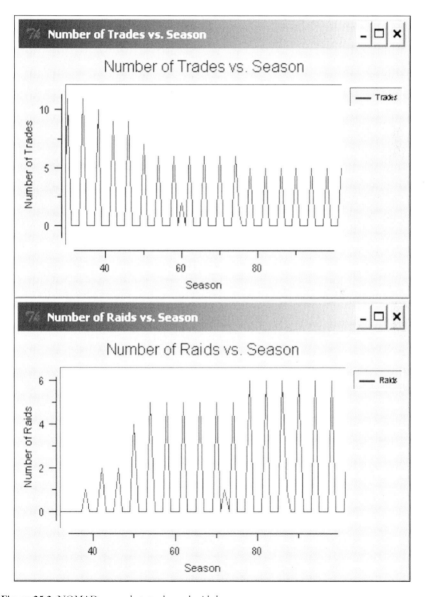

Figure 25.2. NOMAD screenshot: trades and raids by season.

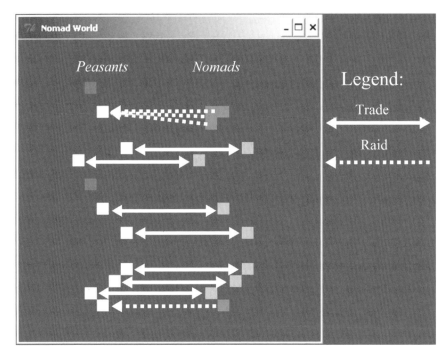

Figure 25.3. NOMAD screenshot: trade and raid graphics.

interactions as observed ethnographically (Barth 1961:99; Sweet 1969; Nielsen 2001). Interestingly, the average number of raids/year (0.6) was within the order of magnitude of what Gray et al. (2003) indicate.

The runs provide insight into dimensions on which the model was particularly sensitive. First, the productivities of labor in agricultural and pastoral production easily tip prices to extremes. We found that agriculture was particularly productive, devaluing Kcals and increasing the value of protein. The price imbalance typically led to nomads practicing predatory pricing and preventing agriculturalists from amassing wealth. Agriculturalists were therefore constantly vulnerable to starvation. We had to allot agriculturalists a modest protein supplement derived from their own wheat production, reasonable enough, in order to keep their own Kcal/protein ratio from becoming too imbalanced and driving down the value of their Kcals. This allotment prevented the agriculturalists' minimal rate of substitution from becoming too large. Similarly, the Kcals derived from dairy production by nomads was essential in preventing the nomadic Kcal/protein ratio from becoming overly imbalanced. The need for not becoming too impoverished in what one's trading partner produces leads to the paradox that, although agriculturalists and nomads are economic specialists, they must provide some small measure of what the other produces so that they do not enter trade negotiations too weakly. This necessary modest economic diversification could be one reason that the myths of the carnivorous pure pastoralist and vegetable-eating agriculturalist are untrue (Barfield 1993:3): real pastoralists have access to Kcal supplements, and real agriculturalists have access to protein supplements.

Another implication of behavioral sensitivity to pricing is that, if prices became overly favorable to one party (usually the nomads), then a pattern of frequent raiding emerged. In runs where this took place, nomads raided mercilessly and never traded with agriculturalists, eventually driving the agriculturalists to extinction. Our results were probably extreme, a result of the artificial lack of economic alternatives or state protection for agriculturalists. We think, however, that we have gained insight into one factor that might lead to cycles of intense raiding by pastoral nomads. The most intense raiding occurred when agriculturalists were unusually wealthy in Kcals, their primary product, but very poor in stores of protein. In this situation nomads found the most profitable course of action to be intense raiding, since agriculturalists could not afford pastoral products, despite their absolutely high wealth in Kcals. We think that this result is reminiscent of Barfield's (1989:9) observation that cycles of nomadic warfare in Asia coincided with periods of agrarian prosperity. While food goods may not necessarily have been the economically deciding factor, imbalances between agrarian stores of nomadic and agricultural goods could have sparked a cycle of intense raiding. We think that this proposition is worth further investigation.

Another implication of the sensitivity of behavior to pricing is the indication that cultural norms like customary pricing, and markets, are probably necessary for stable and profitable pastoral-agricultural specialization. We found much more stable trading behavior when a customary set price was used instead of the negotiated price based on marginal rates of substitution. Without a market agriculturalists were occasionally, and in some runs frequently, wiped out through predatory pricing, which in turn led to the eventual extinction of nomads because of the lack of agriculturalist trading partners. A market would permit agriculturalists to collectively dump their Kcals and stabilize a market price, even a negotiated one, for nomad protein. In this way agriculturalists could sell their goods at a more stable price, reducing price fluctuations and preventing their extinction, as well as that of the nomads. Interestingly, archaeologists have noted that the fully nomadic pastoral specialization did not emerge until after the emergence of towns and cities in Asia and the Middle East (Lattimore 1951; Cribb 1991).

Although a pattern of intense raiding emerged in some runs, we failed to detect major cycles of trading and raiding. Furthermore, pastoralists were not reproducing quite fast enough to produce demographic pressure on resources and to create new families. Without this pressure there could be no relative impoverishment or enrichment of nomads. More fully specifying the model will allow us to test whether raiding and trading cycles can emerge from the interactions between nomads and agriculturalists or whether external political influences drive such cycles, as some researchers suggest.

DISCUSSION

ABMs can provide insights into the value of anthropological theories by allowing researchers to test whether their theories could logically lead to the phenomena they purport to explain. Using important theoretical concepts in nomadic studies, we were able to generate a facsimile of pastoralist-agriculturalist interactions between individual families in an arid environment. Our analysis of the ABM highlighted the need for modest diversification in pastoral and agricultural economies, despite their respective economic emphases. The sensitivity of behavior to pricing also highlights the potential long-term value of markets and normative pricing for both agriculturalists and nomads. A relationship between balancing complimentary goods, the volatility of pricing and raiding was also observed, suggesting a possible influence on ancient cycles. More research is necessary, however, to explore the basis for raiding and trading cycles.

We have provided a generic example for purposes of illustrating the potential use of ABMs for exploring theories of pastoralist-agriculturalist interactions. The model's sensitivity to some parameters, however, especially pastoral and agricultural productivity, underscores the importance that local environmental, economic and social context will have on the performance of any simulation. Therefore, we encourage application of this tool to specific instances (see our application to Darfur in Kuznar and Sedlmeyer 2005). General patterns may emerge from such research, but they will be valid only after varied settings have been modeled, providing a cross-simulation (analogous to a cross-cultural) analysis.

Finally, our experience in developing the NOMAD ABM reinforced the need for quality empirical data collected through traditional ethnography. ABMs can reflect the world only to the extent that their logic parallels real-world relationships and their parameters are grounded in actual data. Simulations are not an alternative but a complement to traditional anthropological research. Developing ABMs can enhance empirical data gathering as well. It becomes clear, once one begins developing the logic for a simulation, what data are required and what relationships need to be known in order to complete the construction of a functioning simulation. Attempts at simulation before field-work can guide researchers to the kinds of data that they need to gather to address a particular research question.

REFERENCES

Adano, W. R. and K. Witsenburg

2003   *Surviving Pastoral Decline in Marsabit District*. Amsterdam, Research Institute for Global Issues and Development Studies.

Asad, T.

1973   The Beduin as a Military Force: Notes on Some Aspects of Power Relations Between Nomads and Sedentaries in Historical Perspective. In C. Nelson (ed.), *The Desert and the Sown: Nomads in the Wider World*. Berkeley, University of California Press: pp. 61–73.

Axelrod, R.

1997   *The Complexity of Cooperation: Agent-Based Models of Conflict and Cooperation*. Princeton, Princeton University Press.

Axtell, R. L., J. M. Epstein, J. S. Dean, G. J. Gumerman, A. C. Swelund, J. Harburger, S. Chakravarty, R. Hammond, J. Parker and M. T. Parker

2002   Population Growth and Collapse in a Multiagent Model of the Kayenta Anasazi in Long House Valley. In *Proceedings of the National Academy of Sciences 99, Supplement 3*, pp. 7275–7279.

Barfield, T. J.

1989   *The Perilous Frontier: Nomadic Empires and China*. Cambridge, Blackwell.

1993   *The Nomadic Alternative*. Englewood Cliffs, Prentice-Hall.

2004   *Nomadic Pastoralists in Afghanistan: Reconstruction of the Pastoral Economy*. Washington, Bank Information Center.

Barth, F.

1961   *Nomads of South Persia*. New York, Holt, Rinehart and Winston.

1973   A General Perspective on Nomad-Sedentary Relations in the Middle East. In C. Nelson (ed.), *The Desert and the Sown: Nomads in the Wider World*. Berkeley, University of California Press: pp. 11–21.

Bates, D. G.

1971   The Role of the State in Peasant-Nomad Mutualism. *Anthropological Quarterly 44*: 3, pp. 109–131.

Beck, L.

1991   *Nomad: A Year in the Life of a Qashqa'i Tribesman in Iran*. Berkeley, University of California Press.

1998   Use of Land by Nomadic Pastoralists in Iran, 1970–1998. *Bulletin of the Yale School of Forestry and Environmental Science 103*: pp. 58–80.

Ben-David, J.

1990   The Negev Bedouin: From Nomadism to Agriculture. In R. Kark (ed.), *The Land That Became Israel*. Jerusalem, Magnes Press: pp. 181–195.

Berntsen, J. L.

1976   The Maasai and Their Neighbors: Variables of Interaction. *African Economic History 2*: pp. 1–11.

Browman, D. L.

1987   Pastoralism in Highland Peru and Bolivia. In D. L. Browman (ed.), *Arid Land Use Strategies and Risk Management in the Andes*. Boulder, Westview Press: pp. 121–149.

Burnham, P.

1979   Spatial Mobility and Political Centralization in Pastoral Societies. In *Pastoral Productivity and Society*. Cambridge, Cambridge University Press: pp. 349–360.

Casimir, M. J.

1988   Nutrition and Socio-economic Strategies in Mobile Pastoral Societies in the Middle East with Special Reference to West Afghan Pashtuns. In I. de Garine and G. A. Harrison (eds.), *Coping with Uncertainty in Food Supply*. Oxford, Clarendon Press: pp. 337–359.

Chagnon, N.

1992   *Yanomamö*. Fort Worth, Harcourt Brace.

Cook, C. W. and P. L. Sims

1975   Drought and Its Relationship to Dynamics of Primary Productivity and Production of Grazing Animals. Paper presented at the *Conference on Evaluation and Mapping of Tropical African Rangelands*, Bomako(Mali).

Cribb, R.

1991   *Nomads in Archaeology*. Cambridge, Cambridge University Press.

Cronk, L.

1998   Ethnographic Formation Processes. S*ocial Science Information 37*: 2, pp. 321–349.

Dahl, G.

1979   Ecology and Equality: The Boran Case. In L'Equipe écologie et anthropologie des sociétés pastorales (ed.), *Pastoral Production and Society/Production pastorale et société*. Cambridge, Cambridge University Press: pp. 261–282.

Dahl, G. and A. Hjort

1976   *Having Herds: Pastoral Herd Growth and Household Economy. Stockholm Studies in Social Anthropology 2*. Stockholm, University of Stockholm.

Dean, J. S., G. J. Gumerman, J. M. Epstein, R. L. Axtell, A. C. Swedlund, M. T. Parker and S. McCarroll

1999   Understanding Anasazi Culture Change Through Agent-Based Modeling. In T. A. Kohler and G. J. Gumerman (eds.), *Dynamics in Human and Primate Societies*. New York, Oxford University Press: pp. 179–205.

Devendra, C.

1978   Goats. In G. Williamson and J. W. Payne (eds.), *Animal Husbandry in the Tropics*. New York, Longman: pp. 465–483.

Diarra, L. and H. Breman

1975   Influence of Rainfall on the Productivity of Grasslands. Paper presented at the *Conference on Evaluation and Mapping of Tropical African Rangelands*, Bomako, (Mali).

Dyson-Hudson, R. and N. Dyson-Hudson

1980   Nomadic Pastoralism. *Annual Review of Anthropology 9*: pp. 15–61.

Epstein, J. M. and R. L. Axtell

1996   *Growing Artificial Societies: Social Science from the Bottom Up*. Washington, Brookings Institution Press.

Fratkin, E. and J. T. McCabe

1999   East African Pastoralism at the Crossroads: An Introduction. *Nomadic Peoples 3*: 2, pp. 5–15.

Fratkin, E., M. A. Nathan and E. A. Roth

1999   Health Consequences of Pastoral Sedentarization Among Rendille of Northern Kenya. In D. M. Anderson and V. Broch-Due (eds.), *The Poor Are Not Us: Poverty and Pastoralism in Eastern Africa*. Athens, Ohio University Press: pp. 149–162.

Gatenby, R.

1986   *Sheep Production in the Tropics and Sub-Tropics*. New York, Longman.

Gellner, E.

1973   Introduction. In C. Nelson (ed.), *The Desert and the Sown: Nomads in the Wider World*. Berkeley, University of California Press: pp. 1–9.

Glatzer, B.

1982   Processes of Nomadization in West Afghanistan. *Studies in Third World Societies 18*: pp. 61–86.

Glatzer, B. and M. J. Casimir

1983   Herds and Households Among Pashtun Pastoral Nomads: Limits of Growth. *Ethnology 22*: pp. 307–325.

Goldschmidt, W.

1979   A General Model for Pastoral Social Systems. In L'Equipe écologie et anthropologie des sociétés pastorales (ed.), *Pastoral Production and Society/Production pastorale et société*. Cambridge, Cambridge University Press: pp. 15–27.

Gray, S., M. Sundal, B. Wiebusch, M. A. Little, P. Leslie and I. L. Pike

2003   Cattle Raiding, Cultural Survival, and Adaptability of East African Pastoralists. *Current Anthropology 44*: pp. S3–S30.

Handwerker, W.

1983   The First Demographic Transition: An Analysis of Subsistence Choices and Reproductive Consequences. *American Anthropologist 85*: pp. 5–27.

Hannoyer, J. and J.-P. Thieck

1982   Observations sur l'élevage et le commerce du Mouton dans la région de Raqqa
        en Syrie.' *Production Pastorale et Société 14*: pp. 47–63.

Hillman, G. and M. S. Davies

1990   Measured Domestication Rates in Wild Wheats and Barley Under Primitive
        Cultivation, and Their Archaeological Implications. *Journal of World Prehistory*
        4: 2, pp. 157–222.

Hole, F.

1978   Pastoral Nomadism in Western Iran. In R. A. Gould (ed.), *Explorations
        in Ethnoarchaeology*. Albuquerque, University of New Mexico Press: pp.
        127–179.

Iannelli, P.

1984   *The Principles of Pasture Improvement and Range Management and Their
        Application in Somalia*. Rome, FAO.

Ibn Khaldun (translated by F. Rosenthal)

1967   *The Muqaddimah: An Introduction to History*. Princeton, Princeton University
        Press.

Irons, W.

1965   Livestock Raiding Among Pastoralists: An Adaptive Interpretation. *Papers of
        the Michigan Academy of Science, Arts, and Letters 1*: pp. 393–414.

1972   Variation in Economic Organization: A Comparison of the Pastoral Yomut
        and the Basseri. In W. Irons and N. Dyson-Hudson (eds.), *Perspectives on
        Nomadism*. Leiden, E. J. Brill: pp. 88–104.

1979   Political Stratification Among Pastoral Nomads. In L'Equipe écologie et
        anthropologie des sociétés pastorales (ed.), *Pastoral Production and Society/
        Production pastorale et société*. Cambridge, Cambridge University Press: pp.
        361–374.

Kahn, P. (ed.)

1998   *The Secret History of the Mongols: The Origin of Chingis Kahn*. Boston, Cheng
        and Tsui.

Khazanov, A.

1994   *Nomads and the Outside World*. Madison, University of Wisconsin Press (second
        edition).

Kohler, T. A., J. Kresl, C. Van West, E. Carr and R. H. Wilshusen

1999   Be There Then: A Modeling Approach to Settlement Determinants and
        Spatial Efficiency Among Late Ancestral Pueblo Populations of the Mesa
        Verde Region, U.S. Southwest. In T. A. Kohler and G. J. Gumerman (eds.),
        Dynamics in Human and Primate Societies. New York, Oxford University Press:
        pp. 145–178.

Krader, L.

1979 The Origin of the State Among the Nomads of Asia. In L'Equipe écologie et anthropologie des sociétés pastorales (ed.), *Pastoral Production and Society/ Production pastorale et société*. Cambridge, Cambridge University Press: pp. 231–234.

Kuznar, L. A.

1991a El medio ambiente y la capacidad de carga de la Sierra Alta de los Andes sur central en el departamento de Moquegua, Perú [in Spanish]. *Diálogo Andino 10*: pp. 100–112.

1991b Herd Composition in an Aymara Community of the Peruvian Altiplano as a Linear Programming Problem. *Human Ecology 19*: pp. 369–387.

1995 *Awatimarka: The Ethnoarchaeology of an Andean Herding Community*. Fort Worth, Harcourt Brace.

1999 Traditional Pastoralism and Development: A Comparison of Navajo and Aymara Grazing Ecology. In T. L. Gragson and B. G. Blount (eds.), *Ethnoecology: Knowledge, Resources, and Rights*. Athens, University of Georgia Press: pp. 74–89.

2001 Risk Sensitivity and Value Among Andean Pastoralists: Measures, Models, and Empirical Tests. *Current Anthropology 42*: 3, pp. 432–440.

2006 Hi Fidelity Computational Social Science in Anthropology: Prospects for Developing a Comparative Framework. *Social Science Computer Review 24*: 1, pp. 1–15.

Kuznar, L. A. and R. Sedlmeyer

2005 Collective Violence in Darfur: An Agent-Based Model of Pastoral Nomad/ Sedentary Peasant Interaction. *Mathematical Anthropology and Culture Theory 1*: 4, pp. 1–22 (on-line at http://www.mathematicalanthropology.org/)

Lattimore, O.

1951 *Inner Asian Frontiers of China*. Boston, Beacon Press (second edition).

1979 Herdsmen, Farmers, Urban Culture. In L'Equipe écologie et anthropologie des sociétés pastorales (ed.), *Pastoral Production and Society/Production pastorale et société*. Cambridge, Cambridge University Press: pp. 479–490.

Lazar, A. and R. G. Reynolds

2002 Computational Framework for Modeling the Dynamic Evolution of Large-Scale Multi-agent Organizations. Paper presented at the *Computational Analysis of Social and Organizational Systems Proceedings*, Pittsburgh.

Lewis, O.

1965 *Village Life in Northern India*. New York, Random House.

Martin, M. and B. Voorhies

1975 *Female of the Species*. New York, Columbia University Press.

McCorriston, J.
1997   The Fiber Revolution: Textile Extensification, Alienation, and Social Stratification in Ancient Mesopotamia. *Current Anthropology 38*: 4, pp. 517–549.

McElreath, R., R. Boyd and P. J. Richerson
2003   Shared Norms and the Evolution of Ethnic Markers. *Current Anthropology 44*: 1, pp. 122–129.

Nielsen, A. E.
2001   Ethnoarchaeological Perspectives on Caravan Trade in the South-Central Andes. In L. A. Kuznar (ed.), *Ethnoarchaeology of Andean South America: Contributions to Archaeological Method and Theory*. Ann Arbor, International Monographs in Prehistory: pp. 163–201.

Roth, E. A.
1986   The Demographic Study of Pastoral Peoples. *Nomadic Peoples 20*: pp. 63–76.

Salzman, P. C.
1972   Multi-resource Nomadism in Iranian Baluchistan. In W. Irons and N. Dyson-Hudson (eds.), *Perspectives on Nomadism*. Leiden, E. J. Brill: pp. 60–68.

1979   Inequality and Oppression in Nomadic Society. In L'Equipe écologie et anthropologie des sociétés pastorales (ed.), *Pastoral Production and Society/ Production pastorale et société*. Cambridge, Cambridge University Press: pp. 429–446.

Schneider, H. K.
1979   *Livestock and Equality in East Africa: The Economic Basis for Social Structure*. Bloomington, Indiana University Press.

Shepardson, M. and B. Hammond
1970   *The Navajo Mountain Community*. Berkeley, University of California Press.

Sidky, H.
1995   *Hunza: An Ethnographic Outline*. Jaipur, Illustrated Book Publishers.

Simon, R.
1981   Symbiosis of Nomads and Sedentaries on the Character of the Middle Eastern Civilization. *Acta Orientalia Academiae Scientiarum Hungary 35*: 2–3, pp. 229–242.

Spooner, B.
1972   The Status of Nomadism as a Cultural Phenomenon in the Middle East. In W. Irons and R. Dyson-Hudson (eds.), *Perspectives on Nomadism*. Leiden, E. J. Brill: pp. 122–131.

Sweet, L.
1969   Camel Pastoralism in North Arabia and the Minimal Camping Unit. In A. P. Vayda (ed.), *Environment and Cultural Behavior*. Austin, University of Texas Press: pp. 157–180.

Swidler, W. W.

1972   Some Demographic Factors Regulating the Formation of Flocks and Camps Among the Brahui of Baluchistan. In W. Irons and N. Dyson-Hudson (eds.), *Perspectives on Nomadism*. Leiden, E. J. Brill: pp. 69–75.

Swift, J.

1979   The Development of Livestock Trading in Nomad Pastoral Economy: The Somali Case. In L'Equipe écologie et anthropologie des sociétés pastorales (ed.), *Pastoral Production and Society/Production pastorale et société*. Cambridge, Cambridge University Press: pp. 447–465.

Terna, P.

1998   Simulation Tools for Social Scientists: Building Agent Based Models with SWARM. *Journal of Artificial Societies and Social Simulation. Volume 1, Number 2* (on-line at http://www.soc.surrey.ac.uk/JASSS/1/2/4.html).

Thomas, R. B.

1973   *Human Adaptation to a High Andean Energy Flow System. Department of Anthropology Occasional Paper No. 7*. University Park, Pennsylvania State University.

LIST OF CONTRIBUTORS

Abbas Alizadeh (Chapter 4)
Director of Iranian Prehistoric Project
Oriental Institute, University of Chicago (USA)

Hans Barnard (Chapters 1 and 19)
Research Associate, Cotsen Institute of Archaeology
University of California, Los Angeles (USA)

Reinhard W. Bernbeck (Chapter 3)
Professor, Department of Anthropology
Binghamton University (USA)

Alison Betts (Chapter 2)
Associate Professor and Chair, Department of Archaeology
University of Sydney (Australia)

Alexander V. Borisov (Chapter 10)
Senior Researcher,
Institute of Physical and Biological Problems in Soil Science
Russian Academy of Science (Russia)

David L. Browman (Chapter 7)
Professor of Archaeology, Department of Anthropology
Chair, Interdisciplinary Program in Archaeology
Washington University in Saint Louis (USA)

Giorgio Buccellati (Chapter 6)
Director, Mesopotamian Laboratory, Cotsen Institute of Archaeology
Professor Emeritus of Near Eastern Languages and Cultures
Professor Emeritus of History
University of California, Los Angeles (USA)

Stanley M. Burstein (Chapter 11)
Professor Emeritus of History
California State University, Los Angeles (USA)

Claudia Chang (Chapter 15)
Professor, Department of Anthropology and Sociology
Sweet Briar College (USA)

Roger L. Cribb † (Chapter 24)
Adjunct Research Fellow, Department of Anthropology, Archaeology and Sociology, School of Arts and Social Sciences at the Cairns Campus of James Cook University (Australia)

Jelmer W. Eerkens (Chapter 14)
Associate Professor, Department of Anthropology
University of California, Davis (USA)

Michael D. Frachetti (Chapter 17)
Assistant Professor, Department of Anthropology
Washington University in Saint Louis (USA)

Eugeny I. Gak (Chapter 10)
Researcher, Department of Complex Archaeological Investigation
State Historical Museum, Moscow (Russia)

Margaret B. Holman † (Chapter 13)
Research Associate, Anthropology
Michigan State University Museum (USA)

Esther Jacobson-Tepfer (Chapter 9)
Maude I. Kerns Professor of Asian Art
Department of Art History, Architecture, and Allied Arts
University of Oregon (USA)

Lawrence A. Kuznar (Chapter 25)
Professor, Department of Anthropology
Indiana University–Purdue University at Fort Wayne (USA)

William A. Lovis (Chapter 13)
Professor, Department of Anthropology
Curator at the Michigan State University Museum
Michigan State University (USA)

Anwar Abdel-Magid (Chapter 20)
Academic Adviser for Sudan Cooperation
Senior Professor, Center for Africa Studies
University of the Free State (South Africa)

S. Brooke Milne (Chapter 8)
Assistant Professor Archaeology, Department of Anthropology
University of Manitoba, Winnipeg (Canada)

Alan G. Roe (Chapter 22)
Senior Researcher,
Afghanistan Research and Evaluation Unit (Kabul, Afghanistan)

Steven A. Rosen (Chapter 5)
Professor, Department of Bible, Archaeology, and Ancient Near Eastern
Studies, Ben-Gurion University of the Negev (Israel)

Benjamin A. Saidel (Chapter 21)
Assistant Professor, Department of Anthropology
East Carolina University (USA)

Robert Sedlmeyer (Chapter 25)
Associate Professor, Department of Computer Sciences
Indiana University–Purdue University at Fort Wayne (USA)

Natalya I. Shishlina (Chapter 10)
Senior Researcher, Archaeology Department
State Historical Museum, Moscow (Russia)

Andrew B. Smith (Chapter 12)
Associate Professor, Department of Archaeology
University of Cape Town (South Africa)

Stuart T. Smith (Chapter 16)
Associate Professor, Department of Anthropology
University of California, Santa Barbara (USA)

Jeffrey J. Szuchman (Chapter 18)
Post-Doctoral Scholar, Oriental Institute
University of Chicago (USA)

Willeke Z. Wendrich (Chapters 1 and 23)
Associate Professor of Egyptian Archaeology, Department of Near Eastern
Languages and Cultures, University of California, Los Angeles (USA)

LIST OF FIGURES

LIST OF TABLES

INDEX